PUBLIC AND PRIVATE ENFORCEMENT OF SECURITIES LAWS

This book undertakes unique case studies – including interviews with participants and empirical analysis – of public and private enforcement of Australian securities laws addressing continuous disclosure.

Enforcement of laws is crucial to effective regulation. Historically, enforcement was the province of a government regulator with significant discretion (public enforcement). However, more and more citizens are being expected to take action themselves (private enforcement). Consistent with regulatory pluralism, public and private enforcement exist in parallel, with the capacity to both help and hinder each other, and the achievement of the goals of enforcement in a range of areas of regulation. The rise of the shareholder class action in Australia, backed by litigation funding or lawyers, has given rise to enforcement overlapping with that of the government regulator, the Australian Securities and Investments Commission. The ramifications of overlapping enforcement are explained based on detailed analysis. The analysis is further bolstered by the regulator's approach to enforcement changing from a compliance orientation to a 'Why not litigate?' approach.

The analysis and ramifications of the Australian case studies involve matters of regulatory theory and practice that apply across jurisdictions. The book will appeal to practitioners, regulators and academics interested in regulatory policy and enforcement, and the operation of regulators and class actions, including their interaction.

Volume 12 in the series Civil Justice Systems

Civil Justice Systems

Series General Editor: Christopher Hodges, Director, Swiss Re/CMS Research Programme, Centre for Socio-Legal Studies, University of Oxford

This series covers new theoretical and empirical research on the mechanisms for resolution of civil disputes, including courts, tribunals, arbitration, compensation schemes, ombudsmen, codes of practice, complaint mechanisms, mediation and various forms of Alternative Dispute Resolution. It examines frameworks for dispute resolution that comprise combinations of the above mechanisms, and the parameters and conditions for selecting certain types of techniques and procedures rather than others. It also evaluates individual techniques, against parameters such as cost, duration, accessibility, and delivery of desired outcomes, and illuminates how legal rights and obligations are operated in practice.

Volume 1: *The Costs and Funding of Civil Litigation: A Comparative Perspective*
edited by Christopher Hodges, Stefan Vogenauer and Magdalena Tulibacka

Volume 2: *Consumer ADR in Europe*
Christopher Hodges, Iris Benöhr and Naomi Creutzfeldt-Banda

Volume 3: *Law and Corporate Behaviour: Integrating Theories of Regulation, Enforcement, Compliance and Ethics*
Christopher Hodges

Volume 4: *A Comparative Examination of Multi-Party Actions*
Joanne Blennerhassett

Volume 5: *Redress Schemes for Personal Injuries*
Sonia Macleod and Christopher Hodges

Volume 6: *Ethical Business Practice and Regulation: A Behavioural and Values-Based Approach to Compliance and Enforcement*
Christopher Hodges and Ruth Steinholtz

Volume 7: *Delivering Collective Redress: New Technologies*
Christopher Hodges and Stefaan Voet

Volume 8: *Pharmaceutical and Medical Device Safety: A Study in Public and Private Regulation*
Sonia Macleod and Sweta Chakraborty

Volume 9: *Delivering Dispute Resolution: A Holistic Review of Models in England and Wales*
Christopher Hodges

Volume 10: *Regulatory Delivery*
Graham Russell and Christopher Hodges

Volume 11: *Access to Justice for the Chinese Consumer: Handling Consumer Disputes in Contemporary China*
Ling Zhou

Volume 12: *Public and Private Enforcement of Securities Laws: The Regulator and the Class Action in Australia's Continuous Disclosure Regime*
Michael Legg

Public and Private Enforcement of Securities Laws

The Regulator and the Class Action in Australia's Continuous Disclosure Regime

Michael Legg

•HART•

OXFORD • LONDON • NEW YORK • NEW DELHI • SYDNEY

HART PUBLISHING

Bloomsbury Publishing Plc

Kemp House, Chawley Park, Cumnor Hill, Oxford, OX2 9PH, UK

1385 Broadway, New York, NY 10018, USA

29 Earlsfort Terrace, Dublin 2, Ireland

HART PUBLISHING, the Hart/Stag logo, BLOOMSBURY and the Diana logo are trademarks of Bloomsbury Publishing Plc

First published in Great Britain 2022

A catalogue record for this book is available from the British Library.

Library of Congress Cataloging-in-Publication data

Names: Legg, Michael, author.

Title: Public and private enforcement of securities laws : the regulator and the class action in Australia's continuous disclosure regime / Michael Legg.

Description: Oxford ; New York : Hart, 2022. | Series: Civil justice systems ; volume 12 | Based on author's thesis (doctoral - University of Melbourne, 2019) issued under title: Public and private enforcement of securities laws in Australia : an examination of the continuous disclosure regime. | Includes bibliographical references and index.

Identifiers: LCCN 2021044668 (print) | LCCN 2021044669 (ebook) | ISBN 9781509941513 (hardback) | ISBN 9781509956784 (paperback) | ISBN 9781509941520 (pdf) | ISBN 9781509941537 (Epub)

Subjects: LCSH: Securities—Australia. | Disclosure of information—Law and legislation—Australia.

Classification: LCC KU956.5 .L44 2021 (print) | LCC KU956.5 (ebook) | DDC 346.94/0666—dc23/eng/20211105

LC record available at https://lccn.loc.gov/2021044668

LC ebook record available at https://lccn.loc.gov/2021044669

ISBN: HB: 978-1-50994-151-3
ePDF: 978-1-50994-152-0
ePub: 978-1-50994-153-7

Typeset by Compuscript Ltd, Shannon

To my grandparents, Ronald and Emma Dobney

PREFACE

Who rights wrongs better, deterring misconduct and obtaining compensation? And who promotes the regulatory process, pursuing the public interest in an accountable and efficient manner? The sheriff (government regulator) or the bounty hunter (class action lawyers and litigation funders), or some combination of both?

Enforcement of laws is crucial to effective regulation. Historically, enforcement of regulation was the province of a government regulator – public enforcement. However, citizens are being expected to take action themselves – private enforcement. Government grants citizens standing to pursue statutory remedies and the means to do so, the class action and third-party litigation funding. Consistent with regulatory pluralism, public and private enforcement exist in parallel, with the capacity to both help and hinder each other, and the achievement of the goals of enforcement in a range of areas of regulation.

This monograph examines the public and private enforcement of securities laws, and in particular, Australia's continuous disclosure regime. Continuous disclosure requires regulated entities to immediately disclose material information that is not generally available to the market. The objective of the continuous disclosure regime is to ensure market integrity and efficiency, as well as protecting investors. The text focuses on a particular regulatory regime because that regime creates specific incentives and requirements for the regulator and the class action's proponents. This includes the available enforcement tools, the elements of causes of action and the possible outcomes, such as levels of penalties and available compensation, that may follow.

Australia has traditionally relied on a public regulator to enforce its securities laws and, since 1994, the enforcement of its continuous disclosure regime. However, shareholder class actions have become a growing phenomenon in the Australian legal landscape since around 2002–03. The rise of the shareholder class action has given rise to overlapping enforcement of the continuous disclosure laws by the public regulator, the Australian Securities and Investments Commission (ASIC), and private citizens with the assistance of lawyers and litigation funders. Shareholder class action activity peaked in 2017–18 with billions of dollars having already been paid out and more being sought. This prompted the adoption of a stricter regulatory regime for litigation funding. At around the same time, ASIC's willingness to litigate, resourcing and available penalties increased with the aim of enhancing enforcement. These changes were driven by the significance of regulatory enforcement and the class action for Australian businesses and consumers.

The above developments have been the motivation for four questions examined in this monograph.

The first question is to inquire as to the effectiveness of ASIC and the shareholder class action in achieving deterrence and compensation in relation to the continuous disclosure regime. The focus on deterrence and compensation is chosen because these are the areas where ASIC and the class action overlap.

The second question is to ask what the ramifications are of ASIC and class actions co-existing in relation to the continuous disclosure regime from the perspective of regulatory process and the desired values that underly that process. Moreover, consideration is given to how ASIC and the class action may impact each other, ie whether the class action and ASIC help or hinder each other.

In summary, the first question focuses on outcomes and the effectiveness of ASIC enforcement and the class action in achieving deterrence and compensation. The second question focuses on process and process values. The answers to these questions are addressed through the development of an analytical framework and the creation of case studies, including interviews with participants. The text does not seek to give a single answer to each of the research questions, but rather to produce a sophisticated account of the various factors that interact and mediate both outcomes and processes, so as to demonstrate that any answer is complex and contingent on a number of influences and circumstances.

The third question is whether changes in policy settings and legal requirements can encourage or discourage public and private enforcement, and consequently impact the effectiveness of public and private enforcement in achieving deterrence and compensation. This is a re-examination of the first question through the lens of actual policy changes in Australia post-31 December 2017, including changes to ASIC's resourcing and enforcement approach, and regulation of litigation funding. This analysis includes further empirical examination of the enforcement undertaken by ASIC and class action activity.

The fourth question asks how the coexistence of public and private enforcement may be more effectively addressed through some form of coordination. Having identified that ASIC and the class action may impact each other, and the achievement of desirable regulatory values, the text draws on a range of coordination mechanisms from other regulatory regimes to design strategies for coordination.

The analysis of the Australian continuous disclosure regime and its enforcement by ASIC and class actions involves matters of regulatory policy and practice that are of general interest, namely deterrence, compensation, regulatory processes, and the mix of public and private enforcement. The text provides specific findings drawn from the subject of study, but those findings may be extrapolated across jurisdictions and into other regulatory settings.

ACKNOWLEDGEMENTS

This monograph is the outcome of a research interest that has spanned at least 10 years. Class actions and regulatory enforcement have been of interest since I was a legal practitioner in Australia and the United States, having acted in numerous investigations and litigation in these areas. It is an interest that I carried into academia when I joined the Faculty of Law at the University of New South Wales (UNSW) in Sydney, Australia in 2009. In 2011 I spoke on 'The Sheriff and the Bounty Hunter: Gunfight at the Regulatory Corral?' at the Centre for Law, Markets and Regulation Workshop on The Role of Regulators and Class Actions in Sydney, and authored a chapter, 'Public and Private Enforcement: ASIC and the Shareholder Class Action' in the edited collection *Regulation, Litigation and Enforcement* (Thomson Reuters, 2011). However, the subject matter required greater and deeper analysis, which was achieved through undertaking a PhD part-time from 2013 to 2019 at the University of Melbourne Law School. The text is based on the PhD thesis but with additional chapters. One takes account of reforms aimed at both ASIC enforcement and class actions that occurred after the period addressed in the thesis. Policy settings and laws that had been unchanged for years were in line for reform because of the significance of regulatory enforcement and the class action for Australian businesses and consumers. Another chapter examines an area that I could not address in the thesis due to the word limit: the concept of coordination between the regulator and class action proponents. I see this as a productive way forward for public and private enforcement, although there are trade-offs to be managed and much depends on implementation not just policy settings.

Special thanks to

- My PhD supervisors, Professor Helen Andersen and Professor Ian Ramsay, University of Melbourne Law School for their guidance and advice on both the big picture and the detail.
- The participants in the interviews that formed part of the case studies. All were busy with important undertakings and in some cases had moved on to new careers and responsibilities. Without their willingness to find time to be interviewed the depth of the study would not have been possible.
- The PhD examiners who provided feedback on the thesis, which could be addressed in the text.
- Professor Christopher Hodges OBE, University of Oxford, who has been a source of advice for many years and supported the publication of this text in the Hart Civil Justice Systems series, which enabled the text to have a global audience.
- The Hart Publishing team of Roberta Bassi, Rosemarie Mearns, Linda Staniford and Vicki Hillyard for their professionalism and care in bringing this publication to fruition.
- My family, Laëtitia, Maxime and Alexandre, for their love, support and encouragement over the lengthy period that undertaking this research took, but especially during the final drafting stages of this text which was during the operation of stay-at-home orders due to the COVID-19 pandemic.

CONTENTS

ABBREVIATIONS

$	Australian dollars
AFSL	Australian Financial Services Licence
ALRC	Australian Law Reform Commission
ASIC	Australian Securities and Investments Commission
ASIC Act	Australian Securities and Investments Commission Act 2001 (Cth)
ASX	Australian Securities Exchange
CEO	Chief executive officer
CFO	Chief financial officer
Corporations Act	Corporations Act 2001 (Cth)
D&O insurance	Directors' and officers' insurance
ED securities	Enhanced disclosure securities
FCA Act	Federal Court of Australia Act 1976 (Cth)
Financial Services Royal Commission	Royal Commission into Misconduct in the Banking, Superannuation and Financial Services Industry
FMA Act	Financial Management and Accountability Act 1997 (Cth)
IOSCO	International Organization of Securities Commissions
MIS	Managed investment scheme
PGPA Act	Public Governance, Performance and Accountability Act 2013 (Cth)
SEC	United States Securities and Exchange Commission
Trade Practices Act	Trade Practices Act 1974 (Cth)
VLRC	Victorian Law Reform Commission

TABLE OF CASES

1

Introduction

I. Research Questions

The proper functioning of financial markets, with spillover effects on the economy and a population's wellbeing, is a matter of significant concern. Australia's continuous disclosure regime has been identified as 'critical to protecting shareholders, promoting market integrity and maintaining the good reputation of Australia's financial markets ($1.84 trillion market capitalisation with an average turnover of $5.9 billion a day)' with the result that there is 'increased investor participation and investment, higher liquidity, and lower transaction costs'.[1] Central to the proper functioning of the continuous disclosure regime is the manner in which it is enforced.[2]

Australia has traditionally relied on a public regulator, the Australian Securities and Investments Commission (ASIC), to enforce its securities laws,[3] and since 1994, the enforcement of its continuous disclosure regime which has been regulated by the Corporations Act 2001 (Cth) ('Corporations Act') and its predecessor, the Corporations Law. However, shareholder class actions whereby private litigants pursue claims for contravention of the securities laws, including the continuous disclosure regime, have become a growing phenomenon in the Australian legal landscape since around 2002–03.[4] The advent of the shareholder class action, driven in part by litigation funding, has given rise to overlapping enforcement of the continuous disclosure laws by the public regulator and private citizens.[5]

Because the continuous disclosure regime is subject to both public and private enforcement, there is a pressing need to understand the ramifications of both ASIC and the class action operating in the same regulatory field. The above developments have motivated four main questions for examination in this text.

[1] Australian Securities and Investments Commission (ASIC), Submission No 72 to Australian Law Reform Commission, 'Inquiry into class action proceedings and third-party litigation funders' (September 2018) [4]–[5].

[2] International Organization of Securities Commissions (IOSCO), 'Methodology For Assessing Implementation of the IOSCO Objectives and Principles of Securities Regulation' (May 2017) 69–70 (recommending that a regulator should have 'comprehensive enforcement powers' to give effect to the securities laws but that 'Enforcement powers should not compromise private rights of action').

[3] See Robert Austin and Ian Ramsay, *Ford, Austin and Ramsay's Principles of Corporations Law* (LexisNexis Online, 2018) [2.170] (describing the history of corporate and securities regulation in Australia).

[4] Vince Morabito, 'An Empirical Study of Australia's Class Action Regimes – First Report' (December 2009) 22–27 (finding an 'unambiguously clear' increase in the importance of disputes concerning investors and shareholders as class actions); Vince Morabito, 'An Empirical Study of Australia's Class Action Regimes – Fifth Report' (July 2017) 27–29 (finding that shareholder class actions were the second most common type of class action in the 25 years since class actions came into existence. There were 81 shareholder class actions in total, of which 11 (5.1%) were filed in the first half of the period and 70 (23.4%) were filed in the second half of the period, and in the last five years of the period 43 shareholder class actions had been filed, making them the most common claim).

[5] Michael Legg, 'Public and Private Enforcement: ASIC and the Shareholder Class Action' in Michael Legg, *Regulation, Litigation and Enforcement* (Thomson Reuters, 2011) 151; Michelle Welsh and Vince Morabito, 'Public v Private Enforcement of Securities Laws: An Australian Empirical Study' (2014) 14 *Journal of Corporate Law Studies* 39.

The first question is to inquire as to the effectiveness of ASIC enforcement and the shareholder class action in achieving deterrence and compensation in relation to a particular category of Australia's securities law: the continuous disclosure regime. Effectiveness seeks to ascertain if a desired state of affairs is achieved. As the thesis is interested in the coexistence of ASIC enforcement and the class action, the approach to effectiveness is comparative rather than absolute. Put another way, the question is: 'Is ASIC enforcement more or less effective at achieving deterrence and compensation than the shareholder class action?' The focus on deterrence and compensation is chosen because these are the areas where ASIC and the class action overlap. The overlap is derived from an examination of the objectives of ASIC and the role of the class action, discussed in chapter two, that puts forward deterrence and compensation for both. As will be explained, the emphasis varies between ASIC and the class action.

The second question asks what the ramifications are of ASIC enforcement and class actions coexisting in relation to the continuous disclosure regime from the perspective of regulatory process and the values of a 'good' regulatory process. The consideration of the regulatory process is necessary to determine if desirable regulatory values or norms are complied with or promoted by ASIC enforcement and the class action. Moreover, consideration is given to how action by ASIC and the class action may impact each other; that is, whether they help or hinder each other.

In summary, the first question focuses on outcomes and the effectiveness of ASIC enforcement and the class action in achieving deterrence and compensation. The second question focuses on process and process values.

The answers to these questions are addressed in chapters five and six after the development of an analytical framework in chapter three and the creation of case studies in chapter four The case studies and associated analysis is based on the state of the law as at 31 December 2017. The text presents a multi-dimensional understanding of deterrence, compensation and regulatory process; these are explored through the detail and nuance of the in-depth case studies, including interviews with participants. The text does not seek to give a single answer to each of the research questions, but rather to produce a sophisticated account of the various factors that interact and mediate both outcomes and processes, so as to demonstrate that any answer is complex and contingent on a number of influences and circumstances.

The third question is whether changes in policy settings and legal requirements can encourage or discourage public and private enforcement, and consequently impact the effectiveness of public and private enforcement in achieving deterrence and compensation. This is a re-examination of the first question through the lens of actual policy changes in Australia post-31 December 2017, including changes to ASIC's resourcing and enforcement approach, regulation of litigation funding and changes to the requirements for there to be a contravention of the substantive law. This analysis, including drawing on further empirical examination of the enforcement undertaken by ASIC and class action activity, is set out in chapter seven.

The fourth question asks how the coexistence of public and private enforcement may be more effectively addressed through some form of coordination. Having identified that ASIC and the class action may impact each other, and the achievement of desirable regulatory values, the text draws on a range of coordination mechanisms from other regulatory regimes to design strategies for coordination.

II. Structure of the Text

A. Background (Chapter Two)

Chapter two provides the background to the relevant substantive law, namely the continuous disclosure regime and the related prohibition on misleading conduct, with an emphasis on the enforcement options or causes of action that the legislature has created. Significantly, both ASIC and the private citizen have standing to pursue actions which allows for overlapping enforcement. This chapter also explains the operation and function of ASIC and the shareholder class action. The literature on the objectives of ASIC and the role of the class action identifies deterrence and compensation as being outcomes that both may achieve. Consequently, ASIC enforcement and the class action can overlap in relation to deterrence and compensation.

B. Analytical Framework (Chapter Three)

Chapter three develops the analytical framework which is applied throughout the text, and in particular to the case studies in chapters five and six. The first part of the framework critically unpacks the literature on deterrence and compensation, including the definition and dimensions of each. It also includes a discussion of the conditions for effectiveness and limitations. This multi-faceted perspective on deterrence and compensation allows for an in-depth analysis of both. The second part of the framework draws on regulatory theory to develop the process values or norms that inhere in a 'good' regulatory process. The values identified are: legislative authority; the public interest; accountability; and efficiency. The values provide criteria for evaluating the operation of ASIC action and the shareholder class action, both separately and in relation to each other.

C. Case Studies (Chapter Four)

The thesis employs four case studies. Chapter four explains the case study approach and its use of interviews and document analysis. The choice of case studies is also explained. Chapter four explains the background facts, ASIC enforcement action and class action outcomes for each case study. The case studies are then summarised in Tables 4.3, 4.4 and 4.5 for ease of reference. An overview of each case study examined by the thesis is set out below.

D. Application of the Analytical Framework (Chapter Five)

This chapter then examines the case studies through the lens of the analytical framework: deterrence and compensation; and the regulatory process. The application of the analytical framework involves drawing on the detailed interviews and documentary analysis undertaken for each case study as the primary source of information for evaluating the elements of the framework.

E. Effectiveness and Coexistence of Regulatory Enforcement and Class Actions (Chapter Six)

Chapter six draws together the analytical framework from chapter three and its application to the case studies in chapter five, to answer the first two questions posed for examination in this chapter. The findings are situated within the broader context of all of the publicly reported actions taken by ASIC and by shareholders through the class action in relation to continuous disclosure as at 31 December 2017. The key findings are set out below in section V and summarised in chapter 6, Tables 6.2 and 6.3.

F. Public and Private Enforcement Recalibrated (Chapter Seven)

The extended time period covered by the text provides the opportunity to examine if and how changes to policy settings and legal requirements alter the operation of public and private enforcement. Chapter seven chronicles a range of changes that took place in relation to both ASIC enforcement and class actions from 2018 to 2021 which altered, or provided incentives to alter, the effectiveness of ASIC enforcement and class actions in achieving deterrence and compensation and the ramifications of coexistence.

G. Coordination of Public and Private Enforcement (Chapter Eight)

The logical next step from the coexistence of public and private enforcement and their impact on the regulatory process, and each other, is to consider if they can be more effective through some form of coordination. This chapter examines the existing mechanisms for coordinating enforcement in Australia, which are largely court procedures, and coordination mechanisms from four regulatory regimes in the United States.

The chapter then develops two potential coordination strategies for the public and private enforcement of securities regulation generally, and the continuous disclosure regime specifically.

III. Scope of Study and Text

The focus of the research set out in this text is an investigation of public and private enforcement in a single area of Australian securities law: the continuous disclosure regime. This is a considered choice. Examinations of public and private enforcement in other areas of regulation have warned against the 'abstract speculation on the functioning or desirability of [private enforcement]'.[6] This is because:

> [T]he desirability of authorizing private actions involves difficult policy judgments and is likely to depend on a number of context-specific factors. Making such determinations therefore requires familiarity with the nature of the particular policy problem, the substantive goals of the regulatory scheme, and the likely interaction of private lawsuits with other elements of the government's enforcement strategy.[7]

The regulatory regime creates specific incentives and requirements for the regulator and the class action's proponents. This includes the available enforcement tools, the elements of causes of action and the possible outcomes, such as levels of penalties and available compensation, that may follow. These are important to understanding the 'how' and 'why' embedded in the research questions.

As this study is interested in the overlapping enforcement of the continuous disclosure laws, the text focuses on those areas where ASIC enforcement and the class action intersect, namely deterrence and compensation. While ASIC has additional objectives to deterrence and

[6] Barry Boyer and Errol Meidinger, 'Privatizing Regulatory Enforcement: A Preliminary Assessment of Citizen Suits Under Federal Environmental Laws' (1985) 34 *Buffalo Law Review* 833, 964.

[7] Matthew Stephenson, 'Public Regulation or Private Enforcement: The Case for Expanding the Role of Administrative Agencies' (2005) 91 *Virginia Law Review* 93, 106. See also Stephen Burbank, Sean Farhang and Herbert Kritzer, 'Private Enforcement' (2013) 17 *Lewis & Clark Law Review* 637, 640.

compensation, which are identified in chapter two, the text does not develop an analytical framework in relation to those other objectives. The analytical framework draws on a wide array of literature, including a heavy reliance on literature from the United States where the study of the interaction of public and private enforcement is highly developed due to the longstanding existence of the class action. However, the text does not compare jurisdictions, but focuses solely on the Australian continuous disclosure regime. Nonetheless, the arguments and findings made in the text can be extrapolated, or contested, by the reader in relation to other regulatory regimes with which they are familiar.

For the case studies, the population of interest was comprised of entities that had been subject to both ASIC enforcement activity and a class action where the underlying factual matrix included allegations of non-compliance with the continuous disclosure regime. Moreover, as the focus of the research questions is a comparison of ASIC enforcement and the class action, the text does not consider actions brought by the Australian Securities Exchange or individual shareholder actions.

The scope of the case studies and associated analysis is delimited by time in two respects. First, the choice of case studies needed to occur prior to an ethics approval application for the conduct of interviews. As a result, the case studies could only be chosen from a field of ASIC enforcement and class actions that had been completed prior to 17 September 2015 when the ethics application was lodged.[8] This is explained in chapter four. Second, to enable analysis of the case study findings in the broader context of all of the publicly reported actions taken by ASIC and class actions in relation to continuous disclosure, an end date of 31 December 2017 was chosen for identifying publicly reported actions. However, the text takes account of later developments relevant to the conclusions reached through chapter seven, which examines subsequent changes to policy settings and legal requirements, including changes to ASIC's enforcement approach, funding and available penalties. Chapter seven also incorporates all publicly reported actions taken by ASIC and class actions in relation to continuous disclosure up to 30 June 2021.

IV. Case Studies

Case studies are employed to understand complex social phenomena or processes, including why or how something occurs. In the current text the phenomena under study is enforcement of the continuous disclosure regime and how that occurs when both ASIC action and class actions are operating, and with what results or effects. The case studies, including interviews with the main participants, are central to the original insights that the text contributes to knowledge.

Four case studies were chosen for examination: Telstra; Multiplex; Centro; and Leighton. The detailed explanation for the choice is set out in chapter four. In short, they involved overlapping ASIC enforcement action and class action activity. They also provided a diversity of ASIC enforcement action and class action outcomes.

Telstra Corporation Limited was Australia's largest telecommunications provider which, at a time when it was still part owned by government but also publicly listed, was alleged to have

[8] Application for Human Research Ethics Approval No 1545406.1 (17 September 2015). Ethics approval was granted on 9 October 2015.

made selective briefings and inaccurate profit downgrades. Telstra received a warning from ASIC in relation to potential contraventions of the continuous disclosure regime. The alleged breach also led to one of the earliest class actions which ultimately settled for $5 million.

Multiplex Limited was a construction company that was alleged to have failed to inform the market of profit downgrades due to losses on the construction of the Wembley Stadium. ASIC secured an enforceable undertaking which included a compensation fund of $32 million. Two class actions pursued damages for the share price fall associated with alleged late disclosure of losses from three construction projects, including Wembley Stadium. A settlement for $110 million followed.

Centro Properties Group was involved in retail property and funds management. It suffered a spectacular share price fall during the global financial crisis. Three shareholder class actions were commenced for contravention of the continuous disclosure regime. These were stayed while ASIC brought civil penalty proceedings against the company directors and officers for breach of directors' duties. ASIC was successful at trial. The class actions subsequently settled for $200 million, the largest shareholder class action settlement in Australian history.

Leighton Holdings Limited was a construction, mining and engineering company. Leighton reported an unexpected loss due to profit downgrades on three projects. ASIC and Leighton entered into an enforceable undertaking and Leighton also paid three $100,000 infringement notices, one for each project, in relation to allegations of continuous disclosure violations. A subsequent continuous disclosure class action resulted in a $69.45 million settlement.

The case studies of these four entities form the basis of the empirical work undertaken for the text and are analysed in chapter five.

V. Key Findings

This text develops novel findings in two main ways. The first is through the development of an analytical framework in chapter three. The analytical framework deconstructs the concepts of deterrence and compensation so as to elucidate the elements of each that need to be examined to determine whether and how they are attained. The analytical framework also develops a number of regulatory norms or values that allows for the evaluation of the regulatory process that results from the coexistence of ASIC enforcement and class actions.

Deterrence is broken down into a number of dimensions: formal sanctions; indirect costs; reputational harm; as well as specific and general deterrence. The factors that impact the effectiveness of deterrence are elucidated. Traditional elements such as certainty, severity and celerity are explained, as well as the theories of perceptual deterrence and optimal deterrence, and practical considerations such as who is the object of deterrence and the need to avoid the dispersion of deterrence. The limitations of deterrence are also explored. Likewise, the analysis of compensation goes beyond the headline figure and explains the need to compare recoveries with losses, factoring in the effect of settlement, incomplete recovery, transaction costs and consideration of the circularity problem.

The analytical framework also focuses on regulatory process values or norms through four perspectives: legislative authority; the public interest; accountability; and efficiency. This framework allows for an assessment of how ASIC enforcement and the class action each function and whether the process is consistent with the values that are equated with a legitimate regulatory process. The framework also provides a means by which to examine how actions by ASIC and the class action, public and private enforcement, impact on each other.

The second way in which the text adds to knowledge is through the use of in-depth, detailed case studies in chapters four and five, in particular through the interviews with participants, which have not previously been undertaken.[9] The text draws upon the observations and experiences of the regulator, the lawyers and a funder for the class action, and the lawyers and corporate officers for the defendants.[10] Interviews with the key participants in each case study allowed for both access to information beyond the public record, but also for investigating and testing of the intricacies of that information.

The combination of the analytical framework and the use of case studies allows for a better understanding and analysis of the multiple factors at play in relation to deterrence, compensation and the functioning of the regulatory process. This study disentangles the multiple causes and mediating factors that result in ASIC enforcement and the class action being successful or not in relation to deterrence and compensation, and in fostering a legitimate regulatory process, including helping or hindering each other.

A. Outcomes – Deterrence and Compensation

Deterrence is a key objective for ASIC. The text finds that ASIC seeks to achieve deterrence through impacting reputation and using direct sanctions. However, the analysis of the enforcement tools used by ASIC in the continuous disclosure area prior to 31 December 2017 demonstrates that ASIC relied heavily on administrative enforcement tools (infringement notices, disallowing the use of a reduced content prospectus and enforceable undertakings) rather than the litigation tools of civil penalty and criminal proceedings as set out in chapter six, Table 6.1.

ASIC's objective does not appear to align with its actual conduct in terms of the choice of enforcement tools. Indeed, the text finds that choice of enforcement tools was crucial to whether and how deterrence could be achieved. The case studies find that ASIC is able to be effective in achieving deterrence through reputational sanctions because it is an independent statutory body that is accountable to the Australian Parliament. However, the extent of the impact on reputation appears to vary depending on the enforcement tool employed and the outcome achieved. Tools that have no finding of wrongdoing, such as the much-used administrative tools, seem to have less impact than those that do, namely the litigation tools. But administrative tools are not completely without impact because reputation is important to corporations and individuals, and ASIC, as an independent, accountable body, is able to communicate its findings and concerns to the market in an authoritative manner.

The text also finds that ASIC's achievement of deterrence through direct sanctions, such as fines, civil penalties and criminal penalties, was seen as less effective than that of the class action. This was because ASIC rarely used the litigation tools which could result in the imposition of criminal and civil penalties. In classical deterrence terms, ASIC appears to have preferred detection of a contravention and timely imposition of sanctions, that is, certainty and celerity, over severity of sanctions.

[9] A number of commentators have addressed the Multiplex case study, but none with the benefit of interviews with the main participants, including those that attended the meeting between ASIC and the corporation where the regulatory tool to be employed was negotiated. See, eg, Welsh and Morabito (n 5); Camille Cameron, 'Litigation as "core business": Analysing the access to justice and regulatory dimensions of commercially funded class actions in Australia' in Deborah Hensler, Christopher Hodges and Ianika Tzankova (eds), *Class Actions in Context* (Edward Elgar, 2016) 189.

[10] The interviews that were undertaken are set out in Appendix 1.

ASIC's choice of enforcement tools to achieve the deterrence objective necessitated consideration as to how this approach arises. The conclusion reached is that ASIC's approach to deterrence is subject to a number of self-imposed and external constraints that influence how ASIC operationalises its objective.

In the continuous disclosure area, ASIC places significant importance on achieving deterrence to ensure market integrity. As chapter two explains, continuous disclosure is designed to ensure that price-sensitive information is made public so that the market is informed. When ASIC detects conduct that is antithetical to prompt disclosure of price-sensitive information it has determined that it needs to act quickly. The focus on a swift response is to inform the particular entity, but also other participants in the market, that it regards the conduct as contrary to the law. This approach is supported by using enforcement tools that can be promptly applied, which supports the use of administrative remedies. Litigation-based enforcement tools by their nature involve greater delay.

ASIC must also operate with the regulatory resources at its disposal so that the cost of regulatory tools also plays a role. Administrative tools at the bottom of the enforcement pyramid are cheap, compared to the cost of higher order tools involving hard fought, adversarial litigation with its various procedural protections for defendants. ASIC's achievement of deterrence through the use of litigation-based enforcement tools may also be hampered by low penalties.

The text also finds that the continuous disclosure regime is structured so as to make the use of higher order sanctions against individuals difficult due to additional elements that must be proved compared to proceedings against the corporation. Accordingly, individuals are not typically targeted for enforcement action despite recognition that the threat of personal liability, especially criminal sanctions, can achieve effective deterrence. In addition, civil penalty and compensation claims against directors may be alleviated through directors' and officers' (D&O) insurance so that the director does not feel the financial cost directly.

Turning to compensation, the text found that ASIC rarely seeks compensation. ASIC appears to give this goal lower importance in relation to continuous disclosure for two main reasons: first, the focus on market integrity discussed above; and second, the presence of the class action. ASIC places greater importance on achieving market integrity through deterrence than obtaining compensation, and shareholders have a route to compensation through the class action. However, in relation to the latter, class actions may not always be commenced, especially if the claim is uneconomic for a litigation funder to finance.

The main goal of the proponents of class actions is to pursue compensation which often results in large monetary payments. Class action litigation can achieve access to justice that would not otherwise be possible, including because ASIC makes compensation a low priority. However, the headline compensation payment obscures the true outcome which needs to factor in that the compensation recovered is rarely equivalent to the losses suffered and there are significant deductions for legal fees and litigation funding fees. Class actions have also been subject to criticism due to the circularity problem, which 'in shorthand' is shareholders paying themselves compensation. The criticism is a concern at a theoretical level, but the text finds that the extent of its application in practice is difficult to ascertain, and it can be avoided through the participation of non-diversified shareholders in the class action and by the inclusion of claims that go beyond the corporation to include directors and advisers. However, the proponents of a class action may have little incentive to pursue directors as they can access their D&O insurance through pursuing the company, as the coverage from the insurance policy responds to securities claims against both directors and the company. Compensation is a worthy goal, as established by both the objective of the legislation and corrective justice, but in practice the person may not receive full compensation.

A further finding is that class actions, in contrast to actions by ASIC, typically impose significant financial sanctions on defendants through the effect of compensation payments. Class actions also impose significant indirect costs through the use of civil litigation. From a deterrence perspective it does not matter where the money extracted from a defendant – compensation or costs – goes, only that the defendant pays it. D&O insurance can relieve the defendant from paying some or all of a compensation payment. In financial terms, the class action imposes greater sanctions and therefore deterrence than enforcement actions by ASIC, subject to the effect of insurance. However, the class action is a blunter tool than ASIC enforcement, as the class action only has costs to impose. Further, as the class action's real goal is to maximise compensation, it has little concern in trying to calibrate the deterrence achieved with the seriousness of the wrong committed. The private nature and financial incentives embedded in class actions, as well as the focus on settlement, may undermine deterrence through impact on reputation compared to ASIC action.

B. Regulatory Process

The text concludes that the coexistence of ASIC enforcement and the class action complicates the regulatory landscape and offers both benefits and detriments, including in relation to their impact on each other.

The benefits are greater resources for enforcement, multiple viewpoints on desirable responses to contraventions, and an additional or replacement source of deterrence and compensation. The detriments are largely for the regulator, who loses its dominant position, its ability to define the public interest, its exercise of discretion, including being able to deploy enforcement tools consistent with responsive regulation, and its development of a consistent regulatory framework.

These advantages and disadvantages also illustrate the societal calculus that government and the legislature have made, perhaps without expressly knowing that they were. The shareholder class action was borne from a combination of the grant of standing to shareholders to pursue their losses from a contravention of the continuous disclosure regime, enactment of a class action procedure and the advent of litigation funding. Private citizens were given the means, albeit at considerable cost, to take action to pursue compensation and, indirectly, deterrence. The state is relieved, to some degree, from the provision of what was previously a public good – enforcement – especially in relation to obtaining compensation, and instead a user-pays principle applies. However, societal consumption of resources to obtain compensation may actually be higher due to the cost of lawyers in private practice and litigation funding. Enforcement also has an entrepreneurial element with class action lawyers and litigation funders, although primarily concerned with access to compensation for group members, also determining what cases are brought and where duplication may occur with ASIC actions, based on their own financial imperatives. In summary, the shareholder class action may advance or harm the public interest, depending on the particular circumstances in which it is brought.

The regulatory process is no longer a straight line between regulator identification of contraventions and the choice of a suitable enforcement tool based on the regulator's objectives and interactions with the regulated entity. Regulation of continuous disclosure is now a triangle of interactions between the regulator, the regulated entity and the proponents of the class action. Each is trying to take account of, or pre-empt, what another may do. Although ASIC's enforcement approach appears to be affected to a greater extent by the class action than the proponents of class actions are affected by ASIC and its enforcement strategy.

The ramifications of coexistence may have received scant consideration when class actions were enacted; however, in light of the findings in the text it is necessary to take a more considered and structured approach to factoring coexistence into the operation of the regulatory process for the enforcement of the continuous disclosure regime.

C. Public and Private Enforcement Recalibrated

Subsequent to 31 December 2017 some of the policy settings and legal requirements that formed part of the background to the above findings changed. In particular, ASIC's enforcement was invigorated through a new 'Why not litigate?' approach, the adoption of an industry funding model and increased powers and penalties. In the case of litigation funding, the previous light-touch regulatory approach was replaced with more stringent regulation. At around the same time the State of Victoria enacted 'group costs orders' which permitted lawyers to receive a percentage of the class action group's recovery. The continuous disclosure laws that were the basis for both ASIC action and class actions were also subject to reform with an intention or fault requirement added.

Through analysing the number and type of ASIC enforcement actions the text found public enforcement, especially through civil penalty proceedings, had been promoted. If the public regulator is more active, more likely to utilise litigation and is able to seek higher penalties then it may more effectively achieve deterrence, both through direct sanctions and impact on reputation. However, this needs to be balanced with ASIC's concern for timely correction of inadequate disclosure to protect market integrity. There was no change in ASIC's preparedness to seek compensation. The analysis of reforms also points to an attempt to discourage class actions, albeit through indirect measures, to make them less profitable such as through increased regulation of litigation funding. However, no clear empirical picture arose, especially as the group costs order reform may encourage class actions. It was clear though that the class action remains central to, and more effective than ASIC at, seeking compensation.

Existence of these reforms and their impacts is of significance because it illustrates that the mix of public and private enforcement is not fixed but rather can be altered based on the settings of a range of policy levers and legal developments.

D. Coordination of Public and Private Enforcement

To address the coexistence of public and private enforcements impact of the regulatory process and each other the text puts forward two potential coordination strategies. They are an information-sharing approach and a regulator as gatekeeper approach.

The information-sharing approach requires a person who is proposing to commence a class action to notify ASIC of that intention and to provide specified information. ASIC is then able to use that information to assist in determining the enforcement action it will take. ASIC can take account of the class action in relation to the availability of compensation and the associated indirect deterrence that may follow. This approach does not restrict the commencement of a class action or subject it to conditions so that this strategy does not address the detrimental effects on the regulatory process, such as the class action's impact on regulatory discretion.

The gatekeeper approach provides ASIC with the authority to determine if a class action may be commenced. ASIC performs the role of enforcement coordinator and needs to determine the combination of enforcement tools that should be employed, including potentially permitting a class action, to achieve both deterrence and compensation. This approach addresses the negative impacts of the class action on the regulatory process. However, such an approach creates a risk that additional and different viewpoints as to what the public interest requires in relation to how enforcement should be configured may be lost.

The coexistence of ASIC enforcement action and class actions has ramifications for deterrence, compensation and regulation that can be addressed through the coordination approaches put forward in the text. However, each approach brings with it its own advantages and disadvantages that may be ameliorated or accentuated depending on their actual implementation.

VI. Conclusion

The aim of this text is to examine public and private enforcement of securities law through a comparison and critique of ASIC enforcement and shareholder class actions in relation to the continuous disclosure regime using a case study methodology. This chapter has set out the research questions that will be examined.

The next chapter provides the necessary background for this text. Chapter two reviews the substantive law on continuous disclosure regime and the related prohibition on misleading or deceptive conduct. It also explains the function and operation of ASIC and class actions. Chapter two demonstrates that the literature has identified ASIC enforcement and shareholder class actions as achieving, or being able to achieve, compensation and deterrence. ASIC and the shareholder class action, therefore, may overlap or intersect in relation to the enforcement of the continuous disclosure regime.

Chapter three then develops the analytical framework that was outlined above. Chapter four addresses the case study methodology adopted in the text. Chapter five applies the analytical framework to the case studies. Chapter six answers the first and second questions posed in this chapter by drawing on the findings from chapter five and situating the analysis in the broader context of all of the publicly reported actions taken by ASIC and through the class action in relation to continuous disclosure as at 31 December 2017.

Chapter seven discusses a range of changes that took place in relation to both ASIC enforcement and class actions from 2018 to 2021 to demonstrate how the settings of a range of policy levers and legal developments can promote or dissuade public and private enforcement, and in turn the effectiveness of each. Chapter eight examines the idea of improving public and private enforcement through coordination.

2

Background

I. Introduction

This chapter performs three important background roles. First, it sets out the necessary context for understanding how the public and private enforcement of the continuous disclosure regime has arisen in Australia. To that end this chapter reviews the substantive law on continuous disclosure, with an emphasis on the enforcement options or causes of action that the legislature has created. Significantly, both ASIC and the private citizen have standing to pursue actions. This chapter also explains the related prohibition on misleading conduct which augments the continuous disclosure regime by prohibiting disclosures to shareholders that could undermine the goals of the continuous disclosure regime. The misleading conduct prohibition may be enforced by both ASIC and the private citizen.

Second, the chapter focuses on ASIC's approach to enforcement and the enforcement options it employs in relation to the continuous disclosure regime. The aim here is to explain ASIC's objectives and how the enforcement options are used to achieve those objectives.

Third, the chapter discusses private enforcement through the class action. This part of the chapter seeks to outline why shareholder class actions were adopted while at the same time explaining the operation and role of the shareholder class action. Consequently, the chapter proceeds by explaining the role of the class action, summarising the resulting legislative regime that governs class actions in Australia, and introducing litigation funding.

The chapter sets out the law, ASIC's approach to enforcement and the class actions procedure as at 31 December 2017, although subsequent developments elucidating each are drawn on. This approach is taken because this was the context in which the case studies developed in chapter four occurred. Changes to policy settings and legal requirements discussed in this chapter that occurred after this date are addressed in chapter seven.

II. Continuous Disclosure

A. Background

Continuous disclosure requires relevant regulated entities to promptly disclose material information as it arises, that is, on a continuing basis. It is usually contrasted with periodic disclosure which requires relevant regulated entities to disclose at fixed intervals, such as annually, semi-annually or quarterly.[1]

[1] Greg Golding and Natalie Kalfus, 'The Continuous Evolution of Australia's Continuous Disclosure Laws' (2004) 22 *Company and Securities Law Journal* 385, 385; Elizabeth Boros, 'Public and Private Enforcement of Disclosure Breaches in Australia' (2009) 9 *Journal of Corporate Law Studies* 409, 410.

The main aim of continuous disclosure is to enhance confident and informed participation by investors in secondary securities markets.[2] Continuous disclosure does this by mandating disclosure of price-sensitive information, subject to certain exceptions discussed below, and by establishing a level playing field where all investors have the same information with which to make investment decisions. As the following demonstrates, the desirability of continuous disclosure and its goals have been elaborated on at both the international and domestic levels.

i. *International Standards*

The International Organization of Securities Commissions (IOSCO)[3] has set out three core objectives of securities regulation:[4]

(1) the protection of investors;
(2) ensuring that markets are fair, efficient and transparent; and
(3) the reduction of systemic risk.

IOSCO's Principle 16 requires 'full, accurate and timely disclosure of financial results, risk and other information which is material to investors' decisions'.[5] IOSCO then explains that Principle 16 'is directly related to the objectives of investor protection and fair, efficient and transparent markets'.[6]

The continuous disclosure regime achieves IOSCO's objectives (1) and (2) directly, and in doing so then facilitates objective (3) because investors have accurate information and confidence in the operation of the market.

IOSCO expands on objective (1) by explaining that investors should be protected from misleading, manipulative or fraudulent practices and that full disclosure of material information to investors is the most important means for ensuring investor protection.[7] This then ties into fair, efficient and transparent markets as IOSCO states that investors should be given fair access to market or price information about a security.[8]

IOSCO also recommends that a regulator should have 'comprehensive enforcement powers' to give effect to the securities laws.[9] This is to both maintain fair and efficient markets but also to protect investors.[10] However, 'Enforcement powers should not compromise private rights of action' and private individuals should be able to seek their own remedies such as compensation.[11]

[2] Companies and Securities Advisory Committee, 'Report on an Enhanced Statutory Disclosure System' (1991) 6–7 ('CSAC Enhanced Disclosure Report'); Corporate Law Economic Reform Program, 'Corporate Disclosure: Strengthening the Financial Reporting Framework' (Paper No 9, 2002) 129 ('CLERP 9'); IOSCO, 'Objectives and Principles of Securities Regulation' (May 2003) 23.

[3] IOSCO is the international body that brings together the world's securities regulators and is recognised as the global standard-setter for the securities sector. IOSCO's membership regulates more than 95% of the world's securities markets. See IOSCO, 'Fact Sheet '(November 2017) 2.

[4] IOSCO, 'Objectives and Principles of Securities Regulation' (May 2017) 3. The IOSCO Objectives and Principles of Securities Regulation have been endorsed by both the G20 and the Financial Stability Board as the relevant standards in this area.

[5] ibid 8.

[6] IOSCO, 'Methodology For Assessing Implementation of the IOSCO Objectives and Principles of Securities Regulation' (May 2017) 104.

[7] ibid 10.

[8] ibid 11.

[9] ibid 69.

[10] ibid 63.

[11] ibid 70.

The global standard-setter for securities regulation recommends a system of regulation that combines investor protection and market integrity, as well as public and private enforcement. The Australian system of securities regulation embraces these recommendations.[12]

ii. Australian Approach

In Australia securities regulation is dealt with by the Corporations Act and the Australian Securities and Investments Commission Act 2001 (Cth) ('ASIC Act'). In Australia, continuous disclosure aims to ensure that market participants act with integrity and provide adequate disclosure. Due to the market providing insufficient incentive to ensure adequate disclosure, it is mandated by law.[13] Regulation is also supported by the need for consumer protection.[14] The Inquiry into Australia's Financial System observed that: 'There are close links and no clear dividing line between consumer protection and market integrity regulation in retail markets since both use the same regulatory tools, namely disclosure and conduct rules'.[15]

Continuous disclosure is also fundamental to investor protection through preventing insider trading and market manipulation.[16] The need to disclose may also discourage questionable corporate conduct where the disclosure regime would require that the conduct be made public.[17] The policy objective of Australia's continuous disclosure regime has been described judicially as:

> [T]o enhance the integrity and efficiency of Australian capital markets by ensuring that the market is fully informed. The timely disclosure of market sensitive information is essential to maintaining and increasing the confidence of investors in Australian markets, and to improving the accountability of company management.[18]

The regulator responsible for securities regulation generally, and continuous disclosure specifically, is ASIC. ASIC is created by the ASIC Act, which also specifies its objectives, functions and powers. ASIC is required to 'promote the confident and informed participation of investors and consumers in the financial system' and has the function of 'monitoring and promoting market integrity and consumer protection in the Australian financial system'.[19] ASIC has acknowledged

[12] See International Monetary Fund, 'Australia: IOSCO Objectives and Principles of Securities Regulation – Detailed Assessment of Implementation', IMF Country Report No 12/314 (November 2012).

[13] Commonwealth of Australia, 'Financial System Inquiry Final Report' (1997) 177, 188 ('FSI Report'); CLERP 9 (n 2) 129 ('The existence of a mandatory continuous disclosure regime recognises that entities will not always have incentives to voluntarily disclose price sensitive information to investors. This is most relevant in relation to information that may have adverse implications for the price of an entity's securities.'); *ASIC v Newcrest Mining Limited* (2014) 101 ACSR 46, 52 [39]–[40] (Middleton J). See also Golding and Kalfus (n 1) 387 (summarising the literature on mandatory disclosure).

[14] FSI Report (n 13) 188.

[15] ibid.

[16] CLERP 9 (n 2) 129; *Grant-Taylor v Babcock & Brown Limited (in liq)* (2016) 245 FCR 402, 418 [92] (Allsop CJ, Gilmour and Beach JJ).

[17] Second Reading Speech, Corporate Law Reform Bill (No 2) 1992 (Cth), 26 November 1992; *ASIC v Chemeq Ltd* (2006) 234 ALR 511, 523 [45] (French J).

[18] *James Hardie Industries NV v ASIC* (2010) 274 ALR 85, 162 [355] (Spigelman CJ, Beazley and Giles JJA). See also *National Australia Bank Ltd v Pathway Investments Pty Ltd* (2012) 265 FLR 247, 260 [61] (Bell AJA); *Grant-Taylor v Babcock & Brown Limited (in liq)* (2016) 245 FCR 402, 418 [92] (Allsop CJ, Gilmour and Beach JJ). The ASX while endorsing the court's statement has observed that it prefers the term 'reasonably informed' rather than 'fully informed'. See ASX, 'ASX Listing Rules Guidance Note 8 – Continuous Disclosure: Listing Rules 3.1–3.1B' (11 May 2018) 6. Guidance Note 8 has been amended on numerous occasions, with versions issued in 11/98, 09/01, 03/02, 01/03, 06/05, 05/13, 01/14, 07/15, 08/15, 12/16, 03/18, 05/18, 08/18, 08/19 and 02/20.

[19] Australian Securities and Investments Commission Act 2001 (Cth), ss 1(2)(b), 12A(2). See also 'ASIC Annual Report 2016–2017' (2017) 14 (describing ASIC as 'promoting investor and consumer trust and confidence' and 'ensuring fair and efficient markets').

that its role as a conduct and disclosure regulator is vital for market integrity and consumer protection.[20]

To understand the structure of the continuous disclosure regime and how ASIC performs its role, it is necessary to review the relevant stock exchange listing rules and provisions in the Corporations Act. After reviewing the substantive legal requirements, the chapter examines how those requirements may be enforced by ASIC and private citizens.

B. Stock Exchange Listing Rules

Historically, continuous disclosure was mandated and enforced by stock exchange listing rules.[21] Generally, the listing rules required the immediate disclosure of any information likely to materially affect the price of a corporation's securities.[22] Failure to comply was policed by the stock exchange which could make inquiries, issue press releases, suspend or delist companies.[23]

The Australian Securities Exchange (ASX) Listing Rules today contain several provisions addressing when listed bodies must make immediate disclosure of information to the market.[24] Listing Rule 3.1 provides:

> Once an entity is or becomes aware of any information concerning it that a reasonable person would expect to have a material effect on the price or value of the entity's securities, the entity must immediately tell ASX that information.

Listing Rule 3.1A sets out a number of exceptions, namely the information is confidential, a reasonable person would not expect the information to be disclosed and one of the following five situations applies: (1) it would be a breach of a law to disclose the information; (2) the information concerns an incomplete proposal or negotiation; (3) the information comprises matters of supposition or is insufficiently definite to warrant disclosure; (4) the information is generated for the internal management purposes of the entity; or (5) the information is a trade secret. However, Listing Rule 3.1B provides that if the ASX considers that a false market in an entity's securities exists, and asks the entity to give it information to correct or prevent a false market, the entity must provide the information.

Guidance on compliance with Listing Rules 3.1 to 3.1B is provided in ASX Guidance Note 8. In the Guidance Note, the ASX recognises that compliance with Listing Rule 3.1 'is critical to the integrity and efficiency of the … market'.[25] The Guidance Note further explains:

> Listing Rules 3.1, 3.1A and 3.1B form an integrated set of rules intended to strike an appropriate balance between the interests of the market in receiving information that will affect the price or value of, or

[20] Letter from Tony D'Aloisio, Chairman, ASIC to Peter Costello, Treasurer, 'ASIC Statement of Intent', 27 June 2007; ASIC, 'Senate' Inquiry into the Performance of the Australian Securities and Investments Commission – Main Submission by ASIC (October 2013) [161]–[164] ('ASIC Senate Inquiry Submission'); ASIC, 'Review of Australian equity market cleanliness – Report 487' (August 2016) [3].

[21] Marina Nehme, Margaret Hyland and Michael Adams, 'Enforcement of Continuous Disclosure: The Use of Infringement Notice and Alternative Sanctions' (2007) 21 *Australian Journal of Corporate Law* 112, 112; Merav Bloch, James Weatherhead and Jon Webster, 'The Development and Enforcement of Australia's Continuous Disclosure Regime' (2011) 29 *Company and Securities Law Journal* 253, 254–55.

[22] CSAC Enhanced Disclosure Report (n 2) 4; House of Representatives Standing Committee on Legal and Constitutional Affairs, Parliament of the Commonwealth of Australia, 'Corporate Practices and the Rights of Shareholders' (1991) 92.

[23] House of Representatives Standing Committee on Legal and Constitutional Affairs (n 22) 30.

[24] ASX Listing Rules 3.1, 3.1A and 3.1B.

[25] ASX (n 18) 4.

> which is needed to correct or prevent a false market in, an entity's securities at the earliest reasonable time, and the interests of the entity in not having to disclose information prematurely or where it would clearly be inappropriate to do so.[26]

The current tools for enforcement by the ASX are largely the same as have existed historically,[27] but the Corporations Act provides for the ASX to be able to institute proceedings to enforce compliance with the rules.[28] The ASX may issue price 'query letters' or 'aware letters'. The former is used where the ASX detects abnormal trading in a listed entity's securities and the entity states that it is not aware of any information not announced which could explain the abnormal trading. The latter is used to ascertain when a listed entity was aware of information to enable a comparison with when the information was disclosed. Usually the letters and the response from the listed entity are made publicly available through the ASX Market Announcements Platform.[29] Consequently they are public documents and may be used in legal proceedings. The ASX may suspend quotation of an entity's securities for non-compliance with the listing rules, or in extreme situations, delist the entity.[30] The ASX must also notify ASIC if the ASX takes disciplinary action against a market participant or suspects a market participant will breach the Corporations Act.[31] The ASX has an obligation to assist ASIC in relation to the performance of ASIC's functions.[32]

C. Corporations Act, Ch 6CA

In 1994, the statutory requirement for continuous disclosure was enacted.[33] The statutory requirements are now in Chapter 6CA of the Corporations Act, which gives the ASX Listing Rules legislative backing.[34] Section 674 of the Corporations Act[35] provides:

> (1) Subsection (2) applies to a listed disclosing entity if provisions of the listing rules of a listing market in relation to that entity require the entity to notify the market operator of information about specified events or matters as they arise for the purpose of the operator making that information available to participants in the market.
>
> (2) If:
>
> (a) this subsection applies to a listed disclosing entity; and
>
> (b) the entity has information that those provisions require the entity to notify to the market operator; and
>
> (c) that information:
>
> (i) is not generally available; and
>
> (ii) is information that a reasonable person would expect, if it were generally available, to have a material effect on the price or value of ED securities of the entity;
>
> the entity must notify the market operator of that information in accordance with those provisions.

[26] ibid 7.

[27] ibid 56–63.

[28] Corporations Act 2001 (Cth), ss 793C, 1101B; Josephine Coffey, 'Enforcement of Continuous Disclosure in the Australian Stock Market' (2007) 20 *Australian Journal of Corporate Law* 301, 313–14. ASIC and a 'person aggrieved' also have standing to approach the court for an order to enforce the listing rules.

[29] ASX (n 18) 57–60.

[30] ASX Listing Rules 17.3.1, 17.3.2 and 17.12; ASX (n 18) 57, 62.

[31] Corporations Act 2001 (Cth), s 792B.

[32] ibid s 792D.

[33] Corporate Law Reform Act 1994 (Cth).

[34] *Jubilee Mines NL v Riley* (2009) 40 WAR 299, 315 [55] (Martin CJ). The background to the creation of the statutory regime is discussed in Golding and Kalfus (n 1) 386–87; Bloch, Weatherhead and Webster (n 21) 255–57.

[35] Corporations Act 2001 (Cth), s 675 is in the same form but applies to other disclosing entities.

As a result, s 674 requires disclosing entities to notify the market operator (ie the ASX) of information required to be disclosed by the Listing Rules where that information is not generally available and is information that a reasonable person would expect, if it were generally available, to have a material effect on the price or value of enhanced disclosure (ED) securities[36] of the entity. When information is generally available is defined in s 676 and the meaning of material effect on price or value of ED securities of the entity is defined in s 677.

Information is generally available when either it 'consists of readily observable matter'[37] or 'it has been made known in a manner that would, or would be likely to, bring it to the attention of persons who commonly invest in securities of a kind whose price or value might be affected by the information' and a reasonable period of time has elapsed.[38] Further, information will be generally available if it 'consists of deductions, conclusions or inferences made or drawn from' either or both of the above sources of information.[39]

A material effect on the price or value of ED securities of a disclosing entity is taken to arise 'if the information would, or would be likely to, influence persons who commonly invest in securities in deciding whether to acquire or dispose of the ED securities'.[40] This definition has been described as analogous to a deeming provision so that information having the characteristics referred to by the definition is taken to be within the scope of s 674(2)(c)(ii).[41] To be material it is insufficient if the information 'may' or 'might' influence a decision as the statute specifically uses 'would' or 'would be likely to'. The Full Federal Court has stated that 'Materiality may also then depend upon a balancing of both the indicated probability that the event will occur and the anticipated magnitude of the event on the company's affairs'.[42]

The expression 'persons who commonly invest in securities' signifies that materiality is determined by reference to a hypothetical class of persons who invest in securities. Large or small, frequent or infrequent, sophisticated or unsophisticated investors are included.[43]

Whether information is 'not generally available' or is material information are questions of fact to be determined on an objective and hypothetical basis.[44] They are not questions to be answered by the subjective belief of the company or by reference to actual share price movements once disclosure occurs. However, such evidence may be relevant to answering the objective, hypothetical question.[45]

[36] ED securities are defined in Corporations Act 2001 (Cth), s 111AD. Where all or any ED securities of the entity are quoted ED securities, ie the entity is included on the official list of a prescribed financial market and the markets listing rules apply to the entity, then the entity is a listed disclosing entity: ss 111AE, 111AL(1). Section 674 applies to a listed disclosing entity subject to a market's continuous disclosure listing rules. Other disclosing entities are unlisted disclosing entities: s 111AL(2). Section 675 applies to unlisted disclosing entities and a listed disclosing entity that is not subject to a market's continuous disclosure listing rules. See generally *Grant-Taylor v Babcock & Brown Limited (in liq)* (2016) 245 FCR 402, 412 [50] (Allsop CJ, Gilmour and Beach JJ).

[37] *National Australia Bank Ltd v Pathway Investments Pty Ltd* (2012) 265 FLR 247, 261 [65] (Bell AJA) citing *ASIC v Citicorp Global Markets Australia Pty Ltd (No 4)* (2007) 160 FCR 35, 107 [551] (Jacobson J) (readily observable matter means 'not whether the particular matter was widely observed but whether it could have been'); *Grant-Taylor v Babcock & Brown Limited (in liq)* (2016) 245 FCR 402, 424 [119] (Allsop CJ, Gilmour and Beach JJ).

[38] Corporations Act 2001 (Cth), s 676(2). See also Robert Austin and Ian Ramsay, *Ford, Austin and Ramsay's Principles of Corporations Law* (LexisNexis Online, 2018) [11.310.3].

[39] Corporations Act 2001 (Cth), s 676(3).

[40] ibid s 677.

[41] *National Australia Bank Ltd v Pathway Investments Pty Ltd* (2012) 265 FLR 247, 262 [68] (Bell AJA) citing *Jubilee Mines NL v Riley* (2009) 40 WAR 299, 316 [57]–[58] (Martin CJ).

[42] *Grant-Taylor v Babcock & Brown Limited (in liq)* (2016) 245 FCR 402, 420 [96] (Allsop CJ, Gilmour and Beach JJ).

[43] ibid 423 [115]–[116], 426 [131]. When the expression is used in s 676 it is read more narrowly than in s 677 due to the addition of the words 'of a kind'.

[44] *National Australia Bank Ltd v Pathway Investments Pty Ltd* (2012) 265 FLR 247, 267 [87] (Bell AJA); *Grant-Taylor v Babcock & Brown Limited (in liq)* (2016) 245 FCR 402, 423 [117], 424 [119] (Allsop CJ, Gilmour and Beach JJ).

[45] *National Australia Bank Ltd v Pathway Investments Pty Ltd* (2012) 265 FLR 247, 267 [88] (Bell AJA).

Section 675 imposes the requirements for continuous disclosure in the Corporations Act on disclosing entities not subject to s 674, ie where no stock exchange listing rules for continuous disclosure apply to the disclosing entity. Rather than requiring the information to be disclosed to the stock exchange, it must be disclosed to ASIC. Sections 674(2A) and 675(2A) extend liability to any person involved in the entity's contravention. However, a due diligence defence is available.[46]

As the focus of the text is on public and private enforcement, this chapter now outlines the enforcement action or tools available to ASIC and to private persons.

D. Public Enforcement

An entity that does not disclose accurately and when required may be subject to enforcement action by ASIC. The following sets out the enforcement options available to ASIC for a contravention of the continuous disclosure regime: criminal offence, civil penalty, administrative penalty through infringement notices, injunctions, compensation and other remedial orders. These are discussed in turn below.

i. Criminal Offence

A contravention of Chapter 6CA can give rise to criminal liability for the listed disclosing entity pursuant to s 1311 of the Corporations Act. The applicable penalties are set out in Schedule 3 to the Corporations Act, which for a contravention of s 674(2) were 200 penalty units[47] and/or five years' imprisonment (as at 31 December 2017). Section 1312 of the Corporations Act provides for a court to be able to impose on a body corporate a penalty of five times the maximum amount specified in Schedule 3. Section 678 of the Corporations Act states that the general principles of criminal liability under Chapter 2 of the Criminal Code[48] apply to an offence based on s 674(2). Because s 674(2) does not specify a fault element, the default fault element applies. Where the physical element of an offence is 'conduct', the default fault element is 'intention'. Where the physical element of an offence is 'circumstances' or 'results', the default fault element is 'recklessness'. Which physical element applies is currently unclear, meaning that the standard of fault is also unclear.[49] However, as a criminal offence, some element of fault is clearly required. Directors, officers and advisers may also be criminally liable if they aid, abet, counsel or procure the disclosing entity's contravention.[50]

[46] Corporations Act 2001 (Cth), ss 674(2B) and 675(2B). Contravention of these provisions does not give rise to any criminal offence because s 1311(1A) says that in Ch 6CA there is an offence only if a penalty is prescribed by Sch 3, and there is no penalty in Sch 3 for contravention of s 674(2A).

[47] A penalty unit is used to specify fines so that numerous amendments to multiple sections in multiple pieces of legislation are avoided. Instead the value of a penalty unit is specified in the Crimes Act 1914 (Cth). The amount of a penalty unit as at 1 July 2017 was $210. The amount of a penalty unit is increased by an indexation factor every three years. See Crimes Act 1914 (Cth), s 4AA; Crimes Legislation Amendment (Penalty Unit) Act 2017 (Cth).

[48] The Criminal Code is a schedule to the Criminal Code Act 1995 (Cth). Ch 2 of the Code introduced mandatory statutory concepts of physical elements and fault elements to replace the common law concepts of *actus reus* and *mens rea*: *ASIC v Whitebox Trading Pty Ltd* (2017) 251 FCR 448, 465 [61] (Allsop CJ, Middleton and Bromwich JJ).

[49] Golding and Kalfus (n 1) 394; Bloch, Weatherhead and Webster (n 21) 265–66.

[50] Accessorial liability arises from the Criminal Code s 11.2, not Corporations Act 2001 (Cth), ss 674(2A), 675(2A). See Austin and Ramsay (n 38) [11.320.3], [11.323.6].

ii. Civil Penalties

The substantive sections of Chapter 6CA, namely ss 674(2), (2A), 675(2), (2A), are also financial services civil penalty provisions.[51] Only ASIC may apply to the court for a declaration of contravention of one of the substantive sections of Chapter 6CA.[52] Since the Financial Services Reform Act 2001 (Cth), which took effect from 11 March 2002, unlike criminal offences, it is not necessary to prove intent or fault as a prerequisite to establishing a contravention.[53] ASIC alone may also apply for a pecuniary penalty order.[54] Where the court has made a declaration of contravention, it may order the payment of a pecuniary penalty of $200,000 for an individual and $1 million for a corporation (as at 31 December 2017) if the contravention:

- materially prejudices the interests of acquirers or disposers of the relevant financial products; or
- materially prejudices the issuer of the relevant financial products or, if the issuer is a corporation or scheme, the members of that corporation or scheme; or
- is serious.[55]

The proceedings for a declaration of contravention and civil penalty orders are treated as civil proceedings for the purposes of the application of the rules of evidence and procedure. The standard of proof is proof on the balance of probabilities, established to the *Briginshaw* standard. This means that the strength of the evidence necessary to meet the civil standard may vary according to the nature of what it is being sought to prove.[56] The more serious the allegation is, the stronger the evidence needed.

A pecuniary penalty is a civil debt payable to ASIC on the Commonwealth of Australia's behalf.[57] It is not available to compensate those who have suffered loss or damage.

iii. Compensation Orders

ASIC may apply for a compensation order.[58] A court may order a person (the liable person) to compensate another person (including a corporation) for damage suffered by the person if: '(a) the liable person has contravened a financial services civil penalty provision; and (b) the damage resulted from the contravention'.[59] Where compensation is sought it is necessary

[51] Corporations Act 2001 (Cth), ss 1317DA and 1317E. Pt 9.4B deals with civil penalties generally.

[52] ibid s 1317J(1).

[53] See WJ Koeck, 'Continuous Disclosure' (1995) 13 *Company and Securities Law Journal* 485, 489; Revised Explanatory Memorandum, Financial Services Reform Act 2001 (Cth) [18.3]; *ASIC v Chemeq Ltd* (2006) 234 ALR 511, 523 [46] (French J); *Jubilee Mines NL v Riley* (2009) 40 WAR 299, 315 [51] (Martin CJ). Originally, a contravention could only be found on proof of intention, recklessness or negligence by the listed entity. See Corporations Law 2001 (Cth), s 1005; *Jubilee Mines NL v Riley* (2009) 40 WAR 299, 318–19 [69]–[71] (Martin CJ); *Grant-Taylor v Babcock & Brown Limited (in liq)* (2016) 245 FCR 402, 421 [102] (Allsop CJ, Gilmour and Beach JJ). The issue of fault or intent was enlivened in 2020 as part of interim measures to address COVID-19 and then permanent measures and are discussed in ch 7.

[54] Corporations Act 2001 (Cth), s 1317J(4). The level of penalties was increased by the Treasury Laws Amendment (Strengthening Corporate and Financial Sector Penalties) Act 2019 (Cth) discussed in ch 7.

[55] ibid s 1317G(1A), (1B).

[56] ibid ss 1317L, 1332; *Briginshaw v Briginshaw* (1938) 60 CLR 336; *ASIC v Rich* (2009) 236 FLR 1, 83–6 [401]–[412] (Austin J).

[57] Corporations Act 2001 (Cth), s 1317G(2).

[58] ibid s 1317J(1).

[59] ibid s 1317HA(1).

to prove both damage and causation. The words 'resulted from' in particular have been held to connote causation.[60] However, like an action for a declaration of contravention, it is not necessary to prove intent or fault as a prerequisite to recovering compensation.

iv. Infringement Notices

Infringement notices were introduced into Part 9.4AA of the Corporations Act by the Corporate Law Economic Reform Program (Audit Reform and Corporate Disclosure) Act 2004 (Cth) ('CLERP 9 Act'), which came into effect on 1 July 2004. The mechanism allows ASIC to issue an infringement notice wherever it 'has reasonable grounds to believe that a disclosing entity has contravened subsection 674(2) or 675(2)' of the Corporations Act.[61] ASIC must provide reasons for the belief and provide an opportunity for the disclosing entity to appear at a hearing before ASIC, give evidence and make submissions to ASIC.[62] Infringement notices were intended to act as an alternative to civil penalties.[63] An infringement notice specifies a penalty of either $100,000, $66,000 or $33,000 (as at 31 December 2017), depending on the market capitalisation of the entity and whether that entity has previously contravened s 674(2) or s 675(2).[64] The entity can choose to pay the penalty and no further action is taken, or if the penalty is not paid, ASIC can commence court proceedings.[65] Payment of the penalty does not amount to an admission or a finding of contravention.[66]

v. Injunction

ASIC may also seek an injunction and an order for damages. Section 1324(1) grants the court power to grant an injunction on appropriate terms where a person has engaged, or is proposing to engage in conduct that constituted, constitutes or would constitute a contravention, or attempt at contravention, of the Act, as well as conduct that would amount to accessorial liability. Section 1324(10) stipulates that where the court has power to grant an injunction, it may, either in addition to, or substitution for the grant of that injunction, make an order for damages.[67] The court may make such orders on the application of ASIC or 'a person whose interests have been, or would be affected by the conduct'.[68] Section 1324B allows for ASIC to seek a court order for the publication of information.

[60] *Adler v ASIC* (2003) 179 FLR 1, 156 [709] (Giles JA).

[61] Corporations Act 2001 (Cth), s 1317DAC. The procedure is described in detail in Michelle Welsh, 'Enforcing contraventions of the continuous disclosure provisions: Civil or administrative penalties' (2007) 25 *Company and Securities Law Journal* 315, 320–23.

[62] Corporations Act 2001 (Cth), s 1317DAD.

[63] ibid s 1317DAB(1).

[64] ibid s 1317DAE.

[65] ibid ss 1317DAF, 1317DAG.

[66] ibid s 1317DAF(3).

[67] *Jovanovic v Commonwealth Bank of Australia* (2004) 87 SASR 570; *Waterhouse v Waterhouse* (1998) 46 NSWLR 449. There have been conflicting judgments on whether damages pursuant to s 1324(10) can be obtained when no injunction is sought. However, recent judgments have taken the view that damages can only be obtained when an injunction is sought. See Austin and Ramsay (n 38) [10.310.18].

[68] *Allen v Atalay* (1993) 11 ACSR 753, *QIW Retailers Ltd v Davids Holding Pty Ltd (No 2)* (1992) 37 FCR 57; *Waterhouse v Waterhouse* (1998) 46 NSWLR 449.

vi. Other Remedial Orders

Section 1325 provides that the court may make 'other orders' in relation to proceedings instituted under, or for a contravention of, inter alia, Chapter 6CA (continuous disclosure) of the Corporations Act. The power exists regardless of whether or not the court makes an order under another provision of the Corporations Act. Standing to apply for these orders is conferred on ASIC and a person who has suffered, or is likely to suffer, loss or damage because of conduct of another person in contravention of the aforementioned provisions.[69] In addition, ASIC may bring the application on behalf of the persons who have suffered, or are likely to suffer, loss, and must have the consent of each of them.[70] Causation and loss must be established in addition to the contravention.[71]

Section 1325(5) sets out the types of orders that may be made, namely: an order declaring the whole or any part of a contract to be void and, if the court thinks fit, to have been void *ab initio* or at all times on and after a specified day before the order is made; an order varying a contract or arrangement; an order refusing to enforce any or all of the provisions of a contract; an order directing the contravening party to refund money or return property to the person who suffered the loss or damage; an order directing the contravening party to pay the person who suffered the loss or damage the amount of the loss or damage; and an order directing the contravening party, at the person's own expense, to supply specified services to the person who suffered, or is likely to suffer, the loss or damage.

vii. Reduced Content Prospectus Ban

ASIC also has the power pursuant to s 713(6) of the Corporations Act to exclude a company that has securities quoted on an exchange and has failed to comply with its continuous disclosure obligations in the past 12 months from issuing a prospectus with reduced content relating to those securities.

viii. Disqualification from Managing Corporations

Pursuant to s 206E of the Corporations Act, ASIC may apply to the court to disqualify a person from managing corporations for a period of time that the court considers appropriate. This is not an enforcement tool directly linked to the continuous disclosure regime. Rather, an order may be made if the person has at least twice been an officer of a body corporate that has contravened the Corporations Act and the person has failed to take reasonable steps to prevent the contravention, or they have at least twice contravened the Corporations Act while they were an officer of a body corporate.

E. Private Cause of Action for Compensation

The legislature has also provided for private causes of action through granting standing to persons who suffer loss or damage. Any person who suffers damage in relation to a contravention

[69] Corporations Act 2001 (Cth), s 1325(2).

[70] ibid s 1325(3).

[71] See *Wealthsure Pty Ltd v Selig* (2014) 221 FCR 1, 48 [255] (White J) ('The words "because" and "by" indicate the requirement for a causal connection between the contravention in question and an applicant's loss and damage.').

of a financial services civil penalty provision (ss 674(2), (2A), 675 (2), (2A)), may apply for a compensation order.[72] A court may order a person (the liable person) to compensate another person (including a corporation) for damage suffered by the person if: (1) the liable person has contravened a financial services civil penalty provision; and (2) the damage resulted from the contravention.[73] Consequently, in addition to needing to prove a contravention of the continuous disclosure regime, albeit without needing to show some intent or fault on the part of the contravenor, it is necessary to prove damage and causation.[74]

Alternatively, as noted above, a person may seek damages pursuant to s 1324(10) when an injunction is sought in relation to a contravention of the Corporations Act[75] or compensation pursuant to s 1325 for a contravention of Chapter 6CA of the Corporations Act.

Further, where ASIC uses the infringement notice regime in Part 9.4AA of the Corporations Act, 'compensation proceedings' may also be instituted by a person in relation to the entity's contravention of the continuous disclosure requirements.[76] Compensation proceedings are defined to mean:[77]

(a) proceedings under s 1317HA (compensation order for contravention of a financial services civil penalty provision); and
(b) proceedings under s 12GF of the ASIC Act in relation to a contravention of s 12DA of that Act (misleading or deceptive conduct, discussed below); and
(c) any other proceedings by a person for compensation for loss or damage suffered by the person.

In addition to claims for compensation, a private citizen may have standing to seek an injunction pursuant to s 1324 or other relief pursuant to s 1325 as discussed above.

Enforcement of continuous disclosure breaches may also be augmented through reliance on the prohibitions on misleading or deceptive conduct that exist in the Corporations Act and the ASIC Act. This is now considered.

III. Misleading or Deceptive Conduct

A. Background

The provisions prohibiting misleading and deceptive conduct in the securities area are based upon the now repealed s 52 of the Trade Practices Act 1974 (Cth) ('Trade Practices Act').[78]

[72] Corporations Act 2001 (Cth), s 1317J(3A). This can be contrasted with corporation/scheme civil penalty provisions where only ASIC or a corporation can apply for a compensation order: Corporations Act 2001 (Cth), s 1317J. See *ASIC v Sigalla* (2009) 74 ACSR 710, 715 [30] (Barrett J); *Fuller v Toms* (2012) 247 FCR 440, 452 [49]–[52] (Barker J).

[73] Corporations Act 2001 (Cth), s 1317HA(1).

[74] The tests for causation and calculation of damages remain uncertain due to a dearth of decided cases: John Emmerig and Michael Legg, 'Twenty Five Years of Australian Class Actions – Time for Reform' (2017) 36 *Civil Justice Quarterly* 164, 174–76.

[75] In *McCracken v Phoenix Constructions (Qld) Pty Ltd* [2013] 2 Qd R 27, 33–39 [21]–[40] the Court of Appeal of the Supreme Court of Queensland found that s 1324(10) was not applicable to the civil penalty provisions in the Corporations Act. The Court's finding arose because standing is not conferred on persons other than ASIC and the corporation to apply for a compensation order and s 1324(10) would have circumvented the operation of the civil penalty provisions. The reasoning does not apply to financial services civil penalty provisions where shareholders are given standing.

[76] Corporations Act 2001 (Cth), s 1317DAF(6). ASIC, 'Regulatory Guide 73 – Continuous disclosure obligations: infringement notices' (October 2017) [31] ('ASIC Regulatory Guide 73').

[77] Corporations Act 2001 (Cth), s 1317DAA.

[78] The Trade Practices Act 1974 (Cth) was replaced by the Competition and Consumer Act 2011 (Cth) with section 52 moved to s 18 of Sch 2, which contains the Australian Consumer Law.

The Trade Practices Act was extended to securities through judicial decisions, until specific securities legislation was enacted in 1998.[79] The misleading or deceptive conduct prohibitions in relation to securities are now embodied in ss 670A, 728 and 1041H of the Corporations Act and s 12DA of the ASIC Act. However, the extensive case law on s 52, and s 82, which provides the regime for compensation, remains applicable.[80]

The reason for extending prohibitions on misleading conduct to securities is that misleading conduct 'may distort the price discovery system, distort prices and unfairly disadvantage investors'.[81] Misleading or deceptive conduct is contrary to the notion that markets should be fair, efficient and transparent, which in turn may lead to harm to investors. The prohibitions on misleading conduct reinforce the requirements of the continuous disclosure regime and provide an additional cause of action that is somewhat easier to prove.[82]

B. Securities and Misleading Conduct

The main provisions relied on in conjunction with alleged contraventions of the continuous disclosure regime are Corporations Act s 1041H and the ASIC Act s 12DA. Section 1041H(1) provides: 'A person must not, in this jurisdiction, engage in conduct, in relation to a financial product or a financial service, that is misleading or deceptive or is likely to mislead or deceive'. 'Financial product' is defined in Part 7.1, Division 3. The definition includes a security.[83] The Full Court of the Federal Court has specifically found that an ASX release by a company was 'in relation to a financial product', namely shares in the company.[84] Section 12DA provides: 'A person must not, in trade or commerce, engage in conduct in relation to financial services that is misleading or deceptive or is likely to mislead or deceive'. 'Financial services' is defined to include providing 'financial product advice', which means a recommendation or opinion or a report of either, intended to influence a person's decision making in relation to a particular financial product. Securities are financial products.[85]

Misleading or deceptive conduct may be constituted by the making of oral or written representations or statements, acts or omissions.[86] Silence may amount to misleading or deceptive conduct where the context requires disclosure to avoid a person being misled or deceived.[87]

[79] See, eg, *Poseidon Ltd v Adelaide Petroleum NL* (1991) 105 ALR 25 (takeover) and *Fraser v NRMA Holdings Ltd* (1995) 55 FCR 452 (prospectus). The Trade Practices Act 1974 (Cth) ceased to apply to financial services after 1 July 1998 when the ASIC Act, s 12DA and other provisions mirroring the Trade Practices Act were enacted. See Trade Practices Act 1974 (Cth), s 51AF(2)(a). The equivalent provision in the Competition and Consumer Act 2010 (Cth), effective from 1 January 2011, is s 131A.

[80] See *National Exchange Pty Ltd v ASIC* (2004) 49 ACSR 369, 373–74 [18] (Dowsett J); *Rawley Pty Ltd v Bell (No 2)* (2007) 61 ACSR 648, 662 [37] (Finn J).

[81] IOSCO (n 6) 241.

[82] Michael Legg, 'Shareholder Class Actions in Australia – The Perfect Storm?' (2008) 31 *UNSW Law Journal* 669, 678–80; John Humphrey and Stephen Corones, 'Forrest v ASIC: A "perfect storm"' (2014) 88 *Australian Law Journal* 26, 26, 37.

[83] *ASIC v Narain* (2008) 169 FCR 211, 212 [1] (Finkelstein J), 219 [40] (Jacobson and Gordon JJ).

[84] ibid 216–17 [19]–[22] (Finkelstein), 222–24 [66]–[87] (Jacobson and Gordon JJ).

[85] Australian Securities and Investments Commission Act 2001 (Cth), ss 12BAB(1)(a), (5), 12BAA(7)(a). Australian Securities and Investments Commission Act 2001 (Cth), s 12BAB (1)(g) also defines a financial service as 'a service that it is otherwise supplied in relation to a financial product'. See also *ABN AMRO Bank NV v Bathurst Regional Council* (2014) 224 FCR 1, 143–45 [758]–[764] (Jacobson, Gilmour and Gordon JJ).

[86] *Campbell v Backoffice Investments Pty Ltd* (2009) 238 CLR 304, 321 [32] (French CJ), 341[102] (Gummow, Hayne, Heydon and Kiefel JJ).

[87] See *Rhone-Poulenc Agrochimie S A v UIM Chemical Services Pty Ltd* (1986) 12 FCR 477; *Henjo Investments Pty Ltd v Collins Marrickville Pty Ltd* (1988) 39 FCR 546, 557 (Lockhart J).

Whether or not conduct amounts to a misrepresentation is a question of fact to be decided by considering what is said and done against the background of all surrounding circumstances.[88] The court must consider whether the impugned conduct viewed as a whole has a tendency to lead a person into error.[89]

In the securities context, the continuous disclosure regime, discussed above, will frequently create the need to disclose.[90] Disclosures that are inaccurate, or a failure to disclose when obligated to (that is, silence), may provide key evidence of misleading or deceptive conduct. The mandating of disclosure by the continuous disclosure regime means that shareholders will receive regular representations, any one of which, if misleading and causing loss, will ground the commencement of proceedings based upon the statutory causes of action prohibiting misleading and deceptive conduct.[91] Intention is irrelevant. The provisions are drafted so as to be concerned with consequences and not the contravener's state of mind.[92] It is therefore incorrect to refer to the provisions as addressing securities 'fraud' as there is no requirement of fraudulent conduct. Liability may be extended to accessories.[93]

The scope of the general provisions – s 1041H of the Corporations Act and s 12DA of the ASIC Act – is very broad, but conduct that contravenes a specific provision against misleading or deceptive statements in takeover documents[94] or a fundraising document[95] is excluded from the general provisions.[96] This is significant because while there are no defences to the general provisions, a suite of defences apply to the specific provisions.[97] This demarcation was first introduced to reflect the different philosophies of consumer protection that applied in relation to s 52 of the Trade Practices Act and investor protection that applied to fundraising, but which had been lost when s 52 was extended to securities.[98] The defences are an acknowledgment that investments provide a return to investors based on them bearing a share of the risks which are intrinsic to financial activity, particularly due to imperfect information. Consequently, Treasury proposed that liability rules should not shift to fundraisers the investment risk properly accepted by investors in efficient securities markets.[99] The general provisions, in contrast, reflect a consumer protection approach.

[88] *Campbell v Backoffice Investments Pty Ltd* (2009) 238 CLR 304, 341 [102] (Gummow, Hayne, Heydon and Kiefel JJ).

[89] ibid 319 [25] (French CJ).

[90] *GPG (Australia Trading) Pty Ltd v GIO Australia Holdings Ltd* (2001) 117 FCR 23, 70 [103] (Gyles J).

[91] Michael Legg and Dean Jordan, 'Disclosure Needs Special Care', *The Australian Financial Review* (14 February 2007) 55. See also Andrew Cassidy and Larelle Chapple, 'Australia's Corporate Disclosure Regime: Lessons from the US model' (2003) 15 *Australian Journal of Corporate Law* 1, 5–6.

[92] *Hornsby Building Information Centre Pty Ltd v Sydney Building Information Centre Ltd* (1978) 140 CLR 216, 228 (Stephen J) ('As I read s 52(1) … it is concerned with consequences as giving to particular conduct a particular colour. If the consequence is deception, that suffices to make the conduct deceptive'); *ABN AMRO Bank NV v Bathurst Regional Council* (2014) 224 FCR 1, 308 [1570] (dealing with *Corporations Act 2001* (Cth) s 1041H(1)), 309 [1578] (dealing with Australian Securities and Investments Commission Act 2001 (Cth), s 12DA(1)) (Jacobson, Gilmour and Gordon JJ).

[93] Corporations Act 2001 (Cth), s 1041I(1), Australian Securities and Investments Commission Act 2001 (Cth), s 12GF(1). Both are modelled on the Trade Practices Act 1974 (Cth), s 82. See also Corporations Act 2001 (Cth), s 79 which is modelled on the Trade Practices Act 1974 (Cth), s 75B. The Australian Securities and Investments Commission Act 2001 (Cth), s 5(3) makes Corporations Act 2001 (Cth), s 79 applicable to the Australian Securities and Investments Commission Act 2001 (Cth).

[94] Corporations Act 2001 (Cth), s 670A.

[95] ibid s 728.

[96] ibid s 1041H(3); Australian Securities and Investments Commission Act 2001 (Cth), s 12DA(1A).

[97] Austin and Ramsay (n 38) [22.440], [23.640].

[98] *Fraser v NRMA Holdings Ltd* (1995) 55 FCR 452; Michael Legg, 'Misleading and Deceptive Conduct in Prospectuses' (1996) 14 *Company and Securities Law Journal* 47.

[99] Corporate Law Economic Reform Program, 'Fundraising – Capital Raising Initiatives to Build Enterprise and Employment' (1997) 41.

C. Public Enforcement

A contravention of s 1041H of the Corporations Act or s 12DA of the ASIC Act gives rise to civil liability only. Neither is a criminal offence or a civil penalty provision.[100] However, ASIC can seek an injunction or a declaration in relation to misleading conduct.[101] ASIC may also pursue a banning order for contravention of s 12DA.[102]

ASIC may use the prohibitions on misleading conduct as an alternative to proceeding under the continuous disclosure regime or as a component to proving contravention of the continuous disclosure regime. In *ASIC v Narain*,[103] ASIC chose to pursue the managing director/chief executive officer for incorrect statements made to the ASX by the company through s 1041H, which then grounded a breach of director's duties. The misleading statements demonstrated that Mr Narain had not exercised his duties with the requisite degree of care and diligence. ASIC could have, but did not, proceed under the continuous disclosure regime by employing s 674(2A), which imposes accessorial liability. In ASIC's case against Fortescue Metals Group Ltd, ASIC alleged misleading conduct as a stepping stone to establish that the corporation needed to make a correcting disclosure so as to comply with the continuous disclosure regime.[104]

D. Private Cause of Action for Compensation

The Corporations Act, s 1041I and ASIC Act, s 12GF(1) provide that a person who suffers loss or damage by conduct in contravention of s 1041H or s 12DA respectively may recover the amount of loss or damage by action against the person contravening the section or against any person involved in the contravention. This means that the person who suffers loss or damage has standing to sue.

However, a claim for compensation is premised on being able to establish causation.[105] As Corporations Act, s 1041I and ASIC Act, s 12GF(1) are based on s 82 of the Trade Practices Act, detailed consideration has been given to the causation requirement in that section by the courts.

[100] *ASIC v Narain* (2008) 169 FCR 211, 216 [18] (Finkelstein J); *ABN AMRO Bank NV v Bathurst Regional Council* (2014) 224 FCR 1, 301 [1535] (Jacobson, Gilmour and Gordon JJ).

[101] See Corporations Act 2001 (Cth), s 1324; *ASIC v Fortescue Metals Group Ltd* (2011) 190 FCR 364, 370 [10] (Keane CJ) ('Only declaratory relief was sought against FMG for the alleged contraventions of s 1041H. That is because s 1041H is not a civil penalty provision: see s 1317E.').

[102] Corporations Act 2001 (Cth), s 920A (banning orders are available for contravention of, or involvement in a contravention of, a 'financial services law', which is defined in Corporations Act 2001 (Cth), s 761 to include a provision of Australian Securities and Investments Commission Act 2001 (Cth), Pt 2, Div 2, which includes s 12DA).

[103] *ASIC v Narain* (2008) 169 FCR 211; *ASIC v Citrofresh International Ltd* (No 2) (2010) 77 ACSR 69. For a similar strategy in another context see *ASIC v Cassimatis (No 8)* (2016) 336 ALR 209 employing a breach of financial advice provisions to support a breach of directors' duties.

[104] *ASIC v Fortescue Metals Group Ltd* (2011) 190 FCR 364, 370 [10] ('the contraventions of s 1041H are alleged against FMG as a stepping stone toward the conclusion that FMG contravened s 674(2).'), 425 [189] ('Once it is accepted that FMG's announcements contravened s 1041H of the Act, FMG, having made misleading statements to the ASX, was obliged by s 674(2) to correct the position.') (Keane CJ). However, in *Forrest v ASIC* (2012) 247 CLR 486, 513 [61]–[62] (French CJ, Gummow, Hayne and Kiefel JJ) the High Court overturned the Full Federal Court as the statements were not misleading and therefore could not be a contravention of the continuous disclosure regime. See generally Abe Herzberg and Helen Anderson, 'Stepping Stones – From Corporate Fault to Directors' Personal Civil Liability' (2012) 40 *Federal Law Review* 181.

[105] Corporations Act 2001 (Cth), s 1041I(1) and Australian Securities and Investments Commission Act 2001 (Cth), s 12GF(1) use the expression 'by' which the High Court in *Wardley Australia Ltd v Western Australia* (1992) 175 CLR 514, 525 (Mason CJ, Dawson, Gaurdon and McHugh JJ) interpreted as expressing the notion of causation.

Under s 82 of the Trade Practices Act, an applicant must show that he or she has been induced by misleading or deceptive conduct to do something or to refrain from doing something which gives rise to damage.[106] However, it is sufficient to prove that the misleading or deceptive conduct was but one of a number of causes of the damage.[107] The law acknowledges that people are often swayed by several considerations. It attributes causality to a single one of those considerations if it makes a material contribution or has had a substantial rather than a negligible effect.[108]

Section 1325 provides that the court may make 'other orders' in relation to proceedings instituted under, or for a contravention of, inter alia, Part 7.10 of the Corporations Act which contains s 1041H. As explained above in relation to continuous disclosure, s 1325 gives a person standing to claim damages as well as other relief. Further a person whose interests have been or would be affected may seek an injunction pursuant to s 1324, and damages pursuant to s 1324(10) when an injunction is sought, in relation to a contravention of the Corporations Act.

The foregoing discussion has set out the continuous disclosure and misleading conduct provisions with their applicable causes of action for both public and private enforcement. The next section explains how ASIC has administered these provisions from the perspective of public enforcement. The following section continues the explanation of private enforcement through elucidating the operation and role of class actions and litigation funding.

IV. ASIC Enforcement

This section builds on the above discussion of the substantive law by examining ASIC's approach to enforcement of the continuous disclosure regime. It further explains the enforcement tools available to ASIC and the manner in which they have been employed.

A. ASIC's Approach to Enforcement

ASIC employs 'a range of regulatory tools to enforce, and promote compliance with the laws that ASIC administers, as well as to improve consumer understanding and decision making'.[109] ASIC accepts that 'Effective enforcement is … critical for ASIC in pursuing [its] strategic priorities of promoting fair and efficient financial markets, and ensuring confident and informed investors and financial consumers'.[110] The regulatory tools available to ASIC include education, guidance, surveillance, enforcement action (criminal, civil penalty, compensatory and administrative actions) and negotiated outcomes.[111]

To these tools may be added ASIC's ability to intervene in litigation begun by other persons in relation to matters arising under the Corporations Act.[112] ASIC's use of the enforcement tools

[106] *Argy v Blunts & Lane Cove Real Estate Pty Ltd* (1990) 26 FCR 112, 138 (Hill J).

[107] *I & L Securities Pty Ltd v HTW Valuers (Brisbane) Pty Ltd* (2002) 210 CLR 109, 128 [57] (Gaudron, Gummow and Hayne JJ).

[108] *Henville v Walker* (2001) 206 CLR 459, 482–3 [68]–[70] (Gaudron J), 494 [109] (McHugh J).

[109] ASIC Senate Inquiry Submission (n 20) [394].

[110] ASIC, 'Penalties for Corporate Wrongdoing – Report 387' (March 2014) [1] ('ASIC Penalties Report').

[111] ASIC Senate Inquiry Submission (n 20) [395]; ASIC, 'Information Sheet 151 – ASIC's approach to enforcement' (September 2013) 4–7 ('ASIC Information Sheet 151').

[112] See Corporations Act 2001 (Cth), s 1330; ASIC, 'Information Sheet 180 – ASIC's approach to involvement in private court proceedings' (June 2013); Austin and Ramsay (n 38) [3.280].

in relation to continuous disclosure is discussed further below, including how frequently they are used. The enforcement tools are also discussed in chapter four to the extent they feature in the case studies.

The regulatory tool or tools ASIC chooses to use in response to a potential breach of the law will depend on the objectives that ASIC is seeking to achieve. ASIC has explained that its objectives include:

(a) punishment;
(b) improving compliance;
(c) protecting the public;
(d) compensation for investors; and
(e) deterrence.[113]

Significantly, ASIC has multiple objectives to achieve, which in turn necessitate the use of different regulatory tools. ASIC may also seek to achieve a number of objectives at the same time.[114]

In chapter three the regulatory objectives common to ASIC and class actions, namely deterrence and compensation, will be examined in greater detail so as to develop an analytical framework for application to the case studies.

B. Responsive Regulation – The Enforcement Pyramid

In the continuous disclosure regime, supported by prohibitions on misleading conduct, ASIC's enforcement powers allow for the employment of the classic enforcement pyramid approach championed by 'responsive regulation'.[115]

The responsive regulation thesis is that regulatory agencies are best able to secure compliance when they are 'benign big guns', that is, regulators will be more able to 'speak softly when they carry big sticks (and [have access to] a hierarchy of lesser sanctions)'.[116] Responsive regulation is based on the following assumptions. A corporate actor's decision as to whether to comply with the law may be driven by whether it is economically rational to do so (ie, a weighing of potential costs and benefits), but also by their concern to do what is right because of their own perception of themselves as law abiding citizens who are socially responsible. A strategy based totally on persuasion and self-regulation will be exploited by those corporations who are making decisions based on economic rationality. As persuasion and self-regulation do not have the same sort of costs as civil litigation or criminal prosecution, it may be rational to not comply. However, a strategy based mostly on punishment will undermine the goodwill of those actors who are motivated to comply because of their self-perception as responsible, law-abiding citizens. Further, punishment is expensive as contraventions need to be proven and due process followed, usually in a court. Persuasion is cheap as the corporate actor will voluntarily comply. However, compliance

[113] ASIC Senate Inquiry Submission (n 20) [396]; ASIC Penalties Report (n 110) [2]. See also Australian Securities and Investments Commission Act 2001 (Cth), ss 1(2), 12A(2).

[114] ASIC Penalties Report (n 110) [31].

[115] Ian Ayres and John Braithwaite, *Responsive Regulation* (Oxford University Press, 1992); Nehme, Hyland and Adams (n 21) 116; Coffey (n 28) 304–06; Boros (n 1) 416–17; Aakash Desai and Ian Ramsay, 'The Use of Infringement Notices by ASIC for Alleged Continuous Disclosure Contraventions: Trends and Analysis' (2011) 39 *Australian Business Law Review* 260, 272–73. ASIC's enforcement approach, including responsive regulation, is revisited in ch 7.

[116] Ayres and Braithwaite (ibid) 19.

will be more forthcoming if it is supported by a hierarchy of sanctions so that a more costly and punitive response is available if needed.[117]

The regulator needs to establish a synergy between punishment and persuasion so that the threat of punishment underwrites persuasion as something to be preferred. The aim is to give regulatory agencies the maximum capacity to lever cooperation by allowing them to escalate their response in a way that responds to the degree of uncooperativeness of an individual or corporation, whilst also taking account of the moral and political acceptability of the response.[118] A regulator needs to have not just a hierarchy of enforcement steps or sanctions it can invoke, but also a sufficient number of enforcement steps so that it is not placed in a position where non-cooperation at one level leads to it needing to escalate the response to a level that is considered unacceptable from a political perspective.

In the area of continuous disclosure, ASIC's enforcement pyramid would have guidance, education and warnings or persuasion at the base. The next level as ASIC moved up the hierarchy would be either infringement notices or enforceable undertakings.[119] This level could also include the s 713 power to prevent a listed entity from using a prospectus with reduced content. Next would be civil penalties and disqualification/banning orders, with criminal penalties at the apex of the pyramid.

As explained above, ASIC also has the ability to seek injunctions, compensation, or other orders such as varying or voiding a contract, refund of money or return of property and awards of damages. ASIC has recognised that corrective action and compensatory action are forms of civil enforcement.[120] They would seem to sit in the middle of the pyramid. They sit above infringement notices and enforceable undertakings (explained below in section IV.C.ii) because they are coercive and court-sanctioned. They would sit below criminal penalties which must be proven to a higher standard of proof and can include imprisonment. They are also below disqualification and banning orders which, like imprisonment, act as a form of incapacitation. They probably also sit below civil penalties which are in the form of fines if actions aimed at deterrence are regarded as involving greater escalation than remedial actions.

ASIC has also indicated that in a particular situation it may combine a number of levels in the enforcement pyramid.[121] For example, it may ban a person to achieve specific deterrence (deter the person from repeating the conduct) and general deterrence (deter other similarly situated persons from engaging in such conduct), enter into an enforceable undertaking to improve conduct and provide guidance to assist with compliance.[122]

It should also be noted that the ASX's tools for enforcing the listing rules may also be part of the enforcement pyramid. Price 'query' and 'aware' letters, as well as mandating compliance with the listing rules, would be at the base of the pyramid. Delisting or suspending quotation of an entity's securities would be towards the top of the pyramid as it would be similar to banning or disqualifying persons and incapacitates the company.

ASIC's use of each of the enforcement pyramid levels or steps in the continuous disclosure regime is discussed next.

[117] ibid 19, 20, 22, 24. See also Neil Gunningham, 'Enforcement and Compliance Strategies' in Robert Baldwin, Martin Cave and Martin Lodge (eds), *The Oxford Handbook of Regulation* (Oxford University Press, 2010) 125–26.

[118] ibid 36.

[119] See Desai and Ramsay (n 115) 273, 278–79 observing that commentators disagree on the order of infringement notices or enforceable undertakings and that ASIC may move one above the other or combine them.

[120] ASIC Senate Inquiry Submission (n 20) [395].

[121] ASIC Penalties Report (n 110) [31]–[32].

[122] ibid.

C. ASIC and Enforcement of the Continuous Disclosure Regime

i. *Guidance, Education and Persuasion*

ASIC has provided considerable guidance and education to listed entities as to the operation of the continuous disclosure regime and a number of its enforcement tools. ASIC has the ability to issue regulatory guides which explain when and how ASIC will exercise specific powers under legislation, how ASIC interprets the law, the principles underlying ASIC's approach, and/or giving practical guidance.[123] In 2000, ASIC released a publication entitled 'Better disclosure for investors'.[124] The publication contained practical steps to assist listed entities meet both the letter and the spirit of the continuous disclosure requirements. The publication stated:[125]

> The principles are intended to assist company directors and executives to manage their disclosure obligations and minimise the risk of breaching the law. … The objective of these principles is to outline what ASIC considers to be good disclosure practice, not to impose regulatory requirements.

In 2004, ASIC issued a guide entitled 'Continuous Disclosure Obligations: Infringement Notices', which set out how ASIC would use the regime and provided information on the steps in the infringement notice process.[126] ASIC's Chairman and Commissioners have also made numerous speeches at various conferences and seminars.[127]

ASIC also has the ability to issue warning letters.[128] ASIC can use a warning letter to advise an entity of practices by that entity which the regulator regards as sub-optimal and should be corrected. The aim is to address potential risks to the entity's ability to meet its continuous disclosure obligations in the future. The warning letter has been characterised as a 'yellow card'.[129]

ii. *Infringement Notices, Enforceable Undertakings and Disallowing Use of Reduced Content Prospectuses*

Since their introduction in 2004, infringement notices have been the enforcement tool most used by ASIC in relation to continuous disclosure.[130] ASIC's Regulatory Guide on Infringement Notices explains:[131]

> Infringement notices provide a regulatory tool for ASIC to address less serious breaches of the continuous disclosure obligations. They are designed to provide a fast and effective regulatory response that is proportionate and proximate in time to the alleged breach.

[123] ASIC, 'ASIC: A guide to our regulatory documents' (June 2007) 5.

[124] ASIC, 'Regulatory Guide 62 – Better disclosure for investors' (August 2000).

[125] ibid 2.

[126] ASIC, 'Continuous Disclosure Obligations: Infringement Notices, An ASIC Guide' (May 2004). The guide is now ASIC Regulatory Guide 73 (n 76).

[127] See, eg, Belinda Gibson, ASIC Commissioner, 'Disclosure and the Role of ASX and ASIC', Listed Companies Conference, 26 March 2008; John Price, ASIC Commissioner, 'Continuous Disclosure' Chartered Secretaries Australia 2012 Annual Conference, 3 December 2012; Belinda Gibson, Deputy Chair, and John Price, ASIC Commissioner, 'Speech to ASX Forum: Continuous disclosure: Guidance Note 8 rewrite' ASX Forum (April 2013).

[128] Nehme, Hyland and Adams (n 21) 116; Luke Hastings, 'Enforcing the Continuous Disclosure Regime' in Michael Legg, *Regulation, Litigation and Enforcement* (Thomson Reuters, 2011) 139–40.

[129] Hastings (n 128) 140.

[130] Ian Ramsay, 'Enforcement of Continuous Disclosure Laws by the Australian Securities and Investments Commission' (2015) 33 *Company and Securities Law Journal* 196, 204.

[131] ASIC Regulatory Guide 73 (n 76) [3].

If the disclosing entity complies with an infringement notice, ASIC will publish details of the notice.[132] A list of 37 successful infringement notices for the period 1 July 2004 (when infringement notices were introduced) to 31 December 2017 is set out in Appendix 2, Table 1. Publication assists in educating the market and deterring contraventions by demonstrating that ASIC is actively enforcing the continuous disclosure regime. ASIC's aim is to encourage voluntary compliance.[133]

Enforceable undertakings provide another form of enforcement towards the lower end of the enforcement pyramid. An enforceable undertaking is an administrative settlement whereby ASIC and the alleged wrongdoer resolve the allegations through a public written settlement, the terms of which can be enforced by ASIC in court.[134] ASIC utilises enforceable undertakings as an alternative to civil court actions and administrative actions. ASIC has stated that it will not use an enforceable undertaking for trivial matters or for matters that it believes should be dealt with as criminal contraventions or through civil penalty provisions.[135]

ASIC has observed that 'Negotiated outcomes, such as EUs, can offer a faster, more flexible and effective regulatory outcome than could otherwise be achieved through administrative or civil action'.[136] The flexibility of an enforceable undertaking means it can be used to compensate persons who have suffered loss, restrict the activities of a person or company and compel improved compliance arrangements including monitoring by an independent expert.[137] ASIC considers an enforceable undertaking to be an effective regulatory outcome if it:

- promotes the integrity of, and public confidence in, our financial markets and corporate governance;
- specifically deters the person from future instances of the conduct which gave rise to the undertaking;
- promotes general deterrence in making the business community aware of the conduct and the consequences arising from engaging in that conduct; or
- provides an ongoing benefit by way of improved compliance programs.[138]

ASIC has accepted enforceable undertakings in relation to alleged continuous disclosure failures, but they have been a small proportion of the total number of enforceable undertakings for corporate law breaches in general, and have been used less than infringement notices in the continuous disclosure area.[139] A list of 11 enforceable undertakings for the period 1998 (the year of the first undertaking) to 31 December 2017 dealing with continuous disclosure is set out in Appendix 2, Table 2.

Infringement notices and enforceable undertakings are similar in that the alleged wrongdoer must voluntarily accept the penalty, there is no admission of liability,[140] and the sanctions are made public. Neither inhibits third parties, such as shareholders, from seeking remedies. However, they differ in that the enforceable undertaking outcome is more transparent, especially

[132] ibid [39].

[133] Cassidy and Chapple (n 91) 88; Jeremy Cooper, 'Corporate wrongdoing: ASIC's enforcement role', International Class Actions Conference 2005, Melbourne. 2 December 2005, 12 ('The purpose of the [infringement notice] regime is substantially "educative" because compliance is effectively voluntary'); Welsh (n 61) 324.

[134] Australian Securities and Investments Commission Act 2001 (Cth), s 93AA; *Liu v Fairfax Media Publications Pty Ltd* (2012) 84 NSWLR 547, 563 [102] (Beech-Jones J).

[135] ASIC, 'Regulatory Guide 100 – Enforceable Undertakings' (February 2015) [3], [16], [21] ('ASIC Regulatory Guide 100).

[136] ASIC, 'ASIC enforcement report – July to December 2013' (Media Release 14-018MR, 31 January 2014).

[137] ASIC Regulatory Guide 100 (n 135) [19].

[138] ibid [25].

[139] Nehme, Hyland and Adams (n 21) 129; Gill North, 'A Call for Bold and Effective Corporate Disclosure Regulatory Framework' (2010) 28 *Company and Securities Law Journal* 331, 339–40; Desai and Ramsay (n 115) 274–77.

[140] For an enforceable undertaking, although liability does not have to be admitted it cannot be denied and it must be accepted that ASIC's views are reasonably held: see ASIC Regulatory Guide 100 (n 135) [39]–[40].

as ASIC maintains a public register of undertakings. Further the infringement notice can only impose fines at predetermined levels while the enforceable undertaking can be much more flexible by including changes to corporate governance, compliance regimes, corrective notices and compensation.[141]

An infringement notice seeks to achieve education and deterrence through imposing a fine because a contravention has occurred. The enforceable undertaking also deters, not through the threat of a fine being imposed, but through imposing costs through directing changes to corporate governance and compliance regimes, although these costs should benefit the entity and its shareholders.

ASIC has combined infringement notices and enforceable undertakings on the basis that it believes that the fine indicates the gravity of the breach while the undertaking can assist in the adoption of procedures to improve compliance in the future.[142]

As noted in section II.D above, s 713(6) grants power to ASIC to disallow the use of a reduced content prospectus where in the previous 12 months the issuer has not complied with its continuous disclosure obligations. The power has been used in response to failures to comply with continuous disclosure at least ten times.[143] In addition, the power has also been referred to three times within an enforceable undertaking where the company agreed not to seek to rely on s 713 to issue a reduced content prospectus until other undertakings had been complied with or a period of 12 months had expired.[144] The inability to use a reduced content prospectus imposes additional costs on the company that it could otherwise have avoided.

iii. Civil and Criminal Penalties

The role of a pecuniary penalty is principally to act as a specific and general deterrent to prevent the corporate structure from being used in a manner contrary to commercial standards.[145] The introduction of civil penalties for contraventions of Chapter 6CA was supported on the basis that because it would be easier for ASIC to succeed than on the criminal standard, greater deterrence could be achieved.[146] The reasoning presumably is that more listed entities would be at risk of enforcement action and so would respond with greater efforts to avoid contraventions.

As at 31 December 2017 ASIC has commenced eight civil penalty proceedings and been successful in seven of those. The first two companies which were subject to ASIC civil penalty action – Southcorp Ltd and Chemeq Ltd – both admitted liability and the penalty was approved by the Federal Court.[147] The third was against James Hardie where ASIC was successful after trial.[148] The fourth was against Fortescue Metals Group Ltd where ASIC was ultimately

[141] Nehme, Hyland and Adams (n 21) 126–29.

[142] Price (n 127) 9 (referring to this approach in relation to Nufarm and Leighton Holdings).

[143] Ramsay (n 130) 201, 202 (referring to eight instances between 2001 and 31 January 2015); ASIC, 'ASIC restricts Continental Coal from issuing reduced content prospectus following disclosure and financial reporting failures' (Media Release 16-061, 4 March 2016); ASIC, 'ASIC restricts Axiom Mining from issuing a reduced content prospectus' (Media Release 17-210, 28 June 2017).

[144] Ramsay (n 130) 201, 202; ASIC, Enforceable Undertaking: Rhinomed Ltd, Document No 029622129, 9 June 2016, varied on 23 December 2016.

[145] *ASIC v Adler* (2002) 42 ACSR 80, 114–16 [126] (Santow J).

[146] Explanatory Memorandum to the Financial Services Reform Bill 2001 (Cth), [2.79]; Department of Treasury, Commonwealth of Australia, Corporate Disclosure Strengthening the Financial Reporting Framework (2002) 133, 147.

[147] *ASIC v Chemeq Ltd* (2006) 234 ALR 511; *ASIC v Southcorp Ltd (No 2)* (2003) 130 FCR 406.

[148] *ASIC v Macdonald (No 11)* (2009) 256 ALR 199. An appeal to the New South Wales Court of Appeal by the corporation was unsuccessful: *James Hardie Industries NV v ASIC* (2010) 274 ALR 85.

unsuccessful after the matter was appealed to the High Court.[149] The fifth was against Newcrest Mining Limited for briefing analysts on market-sensitive information ahead of it being disclosed to the market. Newcrest Mining admitted liability for two contraventions and a fine of $1.2 million was imposed.[150] The sixth was ASIC's proceeding against Padbury Mining Ltd and two of its executives, Mr Stokes and Mr Quinn. Liability was admitted. For contravention of their directors' duties and s 674(2A) of the Corporations Act both Mr Stokes and Mr Quinn received a civil penalty in the sum of $25,000. Both were also prohibited from managing a corporation for a period of three years for breach of their directors' duties.[151] The seventh was ASIC obtaining declarations of contravention and a civil penalty of $800,000 against Sino Australia Oil and Gas Ltd. ASIC also obtained declarations of contravention against the CEO, Mr Tianpeng Shao, and an order that he be disqualified from managing corporations for a period of 20 years, but this stemmed from breach of his director's duties.[152] The eighth proceedings against MG Responsible Entity Limited settled with a penalty of $650,000 to be paid.[153]

ASIC is also able to address conduct that contravenes the continuous disclosure regime and prohibition on misleading conduct indirectly through other causes of action, including breach of director's duties. A key case in this regard was the civil penalty proceedings against the directors of Centro Properties Ltd, which is discussed in chapter four.

Although a criminal prosecution is available for a contravention, it has only been successfully utilised once. The former executive chairman of Waratah Resources Ltd was convicted after pleading guilty to a charge under the Criminal Code of aiding and abetting Waratah Resources to breach its continuous disclosure obligations. The court imposed a sentence of 12 months' imprisonment, to be served as a 12-month Intensive Correction Order (ICO).[154] ICOs allow for a sentence of imprisonment of no more than two years to be served by way of intensive correction in the community with the offender to comply with mandatory conditions such as being of good behaviour, undertaking community service and meeting with a supervisor.[155] An earlier prosecution of two directors of Hart Australasia Limited for failing to keep the market informed of the group's unexpected loss of $9.7 million in 2001 was unsuccessful.[156]

ASIC has explained that it pursues criminal remedies for the most serious misconduct. This includes conduct that has a widespread negative impact on investors or creditors and offences involving conduct that is dishonest, intentional or highly reckless. Criminal proceedings are punitive and aim to punish a wrongdoer.[157] They also have a powerful deterrent effect, especially on individuals who may be imprisoned.[158]

[149] *Forrest v ASIC* (2012) 247 CLR 486.

[150] *ASIC v Newcrest Mining Limited* (2014) 101 ACSR 46.

[151] *ASIC v Padbury Mining Ltd* (2016) 116 ACSR 208.

[152] *ASIC v Sino Australia Oil and Gas Ltd (in liq)* (2016) 118 ACSR 43. The liquidator also obtained a compensation order against Mr Shao in the amount of $5,539,758 pursuant to ss 729, 1041I, 1317H, 1317HA and/or 1325 of the Corporations Act 2001 (Cth).

[153] *ASIC v MG Responsible Entity Limited* [2017] FCA 1531.

[154] ASIC, 'Waratah Resources' former executive chairman convicted and sentenced for misleading the market' (Media Release 17-018MR, 30 January 2017); ASIC, 'ASIC enforcement outcomes: January to June 2017 – Report 536' (August 2017) 15.

[155] Crimes (Sentencing Procedure) Act 1999 (NSW) (Crimes Regulations 1990 (Cth) allows for an ICO to be applied to federal offences prosecuted in New South Wales courts); *R v Pogson* (2012) 82 NSWLR 60.

[156] ASIC, 'Former Harts executives charged with continuous disclosure breach' (Media Release 06-176, 2 June 2006); ASIC, 'Verdict on charges against former Hart executives' (Media Release AD08-26, 25 September 2008); ASIC, 'Prosecution of Brisbane man discontinued' (Media Release AD09-06, 22 January 2009).

[157] ASIC Information Sheet 151 (n 111) 5.

[158] ASIC Senate Inquiry Submission (n 20) [432].

iv. Redress and Compensation

ASIC may also pursue redress for harmed consumers including seeking compensation, injunctions or other orders such as varying or voiding a contract, refund of money or return of property and awards of damages.[159] This includes being specifically empowered to bring proceedings on behalf of a person or company to recover damages for fraud, negligence, default, breach of duty or other misconduct connected with the matter to which the investigation or examination related, or proceedings for recovery of property.[160] However, it must appear to ASIC that it is in the 'public interest' for the person or company to bring proceedings, and where the applicant is not a company, ASIC must obtain the person's consent.[161] ASIC has utilised this procedure in a number of matters,[162] such as in relation to financial advisers who recommended investment in the Westpoint group, which subsequently collapsed,[163] and against banks which provided loans to fund investments advised by Storm Financial Limited that were lost during the global financial crisis.[164]

While ASIC accepts that a failure to comply with the continuous disclosure regime can cause 'serious damage to individual investors',[165] ASIC's current position on seeking compensation is:

> We will ordinarily only take action to recover damages or property on a person's behalf if this would be in the public interest, beyond the interests of the affected consumers. We encourage investors to consider alternative options to recover damages or property from wrongdoers where possible, such as by lodging a dispute with the Financial Ombudsman Service or taking private legal action.[166]

While ASIC has the power to obtain compensation for continuous disclosure breaches, it has been reluctant to do so. It is not surprising therefore that class actions have emerged as an alternative approach to obtaining compensation for investors. This chapter now turns to the shareholder class action which is the focus of comparison with ASIC in assessing public and private enforcement of the continuous disclosure regime.

V. Shareholder Class Actions

A. Background

The availability of private enforcement in the form of the shareholder class action is the result of the accretion of three developments in the Australian legal system. The first is Parliament's determination to grant standing to private litigants in relation to contraventions of the continuous disclosure regime and the prohibitions on misleading and deceptive conduct where loss or

[159] See, eg, Corporations Act 2001 (Cth), ss 1317HA/1317J (compensation orders for breach of financial services civil penalty provision); 1324 (statutory injunctions), 1325 (other orders) and Australian Securities and Investments Commission Act 2001 (Cth), s 12GM (other orders) discussed above at section II.D.

[160] Australian Securities and Investments Commission Act 2001 (Cth), s 50.

[161] ibid. See also Janet Austin, 'Does the Westpoint litigation signal a revival of the ASIC s 50 class action?' (2008) 22 *Australian Journal of Corporate Law* 8.

[162] Austin (ibid) 28–30 (listing ASIC's use of s 50 from 1992 to 2007).

[163] See, eg, *Rikys v Bongiorno Financial Advisers (Aust) Pty Ltd* [2009] FCA 1603, *Casey v State Trustees Ltd* [2010] FCA 163; *Markov v Dukes* [2010] FCA 1419.

[164] See, eg, *Australian Securities and Investments Commission v Bank of Queensland Ltd* (2011) 211 FCR 412: ASIC 'ASIC settles in Storm Financial proceedings' (Media Release 13-122MR, 29 May 2013).

[165] Price (n 127) 9.

[166] ASIC Information Sheet 151 (n 111) 6. See also Cooper (n 133) 4.

damage is caused by the contravention. Second is the introduction of a class action regime which provided the procedural framework for the claims of numerous shareholders to be aggregated and pursued by a representative party. The third is a mechanism for financing the class action and bearing the risk of failure so that shareholders would be willing to participate – third-party litigation funding.[167] The first of these has already been outlined, and the second and third developments are discussed below.

B. The Role of Class Actions

The ability of class actions to achieve both compensation and deterrence has been recognised since the procedure was first examined by the Australian Law Reform Commission (ALRC) in its 1988 report on the subject. This section will demonstrate that while achieving compensation for persons who suffered harm was the Government's dominant objective, class actions were also considered to play a part in deterring contraventions of the law. However, more recently, both the compensation and deterrence rationales for the shareholder class action have been invoked.

On 1 February 1977 the Federal Attorney-General instructed the ALRC to examine the adequacy of the existing law in relation to class actions.[168] The ALRC set about determining whether it was appropriate or desirable to introduce a new form of procedure that would allow for class actions. It determined:

> An effective grouping procedure is needed as a way of reducing the cost of enforcing legal remedies in cases of multiple wrongdoing. Such a procedure could enable people who suffer loss or damage in common with others as a result of a wrongful act or omission by the same respondent to enforce their legal rights in the courts in a cost effective manner.[169]

The ALRC went on to observe that the class action was not being recommended 'to punish respondents or to deter behaviour to any greater extent than can be achieved by enforcement of the law'. The expansion of access to legal remedies 'may have a deterrent effect on the respondent's behaviour, but that is incidental'.[170]

The focus of the ALRC was on facilitating compensation of persons who might otherwise be discouraged from seeking recompense due to such factors as cost, and promoting the efficient resolution of claims in the courts. The ALRC envisaged the new class action procedure being used for securities claims by putting forward the following scenario:

> A group of small shareholders suffer considerable financial loss as a result of misleading advice received from stockbrokers and the directors of the company in which significant amounts of their savings were invested. The shareholders also claim that the company failed to comply with the Australian Stock Exchange listing rules by neglecting to inform the market of factors likely to materially affect the market price of shares. … A grouping procedure could facilitate the recovery of loss by those affected and would offer the advantage of helping to ensure that all concerned were informed of the claim and shared in the result without having to commence individual proceedings.[171]

[167] Legg (n 82) 705–07; Robert Baxt, Ashley Black and Pamela Hanrahan, *Securities and Financial Services Law*, 9th edn (LexisNexis, 2017) [9.28]; Damian Grave, Ken Adams and Jason Betts, *Class Actions in Australia*, 2nd edn (Thomson Reuters, 2012) 891; Australian Law Reform Commission, 'Integrity, Fairness and Efficiency – An Inquiry into Class Action Proceedings and Third-Party Litigation Funders', Report No 134 (2018) 263 ('ALRC 2018 Report').

[168] Australian Law Reform Commission, 'Grouped Proceedings in the Federal Court', Report No 46 (1988), [1] ('ALRC 1988 Report').

[169] ibid [69].

[170] ibid [323].

[171] ibid [65].

This demonstrates that at even this very early stage in the gestation of the class action mechanism, the continuous disclosure regime and prohibitions on misleading conduct, albeit not in their current form, were considered as potential causes of action for shareholders in class actions.

Class actions were introduced into Australia through the enactment of the Federal Court of Australia Amendment Act 1991 (Cth) which provided for 'representative proceedings' through inserting Part IVA into the Federal Court of Australia Act 1976 (Cth) (FCA Act). Part IVA commenced on 4 March 1992.[172]

The objectives of class action litigation, according to the Minister's Second Reading Speech, were:

> [To] enhance access to justice, reduce the costs of proceedings and promote efficiency in the use of court resources. …
>
> to provide a real remedy where, although many people are affected and the total amount at issue is significant, each person's loss is small and not economically viable to recover in individual actions. It will thus give access to the courts to those in the community who have been effectively denied justice because of the high cost of taking action. …
>
> The new procedure will mean that groups of persons, whether they be shareholders or investors, or people pursuing consumer claims will be able to obtain redress and do so more cheaply and efficiently than would be the case with individual actions.[173]

These objectives have been repeated by the courts on a number of occasions.[174] More recently the Federal Government has stated that it 'supports class actions and litigation funders as they can provide access to justice for a large number of consumers who may otherwise have difficulties in resolving disputes'.[175]

As part of the second reading debate in the Senate, the Minister for Justice and Consumer Affairs observed:

> The enhancement of the rights of many shareholders to take this sort of representative proceeding will be a great aid to the more formal regulators, such as the Australian Securities Commission, [now ASIC] in ensuring compliance with the corporations law …. this procedure will be of great assistance in ensuring that, in the area of the corporations law, not only the Australian Securities Commission but shareholders will be given an enhanced capacity to ensure that they can get those remedies which flow from contravention of the corporations law.[176]

The Minister for Justice and Consumer Affairs, while also seeing the class action as facilitating access to remedies under the corporation's legislation, points to the class action encouraging compliance with corporate law requirements. The compliance rationale suggests a further role or objective for the class action. The idea of a regulatory role has been identified by the Federal

[172] Class action procedures also exist in Victoria, New South Wales, Queensland and Tasmania: Supreme Court Act 1986 (Vic), Pt 4A (commenced 1 January 2000); Civil Procedure Act 2005 (NSW), Pt 10 (commenced 4 March 2011); Civil Proceedings Act 2011 (Qld), Pt 13A (commenced 1 March 2017); Supreme Court Civil Procedure Act 1932 (Tas), Pt VII (commenced 9 September 2019).

[173] Commonwealth of Australia, *Parliamentary Debates*, House of Representatives (14 November 1991) 3176–77 (Michael Duffy, Attorney-General).

[174] See, eg, *Wong v Silkfield Pty Ltd* (1999) 199 CLR 255, 264 [20] (Gleeson CJ, McHugh, Gummow, Kirby and Callinan JJ); *Femcare Ltd v Bright* (2000) 100 FCR 331, 334 [10] (Black CJ, Sackville and Emmett JJ); *Dorajay Pty Limited v Aristocrat Leisure Limited* (2005) 147 FCR 394, 422–23 [97] (Stone J); *Guglielmin v Trescowthick (No 2)* (2005) 220 ALR 515, 518 [9] (Mansfield J).

[175] Explanatory Statement, Select Legislative Instrument 2012 (No 172) 1. See also Senate Economics References Committee, *Performance of the Australian Securities and Investments Commission* (June 2014) 261.

[176] Commonwealth of Australia, *Parliamentary Debates*, Senate (13 November 1991) 3023 (Michael Tate, Minister for Justice and Consumer Affairs).

Attorney-General's Access to Justice Taskforce which has observed that 'class actions may have a strong regulatory impact with the potential scale of the pecuniary damages providing a strong incentive to abide by existing laws'.[177] However, the Taskforce went on to raise for further consideration, whether Part IVA of the FCA Act 'appropriately takes account of the behaviour modification aspects of class actions'.[178] The Australian Senate Economics References Committee in its report into the performance of ASIC also recognised that class actions provided access to the courts and facilitated the deterrence of future securities laws violations.[179]

Australian commentators, drawing largely on US experience but consistent with the identified need for the creation of class actions in Australia above, have viewed the shareholder class action as providing compensation to shareholders and acting as a deterrent to contravention of the continuous disclosure laws.[180] The compensation and deterrence rationales for shareholder class actions have also been identified by the Federal Court of Australia:

> [I]t must, I think, be accepted that [shareholder class actions] serve a useful function. It is often said that these actions promote investor confidence in the integrity of the securities market. They enable investors to recover past losses caused by the wrongful conduct of companies and deter future securities laws violations.[181]

The ALRC in its 2018 review of the functioning of class actions observed that 'It is generally accepted that there are two goals that shareholder class actions are expected to deliver: compensation for shareholders harmed by breaches of the rules, and deterrence against future breaches'.[182]

C. Federal Court of Australia Act, Part IVA

The above section sets out the role of the class action. This section will consider the specific legislative requirements that govern when class actions may be commenced and how they are conducted and concluded. A class action is 'a procedure whereby the claims of many individuals

[177] Access to Justice Taskforce, Federal Attorney-General's Department, 'A Strategic Framework for Access to Justice in the Federal Civil Justice System' (September 2009) 114.

[178] ibid 117, Recommendation 8.11.

[179] Senate Economics References Committee (n 175) 261.

[180] See, eg, Julian Donnan, 'Class Actions in Securities Fraud in Australia' (2000) 18 *Company and Securities Law Journal* 82, 84; Peta Spender, 'Securities Class Actions: A View from The Land of the Great White Shareholder' (2002) 31 *Common Law World Review* 123, 127; Bernard Murphy and Camille Cameron, 'Access to Justice and the Evolution of Class Action Litigation in Australia' (2006) 30 *Melbourne University Law Review* 399, 404; Cara Waters, 'The new class conflict: The efficacy of class actions as a remedy for minority shareholders' (2007) 25 *Company and Securities Law Journal* 300, 313–14; Legg (n 82) 707; Michael Legg, 'The Aristocrat Leisure Ltd shareholder class action settlement' (2009) 37 *Australian Business Law Review* 399, 409; James Mayanja, 'Enhancing Private Enforcement of Australia's Corporate Continuous Disclosure Regime: Why Unshackling Litigation Funders Makes Eminent Sense' (2010) 25 *Australian Journal of Corporate Law* 48, 61; Michael Legg, 'Public and Private Enforcement: ASIC and the Shareholder Class Action' in Michael Legg, *Regulation, Litigation and Enforcement* (Thomson Reuters, 2011) 151; Shueh Hann Lim, 'Do Litigation Funders Add Value to Corporate Governance in Australia?' (2011) 29 *Company and Securities Law Journal* 135, 150–51; Michelle Welsh and Vince Morabito, 'Public v Private Enforcement of Securities Laws: An Australian Empirical Study' (2014) 14 *Journal of Corporate Law Studies* 39, 68; Michael Duffy, 'Australian Private Securities Class Actions and Public Interest – Assessing the Private Attorney-General by Reference to the Rationales of Public Enforcement' (2017) 32 *Australian Journal of Corporate Law* 162; Michael Legg, 'Securities Regulation in Australia: The Role of the Class Action' in Robin Huang and Nicholas Howson (eds), *Enforcement of Corporate and Securities Law: China and the World* (Cambridge University Press, 2017) 312.

[181] *Kirby v Centro Properties Limited* (2008) 253 ALR 65, 67–68 [8] (Finkelstein J) citing *Bateman Eichler, Hill Richards Inc v Berner*, 472 US 299, 310 (1985); *J I Case Co v Borack*, 377 US 426, 432 (1964). See also *Perera v GetSwift Limited* (2018) 357 ALR 586, 593–94 [14] (Lee J).

[182] ALRC 2018 Report (n 167) 266.

against the same defendant can be brought or conducted by a single representative'.[183] The class action provides a procedure that both aggregates claims and allows for a representative to prosecute those claims.

i. *Commencement of Proceedings*

The requirements to commence a class action in the Federal Court are set out in the FCA Act, s 33C, which provides that if:

> (a) 7 or more persons have claims against the same person; and
> (b) the claims of all those persons are in respect of, or arise out of, the same, similar or related circumstances; and
> (c) the claims of all those persons give rise to a substantial common issue of law or fact; a proceeding may be commenced by one or more of those persons as representing some or all of them.

Section 33C has been described by the High Court as 'central' to the class action regime.[184] It not only sets the requirements for commencement of a class action, but provides the criteria that determine the level of cohesiveness within the group that is required. There must be at least seven group members, who do not need to be named, but the applicant must be able to show that they are likely to be seven or more based on the nature of the proceedings.[185] The 'claims against the same person' requirement means that there need only be seven group members with a claim against one respondent for the proceedings to be commenced. The addition of other group members and other respondents once the initial requirement is met is not prohibited.[186] The 'same, similar or related circumstances' requirement has been interpreted liberally so that some relationship must exist but they certainly need not be identical.[187] Equally, the 'substantial common issue of law or fact' requirement is not an onerous one, as 'substantial' does not indicate a large or significant issue but instead is 'directed to issues which are "real or of substance"'.[188]

These requirements are readily met in the context of a claim for contravention of the continuous disclosure regime. The group of shareholders will all allege a claim against the corporation, and possibly directors or advisors, that the continuous disclosure regime was not complied with, and commonly that the non-compliance was also misleading conduct.[189] The nature of shareholder claims against listed entities means that there will be more than seven group members. The focus on the same corporation and the same misleading disclosure or omission usually means that the claims are in respect of, or arise out of, the same, similar or related circumstances. The common questions of law or fact will include questions aimed at elements of the law or factual matters that all group members must prove as part of a successful cause of action. This may include determinations as to the existence of information that was not generally available, materiality, awareness, and whether there was a contravention. Compliance with s 33C only becomes difficult when the class action seeks to include multiple misleading disclosures or omissions over

[183] ALRC 1988 Report (n 168) [1].

[184] *Mobil Oil Australia Pty Ltd v Victoria* (2002) 211 CLR 1, 30–31 [35] (Gaudron, Gummow and Hayne JJ).

[185] *Symington v Hoechst Schering Agrevo Pty Ltd* (1997) 78 FCR 164, 166 (Wilcox J); *Au Domain Administration Ltd v Domain Names Australia Pty Ltd* (2003) 202 ALR 127, 129 [8] (Finkelstein J).

[186] *Cash Converters International Limited v Gray* (2014) 223 FCR 139.

[187] *Zhang v Minister for Immigration, Local Government & Ethnic Affairs* (1993) 45 FCR 384, 404 (French J).

[188] *Wong v Silkfield Pty Ltd* (1999) 199 CLR 255, 267 [28] (Gleeson CJ, McHugh, Gummow, Kirby and Callinan JJ).

[189] *P Dawson Nominees Pty Ltd v Multiplex Ltd* (2007) 242 ALR 111, 112–14 [4]–[8] (Finkelstein J); *Perera v GetSwift Limited* (2018) 357 ALR 586, 593–94 [10]–[14] (Lee J); Bernard Murphy, 'Shareholder class actions: are you vulnerable?' (June 2007) *Keeping Good Companies* 275, 278–79; Grave, Adams and Betts (n 167) 893.

an extended time period so that some group members may be relying on different disclosures or omissions. However, as long as the circumstances are 'related' and there is at least one common question, the proceedings will usually be permitted to be commenced as a class action.[190] The difficulty with a less cohesive group of claims is that the proceedings may be longer and more cumbersome. There are matters which may be raised as grounds for discontinuing the proceedings pursuant to s 33N, which is discussed below.

ii. Standing and Adequacy of Representation

Section 33D(1) addresses standing and requires a representative party to have a sufficient interest to commence a proceeding on his or her own behalf against a particular person before they can commence proceedings on behalf of group members.[191] Section 33D(1) is designed to abrogate the common law standing rule that a person can only bring an action for damages on his or her own behalf,[192] so as to allow an applicant to have the representative capacity needed for a class action to function.

In addition, s 33T allows for group members to apply to the court for a representative party to be replaced if they are not able to adequately represent the interests of the group members. Adequacy of representation is not a requirement for commencing the class action by the representative party, but inadequacy does allow for the subsequent replacement of the representative party. Adequate representation embodies the ideals of loyalty and common – not conflicting – interests.[193]

iii. Group Definition and the Right to Opt Out

Section 33H requires the pleadings to 'describe or otherwise identify the group members to whom the proceeding relates'. This allows shareholders to know whether they are included in a class action and defines those group members who will be bound by a settlement or judgment.[194]

There are three ways in which group membership can be identified or designed. The first is the 'opt out' procedure embodied in s 33J, which permits group members to inform the court that they do not wish to be part of the proceedings. An opt-out class action is commenced without the express consent of group members.[195] All persons whose claims fall within the group definition are automatically part of the class action. However, the right to opt-out is given effect by s 33X(1)(a), which imposes the requirement that group members receive notice of the right and of the commencement of the proceedings. If a group member falling within the defined class does not opt out then they are bound by the outcome of the proceedings.[196]

The second approach is an opt-in class action where a group member must expressly consent to participation in the class suit. Only those group members who opt in are bound or entitled to

[190] *Guglielmin v Trescowthick (No 2)* (2005) 220 ALR 515.

[191] *Ryan v Great Lakes Council* (1997) 78 FCR 309, 312 (Wilcox J); *Dorajay Pty Ltd v Aristocrat Leisure Ltd* (2005) 147 FCR 394, 420 [90] (Stone J).

[192] *Symington v Hoechst Schering Agrevo Pty Ltd* (1997) 78 FCR 164, 167 (Wilcox J).

[193] Michael Legg, 'Judge's role in settlement of representative proceedings: Lessons from United States class actions' (2004) 78 *Australian Law Journal* 58, 63.

[194] *Petrusevski v Bulldogs Rugby League Club Ltd* [2003] FCA 61 [19]–[23] (Sackville J).

[195] Federal Court of Australia Act 1976 (Cth), s 33E specifies that consent of a person to be a group member is not required, except for certain government entities.

[196] ibid s 33ZB.

the benefit of the judgment on the common questions.[197] Australia's Part IVA does not permit an opt-in class action.[198]

However, Australia has permitted a third approach with the recognition of the 'closed class'. The Full Federal Court held that s 33C(1) permits a representative party to commence a proceeding where they are representing 'some or all' of the group members. This allows for a proceeding on behalf of less than all of the potential members of the group.[199] Before the class action is commenced the group can be defined by a criteria that limits membership in some manner, usually by reference to entry into a litigation funding agreement. This was done to ensure that the group member was obligated to pay a funding fee to the litigation funder.[200] Litigation funding is discussed below. However, the right to opt out must be maintained and the group cannot be defined to allow putative group members to opt into the proceedings once they have been commenced.[201]

To illustrate the closed class approach in a continuous disclosure class action, the group will usually be defined as follows:[202]

> The Group Members to whom this proceeding relates are persons who:
>
> - between 11 March 2006 and 15 September 2006 acquired an interest in the securities of A Limited; and
> - suffered loss or damage by or as a result of the wrongful conduct of the respondent pleaded in the Statement of Claim, and
> - as at the date of the commencement of this proceeding have entered into a funding agreement with Funder Co.

If the group was to be structured as a traditional opt-out class action then the last criterion would be deleted so that the group would not be limited to those group members who were clients of the litigation funder. Rather, the group would comprise all shareholders who purchased securities in A Limited during the specified time period and had suffered loss.

iv. Discontinuing a Class Action

Under s 33N, the court of its own motion or on application by the respondent may order that the proceeding not continue as a class action where it is in the interests of justice to do so because:

> (a) the costs that would be incurred if the proceeding were to continue as a class action are likely to exceed the costs that would be incurred if each group member conducted a separate proceeding; or
> (b) all the relief sought can be obtained by means of a proceeding other than a class action under Part IVA; or
> (c) the class action will not provide an efficient and effective means of dealing with the claims of group members; or
> (d) it is otherwise inappropriate that the claims be pursued by means of a class action.[203]

[197] Michael Legg, 'Funding a Class Action through Limiting the Group: What does Part IVA of the Federal Court of Australia Act 1976 (Cth) permit?' (2010) 33 *Australian Bar Review* 17, 18.

[198] *Multiplex Funds Management Ltd v P Dawson Nominees Pty Ltd* (2007) 164 FCR 275, 295 [142] (Jacobson J).

[199] ibid 291 [111] (Jacobson J).

[200] Michael Legg, 'Reconciling Litigation Funding and the Opt Out Group Definition in Federal Court of Australia Class Actions – The Need for a Legislative Common Fund Approach' (2011) 30 *Civil Justice Quarterly* 52, 53.

[201] *Multiplex Funds Management Ltd v P Dawson Nominees Pty Ltd* (2007) 164 FCR 275, [142] (Jacobson J).

[202] See, eg, *Clime Capital Ltd v Credit Corp Group Ltd (No 3)* [2012] FCA 218 [3] (Nicholson J); the Applications in *P Dawson Nominees Pty Ltd v Brookfield Multiplex Limited* VID 1380 of 2006, *Watson v AWB Ltd* NSD 2020 of 2007 and *Hobbs Anderson Investments Pty Ltd v Oz Minerals Ltd* NSD 1127 of 2009.

[203] Federal Court of Australia Act 1976 (Cth) s 33M also provides for the discontinuance of a class action where, if judgment were to be given in favour of the representative party, the cost to the respondent of identifying the group members and distributing to them the amounts ordered to be paid to them would be excessive having regard to the likely total of those amounts.

Therefore even when the threshold requirements of s 33C are met, a court may still use its discretion under s 33N to order the discontinuance of a class action.[204] However, the Federal Court's general approach to class actions is to try to use case management techniques, consistent with the purpose of Part IVA, to enable a class action to at least continue to the stage of resolution of the common issues before relying on s 33N or the use of sub-groups or individual determinations.[205] This approach has carried over to the continuous disclosure context. Individual issues such as causation and damages have not resulted in class actions being discontinued prior to the determination of the common issues.[206]

v. Remaining Issues, Sub-groups and Individual Issues

Where the determination of issues common to all group members does not finally determine the claims of all group members, the court may give directions in relation to the determination of the remaining issues.[207] The directions can include the establishment of subgroups or provision for an individual group member to apply for the determination of an issue relating to that member.[208] If an issue cannot be conveniently dealt with through sub-groups, individual determinations or other case management technique, the court may give directions relating to the commencement and conduct of a separate individual or representative proceeding.[209]

vi. Settlement

It is important to consider that class action settlements as settlement rather than trial is the norm in continuous disclosure class action proceedings.[210] A representative proceeding may not be settled or discontinued without the approval of the court.[211] Further, unless the court is satisfied that it is just to do so, an application for approval of a settlement must not be determined unless notice has been given to group members.[212] The court's approach to the approval of a settlement involves the parties persuading the court that: the proposed settlement is fair and reasonable having regard to the claims made on behalf of the group members who will be bound by the settlement; and the proposed settlement has been undertaken in the interests of group members, as well as those of the applicant, and not just in the interests of the applicant and the respondent/s.[213]

Consequently, the quantum of the settlement and the fees paid to lawyers are usually publicly available as part of the settlement approval process.[214] This means that through the media they are likely to be known to the public and other corporations.

[204] *Bright v Femcare Ltd* (2002) 195 ALR 574, 601 [128] (Kiefel J); *Multiplex Funds Management Ltd v P Dawson Nominees Pty Ltd* (2007) 164 FCR 275, 279–80 [13]–[15] (Lindgren J), 298–99 [179]–[192] (Jacobson J).

[205] *Bright v Femcare Ltd* (2002) 195 ALR 574, 580 [18] (Lindgren J).

[206] See *Dorajay Pty Ltd v Aristocrat Leisure Ltd* (2005) 147 FCR 394, 431–32 [127]–[132] (Stone J). See also Jonathan Beach, 'Class Actions: Some Causation Questions' (2011) 85 *Australian Law Journal* 579, 581.

[207] Federal Court of Australia Act 1976 (Cth), s 33Q(1).

[208] ibid ss 33Q(2), 33R.

[209] ibid s 33S.

[210] See Appendix 2 Table 3; ALRC 2018 Report (n 167) 273.

[211] Federal Court of Australia Act 1976 (Cth), s 33V.

[212] ibid s 33X(4).

[213] Federal Court of Australia, Class Actions Practice Note (GPN-CA), 25 October 2016, [14.3]. See also *Jarra Creek Central Packing Shed Pty Ltd v Amcor Ltd* [2011] FCA 671, [68]–[77] (Jacobson J); *Pharm-a-Care Laboratories Pty Ltd v Commonwealth (No 6)* [2011] FCA 277, [20]–[27], [37] (Flick J).

[214] The exceptions to class action settlement information being publicly available are where the settlement occurs prior to the formal commencement of a class action (eg Downer EDI Ltd and Trans Pacific Industries Group Pty Ltd) or

D. Typical Shareholder Class Action

The combination of substantive law and class action procedure typically leads to shareholder class actions arising from the following factual scenario:

(1) At date A, the defendant company either becomes aware of information which it fails to disclose to the ASX or makes a positive statement to the ASX which the group members allege is misleading and/or fails to reveal the company's true position.
(2) At date B, the ASX becomes aware of the undisclosed information or the alleged misrepresentation, usually through the defendant company making a corrective disclosure to the ASX which reveals its true position, causing a decline in the share price.
(3) The group members are shareholders who brought shares in the defendant company between dates A and B and continue to hold the shares as at date B.
(4) The group members allege that the defendant company: (a) acted in breach of its continuous disclosure obligations contained in Chapter 6CA of the *Corporations Act* and the ASX Listing Rules; and/or (a) engaged in misleading or deceptive conduct in breach of the provisions primarily contained in section 1041H of the Corporations Act and section 12DA of the ASIC Act.
(5) The group members seek compensation from the defendant company for their loss, which is usually the difference between the value of the shares at the date they purchased them and their value after date B, although other measures of loss may be pleaded.[215]

E. Litigation Funding

Litigation funding is typically a contractual arrangement between a third-party funder (usually a commercial entity) and one or more potential litigants. The funder pays the costs of the litigation (such as the lawyer's fees, disbursements, project management and claim investigation costs) and usually accepts the risk of paying the other party's costs in the event that the claim fails through providing the plaintiff with an indemnity. In return, if the claim is successful, the funder will receive a certain percentage of any funds recovered by the litigants either by way of settlement or judgment, and the litigants will assign the funder the benefit of any costs order they receive. The share of the proceeds is agreed with the litigants, or awarded to the funder by court order and is typically between 25 and 40 per cent of the proceeds (usually after reimbursement of costs).[216]

In *Campbells Cash and Carry Pty Limited v Fostif Pty Ltd* (2006) 229 CLR 386, the High Court considered the legality of litigation funding for the first time. The majority held that litigation funding was not an abuse of process or contrary to public policy.[217] As a consequence, the

the court does not publish a judgment approving the settlement (eg AWB Limited) or the information is not stated in the judgment.

[215] Corey Byrne and Michael Legg, 'Market-based causation after TPT Patrol Pty Ltd v Myer Holdings Limited' (2020) 37 *Companies and Securities Law Journal* 295, 296.

[216] Vicki Waye, 'Conflicts of Interests Between Claimholders, Lawyers and Litigation Entrepreneurs' (2007) 19 *Bond Law Review* 225, 297; Legg (n 200) 56; *Earglow Pty Ltd v Newcrest Mining Limited* [2016] FCA 1433, [166]–[177] (Murphy J) (setting out funding fees); Michael Legg, 'Ramifications of the Recognition of a Common Fund in Australian Class Actions: An Early Appraisal' (2017) 91 *Australian Law Journal* 655.

[217] *Campbells Cash and Carry Pty Ltd v Fostif Pty Ltd* (2006) 229 CLR 386, 433–6 [88]–[96] (Gummow, Hayne and Crennan JJ). The joint judgment indicated that existing doctrines of abuse of process and the courts' ability to protect

uncertainty around whether litigation funding was permitted in Australian courts was removed, setting the stage for it to become an accepted part of civil litigation. The approach in *Fostif* was considered and confirmed by the High Court three years later.[218]

Litigation funding is advocated on the basis that it provides access to justice for those who could not otherwise afford to enforce their rights. The attraction or need for litigation funding is closely linked to the costs rule that operates in Australian litigation. The usual costs rule in Australian litigation is that a losing party is liable for the other side's costs.[219] This is referred to as 'the loser pays' or 'costs follow the event' and is usually given effect procedurally through an adverse costs order. The rule is modified in relation to class actions as the costs rule applies to the representative party only and not to the group members.[220] This approach to costs has been raised as a disincentive to the commencement of class action litigation as the representative party is liable for their own costs (which are arguably incurred for the benefit of the entire group) and, if they are unsuccessful, the costs of their opponent.[221] The funder in paying the costs of the litigation and indemnifying the litigant against the risk of paying the other party's costs if the case fails, overcomes the disincentive. While the FCA Act protects group members from a costs exposure, the indemnity may still be of benefit in the event that a group member becomes a sub-group representative or has individual issues that need to be determined by the court.[222]

The rise of litigation funding may also be linked to the restriction on fee arrangements between lawyers and clients as fees determined as a percentage of the client's recovery (ie contingency fees) were disallowed.[223] Australian lawyers typically charge based on the time undertaken to complete a matter, ie time-based billing. Australian lawyers may take cases on a conditional or 'no win no fee' basis whereby the fee only becomes payable by the client if a successful outcome is achieved. It is also permissible for a lawyer to charge their usual legal fee multiplied by some factor or a specified additional amount, to a maximum of 25 per cent, as part of a conditional fee.[224] This provides a mechanism to address the disincentive to commencing legal proceedings because an applicant cannot afford to pay their own legal costs. However, it requires a lawyer to be willing to bear non-payment throughout the litigation until a successful settlement or judgment is achieved. Litigation funding, in contrast, covers

their processes would be sufficient to deal with a funder conducting themselves in a manner 'inimical to the due administration of justice'. Gleeson CJ and Kirby J agreed with the reasoning of the joint judgment: 407 [1] (Gleeson CJ), 451 [146] (Kirby J). Callinan and Heydon JJ dissented on this issue: 496 [287].

[218] *Jeffery & Katauskas Pty Limited v SST Consulting Pty Ltd* (2009) 239 CLR 75, 94 [29]–[30] (French CJ, Gummow, Hayne and Crennan JJ), 124 [111] (Heydon J). See also *Gladstone Ports Corporation Limited v Murphy Operator Pty Ltd* [2020] QCA 250, an application for special leave to the High Court was dismissed: *Gladstone Ports Corporation Limited v Murphy Operator Pty Ltd & Ors* [2021] HCATrans 114 (25 June 2021).

[219] *Latoudis v Casey* (1990) 170 CLR 534, 567 (McHugh J); *Ruddock v Vadarlis (No 2)* (2001) 115 FCR 229, 235 [11] (Black CJ and French J).

[220] Federal Court of Australia Act 1976 (Cth), s 43(1A).

[221] Donnan (n 180) 90; Spender (n 180) 143, 160; Vince Morabito, 'Contingency Fee Agreements with Represented Persons in Class Actions – An Undesirable Australian Phenomenon' (2005) 31 *Common Law World Review* 201, 206.

[222] See Federal Court of Australia Act 1976 (Cth), ss 33Q, 33R and 43(1A).

[223] See, eg, Legal Profession Uniform Law 2015 (Vic), s 183; Legal Profession Uniform Law 2015 (NSW), s 183 prohibit the amount payable to a law practice to be calculated by reference to 'the amount of any award or settlement or the value of any property that may be recovered in any proceedings to which the agreement relates'. However, in the State of Victoria legislation has been enacted that provides that in a class action the court may order that the legal costs payable to the plaintiff's lawyers be a percentage of the amount recovered in the proceedings which is discussed further in chapter 7.

[224] See, eg, Legal Profession Uniform Law 2015 (Vic), ss 181, 182; Legal Profession Uniform Law 2015 (NSW), ss 181, 182; *Johnson Tiles Pty Ltd v Esso Australia Ltd* (1999) 94 FCR 167, 173–75 [27]–[31] (Merkel J); *Cook v Pasminco Ltd (No 2)* (2000) 107 FCR 44, 53–54 [52]–[54] (Lindgren J).

an applicant's legal costs by paying the lawyers as the case proceeds and is not inhibited by the prohibition on contingency fees.

While litigation funding is usually examined from the perspective that it makes available the financing needed for identifying and prosecuting potential law suits, it also performs an entrepreneurial or management role. For example, the funder may assist in the identification of the potential lawsuit, undertake the due diligence to determine the feasibility of litigation, organise a representative party and group members, and coordinate the resources needed to achieve a favourable settlement or judgment.[225] The funder's role and its impact on the class action is considered further in chapter five.

The centrality of litigation funding to continuous disclosure shareholder class actions is illustrated by the proceedings listed in Appendix 2, Table 3. Apart from the early proceedings, all continuous disclosure class actions up until 31 December 2017 have been brought with the aid of litigation funding.[226]

VI. Conclusion

The continuous disclosure regime, aided by the prohibitions on misleading conduct, seeks to enhance confident and informed participation by investors in secondary securities markets. It is a crucial component of securities regulation for establishing a level playing field where all investors have the same information with which to make investment decisions. It speaks to both market integrity and investor protection.

This chapter has provided the necessary background needed for the text, namely the substantive law on continuous disclosure and misleading conduct, the objectives and operation of ASIC, and the role of the shareholder class action in relation to continuous disclosure.

The background discussion explained that the public regulator is empowered with a number of causes of action and enforcement tools to administer the continuous disclosure regime. In particular, ASIC has at its disposal a range of responses, including criminal, civil and administrative actions. This chapter has demonstrated that ASIC employs those responses in aid of achieving a range of objectives in regulating continuous disclosure, including deterrence and, to a lesser extent, compensation.

This chapter has also shown that enforcement may be pursued by private citizens through a combination of standing to bring statutory causes of action, a class action procedure and the availability of litigation funding. Shareholder class actions have two roles or outcomes, compensation and deterrence, both of which it shares with ASIC. Consequently, there is an overlap or intersection between ASIC and the shareholder class action, or expressed more broadly, between public and private enforcement. This suggests that ASIC and the shareholder class action may be complimentary or they may be in conflict.

Chapter three develops an analytical framework for use in the text through focusing on the two common areas of ASIC enforcement and the shareholder class action – deterrence and compensation. Each of deterrence and compensation is elucidated in detail so as to allow for an

[225] Legg (n 82) 707.

[226] See also ALRC 2018 Report (n 167) 76–77 (from 2013 to 2018 all shareholder claims received third-party litigation funding).

examination later in the thesis of how, and to what degree, ASIC action and the shareholder class action achieve deterrence and compensation vis-a-vis each other.

Chapter three also develops a framework for considering the interaction of ASIC enforcement and the class action by drawing on regulatory theory to devise a number of values or norms that depict a legitimate or 'good' regulatory process. Chapter three's framework then provides a basis for exploring how public and private enforcement may assist or hamper each other, and the regulatory process.

3

Analytical Framework

I. Introduction

This chapter develops an analytical framework to allow for the comparison of ASIC and shareholder class actions in relation to the enforcement of the continuous disclosure regime. The first part of the analytical framework addresses deterrence and compensation, being the areas identified in chapter two where public securities regulation and private shareholder class actions intersect. This may be viewed as a focus on outcomes. The second part of the framework builds on this intersection by developing criteria for evaluating public and private enforcement of the securities laws from the perspective of the functioning of the regulatory process. In contrast to the first framework, it is a comparison built around process values. In other words, the first framework looks at ends and the second framework looks at means.

This chapter proceeds by critically unpacking two key comparators for public and private enforcement in the area of securities law: deterrence and compensation. The critical assessment of deterrence and compensation means elucidating a definition, or definitions, and the dimensions of each. It also includes a discussion of the conditions for effectiveness and limitations.

The discussion of deterrence provides an overview of its evolution from crime and criminology to white-collar crime and regulation so as to show its relevance to the current research aimed at ASIC enforcement and shareholder class actions. The rich analysis of deterrence from these various perspectives then allows for the concept to be fleshed out through discussions of formal sanctions, indirect costs and reputational harm, as well as specific and general deterrence. These dimensions of deterrence provide for a greater understanding of the goals of deterrence and the nuances around how it may operate. The chapter then discusses the factors that impact on the effectiveness of deterrence. This includes the traditional factors of certainty, severity and celerity, but also the theories of perceptual deterrence and optimal deterrence. The chapter also discusses practical considerations such as who is the object of deterrence and the need to avoid the dispersion of deterrence. Lastly, the chapter reviews the limitations of deterrence such as the focus on imposing costs, the assumption of rationality and the difficulty in measuring if deterrence is successful.

The goal of compensation arises from the principles of corrective justice, a person who is wronged is entitled to be compensated, and consumer protection which is reflected in the text of the Corporations Act. This chapter then examines the need for assistance in accessing compensation and how that access may be facilitated – by the regulator on a person's behalf or, alternatively through the person participating in a class action.[1] The analysis continues by explaining that compensation is achieved when a recovery equivalent to the loss sustained from the misconduct,

[1] An individual with sufficient resources, such as an institutional investor, may also seek compensation alone but this is rare and is not addressed by the text, as explained in ch 1.

namely full compensation, is attained. However, full compensation may not be attained when compensation is reduced due to settlements and transaction costs, such as lawyer and litigation funder fees. In addition, of particular relevance to securities enforcement, is the circularity or pocket-shifting problem. This arises because the shareholders who traded based on flawed disclosure are paid by the shareholders who did not, less substantial transaction costs. When shareholders are diversified this means that over the long term they are as likely to be paying compensation as receiving compensation and are systematically worse off.

This chapter then turns to the second part of the analytical framework, which advances a number of values or norms that depict a legitimate or 'good' regulatory process. The features of the process employed to achieve deterrence and/or compensation are evaluated because the values are crucial to regulatory decisions and outcomes being seen as valid and accepted by regulated entities, the persons who the regulation is meant to benefit, and society at large. Those values are examined from four perspectives: legislative authority; the public interest; accountability; and efficiency. The values are drawn from regulatory theory and applied to both ASIC and the class action on the basis that they are both performing a regulatory role, respectively, public and private enforcement.

The theory in this chapter directs the case study analysis and assessment in chapters five and six of how ASIC action and the class action performed by comparison with each other in relation to specific contraventions, or allegations of contraventions, of the continuous disclosure regime. It also informs the analysis that is undertaken in chapter seven in relation to changes in policy settings and legal requirements, and evaluating strategies for coordination in chapter eight.

II. Deterrence

A. Definition

Deterrence may be defined as the avoidance of a given action through fear of the perceived consequences.[2] Those consequences are usually sanctions of some form, which are unpleasant or costly, and aim to control or shape behaviour. The thinking behind deterrence may be simply put: people seek reward and avoid loss. Sanctions reduce or eliminate reward and impose loss.[3]

B. Why is it an Objective?

The classical theory of deterrence is a systematic approach to the study of crime and criminality that developed in the late eighteenth and early nineteenth century. Its proponents, Cesare Beccaria and Jeremy Bentham, focused on individuals acting rationally and with self-interest so that the pain of punishment should be greater than the potential pleasure or gain from committing the crime. Punishment was to be proportionate and to act as a deterrent.[4]

[2] Arie Freiberg, *Regulation in Australia* (The Federation Press, 2017) 426.
[3] David Kennedy, *Deterrence and Crime Prevention* (Routledge, 2009) 1.
[4] Rob White and Fiona Haines, *Crime & Criminology*, 4th edn (Oxford University Press, 2008) ch 2; Eugene McLaughlin and John Muncie, *The Sage Dictionary of Criminology*, 2nd edn (Sage, 2006) 40, 124–25. The classical approach was a response to the arbitrary system of criminal punishment based on terror, control and paternal benevolence.

Basic to this theory of deterrence is the causal assumption that the cost of punishment and its threat, or its cost relative to any gains, has the power to inhibit unlawful behaviour by encouraging potential offenders to minimise loss.[5] The power to inhibit or deter behaviour in the classical theory is based on the certainty, severity and celerity of the punishment. Certainty refers to the probability that the person is punished for their wrongdoing. Severity refers to the amount of pain administered. Celerity is a term for how swiftly punishment follows after the wrongdoing.[6] The 'stiffer, quicker and more reliable the penalty, the less attractive the act will be'.[7]

Deterrence has found its way from criminal law and criminology to white-collar crime and then to approaches to regulation more generally.[8] In the process, corporate crime has been defined far more broadly than simply breaches of criminal law. Rather, it includes organisational behaviour that attracts criminal, civil, and regulatory sanctions.[9]

In criminal law, deterrence was one objective among others, such as retribution, prevention and rehabilitation.[10] Deterrence is seen as being a particularly effective way to reduce white-collar crime because corporate offenders have more to lose than traditional blue-collar offenders, such as income and reputation, and their crimes are aimed at economic gain.[11] Professor John Braithwaite describes corporate offenders as 'inherently more deterrable'.[12] Deterrence is also seen as being particularly effective in dealing with the corporation as 'an amoral profit seeking organization whose actions are motivated by rational calculation of costs and opportunities'.[13]

[5] Albert Reiss Jr , 'Consequences of Compliance and Deterrence Models of Law Enforcement for the Exercise of Police Discretion' (1984) 47 *Law and Contemporary Problems* 83, 94.

[6] Ray Paternoster and Ronet Bachman, 'Perceptual Deterrence Theory' in Francis Cullen and Pamela Wilcox, *The Oxford Handbook of Criminological Theory* (Oxford University Press, 2013) 650.

[7] Kennedy (n 3) 1.

[8] Keith Hawkins and John Thomas, 'The Enforcement Process in Regulatory Bureaucracies' in Keith Hawkins and John Thomas (eds), *Enforcing Regulation* (Kluwer-Nijhoff Publishing, 1984) 4–5.

[9] Edwin Sutherland, 'White-Collar Criminality' (1940) 5 *American Sociological Review* 1; Edwin Sutherland, *White Collar Crime* (Holt, Rinehart and Winston Inc, 1949).

[10] Simon Bronitt and Bernadette McSherry, *Principles of Criminal Law*, 3rd edn (Thomson Reuters, 2010) 17.

[11] Ray Paternoster and Sally Simpson, 'Sanction Threats and Appeals to Morality: Testing a Rational Choice Model of Corporate Crime' (1996) 30 *Law & Society Review* 549, 550–51; Brian Payne, 'Effects on White-Collar Defendants of Criminal Justice Attention and Sanctions' in Shanna Van Slyke, Michael Benson and Francis Cullen (eds), *The Oxford Handbook of White-Collar Crime* (Oxford University Press, 2016) 605–06. See, eg, *R v Craven* (1995) 17 ACSR 368, 377 (Abadee J) ('The evidence thus reveals that the prisoner has fallen from a successful, respectable and well-rewarded position in the community to one where he has no wealth, no money, no job and to say the least, a damaged or destroyed commercial reputation and "few" prospects.'); *R v Rivkin* (2003) 198 ALR 400, 413 [54] (Whealy J) ('First, there is the undoubted disgrace and humiliation which must accompany the jury's verdict so far as the offender is concerned. Secondly, there is the impact on his wife and family, so eloquently conveyed by Mrs Rivkin. Thirdly, there is the loss of his previous good standing in the community and in his profession as a stockbroker. It is true that many have rallied to his side and have expressed their continued support for him and their belief in him. There will undoubtedly be others who will think considerably less of him as a consequence of the jury's verdict. Fourthly, there is the unquantifiable but real economic impact the conviction may have upon his livelihood and business calling.').

[12] John Braithwaite, *Corporate Crime in the Pharmaceutical Industry* (Routledge & Kegan Paul, 1984) 290.

[13] 'Developments in the Law-Corporate Crime: Regulating Corporate Behavior Through Criminal Sanctions' (1979) 92 *Harvard Law Review* 1227, 1235–36; Robert Kagan and John Scholz, 'The Criminology of the Corporation and Regulatory Enforcement Strategies' in Keith Hawkins and John Thomas (eds), *Enforcing Regulation* (Kluwer-Nijhoff Publishing, 1984) 69. See also *Singtel Optus Pty Ltd v Australian Competition and Consumer Commission* [2012] FCAFC 20, [62] (Keane CJ, Finn and Gilmour JJ) ('There may be room for debate as to the proper place of deterrence in the punishment of some kinds of offences, such as crimes of passion; but in relation to offences of calculation by a corporation where the only punishment is a fine, the punishment must be fixed with a view to ensuring that the penalty is not such as to be regarded by that offender or others as an acceptable cost of doing business. The primary judge was right to proceed on the basis that the claims of deterrence in this case were so strong as to warrant a penalty that would upset any calculations of profitability.').

Regulation seeks to 'govern, direct or alter human behaviour in particular areas of endeavour'.[14] One way in which behaviour may be altered is through an enforcement approach that uses deterrence.[15] The aim is to impose sanctions in a way that incentivises regulated persons to follow the law.[16] The classical theory of deterrence lives on in approaches to regulation. As explained in chapter two, ASIC has adopted deterrence as an objective when enforcing the securities laws and this has been recognised by the courts.

In the class action, the recognition of deterrence as an objective comes mainly from the United States,[17] although, as chapter two explains, it has been adopted in Australia. The United States is seen as having a deterrence-oriented system of enforcement because it is legalistic, adversarial and focused on sanctions.[18] This approach carries over to the way in which the goals of shareholder class actions, a feature of US civil justice, have been depicted and evaluated. The US Congress when enacting the Private Securities Litigation Reform Act of 1995, 15 USC § 78u-4 stated that private lawsuits 'help to deter wrongdoing'.[19] The thinking is that the payment of damages by defendants deters wrongdoing because 'Corporate decision makers who anticipate bearing the costs of securities fraud, will, ex ante, internalize those costs and engage in efficient levels of care to ensure that their disclosures are accurate'.[20] In other words, the extraction of money from a wrongdoer to pay compensation acts as a sanction which the wrongdoer will seek to avoid.[21]

C. Dimensions of Deterrence

i. *Formal Sanctions, Indirect Costs and Reputational Harm*

Sanctions are at the heart of deterrence and 'can include, in principle, anything that exacts a cost'.[22] Consequently sanctions can include formal or direct sanctions such as fines or civil penalties[23] or an extraction of financial resources such as paying damages by way of providing compensation.[24] There may also be indirect financial costs. For a corporation this may mean the costs of investigating allegations and responding to regulators and litigation, including class actions. Indirect costs include the diversion of management from profit-seeking activities to dealing with enforcement. Indirect costs may also include a decline in the share price or

[14] Michael Legg, 'Regulatory Theory, Litigation and Enforcement' in Michael Legg (ed), *Regulation, Litigation and Enforcement* (Thomson Reuters, 2011) 1.

[15] Robert Baldwin, Martin Cave and Martin Lodge, *Understanding Regulation*, 2nd edn (Oxford University Press, 2012) 238–39; Neil Gunningham, 'Enforcement and Compliance Strategies' in Robert Baldwin, Martin Cave and Martin Lodge (eds), *The Oxford Handbook of Regulation* (Oxford University Press, 2010) 121.

[16] Gunningham (ibid) 121.

[17] *J I Case Co v Borack*, 377 US 426, 432 (1964); *Bateman Eichler, Hill Richards Inc v Berner*, 472 US 299, 310 (1985).

[18] Baldwin, Cave and Lodge (n 15) 239.

[19] Private Securities Litigation Reform Act of 1995, House of Representatives Conference Report No 104-369 (1995) reprinted in 1995 USCCAN 730 (28 November 1995) 730. For similar sentiments in US judicial statements see *JI Case Co v Borak*, 377 US 426, 432 (1964); *Tellabs, Inc v Makor Issues & Rights Ltd*, 551 US 308, 313 (2007); *Amgen Inc v Connecticut Retirement Plans and Trust Funds* 568 US 455, 477–78 (2013).

[20] Jill Fisch, 'Confronting the Circularity Problem in Private Securities Litigation' [2009] *Wisconsin Law Review* 333, 336. See also Amanda Rose, 'Reforming Securities Litigation Reform: Restructuring the Relationship Between Public and Private Enforcement of Rule 10B-5' (2008) 108 *Columbia Law Review* 1301, 1325.

[21] Australian Competition & Consumer Commission, 'Submission to the Competition Policy Review – Draft Report', (26 November 2014) 79; Russell Gold, 'Compensation's Role in Deterrence' (2016) 91 *Notre Dame Law Review* 1997, 2005–06.

[22] Kennedy (n 3) 32.

[23] ibid.

[24] See section II.B.i below.

unfavourable effects on other financial indicia. For an individual it may be loss of employment or loss of bonuses or promotions.

There are also informal sanctions such as social stigmatisation or reputational harm.[25] These informal sanctions are particularly significant for white-collar workers who have more to lose in terms of social capital, ie the standing and respect afforded to them by their peers, family and society more broadly. Consequently, embarrassment and shame can be effective reputational sanctions for white-collar workers.[26] Reputational harm may also operate in relation to corporations when customers or other constituents alter the way they deal with the company. Employee morale may decline and prospective employees may be dissuaded from joining the corporation.[27] Customers may decline to purchase products or services from a company that is seen as breaching the law.[28]

In determining whether to employ formal and/or informal sanctions, it has been observed that for sanctions to be effective they need to be aimed at what is important to the potential offender. Formal sanctions matter, but informal sanctions may matter more.[29]

ii. Specific and General Deterrence

The classical theory of deterrence focuses not just on the current offender who should be deterred from reoffending, but on the general population so as to deter future or potential criminal activity.[30] The first focus is specific deterrence and the second focus is general deterrence. Both have been specifically adopted in relation to the goals of ASIC in undertaking enforcement.[31] The Australian courts have stated that specific deterrence aims to deter 'the particular contravenor who might be tempted to re-offend' while general deterrence is aimed at deterring others 'who might be tempted not to comply with the law'.[32]

General deterrence has particular significance in securities regulation due to the stated goals of protecting and maintaining market integrity.[33] More generally, investment in public companies depends on the public having confidence in the operation of those companies.[34] It has also been recognised that shareholders are vulnerable to the conduct of management as the shareholder is dependent on management to provide accurate information.[35]

[25] Brent Fisse and John Braithwaite, *The Impact of Publicity on Corporate Offenders* (State University of New York Press, 1983) 232–33; Kennedy (n 3) 38–39; Robert Apel and Samuel DeWitt, 'Informal and Formal Sanctions' in Daniel Nagin, Francis Cullen and Cheryl Lero Jonson (eds), *Deterrence, Choice, and Crime: Contemporary Perspectives* (Routledge, 2018) 144–45.

[26] Harold Grasmick and Robert Bursik, 'Conscience, Significant Others and Rational Choice: Extending the Deterrence Model' (1990) 24 *Law & Society Review* 837; Ian Ayres and John Braithwaite, *Responsive Regulation* (Oxford University Press, 1992) 22; Paternoster and Simpson (n 11); Aaron Chalfin and Justin McCrary, 'Criminal Deterrence: A Review of the Literature' (2017) 55 *Journal of Economic Literature* 5, 39.

[27] Fisse and Braithwaite, *The Impact of Publicity* (n 25) 232, 248.

[28] ibid 248; VS Khanna, 'Corporate Criminal Liability: What Purpose Does it Serve?' (1996) 109 *Harvard Law Review* 1477, 1500.

[29] Fisse and Braithwaite, *The Impact of Publicity* (n 25) 243; Kennedy (n 3) 182; Apel and DeWitt (n 25) 147.

[30] McLaughlin and Muncie (n 4) 125; Gunningham (n 15) 122.

[31] See, eg, ASIC, 'Statement of Intent – Australian Securities and Investments Commission' (July 2014).

[32] *ASIC v Chemeq Ltd* (2006) 234 ALR 511, 532 [90] (French J). See also *ASIC v Newcrest Mining Limited* (2014) 101 ACSR 46, 55–56 [59] (Middleton J).

[33] *R v Doff* (2005) 54 ACSR 200, 212 [56] (Wood CJ at CL, Adams and Bell JJ); *R v Glynatsis* (2013) 230 A Crim R 99, 106 [39] (Hoeben CJ at CL) (sentencing in relation to insider trading).

[34] *R v Craven* (1995) 17 ACSR 368, 377–78 (Abadee J) (sentencing in relation to breach of directors' duties).

[35] Maria Nicolae, 'The Liability-Sanction Relationship: A Case Study in the Effectiveness of the Corporate Regulatory Regime' (2013) 31 *Company and Securities Law Journal* 365, 371.

D. What Makes Deterrence Effective?

i. Certainty, Severity and Celerity

Deterrence theorists have examined what makes deterrence effective and determined that it includes the severity of sanctions, the speed of imposition or celerity of sanctions, the certainty of sanctions being imposed, and potential offenders' perceptions of these factors.[36] Deterrence scholarship has found that the certainty of being punished has a greater deterrent effect than the severity or celerity of the punishment.[37] In the criminal law, courts have also recognised that deterrence is achieved not by harsher sentences but by 'the impression on the minds of those who are persisting in a course of crime that detection is likely and punishment will be certain'.[38] However, the deterrence effect of certainty may be less when a strict liability offence is in issue as the greater ease of enforcement action (usually with a small fine) is coupled with an absence of moral blameworthiness.[39]

Although scholars often refer to a singular likelihood of punishment, the certainty of enforcement is a composite of several probabilities, including the likelihood of: (1) detection; (2) subsequent apprehension; (3) the finding of a contravention by a court; and (4) sanctions.[40] This means that there may be a difference between the 'law on the books' creating obligations and how that law is enforced. A focus on the constituent steps in arriving at punishment allows for consideration of the various factors that impact certainty, and as a result, the effectiveness of deterrence.

The first factor impacting certainty of each of the above constituent steps in enforcement is the complexity of the modern business environment.[41] Complexity arises from factors including globalisation, corporate structures, transaction structures, accounting requirements and technology. Complexity may impact whether a contravention is detected and whether non-compliance can be proved to the requisite standard.

A second factor impacting certainty is insufficient resources, including personnel, that can mean that contraventions are not detected, or if detected are not pursued, or if pursued are resolved without the sanction of a court.[42] An underfunded regulator may not be able to promote deterrence effectively because the regulated population may know that the chances of detection are low, and even if detected, may be dealt with through a warning, administrative sanction or strict liability offence so as to avoid the cost of formally proving a contravention. Complexity and insufficient resourcing can be offset by the fact that detection is aided by the regulator having expertise in the subject matter it regulates, as well as coercive investigatory powers for obtaining information.[43]

[36] Kennedy (n 3) 32.

[37] George Gilligan, Helen Bird and Ian Ramsay, 'Civil Penalties and the Enforcement of Directors' Duties' (1999) 22 *UNSW Law Journal* 417, 439; Miriam Baer, 'Linkage and the Deterrence of Corporate Fraud' (2008) 94 *Virginia Law Review* 1295, 1306; Freiberg (n 2) 427–28; Chalfin and McCrary (n 26) 37–38.

[38] *Griffiths v The Queen* (1977) 137 CLR 293, 327 (Jacobs J).

[39] Paul Robinson, 'Strict Liability's Criminogenic Effect' (2018) 12 *Criminal Law and Philosophy* 411.

[40] Baer 'Linkage' (n 37) 1306; Daniel Nagin, 'Deterrent Effects of the Certainty and Severity of Punishment' in Daniel Nagin, Francis Cullen and Cheryl Lero Jonson (eds), *Deterrence, Choice, and Crime: Contemporary Perspectives* (Routledge, 2018) 158.

[41] Albert Reiss Jr , 'Selecting Strategies of Social Control Over Organizational Life' in Keith Hawkins and John Thomas (eds), *Enforcing Regulation* (Kluwer-Nijhoff Publishing, 1984) 34; Jennifer Chawla, 'Criminal Accountability and Wall Street Executives: Why the Criminal Provisions of the Dodd-Frank Act Fall Short' (2014) 44 *Seton Hall Law Review* 937, 947.

[42] Robert Kagan, 'On Regulatory Inspectorates and Police' in Keith Hawkins and John Thomas (eds), *Enforcing Regulation* (Kluwer-Nijhoff Publishing, 1984) 40; Chalfin and McCrary (n 26) 38–39.

[43] See Michael Legg, 'Coercive Investigatory Powers of ASIC, ACCC and ATO' in Michael Legg (ed), *Regulation, Litigation and Enforcement* (Thomson Reuters, 2011) 31.

The certainty of enforcement may also be affected by a third factor: the requirements of litigation and trial. Formal enforcement is slow, labour-intensive and subject to a range of procedural steps to protect the rights of the accused or defendant such as the right to silence, the presumption of innocence, burdens of proof, and rules of procedure and evidence.[44] To the extent that a court sanction is required to achieve deterrence, the formalities of litigation may discourage resort to the court. Further, difficulties in proof can provide an alleged contravenor with the ability to bargain over the penalty imposed.[45]

A fourth factor is that corporate defendants may have significant resources that can be devoted to resisting detection, apprehension and findings of contravention. The corporation and its officers will usually be well-educated, knowledgeable about their business and able to afford expert legal services.[46] As a result they may be able to oppose the regulator every step of the way. This can make each step more expensive and time-consuming which can then act as a disincentive to the regulator pursuing each of those steps.[47]

ii. Perceptions

General deterrence may be elaborated on by reference to perceptual deterrence theory which states that people are influenced by what they think or perceive the certainty of being apprehended is, the sanctions that will follow and the swiftness of the imposition of those sanctions, regardless of what each of these elements of deterrence actually are.[48] In keeping with the significance of certainty, a focus on perceptions means that those who think they are likely to get caught are less likely to engage in various acts of corporate crime.[49] There may be a number of sources of information about the costs of contravening the law: the law itself, the enforcement of the law, coworkers and social networks, and the media, some or all of which may impact on the individual's knowledge.[50]

Consequently, it may be that it is the benefits and costs as understood and weighed by the potential offender that determines how, or if, deterrence works.[51] If deterrence is not working, it may be because the underlying law or its enforcement are not effective. However, it may also be the case that it is the subjective response of the potential offender, including not knowing what sanctions they face, that is preventing effective deterrence.[52]

Perception may also be affected by the 'experiential effect'. As time passes the potential offender becomes more informed about the prospects of being caught by seeing what happens to themselves and others. In particular, if an offender contravenes the law and is not apprehended, they may adjust their estimate of the certainty of getting caught downwards.[53]

[44] Kagan (n 42) 41; Kenneth Arensen and Mirko Bagaric, *Criminal Processes and Investigative Procedures: Victoria and Commonwealth*, 4th edn (LexisNexis, 2019) 3–4.

[45] Reiss (n 41) 32.

[46] Kagan (n 42) 47.

[47] See section IV.E below where resourcing and efficiency can also be examined from the perspective of the regulatory process.

[48] Kennedy (n 3) 31; Paternoster and Bachman (n 6) 651.

[49] Ray Paternoster, 'How Much do we Really Know About Criminal Deterrence?' (2010) 100 *Journal of Criminal Law and Criminology* 765, 811–18.

[50] Paternoster and Bachman (n 6) 656–57; Chalfin and McCrary (n 26) 10–12.

[51] Kennedy (n 3) 23.

[52] ibid 23, 182; Baldwin, Cave and Lodge (n 15) 241 (some companies may not have the systems to be able to determine the costs or benefits of avoiding contraventions).

[53] Kennedy (n 3) 11, 29.

iii. Economic Theory and Optimal Deterrence

The classical theory of deterrence, particularly as developed by Bentham, has been the foundation for a law and economics approach to deterrence.[54] Economic theory provides two important insights. First, at the individual level the decision to engage in criminal activity is depicted as being the same as any other decision under uncertainty, with the relevant considerations being the probability of being caught, the monetary equivalent of the punishment if convicted, and the gain from the criminal activity.[55] The level of sanctions to achieve the optimal level of deterrence is said to be created by compelling the responsible party to internalise the full social cost of its conduct multiplied by the likelihood of detection. If a contravention causes harm of $100, but it is only likely to be detected 50 per cent of the time then the sanction should be $200.[56]

Second, at the society level the normative question for a legislature is to determine the policy settings for the resources to be devoted to enforcement and the level of sanctions.[57] The efficient allocation of resources for deterring crime is based on the socially optimal amount of deterrence occurring at the point where the marginal social costs of reducing crime equals the marginal social benefit.[58] This is because deterrence is costly and further expenditure to deter crime may be greater than the benefits derived from that deterrence so that society is worse off overall.

The aim of a securities regulatory regime according to an optimal deterrence approach involves balancing the social benefits from compliance against the costs of enforcement.[59] The social benefits include decreasing the cost of capital, increases in liquidity, efficient allocation of resources, and reduced monitoring costs for investors as confidence in the ability to determine the value of corporate securities is promoted.[60] Enforcement costs may be direct or indirect. Direct costs are the resources consumed in detecting, prosecuting, defending and adjudicating cases. Indirect costs are overinvestment in precautionary measures such as compliance regimes or adopting a defensive disclosure policy.[61] In simple terms, under-enforcement can lead to a reduction in the above social benefits and over-enforcement can lead to excessive enforcement costs.

The optimal deterrence approach provides greater guidance, at least theoretically, as to how deterrence should be calibrated by a regulator. It is also of significance because both the resources devoted to enforcement and the level at which sanctions should be set are affected by the introduction of private enforcement, of current interest, the class action. The theory provides a useful analytical tool for examining how public and private enforcement may interact in relation to deterrence. Once combined, do they address a situation of under-deterrence, or do they result in over-deterrence?

[54] See, eg, Richard Posner, 'An Economic Theory of the Criminal Law' (1985) 85 *Columbia Law Review* 1193.

[55] Robert Cooter and Thomas Ulen, *Law and Economics*, 5th edn (Pearson, 2007) 494–98.

[56] Gary Becker, 'Crime and Punishment: An Economic Approach' (1968) 76 *Journal of Political Economy* 169; Kenneth Dam, 'Class Actions: Efficiency, Compensation, Deterrence and Conflict of Interest' (1975) 4 *Journal of Legal Studies* 47, 67; Brian Fitzpatrick, *The Conservative Case for Class Actions* (The University of Chicago Press, 2019) 103. See also Australian Law Reform Commission, 'Principled Regulation', Report No 95 (2002) 791.

[57] Becker (ibid); Michael Perino, 'Enron's Legislative Aftermath: Some Reflections on the Deterrence Aspects of the Sarbanes-Oxley Act of 2002' (2002) 76 *St John's Law Review* 671, 674–76.

[58] Warren Schwartz, 'An Overview of the Economics of Antitrust Enforcement' (1979) 68 *Georgetown Law Journal* 1075, 1075; Cooter and Ulen (n 55) 511–13.

[59] Rose, 'Reforming Securities Litigation Reform' (n 20) 1322; Amanda Rose, 'The Multienforcer Approach to Securities Fraud Deterrence: A Critical Analysis' (2010) 158 *University of Pennsylvania Law Review* 2173, 2178.

[60] Rose, 'The Multienforcer Approach' (n 59) 2179.

[61] ibid 2183–84. See also Commonwealth Treasury, 'Review of Sanctions in Corporate Law' (2007) 9 ('Sanctions Review').

iv. Targeting Deterrence – Corporate Entity or Individual?

Professor John Coffee has observed that 'Deterrence works best when it is focused on the culpable'.[62] An important factor in achieving deterrence in relation to securities law where there are both corporate and individual actors is to determine whether deterrence is better achieved through imposing sanctions on the corporation or on responsible individuals within the corporation.[63] This question overlaps with, but is separate from, the issue of whether a corporation can, or should be, subject to the criminal law.[64] Chapter two demonstrates that there are a number of causes of action, criminal, civil and administrative, available in relation to contravention of the continuous disclosure regime and they may target the corporation and/or individuals.

Sanctions aimed at individuals are supported from a deterrence perspective because the decision to contravene the law is ultimately made by individuals. Further, only individuals act and have a conscience. The threat of personal liability for misconduct provides a direct incentive to ensure compliance as the negative effect of sanctions will be felt by the individual.[65] In contrast, where sanctions are visited upon the corporation the impact on individuals is indirect. Indeed, individuals may not be deterred if their personal gain is greater than the harm they may suffer should the corporation be penalised.[66] For example, a fine imposed on the company for a criminal contravention would be expected to have less deterrent effect than a fine imposed directly on the individual. However, the corporation in responding to sanctions may discipline or dismiss individuals as discussed below.

The conduct of an individual may be characterised from two different perspectives. The illegal conduct of an individual in a corporation may be seen as conduct undertaken for the business or as conduct undertaken based on self-interest.[67] The former may be actions aimed at increasing business profits or reducing costs. An example could be manipulating earnings to prevent a corporation breaching loan covenants. The latter would be actions aimed at achieving financial reward for the individual such as increasing the price of shares held by the individual, bonuses or promotion. It may also include fraud and theft. In the former situation the case for aiming deterrence at the corporation is stronger than in the latter situation. This is because the gains from the conduct accrue to the company and deterrence needs to persuade the company not to seek such gains. However, even conduct that may appear to be undertaken for the corporation may be linked to managerial self-interest.[68] The influences on an individual's behaviour are not clear-cut, and probably numerous.

[62] John Coffee, 'Reforming the Securities Class Action: An Essay on Deterrence and Its Implementation (2006) 106 *Columbia Law Review* 1534, 1536. See also Jennifer Arlen and William Carney, 'Vicarious Liability for Fraud on Securities Markets: Theory and Evidence' [1992] *University of Illinois Law Review* 691, 694, 727.

[63] Sally Simpson, 'Making Sense of White-Collar Crime: Theory and Research' (2011) 8 *Ohio State Journal of Criminal Law* 481, 482.

[64] See Jonathan Clough and Carmel Mulhern, *The Prosecution of Corporations* (Oxford University Press, 2002) 71–122; Olivia Dixon, 'Corporate Criminal Liability: The Influence of Corporate Culture' in Justin O'Brien and George Gilligan, *Integrity, Risk and Accountability in Capital Markets: Regulating Culture* (Hart Publishing, 2013) 252–59 summarising the theories and critiques of corporate criminal liability.

[65] Eliezer Lederman, 'Criminal Law, Perpetrator and Corporation: Rethinking a Complex Triangle' (1985) 76 *Journal of Criminal Law and Criminology* 285, 294–96; Brent Fisse and John Braithwaite, *Corporations, Crime and Accountability* (Cambridge University Press, 1993) 18, 32; Paternoster and Simpson (n 11) 553–54, 577.

[66] Donald Langevoort, 'On Leaving Corporate Executives "Naked, Homeless and Without Wheels": Corporate Fraud, Equitable Remedies and the Debate Over Entity Versus Individual Liability' (2007) 42 *Wake Forest Law Review* 627, 635.

[67] Reinier Kraakman, 'Corporate Liability Strategies and the Cost of Legal Controls' (1984) 93 *Yale Law Journal* 857, 866; James Cox, 'Private Litigation and the Deterrence of Corporate Misconduct' (1997) 60 *Law & Contemporary Problems* 1, 3.

[68] Cox, 'Private Litigation' (ibid) 11 (providing antitrust and environmental contraventions that were driven by managers seeking to meet budgets which affected their advancement within the firm).

It has also been argued that individual liability must be employed because the corporation is a fictional entity.[69] This followed from early English case law typified by the statement that a corporation 'has no soul to be damned, and no body to be kicked'.[70] Consequently the corporation could not be subject to moral retribution or physical punishment. However, deterrence does not require a soul or body, but simply a rational economic actor that responds to costs. Corporations are seen as making decisions along cost-benefit lines so that monetary sanctions on corporations are well suited to achieving deterrence.[71]

The levelling of sanctions on the corporate entity is based on a view that it is the principal and sanctions visited upon it will provide an incentive for company controllers to discipline its agents such as the director.[72] Imposing sanctions on the corporation for the acts of its agents imposes costs and reduces profits. The corporation has the incentive to devise compliance and reward mechanisms to monitor its agents. Moreover, as the complexity of the corporate entity grows it is argued that it becomes better placed, and it is more efficient, to determine which actors within it are to blame.[73]

The corporation may also be the necessary target when wrongdoing is the result of institutional forces and corporate culture.[74] A person's interests are socially constructed in their working environment. The ways in which the corporation communicates what is acceptable conduct in the pursuit of profit impacts on the decision making of employees.[75] For example, the corporation's process for bonuses and promotions aims to influence the individual's behaviour. Similarly, ineffective training, oversight, reporting lines and risk management may promote or condone certain actions.[76] The corporation as a separate legal entity may have a separate culture or ethos to the individuals which compose it. The financial organisation may constitute a 'group' which through situational forces causes individuals to act differently compared to when they are alone.[77] Corporate culture may value law-abiding behaviour or it may tolerate non-compliance. Deterrence needs to take account of corporate culture as it may impact the level of penalty needed.[78] A focus on individuals allows the organisation to avoid responsibility and point at the 'bad apple' – a single individual who is to be held responsible.[79] To put the argument another way,

[69] Khanna (n 28) 1494; Clough and Mulhern (n 64) 5.

[70] The statement is attributed to Lord Chancellor Thurlow in the 18th century. See also *Continental Tyre and Rubber Co (GB) Ltd v Daimler Co Ltd* [1915] 1 KB 893, 916 (Buckley LJ).

[71] See ch 3, section II.B.

[72] Kraakman (n 67) 859; Harvey Pitt and Karl Groskaufmanis, 'Minimizing Corporate Civil and Criminal Liability: A Second Look at Corporate Codes of Conduct' (1990) 78 *Georgetown Law Journal* 1559, 1573; Khanna (n 28) 1495–96.

[73] Christopher Stone, 'The Place of Enterprise Liability in the Control of Corporate Conduct' (1980) 90 *Yale Law Journal* 1, 28–29; John Coffee, '"No Soul to Damn: No Body to Kick": An Unscandalized Inquiry into the Problem of Corporate Punishment' (1981) 79 *Michigan Law Review* 386, 407–08; Clough and Mulhern (n 64) 6.

[74] Wim Huisman, 'Offender Decision Making in Corporate and White-Collar Crime' in Wim Bernasco, Jean-Louis van Gelder, and Henk Elffers (eds), *The Oxford Handbook of Offender Decision Making* (Oxford University Press, 2017) 691–92; Benjamin van Rooji and Adam Fine, 'Toxic Corporate Culture: Assessing Organizational Processes of Deviancy' (2018) 8 *Administrative Sciences* 23.

[75] Peter Cleary Yeager, 'Understanding Corporate Lawbreaking: From Profit Seeking to Law Finding' in Henry Pontell and Gilbert Geis (eds), *International Handbook of White-Collar and Corporate Crime* (Springer, 2007) 32.

[76] See, eg, Financial Crisis Inquiry Commission, 'The Financial Crisis Inquiry Report' (2011) xviii–xix.

[77] See, eg, Neal Kumar Katyal, 'Conspiracy Theory' (2003) 112 *Yale Law Journal* 1307, 1316–24, 1355–58; Philip Zimbardo, *The Lucifer Effect – Understanding How Good People Turn Evil* (Random House, 2008) ch 12.

[78] *ASIC v Chemeq Ltd* (2006) 234 ALR 511, 532–33 [93] (French J).

[79] Michael Legg, 'Class Actions and Regulating Culture in Financial Organisations: Observations from a Comparison of US and Australian Bank Class Actions' in Justin O'Brien and George Gilligan, *Integrity, Risk and Accountability in Capital Markets: Regulating Culture* (Hart Publishing, 2013) 243–44; Vicky Comino, '"Corporate Culture" Is the "New Black" – Its Possibilities and Limits as a Regulatory Mechanism for Corporations and Financial Institutions' (2021) 44 *UNSW Law Journal* 295, 312–13.

contraventions of the law that arise because of the organisational culture influencing individuals requires the organisation be held to account.[80]

v. *Avoiding Dispersion of Deterrence*

Monetary payments, either as fines or civil penalties, or even compensation, would not achieve deterrence if they could be transferred onto third parties. For example, if fines or civil penalties can be passed onto customers without damaging the competitive position of the corporation then deterrence may be undermined.[81] As explained above, the corporate form may allow for this to a significant degree where sanctions are not imposed on a particular wrongdoer but borne by the organisation and ultimately its shareholders. The responsible manager or director may not pay the fine, which instead comes from the corporate treasury.[82] If the amount of the sanction can be dispersed so can the deterrent effect. This concern has been responded to through the argument that informal or non-monetary sanctions may prevent dispersion because they 'transcend the commercial banality of money'.[83]

E. Limitations of the Sanctions Approach to Deterrence

i. *Insufficient Costs and Flexibility*

Deterrence in the regulatory enforcement literature is closely associated with litigation and the courts because it involves proving contraventions and punishing violators. Unsurprisingly, deterrence is linked with criminal sanctions and civil penalties. As a result deterrence has been argued to be inflexible because it deals with a contravention through jail time or monetary sanctions only.[84] Such criticism disregards the breadth of formal and informal sanctions that may be imposed as a result of litigation or otherwise. However, the breadth of formal sanctions will depend on the content of the legislation creating the sanction. Stepping beyond purely monetary penalties allows for both a broader range of sanctions and flexibility in the use of those sanctions.

The Commonwealth Treasury's consultation paper on sanctions in corporate law opined that 'for a penalty to be meaningful as a deterrent it must have an impact on the entity penalised'.[85] The sanctions approach to deterrence has been criticised for imposing insufficient costs, especially on corporations.[86] Sanctions should not simply be a cost of doing business, but rather outweigh the potential benefits from committing the contravention.[87] However, there may be a reluctance to impose large fines because the fine may impact solvency and the ability of the corporation to continue as a going concern, or it may reduce the resources that can be devoted to compliance.[88]

[80] See Memorandum from Larry Thompson, Deputy Attorney General, US Department of Justice to Heads of Department Components, US Department of Justice, 20 January 2003 ('Indicting corporations for wrongdoing enables the government to address and be a force for positive change of corporate culture, alter corporate behavior, and prevent, discover, and punish white collar crime.'); Samuel Buell, 'The Blaming Function of Entity Criminal Liability' (2006) 81 *Indiana Law Journal* 473.

[81] Reiss (n 41) 28.

[82] Kagan (n 42) 48; Fisse and Braithwaite, *The Impact of Publicity* (n 25) 2.

[83] Fisse and Braithwaite, *Corporations* (n 65) 82.

[84] See Kagan and Scholz (n 13) 68; Baldwin, Cave and Lodge (n 15) 242.

[85] Sanctions Review (n 61) 21.

[86] ibid; Baldwin, Cave and Lodge (n 15) 240; ASIC, 'Penalties for Corporate Wrongdoing – Report 387' (March 2014) 15.

[87] IOSCO, 'Credible Deterrence in the Enforcement of Securities Regulation' (June 2015) 35.

[88] Brandon Garrett, *Too Big to Jail* (Harvard University Press, 2014) 42, 59.

Further, the level of sanctions needed to reflect the gravity of the offence and the low risk of detection, consistent with economic theory, may be so high as to not be payable by the corporation leading to insolvency. This is referred to as the deterrence trap.[89] The wrongdoer, especially a corporation, can cause harm far greater than its resources. As a result the response is to use sanctions beyond financial penalties, imprisonment being the classic response.

ii. Beyond Sanctions – An Expressive Theory of Law

Economic analysis views a legal sanction as if it were a market price. Viewed as a price, the actor sees a sanction as an external constraint. A potential wrongdoer is only concerned with the chances of getting caught and the extent of the expected punishment. A punishment therefore deters negative behaviour by imposing a cost on that behaviour.[90] Alternatively, law can be seen as a way to change social understanding of a particular activity by affecting preferences, norms and behaviour. Laws are seen as having the capability to shape social and institutional norms.

The aim of enforcing regulation is not just to punish the particular offender but to educate others as to society's expectations so as to change morality or culture.[91] By having a moral stigma associated with a contravention, people seek to comply with the law. This is because people act in accordance with their perception of what other people – the community – think.[92] Regulation and enforcement, especially through the judgment of a court, act as guideposts to what the community thinks.[93]

An expressive theory of law offers at least two further perspectives or questions for the public/private enforcement debate. The first is a challenge to the sanctions approach to deterrence by suggesting that there is more to decisions about enforcement than creating efficient cost-internalisation incentives. Indeed, the sanctions approach is argued to elide the moral contentions that motivate enforcement decisions.[94] The distinction between the two may be summarised as: expressive theory focuses on meanings, while deterrence focuses on consequences.[95] The concern here is that meanings matter, which leads to the second perspective. The second question is whether public or private enforcement better achieves moral or cultural change in aid of having conduct accepted as wrong. As Professor Dan Kahan has observed:

> The message of condemnation is very clear when society deprives an offender of his liberty. But when it merely fines him for the same act, the message is likely to be different: you may do what you have done, but you must pay for the privilege.[96]

The manner in which deterrence is achieved, or the enforcement tool employed to deter misconduct, is important. The same issue arises with public and private enforcement. The message sent by a criminal prosecution brought by the state is different to a private suit for damages. The state has a monopoly on criminal prosecutions which may be explained, in part, by that form of punishment being equated with moral condemnation for which the state is the most

[89] Coffee, 'No Soul to Damn' (n 73) 390.

[90] Karen Yeung, 'Quantifying Regulatory Penalties: Australian Competition Law Penalties in Perspective' (1999) 23 *Melbourne University Law Review* 440, 457.

[91] Dan Kahan, 'What Do Alternative Sanctions Mean?' (1996) 63 *University of Chicago Law Review* 591, 593.

[92] Dan Kahan, 'The Secret Ambition of Deterrence' (1999) 113 *Harvard Law Review* 413, 486–87.

[93] Cass Sunstein, 'On the Expressive Function of Law' (1996) 144 *University of Pennsylvania Law Review* 2021, 2032.

[94] Kahan, 'The Secret Ambition of Deterrence' (n 92) 483, 485.

[95] ibid 425.

[96] Kahan, 'Alternative Sanctions' (n 91) 593.

appropriate proxy for society.[97] This is not to say that private actors cannot alter moral or cultural norms. There are a range of 'norm entrepreneurs' who seek to identify the negative consequences of particular actions and seek to shift the community's understanding of those actions.[98] For example, environmental campaigners seek to deter corporations from harming the environment through shame and reputational damage, even if their conduct is not illegal.

iii. Rationality

The sanctions approach to deterrence has also been questioned on the basis that its assumption of rationality does not hold.[99] This must be considered in relation to both individuals and corporations.

First, from an individual perspective, a person may act on impulse such as with a crime of passion or because of the effect of alcohol or drugs, or some personality trait or mental defect may make them act in a criminal manner. Alternatively, crime is seen as the result of socio-economic factors such as lack of education and minimal job opportunities.[100] Without entering into the debate as to whether these critiques of deterrence are valid, it can be observed here that they have less salience in the sphere of securities regulation where the population to be deterred are likely to be educated and highly paid to deal with legal requirements in an orderly and considered manner.[101] Indeed, corporate executives are often referred to as 'bean counters' because of their focus on the costs and benefits that result from particular courses of action.[102] General deterrence in particular is most effective in relation to planned rather than impulsive conduct, with contravention of securities laws usually requiring calculation and preparation.[103]

Second, rationality, particularly in terms of economics' rational choice theory and a person's expected utility, has been criticised because people cannot or do not accurately weigh the costs and benefits of engaging in illegal conduct, let alone the probabilities of being caught and punished.[104] The criticism may be responded to by pointing out that rationality does not require accurate knowledge or precision in probabilities to be effective. Rather, rationality involves only a person being sensible or employing some form of reasoning.[105] Cognitive biases prevent humans from achieving the level of rationality assumed in economics.[106] This does not mean that deterrence through the impositions of sanctions is ineffective, but rather that deterrence needs to take account of these human limitations. Another approach is to view a person's utility, consistent with

[97] Edwin Sutherland, 'Is "White Collar Crime" Crime?' (1945) 10 *American Sociological Review* 132, 136: Miriam Baer, 'Choosing Punishment' (2012) 92 *Boston University Law Review* 577, 603; *ASIC v Vizard* (2005) 145 FCR 57, 64 [30] (Finkelstein J).

[98] Sunstein, 'Expressive Function' (n 93) 2030–01.

[99] Christopher Hodges and Stefaan Voet, *Delivering Collective Redress* (Hart, 2018) 273.

[100] Mirko Bagaric, 'Incapacitation, Deterrence and Rehabilitation: Flawed Ideals or Appropriate Sentencing Goals?' (2000) 24 *Criminal Law Journal* 21, 37; Kennedy (n 3) 16–17.

[101] *Director of Public Prosecutions (DPP) (Cth) v Gregory* (2011) 34 VR 1, 16 [53] (Warren CJ, Redlich JA, Ross AJA) ('White collar criminals are likely to be rational, profit-seeking individuals who can weigh the benefits of committing a crime against the costs of being caught and punished.').

[102] Fitzpatrick (n 56) 104.

[103] Nicolae (n 35) 372; *ASIC v Vizard* (2005) 145 FCR 57, 65 [35] ('Few corporate crimes are spontaneous.'), 66 [37] ('Corporate crimes are … almost always the result of deliberate and calculated conduct.') (Finkelstein J).

[104] Russell Korobkin and Thomas Ulen, 'Law and Behavioral Science: Removing the Rationality Assumption from Law and Economics (2000) 88 *California Law Review* 1051; Kennedy (n 3) 15–19.

[105] See *Oxford English Dictionary* (online) 'rationality'.

[106] Korobkin and Ulen (n 104); Paul Robinson and John Darley, 'Does Criminal Law Deter? A Behavioral Science Investigation' (2004) 24 *Oxford Journal of Legal Studies* 173, 174.

perceptual deterrence theory, as being self-defined or subjective. What then becomes important for achieving deterrence is understanding what factors go into the calculation and directing deterrence at those factors: 'It is benefits and costs as [potential offenders] understand them and define them, and their thinking in weighing those benefits and costs, that are dispositive'.[107]

Corporations are depicted as being rational profit-maximisers, but the corporation may suffer from ignorance or incompetence that result in irrational decisions that expose the corporation to sanctions.[108] This may occur because corporations are composed of individuals who have limitations on their capacity to make rational decisions, as discussed above. But if the individual is deterred, then the corporation may also be deterred. Alternatively, it may be corporate culture or institutional forces that shape behaviour, as discussed above. Fisse and Braithwaite illustrate this point through drawing on organisational theory which suggests that corporate decisions may be made through following standard operating procedures or through bargaining as part of bureaucratic power struggles.[109] This suggests that changing or deterring behaviour requires an understanding of how the corporation operates.[110] The difficulty is that each corporation may operate differently giving rise to a great deal of diversity in the responses required.[111]

iv. Measuring Deterrence

While the reasoning behind deterrence is intuitively appealing, it is much more difficult to determine if, or to what degree, deterrence has been achieved, and how such deterrence occurred.[112] The operation of deterrence has been described as a 'black box'[113] and that it is unclear 'How much deterrence we get from a combination of sanctions for what sorts of offenses in what kinds of industries'.[114] Indeed, the number of moving parts, including those discussed above such as the type of sanction, the value or impact of the sanction (actual and perceived), the likelihood of apprehension (actual and perceived), the gain from the misconduct (actual and perceived) all effect the calculations of the regulated entity, assuming rational calculations are possible and undertaken. Empirical examinations of deterrence have shown that 'deterrence matters a lot', but the failures of deterrence are also clearly visible.[115] Moreover, the inability to measure deterrence also arises because effective deterrence involves proving a negative, that is, that a person or entity refrained from misconduct because of the fear of sanctions. Further, interpreting the effect of enforcement actions is fraught. The number of actions taken by a regulator does not necessarily equate with an increase or decrease in misconduct, but may reflect the focus and efforts of the regulator, such as directing resources elsewhere or preventing misconduct through education.[116] Central to measuring deterrence is establishing the causal link between sanctions and conduct, but that causal link is difficult to directly observe, let alone measure.

[107] Kennedy (n 3) 23.
[108] Kagan and Scholz (n 13) 72; Fisse and Braithwaite, *Corporations* (n 65) 219.
[109] Fisse and Braithwaite, *Corporations* (n 65) 102–03.
[110] ibid 120–21.
[111] ibid 131.
[112] IOSCO (n 87) 51; Hodges and Voet (n 99) 269.
[113] Chalfin and McCrary (n 26) 13.
[114] Peter Cleary Yeager, 'The Practical Challenges of Responding to Corporate Crime' in Shanna Van Slyke, Michael Benson and Francis Cullen (eds), *The Oxford Handbook of White-Collar Crime* (Oxford University Press, 2016) 654. See also Kennedy (n 3); Peter Cleary Yeager, 'The Elusive Deterrence of Corporate Crime' (2016) 15 *Criminology & Public Policy* 439, 439.
[115] Kennedy (n 3); Nagin (n 40) 181; Fitzpatrick (n 56) 110–113 (summarising empirical studies of deterrence).
[116] Yeager, 'Practical Challenges' (n 114) 648, 656.

III. Compensation

A. Definition

Compensation is the reparation of a wrong through the delivery of an equivalent – usually a sum of money.[117] The wrong is specified by the Corporations Act – failure to comply with the continuous disclosure regime or misleading conduct. The Corporations Act also specifies that where that wrong causes loss or damage, the person harmed may seek compensation. Access to that compensation may be facilitated by a regulator being able to obtain compensation on behalf of the harmed person. Alternatively, access to the compensation may be sought through private suit, including the class action. Consequently, enforcement of the continuous disclosure provisions involves both creating the remedy of compensation and assisting those harmed to access the remedy.

B. Why is it an Objective?

The objective of providing investors with access to compensation arises from the theories of corrective justice and consumer protection which require compensation as a matter of fairness when a contravention of an obligation by one actor causes another actor loss. The compensation objective also clearly arises from the text and intention of the legislation. Each of these sources of the compensation objective is explained below.

i. Corrective Justice

Compensation may be approached from either a utilitarian or deontological perspective.[118] A utilitarian approach draws on economic analysis with the focus of maximising aggregate social utility through distributing losses and allocating risks. The payment of compensation is a tool for utilitarians to transfer costs. The reason for transferring a cost may be to ensure an externality is internalised so that the cost of an action is accurately priced or to make the cheapest cost-avoider take socially desirable precautions to avoid the cost.[119] Compensation is not the goal per se; rather, it is a tool for achieving other goals. In the area of securities regulation compensation payments may be used to deter wrongdoing. This perspective has been discussed above in relation to compensation as a part of sanctions.

A deontological approach involves adherence to a moral rule or duty for its own sake and is embodied in the idea of corrective justice.[120] Corrective justice requires compensation as a matter

[117] Michael Tilbury, *Civil Remedies – Volume 1 Principles of Civil Remedies* (Butterworths, 1990) 35–36. See also Peter Cane, *Atiyah's Accidents, Compensation and the Law*, 8th edn (Cambridge University Press, 2013) 4, 406.

[118] David Owen, 'Why Philosophy Matters to Tort Law' in David Owen (ed), *Philosophical Foundations of Tort Law* (Clarendon Press, 1995) 1–6; Richard Wright, 'Right, Justice and Tort Law' in David Owen (ed), *Philosophical Foundations of Tort Law* (Clarendon Press, 1995) 160.

[119] George Fletcher, 'Fairness and Utility in Tort Theory' (1972) 85 *Harvard Law Review* 537, 537–38; David Shapiro, 'Class Actions: The Class as Party and Client' (1998) 73 *Notre Dame Law Review* 913, 924; Cane (n 117) 413–14.

[120] Corrective justice draws on Aristotle's Nicomachean Ethics and Immanuel Kant's philosophy of rights: James Gordley, 'Tort Law in the Aristotelian Tradition' in David Owen (ed), *Philosophical Foundations of Tort Law* (Clarendon Press, 1995) 132; Wright (n 118) 162.

of justice or morality. The payment of compensation aims to 'restore and redress the balance of fairness or justice' that has been upset by the wrongdoer's contravention of the law.[121]

Compensation may be seen as a requirement of corrective justice.[122] The payment of compensation by one party to another is the justice system identifying a wrong and seeking to undo it.[123] Corrective justice 'requires those who have without justification harmed others by their conduct to put the matter right'[124] or as the principle that wrongfully caused harms ought to be repaired.[125] Compensation is the way in which matters are put right or harms repaired.

The American Law Institute's *Principles of the Law of Aggregate Litigation* observes: 'Normatively, compensation is an important objective of most lawsuits brought to obtain monetary relief. The procedural system achieves corrective civil justice by requiring wrongdoers to pay compensation and by enabling victims to obtain it'.[126]

It is important to note that while discussions of corrective justice usually focus on the substantive law,[127] the American Law Institute goes further and adds the idea of the procedural law acting as an enabler. Corrective justice is extended beyond specifying what is a wrong or explaining why compensation is required and includes procedures for those harmed to be able to access the compensation that flows from a wrong having been committed. In relation to continuous disclosure, the legislature has provided mechanisms for that harm to be repaired – the regulator who may seek compensation on behalf of those harmed and the class action which are discussed further in section C.iii below.

ii. Consumer Protection

Consumerism is multifaceted, including both the ethos of consumption[128] and the movement aimed at educating consumers as to their rights and protecting their interests.[129] The occurrence of the former led to the need for the latter, which is of central concern here. Consumerism arose as a response to the metamorphosis of society from one based primarily on individual relationships to one in which production, distribution and consumption have become mass phenomena.[130] Consumerism focuses on how the consumer's lack of bargaining power and the existence of information asymmetry expose the consumer to certain risks, such as receiving a defective or unsuitable product. Consumerism advocates for regulation to address those issues.[131]

[121] Cane (n 117) 403, 416–17.

[122] Kent Roach and Michael Trebilcock, 'Private Enforcement of Competition Laws' (1996) 34 *Osgood Hall Law Journal* 461, 496.

[123] Ernest Weinrib, 'Corrective Justice in a Nutshell' (2002) 52 *University of Toronto Law Journal* 349, 350.

[124] Tony Honore, 'The Morality of Tort Law – Questions and Answers' in David Owen (ed), *Philosophical Foundations of Tort Law* (Clarendon Press, 1995) 78–79.

[125] Jules Coleman, 'The Practice of Corrective Justice' in David Owen (ed), *Philosophical Foundations of Tort Law* (Clarendon Press, 1995) 56.

[126] The American Law Institute, *Principles of the Law of Aggregate Litigation* (2010) § 1.04 comment f.

[127] See, eg, Stephen Perry, 'The Moral Foundations of Tort Law' (1992) 77 *Iowa Law Review* 449; Coleman (n 125) 57.

[128] Teresita Majewski and Michael Brian Schiffer, 'Beyond Consumption: Toward an Archaeology of Consumerism' in David Gaimster and Teresita Majewski (eds), *International Handbook of Historical Archaeology* (Springer, 2009) 192; Daniel Miller, 'Consumption as the Vanguard of History: A Polemic by Way of an Introduction' in Daniel Miller (ed), *Acknowledging Consumption: A Review of New Studies* (Routledge, 1995) 1–57.

[129] *Oxford English Dictionary* (online) 'consumerism'; *Merriam-Webster Online Dictionary* (online) 'consumerism'.

[130] Mauro Cappelletti, 'Alternative Dispute Resolution Processes Within the Framework of the World-Wide-Access-To-Justice Movement' (1993) 56 *Modern Law Review* 282, 284; Geraint Howells, Iain Ramsay and Thomas Wilhelmsson, 'Consumer Law in its International Dimension' in Geraint Howells, Iain Ramsay and Thomas Wilhelmsson with David Kraft, *Handbook of Research on International Consumer Law* (Edward Elgar, 2010) 4–8.

[131] Jason Cornwall-Jones, 'Breach of Contract and Misleading Conduct: A Storm in a Teacup' (2000) 24 *Melbourne University Law Review* 249, 251; Iain Ramsay, 'Consumer Law, Regulatory Capitalism and the "New Learning" in Regulation' (2006) 28 *Sydney Law Review* 9, 9; Iain Ramsay, *Consumer Law and Policy*, 3d edn (Hart Publishing, 2012) ch 2.

It also involves empowerment whereby a remedy is expected if a product or service does not operate as represented.[132]

The thinking behind consumerism has been transferred to securities ownership and financial investment in general.[133] The consumer–investor phenomenon in Australia has been argued to be linked to three key events:

- the Federal Government's decision to promote private superannuation as a substitute for government-funded age pensions;
- the privatisation of major government entities such as Telstra, Qantas and the Commonwealth Bank, and the wave of demutualisations that began in the late 1980s, including AMP and NRMA, and more recently Medibank; and
- the reduction in the cost of securities transactions and access to online securities trading as a result of the internet.[134]

Consequently, securities ownership became accessible to, and desirable for, the general public. Securities ownership also became a key source of investment for retirement. This may be illustrated by looking at changes in share ownership in Australia. In 1991, 10 per cent of Australian adults held securities exchange listed investments. By 2004, that had grown to 44 per cent of Australian adults, but then fell to 39 per cent in 2010, 33 per cent in 2014 and then increased slightly to 35 per cent in 2020.[135] Further, Australia's superannuation system as at December 2019 was the fourth largest pool of superannuation savings in the world, comprising assets of $2.1 trillion.[136] A substantial portion of these funds is invested in Australian equities.[137] According to Australian Prudential Regulation Authority data, direct super fund investments in Australian Securities Exchange (ASX) 200 companies have increased from $16 billion in 2008 to $40 billion in 2014 to $78.3 billion in 2018. If the rate of growth continues then by 2023 the level of investment will be $157 billion.[138]

The exposure of the general population to the securities market has seen consumer protection laws enacted in securities legislation[139] and ASIC given the role of protecting the investor-consumer.[140] If Australian workers and retirees are to be expected to put their financial wellbeing in the hands of listed corporations then there is a need to inspire confidence in such investments,

[132] Dimity Kingsford Smith, 'Financial Services Regulation and the Investor as Consumer' in Geraint Howells, Iain Ramsay and Thomas Wilhelmsson with David Kraft, *Handbook of Research on International Consumer Law* (Edward Elgar, 2010) 434.

[133] ibid 431; Gail Pearson, 'Risk and the Consumer in Australian Financial Services Reform' (2006) 28 *Sydney Law Review* 99, 102; Amy Edwards, '"Financial Consumerism": citizenship, consumerism and capital ownership in the 1980s' (2017) 31 *Contemporary British History* 210, 212 ('the world of finance and stocks and shares entered the "everyday" culture of the 1980s, and consequently, encouraged the individual to assume personal responsibility for financial decisions.').

[134] Michael Legg, 'Shareholder Class Actions in Australia – The Perfect Storm?' (2008) 31 *UNSW Law Journal* 669, 672–73. See also Robert White, Bruce Tranter and Dallas Hanson, 'Share Ownership in Australia – The Emergence of New Tensions?' (2004) 40 *Journal of Sociology* 99; Pearson (n 133); Dimity Kingsford Smith, 'Regulating Investment Risk: Individuals and the Global Financial Crisis' (2009) 32 *UNSW Law Journal* 514, 518–19.

[135] Australian Securities Exchange, 'Australian Investor Study 2020', 14–15. The Australian Securities Exchange has a total market capitalisation of around $2.2 trillion: Australian Securities Exchange, Historical market statistics, December 2020.

[136] Edmund Tang, 'Sound fundamentals: Australia now home to world's 4th largest pension assets', Australian Trade and Investment Commission, 14 April 2020.

[137] See Senate Economics Reference Committee, 'Performance of the Australian Securities and Investments Commission' (June 2014) 9, 14.

[138] '9 trends that are changing Australia's equity markets', *Company Director Magazine* (1 September 2019) 22–23.

[139] Kingsford Smith (132) 431.

[140] Australian Securities and Investments Commission Act 2001 (Cth), ss 1(2), 12A(2).

which in turn requires mechanisms 'to compensate shareholders from losses that might be suffered from undisclosed facts and the need to reduce the incidence of such losses'.[141] Modern consumer law focuses on prohibitions on misleading consumers and on ensuring the disclosure of information about a product or service.[142] The prohibitions on misleading or deceptive conduct and the continuous disclosure regime discussed in chapter two are examples of securities laws that perform a consumer protection role, as pointed out by the High Court in *Sons of Gwalia Ltd v Margaretic* below.[143] Compensation forms part of consumerism and consumer protection.[144] However, while the securities laws make provision for compensation it only applies where there is a failure to disclose when required, or a disclosure is misleading. The consumer still bears performance or market risk that leads to securities losing value or corporations failing.[145]

It should also be noted that the ability to seek compensation from the corporation and/or its directors also appears to arise because government and its regulator have determined that it is not its role to act as an insurer or guarantor of investments.[146] Rather, government has enacted legislation to protect the consumer–investor and provided mechanisms for compensation to be sought.

iii. Legislation: Text and Intent

The urgings of IOSCO and the legislature's decision to make compensation available for breach of continuous disclosure obligations, as explained in chapter two, reflects a view that omissions or misleading statements that give rise to an uninformed market may also lead to individual investors suffering loss. The legislature created an obligation and a remedy for when harm was caused. The legislative intention that persons who had suffered loss as a result of a failure to disclose should be entitled to recover by legal proceedings was expressed by Parliament at the time of introduction of s 1001A, the predecessor to s 674:

> As a result of existing section 1005,[147] a person who suffers loss or damage by conduct of a listed disclosing entity that contravened proposed section 1001A will be able to recover the amount of the loss or damage by action against the entity or against any person involved in the contravention.[148]

In *Sons of Gwalia Ltd v Margaretic*, Gleeson CJ, in dealing with claims for compensation based on contraventions of the continuous disclosure regime and prohibition on misleading conduct, observed:

> Corporate regulation has become more intensive, and legislatures have imposed on companies and their officers obligations, breach of which may sound in damages, for the protection of members of the public who deal in shares and other securities.[149]

[141] Anil Hargovan and Jason Harris, 'Sons of Gwalia and statutory debt subordination: An appraisal of the North American experience' (2007) 20 *Australian Journal of Corporate Law* 265, 296.

[142] Howells, Ramsay and Wilhelmsson (130) 5.

[143] Hargovan and Harris (141) 294–96.

[144] Eilis Ferran, 'Dispute resolution mechanisms in the U.K. financial sector' (2002) 21 *Civil Justice Quarterly* 135, 149.

[145] Pearson (n 133) 104–05; Kingsford Smith (n 132) 439–42.

[146] Kingsford Smith (n 132) 440–41. See also ASIC, 'Information Sheet 151 – ASIC's approach to enforcement' (September 2013) 6; ASIC, 'Statement of Intent – Australian Securities and Investments Commission' (July 2014), discussed in ch 2.

[147] Corporations Law (Cth), s 1005 stated 'a person who suffers loss or damage by conduct of another person that was engaged in contravention of a provision of this Part or Part 7.12 may recover the amount of the loss or damage by action against that other person or against any person involved in the contravention, whether or not that other person or any person involved in the contravention has been convicted of an offence in respect of the contravention.'

[148] Explanatory Memorandum, Corporations Law Reform Bill 1993 (Cth) [231]. See also HAJ Ford and RP Austin, *Principles of Corporations Law*, 7th edn (Butterworths, 1995) [10.320]; *Camping Warehouse Australia Pty Limited v Downer EDI Limited* [2014] VSC 357, [34] (Sifris J).

[149] *Sons of Gwalia Ltd v Margaretic* (2007) 231 CLR 160, 180 [18].

Similarly, Kirby J stated:

> The obligation of continuous disclosure, introduced by the Act, was specifically designed and enacted to protect shareholders and potential shareholders from losses that might be suffered from undisclosed facts and to afford a foundation that would prevent, compensate for and reduce the incidence of such losses. …
>
> [T]he type of claim brought by the respondent is not atypical or unexpected. It is a claim by a shareholder for deceptive and misleading conduct, so far as it affected potential shareholders for which the Federal Parliament, by its enactment, has provided for new remedies that are designed, ultimately, to improve the protection of (and remedies available to) Australian shareholders as such.[150]

The New South Wales Court of Appeal in dealing with proceedings brought by ASIC for contravention of the continuous disclosure regime and misleading conduct observed:

> It is also to be noted that s 674 is remedial legislation to enhance the public interest and to protect individual investors. It should be construed beneficially 'so as to give the fullest relief which the fair meaning of its language will allow'.[151]

C. How should Compensation be Accessed?

Compensation is traditionally seen as being part of private law, and it is the injured plaintiff that may seek the remedy.[152] However, two developments have altered the traditional position. First, the legislature has created numerous statutory rights to compensation. The legislative provisions discussed in chapter two are examples. Second, the ability of a plaintiff to seek compensation has been recognised as facing a number of barriers, most notably the cost of enforcing a right, which has led to the development of procedures to overcome these barriers. The two procedures relevant here which overcome these barriers are action by the securities regulator and the class action. However, other alternatives exist such as actions by not-for-profit organisations or industry-funded bodies such as an ombudsman, and individual claims resolved through small claims courts/tribunals and alternative dispute resolution mechanisms.[153]

i. *Class Actions*

Class actions in a range of fields have been justified on the basis that they perform the valuable function of compensating large numbers of victims in an efficient manner.[154] Modern society is characterised by mass wrongs but individuals suffering harm may be unable to seek compensation acting alone due to the costs of litigation compared to the losses they seek to recover.[155]

Shareholder class actions change the traditional cost-benefit analysis that applies when an individual shareholder must decide whether to commence legal proceedings. The pooling of claims

[150] ibid 206 [106]–[107]. See also 216 [141] (Hayne J).

[151] *James Hardie Industries NV v Australian Securities and Investments Commission* (2010) 274 ALR 85, 163 [356] (Spigelman CJ, Beazley JA and Giles JA).

[152] Tilbury (n 117) 17; Sanctions Review (n 61) 17.

[153] Michael Legg, 'A Comparison of Regulatory Enforcement, Class Actions and Alternative Dispute Resolution in Compensating Financial Consumers' (2016) 38 *Sydney Law Review* 311; Hodges and Voet (n 99).

[154] Martin Redish, 'Class Actions and the Democratic Difficulty: Rethinking the Intersection of Private Litigation and Public Goals' (2003) *University of Chicago Legal Forum* 71, 89.

[155] Vivien Goldwasser, 'The Enforcement Dilemma in Australian Securities Regulation' (1999) 27 *Australian Business Law Review* 482, 509.

allows for the sharing of costs and gives rise to economies of scale so that a claim that may be uneconomic to pursue alone, can when combined with other claims, become a viable lawsuit.[156] In the area of shareholder claims the class action is an attractive procedural vehicle because many of the claims are small and the class action allows for them to be aggregated to create a single substantial claim.[157] The class action procedure may also be relied upon by large shareholders, such as superannuation funds and institutional investors, even though they have the resources to be able to bring litigation, as they may be able to reduce costs and share in any recovery.[158]

The ability to aggregate claims, share costs and obtain economies of scale is also important because it attracts lawyers and litigation funders who see the ability to make profitable returns from investing in the litigation. The class action needs to provide sufficient incentives to attract the legal expertise and resources needed to prosecute the action.[159] In *Amchem Products Inc v Windsor* the US Supreme Court recognised that a class action solves the problem of small claims being uneconomical to pursue 'by aggregating the relatively paltry potential recoveries into something worth someone's (usually an attorney's) labor'.[160] Class actions introduce a third party into the regulatory equation. This has prompted concerns about who initiates, controls and directs the litigation. The lawyers and funders may have a greater interest in the outcome of the class action than any individual shareholder.[161] As a result the class action has been referred to as lawyer-driven.[162] These third parties also need to be paid which gives rise to transaction costs which are discussed further below.

ii. *The Regulator*

While regulators have traditionally employed enforcement strategies that use penalties, those strategies have become more multi-faceted and compensation has been recognised as an acceptable, even desirable, regulatory response.[163] As explained in chapter two, ASIC has the ability to apply for a compensation order in relation to a breach of the continuous disclosure regime,[164] can with the consent of a shareholder bring proceedings on their behalf for breach of the continuous disclosure regime and for misleading conduct[165] or include compensation schemes as a term of an enforceable undertaking.[166]

[156] *Deposit Guaranty Bank v Roper*, 445 US 326, 339 (1980); *Phillips Petroleum Co v Shutts*, 472 US 797, 809 (1985).

[157] Peta Spender, 'Securities Class Actions: A View from The Land of the Great White Shareholder' (2002) 31 *Common Law World Review* 123, 124.

[158] Michael Legg, 'Institutional Investors and Shareholder Class Actions: The Law and Economics of Participation' (2007) 81 *Australian Law Journal* 478.

[159] John Coffee, 'Understanding the Plaintiff's Attorney: The Implications of Economic Theory for Private Enforcement of Law Through Class and Derivative Actions' (1986) 86 *Columbia Law Review* 669; Samuel Issacharoff, 'Governance and Legitimacy in the Law of Class Actions' [1999] *Supreme Court Review* 337, 341; Sean Farhang, *The Litigation State* (Princeton University Press, 2010) 8.

[160] *Amchem Products Inc v Windsor*, 521 US 591, 617 (1997) citing *Mace v Van Ru Credit Corp*, 109 F3d 338, 344 (7th Cir 1997). See also *Deposit Guaranty Bank v Roper*, 445 US 326, 338 (1980).

[161] Elliott Weiss and John Beckerman, 'Let the Money Do the Monitoring: How Institutional Investors Can Reduce Agency Costs in Securities Class Actions' (1995) 104 *Yale Law Journal* 2053, 2058–60; *Mobil Oil Australia Pty Ltd v Victoria* (2002) 211 CLR 1, 77 [183] (Callinan J) ('the lawyers are often as much the litigants as the plaintiffs themselves, and with the same or even a greater stake in the outcome than any member of a group.').

[162] See *Kirby v Centro Properties Ltd* (2008) 253 ALR 65, 67 [4] (Finkelstein J); *Melbourne City Investments Pty Ltd v Treasury Wine Estates Limited (No 3)* [2014] VSC 340, [63] (Ferguson J). See also *Treasury Wine Estates Ltd v Melbourne City Investments Pty Ltd* (2014) 45 VR 585, 590 [21] (Maxwell P and Nettle JA) observing that the advent of the class action had created the possibility of litigation being commenced so as to enrich the solicitor.

[163] See, eg, Baldwin, Cave and Lodge (n 15) 128–30.

[164] Corporations Act 2001 (Cth), s 1317J(1).

[165] ibid s 1325(2), (3); Australian Securities and Investments Commission Act 2001 (Cth), s 50.

[166] See, eg, ASIC, 'Enforceable Undertaking: Multiplex Ltd', Document No 017 029 205 (20 December 2006).

However, a regulator may not pursue compensation, or may pursue compensation at a lower-than-optimum level, for a range of reasons. The regulator, unlike the lawyer or funder in a class action, does not profit from bringing proceedings to recover compensation.[167] Indeed, the time and cost to pursue compensation may open the regulator to criticism if it is unsuccessful, and give rise to a loss of opportunity to pursue other cases. The regulator may also have a preference for criminal sanctions, civil penalties or administrative remedies because they better achieve regulatory goals such as deterrence or cooperation. Further, as part of its enforcement discretion ASIC may not pursue formal remedies in a particular case as a way to coax or reward cooperation and compliance.[168]

D. When is Compensation Achieved?

The aim of compensation is to make the injured person whole.[169] Put another way, to compensate someone for something is to provide that person with 'a full and perfect equivalent' for that thing. If they are given more than that, they have been over-compensated, and if given less, under-compensated. The idea of over- or under-compensation implies that the notion of compensation is to provide an exact equivalent – neither more nor less.[170]

The view that compensation requires a payment equivalent to the harm suffered is accepted by the common law. The High Court of Australia has stated:

> The settled principle governing the assessment of compensatory damages, whether in actions of tort or contract, is that the injured party should receive compensation in a sum which, so far as money can do, will put that party in the same position as he or she would have been in if the contract had been performed or the tort had not been committed. Compensation is the cardinal concept. It is the 'one principle that is absolutely firm, and which must control all else'.[171]

More recently Edelman J has explained that the 'goal of putting the plaintiff in the position they would have been in if the wrongful act had not occurred, is [about] rectifying the consequences of the wrong'.[172] Those consequences are typically a loss which is 'some adverse effect experienced

[167] Steven Shavell, 'The Fundamental Divergence Between the Private and the Social Motive to Use the Legal System' (1997) 26 *Journal of Legal Studies* 575; Margaret Lemos and Max Minzner, 'For-Profit Public Enforcement' (2014) 127 *Harvard Law Review* 853, 863. Lemos and Minzer also suggest that in the US regulators may be given financial incentives to seek compensation such as being able to retain a share of any recovery.

[168] Michael Legg, 'Public and Private Enforcement – ASIC and the Shareholder Class Action' in Michael Legg (ed), *Regulation, Litigation and Enforcement* (Thomson Reuters, 2011) 155.

[169] *Registrar of Titles (WA) v Spencer* (1909) 9 CLR 641, 645 (Griffith CJ) (referring to 'damages commensurate with the loss he sustained' and being 'entitled to full compensation'); *Livingstone v Raywards Coal Co* (1880) 5 App Cas 25, 39. See also Benjamin Zipursky, 'Civil Recourse, not Corrective Justice' (2003) 91 *Georgetown Law Journal* 695, 695 ('Corrective justice theory is based on a simple and elegant idea: when one person has been wrongfully injured by another, the injurer must make the injured party whole'.)

[170] Robert Goodin, 'Theories of Compensation' (1989) 9 *Oxford Journal of Legal Studies* 56, 59. See also Zipursky (ibid) 701 ('The defendant must pay not just any amount, but the amount of the plaintiff's injury, because the payment is not a penalty per se, but the rectification of an injury that the defendant inflicted.').

[171] *Haines v Bendall* (1991) 172 CLR 60, 63 (Mason CJ, Dawson, Toohey and Gaudron JJ) (footnotes omitted). See also *Butler v Egg and Egg Pulp Marketing Board* (1966) 114 CLR 185, 191 (Taylor and Owen JJ); *Commonwealth v Amann Aviation Pty Ltd* (1991) 174 CLR 64, 98 (Brennan J), 116 (Deane J), 161 (McHugh J dissenting); *Clark v Macourt* (2013) 253 CLR 1, 11 [26] (Crennan and Bell JJ), 18–9 [59] (Gageler J); *Lewis v Australian Capital Territory* [2020] HCA 26, [30] (Gageler J), [65] (Gordon J), [139] (Edelman J). In the United Kingdom the 'compensation principle' has been modified by the legislation creating the collective proceeding permitted in the Competition Appeal Tribunal where aggregate damages may be awarded: *Mastercard Inc v Merricks* [2020] UKSC 51, [58], [76]–[77] (Lord Briggs), [94]–[97] (Lord Sales and Leggatt). While the Australian class action allows for an award of aggregate damages (*Federal Court of Australian Act 1976* (Cth) s 33Z) it does not alter the compensation principle: *Mobil Oil Australia Pty Ltd v Victoria* (2002) 211 CLR 1, 27–28 [23] (Gleeson CJ).

[172] *Lewis v Australian Capital Territory* [2020] HCA 26, [150] (Edelman J).

by the plaintiff either on their mind, on the way they conduct their business or live their life, or on their financial position'.[173] In the context of the shareholder claims under discussion here the loss that is to be rectified is usually a diminution in the financial position of the shareholder.

In relation to statutory causes of action, such as those applicable to contravention of the prohibition on misleading or deceptive conduct, it is clear that compensation is not limited to measures of damages provided by the common law.[174] However, while different causes of action may give rise to different measures of damages, the underlying goal is the same: complete compensation.[175]

Section 1317HA of the Corporations Act, which allows the court to order a person who has contravened the continuous disclosure regime to compensate another person for damage suffered resulting from the contravention, would also most likely require complete compensation.[176] Indeed, the pleadings in shareholder class actions typically seek to recover the difference between the price at which a security traded and the true value of the security.[177] However, the court has a discretion whether to order compensation.[178]

Compensation is effective when it puts the injured person back in the position they were in prior to the contravention. While some forms of harm, most notably personal injury, require a harm to be translated into a monetary value that can only ever approximate the harm, financial losses as occur with continuous disclosure contraventions can more readily be equated with a particular amount of monetary compensation.

It should also be noted that full or complete compensation is also said to support the deterrence objective discussed above. If compensation equates with the harm caused then the entity causing the harm is incentivised to avoid it.[179]

E. Limits on Achieving Complete Compensation

i. Claims Not Made and Incomplete Recovery

An important criterion for measuring the success of compensation is that all of those 'who are entitled to compensation … actually receive compensation and in the amount to which they are entitled'.[180] There are three reasons that compensation may not be achieved: an action is not brought; those people with valid claims are excluded from compensation; or upon being included do not receive the compensation owed, as defined above, because funds are not available.

First, the regulator and the class action proponents (lawyers and/or litigation funders) both assist those entitled to compensation to receive it by facilitating claiming through financing and

[173] ibid [146].

[174] *Wardley Australia Ltd v Western Australia* (1992) 175 CLR 514, 526 (Mason CJ, Dawson, Gaudron and McHugh JJ); *Henville v Walker* (2001) 206 CLR 459, 470 [18] (Gleeson CJ) (both cases discuss s 82 of the Trade Practices Act 1974 (Cth) which is analogous to Corporations Act 2001 (Cth), s 1041I (misleading or deceptive conduct)).

[175] *Marks v GIO Australia Holdings* (1998) 196 CLR 494, 503–04 [17] (Gaudron J), 510 [38] (McHugh, Hayne and Callinan JJ), [95] (Gummow J); *Henville v Walker* (2001) 206 CLR 459, 482 [66], [68] (Gaudron J), 509 [164] (Hayne J); *Berry v CCL Secure Pty Ltd* [2020] HCA 27, [64] (Gageler and Edelman JJ).

[176] *ASIC v Sino Australia Oil and Gas Limited (in liq)* (2016) 118 ACSR 43, 55–56 [41]–[42] (Davies J). See also *V-Flow Pty Ltd v Holyoake Industries (Vic) Pty Ltd* (2013) 296 ALR 418, 429 [53]–[55] (Emmett, Edmonds and Rares JJ) which interprets the analogous s 1317H.

[177] See, eg, *Crowley v WorleyParsons Limited* [2017] FCA 3, [35] (Foster J).

[178] Corporations Act 2001 (Cth), s 1317HA(1) states that a court 'may' order.

[179] Richard Stewart and Cass Sunstein, 'Public Programs and Private Rights' (1982) 95 *Harvard Law Review* 1195, 1298–99.

[180] Cane (n 117) 409.

commencing litigation. However, this facilitation may not occur for a number of reasons. For example, commencing litigation may not be an attractive proposition for the regulator or class action proponents. The return, whether financial or non-financial (such as achieving regulatory goals), may be insufficient. Perhaps there are insufficient lawyers or regulatory resources with the necessary expertise to evaluate a claim and commence it. Other disincentives may play a role such as views as to the strength of a claim, the quantum of compensation owed or the solvency of the potential defendants.[181] One commentator has stated that there has probably been insufficient employment of the federal class action regime, suggesting that compensation is not sought on every occasion when it may be owed.[182] A similar statement could be made in relation to ASIC.[183]

Second, compensation may fail to be achieved because even when proceedings are commenced, persons with valid claims do not participate. Little has been written about how regulators contact those harmed or distribute compensation that they obtain. Class actions, on the other hand, have been subject to much greater analysis as to whether injured persons participate in the class action. The Australian class action in utilising an opt-out approach does not require claimants to come forward at the time proceedings are commenced. However, the opt-out nature of the class action creates other problems that may see claimants not participate. First, when litigation funders are involved, the class action may be structured so that it uses a 'closed class'. This means the class action is only brought on behalf of group members who sign litigation funding agreements so that the funder can ensure a contractual right to a percentage of each group member's claim. It also has the effect that some putative group members may be excluded.[184] However, the adoption of court orders so that the funder can recover from all group members without a funding agreement, may reduce the use of a closed class.[185] Second, claimants receive a notice about the proceedings being commenced and are able to exclude themselves through returning a form to the court. A review of opt-out forms suggests that some people misunderstand the procedure and exclude themselves inadvertently.[186] Third, a prerequisite for settlement of some opt-out class actions will be the 'closing of the class' to identify group members. This is necessary because until the participating group members are identified there can be no allocation or distribution of settlement monies to members of the class.[187] Identification of the group members will require notices which may be distributed by a number of mechanisms, for example, mail, electronic mail, publication in newspapers and web pages. The effect of a group member not identifying themselves and providing the necessary information is that they are ineligible to participate in the

[181] See John Walker, Susanna Khouri and Wayne Attrill, 'Funding Criteria for Class Actions' (2009) 32 *UNSW Law Journal* 1036, 1041–45 (setting out disqualifying factors and risks that result in litigation funding being denied); ASIC, 'Information Sheet 151 – ASIC's approach to enforcement' (September 2013) (discussing how matters are selected for investigation and how the choice of enforcement tools is made).

[182] Vince Morabito, 'An Empirical Study of Australia's Class Action Regimes, Third Report: Class Action Facts and Figures – Five Years Later' (November 2014) 1.

[183] See, eg, Michelle Welsh, Peta Spender, Irene Lynch Fannon and Kath Hall, 'The end of the "End of History for Corporate Law"?' (2014) 29 *Australian Journal of Corporate Law* 147, 165–66 (finding that in the area of director's duties and the civil penalty regime that although compensation orders were available they were only sought in 11 of 38 cases).

[184] Michael Legg, 'Reconciling Litigation Funding and the Opt Out Group Definition in Federal Court of Australia Class Actions – The Need for a Legislative Common Fund Approach' (2011) 30 *Civil Justice Quarterly* 52, 59–60; *Money Max Int Pty Ltd (Trustee) v QBE Insurance Group Limited* (2016) 245 FCR 191, 229 [193] (Murphy, Gleeson and Beach JJ).

[185] *BMW Australia Ltd v Brewster; Westpac Banking Corporation v Lenthall* [2019] HCA 45 (finding that common fund orders could not be made at the beginning of proceedings, endorsing funding equalisation orders and not deciding if common fund orders could be made at the end of proceedings); Michael Legg 'Litigation Funding of Australian Class Actions after the High Court Rejection of Common Fund Orders' (2020) 39 *Civil Justice Quarterly* 305.

[186] Vince Morabito, 'An Empirical Study of Australia's Class Action Regimes – Second Report' (September 2010) 33.

[187] *Dorajay Pty Ltd v Aristocrat Leisure Ltd* (2008) 67 ACSR 569, 574 [13] (Stone J).

settlement and their claim for compensation may be extinguished.[188] In some situations, it may prove impossible to identify the harmed person so that they make no recovery.[189]

Third, claimants may find that they do not recover the amount to which they are entitled when there are insufficient available funds to pay compensation. This frequently occurs when the wrongdoer is insolvent, or the quantum of the compensation required to be paid is greater than the wrongdoer's resources, meaning that funds are not available for compensation.[190] There may also be situations where the wrongdoer deliberately seeks to defeat successful suits for compensation through corporate structuring (operating through an insufficiently resourced subsidiary), by dissipating assets or transferring assets outside the jurisdiction of the court.[191] The ability of corporations to avoid full responsibility, including paying full compensation, for the consequences of their operations through having insufficient assets to cover their liability has been referred to as the 'judgment-proof' problem.[192] In some circumstances the judgment-proof problem may be overcome through piercing the corporate veil so as to access a parent company's assets or through freezing orders (also called Mareva injunctions) which prevent the disposal of assets.[193]

An important method for ameliorating the situation where a wrongdoer lacks sufficient assets to pay compensation is insurance which makes funds available where the insured party has committed a contravention covered by the insurance policy.[194] Insurance allows for risk of paying damages to be spread across many people, thus allowing for a larger pool of funds to be available when one of the insured is called upon to compensate a person they have injured.[195]

ii. Settlement

The resolution of disputes without recourse to the courts is advocated because litigation is too costly, too slow, too adversarial, too uncertain, too damaging to relationships and too inflexible.[196] Both shareholder class actions and regulator initiated claims either voluntarily, or at the encouragement of the court, will engage in mediation, or other forms of alternative dispute resolution.[197] However, from a compensation perspective, settlement necessitates compromise which may mean accepting something less than full compensation.

[188] *Inabu Pty Ltd v Leighton Holdings Ltd* [2014] FCA 622, [17] (Jacobson J). A previous practice of closing the class to facilitate settlement negotiations or mediation which also had the effect of barring claims by group members who did not register prior to the approval of a settlement or following a judgment was found to be beyond power by the State of New South Wales Court of Appeal: *Haselhurst v Toyota Motor Corp Australia Ltd t/as Toyota Australia* [2020] NSWCA 66. However, courts have sought to adopt practices permitted by the legislation through requiring group member registration but deferring any barring of claims until and unless a settlement is approved by the court: *Wetdal Pty Ltd as Trustee for the BlueCo Two Superannuation Fund v Estia Health Limited* [2021] FCA 475, [67]–[96] (Beach J).

[189] Cass Sunstein, 'The Limits of Compensatory Justice' in John Chapman (ed), *Compensatory Justice – NOMOS XXXIII* (New York University Press, 1991) 288.

[190] Steven Shavell, 'Liability for Harm versus Regulation of Safety' (1984) 13 *Journal of Legal Studies* 357, 360–61.

[191] See, eg, *Briggs v James Hardie & Co Pty Ltd* (1989) 16 NSWLR 549; Hugh Collins, 'Ascription of Legal Responsibility to Groups in Complex Patterns of Economic Integration' (1990) 53 *Modern Law Review* 731, 737; Lynn LoPucki, 'The Death of Liability' (1996) 106 *Yale Law Journal* 1.

[192] Steven Shavell, 'The Judgment-Proof Problem' (1986) 6 *International Review of Law and Economics* 45.

[193] Robert Austin and Ian Ramsay, *Ford, Austin and Ramsay's Principles of Corporations Law* (LexisNexis Online, 2018) [4.250.12]–[4.250.15]; Bernard Cairns, *Australian Civil Procedure*, 10th edn (Thomson Reuters, 2014) 551–55.

[194] Paul Latimer, 'Compensation of investors for failure of a securities industry licensee' (1997) 15 *Company and Securities Law Journal* 495, 502; Cane (n 117) 233. Directors' and officers' insurance, which responds to claims based on continuous disclosure contraventions, is discussed in ch 5, section II.B.vi.

[195] Gary Schwartz, 'The Ethics and the Economics of Tort Liability Insurance' (1990) 75 *Cornell Law Review* 313, 360.

[196] See Victorian Law Reform Commission, 'Civil Justice Review', Report No 14 (2008) 214.

[197] Michael Legg, 'ADR and Class Actions Compared' in Michael Legg (ed), *The Future of Dispute Resolution* (LexisNexis, 2013) 190.

Settlement has been advocated in class actions because of litigation risk, uncertainty of outcome, cost and delay.[198] In claims based on contravention of the continuous disclosure regime or prohibition on misleading or deceptive conduct seeking compensation, litigation risk is exacerbated as the law in relation to causation and damages is unsettled.[199] There is also the prospect of cost and delay because novel points of law are likely to be appealed.[200] Indeed, there may be additional stages of litigation beyond appeals as large-scale claims may involve determination of liability followed by individual proof of damages before compensation can be awarded.[201]

A settlement can be an attractive outcome because it provides certainty as to recovery and can meet other concerns such as cost and delay. Nonetheless the resolution of claims through settlement will almost inevitably result in compensation lower than the losses suffered.

iii. Transaction Costs

Another important criterion for evaluating the compensation achieved is to look at the transaction or administrative costs of the system.[202] Transaction costs are the cost incurred in undertaking an economic exchange.[203] The exchange at issue here is the seeking and obtaining of compensation which requires various steps to be taken such as lodging a claim, proving a claim or negotiating a payment.

In many compensation systems, the question focuses on the efficiency with which compensation is obtained; for example, litigation compared to a no-fault administrative system in relation to motor vehicle or work place injuries. Here the comparison is between the class action, which by nature involves litigation and regulatory action that also uses litigation, but in addition has non-curial approaches such as enforceable undertakings that can provide compensation. The class action through aggregating claims may reduce the costs faced by the courts as they have one rather than many disputes to resolve. The regulator through drawing on administrative procedures or alternative dispute resolution mechanisms may be able to provide compensation through a system that has less administrative costs which is to the benefit of society and taxpayers.[204] However, the person seeking compensation is not directly affected by this type of administrative cost as they are not asked to bear those costs.

Of greater significance in assessing the achievement of the goal of compensation are transaction costs that directly reduce the amount of compensation received by the harmed person. In private litigation these costs are legal fees and disbursements (for example, court filing fees and expert witness fees), and in some situations, litigation funder's fees.[205] In the class action context this has led to the observation: 'As both lawyers and funders seek to make a profit, the overall

[198] *P Dawson Nominees Pty Ltd v Brookfield Multiplex Ltd (No 4)* [2010] FCA 1029, [2] (Finkelstein J). See also *Perera v GetSwift Limited* (2018) 357 ALR 586, 599 [31] (Lee J).

[199] See, eg, *P Dawson Nominees Pty Ltd v Brookfield Multiplex Ltd (No 4)* [2010] FCA 1029, [15]–[17] (Finkelstein J); *Kirby v Centro Properties Ltd (No 6)* [2012] FCA 650, [4] (Middleton J); *Perera v GetSwift Limited* (2018) 357 ALR 586, 599 [31] (Lee J). The law in relation to causation in a continuous disclosure class action has been the subject of a judgment at first instance: *TPT Patrol Pty Ltd as trustee for Amies Superannuation Fund v Myer Holdings Limited* [2019] FCA 1747, which is addressed in ch 7.

[200] *Kirby v Centro Properties Ltd (No 6)* [2012] FCA 650, [4] (Middleton J).

[201] *Matthews v AusNet Electricity Services Pty Ltd* [2014] VSC 663, [309] (Osborn JA).

[202] Cane (n 117) 409.

[203] John Black, Nigar Hashimzade, and Gareth Myles, *A Dictionary of Economics*, 4th edn (Oxford University Press, 2013) 'transaction cost'. Practical examples of transaction costs include the commission paid to a stockbroker for completing a share deal and the booking fee charged when purchasing concert tickets.

[204] Legg, 'ADR' (n 197) 186–88.

[205] Schwartz (n 195) 351; Jasminka Kalajdzic, Peter Cashman and Alana Longmoore, 'Justice for Profit: A Comparative Analysis of Australian, Canadian and U.S. Third Party Litigation Funding' (2013) 61 *American Journal of Comparative Law* 93, 104.

transaction costs increase and the net return to the class members decreases'.[206] In contrast, when the regulator takes action to obtain compensation they usually do not charge the person who will be the beneficiary of the compensation for their legal services.[207] The greater the transaction costs in obtaining compensation, the less actual compensation that is received. This in turn undermines the effectiveness of compensation.

iv. Circularity Problem/Pocket-shifting

Two important questions in understanding and assessing how a compensation system operates are: who should be paid? And who should pay?[208] In the situation of shareholders making claims against a corporation, this raises a particular concern known as the circularity problem or pocket-shifting that applies to the purchase of shares on-market. The concern may be understood by considering three groups of shareholders:

> [T]he first are those who suffer loss because of the effect that the company's breach has on the share price (the victims), the second are those who sold their shares (at the necessarily inflated price) to those who bought at the inflated price (the winners) and the third are those who are shareholders of the company at the time that it is targeted in the shareholder class action (the targets).[209]

Where the victim shareholders who purchased shares at an inflated price in the relevant period seek to recover their loss from the assets of the corporation, this has the effect that the reduction in corporate value falls on the target shareholders who are not responsible for the corporation's disclosure, or lack thereof. There is therefore a concern at the utility and fairness of seeking compensation from the corporation or the target shareholders.[210] The pocket-shifting occurs because most shareholder class actions do indeed involve settlements funded by the corporate defendant or an insurance policy. Rarely are individual wrongdoers required to contribute financially to a settlement.[211]

The concern about the utility of compensation in the on-market situation has also led to analysis that suggests that diversified shareholders, such as an institutional investor, is equally likely to be the shareholder who traded (the victim) as the shareholder who did not trade (the target) over the long term, but with large transaction costs, being the lawyer's fees and the litigation funder's share of any recovery.[212] The 'pocket-shifting' exercise in relation to diversified shareholders has been illustrated by the following example from Professor John Coffee:

> [A] hypothetical [superannuation/investment] fund owns a portfolio of companies of which, over a period of time, 100 become defendants in securities class actions. In 50 of these cases, the

[206] Kalajdzic, Cashman and Longmoore (ibid) 104.

[207] Joachim Dietrich and Thomas Middleton, 'Statutory remedies and equitable remedies' (2006) 28 *Australian Bar Review* 136, 142; Robert Kagan, 'Regulators and Regulatory Processes' in Austin Sarat (ed), *The Blackwell Companion to Law and Society* (John Wiley & Sons Ltd, 2008) 213.

[208] Cane (n 115) 405.

[209] Australian Law Reform Commission, 'Integrity, Fairness and Efficiency – An Inquiry into Class Action Proceedings and Third-Party Litigation Funders', Report No 134 (2018) 276–77 ('ALRC 2018 Report') citing Paul Miller, 'Shareholder class actions: Are they good for shareholders?' (2012) 86 *Australian Law Journal* 633, 636–37.

[210] Coffee, 'Reforming the Securities Class Action' (n 62) 1556–7; Note, 'Congress, The Supreme Court, and the Rise of Securities-Fraud Class Actions' (2019) 132 *Harvard Law Review* 1067, 1080 ('Note on Securities Fraud'). Cf Lawrence Mitchell, 'The "Innocent Shareholder": An Essay on Compensation and Deterrence in Securities Class-Action Lawsuits' [2009] *Wisconsin Law Review* 243 (arguing that shareholders have the power to select and monitor directors and should be responsible for market integrity because of that power).

[211] Janet Cooper Alexander, 'Rethinking Damages in Securities Class Actions' (1996) 48 *Stanford Law Review* 1487, 1499; Bernard Black, Brian Cheffins and Michael Klausner, 'Outside Director Liability' (2006) 58 *Stanford Law Review* 1055, 1068; Fisch (n 20) 337.

[212] James Cox, 'Making Securities Fraud Class Actions Virtuous' (1997) 39 *Arizona Law Review* 497, 509; Howell Jackson and Mark Roe, 'Public and Private Enforcement of Securities Laws: Resource-Based Evidence' (2009) 93 *Journal of Financial Economics* 207, 209; Note on Securities Fraud (n 210) 1081.

> [superannuation/investment] fund is in the plaintiff class and shares in the recovery; in the other 50, it is not in the plaintiff class and thus bears some of the recovery. The payments would thus balance out, except for the fact that the recovery received in the 50 cases in which the [superannuation/investment] fund is a plaintiff is diminished by the legal fees of the plaintiffs' attorneys …, the fees of the defense attorneys, and other related costs (including increased liability insurance premiums).[213]

This analysis suggests that it only applies to diversified shareholders and only over the long term. It might therefore be suggested that non-diversified shareholders, usually small retail shareholders, would make a worthwhile recovery through a shareholder class action as they are unlikely to be both within and outside the group definition in any single case, nor in a number of cases over time. However, as small investors usually do not trade actively but rather 'buy and hold' they may buy the shares before any contravention (therefore not purchasing as a result of a contravention) and still be holding them once the contravention comes to light. Consequently, the retail shareholder may only fund (be targets), but not participate in, a settlement or verdict.[214] The payment of compensation by the corporation may actually make a portion of its shareholders, the ones that most need assistance in accessing compensation, worse off.

While this argument has been chiefly raised in relation to securities class actions, it can apply equally to regulator actions.[215] However, it may be possible to break the circle by recovering funds from individual offenders, including those that aid and abet a violation, so that the source of the funds is not limited to the corporation whose shareholders have suffered loss.[216] Of course, the individual must have the ability to pay the compensation.

IV. The Regulatory Process

A. Why Assess the Regulatory Process?

This section identifies and develops criteria for evaluating public and private enforcement of the securities laws from the perspective of the functioning of the regulatory process. The aim here is to go beyond the usual comparators of deterrence and compensation that might be seen as end goals and consider how a regulatory regime with public and private enforcers operates by focussing on process goals.[217] The consideration of the regulatory process is necessary to determine if desirable regulatory values or norms are complied with or promoted by a particular regulator, approach or tool. This then allows for an assessment of whether the regulator, approach or tool is seen as legitimate.[218] Legitimacy means 'social credibility and acceptability … the actions of an entity are desirable, proper, or appropriate'.[219] Legitimacy is bestowed because the process

[213] John Coffee, 'Law and the Market: The Impact of Enforcement' (2007) 156 *University of Pennsylvania Law Review* 229, 304. See also Merritt Fox, 'Why Civil Liability for Disclosure Violations When Issuers Do Not Trade?' [2009] *Wisconsin Law Review* 297, 302–3; William Bratton and Michael Wachter, 'The Political Economy of Fraud on the Market' (2011) 160 *University of Pennsylvania Law Review* 69, 94–6.

[214] Coffee, 'Reforming the Securities Class Action' (n 62) 1559–60; Bratton and Wachter (n 213) 97.

[215] Bratton and Wachter (n 213) 139–40; Urska Velikonja, 'Public Compensation for Private Harm: Evidence from the SEC's Fair Fund Distributions' (2015) 67 *Stanford Law Review* 331, 374–75.

[216] Securities Exchange Commission, 'Statement of the Securities Exchange Commission Concerning Financial Penalties' (4 January 2006); Velikonja (n 215) 376.

[217] Robert Summers, 'Evaluating and Improving Legal Processes – A Plea for "Process Values"' (1974) 60 *Cornell Law Review* 1, 1 ('It is possible to evaluate not only the *results* of a process, but the *process*, too.').

[218] Baldwin, Cave and Lodge (n 15) 26.

[219] Julia Black, 'Constructing and Contesting Legitimacy and Accountability in Polycentric Regulatory Regimes' (2008) 2 *Regulation & Governance* 137, 144.

employed conforms to certain norms. Equally, where the process does not conform to the desired norms, its legitimacy is undermined and it may need to be reformed.

The text identifies four values or norms that are developed below. First, legislative authority is important because it explains that both the regulator and the class action process are endorsed by the legislature and the democratic process. The second value is the goal of regulation, namely to advance the public interest. The third value is accountability. Efficiency is the fourth value.

The above values are drawn from regulatory theory and therefore are criteria that ASIC has been measured against before.[220] They are also applied to the class action on the basis that it may be seen as performing a regulatory role. This is a view reinforced by regulatory pluralism, which is discussed below. However, the class action is also a tool or mechanism of civil procedure. Some of the above values have a meaning in that context which are also explained below because the requirements of civil litigation may provide additional or competing norms for legitimacy. Further, while the class action may not adhere to all of the regulatory process values because of its civil procedure heritage, a question still arises as to how it interacts, positively or negatively, with the regulator and on the regulator's compliance with the process values.

B. Legislative Authority

i. The Legislative Mandate

The decision to adopt public or private enforcement in a particular area of regulation is a determination made by the legislature when it enacts laws.[221] The legislature may limit enforcement to specific regulators or allow private citizens to bring suit to enforce the law. The legislature is able to promote private enforcement by specifying who has standing, the remedies available and may even create economic incentives for litigation to be commenced.[222] The overlapping enforcement of the continuous disclosure laws by the public regulator, ASIC, and private citizens through the class action, arises to a large extent due to the Australian Parliament granting standing to both ASIC and private citizens.[223]

Baldwin, Cave and Lodge argue that 'regulatory action deserves support when it is authorized by Parliament' and the action fulfils the mandate prescribed by the Parliament.[224] As noted in chapter two, ASIC is required to 'promote the confident and informed participation of investors and consumers in the financial system' and has the function of 'monitoring and promoting market integrity and consumer protection in the Australian financial system'.[225] Further, ASIC is

[220] Australian Government, 'Statement of expectations: Australian Securities and Investments Commission' (February 2007) ('2007 statement of expectations'); Australian Government, 'Statement of expectations: Australian Securities and Investments Commission' (July 2014) ('2014 statement of expectations'); Australian Government, 'Statement of expectations: Australian Securities and Investments Commission' (April 2018) ('2018 statement of expectations').

[221] An exception to the legislature determining how regulation will be enforced is the US situation where the judiciary has implied a private right of action. The legislature's inaction in not overriding the judiciary is seen as endorsement. See *Blue Chip Stamps v Manor Drug Stores*, 421 US 723, 730 (1975); Joseph Grundfest, 'Disimplying Private Rights of Action Under the Federal Securities Laws: The Commission's Authority' (1994) 107 *Harvard Law Review* 961, 985–98.

[222] Stephen Burbank, Sean Farhang and Herbert Kritzer, 'Private Enforcement' (2013) 17 *Lewis & Clark Law Review* 637, 675–80.

[223] See ch 2, section V.A, where the advent of the shareholder class action is explained as occurring due to standing, the introduction of a class action procedure and litigation funding.

[224] Baldwin, Cave and Lodge (n 15) 27.

[225] Australian Securities and Investments Commission Act 2001 (Cth), ss 1(2)(b), 12A(2). See also 'ASIC's Corporate Plan 2018–22' 18.

required to 'take whatever action it can take, and is necessary, in order to enforce and give effect to the laws of the Commonwealth that confer functions and powers on it'.[226] ASIC clearly has a mandate to enforce the securities laws, including the continuous disclosure regime.

Private enforcement that depends on grants of standing by the legislature may also be said to be deserving of support. The review of the continuous disclosure regime and prohibitions on misleading conduct in chapter two demonstrated that the Parliament has authorised private enforcement. Consequently, private enforcement may be seen as another regulatory approach with associated advantages and disadvantages, which are discussed further below and in subsequent chapters. Further, from this perspective it is legitimate to evaluate the class action as not simply a private litigation procedural tool but as a public regulatory tool.

However, the existence of a legislative mandate or authorisation by Parliament does not conclude the analysis. Rather, it is the starting point. Most regulatory statutes provide the regulator with considerable discretion, specify goals at a high level of abstraction and often will include goals that are conflicting or require trade-offs.[227] Equally, exactly what mandate is given to private enforcement is unclear as there are no accompanying statutory objectives. As a result, while compliance with a legislative mandate is necessary, it is unlikely to be sufficient for determining legitimacy or assessing the regulatory process alone. Resort needs to be made to other regulatory values: the public interest, accountability, and efficiency.

ii. Why Give a Legislative Mandate to a Public Regulator?

The legislature may create a public regulator for a number of reasons. It allows for regulation and oversight of an important component of the economy, but through a non-political or bi-partisan body.[228] The regulator is tasked, implicitly if not explicitly, with carrying out its functions in the public interest and given wide discretion to develop an appropriate response to regulatory issues. Equally, the legislature or Government can hold the regulator accountable for its performance, including its use of resources. The public interest, accountability and efficiency are explored further below.

The legislature may wish to draw on, or develop expertise, knowledge and experience in a regulator.[229] Continual collection of data and repetition of a function allows for superior information and competence.[230] A regulator can also draw on the power of the state for enforcement, including being able to bring criminal prosecutions and seek criminal penalties such as imprisonment.[231] The regulator may also employ coercive investigatory powers such as search warrants.[232]

The enforcement of regulation by public regulators also overcomes the obstacles that individuals may face in pursuing entities that breach regulatory requirements. In particular, the individual

[226] Australian Securities and Investments Commission Act 2001 (Cth), s 1(2)(g). See also Corporations Act 2001 (Cth), s 1317J, which provides that ASIC 'may' apply for a declaration of contravention, a pecuniary penalty order or a compensation order.

[227] Baldwin, Cave and Lodge (n 15) 27–28.

[228] Joanna Bird, 'Regulating the Regulators: Accountability of Australian Regulators' (2011) 35 *Melbourne University Law Review* 739, 743.

[229] ibid; Baldwin, Cave and Lodge (n 15) 29.

[230] Matthew Stephenson, 'Public Regulation or Private Enforcement: The Case for Expanding the Role of Administrative Agencies' (2005) 91 *Virginia Law Review* 93, 129.

[231] Vicky Comino, 'Australia's "Company Law Watchdog" – ASIC and Corporate Regulation' (Thomson Reuters, 2015) 274–75.

[232] Legg, 'Coercive Investigatory Powers' (n 43) 31.

may have insufficient knowledge, expertise or resources, while the public regulator can overcome these obstacles through government funding, employing individuals with expertise in the regulatory subject matter and using coercive investigatory powers for obtaining information.[233] Regulation is a public good. The regulator is an institution designed to allow for the sharing of the regulatory burden across all citizens and to overcome collective action barriers.[234] However, the provision of a public regulator comes at a cost as it must be funded by the state, or as discussed below, by industry.

iii. Why Enable Private Enforcement?

The adoption of private enforcement by the state through granting standing and facilitating enforcement through class actions and litigation funding may be situated within the 'regulatory pluralism' or 'new governance' scholarship.[235] The intellectual history of regulatory pluralism is linked to the failure of both traditional command and control regulation and reliance on the free market.[236] In terms of regulatory enforcement, a public regulator may not act or take sufficient steps due to lack of resources, capture or ineptitude.[237] Equally, the state may deliberately 'retreat' from an area of regulation.[238] As a result, additional regulatory mechanisms may be needed as a replacement or supplement for the regulator.

Regulatory pluralism scholarship has a range of diverse strands but also a number of commonalities.[239] A core belief is that the state no longer has a monopoly on governance and recognition should be given to the diverse ways in which entities may be regulated. This approach to regulation embraces forms of social control which seek to harness not just governments but also business and third parties as regulatory agents. While regulators have traditionally developed and combined knowledge in a centralised space, knowledge, particularly case specific knowledge, may also exist outside regulators.[240] Regulatory pluralism recognises that expertise exists in a range of actors not just the regulatory agency – 'no single actor has all the knowledge required to solve complex, diverse and dynamic problems'.[241] However, the expertise needs to be shared and coordinated.[242] The central argument is that a broader range of regulatory actors will produce

[233] Harry Kalven Jr and Maurice Rosenfield, 'The Contemporary Function of the Class Suit' (1940–41) 8 *University of Chicago Law Review* 684, 686; Edward Brunet, 'Debunking Wholesale Private Enforcement of Environmental Rights' (1992) 15 *Harvard Journal of Law & Public Policy* 311, 321; Colin Scott, 'Enforcing Consumer Protection Laws' in Geraint Howells, Iain Ramsay and Thomas Wilhelmsson with David Kraft, *Handbook of Research on International Consumer Law* (Edward Elgar, 2010) 544.

[234] Stewart and Sunstein (n 179) 1236–37; Issacharoff, 'Governance and Legitimacy' (n 159) 338; Samuel Issacharoff, 'Class Actions and State Authority' (2012) 44 *Loyola University Chicago Law Journal* 369, 371.

[235] Neil Gunningham and Peter Grabosky, *Smart Regulation* (Oxford University Press, 1998) 12, 96–98; Orly Lobel, 'The Renew Deal: The Fall of Regulation and the Rise of Governance in Contemporary Legal Thought' (2004) 89 *Minnesota Law Review* 342, 375; Issacharoff, 'Class Actions' (n 234) 390.

[236] Gunningham (n 15) 132.

[237] Barry Boyer and Errol Meidinger, 'Privatizing Regulatory Enforcement: A Preliminary Assessment of Citizen Suits Under Federal Environmental Laws' (1985) 34 *Buffalo Law Review* 833, 838, 870; Stephenson (n 230) 108–10; Issacharoff, 'Class Actions' (n 234) 385–6.

[238] Peter Grabosky, 'Beyond Responsive Regulation: The Expanding Role of Non-State Actors in the Regulatory Process' (2013) 7 *Regulation & Governance* 114, 115.

[239] Lobel (n 235) 346–47; Cristie Ford, 'New Governance in the Teeth of Human Frailty: Lessons from Financial Regulation' [2010] *Wisconsin Law Review* 441, 444 ('The term "new governance" is something of a big tent that captures several discrete but related approaches').

[240] Scott (n 233) 540.

[241] Julia Black, 'Decentring Regulation: Understanding the Role of Regulation and Self-Regulation in a "Post-Regulatory" World' (2002) 54 *Current Legal Problems* 103, 107.

[242] ibid 106–07; Lobel (n 235) 373.

better regulation than a government only approach. Regulation is no longer a bi-partite process involving government as the regulator and business as the regulatee. Other actors such as standard setting organisations, peer entities, commercial or industry associations, non-government organisations (NGOs), markets and the people the law is intended to benefit – operating at local, regional and global levels – may all play a regulatory role. Self-regulation, either on an individual or industry level, and coregulation with NGOs have been the most prominent example of regulatory pluralism in action.[243]

Professors Neil Gunningham and Peter Grabosky illustrate the operation of regulatory pluralism through building on the enforcement pyramid concept that forms part of responsive regulation, discussed in chapter two. They conceptualise the pyramid as being three-dimensional so that the three sides of the pyramid represent the Government acting as regulator, business acting as a self-regulator and the third side being commercial and non-commercial third parties.[244] Regulatory responses may come from any or all of the three groups/sides described.

The class action may be conceived of as belonging to the third side and be seen as either a commercial or non-commercial third party. It is commercial in the sense that there are lawyers and litigation funders involved who facilitate litigation to advance their commercial interests. But it is also non-commercial in the sense that the shareholders who are claiming are the persons that the laws are designed to protect. The above discussion of deterrence and compensation demonstrated how the class action can act as a regulatory agent.

C. The Public Interest

i. Definition

The public interest has been defined as 'for the benefit or advantage to a whole community, as opposed to the individual',[245] 'the benefit or advantage of the community as a whole; the public good'[246] and 'a concern common to the public at large, or a significant portion of the public, which may or may not involve the personal or proprietary rights of individual people'.[247]

Regulation and its enforcement by a public regulator may be conceived of as involving the pursuit of the public interest or common good through 'deliberative, disinterested, and expert decision making that does not merely serve the interests of a special few'.[248] The regulator seeks to achieve publicly desirable outcomes.[249] The desired outcomes are determined by reference to Parliament's conception of the public interest as expressed in the legislative scheme.[250] The public

[243] See Gunningham and Grabosky (n 235); Black, 'Decentring' (n 241); Lobel (n 235); Bradley Karkkainen, '"New Governance" in Legal Thought and the World: Some Splitting as Antidote to Overzealous Lumping' (2004) 89 *Minnesota Law Review* 471; Scott Burris, Michael Kempa and Clifford Shearing, 'Changes in Governance: A Cross-Disciplinary Review of Current Scholarship' (2008) 41 *Akron Law Review* 1; Gunningham (n 15) 131–35; Neil Gunningham and Darren Sinclair, 'Smart Regulation' in Peter Drahos (ed), *Regulatory Theory: Foundations and Applications* (ANU Press, 2017) 133–35.

[244] Gunningham and Grabosky (n 235) 398. Responsive regulation did foresee a role for third parties: Ayres and Braithwaite, (n 26) ch 3.

[245] *Macquarie Dictionary* (online) 'the public interest'.

[246] *Oxford English Dictionary* (online) 'public interest'.

[247] *Encyclopaedic Australian Legal Dictionary* (LexisNexis Online) 'public interest'.

[248] Jody Freeman, 'Extending Public Law Norms Through Privatization' (2003) 116 *Harvard Law Review* 1285, 1303.

[249] Baldwin, Cave and Lodge (n 15) 40–41.

[250] Suzanne Le Mire, '"It's Not Fair!": The Duty of Fairness and the Corporate Regulator' (2014) 36 *Sydney Law Review* 445, 469. As a matter of statutory interpretation of provisions requiring an entity to act in the public or common interest,

interest is also understood by contrasting it with a situation where a regulator acts in the interests of a group or sector that it regulates. Further, acting in the public interest means that the regulator does not act in its own self-interest or for political reasons.[251]

The public control of enforcement through a regulator that is accountable to a democratically elected parliament aims to ensure that regulatory decisions are by extension decisions made to further the public interest. In contrast, private enforcement is said to be 'overwhelmingly concerned with the narrow self-interest of the claimant'.[252] However, private enforcement may be supported on the basis that allowing the pursuit of private interests can also advance the public interest through the enforcement of society's laws.[253]

ii. Promoting the Public Interest through Public Enforcement

The regulator is usually directed to act in the public interest explicitly or implicitly in its enabling statute.[254] The High Court of Australia has recognised that ASIC 'seeks the remedy it does for public and not its own private purposes' and that ASIC's 'powers are exercised for the public good'.[255] Similarly, the New South Wales Court of Appeal recognised that the continuous disclosure regime 'is remedial legislation to enhance the public interest and to protect individual investors'.[256] Compliance by the regulator with the goals set for it is monitored through accountability mechanisms discussed below. However, ASIC is also an independent body[257] because independence from political influences increases 'the prospects of [a regulator] fulfilling public interest goals'.[258]

Central to facilitating the serving of the public interest, the regulator is usually given significant discretion as to how it will achieve its responsibilities.[259] The government regulator has an array of regulatory tools enabling it to perform its function in a calibrated manner, depending on the facts and circumstances of the particular case before it. Regulators can adopt a coordinated approach to laws so as to develop interpretations and, if needed, bring litigation

the courts have said that the term derives its content from 'the subject matter and the scope and purpose' of the enactment in which it appears: *Hogan v Hinch* (2011) 243 CLR 506, 548 [69] (Gummow, Hayne, Heydon, Crennan, Kiefel and Bell JJ); *O'Sullivan v Farrer* (1989) 168 CLR 210, 216 (Mason CJ, Brennan, Dawson and Gaudron JJ).

[251] Baldwin, Cave and Lodge (n 15) 41–49; Adam Levitin, 'The Politics of Financial Regulation and the Regulation of Financial Politics: A Review Essay' (2014) 127 *Harvard Law Review* 1991, 2042.

[252] Bryant Garth, 'Conflict and Dissent in Class Actions: A Suggested Perspective' (1982) 77 *Northwestern University Law Review* 492, 498; Shavell, 'The Fundamental Divergence' (n 167) 579; John Beisner, Matthew Shors and Jessica Davidson Miller, 'Class Action "Cops": Public Servants or Private Entrepreneurs' (2005) 57 *Stanford Law Review* 1441, 1443; Scott (n 233) 539.

[253] William Rubenstein, 'On What a "Private Attorney General" Is – And Why It Matters' (2004) 57 *Vanderbilt Law Review* 2129, 2147.

[254] Australian Securities and Investments Commission Act 2001 (Cth), ss 1(2)(b), 12A(2), 50. See also Australian Government, Department of Finance, 'Resource Management Guide No 200 – General duties of accountable authorities' (June 2014) 5 ('In the Commonwealth public sector, where entities are accountable, ultimately, to the Parliament and the people, the legal and accountability requirements for accountable authorities often have a strong public good or public interest element.').

[255] *ASIC v Hellicar* (2012) 247 CLR 345, 408–09 [155] (French CJ, Gummow, Hayne, Heydon, Crennan, Kiefel and Bell JJ), 434–35 [239] (Heydon J). See also Senate Economics Reference Committee (n 137) 292.

[256] *James Hardie Industries NV v ASIC* (2010) 274 ALR 85, 163 [356] (Spigelman CJ, Beazley and Giles JJA).

[257] 2007 statement of expectations (n 220) ('ASIC was established as an independent body to administer the financial and corporate regulatory framework.').

[258] Anthony Ogus, *Regulation – Legal Form and Economic Theory* (Clarendon Press, 1994) 117.

[259] See, eg, Australian Securities and Investments Commission Act 2001 (Cth), s 1(2)(g) ('take whatever action it can take, and is necessary, in order to enforce and give effect to the laws of the Commonwealth that confer functions and powers on it.').

to obtain judicial precedents that result in a cohesive regulatory framework.[260] A government regulator can also adjust its approach to enforcement as circumstances require.[261] For example, where regulators have continuing or frequent engagement with regulated entities, negotiated outcomes may be possible, even desirable, as a way to minimise cost and craft bespoke regulatory responses.[262]

iii. Private Enforcement: Public and/or Private Interests

The granting of standing to private citizens when the Australian legislature first enacted prohibitions on misleading conduct as part of consumer protection was 'inspired by the thinking that private litigation, even if in practice brought principally by traders seeking to protect their own commercial interests, will in principle at the same time serve to assert the public interest'.[263]

Even though the private litigant's main motive in bringing suit is to obtain compensation or other relief there are positive side-effects, or in economic terms, externalities, that benefit the public.[264] The main example, which is discussed above, is deterrence. Others include the spread of information about wrongdoers when litigation is filed and resolved, which may alert ASIC to contraventions it had not previously detected. However, there can also be negative side-effects or externalities because the private litigant only considers their costs and benefits. Private enforcement may be over-zealous because they will litigate whenever their expected return is greater than their expected costs.[265] For example, the private litigant will not consider the social costs associated with using the legal system or the costs imposed on a defendant. Similarly, a private litigant may settle a dispute even if a judgment is in the public interest, and the settlement (or parts thereof) may be confidential even though society may benefit from the full disclosure of the terms of settlement.[266] Public enforcers, on the other hand, are expected to take account of the broader costs and benefits of enforcement.[267]

Another cost or negative externality of relevance here is the impact on the regulator. Private enforcement can undermine the enforcement pyramid and regulatory discretion by always seeking the greatest amount of damages possible.[268] Regulated entities may have no incentive to negotiate or cooperate with a regulator as substantial damages claims may still follow. Consequently, the threat of the regulator being able to move 'up' the enforcement pyramid so as to procure cooperation may be lost or the regulator may need to demonstrate a willingness to use more potent remedies, such as criminal sanctions or increased fines, if they are available. There is

[260] Kalven and Rosenfield (n 233) 719; Stewart and Sunstein (n 179) 1292–93.

[261] Kalven and Rosenfield (n 233) 719; Boyer and Meidinger (n 237) 881–82; Rose, 'Reforming Securities Litigation Reform' (n 20) 1329–30.

[262] Scott (n 233) 553–4.

[263] David Harland, 'The statutory prohibition of misleading or deceptive conduct in Australia and its impact on the law of contract' (1995) 111 *Law Quarterly Review* 100, 104. See also Gunningham and Grabosky (n 211) 125.

[264] Shavell, 'The Fundamental Divergence' (n 167) 578, 584; Elizabeth Chamblee Burch, 'Securities Class Actions as Pragmatic Ex Post Regulation' (2008) 43 *Georgia Law Review* 63, 90.

[265] David Freeman Engstrom, 'Agencies and Litigation Gatekeepers' (2013) 123 *Yale Law Journal* 616, 630–31.

[266] Shavell, 'The Fundamental Divergence' (n 167) 577–78, 605; Michael Legg and Sera Mirzabegian, 'Appropriate Dispute Resolution and the Role of Litigation' (2013) 38 *Australian Bar Review* 55, 57–58.

[267] Lemos and Minzer (n 167) 897.

[268] Richard Nagareda, "Class Actions in the Administrative State: Kalven and Rosenfield Revisted" (2008) 75 *University of Chicago Law Review* 603, 616–18.

then a risk that sanctions are seen as capricious or draconian responses that are not proportionate to the severity of the offence or the harm done.[269] Cooperative relationships between regulators and regulated entities may be disrupted.[270]

A further aspect is the role of lawyers and litigation funders and whether the entrepreneurial behaviour of these private entities in facilitating private enforcement produces litigation that is in the public interest.[271] As the enablers of private enforcement, lawyers and litigation funders do not profit unless there is a dispute. The lawyer may be motivated by the desire for legal fees or the ideological pursuit of certain contraventions or defendants.[272] Litigation funders are driven by the need to make a profitable investment. The financial drivers that affect private enforcement are much less significant in public enforcement because the government enforcer is not compensated based on the result of the enforcement action. On the other hand, the private lawyer's and litigation funder's recovery may be directly linked to the outcome in the litigation.[273] The literature suggests that shareholder class action may advance or harm the public interest depending on the particular circumstances in which it is brought.

D. Accountability

i. *Definition*

'Accountability' generally refers to giving account of one's actions to some other person or body. 'Giving account' means to explain or justify actions.[274] It also involves holding a person responsible for those actions.[275] The need for accountability may be explained by reference to agency theory. The regulator and parliament on the public side and the class action lawyer and client on the private side have both been described as classic principal-agent relationships.[276] Public and private enforcement needs to be accountable because the entities undertaking the enforcement are doing it for the benefit of others. Accountability mechanisms are needed to ensure that the agent acts for the benefit of the principal rather than the regulator/lawyer acting in their own interest (shirking, corruption or profiting at the principal's expense) or for someone else (such as the entities being regulated (regulatory capture) or the litigation funder).

[269] Cooter and Ulen (n 55) 513.

[270] Boyer and Meidinger (n 237) 841; Jody Freeman, 'The Private Role in Public Governance' (2000) 75 *New York University Law Review* 543, 662; Stephenson (n 230) 114; Engstrom, 'Agencies' (n 265) 634; Burbank, Farhang and Kritzer (n 222) 669.

[271] Deborah Hensler, Nicholas Pace, Bonita Dombey-Moore, Beth Giddens, Jennifer Gross and Erik Moller, *Class Action Dilemmas – Pursuing Public Goals for Private Gain* (RAND Institute for Civil Justice, 2000) 72.

[272] Garth (n 252) 533; Michael Legg, 'Was Peter Thiel's funding of the Gawker case an abuse of legal process?' *The Conversation* (31 May 2016).

[273] Beisner, Shors and Miller (n 252) 1443, 1452; Lemos and Minzer (n 167) 856.

[274] Colin Scott, 'Accountability in the Regulatory State' (2000) 27 *Journal of Law and Society* 38, 40; Bird (n 228) 741.

[275] Peter May, 'Regulatory Regimes and Accountability' (2007) 1 *Regulation & Governance* 8, 9; Mark Bovens, 'Analysing and Assessing Accountability: A Conceptual Framework' (2007) 13 *European Law Journal* 447, 450; Black, 'Constructing and Contesting' (n 195) 150.

[276] Mathew McCubbins, Roger Noll and Barry Weingast, 'Administrative Procedures as Instruments of Political Control' (1987) 3 *Journal of Law Economics & Organization* 243, 247; Ogus (n 258) 111–12; Coffee, 'Understanding the Plaintiff's Attorney' (n 159); Jonathan Macey and Geoffrey Miller, 'The Plaintiffs' Attorney's Role in Class Action and Derivative Litigation: Economic Analysis and Recommendations for Reform' (1991) 58 *University of Chicago Law Review* 1.

ii. Regulators – ASIC

Regulatory scholars have developed various classifications for accountability.[277] Professor Colin Scott asks three questions: Who is accountable? To whom? And for what? The 'to whom' question then leads to upward accountability to a higher authority (for example, Parliament and courts), horizontal accountability to parallel institutions (for example, public auditors, Ombudsmen) and downwards accountability to lower-level institutions and groups (for example, consumers and other constituents). The 'for what' question leads to categories of values, including economic/financial (probity/efficiency) and social and procedural (fairness/legality).[278]

The desire for, or obligation of, accountability in a regulatory regime has traditionally arisen due to the discretionary use of delegated powers to the regulator from the legislature.[279] Regulatory power is public power.[280] Consequently, from a democratic perspective, regulators are usually held accountable through being required to report to Parliament, that is, upward accountability to a higher authority. In relation to ASIC, a former Federal Treasurer stated: 'ASIC operates as part of the Australian Government and is accountable to the Parliament, and ultimately to the public, through the Treasury Ministers, the Parliamentary Committee process and the tabling of its annual report'.[281]

ASIC is also subject to upward accountability through its rules or regulations being legislative instruments that are subject to parliamentary scrutiny, the minister being able to give directions to ASIC about policies or priorities it should pursue, the availability of a ministerial Statement of Expectations and the ability of the Executive Government to remove senior regulators on specified grounds such as misbehaviour, absences from duty and failure to disclose conflicts of interest.[282]

Horizontal accountability is sought through the Auditor-General, Ombudsman and the Office of Best Practice Regulation. The Auditor-General conducts financial and performance audits, the latter having included a review of the effectiveness of ASIC's processes for receiving reports of suspected breaches of the Corporations Act. The Ombudsman tends to investigate complaints about allegations of maladministration. The Office of Best Practice Regulation addresses regulation-making and the impact of the regulation by reference to a cost-benefit analysis.[283] To these forms of accountability may be added Royal Commissions, or commissions of inquiry, which are established by the Government on an ad hoc basis. The Commission is able to obtain documents and oral evidence to then report to Parliament with findings and recommendations.[284]

Additionally, the constituents of the agency can be empowered to voice concerns – downwards accountability. This can include Freedom of Information requests, submissions to the Ombudsman, government inquiries or to members of parliament, and media coverage.[285] ASIC's constituents bring issues to the attention of other actors who can achieve accountability.[286]

[277] See, eg, Barbara Romzek and Melvin Dubnick, 'Accountability in the Public Sector: Lessons from the Challenger Tragedy' (1987) 47 *Public Administration Review* 227 (legal, bureaucratic, professional and political accountability); Ogus (n 258) 111 (financial accountability, procedural accountability and substantive accountability).

[278] Scott, 'Accountability' (n 274) 41–43.

[279] Baldwin, Cave and Lodge (n 15) 339.

[280] Jody Freeman, 'Private Parties, Public Functions and the New Administrative Law' (2000) 52 *Administrative Law Review* 813, 838.

[281] 2014 statement of expectations (n 220). See also Bird (n 228) 750–52; Senate Economics Reference Committee (n 137) 419–22.

[282] Bird (n 228) 752–56, 761–62.

[283] ibid 756–61; Senate Economics Reference Committee (n 137) 421, 423.

[284] Royal Commissions Act 1902 (Cth).

[285] Bird (n 228) 763–65.

[286] McCubbins, Noll and Weingast (n 276) 249–50 (describing this as 'fire-alarm' monitoring); Grabosky (n 238) 118 (linking citizen action with the rise of technology such as social media).

Two other accountability mechanisms that have specific relevance to enforcement deserve mention. Regulators as an arm of government are subject to model litigant obligations.[287] This includes limiting the scope of legal proceedings wherever possible and giving consideration to alternative dispute resolution before initiating legal proceedings.[288] Further, a regulator must obtain legal advice that there are reasonable grounds for commencing proceedings.[289] A regulator is required to deal with its mandate efficiently and to consider whether litigation is warranted. Failure to comply with model litigant obligations may be dealt with by the Attorney-General imposing sanctions.[290]

Regulators also need to consider how they approach confidentiality from the perspective of the public interest.[291] The Legal Services Directions 2017 provide that an agency is only to agree that the terms of settlement are confidential and cannot be disclosed where this is necessary to protect the Commonwealth's interests.[292] Further, in particular instances, regulators may take policy positions that a resolution of an enforcement action will not be kept confidential, and indeed must be disclosed.[293]

The above overview of accountability mechanisms demonstrates that public regulators, and ASIC in particular, are subject to numerous forms of accountability.

iii. Class Actions

Accountability in the class action has been examined through two main approaches: class action governance; and the relationship between the lawyer and the client. There are other relationships that call for, or give rise to, accountability but have attracted less study, namely the existence of a litigation funder. Each of these will be explained below.

Class action governance essentially focuses on the procedures within the class action from the perspective of whether they protect or empower the group members, in particular the 'absent' group members whose claims are included in the class action but who have not retained the lawyer bringing the class action.[294] The governance approach has used corporate governance as an analogy and detailed a typology of three mechanisms: 'exit', 'voice' and 'loyalty'.[295] Exit is the ability of group members to exclude themselves from the class action, usually through the right to opt out. Voice is giving group members an ability to participate in the class action. This may include being able to object to a settlement or bring an appeal. Loyalty refers to mechanisms whereby the representative party and the lawyer act in the interests of the group rather than themselves or some other person.[296] The governance framework is closely tied to determining how a class action should operate or be designed so that it is has legitimacy. Legitimacy is used in the sense of explaining why a group member who is not before the court can nonetheless have

[287] See Legal Services Direction 2017 (formerly Legal Services Directions 2005) made under s 55ZF of the Judiciary Act 1903 (Cth), which apply to ASIC: *ASIC v Hellicar* (2012) 247 CLR 345, 435 [240] (Heydon J). See also Senate Economics Reference Committee (n 137) 422.

[288] Legal Services Directions 2017, Appendix B [2(d)].

[289] ibid [4.7].

[290] ibid [14]. Obligations imposed upon Commonwealth agencies by the Legal Services Direction 2005 are not enforceable by a private litigant: *Tarrant v ASIC* (2015) 317 ALR 328, 357 [110] (Rares, Yates and Griffiths JJ).

[291] Beisner, Shors and Miller (n 252) 1456.

[292] Legal Services Directions 2017, [4.5].

[293] See, eg, ASIC, 'Regulatory Guide 100 – Enforceable Undertakings' (February 2015) [43]–[46].

[294] Issacharoff, 'Governance and Legitimacy' (n 159); John Coffee, 'Class Action Accountability: Reconciling Exit, Voice, and Loyalty in Representative Litigation' (2000) 100 *Columbia Law Review* 370.

[295] Coffee, 'Class Action Accountability (n 294) 375–77.

[296] Issacharoff, 'Governance and Legitimacy' (n 159) 366–80.

their claim determined and be subject to *res judicata*. The focus is procedural fairness or due process in a civil litigation context.[297]

Class action governance is enforced through judicial oversight. The court has significant powers in relation to the class action, including being able to order the giving of notices, making orders that it 'thinks appropriate or necessary to ensure that justice is done in the proceeding' and being responsible for approving a settlement or discontinuance of a class action.[298] However, once again the focus is on the fairness of the internal operation of the class action.

The loyalty component of the governance approach may also be examined from the more traditional lawyer-client relationship where the lawyer as the client's agent is expected to be accountable to the client. In Figure 3.1 this is depicted through the left side of the diagram. Lawyers are subject to legal, ethical and professional obligations requiring competence, loyalty and confidentiality.[299] These obligations extend to the representative party and group members who have retained the lawyer. However, some of these obligations, such as contractual obligations, will not extend to a group member who has not retained the lawyer or is unidentified, that is, the 'absent' group member. Other obligations such as the scope and content of fiduciary duties are uncertain.[300] This is why the governance approach above has been a focus of class action scholarship.

Lawyers are also subject to regulation through their role as officers of the court which in requiring candour and independence[301] may indirectly protect group members. Australian courts have inherent jurisdiction to restrain a legal practitioner from acting in proceedings to ensure the integrity of the judicial process.[302] This has been employed in class actions where conflicts of interest were perceived as hampering a lawyer's ability to give independent advice and honour his obligations to the court.[303] Further, in the class action context, the commencement of litigation for the purpose of generating legal fees, rather than vindicating legal rights, has been held to be an abuse of process.[304] Nonetheless, it has been said that class actions are lawyer actions[305] and that 'the solicitors acting for the class representative are usually the persons in control of the class action on the plaintiff's side'.[306]

The other relationships that have attracted less study are first, the interaction between the litigation funder and group members (the right side of Figure 3.1) and second, the interplay between the representative party and group members (the centre of Figure 3.1).

[297] ibid 390; Michael Legg and Samuel Hickey, 'Finality and Fairness in Australian Class Action Settlements' (2019) 41 *Sydney Law Review* 185.

[298] Federal Court of Australia Act 1976 (Cth), ss 33V, 33X(5), 33ZF.

[299] GE Dal Pont, *Lawyers' Professional Responsibility*, 6th edn (Thomson Reuters, 2017) 115.

[300] *Kelly v Willmott Forests Ltd (in liquidation) (No 4)* (2016) 335 ALR 439, 508 [308] (Murphy J); *Dyczynski v Gibson* [2020] FCAFC 120, [209] (Murphy and Colvin JJ), [379] (Lee J). However, see Simone Degeling and Michael Legg, 'Fiduciary Obligations of Lawyers in Australian Class Actions: Conflicts between Duties' (2014) 37 *University of New South Wales Law Journal* 914 arguing that a fiduciary relationship can exist.

[301] Dal Pont (n 299) 548–49.

[302] *Melbourne City Investments Pty Ltd v Treasury Wine Estates Limited (No 3)* [2014] VSC 340, [39] (Ferguson J) citing *Kallinicos v Hunt* (2005) 64 NSWLR 561.

[303] *Melbourne City Investments Pty Ltd v Treasury Wine Estates Limited (No 3)* [2014] VSC 340; *Bolitho v Banksia Securities Limited (No 4)* [2014] VSC 582.

[304] *Treasury Wine Estates Ltd v Melbourne City Investments Pty Ltd* (2014) 45 VR 585.

[305] Edward Cooper, 'The (Cloudy) Future of Class Actions' (1998) 40 *Arizona Law Review* 923, 927; *Mobil Oil Australia Pty Ltd v Victoria* (2002) 211 CLR 1, 77 [183] (Callinan J); *Kirby v Centro Properties Ltd* (2008) 253 ALR 65, 67 [4] (Finkelstein J); *Melbourne City Investments Pty Ltd v Treasury Wine Estates Limited (No 3)* [2014] VSC 340, [63] (Ferguson J).

[306] Vince Morabito, 'Judicial Responses to Class Action Settlements that Provide no Benefits to some Class Members' (2006) 32 *Monash University Law Review* 75, 82. See also Issacharoff, 'Governance and Legitimacy' (n 159) 341; John Coffee, 'The Regulation of Entrepreneurial Litigation: Balancing Fairness and Efficiency in the Large Class Action' (1987) 54 *University of Chicago Law Review* 877, 899.

Figure 3.1 Class actions relationships

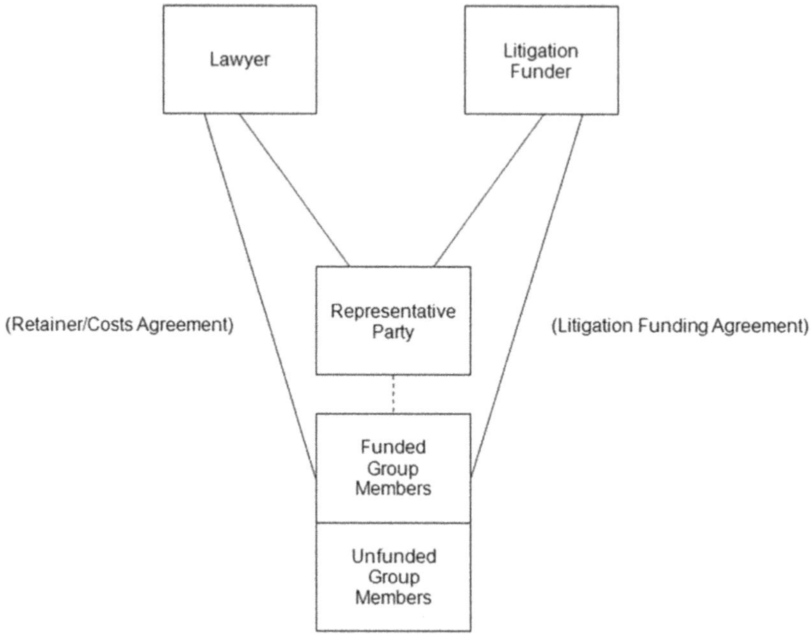

The advent of litigation funding is significant because it transforms the class action so that there is a tri-partite relationship. However, in many ways it raises the same issue as the lawyer–client relationship – how is the funder made accountable to the group members? The answer is that the relationship is primarily commercial and any obligation of accountability flows from the specific terms of the litigation funding agreement.[307] Group members may also be protected through the general law, consumer protection legislation and financial services regulation.[308] There are no ethical obligations as for lawyers. Fiduciary duties may exist but the funder will seek to exclude these through contract.[309] Consumer protection provisions such as prohibitions on misleading conduct, unconscionable conduct and unfair contract terms apply.[310] Australian law has vacillated over the regulation of litigation funding as a financial service or product. For most of its history litigation funding was unregulated, except for a requirement that any conflicts of interest be managed.[311] However further requirements were introduced in 2020, as discussed in chapter seven. Addressing conflicts of interest is important because the funder may prefer their own interests over the interests of group members. Further, the presence of the funder may create additional potential conflicts of interest for the lawyer who may favour the interests of the funder

[307] Damian Grave, Ken Adams and Jason Betts, *Class Actions in Australia*, 2nd edn (Thomson Reuters, 2012) 818.

[308] ALRC 2018 Report (n 209) 155–56.

[309] Michael Legg, 'Entrepreneurs and Figureheads – Addressing Multiple Class Actions and Conflicts of Interest' (2009) 32 *University of New South Wales Law Journal* 909, 926; Simone Degeling and Michael Legg, 'Fiduciaries and Funders: Litigation Funders in Australian Class Actions' (2017) 36 *Civil Justice Quarterly* 244.

[310] See Australian Consumer Law, Competition and Consumer Act 2011 (Cth), Sch 2.

[311] Corporations Regulations, 5C.11.01 exempts funded class actions from the managed investment scheme regime in the Corporations Act 2001 (Cth), Ch 5C. Corporations Regulations, 7.6.01AB requires the funder to maintain 'adequate practices for managing any conflict of interest' and sets out requirements that will give rise to adequate practices. See also ALRC 2018 Report (n 209) 154–55, 177–80.

as a repeat player over group members.[312] Equally the funder may monitor the lawyers on behalf of the group members and therefore assist in achieving accountability.[313]

The analysis of the interplay between the representative party and group members is underdeveloped in Australia. The class action regime is built upon the representative party having interests that are not in conflict with the interests of group members.[314] This is reinforced by a group member being able to move the court for the replacement of an inadequate representative.[315] However, the provision has been rarely used.[316] It is likely that the representative party owes fiduciary obligations to group members, but the scope of those obligations remains unclear.[317] There remains a risk that the representative party may promote their interests over the interests of some or all group members.[318]

In summary, the government regulator, ASIC, is subject to a more extensive regime of accountability than the class action due to the position it occupies within the framework of democratic governance. The class action is not without accountability mechanisms, but they are derived from a focus on private interests and due process, and are therefore narrower in operation.

E. Efficiency

i. Definition

Regulation or enforcement is costly and consumes resources. 'Cost' has been defined as 'an expenditure, usually of money, incurred in achieving a goal'.[319] Expenditure is required to conduct regulation or enforcement. 'Efficiency measures' refer to the relationship between resources and outcomes. An efficient outcome is one that will produced the desired outcome 'at the least net cost or with the greatest net benefit to society, minimising burdens on the regulated community and adverse impacts on the wider community'.[320] Put another way, 'efficiency' means 'obtaining the maximum output for given inputs'.[321] The question in the current context is which of public or private enforcement delivers the desired deterrence or compensation at the lower social cost.[322]

[312] Degeling and Legg, 'Fiduciary Obligations of Lawyers' (n 300) 934.

[313] See, eg, *QPSX Ltd v Ericsson Australia Pty Ltd (No 3)* (2005) 219 ALR 1, 10 [37], 14 [54] (French J). For a contrary view see *Tredrea v KPMG Financial Advisory Services (Australia) Pty Ltd (No 3)* [2019] NSWSC 871, [134]–[135] (Parker J) ('It is well known that funders tend to develop relationships with solicitors who undertake these sorts of proceedings. That is commercially quite understandable. But in practice it must further blunt any incentive for the funder to question the firm's fees.').

[314] Federal Court of Australia Act 1976 (Cth), s 33C(1).

[315] Federal Court of Australia Act 1976 (Cth), s 33T; *Femcare Ltd v Bright* (2000) 100 FCR 331, 352 [86] (Black CJ, Emmett and Sackville JJ).

[316] Vince Morabito, 'Replacing Inadequate Class Representatives in Federal Class Actions: Quo Vadis?' (2015) 38 *University of New South Wales Law Journal* 146, 159.

[317] *Dyczynski v Gibson* [2020] FCAFC 120, [209], [222] (Murphy and Colvin JJ).

[318] See, eg, *Peterson v Merck Sharp & Dohme (Aust) Pty Ltd (No 6)* [2013] FCA 447 (the representative party put forward a settlement where having lost his individual case he would avoid paying the respondent's costs, the settlement would provide 'a windfall' to group members in a similar situation to the representative party but 'would represent an obvious injustice' to other group members).

[319] Jonathan Law (ed), *A Dictionary of Business and Management*, 5th edn (Oxford University Press, 2009) 'cost'; *A Dictionary of Accounting*, 4th edn (Oxford University Press, 2015) 'cost'.

[320] Freiberg (n 2) 481. See also Warwick Funnell and Kathie Cooper, *Public Sector Accounting and Accountability in Australia* (UNSW Press, 1998) 36.

[321] Black, Hashimzade, and Myles (n 203) 'efficiency'.

[322] David Freeman Engstrom, 'Private Enforcement's Pathways: Lessons from Qui Tam Litigation' (2014) 114 *Columbia Law Review* 1913, 1921.

ii. Regulators – ASIC

Regulators are usually funded by the state through an allocation from the consolidated revenue fund and are therefore paid for indirectly by taxpayers. However, some regulators may be able to raise funds through charging for the various services that they operate.[323] Prior to July 2017 ASIC was funded by government but raised funds through service charges (eg obtaining company information). When the regulator took some form of enforcement action the cost was borne by the taxpayer and any revenues from successful actions were paid to government.[324] Since July 2017, ASIC has been funded by the industry participants that it regulates, in addition to charging for services. This change is discussed in chapter seven.

The regulator's ability to draw on government funding means that regulatory responses that benefit the community generally, or a subset of the community, but that would not be paid for by any particular member of the community, can be brought by a government regulator.[325] Adequate resourcing is essential to effective regulation.[326] ASIC has previously stated that 'What we are able to achieve … depends on our level of funding' and 'ASIC can only achieve what it is resourced to do'.[327]

It follows that if an entity is given resources to accomplish a goal, the provider of the resources will expect them to be used efficiently and not wasted.[328] As a result, the financial audit in the public sector has been extended to consider performance and efficiency.[329] Further, the chief executive or head of administrative agencies is required to not just keep records, prepare accounts and provide them for auditing.[330] In addition, the chairman of ASIC must manage the affairs of ASIC in a way that promotes proper use of the Commonwealth resources.[331] The Public Governance, Performance and Accountability Act 2013 (Cth) (PGPA Act), and before it, the Financial Management and Accountability Act 1997 (Cth) (FMA Act), requires the proper use and management of public resources within an entity.[332] 'Proper' is defined in s 8 of the PGPA Act (and previously s 44 of the FMA Act) as 'efficient, effective, economical and ethical'. Efficiency is a hallmark of the proper use of government resources.

The regulator may be well positioned to achieve efficiencies through being a repeat player in its field. For example, economies of scale may apply in the investigative phase due to having dedicated employees and systems (for example, procedures for search warrants and notices for oral examinations and production of documents) for conducting investigations on a continuing basis.[333] Indeed, the ability of regulators to be interconnected and share information may make investigation more efficient. However, the bureaucracy that accompanies a regulator may make

[323] Lemos and Minzer (n 167).

[324] 'ASIC Annual Report 2013–2014' 24, 98.

[325] Tracey Roberts, 'Innovations in Governance: A Functional Typology of Private Governance Institutions' (2011) 22 *Duke Environmental Law and Policy Forum* 67, 125–26.

[326] Martin Lodge and Kai Wegrich, *Managing Regulation: Regulatory Analysis, Politics and Policy* (Palgrave Macmillan, 2012) 249; Burbank, Farhang and Kritzer (n 222) 664; Andrew Keay, 'The Public Enforcement of Directors' Duties: A Normative Inquiry' (2014) 43 *Common Law World Review* 89, 101.

[327] ASIC, 'Senate inquiry into the performance of the Australian Securities and Investments Commission – Main submission by ASIC' (October 2013) [36]–[37].

[328] See, eg, 2018 statement of expectations (n 220) [21].

[329] Funnell and Cooper (n 320) 269, 279; Bovens (n 275) 456; Bird (n 228) 760–61.

[330] Financial Management and Accountability Act 1997 (Cth), ss 48, 49 replaced by the Public Governance, Performance and Accountability Act 2013 (Cth), ss 41, 42 from 1 July 2014.

[331] Senate Economics Reference Committee (n 137) 420.

[332] Public Governance, Performance and Accountability Act 2013 (Cth), s 15; Financial Management and Accountability Act 1997 (Cth), s 44.

[333] William Landes and Richard Posner, 'The Private Enforcement of Law' (1975) 4 *Journal of Legal Studies* 1, 30; A Mitchell Polinsky and Steven Shavell, 'The Economic Theory of Public Enforcement of Law' (2000) XXXVIII *Journal of Economic Literature* 45, 46.

its operations more cumbersome.[334] For example, compliance with accountability requirements may take time and resources.

The focus on costs and efficiency may also have the unintended effect of making a regulator loath to act when positive enforcement outcomes are risky.[335] As a result, a conservative approach to enforcement is taken. Less costly enforcement instruments may be favoured, such as a negotiated settlement (enforceable undertaking), because they do not consume significant amounts of resources. Yet such an approach may not promote the public interest or it may achieve sub-optimal outcomes in terms of deterrence or compensation.

Efficiency may be readily measured when what is provided is something that can be effectively counted. However, where services are provided and quality of the service is important then measurement of efficiency becomes more difficult. In the area of enforcement, while it may be straightforward to measure costs against financial penalties, it is more difficult to assess enforcement outcomes that require changes to policies and procedures (for example, enforceable undertakings) or impose indirect or reputational costs. Nonetheless, efficiency is central to a government entity's legitimacy.

iii. Class Actions

The cost of a class action is borne by the group members if successful, and by the lawyers or litigation funder if unsuccessful. As a result, additional enforcement may be obtained by the state by facilitating private suits but at no additional cost to it. However, unlike the government regulator which is funded by government allocation, private regulation including class actions must develop their own methods for raising funds. Litigation funding has been the primary response to the need for resourcing to cover costs in Australian shareholder class actions.[336] Lawyers may also act on a conditional fee basis, also called a 'no win, no fee' basis, and in addition charge an uplift fee based on their usual fee to a maximum of 25 per cent.[337] As a result of the reliance on private funding for enforcement, there may be too little enforcement action undertaken and therefore less 'public good' produced.[338] This is particularly likely where there are insufficient funds to compensate those harmed, and by extension, to pay the funder of the litigation.

The ability of private actors to fund the enforcement of regulation and insufficient resources for a public regulator to take adequate enforcement action may encourage the use of private enforcement through class actions. In the United States it has been observed that the resources of the Securities and Exchange Commission (SEC) compared to the size of the US securities market means that additional private resources are needed to investigate and litigate contraventions to ensure that misconduct does not escape regulation.[339] According to the United States Supreme Court, class actions are a 'necessary supplement to [Securities Exchange] Commission action'

[334] Stewart and Sunstein (n 179) 1298.

[335] See, eg, Senate Economics Reference Committee (n 137) 257 (ASIC's success rate in litigation from 2006–07 to 2012–13 varied from 90% to 97%); ASIC, 'Annual Report 2016–17' 182 (ASIC's success rate in litigation from 2013–14 to 2016–17 varied from 85% to 96%).

[336] See ch 2, section V.E for a discussion of the operation of litigation funding.

[337] Grave, Adams and Betts (n 307) 771–72.

[338] Keay (n 326) 110.

[339] J Maria Glover, 'The Structural Roles of Private Enforcement Mechanisms in Public Law' (2012) 53 *William and Mary Law Review* 1137, 1159–60, Steven Davidoff and David Zaring, 'Regulation by Deal: The Government's Response to the Financial Crisis' (2009) 61 *Administrative Law Review* 463, 503–04; Howell Jackson, 'Variation in the Intensity of Financial Regulation: Preliminary Evidence and Potential Implications' (2007) 24 *Yale Journal of Regulation* 253; James Cox and Randall Thomas, 'SEC Enforcement Heuristics: An Empirical Inquiry' (2003) 53 *Duke Law Journal* 737, 757–58; Fitzpatrick (n 56) 36–37.

because of limits on the resources available to the SEC.[340] Further, the United States Supreme Court's determination not to overturn the fraud on the market doctrine that is central to US class actions in *Halliburton Co v Erica P John Fund Inc*[341] has been explained as resulting from the recognition that private enforcement is a necessary supplement to criminal and civil enforcement actions brought by the Department of Justice and the SEC.[342]

Efficiency in the class action context has focused on the enhancement of judicial efficiency by encouraging the adjudication of numerous claims through a single proceeding. The idea is that one class action that resolves some or all issues for a group of persons is more efficient than numerous individual suits that all raise the same or similar issues.[343] Efficiency is also indirectly considered through the review of legal costs. A review of legal costs, also called a taxation or assessment of costs, aims to determine if the costs are fair and reasonable.[344] Efficiency arises indirectly because costs may be disallowed where they 'are of an unreasonable amount having regard to, inter alia, the nature of the work performed, the time taken to perform the work'.[345] There is an incentive for the lawyer to be efficient as otherwise their fee may be challenged. However, efficiency is a by-product of the main concern, which is fairness. In contrast, the amount charged by a litigation funder has only become subject to judicial review recently.[346] The power and basis for reviewing a funder's fee is 'unsettled',[347] but the focus is mainly on whether the fee reflects the risk undertaken and is therefore fair, rather than efficient.[348]

V. Conclusion

Chapter two demonstrated that the literature has identified ASIC enforcement and shareholder class actions as achieving, or being able to achieve, compensation and deterrence. Consequently, there is an overlap or intersection between ASIC enforcement and the shareholder class action, or expressed more broadly, between public and private enforcement, in those two areas. The existence of an intersection in relation to enforcement also means that the process of undertaking enforcement is relevant as ASIC and the class action may aid or hinder the other.

Chapter three has built on the identified intersection between ASIC enforcement and the class action through developing an analytical framework for examining that intersection. The first part of the analytical framework provides guidance for assessing the effectiveness of ASIC enforcement and the shareholder class action in achieving deterrence and compensation. Ascertaining the conditions or reasons for ASIC enforcement or the class action achieving or failing to achieve

[340] *J I Case Co v Borack*, 377 US 426, 432 (1964); *Bateman Eichler, Hill Richards Inc v Berner*, 472 US 299, 310 (1985); *Randall v Loftsgaarden*, 478 US 647, 664 (1986); *Dura Pharmaceuticals, Inc v Broudo*, 544 US 336, 345 (2005); *Tellabs, Inc v Makor Issues & Rights Ltd*, 551 US 308, 313, 318 (2007).

[341] *Halliburton Co v Erica P John Fund Inc*, 573 US 258 (2014).

[342] 'Class Actions – Presumption of Reliance Under SEC Rule 10B-5 – Halliburton Co v Erica P John Fund Inc' (2014) 128 *Harvard Law Review* 291, 299 citing *Tellabs, Inc v Makor Issues & Rights Ltd*, 551 US 308, 313 (2007).

[343] See *Bright v Femcare Ltd* (2002) 195 ALR 574, 589 [77] (Lindgren J), 603 [138] (Kiefel J) where applications to discontinue the class action based on efficiency grounds were rejected because the existence of common issues allowed for savings of time and resources.

[344] Dal Pont (n 299) 505–10.

[345] *Modtech Engineering Pty Limited v GPT Management Holdings Limited* [2013] FCA 626, [32], [37] (Gordon J).

[346] *Earglow Pty Ltd v Newcrest Mining Limited* [2016] FCA 1433, [134], [157] (Murphy J); *Blairgowrie Trading Ltd v Allco Finance Group Ltd (Recs & Mgrs Apptd) (In Liq) (No 3)* (2017) 343 ALR 476, 504 [101] (Beach J).

[347] ALRC 2018 Report (n 209) 169.

[348] Michael Legg, 'Ramifications of the Recognition of a Common Fund in Australian Class Actions: An Early Appraisal' (2017) 91 *Australian Law Journal* 655.

deterrence or compensation is of significant importance for the effective regulation of the securities market. The framework takes apart the concepts of deterrence and compensation so as to elucidate the elements of each that need to be examined to determine whether each is attained.

In particular, the framework highlights that deterrence may be achieved through formal sanctions (imprisonment, penalties and compensation payments), indirect costs and reputational harm, and that deterrence operates on two levels: specific deterrence aimed at the particular contravenor; and general deterrence, which is targeted at discouraging the population of regulated entities from offending in the future. Further, the achievement of deterrence is complex: a number of factors play a role in the outcome achieved, namely certainty, severity and celerity, with differing views as to their relative importance, but also as to how the probability of each is perceived by the regulatory population. There are also competing views as to whether corporations or individuals should be the object of deterrence. It also important to keep in mind the limitations of sanctions-based deterrence, because it takes a narrow approach to costs rather than including non-financial sanctions, and may wrongly assume rationality. It is important to recognise the expressive effect that enforcement may have on deterring wrongful behaviour. In any event, determining how, and how much, deterrence has been achieved is problematic. The identification of these influences, incentives and constraints informs the conduct of the case studies by directing attention to the data to collect and questions to ask of interviewees.

The second component of the analytical framework focuses on regulatory process values or norms. The chapter has argued that a legitimate or 'good' regulatory process can be assessed through an analysis of four values: (1) its legislative authority; (2) whether it operates in the public interest; (3) whether it is accountable; and (4) whether it is efficient. This chapter has shown that ASIC, as a traditional regulator, is required to operate in a manner consistent with the regulatory process values. The class action, as a civil procedure vehicle that is used to pursue causes of action created by the legislature, has a hybrid background that gives rise to tensions in some of the process values. How the values are actually given effect by ASIC and the class action in relation to enforcement of the continuous disclosure regime is examined through the case studies. This second component of the analytical framework also allows for consideration of how ASIC and the class action may impact each other in terms of their effect on desirable process values in the other.

These frameworks are employed in subsequent chapters to examine the interaction of ASIC and the shareholder class action.

In summary, the first framework looks at the achievement of goals or ends, and the second framework looks at process or means. Both the result and the process are examined through the case studies that are developed in chapter four with a view to assessing ASIC action and the class action against the criteria developed in the analytical framework and through a comparison with each other.

4

Case Studies

I. Introduction

This chapter explains the case study methodology and describes the case studies that were undertaken. It begins with an explanation for the choice of the case study method, the selection of the case studies and a discussion of the use of documentary analysis and interviews to undertake the case studies. It also sets out the limitations of the research method. This methodology chapter is included to facilitate understanding of the approach utilised in the text to arrive at its conclusions. This facilitates transparency and therefore assessment and critique of the findings. It also aids others who wish to undertake case study research. The chapter describes the four case studies: Telstra, Multiplex, Centro and Leighton. It explains the background facts, and the ASIC enforcement action and class action outcomes for each. The case studies are then summarised in Tables 4.3 to 4.5 by reference to outcomes, costs and time. The case studies provide the 'raw' data for study through the lens of the analytical framework in chapter five.

II. Methodology

A. Why Case Studies?

A case study is an in-depth study, examination or investigation of a single instance – the case.[1] The 'distinctive need for case studies arises out of the desire to understand complex social phenomena'.[2] The case study does not focus on, or goes beyond, 'mere frequencies or incidence' and seeks to understand processes.[3] However, it can include quantitative evidence.[4] The aim is not to study only what happened, but rather why or how it happened.[5] As a result, 'a detailed contextual analysis can often uncover causal and other explanatory mechanisms that statistical correlation cannot capture'.[6] In the current study this means not just recording the outcome of ASIC enforcement or a class action but asking whether, and if so, how deterrence or compensation did or did not result. It further asks how and why the undertaking of action by both ASIC

[1] Lisa Miller, 'The Use of Case Studies in Law and Social Science Research' (2018) 14 *Annual Review of Law and Social Science* 381, 383.

[2] Robert Yin, *Case Study Research: Design and Methods*, 5th edn (Sage, 2014) 4.

[3] ibid 10.

[4] ibid 19.

[5] Miller (n 1) 384.

[6] Jack Goldsmith and Adrian Vermeule, 'Empirical Methodology and Legal Scholarship' (2002) 69 *University of Chicago Law Review* 153, 159. See also Miller (n 1) 383.

and the class action impacted the regulatory process and each other. The aim is to analyse and understand what factors cause or mediate success or failure.

The case study approach is being adopted here with the aim of achieving a deep and detailed examination of the interaction of public and private enforcement of the continuous disclosure regime. A key advantage of the case study is 'thickness' or 'particularisation', meaning it is multi-faceted, detailed, conceptually rich and multi-dimensional.[7] The case study can use multiple research methods, such as interviewing and documentary analysis, which make it better able to focus on qualitative data. These include party information about litigation risks informing settlement, and costs such as reputational damage or organisational dislocation. Significantly, it also allows the identification of the differences between each case study. Furthermore, the use of multiple methods coupled with obtaining information from multiple sources allows for a broader perspective, as well as the testing of perspectives through seeking out consistent or conflicting views of events.

B. Selection of Case Studies

The case study method usually requires the use of non-random selection. This is because the aim is to select a sample of cases that address the features of interest.[8] Consequently, the selection here is non-random and aims to cover a range of situations that are illustrative of the larger population while also dealing with the issues of interest.[9] Although the text is interested in deterrence, compensation and the regulatory process, it is not possible to choose cases based on all of these issues without first analysing the cases. Instead, the selection needs to be made on publicly available information that suggests these issues will exist.

The population of interest is entities that have been subject to both ASIC enforcement activity and a class action stemming from contravention of the continuous disclosure regime. Entities subject to only ASIC action or a class action were not considered, as the interaction and comparison of public and private enforcement is central to the research and is better analysed when an entity is subject to both.[10]

The universe of potential case studies needed to be identified as at September 2015 as an ethics approval application was required to be lodged and approved for the case studies to be undertaken.[11] The potential case studies at that date are set out in Table 4.1. To qualify as a potential case study, there needed to be (1) completed ASIC enforcement action, (2) completed class action proceedings, and (3) the underlying factual matrix needed to involve allegations of non-compliance with the continuous disclosure regime. The AWB, Gunns and Newcrest Mining class

[7] Helen Simons, 'Case Study Research: In-Depth Understanding in Context' in Patricia Leavy (ed), *The Oxford Handbook of Qualitative Research* (Oxford University Press, 2014) 466.

[8] John Gerring, 'Case Selection for Case Study Analysis: Qualitative and Quantitative Techniques' in Janet Box-Steffensmeier, Henry Brady and David Collier (eds), *The Oxford Handbook of Political Methodology* (Oxford University Press, 2008) 645. See also Brent Fisse and John Braithwaite, *The Impact of Publicity on Corporate Offenders* (State University of New York Press, 1983) 4 (using a non-random approach to the case studies chosen).

[9] Gerring (ibid) 652; Fisse and Braithwaite, *The Impact of Publicity* (ibid) 4 (choosing to focus on extreme rather than average cases).

[10] Entities that had been subject to only ASIC enforcement activity or a class action could provide useful material on issues the subject of the study such as deterrence and compensation. There may also be interesting questions about why the entity only attracted the attention of ASIC or the class action. The text has not pursued these questions.

[11] University of Melbourne, Application for Human Research Ethics Approval No 1545406.1 (17 September 2015). Ethics approval was granted on 9 October 2015.

actions were not complete as at September 2015.[12] ASIC did not pursue contraventions of the continuous disclosure regime in all cases. Rather, in a number of cases where it took criminal or civil penalty proceedings, it relied on other causes of action. In Harris Scarfe, AWB and Centro the regulator pursued contraventions of director's duties. In Gunns, the cause of action was insider trading. As a result, there were four potential case studies where continuous disclosure was pursued by both ASIC and the class action: Telstra, Multiplex, Nufarm and Leighton. However, Nufarm and Leighton involved the same enforcement tools; both employed infringement notices and enforceable undertakings. Consequently, it was determined to replace Nufarm with Centro, which utilised civil penalty proceedings.

Table 4.1 Potential case studies as at September 2015

Corporate entity	ASIC action	Class action
Harris Scarfe	Criminal proceedings for breach of director's duties against directors – one successful and others discontinued (2002–06)	Single class action settled for $3m in 2006
Telstra	Continuous disclosure warning (2005)	Single class action settled for $5m in 2007
Multiplex	Enforceable undertaking for alleged continuous disclosure breach including compensation (2006)	Single class action settled for $110m in 2010
AWB	Civil penalty proceedings for breach of director's duties – some successful and others discontinued (2007–2018)	Single class action settled for $39.5m in 2010
Centro	Civil penalty proceedings for breach of director's duties – successful (2011) Enforceable undertaking from auditor – 2012	Three class actions settled for $200m in 2012
Nufarm	Enforceable undertaking and infringement notice for alleged continuous disclosure breach (2010)	Two class actions settled for $43.5m in 2012
Gunns (went into voluntary administration in September 2012)	Criminal proceedings for insider trading action – successful (2013)	Single class action commenced in 2011 but stayed when corporation went into voluntary administration and then liquidation Note: Second class action commenced in 2015 against directors and officers that settled in March 2016 for a confidential amount
Leighton	Enforceable undertaking and three infringement notices for alleged continuous disclosure breach (2012)	One class action settled for $69.45m in 2014
Newcrest Mining	Civil penalty for continuous disclosure breach (2014)	One class action commenced in July 2014 but not settled until November 2016 for $36m

[12] Incomplete proceedings were not selected as the outcomes needed for analysis may not have been available. Furthermore, participants in ongoing proceedings are less likely to be able or willing to participate in interviews.

Consequently, the case studies chosen for examination are: Telstra, Multiplex, Centro and Leighton. In addition to being cases where there is both ASIC and class action activity, the selections allow for a range of ASIC action to be looked at, namely warnings, infringement notices, enforceable undertaking and civil penalty proceedings. It also allows for class actions with a wide range of recoveries – \$5 million, \$69.45 million, \$110 million and \$200 million – to be examined. The aim is to reflect the diversity of ASIC and class action activity.

The issues for investigation and analysis are driven by the analytical framework developed in chapter three and which fall under the broad headings of ends (deterrence and compensation) and means (regulatory process).[13]

C. Documentary Analysis

Both enforcement activity and class actions are well documented. Some of this will be publicly available as it will be in the form of a formal court judgment or a regulatory record (for example, an enforceable undertaking). Other documentation, especially that leading up to the formal record, will be held by participants in the process. This may include evidence filed in court proceedings, board papers or advice or memoranda on decision-making. Some of these will be able to be obtained through a request to a regulator, court, regulated entity or legal representative, but others will not be provided due to confidentiality or being subject to legal professional privilege (also called 'client legal privilege') or public interest immunity. Cost also plays a part as documents like court transcripts must be purchased.[14] There are also likely to be secondary sources, such as media reports (as the subject matter is usually newsworthy), annual reports and the reports or transcripts from Parliamentary inquiries.

Documentary evidence is a valuable source of information because it is usually prepared contemporaneously with the activity that is being studied. In some cases it will be written from a particular perspective or to aid a particular purpose, and the potential for bias must be taken into account. However, by being a contemporaneous record, it is likely to be more accurate than recollections and can therefore serve as a check on information gained through interviews. Furthermore, some records will by their nature aim to be accurate. Court judgments seek to set out facts as accurately possible and rely on evidence given under oath. Some regulatory documents are negotiated, which can lead to an agreed perspective from adversaries as to the facts of what happened.

D. Interviews

A valuable source of information for the case studies are the participants in each enforcement activity and class action. The participants were current or former:

- ASIC officers;
- regulated entity officers;

[13] See Yin (n 2) 14 (stating that the literature should be reviewed to identify the most pressing questions).

[14] Access to transcripts of court hearings from the Federal Court provider of transcription services was sought but could only be obtained through paying the commercial rates of the transcript provider. As it was not possible to identify which transcripts may be of utility and due to the cost of those transcripts, they were not obtained.

- litigation funders; or
- lawyers acting for each of the above.

This information is best obtained by conducting interviews. This method allows for 'deep information and understanding', for others to be able to see the world from the interviewees perspective, 'to make sense of multiple meanings and interpretations of a specific action' and to 'access complex knowledge from an insider'.[15] Interviews can go beyond the public record and elucidate not only more information but also the intricacies of that information. It allows for subjective viewpoints to be gathered and tested. Details can be probed and clarification sought. To encourage full and frank responses, the interviews were conducted on a confidential basis. Interviews are cited in the text by reference to the interviewee's position rather than their name.

The interviews were semi-structured. Case study research frequently uses unstructured interviews as this allows for the greatest flexibility and enables the researcher to respond to interviewees' statements and pursue new lines of investigation. It opens up the research project to unforeseen perspectives and serendipity.[16] However, totally unstructured work may produce little of relevance to the research questions of interest.[17] Consequently, the interviews were based on a series of questions set out in Appendix 1 to the text. However, the questions were open-ended to start with and became more specific as needed. The open-ended nature of the questions allowed for the interviewee to provide their perspective without being unnecessarily 'hemmed in' by the question. The list of questions also acted as a checklist to ensure that an interviewee was asked about all of the issues relevant to the current study. It also ensured consistency across interviews both within a case study and between case studies. This was to assist in allowing for comparison between case studies. A summary of the interviews requested and undertaken, including the short titles identifying the interviews that are used in the text, are included in Appendix 1.

E. Limitations of the Methodology

The trade-off in achieving 'thickness' through the case study method is that there is limited ability to generalise the findings from each one. The focus on the detail of a single instance, or 'sample of one', may mean that explanations depend on case-specific factors.[18] This concern is reduced in the current work as chapter six considers all of the publicly reported actions taken by ASIC and the class action in relation to continuous disclosure up until 31 December 2017, (see chapter two and appendices). Post-31 December 2017 developments are examined in chapter seven. Further, case studies allow for 'analytic generalization'.[19] Analytical generalisation is synonymous with theoretical inference and means that the researcher distils from the case study relationships that are hypothesised to hold for a larger population of cases.[20] Nonetheless, inferences drawn from the four case studies are limited to the product of those case studies.

There are also recognised limitations to the use of an interview process. Potential interviewees may decline to participate in the study; memories fade and recollections become inaccurate;

[15] Pranee Liamputtong, *Qualitative Research Methods*, 3rd edn (Oxford University Press, 2009) 43–44.

[16] Fisse and Braithwaite, *The Impact of Publicity* (n 8) 5–6; Simons (n 7) 462.

[17] Fisse and Braithwaite, *The Impact of Publicity* (n 8) 6.

[18] Simons (n 7) 458.

[19] Yin (n 2) 21, 41–42, 237.

[20] Gregory Mitchell, 'Case Studies, Counterfactuals and Causal Explanations' (2004) 152 *University of Pennsylvania Law Review* 1517, 1584–85.

interviewees may be defensive or unhelpful, or seek to rewrite history, or provide a perspective that places them in the most positive light.[21] To address these limitations a number of steps were taken. Where an interviewee declined to participate, another person who could speak to the relevant issues was sought. However, in some instances no one may be willing to participate. This issue only arose in relation to the Leighton case study where no one representing the company was willing to participate. Interviews were recorded (unless this was objected to, which occurred on two occasions) and transcripts provided to an interviewee for review. Where interviewees were asked whether their actions achieved certain outcomes, deterrence or compensation, or if actions should have been undertaken differently, there was a risk that they would provide self-affirming responses. This predilection towards seeing the actions and outcomes they achieved in a positive light was tested by asking 'why' certain views were held. Further, information from interviews was cross-checked with documentary sources or other interviews to try and attempt to achieve accuracy. However, in some cases there may be no sources to cross-check or there may simply be two conflicting perspectives.

There are also limitations in relation to providing definitive answers to the research questions posed. The first research question examines the effectiveness of deterrence and compensation as between ASIC action and the class action. Measuring effectiveness assumes that a desired state of affairs can be identified and achieved. As explained in chapter three, measuring deterrence is inherently problematic because it is not possible to know that a person or entity refrained from misconduct because they were deterred by their fear of sanctions. While the achievement of full compensation is more measurable, that is, by comparing loss suffered with the compensation achieved less transaction costs, even here there is uncertainty as to the correct measure of loss.

The second research question focusses on process and process values. To address this question, chapter three identified a number of values or norms that the literature regards as the hallmarks of a 'good' or legitimate process. However, other values may exist that could be assessed. The findings on regulatory process are therefore limited to the values selected. Furthermore, while values such as accountability and efficiency may be evaluated, reaching a definitive answer on whether a value was achieved is difficult as such assessments can be subjective and data may not be available. Moreover, ascertaining what was in the public interest was necessarily a contestable notion, and while accountability mechanisms were identified, whether they were effective was more difficult to resolve. In relation to efficiency the costs incurred by ASIC in conducting enforcement was only available for one case study: Leighton. For the other case studies, the amounts needed to be extrapolated from data provided by interviewees and documentary review.

III. Telstra

A. ASIC Action

Telstra Corporation Limited was originally a government department, then a corporation, responsible for telecommunications in Australia. Following the opening of Australia's telecommunications markets to full competition in July 1997, Telstra underwent a partial privatisation (Tranche 1 (T1)) in November 1997 under which the Commonwealth sold approximately 33 per cent of issued shares to the public. At this point Telstra was listed on the ASX. A further

[21] Fisse and Braithwaite, *The Impact of Publicity* (n 8) 3, 8; Liamputtong (n 15) 61.

16.6 per cent of issued shares (Tranche 2 (T2)) were sold to the public in September 1999. Telstra would go on to be fully privatised in 2006–07.[22]

In September 2005, ASIC launched an investigation into whether Telstra had failed to comply with its continuous disclosure obligations in relation to the period 11 August to 6 September 2005. At this time Telstra was only partially privatised and still had reporting obligations to the Australian Government.[23]

ASIC's investigation related to three issues. The first was a selective briefing by webcast to analysts on 11 August 2005. Telstra gave the webcast shortly after it released its full accounts to the ASX. The webcast was alleged to contain guidance about a decline in earnings that was sufficiently specific that those with the benefit of the briefing could quantify the range of that decline. The briefing information should have been provided to the ASX first.[24] However, ASIC took the view that the detriment was limited as the information became public as part of the webcast.[25]

The second issue surrounded a confidential briefing paper to the Commonwealth Government on 11 August 2005. ASIC accepted that the briefing paper did not have to be disclosed as 'the information was confidential, it was incomplete and speculative and a reasonable person would not expect the information to be disclosed' – the exceptions in Listing Rule 3.1.[26] The briefing paper was also protected by the Telstra Corporation Act 1991 (Cth), which required Telstra to keep the minister informed and provided that the provision of such information did not require disclosure pursuant to the Corporations Act or listing rules.[27] However, there was information to suggest that certain parts of this document were disclosed to the market sometime on or around 16 August 2005. ASIC had a particular concern around the information dealing with Telstra's dividend policy. Once confidentiality was lost, ASIC took the view that the listing rule exceptions no longer applied and a reasonable person would expect disclosure. However, the statements about the dividend policy did not entirely accord with Telstra's position. Ultimately the whole of the government briefing paper was disclosed to the market on 7 September 2005.[28]

ASIC's position was that there 'was an argument',[29] that from 16 August until 7 September the market was misinformed about Telstra's dividend policy. But there was also evidence to suggest that the statement was not material and was generally available.[30] However, when the then ASIC chairman, Mr Lucy, was questioned at the Senate Estimates Committee, he stated that the conduct was a breach of the Corporations Act.[31]

[22] www.telstra.com.au/abouttelstra/company-overview/history/telstra-story.

[23] Telstra Corporation Act 1991 (Cth) as amended, taking into account amendments up to Act No 45 of 2005.

[24] See ASX Listing Rule 15.7 ('An entity must not release information that is for release to the market to any person until it has given the information to ASX and has received an acknowledgement that ASX has released the information to the market.').

[25] ASIC, 'ASIC warns Telstra on Disclosure Procedures' (Media Release, 05-391, 14 December 2005) 1 ('ASIC Telstra MR 05-391'); Evidence to Senate Economics Legislation Committee – Estimates, Parliament of Australia, Canberra, 16 February 2006, 22 (Mr Jeffrey Lucy, ASIC Chairman) ('Lucy Evidence to Senate Committee').

[26] Ch 2, section II.B.

[27] Telstra Corporation Act 1991 (Cth), Pt 2, Div 3, s 8AY ('To avoid doubt, the mere fact that particular information was requested, required or given under Division 3 or section 8AQ is not a ground on which Telstra can be required to disclose or notify that, or any other, information under: (a) a provision of the Corporations Act 2001; or (b) if Telstra is a listed disclosing entity – the listing rules of a listing market in relation to Telstra.').

[28] ASIC Telstra MR 05-391 (n 25) 1; Letter from Douglas Gration, Company Secretary, Telstra Corporation Limited to The Manager, Company Announcements Office, ASX, 7 September 2005, 1–2; Tony Boyd and David Crowe, 'Failure to disclose was within the law', *Australian Financial Review* (8 September 2005) 16; Lucy Evidence to Senate Committee (n 25) 22.

[29] Lucy Evidence to Senate Committee (n 25) 22.

[30] ibid.

[31] ibid 23.

The third issue was an earnings downgrade announcement on 5 September 2005 due to an $850 million estimate of costs of regulation. ASIC's investigation found that there was no such direct link and that the wording of the announcement had the potential to confuse ordinary readers.[32]

ASIC issued a media release on 14 December 2005 in which it explained each of the above issues and that it did not propose to take any enforcement action. The media release also reported Mr Lucy as saying: 'I have written to the Board of Telstra summarising ASIC's findings and outlining our concerns to serve as a warning to the board and senior management to lift their game on continuous disclosure'.[33] ASIC's media release was referred to as a warning or 'yellow card'.[34]

B. Class Action

Class actions against Telstra were originally under consideration by two law firms, Slater & Gordon and Maurice Blackburn Cashman.[35] Subsequently, only the former pursued a class action which was commenced on 20 January 2006. The cause of action centred on the briefing paper which Telstra gave on 11 August 2005 to members of the Commonwealth Government, which was not released to the ASX until 7 September 2005. In the briefing, forecasts were provided concerning declining landline or public switched telephone networks (PSTN) revenues, and opinions were expressed regarding the insufficiency of past network expenditure. The second further amended statement of claim refers to these as the 'PSTN Decline Forecast' and the 'Underspend Opinion' respectively. It was alleged that the PSTN Decline Forecast and the Underspend Opinion were information that Telstra was obliged to disclose to the market pursuant to the continuous disclosure regime and that not disclosing it was misleading or deceptive conduct. This in turn caused loss or damage to group members as the PSTN Decline Forecast and the Underspend Opinion conveyed a negative sentiment about the financial position of Telstra.[36] The share price was estimated to have fallen 51 cents and shareholders may have paid $300 million more for shares than their true value.[37] The group members were defined to be those persons who:[38]

- purchased shares in Telstra between (and including) 11 August 2005 and 6 September 2005;
- at the time of purchase in the shares believed that the price paid for shares was not falsely inflated by reason of any non-disclosure to the market by Telstra of material information;
- did not, on or before 6 September, resell those shares at a price equal to or greater than the price for which they were purchased; and
- suffered a loss.

[32] ibid.

[33] ASIC Telstra MR 05-391 (n 25) 1.

[34] Tony Boyd and David Crowe, 'ASIC gives Telstra a yellow card', *Australian Financial Review* (15 December 2005) 4; Evidence to Senate Economics Legislation Committee – Estimates, Parliament of Australia, Canberra, 16 February 2006, 43 (Mr Jeremy Cooper, ASIC Deputy Chairman) ('Cooper Evidence to Senate Committee').

[35] Matthew Charles and Fleur Leyden, 'Two class actions loom against embattled Telstra', *The Courier-Mail* (16 September 2005) 29.

[36] *Taylor v Telstra Corporation Ltd* [2007] FCA 2008 [5]–[12] (Jacobson J); Taylor v Telstra Corporation Ltd, Second Further Amended Statement of Claim, 2 November 2006.

[37] Colin Kruger, 'Investors sue Telstra to recoup $300m', *Sydney Morning Herald* (21 January 2006) 29.

[38] *Taylor v Telstra Corporation Ltd* [2007] FCA 2008 [13] (Jacobson J).

Opt-out notices were issued to group members by sending the notice by prepaid post to each group member who was recorded on the respondent's share register as having purchased shares in the period 11 August 2005 to 6 September 2005. About 33,000 notices were sent to group members and 4073 opt-out notices were received by the court, leaving a group of approximately 29,000 shareholders.[39]

The Telstra class action settled on 12 November 2007, two weeks before it was due to go to trial.[40] The settlement, which was approved by Jacobson J on 13 December 2007, resulted in a $300 million claim being settled for $5 million, or 1.7 per cent of the claim.[41] With $1.25 million of the settlement amount going to the applicants' lawyers, Slater & Gordon, there remained about $3.75 million to be shared by up to 29,000 investors, which equated to 'an amount of less than one cent up to a capped maximum of five cents per share'.[42]

The small settlement compared to the alleged losses is explained by Telstra's lay evidence, which was to the effect that the information conveyed at the briefing to government was at an early stage of an extensive strategic review and thus did not represent a concluded view.[43] The affidavit of a solicitor for the applicant accepted that 'the Information was not required to be disclosed'.[44] The small settlement sum reflected the class action's prospects of success.

IV. Multiplex

A. ASIC Action

Multiplex Limited was listed on the ASX in December 2003. Each share was stapled to a unit in the Multiplex Group Property Trust. The responsible entity for the trust was Multiplex Funds Management Limited.

ASIC commenced an investigation into Multiplex Limited and Multiplex Funds Management Limited (together 'Multiplex') on 22 February 2005. The investigation arose from the profit forecast for the Wembley Stadium project in the UK. The annual accounts for the year ended 30 June 2004 included an estimated profit from the Wembley Stadium of £35.7 million. On 2 February 2005, a Multiplex board meeting was held at which the board decided to adjust the profit forecast from the Wembley project from £35.7 million to zero. This was because the profit could no longer be reliably estimated. The change in financial position was not disclosed to the market until 24 February 2005. When the announcement was made on 24 February, the Multiplex share price dropped from the 23 February price of $5.57 (volume weighted average price, VWAP) to $4.76 on the day of the announcement.[45]

[39] ibid [15].

[40] Susannah Moran, 'Telstra settles class action with investors', *The Australian* (12 November 2007) 1.

[41] *Taylor v Telstra Corporation Ltd* [2007] FCA 2008 [34] (Jacobson J); Telstra Corporation Limited, 'Court asked to approve class action settlement' (Media Release, 263/2007, 12 November 2007) 1 ('Telstra MR263/2007'); Slater & Gordon, 'Court Orders Telstra to pay $5 million to Settle Class Action' (Media Release, 13 December 2007).

[42] *Taylor v Telstra Corporation Ltd* [2007] FCA 2008 [35], [37] (Jacobson J).

[43] ibid [18].

[44] ibid.

[45] ASIC, 'ASIC accepts an enforceable undertaking from the Multiplex Group' (Media Release, 06-443, 20 December 2006) ('ASIC Multiplex MR 16-443').

ASIC's investigation involved a review of over 3,000 documents and an examination of, or statement from, 23 witnesses over about eight months. The investigation concluded in September 2006. ASIC concluded that Multiplex had failed to comply with its continuous disclosure obligations from 3 February 2005 to 23 February 2005. On 20 December 2006 ASIC and Multiplex entered into an enforceable undertaking with the following terms:[46]

- Multiplex to obtain early payment of a $50 million indemnity from the Roberts family, who had originally established the company.
- Multiplex to use its best efforts to procure within 12 months a majority of independent directors on the board.
- Multiplex to establish a $32 million fund to compensate shareholders and provide a report from a third party as to the amount claimed.
- External consultant to review, recommend amendments to, and report on the implementation of recommendations to continuous disclosure policies and procedures.
- Multiplex unable to rely on the Corporations Act, s 713(6)[47] to reduce disclosure obligations in a prospectus until external consultant reviews and reports are completed.

The Multiplex Enforceable Undertaking did not include any admission of wrongdoing by Multiplex, but rather acknowledgement that 'ASIC had reason to be concerned'.[48] ASIC acknowledged that Multiplex had cooperated and worked constructively with ASIC.[49]

As part of its media release, ASIC provided three reasons as to why it regarded the enforceable undertaking as an appropriate regulatory outcome rather than seeking a civil penalty. First, a civil penalty would be confined to a pecuniary penalty order of a maximum $1 million, with compensation not automatically following. Second, the undertaking produced a guaranteed and swift result that offered compensation to those who had suffered loss. In contrast, compensation through litigation would require a court to be convinced that a contravention of the law had occurred and that damage had resulted. Third, the enforceable undertaking provided for Multiplex's disclosures policies to be consistent with industry best practice and monitored by an independent expert.[50] It was subsequently reported that only $20 million of the $32 million in the compensation fund was distributed.[51]

B. Class Actions

The Multiplex shareholder class action involved three streams of proceedings. The first were the class actions proper. The second was related litigation dealing with the class action proponent seeking access to ASIC documents, which ASIC had opposed on the basis of public interest immunity. The third was a claim by Multiplex that the litigation funding arrangements in the class action gave rise to an unregistered managed investment scheme. The third set of proceedings is not of present relevance but initiated the chain of events that would lead to the regulation of litigation funding that is discussed in chapter seven.

[46] ASIC, 'Enforceable Undertaking: Multiplex Ltd', Document No 017 029 205 (20 December 2006).
[47] See ch 2, section II.D.
[48] ASIC Enforceable Undertaking: Multiplex (n 46) [1.19].
[49] ibid [1.20].
[50] ASIC Multiplex MR 16-443 (n 45).
[51] Ben Butler, 'ASIC attacked on Multiplex deal' *The Sydney Morning Herald* (22 July 2010).

i. P Dawson Nominees Pty Limited and Frederick Hart v Multiplex

The class action proper developed over time. Originally, P Dawson Nominees Pty Limited commenced a class action on 18 December 2006 against Multiplex on behalf of about 40 corporations in relation to the construction of the Wembley Stadium in the United Kingdom. The applicants' main contentions were that: (1) there was an overstatement of Multiplex group profits by reason of its failure to recognise a loss on the Wembley Stadium project in its accounts for the six month ended 31 December 2004; and (2) at various dates in 2005, Multiplex failed to disclose that the Wembley Stadium project was forecast to make a loss.[52] The class action adopted a closed class and was funded by International Litigation Funding Partners, Inc.[53]

A further class action was commenced on 10 December 2008 by Frederick Hart in relation to Multiplex's projects known as West India Quay and Qantas Hangar.[54] Both projects were to be carried out under fixed-price contracts. Both projects made losses. It was alleged that Multiplex failed to inform the market of the losses in a timely manner.[55]

A settlement deed for both actions was executed on 14 May 2010 and court approval provided on 21 July 2010.[56] By the time of the settlement of both class actions, the group comprised 109 purchasers of Multiplex securities between 2 August 2004 and 30 May 2005. The losses estimated to have been suffered by the shareholders equated to $220 million.[57] The key elements of the settlement were:[58]

- a total settlement sum of $110 million;
- the amount to be distributed to class members was approximately $100 million, inclusive of interest earned on the settlement sum and after deduction of: (i) the applicants' costs; (ii) administration costs in distributing the settlement; and (iii) reimbursement payments to each of the lead applicants.
- the applicants' costs and administration costs were approximately $11 million;
- the measure of class members' losses was assessed by taking the average of: (i) the price paid for each relevant security less the price received; and (ii) the price paid for the security less its true value, as assessed on an inflation per share basis by an expert economist.
- the settlement represents approximately 62 cents in the dollar for shareholders by reference to the midpoint of a range of what might be assessed as reasonably likely successful outcomes had the matter proceeded.

The amount to be distributed to group members referred to above did not include the fee to be paid to the litigation funder, which was estimated to be about $35 million.[59] The legal costs incurred by Multiplex have been estimated at $15 million.[60] It should also be noted that

[52] *P Dawson Nominees Pty Ltd v Multiplex Ltd* (2007) 242 ALR 111, 112–14, [1]–[9] (Finkelstein J).

[53] ibid [1]; *Multiplex Funds Management Ltd v P Dawson Nominees Pty Ltd* (2007) 164 FCR 275, 284 [44] (Jacobson J).

[54] *P Dawson Nominees Pty Ltd v Brookfield Multiplex Limited (No 4)* [2010] FCA 1029, [1] (Finkelstein J); Mathew Dunckley, 'More join Wider Multiplex action' *The Australian Financial Review* (25 September 2008) 11.

[55] *P Dawson Nominees Pty Ltd v Brookfield Multiplex Limited (No 4)* [2010] FCA 1029 [7]–[10] (Finkelstein J).

[56] ibid.

[57] Dunckley (n 54) 11.

[58] Bernard Murphy and Andrew Watson, 'Negotiations and Settlement – 2010 Multiplex Debrief' LexisNexis Shareholder Class Action Masterclass, Sydney (18 October 2010) 11. See also *P Dawson Nominees Pty Ltd v Brookfield Multiplex Limited (No 4)* [2010] FCA 1029 [12]–[13], [22] (Finkelstein J).

[59] Butler (n 51).

[60] ibid (estimating total legal costs at $25 million and the applicant's legal costs as $10 million); Murphy and Watson, (n 58) 11 (the respondent's estimated their legal costs as exceeding $8 million two years prior to the finalisation of the class action).

Multiplex did not remain as a listed entity. Brookfield Asset Management Inc purchased all of the listed securities of Multiplex and privatised it in November 2007.[61]

ii. *Access to ASIC Documents*

The second stream of proceedings related to a bid to obtain access to documents held by ASIC. ASIC has the power to conduct oral examinations, issue notices to produce books and documents and apply for a search warrant to seize books.[62] ASIC may release transcripts of oral examinations conducted by it under ASIC Act, s 19 and related books to a person's lawyer if the lawyer satisfies ASIC that the person is carrying on, or is contemplating in good faith, a proceeding in respect of a matter to which the examination related.[63] ASIC also has a general power to give any person a transcript of an oral examination and related books, but the power is subject to the confidentiality regime in the ASIC Act.[64] The s 19 transcripts and books may also be obtained through subpoena so that the relevant court's rules would govern the process of obtaining the documents.[65]

On 21 December 2006, solicitors for P Dawson Nominees Pty Ltd applied to ASIC pursuant to s 25 of the ASIC Act for documents in relation to the Multiplex examinations. While ASIC was fulfilling its natural justice obligations[66] to those who were the source of the documents, the solicitors for P Dawson Nominees Pty Ltd sought leave to issue a subpoena to ASIC for the same documents. ASIC did not oppose leave. Multiplex did oppose leave. The Federal Court granted leave on 12 July 2007.[67] ASIC subsequently objected to the inspection of 36 documents obtained from Multiplex and copies of 41 transcripts of witness examinations based on public interest immunity. In particular, ASIC was concerned that the identity of informers/whistleblowers who had alerted ASIC to the issue in relation to Wembley Stadium would be disclosed. This was despite the identity of an informer being known to some officers of Multiplex. The objection was rejected at first instance,[68] but upheld on appeal to the Full Court of the Federal Court.[69]

It subsequently emerged after the appeal that the identity of an informer, Mr Stewart Cummins, Multiplex Accounting Group General Manager, had been disclosed on a television programme called *Four Corners*, broadcast on 5 September 2005. The applicants sought to reopen the application for leave to inspect the documents over which public interest immunity had been claimed. The primary judge allowed the reopening and dealt with the substantive motion by allowing inspection of 18 of the 36 documents, and inspection of 14 more of the 36 documents, but in a masked and redacted form. He refused to permit inspection of the remaining four of the 36 documents. He also refused to permit inspection of any of the transcripts.[70] On appeal, the

[61] Daniel Taub and Fergus Maguire, 'Brookfield Asset Buys Australia's Multiplex for A$4.2 Billion', *Bloomberg* (11 June 2007).

[62] Australian Securities and Investments Commission Act 2001 (Cth), ss 19, 29, 30, 33 and 35.

[63] ibid s 25(1); *Boys v Australian Securities Commission* (1998) 80 FCR 403, 420 (Heerey J).

[64] Australian Securities and Investments Commission Act 2001 (Cth), ss 25(3), 127; *Johns v ASIC* (1993) 178 CLR 408, 425 (Brennan J).

[65] *Maronis Holdings Ltd v Nippon Credit Australia Ltd* (2000) 18 ACLC 609, 615–16; *King v GIO Australia Holdings Ltd* (2001) 116 FCR 509; *Watson v AWB Ltd (No 3)* [2009] FCA 1174.

[66] See *Johns v ASIC* (1993) 178 CLR 408, 430–31 (Brennan J) (ASIC is required to give persons the source of documents or information an opportunity to object to the provision of the documents or information to a third party).

[67] *P Dawson Nominees Pty Ltd v Multiplex Ltd* (2007) 64 ACSR 53.

[68] *P Dawson Nominees Pty Ltd v Multiplex Ltd* (2007) 65 ACSR 239.

[69] *ASIC v P Dawson Nominees Pty Ltd* (2008) 169 FCR 227.

[70] *P Dawson Nominees Pty Ltd v ASIC (No 2)* (2009) 255 ALR 466; *P Dawson Nominees Pty Ltd v ASIC (No 3)* [2009] FCA 779.

Full Court of the Federal Court changed the primary judge's orders slightly by ordering further redactions to five of the documents that were already redacted. The Full Court refused to order inspection of the transcripts on the basis that it was not possible to redact parts of a transcript and be confident that the remaining content could not be used to identify informers other than Mr Cummins.[71] Further claims of public interest immunity arose in relation to subpoenas to KPMG and Mr Cummins, including in relation to the identity of another informer referred to as 'XX'.[72]

V. Centro

A. ASIC Action

i. Civil Penalty Proceedings against Directors

Centro Properties Group (CNP) was a stapled security comprised of Centro Properties Ltd (CPL) and Centro Property Trust (CPT). The responsible entity or trustee for CPT was CPT Manager Ltd (CPTM). Centro Retail Group (CER) was a stapled security comprised of Centro Retail Limited (CRL) and Centro Retail Trust (CRT). The responsible entity or trustee for CRT was Centro MCS Manager Ltd (CMCSM). CPT Manager Ltd and Centro MCS Manager Ltd were both wholly owned subsidiaries of CPL.

The business of CNP comprised two elements. The first part of the business involved investment in and management of retail property, such as shopping centres. The second part of CNP's business was in funds management. CER was a pure retail property trust.[73]

ASIC commenced civil penalty proceedings against eight defendants on 19 October 2009.[74] This was within 13 months of the commencement of ASIC's investigation.[75] Seven defendants were each directors of CPL, CPTM, being the responsible entity of CPT, and CMCSM, being the responsible entity of CRT. The eighth defendant was the chief financial officer of each of CPL, CPT and CMCSM. The allegation which was found to have been proved was that the 2007 annual reports of CNP and CER failed to disclose the following significant matters:

(a) In the case of CNP, the report failed to disclose some $1.5 billion of short-term liabilities by classifying them as non-current liabilities, and failed to disclose guarantees of short-term liabilities of an associated company[76] of about US$1.75 billion that had been given after the balance date.
(b) In the case of CER, the 2007 annual reports failed to disclose some $500 million of short-term liabilities that had been classified as non-current.[77]

[71] *ASIC v P Dawson Nominees Pty Ltd* [2009] FCAFC 183.

[72] *P Dawson Nominees Pty Ltd v ASIC (No 4)* [2009] FCA 1502 (subpoena to KPMG); *P Dawson Nominees Pty Ltd v ASIC (No 5)* [2010] FCA 232 (subpoena to Mr Cummins).

[73] *ASIC v Healey* (2011) 196 FCR 291, 359 [291]–[294] (Middleton J).

[74] ASIC, 'ASIC commences proceedings against current and former officers of Centro' (Media Release 09-202AD, 21 October 2009) attaching Statement of Claim dated 19 October 2009.

[75] Tony D'Aloisio, Chairman, ASIC, 'Responding to the global financial crisis: the ASIC story' (speech delivered at the Trans-Tasman Business Circle, 30 November 2010) 14.

[76] The associated company was Centro Super LLC which was created after the acquisition of New Plan Excel Realty Trust Inc. See Maurice Dunlevy, 'ASIC ramps up Centro probe', *The Australian* (19 November 2010) 21.

[77] *ASIC v Healey* (2011) 196 FCR 291, 297 [9], 313 [87]–[90] (Middleton J).

On 27 June 2011, the court handed down its decision and reasons on liability of the defendants, finding that each of the first to seventh defendants had contravened:

- s 180(1) of the Corporations Act (duty of directors to exercise care and diligence);
- s 344(1) of the Corporations Act (directors of a company to take all reasonable steps to comply with, or secure compliance with, Pt 2M.2 (financial records) or Pt 2M.3 (financial reporting)); and
- s 601FD(3) of the Corporations Act (duty of officers of a responsible entity to exercise care and diligence and ensure the responsible entity complied with the Corporations Act).

Furthermore, the eighth defendant had contravened ss 180 and 601FD(3) of the Corporations Act.[78]

The Centro decision established that the directors of substantial publicly listed companies must:

- apply their own minds to, and carry out a careful review of, the proposed financial statements and directors' report;
- determine whether the information contained in those documents is consistent with the director's knowledge of the company's affairs, and that they do not omit material matters known, or that should have been known, to the director;
- know enough about conventional accounting practice concerning basic accounting concepts in accounts to enable them to carry out their responsibilities adequately, including classifying assets and liabilities as current or non-current and the need to disclose certain events post balance sheet date; and
- make appropriate inquiries if they are uncertain.[79]

Moreover, in relation to delegation and reliance on others, there is a core, irreducible requirement for directors to take all reasonable steps to be in a position to guide and monitor the company. Directors have to undertake a level of scrutiny that befits supervision, rather than detailed direct involvement in operational matters. It is reasonable for directors to rely on advice, without independently verifying the information on which the advice is based, provided that there is no cause for suspicion or circumstances demanding critical and detailed attention. However, directors cannot substitute reliance on advice and management for their own attention and examination of important matters falling within the board's responsibilities.[80]

The proceedings then moved to the next stage: applications for relief from liability and the determination of penalties. ASIC submitted that there should be no relief and the sanctions imposed in respect of each defendant be within the range or in the order of the periods and amounts as set out below.[81] On 31 August 2011, Middleton J declined to grant relief to any of the defendants.[82] For the chief executive officer, Mr Scott, declarations of contravention of the Corporations Act were made and a pecuniary penalty of $30,000, being the lower end of the range, was imposed. For the chief financial officer, Mr Nenna, declarations of contravention of

[78] ibid 296 [5]–[6].

[79] ibid 297 [13], 321 [124]–[128], 341 [211], 426 [567], [573], 428 [583].

[80] ibid 330–33 [166]–[175]. The defences of reliance and delegation in Corporations Act 2001 (Cth), ss 189, 190 are not applicable here because ultimate responsibility for approval of the annual financial statements was imposed upon the directors in a way that they could not delegate: ibid 321 [125], 324 [142].

[81] *ASIC v Healey (No 2)* (2011) 284 ALR 734, 761 [146] (Middleton J).

[82] ibid 764 [168].

the Corporations Act were made and a disqualification ban of two years imposed. For each of the non-executive directors, declarations of contravention of the Corporations Act were made, but no other penalty was imposed.[83]

Table 4.2 ASIC v Healey penalty submissions and sanctions

Name of defendant	ASIC disqualification submission	ASIC pecuniary penalty submission	Court-imposed sanctions
Brian Healey	0.5–1.5 years	$30,000–$60,000	No disqualification or penalty
Andrew Scott	Three years	$100,000	$30,000 penalty
Samuel Kavourakis	0.5–1.5 years	$30,000–$60,000	No disqualification or penalty
James Hall	0.5–1.5 years	$30,000–$60,000	No disqualification or penalty
Paul Cooper	0.5–1.5 years	$30,000–$60,000	No disqualification or penalty
Peter Goldie	0.5–1.5 years	$30,000–$60,000	No disqualification or penalty
Louis Wilkinson	0.5–1.5 years	$30,000–$60,000	No disqualification or penalty
Romano Nenna	Three years	$100,000	Disqualification for two years

Although ASIC's action had dealt primarily with directors' duties, the penalty judgment did draw a link with continuous disclosure. Middleton J observed that the information not disclosed was a matter of significance to the assessment of the risks facing CNP and CER. Middleton J cited expert evidence that the omitted information was information that for the purposes of s 674 of the Corporations Act would be expected by a reasonable person to have a material effect on the price or value of the securities so that there may have been an uninformed market for securities of CNP and CER for at least the period of three months from 18 September 2007 to 17 December 2007. This may have led persons to buy or hold securities that they otherwise would not have.[84]

ii. Suspension of Lead Auditor

When ASIC commenced its civil penalty proceedings against the Centro directors, the media noted that the non-inclusion of the auditor was 'bizarre' or seemed 'a little odd' as the auditor was part of the corporate governance framework relied on by the directors.[85] However, ASIC's approach was to focus on the duties and obligations of the directors. Nonetheless ASIC did subsequently deal with the auditor.

The lead auditor from PriceWaterhouseCoopers (PwC) who was responsible for ensuring compliance with Australian Auditing Standards in the audit of the CNP and CER 2007 financial reports entered into an enforceable undertaking. The conduct which was the subject of the enforceable undertaking related to the same omissions as the civil penalty proceedings against the Centro directors. ASIC found that the audits were not conducted in accordance with Australian Auditing Standards and that the lead auditor had not carried out their duties adequately and properly as required by s 1292(1)(d)(i) of the Corporations Act. The undertakings offered by the lead auditor and accepted by ASIC included a period of suspension from acting as a registered auditor

[83] ibid 768 [191] (non-executive directors), 773 [211]–[214] (Scott), 775 [222]–[225] (Nenna).
[84] ibid 760–61 [139]–[142].
[85] John Durie, 'ASIC has hit the spot this time', *The Australian* (22 October 2009), 32; Matthew Stevens, 'Centro in line to become ultimate testbed for board behaviour', *The Australian* (22 October 2009) 21.

from 19 November 2012 to 30 June 2015, participating in an additional 20 hours of continuing professional education and, subject to client consent, having the first three audits conducted after the period of suspension reviewed by a registered auditor approved by ASIC.[86]

B. Class Actions

Three class actions were filed against Centro entities. Richard Kirby, as the representative party, commenced two actions: one against CPL and CPTM covering a period of 9 August 2007 to 15 February 2008 and another one against CRL and CMCSM relating to a period from 7 August 2007 to 15 February 2008. Both class actions employed a closed class as the group was defined by reference to each group member having entered into a litigation funding agreement. The proceedings comprised 955 members at commencement. The solicitor on the record was Maurice Blackburn Pty Ltd and the proceedings were funded by IMF (Australia) Ltd. The Kirby actions were filed on 9 May 2008.[87]

The third action was filed on 23 May 2008 by Nicholas Vlachos, Monatex Pty Ltd and Ramon Franco, as the representative parties, and had CPL, CPTM, CRL and CMCSM as respondents. This proceeding was a traditional opt-out class action, but it excluded those claimants in the Kirby class actions. It covered shares purchased in the period from 5 April 2007 to 28 February 2008, subsequently amended to a period of 17 July 2007 to 28 February 2008. Slater & Gordon were the solicitors for the applicants and the proceedings were funded by Commonwealth Legal Funding LLC.[88]

The substance of all three proceedings was that the Centro entities were alleged to have engaged in misleading conduct and failed to comply with their continuous disclosure obligations, causing the share price to decline and loss to the group members. The allegations were premised on the 2007 accounts misrepresenting the levels of current liabilities so that the full extent of maturing debt obligations was not disclosed. As with ASIC's proceedings, this included debt for which CNP and CER were directly liable and debt that CNP had guaranteed. Furthermore, it was alleged that there was a failure to disclose the risk of not being able to refinance that debt, or only being able to refinance it at a higher cost, and the risk of profit forecasts no longer being reasonable.[89] The Vlachos proceedings extended the timeframe back to July 2007 in relation to alleged misleading statements by CNP and CER about their ability to finance the acquisition of New Plan Excel Realty Trust Inc, a listed retail property trust in the United States.[90] The inability to refinance debt or obtain new financing occurred at the same time as the collapse of the commercial mortgage backed securities (CMBS) market as part of the subprime mortgage crisis.

The claims were estimated to be worth $1 billion.[91] The share price of CNP fell from above $8 to about 60 cents between August 2007 and February 2008. In the same period CER's share price

[86] ASIC, 'Enforceable Undertaking: Stephen John Cougle', Document No 027 958 710 (19 November 2012). The lead auditor was also subject to disciplinary proceedings by The Institute of Chartered Accountants: www.charteredaccountants.com.au/The-Institute/Member-complaints-and-discipline/Tribunal-decisions/2013/Stephen-John-Cougle-CA-of-Vic.aspx.

[87] *Kirby v Centro Properties Ltd* (2008) 253 ALR 65, 66–67 [1]–[3], 69 [14] (Finkelstein J).

[88] ibid; Slater & Gordon Lawyers, 'New Centro Class Action Issued' (Press Release, 25 May 2008); Vlachos v Centro Properties Ltd, Sixth Amended Statement of Claim, 4 April 2012.

[89] Kirby v Centro Properties Ltd, Fifth Further Amended Statement of Claim, 15 February 2012; Kirby v Centro Retail Ltd, Fifth Further Amended Statement of Claim, 15 February 2012.

[90] Vlachos v Centro Properties Ltd, Sixth Amended Statement of Claim, 4 April 2012.

[91] Carolyn Cummins, 'Centro in court over $1bn class action', *The Age* (25 August 2008) 3; Maurice Dunlevy, 'Centro class action zeroes in on insurance', *The Australian* (6 March 2009) 19 (referring to $432 million in damages

declined from near $10 to less than $2.[92] However, a litigation funder involved in the Centro class actions described the $1 billion figure as being 'at the absolute upper end' of a range of outcomes depending on how loss was calculated.[93] A former Centro senior executive recalled that Centro's calculation was an amount of around $400 million,[94] and other interviewees suggested $800m.[95]

In May 2009, the Centro entities cross-claimed against PwC as the auditors of CNP and CER alleging breach of the retainer, breach of duty of care, misleading or deceptive conduct and seeking contribution and indemnity.[96] PwC then cross-claimed against individual Centro directors and executives.[97] The class action applicants subsequently brought proceedings directly against PwC and PricewaterhouseCoopers Securities Limited (PwC Securities).[98]

It also needs to be noted that CNP was subject to a creditors' scheme of arrangement in the latter half of 2011. Under the arrangement, all of CNP's assets were transferred to a new entity, A-REIT, in exchange for the senior lenders cancelling CNP's debt and receiving 68 per cent of the securities in A-REIT. The proposal also included $100 million for junior stakeholders, which comprised $49 million for CNP equity holders (five cents per security) and $10 million for contingent creditors, that is, group members in the class actions.[99] PwC and Richard Kirby sought to challenge the allocation of $49 million to CNP equity holders. They argued that it should be preserved for contingent creditors but were unsuccessful. The scheme was approved by the Supreme Court of New South Wales on 1 December 2011.[100]

The class actions went to trial in the Federal Court on 5 March 2012. The trial was into its tenth week when the proceedings settled on 9 May 2012 and was approved by the Court on 19 June 2012.[101] The settlement was for $200 million comprised of $85 million from CER, $67 million from PwC, $38 million from Centro's insurance and $10 million from CPL. The settlement was divided as follows: $150 million to the Kirby class action group members, of which there were thought to be 1,000; and $50 million to the Vlachos class action group members, of which there were thought to be about 5,000.[102] The legal costs incurred by the applicants in the Kirby class action were $21.1 million and in the Vlachos class action $10.06 million.[103] The costs of CER were estimated to be $10 million.[104] The litigation funder behind the Kirby class actions, IMF, reported that it earned a profit of $41.8 million from those class actions as well as being reimbursed $18 million that it had spent on legal costs. If the class action had been unsuccessful, IMF estimated that it would have lost the $18 million spent on legal fees and would have faced an

being sought from CNP and $537 million in damages being sought from CER); *Kirby v Centro Properties Ltd* [2009] FCA 695, [8] (Ryan J).

[92] Nick Lenaghan, 'Centro: the mother of class acts', *The Australian Financial Review* (12 May 2012) 54.

[93] Interview Centro funder, 2.

[94] Interview Centro Executive, 7.

[95] Interview Lawyer Participants Centro, 1.

[96] Nick Lenaghan, 'Alarm as Centro moves to sue its auditors', *The Australian Financial Review* (27 May 2009) 50.

[97] Carolyn Cummins, 'Auditors strike back at Centro claim', *The Sydney Morning Herald* (13 June 2009) 3.

[98] *Kirby v Centro Properties Ltd* (2010) 189 FCR 301; Maurice Dunlevy, 'Decision on PwC lawsuit in weeks' *The Australian* (23 September 2010) 31; Leonie Wood, 'Follow-up case launched in Centro class action', *The Age* (2 December 2010) 2.

[99] Centro Properties Group, 'Centro Group announces restructure agreement' (ASX/Media Release, 9 August 2011).

[100] *Re Centro Properties Ltd* (2011) 86 ACSR 584.

[101] *Kirby v Centro Properties Ltd (No 6)* [2012] FCA 650.

[102] Slater & Gordon, 'Thousands of mum and dad investors poised to share in Australia's biggest shareholder class action settlement' (Media Release, 9 May 2012) ('Slater & Gordon Centro MR May 2012'); Centro Retail Australia, 'Conditional Settlement of class actions' (ASX/Media Release, 10 May 2012) 1 ('Centro Retail MR May 2012'); Agnes King, 'Red faces, not red ink at PwC audit', *The Australian Financial Review*, 14 May 2012, 56–57.

[103] Kirby v Centro Properties Ltd, Orders, 19 June 2012; Kirby v Centro Retail Limited, Orders, 19 June 2012, Vlachos v Centro Properties Ltd, Orders, 19 June 2012 accompanying *Kirby v Centro Properties Ltd (No 6)* [2012] FCA 650.

[104] Lenaghan (n 92) 54. See also Leonie Wood, 'Laptop vital evidence, court told', *The Age* (10 August 2011) 5 (reporting that PwC's lawyers had devoted 5500 hours to discovery in the class action).

adverse costs order in the vicinity of $40–50 million.[105] The other funder, Commonwealth Legal Funding LLC, was reported to have received $9 million.[106] A former Centro senior executive estimated that Centro's legal costs were between $40 and $50 million.[107]

VI. Leighton

A. ASIC Action

Leighton Holdings Ltd changed its name to CIMIC Group Limited in April 2015.[108] Before and after the name change it was listed on the ASX. Leighton provided a broad range of contracting and project development services including construction, contract mining and engineering. Leighton's subsidiaries included Thiess (100 per cent owned), John Holland (100 per cent owned until sold in December 2014) and Al Habtoor Leighton Group (45 per cent owned).[109]

On 14 February 2011, Leighton announced that for the 2010–11 financial year it expected to report full year revenue of almost $20 billion and a net profit after tax of around $480 million. Leighton's securities were placed in a trading halt from 7 until 11 April 2011. On 11 April, Leighton announced that it expected to report a loss of $427 million for the 2010–11 financial year, a difference of $907 million. The revision was primarily due to write-backs of expected profit on the Brisbane Airport Link project (BAL Project) and the Victorian Desalination Plant project (VDP Project), and an impairment of Leighton's investment in the Al Habtoor Leighton Group (AHLG).

On 1 July 2011, ASIC commenced an investigation into a breach of the continuous disclosure requirements. As a result of the investigation, ASIC formed the view that by 18 March 2011 Leighton was aware, and should have immediately disclosed, that:

- The previous forecast final profit margin for the BAL Project would not be achieved due to significant cost increases, and that reviews had been carried out which forecast a substantial loss relating to the project, of between $182 million and $610 million.
- The completion date for the VDP Project was likely to be delayed and the costs of the project had increased substantially, so that Thiess's forecast profit on completion for the project would be materially reduced.
- The financial position of AHLG had deteriorated, as it had received (i) a revised cash flow forecast for AHLG; (ii) a request from AHLG for the drawdown of a previously agreed shareholder loan to be accelerated; and (iii) a request from AHLG for further shareholder funding of $230 million.[110]

On 16 March 2012, ASIC and Leighton entered into an enforceable undertaking and Leighton also paid three infringement notices, one for each project.[111] The infringement notices were the

[105] Chris Merritt, 'Funder sitting pretty thanks to Centro suit', *The Australian* (11 May 2012) 34; Alex Boxsell, 'IMF profits from Centro case', *The Australian Financial Review* (24 August 2012) 44.

[106] Sarah Danckert, 'Half of $200m Centro judgment will go in costs', *The Australian* (20 June 2012) 22.

[107] Interview Centro Executive, 10.

[108] CIMIC Group Limited, 'Change of Name to CIMIC Group Limited (CIM)' (ASX Announcement, 22 April 2015) 1.

[109] ASIC, 'Leighton Holdings complies with three ASIC infringement notices for alleged continuous disclosure breaches and ASIC accepts compliance enforceable undertaking' (Media Release 12-53MR, 18 March 2012) ('ASIC Leighton MR 12-53'); Leighton Holdings Ltd, 'Concise Annual Report for the 2011 Transitional Financial Year', 30 March 2012, 4; Leighton Holdings, 'Leighton completes sale of John Holland to CCCI' (ASX Announcement, 20 April 2015) 1.

[110] ASIC Leighton MR 12-53 (ibid).

[111] ibid.

maximum of $100,000 each as the Corporations Act treated Leighton as a Tier 1 entity because it had a market capitalisation exceeding $1,000 million on the relevant day.[112] The enforceable undertaking required Leighton to nominate two independent consultants, of which ASIC would select one, for Leighton to engage to review Leighton's continuous disclosure policies and procedures. The consultant would then prepare a report recommending amendments to the policies and procedures and a timeframe for implementation. The consultant would also provide a report assessing implementation and effectiveness of the recommendations and then for a period of three years carry out an annual review. Leighton was required to provide reasonable assistance to the consultant, provide copies of the above reports to ASIC, implement the recommendations, provide copies of the revised policies and procedures to ASIC and pay the costs of complying with the enforceable undertaking.[113] Ernst & Young was appointed as the external consultant.[114] The cost to ASIC of obtaining the enforceable undertaking was estimated to be $94,000, which was all internal costs such as ASIC staff salaries and overheads.[115]

B. Class Action

Inabu Pty Ltd, as trustee for the Alida Superannuation Fund, commenced a class action in the Federal Court of Australia against Leighton on 30 October 2013. The applicant was represented by Maurice Blackburn Pty Ltd and the class action was funded by International Litigation Funding Partners, Inc. The class action was in relation to the same three matters addressed by ASIC, namely the BAL Project, the VDP Project, and the impairment of Leighton's investment in AHLG.

The class action alleged that in the period 16 August 2010 to 11 April 2011, Leighton had breached its continuous disclosure obligations under s 674 of the Corporations Act and various prohibitions on misleading or deceptive conduct because it:

- failed to disclose that there were material matters arising either individually or collectively from the BAL Project and VDP Project and likely impairments on the AHLG investment which made it likely that Leighton would not achieve its profit forecasts for the 2011 financial year; and
- made statements that misled or deceived shareholders about the profit forecasts and performance for the 2011 financial year and performance.[116]

The class action adopted a much longer period of time for which the market was alleged to be uninformed compared to ASIC. This arose because of an allegation that by 16 August 2010 Leighton know or ought to have known that:

- the forecast profit for the BAL project would be substantially less because it would not achieve the required completion dates, and had expended or would expend significantly more than budgeted amounts;[117] and

[112] Corporations Act 2001 (Cth), s 1317DAE. See also ch 2, section II.A.

[113] ASIC, 'Enforceable Undertaking: Leighton Holdings Limited', Document No 027714755 (16 March 2012).

[114] Leighton Holdings, 'Leighton appoints Ernst & Young as independent reviewer' (ASX Announcement, 17 May 2012), 1.

[115] Interview ASIC Executive Leighton, 11.

[116] Inabu Pty Ltd v Leighton Holdings Ltd, Statement of Claim, NSD 2244 of 2013, 30 October 2013.

[117] ibid [56], [95]–[101].

- the value of Leighton's investment in AHLG had substantially reduced because AHLG was receiving operational funding from Leighton, and that economic conditions in Dubai had deteriorated with the result that AHLG was having difficulty obtaining new work and in receiving payment for completed work.[118]

The date of 16 August 2010 was also significant because Leighton made an ASX announcement on that date which contained representations as to Leighton's profit forecast that allegedly did not take account of the above matters.[119]

The media estimated that the proceedings were for a claim of $400 million.[120] However, a solicitor for the applicant was unable to say where that figure came from but would only advise that it was an overstatement of the quantum at stake.[121]

By mid-May 2014 a settlement, subject to the approval of the Court as required for class actions, had been reached. This was before any defence was filed. The settlement provided for Leighton to pay an amount of $69.45 million, including $4.17 million for the applicant's legal costs.[122] After the class had been closed and group members had registered to participate in the settlement, the Federal Court noted that there were 6,000 participating group members: 2,304 who had entered into a litigation funding agreement; and 3,909 who had not.[123] The amount that each group member would actually receive depended on the number and quantum of claims that participated in the settlement.[124] There would also be a deduction for the litigation funder's fee, estimated to be between 20 and 30 per cent, or using 25 per cent of the recovery less legal costs, $16.32 million.[125] The participating group members would have comprised institutional investors, including superannuation funds, as well as smaller retail investors.[126]

VII. Conclusion – Summary of Case Studies

To aid in the application of the analytical framework, ASIC's enforcement actions and the class action are compared across case studies by reference to outcome, costs and time from commencement to completion.

Table 4.3 Case studies – summary of outcomes

	ASIC	Class action
Telstra	Warning	$5m settlement (estimated $300m claim) ($3.75m to group members and $1.25m in legal costs. No funder)

(continued)

[118] ibid [90], [95]–[101].
[119] ibid [112]–[117].
[120] Adele Ferguson, 'Leighton class action', *The Age* (1 September 2011) 1.
[121] Interview Applicant's solicitor Leighton, 6.
[122] *Inabu Pty Ltd v Leighton Holdings Ltd* [2014] FCA 622 [2] (Jacobson J); *Inabu Pty Ltd v Leighton Holdings Ltd (No 2)* [2014] FCA 911, orders; Interview Applicant's solicitor Leighton, 4.
[123] *Inabu Pty Ltd v Leighton Holdings Ltd (No 2)* [2014] FCA 911 [2], [19] (Jacobson J).
[124] A Loss Assessment Formula was devised to calculate payments to individual group members but was ordered to be treated as confidential by the Court.
[125] The actual amount is not known, but an amount towards the lower end of the average fee would be expected due to the quick settlement.
[126] Philip Wen, 'Big investors in Leighton consider joining class action', *The Age* (2 September 2011) 1; Karina Barrymore, 'Call out to join a Leighton suit', *Herald Sun* (2 September 2011) 71.

Table 4.3 ***(Continued)***

	ASIC	Class action
Multiplex	Enforceable undertaking Early payment of $50m indemnity from Roberts family Corporate governance changes $32m compensation fund (only $20m claimed)	$110m settlement (estimated $220m claim) ($64m to group members, $11m in legal costs and estimated $35m to ligation funder)
Centro	Civil penalty proceedings against directors, CEO and CFO Declarations of contravention for all directors $30,000 penalty for CEO Two-year disqualification ban for CFO Enforceable undertaking from lead auditor Suspension from acting as registered auditor, additional professional education and review of first three audits after conclusion of suspension	$200m settlement (estimated $400m to $1bn claim) Settlement funded $85m from CER, $67m from PwC, $38m from Centro's insurance and $10m from CPL ($119.04m to group members, $31.16m in legal costs and estimated $49.8m to litigation funders)
Leighton	Infringement notices – $300,000 fine Enforceable undertaking Corporate governance changes	$69.45m settlement (estimated $400m maximum claim but lower amounts indicated) ($48.96m to group members, $4.17m in legal costs and estimated $16.32m to litigation funder)

Table 4.4 Case studies – costs

	ASIC	Class action
Telstra	Corporation's internal and legal costs dealing with ASIC unknown	$1.25m in applicant's legal costs Respondent's legal costs unknown
Multiplex	Corporation's internal and legal costs dealing with ASIC unknown	$11m in applicant's legal costs $15m in respondent's legal costs estimated
Centro	Corporation's and directors' internal and legal costs dealing with ASIC and defending litigation unknown	$31.16m in applicants' legal costs $30–$50m in respondents' legal costs estimated
Leighton	ASIC costs $94,000 Corporation's internal and legal costs dealing with ASIC unknown	$3.9m in applicant's legal costs Respondent's legal costs unknown

Table 4.5 Case studies – time

	ASIC	Class action
Telstra	Investigation launched September 2005 Media release containing warning 14 December 2005 Four months	Commenced 20 January 2006 Settlement 12 November 2007 Approval of Settlement 13 December 2007 24 months or two years

(continued)

Table 4.5 ***(Continued)***

	ASIC	Class action
Multiplex	Investigation launched 22 February 2005 Enforceable undertaking executed on 20 December 2006 23 months or almost two years	Commenced 18 December 2006 and 10 December 2008 Settlement 14 May 2010 Approval of Settlement 21 July 2010 44 months or three years and eight months
Centro	Commenced 19 October 2009 Judgment on liability 27 June 2011 Judgment on penalties 31 August 2011 23 months or almost two years (13 months elapsed between the commencement of ASIC's investigation and the commencement of proceedings)	Commenced on 9 May 2008 and 23 May 2008 Trial commenced 5 March 2012 Settlement 9 May 2012 Approval of Settlement 19 June 2012 50 months or four years and two months
Leighton	Investigation launched 1 July 2011 Enforceable undertaking executed and infringement notice fines paid on 16 March 2012 Nine months	Commenced 30 October 2013 Settlement 16 May 2014 Approval of Settlement 15 August 2014 11 months

5

Application of the Analytical Framework to the Case Studies

I. Introduction

This chapter examines the case studies in chapter four through the lens of the analytical framework from chapter three: deterrence; compensation; and regulatory process. The application of the analytical framework involves drawing on the detailed interviews and documentary analysis undertaken for each case study as the primary source of information for evaluating the elements of the framework.

The chapter commences with the application of the deterrence framework. This consists of an analysis of the case studies by reference to the dimensions of deterrence and then the factors that aid or limit the effectiveness of deterrence. The dimensions of deterrence are direct sanctions, indirect costs, reputation, and specific and general deterrence. This chapter will demonstrate that, in terms of financial sanctions and indirect costs, the class actions considered here imposed a greater quantum than action by ASIC, which in turn suggests a larger deterrent effect. In contrast, it will also argue that the impact on reputation due to a finding of a contravention appears to be greater for ASIC enforcement than for class actions. However, even when the dimensions of deterrence are fully accounted for, their impact or effectiveness is mediated by several factors: certainty, severity, timeliness, perceptions, the target of deterrence (corporations or directors) and insurance.

Next, the compensation framework is applied to the case studies. It considers how compensation is accessed and then the factors that aid or limit the achievement of compensation. The source of compensation for shareholders is largely the class action. While ASIC is able to pursue compensation, it is not seen as its main objective in relation to regulating continuous disclosure. The achievement of compensation is examined through a comparison of losses suffered and compensation achieved, incomplete recovery due to investors not claiming or respondents being unable to pay, transaction costs that reduce the compensation received, and the circularity problem – one set of innocent shareholders who did not trade pay another set of innocent shareholders who did trade based on flawed disclosure.

Finally, the regulatory process framework looks at ASIC action and the class action as forms of public and private enforcement respectively in the continuous disclosure regime. ASIC enforcement and the class action are examined through the lens of the case studies in relation to four values that are equated with a legitimate regulatory process: legislative authority; the public interest; accountability; and efficiency.

The above analysis focuses on the first and second research questions so as to allow for conclusions to be drawn in chapter six. The first is the effectiveness of ASIC enforcement and the shareholder class action in achieving deterrence and compensation in relation to the continuous disclosure regime. The second is the ramifications of ASIC enforcement and shareholder class actions coexisting in terms of the values of a 'good' regulatory process and whether they help or hinder each other in the achievement of their objectives.

II. Application of the Analytical Framework – Deterrence

Deterrence was a central objective for ASIC in each of the case studies.[1] However, in terms of financial sanctions and indirect costs, the class action imposed a far greater quantum in each case study than action by ASIC, which in turn suggests a larger deterrent effect. But deterrence is not limited to monetary sanctions and costs. The impact on reputation due to a contravention being alleged and settlement by a party or a finding by a court is very significant to deterrence and appears to be greater for ASIC enforcement actions than for class actions. However, even when the dimensions of deterrence are fully accounted for, their impact or effectiveness is mediated by several factors that are explained below. These are certainty, severity, celerity or timeliness, perceptions, the target of deterrence (corporations or directors) and insurance.

A. Dimensions of Deterrence

i. Direct Sanctions

As explained in chapter three, specific and general deterrence can be achieved through sanctions that impose costs. The sanctions may be formal or direct costs such as fines or civil penalties, or an extraction of financial resources such as paying damages by way of providing compensation.

From a direct sanctions perspective, chapter four, Table 4.3 demonstrates that the class action imposes greater costs on a corporation than do ASIC enforcement actions. The payment of compensation may achieve deterrence on the basis that corporate resources and financial performance are diminished, which the corporation would prefer to avoid.[2] The class action lawyers and litigation funder involved in the four case studies all described class actions as having a deterrent effect, although this was not the primary goal or purpose behind the commencement of the class actions.[3] A significant reason for drawing this distinction was that the instructions from the applicant and group members were to recover compensation.[4] Nonetheless, regardless of the reason for bringing a class action, the compensation payments from the class action were intuited to result in deterrence. Other participants in the class actions agreed that deterrence was a result.[5]

The imposition of greater direct costs on the corporation by the class action rather than by ASIC actions follows from the monetary fines for civil penalties and infringement notices being capped at particular amounts, namely \$1 million and \$100,000 respectively.[6] In contrast, the

[1] Interview ASIC Executive Telstra/Multiplex; Interview ASIC Executive Centro, 2; Interview ASIC Executive Leighton, 9.

[2] See Australian Competition & Consumer Commission, 'Submission to the Competition Policy Review – Response to the Draft Report' (26 November 2014) 79; Russell Gold, 'Compensation's Role in Deterrence' (2016) 91 *Notre Dame Law Review* 1997, 2005–06.

[3] Interview Applicants' solicitors Multiplex, 8; Interview Applicant's solicitor Centro, 2, 21; Interview Applicant's solicitor Leighton, 1.

[4] Interview Applicant's solicitor Centro, 2–3; Interview Applicant's solicitor Leighton, 1.

[5] Interview Lawyer Participants Telstra/Multiplex/Centro.

[6] See ch 2, section II.D. The quantum of the available civil penalties has since increased as discussed in ch 7.

class action can recover an amount up to the actual losses suffered by shareholders. There is no maximum. This has been recognised by ASIC through its own actions in Multiplex, where part of the reason for establishing the $32 million compensation fund was because a civil penalty would have been confined to a maximum of $1 million.[7] While one is compensation for shareholders and the other a fine paid to government, both are sanctions that can impart deterrence. This suggests that ASIC can try to work around the statutory limits, but it involves ASIC seeking an additional or different remedy, that is, seeking a compensation order, or as in Multiplex, the corporation cooperating. The use of compensation by ASIC to deter is discussed further in chapter six.

In relation to individuals, direct costs were only imposed in Centro through ASIC pursuing contraventions of directors' duties rather than contraventions of the continuous disclosure regime. In ASIC's civil penalty litigation, a $30,000 fine was imposed on the CEO of Centro for breach of his director's duties. The Centro directors were part of the class action but did not directly contribute to the settlement. It was reported that $38 million was paid by Centro's insurers, which likely drew on directors' and officers' (D&O) insurance, which also covered the directors. The role of insurance in relation to deterrence is discussed separately below. In Multiplex, the allegations in relation to Wembley Stadium saw the former owners, the Roberts family, be required to make early payment of a $50 million indemnity, which may have been used to pay compensation under the enforceable undertaking or class action.[8] Members of the Roberts family were directors of Multiplex[9] so that the payment might be seen as imposing a direct cost on those directors. However, it may be more accurately characterised as a cost imposed on the vendor of a business where that business fails to perform as expected because the Roberts family had listed Multiplex on the ASX and provided the indemnity to cover losses on the project.[10]

The case studies found that directors were not the focus of either ASIC actions or class actions, and where they were as in Centro, the outcome in terms of direct financial cost was minimal. However, ASIC has other tools that may impact individual deterrence. As explained in chapter two, the continuous disclosure regime only imposes criminal penalties on the corporation. Only recently have directors been subject to successful criminal prosecution using accessorial liability under the Criminal Code. However, ASIC can seek civil penalty orders where a director is 'involved' in a corporation's breach of the continuous disclosure regime. ASIC can also ban a person from providing any financial service if that person has not complied with, or was involved in the contravention of, the prohibition on misleading or deceptive conduct. ASIC may also apply to a court to seek the disqualification of a person from managing a corporation for repeated contraventions of the Corporations Act.[11] Banning and disqualification orders have been identified as achieving deterrence.[12] Equally, ASIC can use the 'stepping stone' approach where it proves a breach of the law by the corporation (for example, misleading conduct) and then uses that breach to demonstrate a breach of a director's duties which can attract a civil penalty or result in

[7] ASIC, 'ASIC accepts an enforceable undertaking from the Multiplex Group' (Media Release, 06-443, 20 December 2006) ('ASIC Multiplex MR 16-443').

[8] Kate Askew, 'ASIC looking under the lid', *The Age* (26 March 2005) (reporting the offer of a $50m indemnity from Multiplex founder John Roberts); ASIC, 'Enforceable Undertaking: Multiplex Ltd', Document No 017 029 205 (20 December 2006); Interview Applicants' solicitors Multiplex, 19.

[9] Andrew Roberts was Chief Executive Officer of Multiplex and Tim Roberts was an Executive Director: Multiplex Group, 'Annual Report 2006' 56–57.

[10] ibid 124.

[11] See ch 2, sections II.C, II.D and III.C.

[12] *ASIC v Adler* (2002) 42 ACSR 80, 97–99 [56], 101 [60] (Santow J); *ASIC v Healey (No 2)* [2011] FCA 1003, [109] (Middleton J); *Panganiban v ASIC* (2016) 338 ALR 119, 122 [15] (Bromwich J).

a banning order.[13] Although not straightforward, ASIC does have avenues to pursue and seek to deter directors, which is discussed further below.

ii. Indirect Costs

There are five types of indirect costs identified in the case studies: legal fees; lost management time; compliance reform costs; corporate going concern/financing costs; and loss of employment and associated opportunities.

Deterrence may be achieved through indirect costs associated with dealing with a regulator or class action. Indirect costs are broader and less measurable than formal sanctions. The most obvious indirect cost is legal fees as corporations will require legal advice and representation in dealing with ASIC and a class action.[14] These are usually not disclosed, but estimates were available for the Multiplex ($15 million) and Centro ($30–$50 million) class actions that demonstrate that they are substantial amounts. It is likely that the legal costs caused by class actions will be greater than those imposed by ASIC actions as the class action usually takes place over a longer period and requires engagement with causation and loss that is not needed where ASIC seeks to only prove a contravention. Nonetheless, legal advice will be needed even in relation to determining whether to accept an infringement notice or to negotiate an enforceable undertaking. The company may also become liable for the legal costs of an opponent when legal proceedings are lost or settled. These amounts are available for class actions, and are set out in Table 4.4 above, as an applicant's legal fees are usually approved by the court as part of the larger class action settlement approval process. ASIC does not usually seek its costs as part of non-litigious outcomes such as infringement notices and enforceable undertakings, but will seek an award of costs when it is successful in litigation.[15] However, 'the costs incurred in a private law firm are pretty much always going to be higher than the kind of costs ASIC would bill for a matter'.[16]

Indirect costs in terms of lost management time because of dealing with ASIC or a class action were not available from any of the corporations in the case studies and are likely to be difficult to measure. However, a former Telstra senior executive opined that 'to the extent we were spending our days worrying about [ASIC's actions] we were not doing whatever else we might have been doing on those days'.[17] Similarly, when a person faces ASIC examinations, 'you've got these highly paid senior executive[s] sitting around getting quizzed by ASIC, rather than doing whatever it is that they're highly paid for'.[18] Further, the Telstra and Leighton media releases at the time the class action settlements were reached referred to a desire to allow management to focus on the main business.[19]

ASIC's ability to use enforceable undertakings provides a particular source of indirect costs where it requires changes to procedures and/or the review of procedures by an external consultant. The Multiplex and Leighton case studies demonstrate that the corporation must incur the internal costs, including management time, of reforming procedures and the payments to the external consultant.

[13] See ch 2, section III.C.
[14] See, eg, Interview Telstra Executive, 4.
[15] Interview ASIC Executive Centro, 4.
[16] ibid 8.
[17] Interview Telstra Executive, 4.
[18] ibid 4.
[19] Telstra Corporation Limited, 'Court asked to approve class action settlement' (Media Release, 263/2007, 12 November 2007) 1 ('Telstra MR263/2007'); Leighton Holdings, 'Conditional Settlement of Leighton Class Action' (Media Release, 16 May 2014) ('Leighton MR May 2014').

The quantum at stake in relation to a class action can also give rise to a range of other indirect costs – 'a shareholder class action has the potential to sink a company, unsettle a share price, devalue a business, or act as a poison pill against a white knight rescue'.[20] In none of the case studies was the class action responsible for causing the company to fail. However, in relation to the Centro class actions the presence of the class action created uncertainty for Centro Properties Group (CNP) and Centro Retail Group (CER) as it gave rise to the prospect of any funds provided to purchase the group or refinance/restructure the debt being paid out in damages.[21] Ultimately, however, CNP and CER were able to restructure through a creditors' scheme of arrangement as explained in chapter four. Usually, class action lawyers and funders are not interested in bringing a case that will render a company insolvent for the simple reason that they then make no recovery or a much smaller recovery because the funds for any claim need to be shared with other creditors.[22]

Indirect costs also arise for individuals. In Centro, the chief financial officer was banned for two years, which presumably imposed indirect costs in the form of lost salary and other forms of executive compensation. The declarations of contravention made against all Centro directors may also have reduced their ability to obtain future directorships, although they were not legally prevented from doing so. In Telstra, Multiplex and Leighton the directors were not pursued by ASIC or a class action. However, some directors did lose their employment. The Centro CEO and CFO were both forced out prior to ASIC's success at trial.[23] Similarly, the Leighton chairman and CEO were replaced.[24] However, it is unclear whether these terminations were the result of ASIC's actions, the class action, or as a result of the decline in corporate performance.[25]

iii. Reputation

Chapter three explained that another important form of deterrence in the corporate world is the sanction of social stigmatisation or reputational harm that imposes intangible costs. This was borne out by the case studies. Reputational impact seems to be greater in relation to a successful ASIC action, although the extent of the impact appears to depend on the enforcement tool used. As one of the solicitors for the applicant in the Telstra class action put it:

> [I]f ASIC come in and get a decision as well, that's a much stronger signal I think, than just simply a settlement in the shareholder class action, … So I think there's still a lot of value in ASIC bringing proceedings, because it's effectively the referee calling you in, rather than the crowd booing.[26]

A similar sentiment was expressed by a former Centro senior executive who opined that an ASIC action 'would be extremely damaging' to reputation and 'boards take … the reputational risk for that incredibly seriously'.[27] This is borne out by the reasoning in the Centro civil penalty

[20] Adele Ferguson, 'Class actions on the increase', *The Australian* (4 January 2008) 15.

[21] ibid; Nick Lenaghan, 'PwC wrangle threatens deal', *The Australian Financial Review* (23 November 2011) 50; Nick Lenaghan, 'Trust seals its recovery', *The Australian Financial Review* (16 April 2013) 29; Interview Centro Executive, 4, 8.

[22] John Walker, Susanna Khouri and Wayne Attrill, 'Funding Criteria for Class Actions' (2009) 32 *UNSW Law Journal* 1036, 1041, 1043, 1046; Interview Multiplex solicitor, 11 ('the plaintiff law firms choose [respondent corporations] because they are not financially imperilled').

[23] Interview Centro Executive, 1.

[24] Adele Ferguson, 'Leighton class action', *The Age* (1 September 2011) 1.

[25] Interview Multiplex solicitor, 9 (drawing a distinction between the impact of ASIC action and what the underlying facts said about certain directors or executives 'business acumen').

[26] Interview Applicant's solicitors Telstra, 16.

[27] Interview Centro Executive, 5.

proceedings. Middleton J supported his orders in relation to disqualification and penalties by focusing on the reputational effects of the liability judgment:

> [I]t is important to appreciate that the liability judgment has attracted widespread publicity. The acts and omissions of the directors, as recorded in the liability judgment, have already been the subject of widespread public dissemination. Against such a backdrop of widespread public analysis and associated embarrassment and reputational damage for each of the directors, the need for the imposition of a disqualification order or pecuniary penalty for reasons of general deterrence is much less than it would otherwise be.[28]

The reputational impact was acknowledged by a former ASIC senior executive who pointed out that 'there was almost front page press, nearly every day on the [Centro] matter', so that when the defence ran many arguments to defend the directors' actions but the court still found a contravention, the result was 'a good outcome in terms of deterrence'.[29]

The ASIC warning, or 'yellow card', to Telstra provides a useful vignette on reputation. The media referred to it as 'naming and shaming'.[30] The difficulty with the warning to Telstra was that the basis for the warning was strongly disputed by Telstra. Nonetheless, the potential impact on reputation was implicitly accepted by Telstra, which expressly rejected 'any suggestion that its continuous disclosure policies and practices are inadequate' and then stated that 'Telstra's standard of corporate governance is widely respected in the Australian corporate community'.[31] One commentator described this as Telstra becoming angry because an allegation of non-compliance remained on the public record.[32] As there were no formal proceedings, Telstra was unable to 'clear its name'. Equally, ASIC's warning may be seen as an attempt to save face after it decided to undertake an investigation. It was suggested that ASIC was concerned that Telstra would refuse to pay the $100,000 calculated for a Tier 1 infringement notice and ASIC would be forced to move to civil penalty proceedings. This, it was suggested, necessitated an approach that extricated ASIC from a continuing confrontation with Telstra on what was a weak case.[33]

Another former senior ASIC executive also saw an enforceable undertaking as impacting reputation as it highlights conduct, shines light on behaviour and obtains an acknowledgement of wrongdoing or at least a failure to live up to the compliance standards that ASIC expects.[34] However, much may turn on the actual terms of the enforceable undertaking. Both the Multiplex and Leighton undertakings had no admission of liability. The Multiplex undertaking included an acknowledgement that 'ASIC had reason to be concerned', while the Leighton undertaking acknowledged 'ASIC's views'.[35] The ASIC officer involved in the Leighton matter stated that there was 'no doubt that [ASIC] taking action has a reputational impact', but 'the tool that we select will have different reputational impacts'.[36] The ASIC officer opined that infringement notices may have less reputational impact than court action. However, this has to be balanced with other objectives, such as achieving a timely outcome.[37]

[28] *ASIC v Healey (No 2)* (2011) 284 ALR 734, 765–66 [177] (Middleton J). See also 766 [180], 767 [188].

[29] Interview ASIC Executive Centro, 2.

[30] Andrew Cornell, 'More than a reprimand needed to appease suspicions' *Australian Financial Review* (15 December 2005) 4.

[31] Telstra Corporation Limited, 'Telstra statement on ASIC' (Media Release, 352/2005, 14 December 2005) 1.

[32] Robert Baxt, 'Infringement Notices – It's Time to Scrap Them' *Company Director* (1 April 2006).

[33] Robert Baxt, 'Editorial' (2006) 24 *Company and Securities Law Journal* 73; Josephine Coffey, 'Enforcement of Continuous Disclosure in the Australian Stock Market' (2007) 20 *Australian Journal of Corporate Law* 301, 311.

[34] Interview ASIC Executive Telstra/Multiplex.

[35] ASIC Enforceable Undertaking: Multiplex (n 8); ASIC, 'Enforceable Undertaking: Leighton Holdings Limited', Document No 027714755, 16 March 2012.

[36] Interview ASIC Executive Leighton, 9.

[37] ibid 9–10.

Class actions have also been linked with reputational impact.[38] Participants in class actions explained that class actions are seen as a serious issue by corporations as such actions attract media attention which then puts the corporate management and decision making in the spotlight.[39]

iv. Specific and General Deterrence

Each of the ASIC executives interviewed spoke in terms of specific and general deterrence. ASIC actions were aimed at deterring the entity the subject of enforcement action from repeating the conduct, but also at educating the market more broadly so as to achieve general deterrence.[40] To the extent that specific deterrence may be evidenced by there being no subsequent enforcement or class actions against the entities in the case studies for further breaches of the continuous disclosure regime, that is the case for three of the entities based on there being no public record of such subsequent actions. The exception is Leighton, which was the subject of two class actions in its new name CIMIC Group Limited for allegedly failing to inform the market that an offshore subsidiary may have been engaged in corrupt conduct in order to secure construction work in Iraq, and then separately, for allegedly employing controversial financing techniques to mislead investors about its cash flows so that it did not fully disclose financial problems in its Middle Eastern joint venture.[41]

In terms of general deterrence, ASIC's actions against Leighton were interpreted by ASIC and the media as causing other companies and directors to change their behaviour.[42] This is consistent with ASIC's regulatory guide on enforceable undertakings, which states that an enforceable undertaking is an effective regulatory outcome if it 'promotes general deterrence in making the business community aware of the conduct and the consequences arising from engaging in that conduct'.[43] The then chairman of ASIC explained the action in relation to Leighton as follows: 'it sends a very clear message to the directors of listed companies that they need to have a close look at what happened in Leighton and make sure that their own governance policies around continuous disclosure are adequate'.[44]

The front page of *The Australian Financial Review* stated that ASIC was getting tougher on disclosure. It was observed that the Leighton fine was the most severe penalty imposed by ASIC for alleged continuous disclosure breaches and put 'directors on notice to release bad news faster'.[45] Two companies, Stockland and David Jones, were thought to have disclosed declines in earnings based on seeing the action against Leighton.[46]

[38] Interview Applicant's solicitors Telstra, 4; Interview Centro funder, 5; Interview Applicant's solicitor Centro, 7; Interview Applicant's solicitor Leighton, 21.

[39] Interview Lawyer Participants Telstra/Multiplex/Centro.

[40] Interview ASIC Executive Telstra/Multiplex; Interview ASIC Executive Centro, 2; Interview ASIC Executive Leighton, 9.

[41] Inabu Pty Ltd v CIMIC Group Limited, Federal Court of Australia, ACD93/2016 filed on 23 November 2016; *Inabu Pty Ltd as trustee for the Alidas Superannuation Fund v CIMIC Group Ltd* [2020] FCA 510; Jenny Wiggins, 'Class action alleges CIMIC misled investors on cash flow' *The Australian Financial Review* (26 August 2020).

[42] Interview ASIC Executive Leighton, 4, 9.

[43] ASIC, 'Regulatory Guide 100 – Enforceable Undertakings' (February 2012) [100.25].

[44] Australian Broadcasting Corporation, 'Corporate watchdog in crackdown on disclosure breaches', *AM* (19 March 2012) (Greg Medcraft, ASIC Chairman) ('Medcraft ABC Interview'). See also Richard Gluyas, 'Corporate regulator urges tougher disclosure penalties', *The Australian* (19 March 2012) 2.

[45] Jenny Wiggins, 'ASIC gets tougher on disclosure', *The Australian Financial Review* (19 March 2012) 1.

[46] Claire Stewart, 'Peril of disclosure rush raised', *The Australian Financial Review* (20 March 2012) 17; Stephen Bartholomeusz, 'Leighton covers its indecent disclosure', *Business Spectator* (online) (27 March 2012).

The Centro case study highlights ASIC seeking to achieve general deterrence through the creation of a binding legal precedent. The liability stage of the proceedings was significant because it continued the evolution of the development of the directors' duty of care in relation to financial information and the extent to which directors could delegate tasks and rely on management under Australian law.[47] The successful prosecution of the case by ASIC in relation to liability meant that ASIC clarified the expectations of directors in relation to financial information and accounts. ASIC labelled the judgment 'as a landmark decision in Australian corporate governance'.[48] Others have questioned whether the Centro decision created new law.[49] However, it has been observed that company directors now devote more time and effort to the review and approval of financial statements.[50] A similar observation was made by a former ASIC senior executive, who was aware of some companies postponing the release of their financial statements so they could reflect on the requirements of the Centro decision and in other cases tasking a company officer with the preparation of a board paper setting out significant events for the past 12 months before financial statements were signed off.[51]

In Centro, the penalties stage required the court to expressly address deterrence. The court accepted that deterrence, general and specific, was an important factor in determining whether to grant relief from liability, disqualification and imposition of penalties.[52] However, in reviewing the relevant case law, Middleton J cited two competing perspectives on general deterrence. The first was that 'No-one should be sacrificed to the public interest' so that a higher sanction on the individual could not be justified by the need for general deterrence.[53] The second was that achieving general deterrence justified a harsher penalty on an individual offender so as to take account of the propensity of others to contravene the law.[54] Courts are expected to balance these two views.[55] These perspectives highlight that what may be required to achieve specific, or personal deterrence as Middleton J expressed it, and general deterrence do not necessarily align. The court determined that the liability judgment, with its associated embarrassment and reputational damage, achieved sufficient specific deterrence. The court went on to explain that the Centro directors had a low likelihood of reoffending and had much to offer corporate Australia in terms of expertise and experience.[56]

On one view, Middleton J's approach undermined the general deterrence of ASIC's successful civil penalty action against the directors, namely the need for all directors to provide sufficient scrutiny of corporate compliance with financial reporting requirements. The courts

[47] *ASIC v Healey* (2011) 196 FCR 291, 297 [13] (Middleton J). See also Kathyrn Tomasic, Australian Securities and Investments Commission v Healey: Implications for the directors' duty of care and diligence' (2011) 26 *Australian Journal of Corporate Law* 234; Philip Crutchfield and Catherine Button, 'Men over board: The burden of directors' duties in the wake of the Centro case' (2012) 30 *Companies and Securities Law Journal* 83, 90.

[48] ASIC, 'Decision in Centro civil penalty case' (Media Release, 11-125, 27 June 2011) 1; Evidence to Senate Economics Legislation Committee – Estimates, Parliament of Australia, Canberra (12 October 2011) 11 (Mr Greg Medcraft, ASIC Chairman) ('Medcraft Evidence to Senate Committee').

[49] Elisabeth Sexton, 'Watchdog ruling shakes up boardrooms', *The Sydney Morning Herald* (8 July 2011) 7; Samantha Bowers and Jason Murphy, 'Centro case makes directors sit up', *The Australian Financial Review* (29 July 2011) 23.

[50] Tim Leung and Jon Webster, 'Directors' duties, financial literacy and financial reporting after Centro' (2012) 30 *Companies and Securities Law Journal* 100, 109.

[51] Interview ASIC Executive Centro, 11.

[52] *ASIC v Healey (No 2)* (2011) 284 ALR 734, 747–48 [91]–[92], 753–54 [112]–[113], 756–57 [120]–[122], 764 [168], 775 [224] (Middleton J).

[53] ibid 747–48 [92].

[54] ibid 749 [99].

[55] *Morley v ASIC (No 2)* (2011) 83 ACSR 620, 645 [126] (Spigelman CJ, Beazley and Giles JJA); *ASIC v Australian Property Custodian Holdings Ltd (recs and mgrs apptd) (in liq)* (2014) 322 ALR 45, 66 [91]–[92] (Murphy J).

[56] *ASIC v Healey (No 2)* (2011) 284 ALR 734, 76–77 [184] (Middleton J).

have recognised that the showing of leniency to corporate offenders can undermine general deterrence, both in relation to other business people and to offenders generally, who may seek to justify their misconduct by pointing to the actions of the white-collar offender.[57] Another view is that Middleton J sought to balance the operation of direct sanctions, indirect costs and reputational harm on the directors in terms of specific deterrence. However, the general deterrence of the director population is still maintained because the declaration of contravention was made and the judgment signalled that a range of sanctions could then follow if the law was not adhered to.

B. Effectiveness and Limitations of Deterrence

This section applies to the case studies those factors that chapter three identified as bearing on whether deterrence is effective or as limiting its operation.

i. Certainty of Detection and Punishment

Deterrence scholarship has found that the certainty or probability of being punished has a greater deterrent effect than the severity or celerity of the punishment. However, as discussed in chapter three, the final point of punishment hinges on a number of earlier steps also occurring, including detection and a finding of contravention.[58]

ASIC's approach in the case studies was to place significant emphasis on detecting a contravention.[59] This was due to a desire to have corporations fix problematic continuous disclosure policies or procedures quickly, in effect specific deterrence. But it was also driven by a need to achieve general deterrence and to provide guidance to the market. As a consequence, warnings (Telstra), enforceable undertakings (Multiplex and Leighton) and infringement notices (Leighton) were seen as effective because they allowed ASIC to indicate that it had identified what it viewed as a contravention, or at least sub-standard practice.[60] ASIC wanted the market to know that it is actively looking to identify problematic disclosure practices. Certainty aids the high reputational impact that ASIC actions are viewed as having by interviewees because regulated entities will have their conduct brought to the attention of the public and their peers. Moreover, the steps between detection and punishment may be less important here because once ASIC detects an alleged contravention it will be able to extract some form of punishment. The lower levels of the enforcement pyramid, such as warnings, infringement notices and enforceable undertakings, give ASIC significant flexibility as to the form of punishment employed.

The generally lower financial sanctions imposed by ASIC actions compared to those imposed by class actions may be less cause for concern if effectiveness of deterrence turns on the certainty of getting caught and being required to correct the identified deficiency rather than on the ultimate punishment. However, it is difficult to assess certainty of detection as undetected contraventions

[57] *ASIC v Vizard* (2005) 145 FCR 57, 65 [33], 66 [37], 68–69 [48] (Finkelstein J).

[58] See ch 3, section II.D.i.

[59] Interview ASIC Executive Leighton, 4. See also ASIC, 'Penalties for corporate wrongdoing', Report 367 (March 2014) 10 ('ASIC Penalties Report') ('ASIC's credibility as an effective regulator depends on our ability to detect corporate wrongdoing.').

[60] Interview ASIC Executive Telstra/Multiplex; Interview ASIC Executive Leighton, 4, 9. See also Australian Law Reform Commission, 'Principled Regulation: Federal Civil and Administrative Penalties in Australia' (Report No 95 December 2002) 426–27 (observing that infringement notices allow offences to be officially 'noticed' and penalised so that risk of detection of non-compliance is real).

are not known.[61] This is in a context where ASIC has more than 2,000 listed companies[62] (as well as other disclosing entities) for which it must seek to detect contraventions.

The existence of class actions and the ability of lawyers and funders to make a return on successful litigation may also assist in increasing the probability of a contravention being detected as there is an incentive to identify and pursue contraventions. Both ASIC and class action lawyers/funders are looking for contraventions. However, this depends on lawyers and litigation funders bringing to light contraventions that ASIC has not acted upon. The case studies selected for this study were based on ASIC enforcement action and class actions both occurring. However, there are examples of class actions being brought where ASIC did not act.[63] This suggests that the class action aids in the certainty aspect of deterrence. Equally, a review of the list of infringement notices issued by ASIC reveals a number of corporations that were not subject to a class action.[64] A litigation funder involved in the Centro class action pointed out that a 'funder is not a public body' and could not 'fund a case that was directed at a nonmonetary goal'.[65] Similarly, an ASIC officer pointed out that class action lawyers and ASIC differ in the cases they bring because 'private litigation needs to be commercial'.[66] As a result, smaller corporations or contraventions with lower shareholder losses may not be attractive class action targets.

While the importance of certainty can be accepted, there is still a need to consider the severity of the sanction. This follows because it may be argued that it is also the size or extent of the sanctions that affects the achievement of deterrence.[67]

ii. Severity – Under- or Over-deterrence

The significance of severity of sanction is contested in the literature reviewed in chapter three. For deterrence scholarship that comes from criminal law and criminology, a sanction is important, but the level or quantum is not expressed with precision because knowledge of the impact of a harsher or more lenient sanction on deterrence is not well understood.[68] In contrast, law and economics theory's optimal deterrence places much greater emphasis on severity of sanction because it requires that the regulated entity internalise the full social cost of its conduct multiplied by the likelihood of detection.

Severity may be looked at from the perspective that the level or quantum of the sanction informs whether an incentive to alter conduct has been created, and also signals the seriousness of the underlying conduct. A significant sanction, even without a trial and judgment, can indicate that there is merit to an allegation and the law has been violated.[69] Equally, a small sanction could

[61] See ch 3, section II.E.iv.

[62] Australian Securities Exchange, 'Historical Market Statistics – Number of Companies and securities listed on ASX' (December 2020), available at www.asx.com.au/about/historical-market-statistics.htm#No%20of%20Companies.

[63] See, eg, *Vernon v Village Life Ltd* [2009] FCA 516; *Clime Capital Ltd v Credit Corp Group Ltd (No 3)* [2012] FCA 218; *Pathway Investments Pty Ltd v National Australia Bank Ltd (No 3)* [2012] VSC 625; *Modtech Engineering Pty Ltd v GPT Management Holdings Ltd* [2013] FCA 626.

[64] See Appendix 2 Table 1 and Table 3 (37 infringement notices were issued from 1 July 2004 to 31 December 2017, but only five of the corporations were subject to class actions: Nufarm, Leighton, Sirtex Medical, Bellamy's and Murray River Organics).

[65] Interview Centro funder, 3.

[66] Interview ASIC Executive Leighton, 22.

[67] Miriam Baer, 'Linkage and the Deterrence of Corporate Fraud' (2008) 94 *Virginia Law Review* 1295, 1306; ASIC Penalties Report (n 59) 11.

[68] David Kennedy, *Deterrence and Crime Prevention* (Routledge, 2009) 34–38.

[69] Samuel Issacharoff and Robert Klonoff, 'The Public Value of Settlement' (2009) 78 *Fordham Law Review* 1177, 1196; James Park, 'Rules, Principles and the Competition to Enforce Securities Laws' (2012) 100 *California Law Review* 115, 160.

indicate a minor contravention. On that reasoning, Telstra would be seen to have committed a minor contravention because of the low level of the sanction from both ASIC and the class action. ASIC accepted that its warning was employed because the contraventions were 'not sufficiently serious'.[70] A former senior Telstra executive described the 'yellow card' as 'probably a little bit effective'.[71]

In the Centro case study, even though there was no sanction imposed on the company by ASIC and minor direct financial sanctions on the directors, it is likely to qualify as an example of a severe penalty for a serious contravention. ASIC took the director's duty route to civil penalties and was successful in proving contraventions. Taking into account the lack of criminal penalties in the continuous disclosure area, participants in the Centro class action described this outcome as: 'personally [for a director] that's really very significant … it's as bad as it gets really as a director'.[72] However, some criticism was directed at the court's findings, describing the penalties as being too low.[73] The class action resulted in a $200 million payout which, at the time, was the largest class action settlement in Australian history.[74] To be added to this was the high level of legal costs because the multiple class actions and multiple parties meant there were 'lawyers everywhere'.[75]

The Multiplex and Leighton case studies demonstrated significant criticism of the severity of the ASIC sanctions and generally praise for the class action. For example, the class action lawyers in Multiplex stated that the 'class action settlement would net its participants about 20 times what they would have got if they had signed up to the ASIC deal', referring to the $32 million compensation fund, and that the class action 'demonstrates in absolutely concrete terms the inadequacy of the ASIC settlement back in December 2006'.[76] ASIC was also criticised for taking the 'easy route of an enforceable undertaking'.[77] This analysis focuses on compensation. However, from a deterrence perspective, where the focus is the cost that the company is made to bear, the compensation fund, secured a sanction that was 32 or 20 times larger (depending on whether the amount agreed to in the enforceable undertaking or the reported payout is used) than if ASIC had successfully pursued a civil penalty, in addition to the impact on internal governance and reputation. It can be said that ASIC could have obtained both a civil penalty order and a compensation order and so could have obtained an even higher amount. However, the context is an enforceable undertaking or settlement so that the distinction may be argued to be less important. From the perspective of deterrence, the focus is on the total sanctions obtained. ASIC's outcome in Leighton was described by one commentator as 'light penalties and small fines … akin to fighting with a piece of wet lettuce'.[78] The same commentator described the 'whopping $400 million class

[70] Evidence to Senate Economics Legislation Committee – Estimates, Parliament of Australia, Canberra, 16 February 2006, 44 (Mr Jeremy Cooper, ASIC Deputy Chairman) ('Cooper Evidence to Senate Committee').

[71] Interview Telstra Executive, 3.

[72] Interview Lawyer Participants Centro, 7.

[73] Jennifer Hill, 'Centro and the Monitoring Board – Legal Duties Versus Aspirational Ideals in Corporate Governance' (2012) 35 *UNSW Law Journal* 341, 342; Patrick Durkin, 'Centro Investors Vent Anger at "Injustice"', *The Australian Financial Review* (1 September 2011) 9; Michael West, 'Off the Hook, With Barely a Slap', *Sydney Morning Herald* (3 September 2011) 2.

[74] Maurice Blackburn, 'Record-Breaking $200m Centro Class Action Win' (Media Release, 9 May 2012) ('Maurice Blackburn Centro MR May 2012'); Slater & Gordon, 'Thousands of mum and dad investors poised to share in Australia's biggest shareholder class action settlement' (Media Release, 9 May 2012) ('Slater & Gordon Centro MR May 2012'); Adam McLean, 'Centro, PwC take record $200m legal hit', *The Australian Financial Review* (9 May 2012).

[75] Interview Centro Executive, 10.

[76] Ben Butler, 'ASIC attacked on Multiplex deal' *The Sydney Morning Herald* (22 July 2010).

[77] Adele Ferguson, 'Multiplex settlement is a bitter-sweet victory', *The Age* (22 July 2010) 9.

[78] Adele Ferguson, 'Wrong signal to let Leighton off lightly', *The Sydney Morning Herald* (19 March 2012) 5.

action' as putting 'the spotlight directly on the company's corporate governance standards [and] its continuous disclosure obligations'.[79] As noted in chapter four, the class action in fact achieved a direct payment of $69.45 million. Further, it was the enforceable undertaking that secured the corporate governance changes, not the class action. The Multiplex and Leighton case studies illustrate a fixation on direct financial sanctions.[80] Indirect costs and reputational impact also need to be taken into account in considering the severity of sanction, as this text has broadly defined it, and deterrence more generally, even if they are more difficult to measure.

Turning to optimal deterrence, the above discussion of the dimensions of deterrence in relation to the case studies demonstrates that it is not possible to precisely quantify the full sanction imposed. While compensation payments and penalties are on the public record, the costs imposed, particularly indirect costs and reputational impact, are unclear. However, the concepts of over- or under-deterrence do have explanatory value. This may be illustrated through two of the case studies: Telstra and Centro.

In Telstra, ASIC determined only to issue a warning, but this was nonetheless followed by a class action. While the settlement payment of $5 million was relatively small, there were significant indirect costs imposed on Telstra. The media reported that Telstra's general counsel described the settlement as having the flavour of 'greenmail' and the settlement was reached because although Telstra was confident of success in the case, $5 million was less than what it expected to pay in legal fees if the case went to trial.[81] If a warning were sufficient to achieve deterrence, the class action would over-deter. Over-deterrence means that resources are wasted or costs unnecessarily incurred, such as overinvestment in precautionary measures such as compliance regimes, or adopting a defensive disclosure policy. But if ASIC had failed to take adequate action, the class action may have addressed this. The actual class action result and reasoning in the settlement judgment discussed above in chapter four, section 3.2 suggests that the warning was adequate.

In Centro, Justice Middleton determined not to impose a disqualification order or pecuniary penalty on the non-executive directors, as specific deterrence had been achieved through the finding of a contravention and the impact on reputation. Yet the class action included claims against the directors through a cross-claim. The directors' conduct was scrutinised for a second time and there was a contribution to the settlement by the D&O insurance policy that was in place. If specific deterrence in the directors' duties case was sufficient, no additional sanctions were necessary from a class action. Equally, if there had been under-deterrence, a class action could correct this. However, the analysis is complicated in the Centro example by the use of different causes of action in the ASIC action and the class action. On one view, different causes of action equate to different instances of wrongdoing with each needing to be deterred. As a result, ASIC and the class action are not seen as cumulative in relation to severity, or over and under deterrence. Alternatively, if the focus is the underlying facts giving rise to the misconduct, misclassification of liabilities, and the aim is to deter that misconduct, then even different causes of action may result in over deterrence.

The case studies illustrate that the class action can correct under-deterrence but also result in over-deterrence. Significantly though, when optimal deterrence is applied to an actual case

[79] Adele Ferguson, '$400m lawsuit turns spotlight on issues of governance', *The Sydney Morning Herald* (1 September 2011) 7.

[80] Michelle Welsh and Vince Morabito, 'Public v Private Enforcement of Securities Laws: An Australian Empirical Study' (2014) 14 *Journal of Corporate Law Studies* 39, 76.

[81] Susannah Moran, 'Telstra class action payout fair, says judge', *The Australian* (14 December 2007) 25; Telstra Corporation Limited, 'Class action dismissed' (Media Release, 296/2007, 13 December 2007) 1 ('Telstra MR 296/2007').

study, it does not yield a single correct answer. Rather, it highlights that there are important ramifications for regulated entities and the public interest in having two mechanisms that impose sanctions that can achieve deterrence. This is considered further in chapter six.

iii. Celerity or Timeliness

Celerity or timeliness refers to how swiftly sanctions follow the wrongdoing. Although not as significant as certainty or severity, the more rapidly sanctions are imposed, the more effective they are likely to be. The time taken to reach a conclusion of ASIC's enforcement actions and the settlement of the class actions is set out in chapter four, Table 4.5. In each case study ASIC actions were concluded in a shorter period than the time taken to resolve the related class action. In Telstra, Multiplex and Centro the difference was substantial, being 20 months, 21 months and 27 months respectively, while in Leighton there was little time difference between the ASIC action and the class action, with the class action only taking two months longer.

Speed is important in the area of continuous disclosure because of the need to ensure that the market is informed and efficient. Whether an individual company or a number of entities have adopted a sub-standard or illegal practice, the unacceptable practices need to be stopped quickly.[82] Prompt ASIC enforcement outcomes communicate to the individual company and the market generally that practices are unacceptable. In relation to Telstra, the then Deputy Chairman of ASIC explained to a Senate Estimates Hearing: 'We took the decision to communicate our findings quickly using the yellow card type language so that business people could see that when irregular behaviour occurred in a large company we would investigate it and communicate our findings quickly'.[83]

Similarly, the former Chairman of ASIC explained the action in relation to Leighton as 'an outcome that is timely and it's efficient'.[84] In Multiplex the enforceable undertaking was employed because ASIC wanted to provide a mechanism for change in a timely manner. The aim was to ensure better procedures in a listed company that had previously been a private company.[85] This approach is supported by the Australian Government's capability review of ASIC, which stated that enforcement actions can achieve general deterrence 'if delivered in a timely way'.[86]

Class actions, needing to rely on litigation or the threat of litigation, are likely to move more slowly than ASIC's non-court enforcement mechanisms. Equally, when ASIC uses litigation as it did in Centro, the time taken is longer. This follows from the court process incorporating various protections for the defendant in criminal or civil penalty cases, but also more generally, including in civil cases, for there to be the gathering and provision of evidence, followed by argument and the delivery of a judgment. However, in the Multiplex and Centro cases, the delay in relation to the class actions was partially due to ASIC. In Multiplex, ASIC prevented access to evidence being obtained due to public interest immunity. In Centro, as in most situations where there are both criminal/civil penalty proceedings and civil proceedings, the civil proceeding was stayed while the former was determined.

[82] Interview ASIC Executive Leighton, 4 ('timeliness of getting that message to market is a key consideration').

[83] Cooper Evidence to Senate Committee (n 70) 44.

[84] Medcraft ABC Interview (n 44). See also Rebecca Urban, 'Leighton fine "a timely message"', *The Australian*, 24 March 2012, 31.

[85] Interview ASIC Executive Telstra/Multiplex.

[86] ASIC Capability Review Panel, 'Fit for the future: A capability review of the Australian Securities and Investments' (December 2015) 114.

iv. Perceptions and Rationality

Perceptual deterrence theory, as explained in chapter three, holds that general deterrence is affected by what the regulated population perceives to be the certainty, severity and celerity of sanctions, rather than what the sanctions actually are. Statements of entities subject to enforcement actions or class actions, media reporting, statements by industry bodies and advice from external advisers can influence perceptions about the likelihood and ramifications of an ASIC action or a class action, and the need to take precautions.

ASIC has expressed the view that public enforcement has greater potential to produce meaningful change than private actions because it tends to attract greater industry awareness.[87] However, in the case studies there was often a suggestion in the media that if an entity were apprehended by ASIC, they would face light sanctions. For example, in relation to Telstra, the then Shadow Communications Minister, Senator Stephen Conroy, was highly critical of ASIC and expressed the view that: 'ASIC's decision not to prosecute Telstra today demonstrates that ASIC isn't a corporate watchdog. It's a corporate chihuahua'.[88] Similar sentiments were expressed above in the discussion about severity in relation to Multiplex and Leighton. However, this needs to be contrasted with the views about reputation expressed above.

There was also a general view that the advent of shareholder class actions has promoted awareness of continuous disclosure obligations.[89] Lawyers for the applicants in the class actions and a litigation funder reported a growing focus on continuous disclosure obligations as a result of shareholder class actions.[90] This was seen as a positive effect of the perception that class action risk had increased. It makes intuitive sense that if an additional enforcement mechanism is added to, and used in, an area of regulation, then certainty and severity are likely to increase. The availability of both class actions and litigation funding had the effect that the standing given to shareholders to bring claims for contravention of the continuous disclosure regime could be translated into actual litigation.[91] However, the perception of the risk may impact whether over- or under-deterrence results. If the actual risk is considered higher than it is, that may mean that the level of deterrence moves closer to an optimal level without needing to incur additional enforcement costs. Equally it may foster over deterrence as regulated entities take excessive steps to prevent a contravention.

The above discussion regarding reputation indicated an awareness by ASIC that 'the tool that [they] select will have different reputational impacts'.[92] Moreover, for both ASIC and class actions there is an issue about what an outcome means in terms of reputation if there is no finding or admission of wrongdoing as occurs where some form of settlement results. The issue arises most clearly in Leighton for both the ASIC action and the class action. The Leighton Chairman's Address to Shareholders at the Annual General Meeting following the infringement notices and enforceable undertaking explained the ASIC action as follows:

> In March this year, the Company accepted three infringement notices issued by the Australian Securities & Investments Commission in relation to the earnings downgrade issued by Leighton on 11 April 2011.

[87] ASIC Penalties Report (n 59) 10.

[88] Australian Broadcasting Corporation, 'ASIC lets Telstra off', *The 7.30 Report* (14 December 2005) (Senator Stephen Conroy).

[89] Gluyas (n 44) 2; Chris Merritt, 'Securities class actions just blackmail suits', *The Australian* (6 June 2014) 33; Chris Merritt, 'Fear of class actions grows', *The Australian* (13 June 2014) 31; Chris Merritt, 'Second wave of litigation looms', *The Australian* (25 July 2014) 27.

[90] Interview Centro funder, 3; Interview Applicants' solicitors Multiplex, 18, 20; Interview Applicant's solicitor Centro, 1, 21; Interview Applicant's solicitor Leighton, 23–24.

[91] Bernard Murphy, 'Shareholder class actions: are you vulnerable?' (2007) 59 *Keeping Good Companies* 275.

[92] Interview ASIC Executive Leighton, 9.

> In total, the three notices required the Company to pay a penalty of $300,000. It is important to emphasise that we have not accepted, nor admitted, liability in this matter. We accepted these infringement notices and paid the penalty as a pragmatic decision which we strongly believe was in the best interests of the Company. This matter would most certainly have taken a long time to finalise, and the Board wished to prevent a major distraction for management at a time when their focus should clearly be on implementing the key initiatives that I have previously outlined. Furthermore, this agreement with ASIC will allow the Company to avoid substantial legal and other costs which would have been incurred in a drawn out process.[93]

Similarly, Leighton stated in its media release dealing with the class action settlement:

> Whilst we continue to deny the claim, the decision to settle the class action was a commercial one, taken in the interests of our shareholders. Resolving the matter permits management to focus on the operations of the business. It is important to note that the settlement is not an admission of any liability or a finding of any breach of law against Leighton or any of our executives.[94]

The position adopted by Leighton is possible because there was no admission of liability in relation to either the ASIC action or the class action settlement. A response to statements such as Leighton's was put forward by an ASIC officer who thought that the public would evaluate what had occurred and would reach their own conclusions.[95] Nonetheless, there is a clear contrast between Leighton's position of a settlement being a cost-benefit analysis and the view that regulatory actions and class actions can impact reputation.

v. Corporations or Directors

Chapter two's review of the continuous disclosure regime demonstrates that it is primarily targeted at the corporation. Accordingly, a director cannot directly contravene the disclosure obligation. Directors may be liable as accessories. An accessory claim faces a higher bar than the claim against the corporation as intention/knowledge and participation must be proved.[96] In contrast, the prohibitions on misleading or deceptive conduct apply to a 'person', and as a result to both corporations and directors, so that direct liability may be pursued. However, such claims can only be civil proceedings.

In all the case studies, except Centro, the focus was on the corporation. No directors were the subject of enforcement action or a class action in the Telstra, Multiplex and Leighton case studies. The focus on the corporation is typical of class actions as it has greater resources than the directors and the intricacies of accessorial liability can be avoided. Directors will usually only be the target of a class action if the corporation is insolvent or lacks the financial resources to meet a judgment or settlement.[97] In the Centro class action the directors were joined in response to

[93] Mr Stephen Johns, Chairman, Leighton Holdings, 'Address to Shareholders' (Presentation to 51st Annual General Meeting of Leighton Holdings Limited, 22 May 2012) 6–7.

[94] Leighton MR May 2014 (n 19).

[95] Interview ASIC Executive Leighton, 10.

[96] For criminal contravention see *Giorgianni v R* (1985) 156 CLR 473; Stephen Odgers, *Principles of Federal Criminal Law*, 3rd edn (Thomson Reuters, 2015) [11.2.340]. For civil penalty and civil claims, see *Yorke v Lucas* (1985) 158 CLR 661; Tim Bednall and Pamela Hanrahan, 'Officers' liability for mandatory corporate disclosure: Two paths, two destinations?' (2013) 31 *Company and Securities Law Journal* 474, 489–94.

[97] Examples of the exception are the Harris Scarfe and Gunns Limited class actions: *Guglielmin v Trescowthick (No 5)* [2006] FCA 1385 (directors sued after corporation placed in voluntary administration in April 2001) and *Foley v Gay* [2016] FCA 273 (directors sued as accessories after corporation went into liquidation).

the company cross-claiming against the auditors. This is unusual and appears to reflect litigation tactics to shift the blame and share the payment of compensation rather than concerns about deterrence.

ASIC approached the conduct in Centro through civil penalty proceedings for a breach of directors' duties. The focus was the individual, not the company. In Centro, it seems that ASIC deliberately chose its enforcement approach so as to educate and deter individuals who are directors by focusing on their obligations in relation to financial reporting. Unlike class actions, which focus on the defendants with assets to pay compensation, ASIC also has the ability to bring proceedings based on a view of what is the better way to achieve deterrence, which means that directors may be targeted. More generally, ASIC has the ability to couch contraventions of corporate laws by a corporation, such as the continuous disclosure regime, as a breach of a director's duty and therefore seek to deter the individual rather than the company.[98]

vi. Dispersion of Deterrence and D&O Insurance

Chapter three explained that the effectiveness of sanctions in achieving deterrence may be undermined where the sanction is dispersed beyond the wrongdoer. In relation to continuous disclosure, that requires consideration of D&O insurance. The usual concern is that insurance undermines deterrence because the wrongdoer is relieved from making payment. Instead, the payment is to be met by the insurance provider.[99] If companies and directors are insulated from the costs of shareholder litigation, these costs are unlikely to inform their decision-making and deter law-breaking behaviour. However, the effect of insurance on deterrence is complicated by provisions in the Corporations Act, the general law, and the specific terms of insurance policies.

The Corporations Act limits the situations in which a company may indemnify a director or pay insurance premiums on behalf of a director. For example, a company cannot indemnify a person (other than for legal costs) against liability incurred as an officer of the company for a liability for a pecuniary penalty order under Corporations Act, s 1317G or a compensation order under s 1317H or 1317HA, or for a liability that is owed to someone other than the company or a related body corporate and which did not arise out of conduct in good faith.[100] In short, no indemnity is available for conduct in bad faith, civil penalties or compensation orders. However, an indemnity may be given in relation to civil liability for misleading or deceptive conduct.[101]

The restriction on paying insurance premiums is narrower than the restriction on indemnification. It only applies to liability incurred by the officer arising out of conduct involving either: a wilful breach of duty in relation to the company; or a contravention of the provisions relating to an officer making improper use of information or improper use of his or her position for his

[98] Abe Herzberg and Helen Anderson, 'Stepping Stones – From Corporate Fault to Directors' Personal Civil Liability' (2012) 40 *Federal Law Review* 181. It should be noted that the elements for a contravention of the director's duty must be proved, not the corporation's contravention of a law, although that is part of the factual matrix to be considered in answering the question whether the director met the standard prescribed: *Cassimatis v Australian Securities and Investments Commission* (2020) 275 FCR 533, 554–55 [77]–[79] (Greenwood J), 641–42 [462]–[465] (Thawley J).

[99] John Fleming, 'The Role of Negligence in Modern Tort Law' (1967) 53 *Virginia Law Review* 815, 823 ('The deterrent function of the law of torts was severely, perhaps fatally, undermined by the advent of liability insurance.'); Tom Baker and Sean Griffith, *Ensuring Corporate Misconduct: How Liability Insurance Undermines Shareholder Litigation* (University of Chicago Press, 2010) 10, 200.

[100] Corporations Act 2001 (Cth), s 199A(2).

[101] Robert Austin and Ian Ramsay, *Ford, Austin and Ramsay's Principles of Corporations Law* (LexisNexis Online, 2018) [8.410].

or her advantage or gain or to the detriment of the company, that is, in breach of ss 183 and 182 respectively.[102]

None of the above restrictions prevent directors themselves from acquiring such insurance provided premiums are paid in their personal capacity with no contribution from the corporation.[103] However, such insurance may not be available.

More generally, insurance may not be available or will be found to be illegal as a matter of public policy in relation to criminal liability or liability for a civil penalty where the conduct was intentional or morally offensive.[104] However, the position is less clear where the criminal offence is established without personal responsibility or moral blame, such as in the case of strict liability. In those situations an indemnity or insurance may be permitted.[105] Similarly, civil penalties that may be imposed without personal responsibility or moral blame may be capable of being insured against.[106]

D&O insurance policies obtained by corporations commonly contain three insuring clauses. 'Side A' covers individual directors and officers in respect of personal liability incurred in their capacity as a director or officer of the company and for which they have not or cannot claim indemnity from the company. 'Side B' reimburses the company in respect of its indemnification of its directors and officers. 'Side C' provides indemnity to listed companies for claims made against them in relation to their securities. While Side A and Side B deal with claims against the directors, Side C provides coverage for the corporation.[107] Side C is significant because it means that the company is able to insure against shareholder class actions.

D&O insurance policies frequently exclude liability in respect of loss arising from a variety of conduct including fraud, dishonesty, criminal act, deliberate breach of legislation, insider trading and gaining an improper personal advantage. However, policies also normally make an exception from the exclusion where the relevant insured person 'had no direct or personal involvement in, or knowledge of, the matters upon which the operation of the exclusions is based'.[108] The exclusions seek to give effect to the statutory and general law restrictions on insurance.

The above matrix of statute, general law and insurance policy terms means that criminal prosecutions of offences requiring some form of *mens rea* do not have their deterrence value reduced. Civil claims fall at the other end of the spectrum, and the imposition of personal liability on the director may provide little deterrence where there is D&O insurance. In between, and subject to uncertainty, are criminal and civil penalties that do not require personal responsibility or moral blame.[109]

[102] Corporations Act 2001 (Cth), s 199B.

[103] Peter Mann, 'Directors' and Officers' Insurance in the Regulatory Litigation Context' in Michael Legg, *Regulation, Litigation and Enforcement* (Thomson Reuters, 2011) 76.

[104] Robert Merkin and Ian Enright, *Sutton on Insurance Law*, 4th edn (Thomson Reuters 2015) [23.1860]; Australian Law Reform Commission, *Compliance With The Trade Practices Act 1974* (Report No 68, 1994) [10.34] citing *Askey v Golden Wine Co Ltd* [1948] 2 All ER 35; *R Leslie Ltd v Reliable Advertising and Addressing Agency Ltd* [1915] 1 KB 652; *Hasledine v Hosken* [1933] 1 KB 822; *Burrows v Rhodes* [1899]1 QB 816.

[105] *Horsell International Pty Ltd v Divetwo Pty Ltd* [2013] NSWCA 368, [272]–[276] (Meagher JA); Austin and Ramsay (n 101) [8.410].

[106] Mann (n 103) 78–79; Chief Justice TF Bathurst, 'Insurance Law – A View from the Bench' (2014) 25 *Insurance Law Journal* 94, 102–04.

[107] *BOS International (Aust) Ltd v Babcock & Brown International Pty Ltd* [2011] NSWSC 1382, [12] (Rein J); Guy Narburgh and Sally-Anne Ivimey, 'Side by Side (A, B and C): Securities Class Actions and D&O Insurance' in Damian Grave and Helen Mould (eds), *25 years of class actions in Australia: 1992–2017* (Ross Parsons Centre, 2017) 372–73.

[108] *Wilkie v Gordian Runoff Ltd* (2005) 221 CLR 522, 532 [27] (Gleeson CJ, McHugh, Gummow and Kirby JJ); LexisNexis, *Halsbury's Laws of Australia* (online at 1 November 2017) 235 Insurance, 'III (4)(E)(II) Directors' and Officers' Liability' [235–1890].

[109] Bathurst (n 106); Merkin and Enright (n 104) [23.1860].

The consequence for deterrence of this situation is that insurance would almost always cover the civil claims against the company or directors for contravention of the continuous disclosure regime brought through a class action. Further insurance is likely to respond to an ASIC action against a director for a civil penalty contravention as no intention is required. However, insurance would not be available in relation to a criminal prosecution. Insurance, therefore, reduces the certainty and severity of the specific deterrence of financial sanctions to the extent it covers the quantum of those sanctions. Insurance is also likely to reduce general deterrence of financial sanctions to the extent that companies and directors are aware that they have coverage from a policy that responds to a continuous disclosure class action and has sufficient coverage. However, insurance cannot ameliorate bans on being a director or reputational sanctions. A litigation funder in the Centro class action opined that the reason reputation was more important than monetary consequences was because insurance was often able to meet those costs.[110]

The effect of insurance was only (partially) visible in the Centro case study. While the position on insurance and civil penalties is not clear, it is likely that D&O insurance would have covered the directors' and officers' legal costs in both the ASIC action and class action and also responded to the CEO Mr Scott's civil penalty of $30,000. Insurance also contributed $38 million to the class action settlement but, due to Side C coverage, this could have been for either or both the corporation and the directors.

III. Application of the Analytical Framework – Compensation

Compensation for shareholders is largely achieved through the class action. While ASIC can pursue compensation, it was not seen as its main focus in relation to regulating continuous disclosure. The achievement of compensation is therefore mainly an analysis of the class action, although the same factors would apply equally to ASIC if it sought to pursue compensation. Those factors are whether full compensation compared to loss is achieved, incomplete recovery due to investors not claiming or respondents being unable to pay, transaction costs that reduce the compensation received, and the circularity problem, that is, diversified shareholders effectively paying themselves.

A. Accessing Compensation

All of the interviewees who had been involved in the class actions from the applicant's side stated that seeking compensation for shareholders was the main reason for commencing a class action.[111] A number of the lawyers for class action applicants reported speaking to the applicant and group members about their goals and motivations in the class action. In relation to Multiplex, 'the primary driver of the applicants and group members was to recover the monies they lost because of the alleged misleading behaviour'.[112] A solicitor for the applicant in the Centro class action explained:

> [Retail investors will] be aggrieved by how they felt that they were misled, how they were surprised by that information being put into the market. They'll be upset about the fact that they've suffered losses,

[110] Interview Centro funder, 5.

[111] Interview Applicant's solicitors Telstra, 3; Interview Centro funder, 1; Interview Applicants' solicitors Multiplex, 1, 7; Interview Applicant's solicitor Centro, 1, 21; Interview Applicant's solicitor Leighton, 1.

[112] Interview Applicants' solicitors Multiplex, 7.

> and they're going to be looking for a way of getting as much of that back as possible. Quite often people do have feelings of vengeance and wanting to see justice done, but for the most part, particularly as the case progresses, people start to configure that sense of justice in terms of a monetary outcome.[113]

In the Leighton class action, Maurice Blackburn issued a media release announcing the settlement and stating that it would 'compensate thousands of investors'.[114] Similarly, the director of Inabu Pty Ltd, the applicant in the class action, stated that he was 'grateful that this class action has given me and others the opportunity to recover compensation for our losses'.[115]

The litigation funder involved in the Centro class action explained that there needed to be sufficient loss for a litigation funder to become involved.[116] In Centro, that was the case due to both CNP and CER being heavily traded over a relatively long time period, from at least August 2007 to February 2008.[117] A litigation funder takes a commercial perspective on funding, which was said by the Centro funder to equate with 'compensation recovery'. A funder could not fund a case directed at a non-monetary goal.[118] A solicitor for the applicant in the Centro class action echoed these thoughts and drew the conclusion that the focus on compensation was not just due to the motivation of group members, but also the economic realities of securing litigation funding, namely that a sufficiently large financial recovery could be achieved so that the funder made a return commensurate with the risk they were undertaking.[119] This suggests that while accessing compensation is the goal of the class action, there needs to be a large enough loss for financing to be provided to assist in the bringing of the class action.

The ASIC interviewees, while acknowledging that compensation could be pursued by ASIC in appropriate situations, stated that it was not ASIC's main objective.[120] This view is borne out by the case studies with ASIC only seeking compensation in relation to Multiplex. The reasons for the view adopted were expressed in terms of ASIC having the responsibility for market integrity and governance, which necessitated prompt actions that deter and educate,[121] ASIC having limited resources making the pursuit of compensation for all persons untenable,[122] and class actions taking on the compensation role.[123] ASIC was only prepared to pursue compensation when it was in the public interest, not just in the private interests of some shareholders. This is discussed further below in relation to regulatory process.

The exception was Multiplex where the enforceable undertaking provided for Multiplex to establish a $32 million compensation fund. Compensation was limited to a group of investors for whom ASIC believed there was clear liability on the part of Multiplex. The former ASIC senior executive involved in the Multiplex enforcement action explained that the thinking was that if there had been a civil penalty procedure then that litigation may have resulted in admissions that could have been used by investors as findings of fact for them to then pursue their own compensation. However, as an enforceable undertaking was utilised rather than the civil penalty procedure, no admissions or findings of fact existed. The compensation scheme was meant to be

[113] Interview Applicant's solicitor Centro, 2.
[114] Maurice Blackburn, 'Leighton reaches swift $69.45m class action settlement' (Media Release, 16 May 2014).
[115] ibid.
[116] Interview Centro funder, 1.
[117] ibid.
[118] ibid 3.
[119] Interview Applicant's solicitor Centro, 3.
[120] Interview ASIC Executive Telstra/Multiplex; Interview ASIC Executive Centro, 3; Interview ASIC Executive Leighton, 3.
[121] Interview ASIC Executive Telstra/Multiplex; Interview ASIC Executive Leighton, 4.
[122] Interview ASIC Executive Leighton, 3.
[123] Interview ASIC Executive Centro, 3; Interview ASIC Executive Leighton, 4.

a replacement for the lack of admissions for private investors.[124] This view was corroborated by the solicitor for Multiplex who explained that ASIC was in favour of an agreed civil penalty, and that a civil penalty may have been acceptable to Multiplex but for the fact that Multiplex would have had to admit to contravening the law, which would 'underwrite the class action' that was expected to follow.[125]

B. Limitations on Achieving Full Compensation

i. Corrective Justice – Loss and Recovery

Chapter three explained that compensation is achieved, from both a corrective justice perspective and in terms of the legal principles governing the assessment of compensatory damages, when full or complete compensation is recovered. The aim of compensation is to make the injured person whole.

Table 4.3 in chapter four summarised the outcomes based on publicly reported figures as follows: Telstra ($5 million settlement and estimated $300 million claim); Multiplex ($110 million settlement and estimated $220 million claim as well as $20 million paid from ASIC created compensation fund); Centro ($200 million settlement and estimated $1 billion maximum claim); Leighton ($69.45 million settlement and estimated $400 million maximum claim). Put in percentage terms: Telstra 1.6 per cent; Multiplex 50 per cent or, with ASIC's fund added, 60 per cent; Centro 20 per cent; and Leighton 17 per cent.

Assessing the loss suffered is difficult because there is no settled law as to the correct methodology for calculating loss.[126] The legal tests put forward for calculating loss may be summarised as follows. The *Potts v Miller* measure is the difference between the price paid and the true value of the shares, that is, the underlying value of the company, at the time of purchase.[127] A variation on *Potts v Miller* occurs where the true value is replaced by the market price that would have prevailed if disclosure had been made. The 'left-in-hand' measure is the difference between the price paid and whatever is left in hand after the actual or assumed sale of the shares by the date on which the share is no longer inflated by the conduct the subject of the action. A further measure of loss is a 'no-transaction' case, which assumes that the shareholder would not have purchased the shares at all had the market been properly informed. There may also be claims for foregone investment returns as the group member lost the opportunity to be able to invest elsewhere.[128]

The uncertainty around calculation of loss was referred to by some interviewees when asked about recovery compared to loss.[129] This uncertainty may assist in understanding why

[124] Interview ASIC Executive Telstra/Multiplex.

[125] Interview Multiplex solicitor, 5.

[126] *P Dawson Nominees Pty Ltd v Brookfield Multiplex Ltd (No 4)* [2010] FCA 1029, [15]–[17] (Finkelstein J); *Hobbs Anderson Investments Pty Ltd v Oz Minerals Ltd* [2011] FCA 801, [9]–[10] (Emmett J); *Earglow Pty Ltd v Newcrest Mining Limited* [2016] FCA 1433, [69] (Murphy J).

[127] *Potts v Miller* (1940) 64 CLR 282, 297–300 (Dixon J).

[128] Damian Grave, Leah Watterson and Helen Mould, 'Causation, Loss and Damage: Challenges for the New Shareholder Class Action' (2009) 27 *Company & Securities Law Journal* 483, 498–502; Justice Jonathan Beach, 'Structural and Forensic Developments in Securities Litigation', International Commercial Law Conference, Inner Temple, Inns of Court, London (29 June 2016) 19–20; Michael Garner and Helen Mould, 'Measuring and Proving Loss in Securities Class Actions' in Damian Grave and Helen Mould (eds), *25 years of class actions in Australia: 1992–2017* (Ross Parsons Centre, 2017) 172–73.

[129] Interview Applicants' solicitors Multiplex, 5–6; Interview Centro funder, 2.

differing estimates of loss may exist. In Multiplex, the Federal Court stated that the recovery was 62 per cent (excluding the ASIC fund).[130] The measure of losses in Multiplex was said to be an average of the *Potts v Miller* measure and the left-in-hand measure with the 62 per cent based on 'the midpoint of a range of … reasonably likely successful outcomes had the matter proceeded'.[131] It should be noted that this is higher than the 50 per cent calculation referred to above.

The Centro figure of a $1 billion loss was thought to have been based on the recovery that the shareholders would make if compensation was calculated using a methodology most favourable to them. This would most likely be a 'no transaction' basis, that is, the investor would not have bought the securities and so would recover the entire amount they invested.[132] Although expert reports were prepared for the Centro class action, the total quantum of the claim was never calculated by an expert.[133] Other figures put forward by interviewees were $400 million[134] and $800 million.[135] This suggests a range of recovery from between 20 and 50 per cent.

The solicitor for the applicant in the Leighton class action stated that the $69.45 million settlement and estimated $400 million maximum claim could not be compared to determine the recovery achieved and that the percentage recovery was 'considerably higher' than that comparison would suggest.[136] However, no alternative loss figure or percentage of recovery was provided.

The variation between large initial assessments of loss and later figures may also arise due to plaintiff lawyers' optimism and seeking to attract group member interest. The possibility of a larger recovery is likely to cause group members to take steps to find out about the class action and enter retainer/funding agreements. Variations may also occur as better and greater knowledge about the claim becomes available. One plaintiff lawyer explained that 'the work by defence lawyers on both liability and quantum meant that the firm's internal assessment of the overall claim value reduced over time, sometimes significantly'.[137] Another plaintiff lawyer expressed a similar view: after access to internal company records and expert reports, 'you have a better appreciation of the various risks that are at play. And so it's quite obvious that what might be a success at the end of litigation is less than you were hoping for at the very beginning'.[138] The nature of litigation means that a proceeding will be commenced without complete knowledge. A further explanation is that the class actions deliberately choose a broader group period in the hope that it expands the potential liability of the respondent for the purposes of negotiating a settlement.[139] The large initial assessment is a litigation tactic that can create greater indirect costs and reputational harm for the respondent by placing more issues in dispute and attracting greater media interest, which may encourage resolution.

Taking account of uncertainty around calculation of loss and variations in estimates, none of the case studies achieved full compensation. Despite this, in all of the case studies, the interviewees who had been involved in the class actions from the applicant's side saw them as a success in terms of compensation.

[130] *P Dawson Nominees Pty Ltd v Brookfield Multiplex Limited (No 4)* [2010] FCA 1029, [22] (Finkelstein J).

[131] Bernard Murphy and Andrew Watson, 'Negotiations and Settlement – 2010 Multiplex Debrief' *LexisNexis Shareholder Class Action Masterclass*, Sydney (18 October 2010) 11.

[132] Interview Lawyer Participants Telstra/Multiplex/Centro. See also *Kirby v Centro Properties Ltd* [2009] FCA 695, [8] (Ryan J).

[133] Interview Lawyer Participants Telstra/Multiplex/Centro.

[134] Interview Centro Executive, 7.

[135] Interview Lawyer Participants Centro, 1.

[136] Interview Applicant's solicitor Leighton, 6.

[137] Interview Applicants' solicitors Multiplex, 1.

[138] Interview Applicant's solicitor Centro, 5.

[139] Interview Lawyer Participants Telstra/Multiplex/Centro; Interview ASIC Executive Leighton, 20.

The solicitors for the applicant in the Telstra class action acknowledged that the recovery compared to a loss of $300 million would not be considered a success.[140] However, they also pointed out that the outcome needed to be assessed in the context where a result was achieved at an early stage of the jurisprudence and 'shareholders got some compensation at no risk'.[141] Furthermore, as ASIC had not sought compensation, shareholders had 'the class action or nothing'.[142] In media reports at the time, the settlement was described as significant by a lawyer for the applicant because it was the first time an Australian company had agreed to pay compensation to investors for alleged breaches of the continuous disclosure requirements.[143] However, as noted above, Telstra's general counsel described the settlement as having the flavour of 'greenmail' and the settlement was reached because although Telstra was confident of success in the case, $5 million was less than what it expected to pay in legal fees if the case went to trial.[144] The Multiplex class action was viewed as a success with a solicitor for the applicant in the class action explaining that a recovery of 60 cents in the dollar was a good result in 'a strenuously contested piece of commercial litigation' where there are a number of complexities and risks.[145] The Centro settlement was described as 'a terrific result'.[146] In media releases and media reports, the main focus in relation to compensation was that the Centro class action payment was the largest shareholder class action settlement in Australian history. Indeed, at the time, it was the largest settlement of any type of class action in Australian history.[147] In the Leighton class action, the solicitor for the applicant stated that the primary goal of compensation was achieved by reference to the following criteria for success: 'compensation that appropriately reflects the losses that have been suffered, having regard to the risks of that particular case, and of litigation generally'.[148]

ii. Incomplete Recovery – Shareholders do not Claim or Respondents cannot Pay

Chapter three raised three issues that could undermine compensation: (1) no action for compensation is commenced; (2) shareholders who have suffered loss but do not seek compensation; and (3) compensation is unavailable due to the financial position of the respondents. The methodology employed in the research meant that class actions were commenced in each case study, and as the thesis has demonstrated, a compensation payment was obtained in each class action. In contrast, ASIC's choice of enforcement tools meant that it only obtained compensation in one instance, being Multiplex. This section focuses on the second and third issues. The second issue was common, and the third rare, in the class actions studied.

The Telstra class action was open to all eligible shareholders. This amounted to about 29,000 group members, but those group members needed to come forward and claim the compensation achieved. Two participants in the Telstra class action advised that not all of the $5 million was

[140] Interview Applicant's solicitors Telstra, 11.

[141] ibid 12–13.

[142] ibid 16.

[143] Susannah Moran, 'Telstra offers 5c to settle class action', *The Australian* (13 November 2007) 3.

[144] Telstra MR 296/2007 (n 81) 1 ('Telstra expected to win the case, but we could not guarantee we would recover our costs, meaning that the small settlement offer put to us by our opponents represented the best outcome for our shareholders, Mr Irving said.').

[145] Interview Applicants' solicitors Multiplex, 6–7.

[146] Interview Centro funder, 7.

[147] Maurice Blackburn Centro MR May 2012 (n 74); Slater & Gordon Centro MR May 2012 (n 74); Ben Butler, Leonie Wood and Georgia Wilkins, 'Centro $200m legal deal a record', *Sydney Morning Herald* (9 May 2012) 2.

[148] Interview Applicant's solicitor Leighton, 3–4.

claimed, suggesting that not all eligible shareholders participated.[149] In relation to Multiplex, the compensation fund was not fully claimed, but that may have been due to shareholders electing to pursue compensation through the class action. The class action was a closed class and therefore only permitted those shareholders who had entered into a litigation funding agreement to participate. This equated to 109 shareholders. In the Centro shareholder class action, two closed class actions comprised of 955 group members recovered $150 million, while a third open class action, which included 5,000 group members, recovered $50 million.[150] In the Leighton shareholder class action, the court recorded that after the class had been closed and group members had registered to participate in the settlement, there were 6,000 participating group members, of whom 2304 had entered into a litigation funding agreement and 4,032 had not.[151] The relative recoveries were not disclosed, but it was reported that the claims of the unfunded group members 'were of a relatively low value compared to those of the funded group members'.[152]

These figures suggest that the number of group members who will participate in a class action are higher when an open rather than a closed class is employed. However, Centro and Leighton suggest that the quantum increases to a far lesser degree. This is likely to be because the closed class usually targets investors with large shareholdings, such as institutional investors and superannuation funds. The additional group members who joined the open class in Centro or were unfunded group members in Leighton were probably retail investors with small shareholdings. The structure of the class action is important in facilitating the recovery of compensation, especially for investors with small shareholdings. However, the Telstra class action illustrates that even when an open class action is employed, group members may still not come forward to claim compensation. Some reasons for this were suggested in chapter three, namely confusion by group members as to what is required, or not being aware of the class action and the need to affirmatively claim.

The second concern in relation to incomplete recovery is that a respondent is unable to pay. In Telstra, Multiplex and Leighton, there were no concerns expressed about the ability of those corporations to meet a compensation payout. However, in the Centro shareholder class action, there was considerable concern about whether the corporate entities would remain as going concerns. One applicant unsuccessfully sought access to the insurance policies to determine if Centro would be able to pay the damages sought in the class action.[153] The solvency of Centro was also a major concern for the litigation funder as it impacted the capacity of the respondents to pay compensation.[154] It subsequently transpired that Centro Properties Ltd (part of CNP) was only able to contribute $10 million as a result of the creditors' scheme of arrangement and insurance was responsible for $38 million of the settlement. The outcome in Centro demonstrates that solvency of respondents is clearly necessary for compensation to be recovered, or in the alternative there is adequate insurance coverage. While insurance may undermine deterrence, it facilitates compensation. Where insolvency or inadequate insurance exists, it is unlikely that full compensation will be possible.

[149] Interview Lawyer Participants Telstra/Multiplex/Centro.

[150] Slater & Gordon Centro MR May 2012 (n 74); Centro Retail Australia, 'Conditional Settlement of class actions' (ASX/Media Release, 10 May 2012) 1; Agnes King, 'Red faces, not red ink at PwC audit', *The Australian Financial Review* (14 May 2012) 56–57.

[151] *Inabu Pty Ltd v Leighton Holdings Ltd (No 2)* [2014] FCA 911, [2], [19], [39]–[45] (Jacobson J).

[152] ibid [26].

[153] *Kirby v Centro Properties Ltd* [2009] FCA 695, [43] (Ryan J) (denying an application for access to insurance policies); Maurice Dunlevy, 'Centro class action zeroes in on insurance', *The Australian* (6 March 2009) 19.

[154] Interview Centro funder, 1.

iii. Transaction Costs

The costs incurred in the class actions are set out in Table 4.4 in chapter four. A comparison of those costs to the compensation recovered in set out in Table 5.1 below. The class action can reduce the legal costs per group member due to the sharing of costs and economies of scale compared to the costs that would be incurred if litigation in a superior court were pursued alone. However, the shareholder class action can also increase cost because of the need to address not just the substantive law but the additional complexities created through aggregating claims to be pursued by a representative party, including notices advising of the right to opt out and approval of a settlement by the court.[155] Class actions can also be subject to greater interlocutory disputation due to the high stakes nature of the dispute so that greater cost ensues.[156] There is also the concern of liability for an adverse costs order against which a litigation funder provides protection.

Table 5.1 Transaction costs and recovery

	Gross Recovery	**Legal fees (% of gross recovery)**	**Funder's Fees (% of gross recovery and % of gross recovery less legal fees)**	**Net Recovery (% of total recovery)**
Telstra	$5m	$1.25m (25%)	None	$3.75m (75%)
Multiplex	$110m	$11m (10%)	$35m (32% and 35%)	$64m (58%)
Centro	$200m	$31.16m (15.5%)	$49.8m (25% and 29.5%)	$119.04 (59.5%)
Leighton	$69.45m	$4.17m (6%)	$16.32m (23.5% or 25%)	$48.96m (70.5%)

Table 5.1 demonstrates that transaction costs clearly reduce the compensation actually received by group members. In the case studies where substantial recoveries were achieved (Multiplex, Centro and Leighton), it can be seen that legal fees take up between six per cent and 16 per cent of the recovery, while funder's fees consume between 25 per cent and 35 per cent of the recovery. If no transaction costs were incurred then the compensation received by group members would be significantly higher.

The impact of transaction costs on the compensation received by shareholders was a concern for class action lawyers. A solicitor for the applicant in a Centro class action stated:

> [W]e obviously try to make sure that as much money goes back into the hands of investors on a net basis. But litigation funding does make that challenging. … when you're looking at a *potential* class action, we're very particular about making sure that you only commence one if you believe that it's sufficiently large that after all of the transaction costs, including litigation funding commission, there is going to be sizable net return to investors. We're very mindful of the fact that there are criticisms out there in the legal community and the business community that this is fundamentally an industry that's intended to benefit the transactors rather than the supposed people who have suffered harm.[157]

Similarly, the solicitor for the applicant in the Leighton class action stated that class action lawyers were concerned about the return to the shareholders versus the lawyers' fees and that the lawyers

[155] Federal Court of Australia Act 1976 (Cth), ss 33J, 33V, 33X.

[156] *Mercedes Holdings Pty Ltd v Waters (No 5)* [2011] FCA 1428, [78] (Perram J) (describing interlocutory disputes as 'a long and drawn out procedural Stalingrad in which no quarter will be given'). See also *Bright v Femcare Ltd* (2002) 195 ALR 574, 607–608 [160] (Finkelstein J).

[157] Interview Applicant's solicitor Centro, 4–5 (emphasis in original).

needed to advise the claimants about whether to pursue a class action within the system of litigation that exists so that there is 'adequate compensation to the applicant and group members relative to what it's going to cost to pursue it'.[158] Equally, lawyers and funders openly acknowledge that class actions are brought for the purpose of them making a fee or profit, in addition to a recovery for the shareholders.[159]

ASIC interviewees, while not wanting to be critical of class action lawyers or funders, were conscious of two key differences between an ASIC action and a funded class action: ASIC did not seek to recover its costs from the people it sought compensation for, nor did it take a portion of their recovery.[160] As a result, while there are still transaction costs, they were borne by the taxpayer rather than the specific people who had suffered loss.[161] However, other groups have been more critical of the above transaction costs, including the Australian Institute of Company Directors, who identify 'the big winners from shareholder class actions [as] litigation funders, class action lawyers and other experts and intermediaries rather than plaintiff shareholders.[162] Similar sentiments have been expressed by new plaintiff's law firms entering the class actions practice area.[163]

While class actions can facilitate claims for compensation, they do so at greater cost than other mechanisms, such as ASIC actions.[164] Large transaction costs can undermine the goal of compensation as the harmed investor does not receive the compensation they are entitled to. The need for class actions to reduce transaction costs so as to improve the amount of compensation paid to group members and the need to reconsider ASIC's approach compensation are discussed in chapter six.

iv. Circularity Problem

As explained in chapter three, the circularity or 'pocket-shifting' problem describes the situation where shareholders who traded in a company's securities based on flawed disclosure and suffered loss, are paid compensation by the shareholders of the same company who did not trade. In certain situations, namely for diversified shareholders over the long term, shareholders are just as likely to have traded, or not, and are effectively paying themselves, but with large transaction costs. As a result, the US literature has concluded that shareholder class actions perform poorly in relation to compensation.[165]

However, the application of the theory may be challenged in certain circumstances, namely: (1) where directors or third parties such as auditors pay for the contravention; or (2) the recipients of the compensation are retail investors who are not diversified. In either of those situations the payment of compensation is not circular.

[158] Interview Applicant's solicitor Leighton, 3.

[159] Interview Applicants' solicitors Multiplex, 1; Interview Centro funder, 1.

[160] Interview ASIC Executive Centro, 8; Interview ASIC Executive Leighton, 19.

[161] Since the ASIC Supervisory Cost Recovery Levy Act 2017 (Cth) came into effect the transaction costs from ASIC enforcement are to be borne by industry. See ch 7.

[162] Chris Merritt, 'Securities class actions just blackmail suits', *The Australian* (6 June 2014) 33.

[163] Chris Merritt, 'Class action 'mates' too powerful', *The Australian* (31 October 2014) 27.

[164] Michael Legg, 'A Comparison of Regulatory Enforcement, Class Actions and Alternative Dispute Resolution in Compensating Financial Consumers' (2016) 38 *Sydney Law Review* 311, 334.

[165] John Coffee, 'Reforming the Securities Class Action: An Essay on Deterrence and Its Implementation' (2006) 106 *Columbia Law Review* 1534, 1545; Amanda Rose, 'Reforming Securities Litigation Reform: Restructuring the Relationship Between Public and Private Enforcement of Rule 10B-5' (2008) 108 *Columbia Law Review* 1301, 1314.

In all instances in the case studies where compensation was paid, only Multiplex and Centro involved payments by directors or third parties. In Multiplex, as discussed above in relation to direct sanctions, the former owners, the Roberts family, paid a $50 million indemnity that may have partially financed the compensation paid under the enforceable undertaking or class action. In Centro, the directors, albeit through insurance, and the auditor were significant contributors to the class action settlement. In those circumstances, the shareholders are not the source of the compensation funds and so do not pay themselves.

In those case studies where compensation was obtained, retail investors participated, albeit to different degrees. The Telstra, Centro and Leighton class actions contained significant numbers of retail investors. Telstra, having been recently privatised through the sale of shares to the public, included about 29,000 group members, many of whom were 'mum and dad shareholders'.[166] In the Centro case study, a separate class action was commenced with the specific goal of including retail investors.[167] It was reported to comprise 5,000 group members.[168] Leighton also included a large number of retail investors, but precise figures were not available. Multiplex, in contrast, was primarily institutional investors. The participation of retail investors in Australian class actions appears to be common practice.[169] Although often numerous, they account for a much smaller dollar value of the class action, as explained above in relation to incomplete recovery. Nonetheless, if retail investors are not diversified investors, then they do recover compensation which is not offset by participation in the payment of compensation.

IV. Application of the Analytical Framework – Regulatory Process

The regulatory process framework looks at ASIC and the class action from the perspective that they are both pursuing enforcement, namely public and private enforcement, in the same area of securities regulation, the continuous disclosure regime. ASIC and the class action are examined through the lens of the case studies in relation to four values that are equated with a legitimate regulatory process: legislative authority; the public interest; accountability; and efficiency.

A. Legislative Authority

Both ASIC and private individuals are authorised to enforce the continuous disclosure and misleading conduct laws. However, ASIC's authority may be seen as broad, compared to the narrower authority of the private class action.

As set out in chapter two, ASIC's legislative authority gives rise to a broad range of objectives: punishment; improving compliance; protecting the public; compensation for investors; and deterrence. In relation to continuous disclosure, ASIC seeks to achieve both market integrity and investor protection. ASIC also has several tools with which to achieve those objectives, which are generally organised by reference to the Responsive Regulation enforcement pyramid, and range from measures such as warnings, enforceable undertakings and infringement notices, to civil proceedings and criminal proceedings.

[166] Interview Applicant's solicitors Telstra, 4.

[167] Interview Applicant's solicitor Centro, 1.

[168] Slater & Gordon Centro MR May 2012 (n 74).

[169] See, eg, *Earglow Pty Ltd v Newcrest Mining Ltd* (2015) 230 FCR 469, 485–87 [68]–[78] (Beach J); *Impiombato v BHP Group Limited (No 2)* [2020] FCA 1720, [43] (Moshinsky J).

The range of objectives and enforcement tools means ASIC has significant discretion as to the way in which it proceeds. The four case studies illustrate this as different approaches were taken in each of the case studies: Telstra involved a warning, Multiplex involved an enforceable undertaking, Centro involved civil penalty proceedings against the directors and an enforceable undertaking for the auditor, while for Leighton an enforceable undertaking and infringement notices were combined.

In contrast, a private individual or individuals that are grouped together in a class action have a more limited statutory authority and, as a result, a more limited set of objectives and narrower set of tools, namely the civil litigation remedies of compensation and injunctions. In each case study, the civil litigation process was employed to obtain compensation. However, as discussed above, while compensation is the main goal of a class action, it is also recognised that a class action has an incidental deterrent effect.

Chapter three explained at a theoretical level why public and private enforcement are adopted and how they may interact. The rest of this chapter utilises the case studies to explore ASIC and the class actions functioning in the regulatory process with a focus on their interactions. The ramifications of this co-existence are explored in chapter six.

B. The Public Interest

As explained in chapter three, a government regulator is expected to act in the public interest, that is, for the community as a whole, not just for a particular individual or group of individuals. This was acknowledged by all of the ASIC interviewees.[170] In relation to continuous disclosure, determining what action is required to promote the public interest was said to involve consideration of a number of factors: the egregiousness of the conduct; the market impact or harm; whether ASIC action will provide a timely message to the market; the level of cooperation and contrition from the entity alleged to have contravened the law; the available evidence; and ASIC's resources.[171] In summary, ASIC considers the public interest in terms of how it can advance the purpose of the continuous disclosure regime, namely a fully informed market and investor protection, with the resources provided to it. The issue of cost and efficiency is discussed separately below.

Class actions involve the pursuit of private interests being the interests of the group members. Indeed, as described in chapter two, the class actions regime in Part IVA of the Federal Court of Australia Act 1976 (Cth) and related jurisprudence focus on the pursuit and protection of group member interests. The class action lawyers interviewed for the case studies reported that the instructions from the applicant and group members were to recover compensation.[172] The lawyers advised on whether pursuing an action was worthwhile, with worth being determined by the monetary recovery that could be achieved in the context of the litigation system and its costs.[173] Factors to be considered are the solvency of the respondent and other sources of compensation, such as insurance policies.[174] The aim was to pursue the applicants' and group members' personal

[170] Interview ASIC Executive Telstra/Multiplex; Interview ASIC Executive Centro, 12; Interview ASIC Executive Leighton, 11. See also Evidence to Joint Committee on Corporations and Financial Services, Parliament of Australia, Canberra, 11 March 2011, 33 (Mr Tony D'Aloisio, ASIC Chairman) (D'Aloisio Evidence to Parliamentary Joint Committee').

[171] Interview ASIC Executive Leighton, 1–4 (referring to ASIC, 'Information Sheet 151 – ASIC's approach to enforcement' (September 2013) ('ASIC Information Sheet 151')).

[172] Interview Applicant's solicitor Centro, 2–3; Interview Applicant's solicitor Leighton, 1.

[173] Interview Applicant's solicitor Centro, 4–5; Interview Applicant's solicitor Leighton, 3.

[174] Interview Applicant's solicitor Leighton, 4.

causes of action and, as a consequence, it is private interests that are the moving force behind class actions. However, when class actions are viewed as a form of private enforcement, the public interest becomes relevant. This then raises for discussion how ASIC and the class action interact in the pursuit of the public interest.

i. The Class Actions Impact on ASIC and the Public Interest

The ASIC interviewees recognised that the prospect or commencement of a class action may implicate how the public interest should be pursued. The former ASIC senior executive involved in Centro stated that while class actions are generally about money, 'the subject matter of the class actions can be argued to deal with public interest considerations'.[175] Other ASIC interviewees accepted that the class action may be relevant to the enforcement action that ASIC would take, but not whether an investigation should be undertaken. One former ASIC senior executive explained that if an investigation into possible misconduct was in the public interest then the possibility or existence of a class action would not prevent ASIC from investigating.[176] Equally, if ASIC was of the view that a particular type of enforcement action should be taken to promote the public interest, such as an enforceable undertaking, because it could achieve the timely correction of a practice in the market, ASIC would take that action.[177] However, in relation to the decision whether ASIC should seek compensation, the ASIC senior executive involved in the Leighton case study opined that:

> We will only assert peoples' private rights where there's a real public interest to do so and there's a lot of factors that will weigh for and against that. And there'll often be well no-one else is able to bring this claim and us bringing this compensatory claim will have a massive regulatory impact or send a targeted message then we might, but … if there's … a class action, we won't be taking compensation action.[178]

If seeking compensation is in the public interest and a class action will perform that role, then the class action is seen by some within ASIC and amongst class action lawyers as relieving ASIC from seeking compensation.[179]

The case studies also suggest that ASIC's consideration of how to factor in the advent of the class action has developed over time. In the early case studies – Telstra and Multiplex – the shareholder class action was only beginning to arise and was not given significant attention by ASIC as it was a novel and uncertain development.[180] Moreover, ASIC officers would have had little experience with how a class action may impact on ASIC and its objectives. In the latter case studies – Centro and Leighton – the shareholder class action was much more established and ASIC could more readily factor in the commencement of private proceedings.

While the class action may be able to pursue compensation for both private and public interests, the Multiplex case study demonstrates how the presence of a class action may impact what approach ASIC takes to further the public interest. In Multiplex, as explained above in relation to compensation, ASIC's original preference for an agreed civil penalty gave way to an enforceable undertaking because of the company's concerns about a class action. The outcome

[175] Interview ASIC Executive Centro, 10.
[176] Interview ASIC Executive Telstra/Multiplex.
[177] ibid; Interview ASIC Executive Leighton, 6–7.
[178] Interview ASIC Executive Leighton, 11.
[179] See, eg, Interview Applicants' solicitors Multiplex, 13; Interview ASIC Executive Centro, 3, 8, 13; Interview ASIC Executive Leighton, 11, 16.
[180] Interview ASIC Executive Telstra/Multiplex.

appears to have been negotiated with both ASIC and Multiplex trading off various objectives in reaching the enforceable undertaking with requirements for governance changes and a compensation scheme. This case study may be seen as illustrating ASIC foregoing the outcome initially thought by it to be in the public interest because the possibility of a class action removed a civil penalty settlement as an option. The company was not prepared to make the necessary admissions because it would have assisted the class action in obtaining compensation. ASIC could have commenced a civil penalty proceeding and gone to trial if it was of the view that this was what the public interest required. However, ASIC did not choose litigation and instead opted for the lower-order negotiated outcome offered by an enforceable undertaking. This course of action may be supported as being in the public interest as it obtained governance changes and a modicum of compensation while reducing cost and delay. Moreover, the courts have recognised that regulatory settlements can be in the public interest.[181] Equally, a regulator that seeks negotiated outcomes may be criticised for failing to enforce the law for the benefit of the public, which in turn may undermine deterrence through reduced sanctions. The Multiplex case study may illustrate ASIC being too willing to alter its view of what the public interest required so as to accommodate Multiplex's concern about a class action. Regardless of whether ASIC is viewed as a canny negotiator or as giving up at the first sign of push-back, the looming class action clearly played a role in how the public interest was actuated through a particular enforcement response.

More generally, a former ASIC senior executive was adamant that the prospect of a class action impacted how regulated entities dealt with ASIC: 'they put a lot of effort into making sure that the longer term prospects of such an action succeeding are not enhanced by anything that happens as part of the ASIC investigation or the ASIC action'.[182] The former senior Telstra executive agreed and pointed out the difficulty between balancing cooperation with ASIC, with whom a company is likely to have ongoing dealings, but not wanting to trigger or assist a class action.[183] However, other interviewees took the position that cooperation with ASIC is paramount and regulated entities have to respond appropriately to ASIC inquiries or notices.[184] Indeed, proactive engagement with ASIC may be the best approach to try and 'cauterize the ASIC process' and keep it within the strictest limits possible.[185]

The Multiplex case study also provides an example of a direct conflict between ASIC and the class action. ASIC wanted to protect the identity of whistleblowers because it is in the public interest to encourage such people to come forward and report potential misconduct to the regulator.[186] To that end ASIC deployed public interest immunity to prevent access to ASIC documents, as explained in chapter four, section IV.B.ii. The lawyers bringing the class action, in comparison, wanted the documentation to be able to assist in the proof of the applicant's case. The aim was to lessen the cost and improve the prospects of the private interests involved in the class action. However, construing these as only involving private interests is to disregard the legislative provisions that allow ASIC to release transcripts of oral examinations and related books to a person's lawyer if the lawyer satisfies ASIC that the person is conducting or contemplating a proceeding in respect of a matter to which the examination related.[187] As Heerey J stated

[181] See, eg, *Commonwealth of Australia v Director, Fair Work Building Industry Inspectorate* (2015) 258 CLR 482, 523 [108]–[109] (Keane J).

[182] Interview ASIC Executive Centro, 10. See also Interview ASIC Executive Leighton, 13–15 (who shared this view).

[183] Interview Telstra Executive, 12.

[184] Interview Centro Executive, 11; Interview Multiplex solicitor, 14.

[185] Interview Lawyer Participants Telstra/Multiplex/Centro.

[186] *ASIC v P Dawson Nominees Pty Ltd* (2008) 169 FCR 227, 237 [48]–[50] (Heerey, Moore and Tracey JJ).

[187] Australian Securities and Investments Commission Act 2001 (Cth), s 25(1).

in *Boys v Australian Securities Commission*: 'The whole point of s 25(1) is to enable the fruits of [ASIC's] compulsory examination to be made available for use in civil litigation'.[188] The private interests in the class action also have a public interest dimension. Access to ASIC documents can promote 'the fair and efficient disposition of civil disputes by the courts'.[189]

ii. ASIC's Impact on the Class Action

While much of the literature reviewed in chapter three focused on how a class action can help or hinder a regulator's ability to pursue actions it saw as being in the public interest, the case studies also raised the opposite effect. ASIC's actions can assist or hinder the proponents of class actions in pursuing compensation. The pursuit of compensation may be seen as pursuing a private interest, but also as promoting the public interest by requiring wrongdoers to compensate those who are harmed by the wrongdoing.

A successful ASIC action is generally seen as strengthening or at least supporting a class action. In relation to Centro, the litigation funder IMF advised clients that ASIC's success in its civil penalty proceedings 'provided important support' to the class action because:

- there is a substantial overlap between allegations and claims made in the ASIC proceedings and some of those made in the class actions;
- ASIC was able to prove a number of allegations which are the same, or very similar, to those made in the class actions;
- the class action claimants will be able to rely on facts referred to in the declarations now made by the Court and will not have to prove those facts again; and
- the ASIC proceedings allowed the claimants' lawyers to observe Centro's and PwC's witnesses under cross-examination and to listen to the arguments the directors and managers used in their attempt to defend ASIC's charges.[190]

IMF also observed:

> The Centro case is a powerful demonstration of the benefits which can arise for the effective enforcement of Australia's securities law when the public regulator, ASIC, chooses to prosecute breaches of those laws, while private class action lawyers and funders combine to allow victims of the breaches to sue for compensation.[191]

A similar sentiment was expressed by then ASIC Chairman Greg Medcraft, who saw class actions as being able to help the regulator by creating an alternative way for investors to recover losses.[192] Similarly, in relation to Leighton, ASIC's action was seen as strengthening the class action.[193] Even in Telstra where ASIC's enforcement action was a warning, the solicitors for the applicant in the class action saw that step as giving them confidence that the class action was 'arguing along the right lines'.[194]

[188] *Boys v Australian Securities Commission* (1998) 80 FCR 403, 420.

[189] *ASIC v P Dawson Nominees Pty Ltd* (2008) 169 FCR 227, 234 [32] (Heerey, Moore and Tracey JJ).

[190] IMF (Australia) Ltd, 'ASIC Centro Win Bolsters Class Actions' (Newsletter, 24 May 2013). See also Alex Boxsell and Samantha Bowers, 'Ruling boosts class actions', *The Australian Financial Review* (1 July 2011) 56.

[191] ibid.

[192] Hannah Low, 'ASIC a class act in Centro case', *The Australian Financial Review* (30 June 2011) 10.

[193] Ben Butler and Adele Ferguson, 'Disclosure rules need more bite – ASIC', *The Sydney Morning Herald* (19 March 2012) 1; Lisa MacNamara, 'Leighton's ASIC penalty more fuel for class action', *The Australian* (20 March 2012) 23; Interview Applicant's solicitor Leighton, 10 (ASIC's action provided 'a little sense of confidence that there's wrongdoing').

[194] Interview Applicant's solicitors Telstra, 6.

Despite these views, there was also a general feeling among interviewees who acted for class action applicants that ASIC was not co-operative in regard to class actions.[195] While this could impact costs and efficiency (discussed below) there were also two examples, including Multiplex, where ASIC was seen as potentially harming the pursuit of compensation by the class action. In Multiplex, as explained above, ASIC did not pursue a civil penalty, which meant there were no findings of liability that could be relied on in the class action. However, the compensation fund was also seen as harming investors because to recover, the investor needed to sign a release which prevented participation in the class action. This then prevented them from recovering on a more favourable basis or as part of the extended time period being pursued in the class action, should the class action be successful.[196]

Concerns were also raised in relation to Leighton and what was described by the lawyer for the applicant in the class action as a 'paperless process' in relation to ASIC's investigation.[197] The class action lawyers were under the impression that there had been no s 19 examinations of Leighton's personnel. The ASIC senior executive involved in Leighton explained that s 19 examinations may not be conducted if statements were provided voluntarily but that the enforcement process is not paperless.[198] This suggests that Leighton cooperated with ASIC to try to limit or expedite the ASIC process and/or to minimise the evidence that ASIC collected which could be used by class action proponents. Either way, when ASIC decides to accept cooperation, it means that material that might otherwise be available for use in a class action through s 25 or a subpoena, does not exist. Of course, ASIC's decision may be justified by not just saving time and cost per se, but in accordance with Responsive Regulation and the idea that ASIC can leverage compliance (which is cheap) from the regulated entity through making it want to avoid the more serious sanctions in the upper level of the enforcement pyramid (which are expensive). Here it might be argued that those more serious sanctions are not just civil penalties, but compensation payments extracted by the class action.

For completeness it should be noted that Leighton and the class action applicant agreed on a document discovery regime so as to facilitate a mediation.[199] As a result, some information was shared. The mediation occurred within five months of commencement and a settlement was reached within seven months of commencement.[200] The voluntary provision of discovery and such a quick settlement suggests that Leighton was not only seeking to bring the ASIC action to an end quickly, but also the class action.

C. Accountability

As one former ASIC executive put it:

> ASIC is highly accountable, …, it's been attending senate hearings, and being accountable for how it spends its money, and having to abide by and follow the charter in the ASIC Act, and so on. And all of that is in contrast to a private class action. I think the accountability is lower in a private action.

[195] ibid 7; Interview Applicants' solicitors Multiplex, 8.
[196] Interview Applicants' solicitors Multiplex, 9.
[197] Interview Applicant's solicitor Leighton, 10–11.
[198] Interview ASIC Executive Leighton, 15.
[199] Interview Applicant's solicitor Leighton, 11.
[200] Michael Legg, 'The Leighton class action settlement: managing a need for speed' (2015) 2 *Australian Alternative Dispute Resolution Bulletin* 19.

> It obviously picks up things like an action having merit, and other things around ethical obligations of lawyers and so on. It's a different species of accountability, but nowhere near as high as ASIC would have.[201]

Another ASIC executive described the requirements for a class action to be commenced and an ASIC action as 'two massively different things'.[202] The mechanisms for ensuring accountability of ASIC are set out in chapter three, section IV.D.ii. The oversight of ASIC is borne out by the case studies. In the Telstra case study, ASIC was questioned at Senate Estimates at length over why a warning was used rather than an infringement notice.[203] In relation to Centro, ASIC reported to the Senate Estimates Committee on the ramification of the Federal Court's decision in relation to the financial literacy expected of directors and reassured the Committee that the decision 'would be unlikely to lead to a flight of directors'.[204] The Centro proceedings were also considered in the 2013–14 inquiry into ASIC's performance, as part of a more general review of ASIC's approach to enforcement.[205] Each of the case studies was also the subject of ASIC reporting and media coverage as demonstrated by the material cited above.[206] The enforceable undertakings are publicly available and listed on an ASIC register. More generally, the Australian National Audit Office conducted a performance audit into ASIC's administration of enforceable undertakings.[207]

In contrast, the class action has no public reporting obligations. Rather, as explained in chapter three section IV.D.iii, the class action mechanisms include requirements to protect or empower group members. Further, the lawyer-client or group member relationship gives rise to various obligations, mainly aimed at protecting the group member. However, the lawyer also has an overriding obligation to the court. There is also a litigation funder-client relationship which creates various obligations. More broadly, there is also to some degree the disciplining effect of the market; group members must be given an opportunity to opt out of a class action, which they may exercise if they have sufficient information to determine that it is not in their interests. However, failure to exercise the opt out right will mean a group member remains part of the class action. Litigation funding agreements may also discourage a group member from choosing to opt out.[208] There are therefore obstacles to the disciplining effect of the market.

The role of the class action lawyer was most clearly explained by the solicitor for the applicant in the Centro class action, who stated:

> We're accountable to the group, and to our clients. And we're accountable to the Court throughout the proceeding and, particularly at the point of settlement approval. There's … also that ultimate accountability of whether clients or group members are happy with the results that we produce, and understand why.[209]

[201] Interview ASIC Executive Centro, 12.

[202] Interview ASIC Executive Leighton, 5.

[203] Evidence to Senate Economics Legislation Committee – Estimates, Parliament of Australia, Canberra (16 February 2006) 2–4 (Mr Jeffrey Lucy, ASIC Chairman); Cooper Evidence to Senate Committee (n 70) 43–48.

[204] Medcraft Evidence to Senate Committee (n 48) 12; Parliamentary Joint Committee on Corporations and Financial Services, 'Statutory oversight of the Australian Securities and Investments Commission' (March 2012) [3.28].

[205] Senate Economics References Committee, 'Performance of the Australian Securities and Investments Commission' (June 2014) 195, 499.

[206] See, eg, ASIC, 'ASIC warns Telstra on Disclosure Procedures' (Media Release, 05-391, 14 December 2005) 1; ASIC Multiplex MR 16-443 (n 7); ASIC, 'Leighton Holdings complies with three ASIC infringement notices for alleged continuous disclosure breaches and ASIC accepts compliance enforceable undertaking' (Media Release 12-53MR, 18 March 2012).

[207] Australian National Audit Office, 'Administration of Enforceable Undertakings' (2 June 2015).

[208] *Multiplex Funds Management Limited v P Dawson Nominees Pty Limited* (2007) 164 FCR 275, 295 [147]–[149] (Jacobson J) (group member liable to pay the funder its fee even if the group member opted out of the class action).

[209] Interview Applicant's solicitor Centro, 19.

Another class actions lawyer explained that 'We care very significantly about what [compensation] goes to our clients'.[210] A key theme was that the class action lawyers are 'agents rather than principals' and are 'creatures of instructions'.[211] Consequently, the lawyer pursues compensation for clients and not broader public policy goals.[212] However, as stated above, there are public policy implications such as deterrence, even if an indirect effect.

An important form of accountability in relation to ASIC enforcement is the procedures in place for the commencement and conduct of litigation, or whether another form of enforcement should be employed. The accountability mechanisms for ASIC and class actions are very different in relation to litigation. For ASIC, the decision to commence litigation includes the need for reasonable prospects of success and consideration of cost. However, as explained by ASIC's former chairman, Tony D'Aloisio, ASIC must also consider additional factors: the significance of wrongdoing, balancing priorities due to limited resources, as well as 'is it in the public interest that you take that case on in that way?'[213] Commencement of litigation is seen by ASIC as 'a strategic decision'.[214] This follows from taking on litigation as being 'critical to deterrence activities and preserving market integrity'.[215]

These factors were also referred to by the ASIC senior executive involved in the Leighton enforcement action. In Leighton, ASIC did not commence litigation, but the considerations as to whether litigation was the correct option in a continuous disclosure case included the need to provide a timely message to the market, the level of cooperation and contrition from the entity alleged to have contravened the law, and ASIC's available resources. Consideration was also given to the available evidence and the evidence that could be obtained.[216]

The key issues for the commencement of a class action are prospects of success and the quantum that can be recovered, considering the cost to run the litigation.[217] Once a lawyer has the necessary instructions from the representative party and financing is in place, the proceedings can be commenced. In chapter three, it was observed that the lawyers and funders control the class action, including commencement, rather than the representative party or group members. This observation was borne out by comments of the lawyers in the Telstra, Multiplex and Centro class actions. The Telstra class action was undertaken to develop a new practice area for the law firm.[218] In Multiplex, the possibility of a class action arose due the lawyers' observations in relation to the share price and litigation funder interest.[219] In Centro, it was the lawyers who identified that losses were likely to be widespread amongst retail investors and that the first two class actions had excluded them, so that a third class action was needed.[220] Although the lawyers may be agents and accountable to the group, the class action is also driven by the lawyers' and funders' commercial interests.

[210] Interview Applicant's solicitor Leighton, 3.

[211] Interview Applicant's solicitor Centro, 1–2. See also Interview Applicant's solicitor Leighton, 1.

[212] Interview Applicant's solicitor Centro, 20.

[213] D'Aloisio Evidence to Parliamentary Joint Committee (n 170) 33. See also Parliamentary Joint Committee on Corporations and Financial Services, 'Statutory oversight of the Australian Securities and Investments Commission' (21 June 2010) [2.36] ('Parliamentary Joint Committee ASIC Oversight June 2010').

[214] Parliamentary Joint Committee ASIC Oversight June 2010 (n 213) [2.36].

[215] ibid.

[216] Interview ASIC Executive Leighton, 1, 2, 4.

[217] Interview Centro funder, 1; Interview Applicant's solicitor Leighton, 3. A number of lawyers set the bar higher and said that there needed to be serious misconduct and significant losses: Interview Applicants' solicitors Multiplex, 1; Interview Applicant's solicitor Centro, 8.

[218] Interview Applicant's solicitors Telstra, 1.

[219] Interview Applicants' solicitors Multiplex, 1–3.

[220] Interview Applicant's solicitor Centro, 1.

There is no express consideration of whether the litigation is otherwise desirable, such as whether it is in the public interest. The group members only need to consider their personal interests and the likely recovery compared to costs exposure, which may be non-existent if a funder is paying the legal fees and providing an indemnity against adverse costs orders. The lawyer and funder similarly consider recovery and costs, but also the fee they may earn.[221] The main discipline on commencement is financial, that is, the compensation that can be recovered and the risk of costs.

Accountability mechanisms also arise for class actions at the time of settlement. The court is concerned to ensure that the proposed settlement is undertaken in the interests of group members, as well as those of the applicant, and not just in the interests of the applicant and the respondent(s).[222] In the Multiplex class action settlement, the court stated that 'there is a need to ensure that the interests of class members are adequately looked after' and that 'it is the court that assumes responsibility for protecting the interests of the class members', although 'the court necessarily places considerable reliance on the parties' lawyers'.[223] The courts also consider if the legal fees and disbursements are reasonable, as occurred in each case study.[224] Litigation funding fees were not considered in the case studies, but this practice has subsequently changed.[225] These accountability mechanisms have been adopted because the group members' claims are resolved on the terms of the class action settlement, but they are not present before the court. While the court looks beyond the parties to the group members in considering fairness, it does not consider the public interest more generally.

For ASIC, court oversight also arises where a civil penalty action is settled as the finding of a contravention and determination of a penalty must be undertaken by a court.[226] In the case studies, this was not one of the outcomes.

The difference between ASIC and class actions in relation to not just accountability but public and private interest is also highlighted by the approach to unsuccessful litigation. For lawyers, litigation funders and group members, a lost class action is a failure. Group members receive no compensation. In the funded litigation situation, the funder loses their investment and is liable for any adverse costs order. For unfunded litigation, it is the lawyer who loses their investment and the representative party that is liable for any adverse costs order. Success and failure are measured by their ramifications on private interests. This risk of loss has been accepted as supporting settlement.[227] In relation to litigation by a regulator, the Parliamentary Joint Committee on Corporations and Financial Services has stated that it accepts that 'lost litigation is not the same thing as failed litigation' as ASIC may need to test and clarify the law through the courts.[228]

[221] Interview Centro funder, 1 (For a funder there is the need 'to recover sufficient damages, or achieve a settlement that's going to be commensurate with the risks, and the cost, and the time involved in running the case'.).

[222] *Taylor v Telstra Corporation Ltd* [2007] FCA 2008, [56] (Jacobson J); *Inabu Pty Ltd v Leighton Holdings Ltd (No 2)* [2014] FCA 911, [21] (Jacobson J).

[223] *P Dawson Nominees Pty Ltd v Brookfield Multiplex Limited (No 4)* [2010] FCA 1029, [4] (Finkelstein J).

[224] *Taylor v Telstra Corporation Ltd* [2007] FCA 2008, [72]–[74] (Jacobson J); *P Dawson Nominees Pty Ltd v Brookfield Multiplex Limited (No 4)* [2010] FCA 1029, [21] (Finkelstein J); *Kirby v Centro Properties Ltd (No 6)* [2012] FCA 650, [9] (Middleton J); *Inabu Pty Ltd v Leighton Holdings Ltd (No 2)* [2014] FCA 911, [32]–[34] (Jacobson J). The method for evaluating the reasonableness of costs has developed as discussed in ch 7, section III.A. i.

[225] See ch 7, section III.A.iii.

[226] *Commonwealth of Australia v Director, Fair Work Building Industry Inspectorate* (2015) 258 CLR 482, 507–508 [59]–[61] (French CJ, Kiefel, Bell, Nettle and Gordon JJ).

[227] *Taylor v Telstra Corporation Ltd* [2007] FCA 2008, [70] (Jacobson J); *P Dawson Nominees Pty Ltd v Brookfield Multiplex Limited (No 4)* [2010] FCA 1029, [15]–[17], [24] (Finkelstein J); *Kirby v Centro Properties Ltd (No 6)* [2012] FCA 650, [3]–[4], [12] (Middleton J); *Inabu Pty Ltd v Leighton Holdings Ltd (No 2)* [2014] FCA 911, [27]–[30] (Jacobson J).

[228] Parliamentary Joint Committee ASIC Oversight June 2010 (n 213) [2.37].

Clarifying the law for the regulator and the regulated entity, and possibly identifying the need for amendment, is part of a regulator's responsibility in dealing with the legislation that it administers. However, the Committee also 'strongly endorses the need for rigorous review of cases, particularly those that are likely to be expensive to litigate'.[229] ASIC is not held accountable by Parliament based on simply winning litigation, but rather on a more nuanced basis, which may be explained as being whether litigation is justified in the public interest. As the next section discusses, the assessment of the public interest and accountability also involve questions of cost and efficiency.

D. Efficiency

Cost in the regulatory process context is viewed from a different perspective than in relation to deterrence or compensation. From a deterrence perspective, costs can add to the level of deterrence and from a compensation perspective costs can reduce the amount of compensation received. Here, costs are the resources consumed to achieve an outcome and efficiency seeks to compare the resources consumed with the outcome achieved. From a regulatory process perspective, the concern is to achieve the outcome at the least cost.[230] This entails assessing ASIC's regulatory enforcement outcomes and the class action outcomes by considering the cost to achieve them.

i. ASIC

As explained in Chapter three, ASIC is required to ensure the proper use of Commonwealth resources. To understand how those resources are utilised, it is necessary to first consider what resources are available and what outcomes can be achieved. ASIC's enforcement budget for market integrity, which includes continuous disclosure but also other matters such as insider trading, was $1.1 million for external expenditure in 2016.[231] This did not include spending on ASIC employees. This did not include the Enforcement Special Account, which provides funding to investigate and/or bring legal or administrative proceedings in relation to suspected breaches of the law that are of 'significant public interest'.[232] If ASIC has a very large piece of litigation that meets the significant public interest test, it can be funded separately. The significance of the budget is explained by the ASIC executive officer involved in Leighton, who stated, 'there's only so many bullets I've got in a gun in a particular year and I've got to try and distribute them as far as possible'.[233]

The available budget and the cost of pursuing particular enforcement actions also need to be weighed against available outcomes. The caps on direct sanctions from monetary fines for corporations for civil penalties and infringement notices, namely $1 million and $100,000 respectively (as at 31 December 2017),[234] when combined with the need to ensure efficient use of resources,

[229] ibid [2.38].

[230] See ch 3, section IV.E.i.

[231] Interview ASIC Executive Leighton, 12–13.

[232] Public Governance, Performance and Accountability Act 2013 (Cth). s 78; 'PGPA Act Determination (Enforcement Special Account 2016) – Establishment' (23 August 2016).

[233] Interview ASIC Executive Leighton, 1. See also Interview ASIC Executive Centro, 4 ('there is an actual cost to running the action, and also there's an opportunity cost' so that using resources on one enforcement action means that they cannot be used on another).

[234] See ch 2, section II.D. The quantum of the available civil penalties has since increased, as discussed in ch 7.

can create an incentive structure that favours quicker and cheaper enforcement tools. This is also reflected in ASIC's information sheet on enforcement where in assessing the 'expected level of public benefit' as part of determining what remedy to take, it is stated that ASIC considers the 'length and expense of a contested hearing and the remedies available compared with other remedies that may be available more quickly (for example, improved compliance under an enforceable undertaking)'.[235]

From the case studies, the cost of ASIC enforcement action was only available for Leighton, where the infringement notices and enforceable undertaking were estimated to cost ASIC $94,000 (chapter four, Table 4.4). However, the ASIC executive officer involved in Leighton was able to provide an indication as to what other enforcement actions may cost as this was necessary to be able to evaluate regulatory options. The ASIC executive officer explained that for civil penalty litigation that was dealt with very efficiently and settled, the cost would be about $2 million. In contrast, the Fortescue case, which was a continuous disclosure and misleading conduct case that involved contested litigation in the Federal Court, the Full Court of the Federal Court, and the High Court of Australia, with ASIC ultimately unsuccessful, the cost was about $20 million, with about half of that being to pay the respondent's legal costs.[236] Using these figures to extrapolate the costs in the other case studies, it is likely that the Centro civil penalty proceeding would have cost more than $2 million but less than $10 million. However, in Centro, the court ordered the defendants to pay ASIC's costs of the action as ASIC was successful.[237] The Multiplex enforceable undertaking probably cost more than Leighton, as the time to reach an outcome was more than double that involved in Leighton (see chapter four, Table 4.5) so an estimate of $200,000 to $500,000 may be made. The Telstra warning was delivered within four months of the investigation commencing (see chapter four, Table 4.5) so that it probably cost the same or less than Leighton.

Cost-effectiveness or efficiency requires that the costs be compared with outcomes, financial and otherwise. As discussed above in relation to the effectiveness and limitations of deterrence, ASIC regarded the regulatory outcomes in all case studies as effective. In contrast, the media (and at times the class action law firms) were critical of ASIC not seeking higher penalties which would have required criminal or civil penalty litigation.[238]

In the four case studies, ASIC took court action only in Centro. ASIC successfully proved contraventions and recovered its costs, but the penalties were minor. From a financial perspective, ASIC effectively broke even, but as explained in relation to deterrence, a number of other outcomes were achieved including specific and general deterrence. In contrast, in Leighton, ASIC saw the outcomes as an effective and efficient use of its resources as it yielded not just $300,000 in fines for $94,000 in costs, but also educated and deterred both Leighton and the market more generally.[239] However, as discussed above in relation to deterrence and perceptions, Leighton explained the outcome as a pragmatic response to save costs as no liability had been admitted. The Centro directors had no such course of action open to them. The court, after a trial in which the directors were able to adduce evidence and argument as to why they had not broken the law, made declarations of contravention. ASIC's expenditure on litigation may be seen as money well

[235] ASIC Information Sheet 151 (n 171) 8.

[236] Interview ASIC Executive Leighton, 11–12. See also Suzanne Le Mire, 'Low penalties, high costs: ASIC needs legislative reform', *The Conversation* (20 February 2014) (reporting that the Fortescue case had cost ASIC $30 million).

[237] ASIC, 'Centro civil penalty proceedings' (Media Release, 11-188, 31 August 2011) 1.

[238] See, eg, Butler (n 76); Adele Ferguson, 'Wrong signal to let Leighton off lightly', *The Sydney Morning Herald* (19 March 2012) 5.

[239] Interview ASIC Executive Leighton, 4, 6.

spent because the directors could not deny their liability, or claim that any settlement/payment was simply a rational cost-benefit analysis. A court decision has value beyond any penalty amount.

For Multiplex, assuming the high end of costs for ASIC, the expenditure of $500,000 resulted in early payment of an indemnity from the former owners of $50 million, corporate governance changes and a $32 million compensation fund. Although ASIC was out of pocket, it achieved a very efficient outcome for the shareholders in terms of compensation and improving the governance of their company. In relation to Telstra, ASIC explained its approach to the Senate's Economics Legislation Committee where the factors in play included 'whether it was a worthwhile use of our budget funds in going through a full litigation process with a major company over relatively minor breaches'.[240] Telstra had made it clear that it would not pay an infringement notice. This left ASIC with the option of either civil penalty litigation or the warning that it used. Based on the cost estimates above, the litigation option would have put at risk multiple millions of dollars. Indeed, ASIC's Deputy Chairman at the time stated, 'We may have spent millions of dollars and lost'.[241]

Infringement notices and enforceable undertakings can be justified on the basis that they allow for contraventions to be acted upon in a timely manner.[242] However, this does not always occur in practice. As shown in Table 4.5 in chapter four, Leighton took nine months, but Multiplex took 23 months. They are also relatively cheap, and utilise less of the budget than the significantly more expensive civil penalty proceedings. There is also an ability to avoid the litigation risk associated with a civil penalty, a failure to prove a contravention to the necessary standard, which due to *Briginshaw v Briginshaw* is higher than the civil standard that applies in civil litigation,[243] and the liability for an opponent's costs. However, they do not result in independent findings by a court and reasons. The determination of how these factors are weighed is through the application of ASIC's regulatory expertise. The cost-benefit analysis described above may hinder the use of litigation because it is almost always more expensive than an infringement notice or an enforceable undertaking. The Enforcement Special Account ameliorates this issue to some extent. The analysis may also underestimate the intangible costs such as reputational impact that litigation imposes on defendants. However, ASIC needs to achieve its regulatory goals across a range of responsibilities with limited resources. ASIC is accountable for how its resources are deployed and must make choices as to how it will balance achieving its objectives with its available resources.

ii. Class Actions

Turning to the class action, the general view is that the costs incurred in a private law firm are going to be higher than the costs ASIC would bill for a matter.[244] Plaintiff law firms in class actions use time-based charging, with the case studies being no exception. Where there is a litigation funder a proportion of the legal fee may be contingent on success or there may be an additional success fee. Where there is no funder, the legal fees will usually be conditional with an uplift applying as explained in chapter two, section V.D.[245]

[240] Cooper Evidence to Senate Committee (n 70) 44.

[241] ibid 47.

[242] Australian National Audit Office (n 207) [5]; ASIC, 'Regulatory Guide 73 – Continuous disclosure obligations: infringement notices' (October 2017) [3].

[243] *Briginshaw v Briginshaw* (1938) 60 CLR 336 discussed in ch 2, section II.D. The Briginshaw standard was subsequently extended to continuous disclosure class actions in *Crowley v Worley Limited* [2020] FCA 1522, which is discussed in ch 7, section III.E.

[244] Interview ASIC Executive Centro, 8.

[245] See ch 7, section III.D discussing changes to how legal fees may be charged in class actions.

For the class actions in the case studies, the costs are set out in chapter 4, Table 4.4 and range from the low end of $1.25 million in Telstra (which was less than the total costs incurred) and $3.9 million in Leighton up to $11 million in Multiplex and $31.16 million in Centro. The comparison between costs and outcome, in terms of compensation achieved, is set out in Table 5.1 above. Centro, Multiplex and Leighton all made large recoveries, but in Centro and Multiplex about 40 per cent of the recovery went in legal or funder costs, while in Leighton about 30 per cent went in legal or funder costs. In Telstra, the settlement was small, especially by reference to the amount of shareholder's recovery per share (five cents). The cost of the class actions may be put another way: in Telstra, the class action recovered $4 for each $1 spent on legal fees; in Multiplex, the class action recovered about $2.40 for each $1 spent on legal fees and litigation funder's fees; in Centro, about $2.50 for each $1 spent on legal fees and litigation funder's fees; and in Leighton, about $3.40 for each $1 spent on legal fees and litigation funder's fees.[246]

From this it can be concluded that Leighton was more efficient than Centro or Multiplex, but that was presumably the result of an early settlement so that fewer legal fees were incurred. However, in all case studies the pursuit of compensation was expensive and if costs could be reduced, the class action could produce compensation more efficiently.

In addition, all class actions settled. However, settlements are justified in class actions because of uncertainty as to outcome (failure to prove a contravention, but also in relation to causation and calculation of loss). This also carries with it the risk of an adverse costs order. In each of the case studies, the court approving the settlement justified it, in part, by reference to litigation risk and saving costs.[247] Indeed, the court in Multiplex stated:

> It goes without saying that the court should encourage the settlement of class actions and other complex cases. Perhaps more than most cases, class actions lend themselves to compromise because of the uncertainty of their result, difficulties of proof, complexities in the assessment of damages, as well as the expense of a long trial.[248]

The cost of litigation not only reduces the outcome that is achieved directly by being deducted from compensation, but also creates an incentive for accepting less than full compensation to avoid the risk of losing and associated costs. However, that same incentive acts upon the respondent to a class action.

V. Conclusion

Chapter four developed four case studies –, Telstra, Multiplex, Centro and Leighton – based on documentary analysis and interviews. This chapter examined the case studies through the lens of the analytical framework from chapter three. This resulted in a detailed elucidation of the multiple dimensions of the framework.

Deterrence was not examined as a single monolithic concept, but rather the dimensions of deterrence that were developed in chapter three, namely direct sanctions, indirect costs and

[246] The calculation is gross recovery divided by cost (legal fees and funder's fees) as set out in Table 5.1, ie for Multiplex a $110 million recovery required expenditure of $46 million.

[247] *Taylor v Telstra Corporation Ltd* [2007] FCA 2008, [70] (Jacobson J); *P Dawson Nominees Pty Ltd v Brookfield Multiplex Limited (No 4)* [2010] FCA 1029, [15]–[17], [24] (Finkelstein J); *Kirby v Centro Properties Ltd (No 6)* [2012] FCA 650, [3]–[4], [12] (Middleton J); *Inabu Pty Ltd v Leighton Holdings Ltd (No 2)* [2014] FCA 911, [27]–[30] (Jacobson J).

[248] *P Dawson Nominees Pty Ltd v Brookfield Multiplex Limited (No 4)* [2010] FCA 1029, [2] (Finkelstein J).

reputation, were considered by reference to the case studies. In terms of financial sanctions and indirect costs, the class action imposed a greater quantum in each case study than ASIC actions, which in turn suggests a larger deterrent effect. In contrast, the impact on reputation due to a finding of a contravention is very significant to deterrence and appears to be greater for ASIC enforcement than class actions. Importantly, deterrence is derived from both ASIC enforcement and class actions. Furthermore, while ASIC enforcement seeks to achieve deterrence as a primary goal, the class action achieves deterrence indirectly.

However, even when the dimensions of deterrence are fully accounted for, their impact or effectiveness is mediated by several factors. In short, the case studies suggest that ASIC tended to focus on the certainty of detection and a timely response due to the need to ensure market integrity. The class action, on the other hand, tended to achieve severity or maximising the quantum of the direct sanctions, but also assisted in detecting contraventions. Perceptions of certainty, severity and timeliness by regulated entities also play a key role in mediating the effectiveness of deterrence. The choice of target for deterrence – corporate entity or individual – was shown to be important in chapter three, but in the case studies the corporation was most commonly targeted. In addition, the effectiveness of deterrence may be undermined by D&O insurance.

Compensation is the primary goal and motivation of the class action's proponents: group members, lawyers and litigation funders. While ASIC is able to pursue compensation, it is not seen as its main objective in relation to regulating continuous disclosure. The achievement of compensation may be undermined where it fails to achieve full compensation, investors do not claim, there are insufficient resources to pay compensation, transaction costs (legal fees and litigation funding fees) reduce the compensation received, and the circularity problem applies. These factors were more or less present in each of the case studies.

The regulatory process framework looks at ASIC action and the class action as forms of public and private enforcement in the continuous disclosure regime. ASIC action and the class action are examined through the lens of the case studies in relation to four values that are equated with a legitimate regulatory process: legislative authority; the public interest; accountability; and efficiency. While both ASIC and private individuals are authorised by legislation to enforce the provisions of the continuous disclosure regime, they do so from different perspectives. The case studies demonstrate that ASIC seeks to act in the public interest and has various procedures and considerations aimed at achieving this, while the class action is about asserting private rights and pursuing private interests, but in doing so it impacts the public interest. Moreover, ASIC action and the class action impact each other, sometimes favourably, but also unfavourably so that the objectives of each may be undermined. In keeping with ASIC's public interest orientation, it is subject to a high level of accountability and must consider how to efficiently utilise the resources available to it. In contrast, while the class action has accountability mechanisms, they are narrower and directed to the group members. Furthermore, class action costs are higher and generally less efficient than ASIC's enforcement actions.

The findings from the application of the analytical framework to the case studies in this chapter, are combined with the broader context of all of the publicly reported actions taken by ASIC and the class action in relation to continuous disclosure as at 31 December 2017 in chapter six to answer the first and second questions posed for examination in this text.

6

Effectiveness and Coexistence of Regulatory Enforcement and Class Actions

I. Introduction

The rise of the shareholder class action has given rise to overlapping enforcement of the continuous disclosure laws by the public regulator, ASIC, and private citizens with the assistance of lawyers and litigation funders. This development prompted the first and second questions for examination in the text.

First, are ASIC enforcement and the shareholder class action, when compared to each other, effective in achieving deterrence and compensation in relation to a particular category of Australia's securities law, the continuous disclosure regime? Second, what are the ramifications of ASIC enforcement and shareholder class actions coexisting? How does their coexistence impact on the values of a 'good' regulatory process? Do they help or hinder each other in the achievement of deterrence and compensation?

The findings in relation to those questions are set out in this chapter. The findings draw on the combination of the analytical framework in chapter three and the analysis of the case studies in chapters four and five, situated within the larger population of ASIC's continuous disclosure enforcement activities and the shareholder class actions undertaken up until 31 December 2017.

As a consequence, the findings are arrived at after a detailed contextual analysis, including interviews with the main participants. The effectiveness of ASIC enforcement and the class action in achieving deterrence and compensation goes beyond merely measuring outcomes – although that is undertaken – but also considers the numerous factors that influence, incentivise and constrain the achievement of deterrence and compensation. Similarly, the regulatory process question results in a 'thick' analysis of why and how ASIC enforcement and the class action interact, with ramifications for the regulatory process and each other.

II. Effectiveness of ASIC Enforcement and Class Actions

The bringing of shareholder class actions for breach of the continuous disclosure regime and the related prohibitions on misleading conduct meant that ASIC and the class action have, upon occasion, been pursuing the same regulated entities. In pursuing those contraventions, ASIC and the class action overlapped in relation to the pursuit of deterrence and compensation as potential outcomes. Chapter three unpacked both deterrence and compensation so as to provide a detailed framework that explained how each functioned, what made them effective, and what limited or undermined their effectiveness. Chapter five then applied the framework to the case studies. Consequently, the text has examined the effectiveness of ASIC enforcement and the class action by reference to both detailed understandings of deterrence and compensation, but also, and more significantly for the accretion of knowledge, through the use of case studies that provide real-world context in which to analyse why and how those outcomes were achieved, or not.

A. ASIC and Deterrence – Reputation

Deterrence is achieved through reputational harm, the imposition of direct sanctions and/or indirect costs. The analysis in chapter five demonstrated that ASIC is thought to be effective in achieving deterrence through the stigma or cost of reputational harm. Regulators, plaintiff lawyers and defence lawyers agreed that successful action by the regulator impacted corporate and individual reputation. The reason for ASIC's ability to impact reputation may be posited as resulting from three factors.

First, as chapter three explained in relation to the regulatory process, ASIC is both an independent statutory body and an arm of government that is accountable to the people through Parliament. Furthermore, ASIC's motives for enforcement action are to give effect to the laws that confer functions and powers on it in aid of the public interest, not to seek personal gain. The case studies found that entities regulated by the continuous disclosure regime and associated actors, such as their lawyers, seem to largely agree that regulatory action that fulfils the mandate prescribed by the Parliament has greater legitimacy and therefore reputation is more adversely affected than when class action lawyers and litigation funders pursue private interests for financial gain.

Second, chapter three in discussing formal and informal sanctions identified that for sanctions to be effective, they need to be aimed at what is important to the potential offender. For entities regulated by the continuous disclosure regime, reputation is important. This is because it speaks to not just compliance with the law, which is undoubtedly important, but also culture, competence and standards of corporate governance. For companies, a sound reputation means they can enjoy economic benefits, including from attracting the best people as employees and engendering and maintaining customer loyalty. Corporations that have their reputation harmed reap fewer such benefits, or none at all. For individuals, reputation is equally or more important as its loss can lead to disgrace and humiliation, the loss of good standing in the community and in their profession, and loss of livelihood and business opportunities. However, ASIC has not generally pursued individuals. This is discussed below.

Third, a further insight drawing on the expressive theory of law, discussed in chapter three, is that laws may make a statement about what is proper or improper conduct with a view to affecting social norms and behaviour.[1] In the corporate law context, this is of importance because corporate law is very much about 'norm management' in relation to how directors and management should interact with other stakeholders, most relevantly here, shareholders.[2] The expressive theory of law differs from traditional sanctions-based deterrence theory in that it does not focus

[1] Ch 3, section II.E.ii.

[2] James Cox, 'The Social Meaning of Shareholder Suits' (1999) 65 *Brooklyn Law Review* 3, 7.

on imposing costs, but rather on the signalling effect of law in relation to society's expectations. It may be argued that ASIC, due to its role as regulator, impacts reputation because its enforcement actions are the signal as to when laws are not being adhered to. It is not just the law as enacted which conveys society's expectations,[3] but what the regulator with responsibility for enforcing that law conveys about compliance with the law.

The signal that ASIC provides, and the reputational impact that follows, may also depend on the nature of the enforcement tool it employs as it conveys differing views as to the conduct: whether criminal, civil or administrative. As Table 6.1 below demonstrates, ASIC has employed administrative enforcement tools (infringement notices, disallowing the use of a reduced content prospectus and enforceable undertakings) on 58 occasions compared to the litigation tools of civil penalty and criminal proceedings which were used on a total of 10 occasions. An enforcement tool such as an infringement notice, where there is no admission of liability, will carry less reputational impact than a judicial acceptance[4] or finding of a contravention or criminal liability. As discussed below, this is because there is less assurance of merit to the action, and the moral or legal culpability varies. However, lower-level enforcement tools may still have a reputational impact. For an infringement notice to be issued, ASIC must have 'reasonable grounds to believe' there is a contravention, provide reasons for the belief, and provide an opportunity for the disclosing entity to appear at a hearing before ASIC, give evidence and make submissions to ASIC.[5] Enforceable undertakings also set out the underlying allegations; liability cannot be denied; and it must be accepted that ASIC's views are reasonably held.[6] Even the warning provided to Telstra included information about ASIC's concerns. Nonetheless, there is no independent judicial ruling on whether a contravention occurred, which is discussed further below.

The signal may also depend on the result achieved with the enforcement tool. For example, reputation may be impacted by the fact of a criminal prosecution or enforceable undertaking, but also the penalty imposed. In the criminal setting, this is the term of imprisonment and/or quantum of any fine, while with an enforceable undertaking, it is the terms of the undertaking and expenditure required. The penalty as well as the tool may have an expressive effect, although the tool selected will dictate what penalties are available. However, it is important to recognise the distinction. This is illustrated by the Centro case study where the court made a finding of contravention of the law by the non-executive directors but imposed no penalty. The court held that the finding of contravention sufficiently impacted reputation so as to achieve deterrence. Some commentators saw the lack of a penalty as undermining or reducing the deterrence achieved.[7] Nonetheless, the expressive effect achieved by ASIC appears to be affected by both the tool chosen and the result achieved.

In short, reputational impact depends on the legitimacy of ASIC as a regulator, actions that impact what matters to the offender, and the outcome (enforcement tool chosen and result) that ASIC achieves.

[3] The original enactment of the continuous disclosure regime and prohibitions on misleading conduct conveyed society's changed expectations as to what information a corporation was required to provide the market.

[4] Civil penalty settlements and a plea of guilty in a criminal action result in findings of contravention.

[5] Ch 2, section II.D.

[6] Ch 2, section IV.C.ii.

[7] Ch 5, section II.A.iii, iv.

Table 6.1 ASIC's usage of enforcement tools as at 31 December 2017

Enforcement tool	**Usage based on completed matters**
Warning	1
Infringement notices (chapter two and Appendix 2 Table 1)	37
Disallowing the use of a reduced content prospectus (chapter two)	10
Enforceable undertakings (chapter two and Appendix 2 Table 2)	11
Civil penalty proceedings (chapter two)	8 (1 unsuccessful)
Criminal proceedings (chapter two)	2 (1 unsuccessful)
Total	69

B. ASIC and Deterrence – Direct Sanctions

The case studies found that ASIC was seen as less effective in achieving deterrence through direct sanctions than through impact on reputation, as direct sanctions are either not used or give rise to minor costs for the regulated entity. ASIC's achievement of deterrence of continuous disclosure contraventions was critiqued because ASIC rarely used the 'peak' of the pyramid, such as criminal penalties, and the quantum of its criminal and civil penalties, when imposed on corporations, was low.[8] ASIC appears to have prioritised a rapid and certain sanction over a severe sanction. Individuals were seldom pursued, which is discussed below. ASIC's patterns of enforcement, as described in chapter two and summarised in Table 6.1, also support the view that ASIC focuses on administrative remedies that impose low direct sanctions. However, a number of explanations exist for ASIC's approach to direct sanctions.

In terms of what makes deterrence effective, chapter three explained that deterrence theorists focused on three elements: severity of sanctions; the speed of imposition or celerity; and the reliability or certainty of sanctions being imposed. Chapters three and five explained that severity is argued to not be as central to the effectiveness of deterrence as the certainty of detection but, in contrast, it is also the case that optimal deterrence theory creates an expectation that a regulated entity will have a penalty imposed commensurate with the full social cost of its misconduct. Optimal deterrence can necessitate a severe penalty.

The case studies suggest that ASIC has a tendency to rely primarily on detection of a contravention and timely imposition of sanctions.[9] This is driven by continuous disclosure being about ensuring that the market is informed and efficient.[10] This is something that needs to be dealt with in a timely way through promptly identifying and responding to misconduct. This focus also means that ASIC saw itself as being effective at achieving general deterrence through using

[8] Ch 4, Table 4.3.

[9] Ch 5, section II.B.i, ii.

[10] ASIC, Submission No 72 to Australian Law Reform Commission, 'Inquiry into class action proceedings and third-party litigation funders' (September 2018), [24]–[25] ('ASIC ALRC Submission') ('The continuous disclosure obligations and misleading or deceptive conduct provisions are critical to the integrity and reputation of Australia's capital markets. Market integrity is fundamental to investor confidence and a well-developed financial market.').

its enforcement tools to signal to the market what is unacceptable conduct. Whether ASIC is in fact effective is difficult to determine due to the problems in measuring deterrence – effective deterrence involves proving a negative, that is, that a person or entity refrained from misconduct because of the fear of sanctions.[11] In contrast, there is in the public mind, reinforced by media reporting, an association between severity and the effectiveness of deterrence. Severity is also more tangible and measurable. This is especially the case when there is a class action for comparison. ASIC and the public appear to focus on different elements of deterrence.

Debate over whether severity of the sanctions should be a focus for ASIC in seeking deterrence must also consider the legislative framework that ASIC administers. A contravention of Chapter 6CA can give rise to criminal liability for the listed disclosing entity pursuant to s 1311 of the Corporations Act. The applicable penalties are set out in Schedule 3 to the Corporations Act, which for a corporation's contravention of s 674(2) is 200 penalty units. Pursuant to s 678 the court may multiply that maximum by five, ie 1,000 penalty units or $210,000 (as at 31 December 2017). There is no direct criminal liability for directors. However, they may be criminally liable if they aid, abet, counsel or procure the disclosing entity's contravention. Liability of individuals is discussed further below. ASIC's ability to impose direct sanctions through civil penalty provisions is also limited by statutory caps. Although civil penalty breaches are easier to prove as it is not necessary to demonstrate intent or fault as a prerequisite to establishing a contravention, the court may only order the payment of a maximum pecuniary penalty of $200,000 for an individual and $1 million for a corporation per contravention (as at 31 December 2017).[12]

When the available sanctions are low and this is combined with the risk of failing to prove the contravention, a regulator may rationally conclude that resorting to the peak of the pyramid is not worth the costs incurred. This finding is consistent with the statement in the Senate Economic References Committee's report into penalties for white collar crime that is attributed to ASIC:

> ASIC noted that one of the factors it considers in determining its enforcement approach in a particular matter is the market impact of an investigation and an enforcement outcome. In cases where only low civil penalties were available (or low criminal penalties in criminal matters), ASIC advised that this might weigh against it pursuing a particular course of enforcement action.[13]

Moreover, as the peak of the pyramid necessitates court action, the accompanying delay may prevent the quick response that ASIC desires to promote market integrity.

Despite ASIC's professed focus on certainty of detection and timely imposition of sanctions, ASIC made recommendations for an increase in civil penalties in 2014 because 'the fines available for breaches of continuous disclosure obligations … are comparatively lower in Australia than … in other jurisdictions'.[14] This suggests that ASIC accepts that severity can be relevant to effective deterrence. The Australian Government responded to the call for stronger penalties for corporate law contraventions with a taskforce in 2016, draft legislation in 2018, and its enactment in 2019.[15]

[11] Ch 3, section II.V.iv.

[12] Ch 2, section II.D.

[13] Senate Economics References Committee, '"Lifting the fear and suppressing the greed": Penalties for white-collar crime and corporate and financial misconduct in Australia' (23 March 2017) [6.7].

[14] ASIC, 'Penalties for Corporate Wrongdoing – Report 387 (March 2014) [56]. See also Commonwealth of Australia, Financial System Inquiry – Final Report' (November 2014) 236 (recommending 'substantially higher criminal and civil penalties').

[15] Commonwealth of Australia, 'ASIC Enforcement Review Taskforce Report (December 2017); Treasury Laws Amendment (Strengthening Corporate and Financial Sector Penalties) Act 2019 (Cth)'. The new penalties regime is explained in ch 7.

The Treasurer of the Commonwealth of Australia commented, upon releasing the draft legislation, that the increase in penalties was 'to ensur[e] ASIC is properly armed to effectively deter, prosecute and punish those who do the wrong thing'.[16] The Australian Government would also seem to accept that the severity of sanctions is important in achieving deterrence.

In the continuous disclosure setting ASIC tends to mainly utilise administrative enforcement tools with a view to promptly informing the market that conduct is not acceptable. The decision-making also appears to have been driven by a cost-benefit analysis where the penalties available are outweighed by the cost of litigation. However, severity of sanctions is accepted as an important component of deterrence. It is not possible to accurately specify what quantum of sanctions is required to achieve effective deterrence, or to be able to state that it is more or less important than certainty or celerity. Severity matters because the costs imposed will impact decision-making.

C. ASIC and Deterrence – Indirect Costs

ASIC achieves deterrence, to some extent, through indirect costs such as lost management time and legal fees associated with dealing with ASIC. ASIC has also taken steps to be able to recover its own costs of investigation from persons subject to successful litigation-based enforcement.[17] These are costs that a rational entity would prefer to avoid. In large matters the costs may also be large, but the need for ASIC to use its resources efficiently means that is incentivised to keep costs down.

D. Class Actions and Incidental Deterrence

Class actions on behalf of shareholders achieve deterrence through the imposition of direct costs in the form of compensation and indirect costs associated with defending and settling litigation. In respect of both direct and indirect financial costs, the quantum imposed by the class action is far greater than that imposed by ASIC. Appendix 2, Table 3 lists the outcome of all shareholder class actions involving an alleged contravention of the continuous disclosure regime as at 31 December 2017. For the purposes of deterrence, the focus is on the total payment borne by the respondent, rather than the amount received by group members. A review of those payments demonstrates that typically the amounts paid by respondents are significantly higher than payments made in relation to action by ASIC. The four case studies also demonstrate this result.

In terms of the three elements that impact effective deterrence: severity of sanctions, speed of imposition and certainty of sanctions, the class action typically relies on severity and certainty. Compensation payments are often large, although as the case studies in chapter four showed, they may only be a fraction of the total harm alleged. Furthermore, some form of payment is almost always needed to conclude a class action. The class action is usually slow in reaching finality. However, the extent of severity and certainty must consider the impact of insurance, as discussed below.

[16] The Hon Josh Frydenberg MP, 'Government consults on stronger penalties for corporate and financial sector misconduct' (Media Release, 26 September 2018).

[17] ASIC has sought to extend its ability to recover costs through ASIC Act 2001 (Cth), s 91: ASIC, 'Information Sheet 204 – Recovery of investigation expenses and costs' (July 2015). However, deterrence is not expressed to be a reason for seeking recovery.

The effectiveness of the class action in achieving deterrence must also be considered in light of deterrence being incidental to seeking compensation. While ASIC and the class action both achieve deterrence as an outcome, only ASIC has deterrence as a specific objective. This has two main ramifications. First, there must be substantial compensation available, as determined by both losses suffered and the respondent's ability to pay, for a class action to be financially viable.[18] This means that even heinous contraventions due to poor systems and culture will not be pursued and therefore not deterred if the loss caused is below the class action viability threshold.[19] Deterrence from class action costs only operates in relation to large corporations where there are large losses.

Second, the decision-making by the class action lawyers and funders does not focus on the finer points of deterrence in the way that a regulator would because that is not the goal. This is also because the class action proponent does not have the range of enforcement tools that a regulator such as ASIC has available. This means that deterrence through a compensation payment as a result of a class action is a blunter instrument compared to the more refined behavioural type changes that can be pursued by ASIC which has access to an enforcement pyramid which includes tools such as an enforceable undertaking. However, there may be scope for a class action to seek changes to corporate governance including policy and procedures as part of the relief sought.[20] This could be through injunctions or possibly the wide relief permitted by s 1325 of the Corporations Act. However, such relief does not achieve the main goal of the class action: compensation for the shareholder. It also does not give rise to a payment from which a litigation funder may recover their fee. Both factors hamper the class action's ability to obtain non-monetary forms of relief.

The class action has also been linked with reputational impact on the basis that a large settlement payment indicates the acceptance of some wrongdoing. However, as discussed below, no finding of contravention means there is no external validation of the claim. The requirement for a class action settlement to be approved by a court for it to be valid offers external oversight but the court considers many factors other than the merits, such as cost and delay. Further, the financial incentives for lawyers and funders in bringing a class action may hinder any reputational impact. This is because those incentives may be viewed, correctly or incorrectly, as driving the commencement and resolution of the class action rather than deterring wrongdoing.

E. Deterrence without Findings of Contravention?

Both actions by ASIC and class actions frequently result in settlements. For ASIC, warnings, the infringement notice and enforceable undertaking all result in no findings of a breach of the law. A civil penalty claim can be settled, but there must be a finding of contravention.[21] Similarly,

[18] John Walker, Susanna Khouri and Wayne Attrill, 'Funding Criteria for Class Actions' (2009) 32 *University of New South Wales Law Journal* 1036, 1041, 1045.

[19] See, eg, IMF (Australia) Ltd, Submission No 103 to Productivity Commission, 'Access to Justice Arrangements' (18 November 2013) 5 ('IMF applies strict investment criteria when deciding which cases to fund and whether to continue funding. IMF will only fund claims which … are likely to be resolved for not less than \$5m for single party matters or \$30m for multi-party litigation.').

[20] Michael Legg, 'Class Actions and Regulating Culture in Financial Organisations: Observations from a Comparison of US and Australian Bank Class Actions' in Justin O'Brien and George Gilligan (eds), *Integrity, Risk and Accountability in Capital Markets* (Hart, 2013) 247–48.

[21] See, eg, *ASIC v Westpac Banking Corporation* (2018) 132 ACSR 230, 236 [29] (Perram J) (judge refused to make declaration of contravention of civil penalty provision where not satisfied that law had been contravened).

a criminal case can be resolved through a plea of guilty but a contravention is found. All class actions brought in relation to continuous disclosure as at 31 December 2017 (Appendix 2, Table 3), including the four case studies, were settled on the basis of no admission of liability.

The propensity for resolution without an admission of liability or without a trial at which liability is found raises for consideration whether deterrence, specific and general, is undermined. Both ASIC and class action proponents see their reliance on settlement as still achieving deterrence. Indeed, the Productivity Commission has noted 'the prevalence of settlements is not unique to shareholder claims … less than 3 per cent of matters that reach supreme and district courts are resolved through final judgment'.[22] Settlement is promoted to reduce uncertainty and cost. However, the general prevalence of settlement does not answer the question of what the effect of settlement is on deterrence.

A payment without a finding of wrongdoing permits the 'alleged' contravenor to claim that the payment was based on a cost-benefit analysis rather any actual wrongdoing. In the case studies, this was most clearly shown through the Leighton Chairman's Address in chapter five. However, it has occurred in relation to other continuous disclosure allegations.[23] The prospect of effective deterrence is limited if the particular corporation views payments to settle regulatory enforcement action and class actions as merely costs of doing business rather than reflecting any sort of moral or legal condemnation.

A settlement also makes it difficult for shareholders and potential investors to evaluate the conduct and what it means. If the underlying conduct was an isolated, one-off event, it would be assessed differently compared to if it were a continuing pattern of conduct. Similarly, whether conduct was an innocent error, negligent or intentional will impact how it is evaluated. Settlements do not provide as much public information as trials because settlements do not resolve allegations, apply the law or make findings public. This opacity then allows a settling entity to influence or shape how their actions are interpreted by outsiders.[24]

From a general deterrence perspective, the question is how the community of regulated entities responds to settlements. Perceptual deterrence theory (see chapter three) assists here, as the question is not what is the actual likelihood of a contravention being detected and sanctions imposed, but rather what does a regulated entity perceive the likelihood and quantum to be. On one view, frequent settlements may suggest to an entity that even if they contravene the law they will be able to negotiate a payment to resolve the issue without the risk of a finding of contravention. The entity can 'buy' their way out of trouble, albeit at considerable inconvenience and likely expense. This is an example of the 'experiential effect' discussed in chapter three. However, it is difficult to accurately estimate the probability of apprehension or quantum of sanctions. This is especially the case where the regulator has resort to an enforcement pyramid that allows it to escalate its response if needed.

The above discussion casts doubt on the effectiveness of deterrence where there are no findings of contravention. However, one would expect the rational corporate decision-maker to still prefer to avoid resources being diverted to penalties and settlements, with the result that they comply with the law.

[22] Productivity Commission, 'Access to Justice Arrangements' (Report No 72, 5 September 2014) vol 2, 620.

[23] See, eg, National Australia Bank, 'Class action Settlement' (ASX Announcement, 9 November 2012) 1 ('The settlement has been reached on a commercial basis and there is no admission of liability by NAB'); Rhinomed Limited, 'Rhinomed accepts ASIC infringement notice' (Company Statement, 10 June 2016) 1 (after paying a $33,000 penalty in relation to an infringement notice stated 'The notice states that payment is not an admission of liability and cannot be regarded as a finding that Rhinomed contravened the *Corporations Act*').

[24] Roy Shapira, 'Reputation Through Litigation: How the Legal System Shapes Behavior by Producing Information' (2016) 91 *Washington Law Review* 1193, 1202, 1206, 1239.

F. Class Actions and Compensation

Class actions brought by shareholders seek compensation and they frequently achieve large monetary payments. Moreover, many shareholders, despite having standing to pursue compensation, would be unlikely to obtain compensation without class actions and litigation funding. Both factors are crucial to access to justice. However, the goal of compensation is undermined by three matters: incomplete recovery; transaction costs; and the circularity problem.

Shareholder class actions (actions based on continuous disclosure as well as other causes of action) in aggregate have resulted in settlements of more than $1.5 billion.[25] Appendix 2, Table 3 lists the outcome of all shareholder class actions involving an alleged contravention of the continuous disclosure regime as at 31 December 2017–43 in total. A review of those outcomes demonstrates that the largest payment is the Centro settlement of $200 million.[26] This is followed by the Aristocrat Leisure settlement of $144.5m,[27] the QBE settlement of $132.5 million,[28] the National Australia Bank settlement of $115 million,[29] and the Multiplex settlement of $110 million.[30] However, there have also been small recoveries (including Telstra),[31] as well as a range of settlements in the $30 million to $60 million range (including Leighton).[32]

Despite the headline settlement sums, recovery may still be incomplete – the first matter undermining compensation. Litigation that proceeds to judgment results in a winner and a loser. The unsuccessful party is liable for the successful party's costs under the Australian costs rules. However continuous disclosure class actions have typically been resolved by settlement,[33] including in all four of the case studies. Settlements typically lead to incomplete recovery because the amount claimed will be reduced to take account of the risk of the litigation being unsuccessful (no recovery and liability for the opponent's costs), or less successful than desired (for example, the court adopts a method for calculating loss that is lower than expected), and the future costs that may be avoided by not continuing to trial. In class actions while the lawyers and funders will be seeking to maximise recovery, they will also want to avoid an unsuccessful outcome. The litigation funder in particular will recover nothing from their investment and be liable for the opponent's legal fees if the class action fails.

The involvement of litigation funders has been welcomed because they 'may inject a welcome element of commercial objectivity [and] efficiency with which the litigation is conducted'.[34] Equally, the litigation funder's commercial drivers and assessment of risk will impact recoveries. It would be sensible for the funder to accept a lower settlement as the price of removing the uncertainty and risk that accompanies litigation. The funder will also have a portfolio of cases so that it needs to make decisions not just based on an individual class action but in relation to its entire portfolio. If a case is settled, then the revenue from the case can be used to invest in

[25] King & Wood Mallesons, 'The Review – Class Actions in Australia 2016/2017' (2018) 7.
[26] *Kirby v Centro Properties Ltd (No 6)* [2012] FCA 650.
[27] *Dorajay Pty Ltd v Aristocrat Leisure Ltd* (2008) 67 ACSR 569; *Dorajay Pty Ltd v Aristocrat Leisure Ltd* [2009] FCA 19.
[28] *Money Max Int Pty Ltd (Trustee) v QBE Insurance Group Limited* (2018) 358 ALR 382.
[29] *Pathway Investments Pty Ltd v National Australia Bank Limited (No 3)* [2012] VSC 625.
[30] *P Dawson Nominees Pty Ltd v Brookfield Multiplex Ltd (No 4)* [2010] FCA 1029.
[31] See, eg, *Guglielmin v Trescowthick (No 5)* [2006] FCA 1385; *Taylor v Telstra Corporation Ltd* [2007] FCA 2008.
[32] See, eg, AWB Limited, Oz Minerals Ltd, Nufarm Limited and Sigma Pharmaceuticals Ltd in Appendix 2, Table 3.
[33] Appendix 2, Table 3 records that all continuous disclosure class actions resolved as at 31 December 2017 were settled. See also Vince Morabito, 'An Empirical Study of Australia's Class Action Regimes – Fifth Report' (July 2017) 30 (64% of shareholder class actions settle, which is a broader classification than continuous disclosure class actions).
[34] *QPSX Ltd v Ericsson Australia Pty Ltd (No 3)* (2005) 219 ALR 1, 14 [54] (French J).

another case. If the return on investment in the instant class action is lower than that forecast, then the correct business decision may be to settle promptly.[35]

In short, the compensation recovered is rarely equivalent to a complete recovery because of the inherent uncertainties and costs of class actions operating within the civil justice system and the business interests of the litigation funder.

Second, the civil justice system and litigation funding also drive transaction costs. The class action will reduce the legal costs per group member due to the sharing of costs and economies of scale.[36] However, high transaction costs persist as shown by the legal fees and litigation funding fees incurred in each of the case studies. As explained in Table 5.1 in chapter five, the case studies illustrated that where substantial recoveries are achieved, legal fees take up 6–16 per cent of the recovery, while funders' fees consume 25–35 per cent of the recovery. More generally, shareholder class actions with substantial recoveries tend to incur similar legal and funding costs to those seen in the case studies.[37] Class actions with smaller recoveries tend to have much higher lawyer fees as a percentage of the recovery.[38] The Federal Court has observed generally that 'the largest single deduction from the recoveries of class members in funded class actions is usually the funding commission'[39] and 'the deduction [for litigating funding fees] will directly impact on the quantum of compensation [group members] will receive "in hand"'.[40]

Complex litigation, such as a shareholder class action, can only be brought with the assistance of sophisticated legal representation. Indeed, the defendant corporation will retain highly skilled lawyers to defeat or minimise the compensation sought. Legal fees are charged by time in Australian class actions. Legal fees will be higher the greater the work that needs to be undertaken. Some cost in litigation is inevitable because of the need to determine disputes according to law and through ensuring procedural fairness.[41] Class actions can generate even greater costs than other litigation as the representative and aggregative character of the class action gives rise to additional steps necessary to ensure fairness, including notices advising of the right to opt out and approval of a settlement by the court. Class actions can also be subject to more interlocutory disputes due to the high-stakes nature of the class action so that greater cost ensues.[42]

In addition to legal fees are the fees to be paid to the litigation funder. The funder is usually necessary because they pay the legal fees as they are incurred and indemnify the representative party against the liability for costs if the litigation is unsuccessful.[43] Without the funder, there would need to be a group member who was prepared to incur these costs, or at least the risk of paying an opponent's costs, if the lawyer were prepared to act on a conditional fee basis. In exchange, the funder charges a success-based fee, typically a percentage of any recovery. Historically, the fee has tended to be relatively standard despite there being a number of factors that impact the fee, such

[35] Justice Patrick Keane, 'Access to Justice and Other Shibboleths' (Speech, JCA Colloquium, 10 October 2009) 7 ('The profit-making expectations of the trader who controls the litigation add a special complication to the risk-benefit calculations which inform settlement negotiations.').

[36] See ch 2, section V.B.

[37] Michael Legg, 'Securities Regulation in Australia: The Role of the Class Action' in Robin Huang and Nicholas Howson (eds), *Enforcement of Corporate and Securities Law: China and the World* (Cambridge University Press, 2017) 318–20.

[38] ibid.

[39] *Money Max Int Pty Ltd v QBE Insurance Group Ltd* (2016) 245 FCR 191, 208 [72] (Murphy, Gleeson and Beach JJ).

[40] *Earglow Pty Ltd v Newcrest Mining Limited* [2016] FCA 1433, [133] (Murphy J).

[41] See *Halpin v Lumley General Insurance Ltd* (2009) 78 NSWLR 265, 287 [93] (Sackville AJA).

[42] Ch 5, section III.B.iii.

[43] See ch 2, section V.D; Appendix 2, Table 3 (only four of the 42 continuous disclosure class actions did not have litigation funding as at 31 December 2017).

as the risk of the litigation.[44] However, the advent of more litigation funders entering the market and competing class actions has seen funding fees reduce in response to competitive pressures, including seeking to attract group members and convince a court that the class action should not be stayed.[45] While obtaining financing is needed to seek compensation, the cost of that finance will reduce the compensation recovered.

High transaction costs can be addressed to a degree through court oversight. The Full Court of the Federal Court has recognised that 'the Court has a supervisory or protective role in relation to legal costs proposed to be charged to class members … and in relation to litigation funding charges', which can be dealt with as part of the settlement approval process.[46] However, all the legal fees and funder's fees in the case studies were subject to the settlement approval process.

Nonetheless, while class actions achieve compensation, they do so through a process that generates significant costs and uses financing that is expensive. Large transaction costs undermine the goal of compensation as the harmed shareholder does not receive a payment equivalent to their loss. However, compensation, even if reduced by large transaction costs, is better than no compensation, which would be the alternative if shareholders had to rely on ASIC and its current policy position.

The third issue is of a different order. The circularity problem has been described by one academic in the US as 'the most damaging securities class action criticism'[47] and is a key reason why compensation as a goal of shareholder class actions has been almost abandoned by American academics.[48] However, the case studies found that in Australia the class action's main purpose is compensation.

The circularity problem describes the situation where shareholders who traded in a company's securities based on flawed disclosure and suffered loss are paid compensation by the shareholders of the same company who did not trade. Over the long term diversified shareholders are just as likely to have traded as not, and are effectively paying themselves, but with large transaction costs.[49] To break the circle, it is necessary that the group members are not diversified, which usually means they are retail investors, or the compensation comes from a source other than the shareholders, such as from advisors, auditors or directors.

The case studies demonstrate that the assumptions for the circularity problem to apply do not always hold. For example, all the case studies had a significant number of retail investors in the group. Furthermore, in the Centro class action the auditor contributed $67 million of the total $200 million settlement. The directors also contributed through their D&O insurance policy. However, the case studies also show that there are indeed large payments from the shareholders at the time of settlement, via the company, to the shareholders who traded, suffered loss and are part of the group. The extent of the circularity problem is, however, not known as the identity of group members, the amount of their shareholdings and whether they are diversified is not usually available. Indeed, determining whether a shareholder is diversified, in addition to being difficult, may not really elucidate whether shareholder class actions compensate. This is because being

[44] *ASIC v Richards* [2013] FCAFC 89, [52] (Jacobson, Middleton and Gordon JJ).

[45] See, eg, *Lenthall v Westpac Life Insurance Services Ltd* [2018] FCA 1422, [19]–[24] (Lee J).

[46] *Melbourne City Investments Pty Ltd v Treasury Wine Estates Limited* (2017) 252 FCR 1, 24 [90] (Jagot, Yates and Murphy JJ).

[47] Elizabeth Chamblee Burch, 'Securities Class Actions as Pragmatic Ex Post Regulation' (2008) 43 *Georgia Law Review* 63, 86.

[48] Amanda Rose, 'Reforming Securities Litigation Reform: Restructuring the Relationship Between Public and Private Enforcement of Rule 10B-5' (2008) 108 *Columbia Law Review* 1301, 1312–14.

[49] See ch 3, section III.E and ch 5, section III.B.

equally likely to be the shareholder paying the compensation or receiving the compensation still leaves the issue at the theoretical level. There would need to be many shareholder class actions for this type of 'on average' reasoning to apply. In Australia, there have been continuous disclosure class actions brought against 43 disclosing entities and/or directors as at 31 December 2017.[50] In comparison, in the United States where the circularity argument has had the greatest traction, the average number of filings per year for the period from 1997–2016 is 193, with a maximum of 271 filings in a year and a minimum of 120 filings in a year.[51] In practice, for the circularity argument to hold, the diversified shareholder needs to actually pay out and receive payments for class actions in an equal amount. In a smaller market with fewer class actions than the United States, this may not be the case. Importantly, however, is the fact that it is not possible to empirically prove or disprove the circularity argument by reference to diversification.

The circularity argument, contrary to the arguments made in the US literature, does not justify the abandonment of compensation as a class action goal. However, it does direct attention to an issue that is attracting more attention in Australia – class actions and enforcement action directed at the corporation are indirectly paid for by the shareholders. The alternative of pursuing individuals is discussed below.

G. ASIC and Compensation

ASIC's policy position is that it does not seek compensation unless it is in the public interest, beyond the interests of the affected shareholders, to do so.[52] Rather, ASIC encourages shareholders to consider alternative options such as private action.[53] The former ASIC Chairman, Greg Medcraft, embraced class actions as a source of compensation because he saw the 'class action industry' as 'quite effective' at achieving compensation and it allowed ASIC to use its resources elsewhere.[54]

In the case studies, the regulator's aversion to compensation was played out, except for the compensation fund that formed part of the enforceable undertaking procured in Multiplex. Previous analysis of Multiplex has focused on simply comparing the quantum paid in the class action and the enforceable undertaking.[55] However, the interviews that were undertaken as part of the case study provide a richer explanation. The establishment of the compensation scheme appears to be a compromise that not only obtained compensation, but allowed ASIC to achieve other goals, such as deterrence and governance changes, while taking account of Multiplex's concerns about admissions from a civil penalty being used in a subsequent class action.[56] The Multiplex experience demonstrates that ASIC can obtain compensation.[57] However, the case

[50] Appendix 2, Table 3.

[51] Cornerstone Research, 'Securities Class Action Filings – 2017 Year in Review' (2018) 1.

[52] ASIC, 'Information Sheet 151 – ASIC's approach to enforcement' (September 2013) 6 ('ASIC Information Sheet 151').

[53] ibid; ASIC ALRC Submission (n 10) [47].

[54] See Alex Boxsell, 'Regulators Praise Private Court Actions', *The Weekend Australian Financial Review* (5–9 April 2012) 59; Evidence to Senate Economics Legislation Committee – Estimates, Parliament of Australia, Canberra, 20 November 2013, 23 (Mr Greg Medcraft, ASIC Chairman).

[55] Ch 5, section II.B.ii.

[56] Ch 4, section IV and Ch 5, section II.A.

[57] ASIC has also achieved compensation in other circumstances as well: Greg Golding, 'Tightening the Screws on Directors: Care, Delegation and Reliance' (2012) 35 *University of New South Wales Law Journal* 266, 289; Helen Bird, George Gilligan and Ian Ramsay, 'The who, why and what of enforceable undertakings accepted by the Australian Securities and Investment Commission' (2016) 34 *Company and Securities Law Journal* 493, 509; Michael Legg, 'A Comparison of Regulatory Enforcement, Class Actions and Alternative Dispute Resolution in Compensating Financial Consumers' (2016) 38 *Sydney Law Review* 311.

studies, and ASIC's continuous disclosure enforcement actions more generally, highlight that ASIC has not sought compensation in a litigation context, despite legislation specifically granting ASIC standing to do so.[58]

The ASIC interviewees raised as reasons for not pursuing compensation the need to focus on other objectives, limited resources and class actions already performing the role.[59] Each of these requires comment.

First, ASIC could seek compensation and use it to achieve deterrence just as class actions do through the indirect effect that the payment of money for shareholder loss imparts on the corporation by imposing costs. The amounts obtained for compensation have been shown to be larger than the monetary penalties obtained and therefore could assert a greater deterrent effect. However, as with the class action, deterrence sought in this way is blunter as it is limited to the imposition of direct sanctions, that is, cost. The behavioural change that ASIC may seek is not as specific in seeking compensation as it may be with other enforcement tools such as an enforceable undertaking. However, if ASIC were to seek compensation, that does not mean it cannot use its other enforcement tools. Unlike the class action, compensation can be paired with other techniques, as it was in Multiplex. Furthermore, a compensation order could be paired with a declaration of contravention and/or a civil penalty.

Second, ASIC's limited resources were clearly a concern at the time ASIC was taking the enforcement actions in the case studies, and consistent with regulatory pluralism (discussed below), the class action provided additional resources that could pursue compensation without ASIC incurring the cost. However, the fact remains that ASIC's incentives to maximise the recovery are not as direct as those of a litigation funder that profits from the litigation.

Third, while class actions are being successfully undertaken in relation to continuous disclosure, their conduct is arguably not optimal due to the large transaction costs involved, as discussed above. ASIC could reduce the transaction costs through it incurring the costs of pursuing compensation using litigation or alternative dispute resolution, such as through seeking or requiring a disclosing entity to offer a redress scheme. Furthermore, the need for there to be substantial losses for a funder to find financing a class action commercially attractive may mean smaller corporations or situations where the level of loss is low may not be pursued by a class action, or the cost of pursuing the claims is disproportionate to the potential recovery.[60] ASIC could fill this gap.

H. Individuals Rarely Pursued

As stated in chapter three, Professor John Coffee has observed that 'Deterrence works best when it is focused on the culpable'.[61] Chapter three went on to explain that sanctions aimed at individuals are supported from a deterrence perspective because the decision to contravene the law is ultimately made by individuals. The threat of personal liability for misconduct provides a direct incentive to ensure compliance as the negative effect of sanctions will be felt by the individual.

[58] Ch 2, section II.D explaining Corporations Act 2001 (Cth), ss 1317J(1), 1317HA, 1325.

[59] Interview ASIC Executive Centro, 3; Interview ASIC Executive Leighton, 3–4.

[60] See *Petersen Superannuation Fund Pty Ltd v Bank of Queensland Limited (No 3)* (2018) 132 ACSR 258, 286 [129] (Murphy J), where it is noted that when claims are for compensation less than $30 million the quantum of legal costs and funding charges can become disproportionate to the recovery made by group members.

[61] John Coffee, 'Reforming the Securities Class Action: An Essay on Deterrence and Its Implementation' (2006) 106 *Columbia Law Review* 1534, 1536.

In contrast, where sanctions are visited upon the corporation, the impact on individuals is indirect, although that indirect effect can see individuals dismissed from their positions or subject to criticism.[62] Furthermore, as discussed above, shareholder class actions directed at corporations can give rise to the circularity problem. If individual directors are the subject of the class action, then the circle of one group of shareholders paying another may be broken. Despite there being clear reasons for pursuing the individual, this rarely occurs in relation to continuous disclosure breaches that attract ASIC or class action attention, for two reasons.

The first is the structure and requirements for proof of a contravention in the legislation. The continuous disclosure regime is primarily aimed at the corporation, the 'disclosing entity'. It follows that both ASIC and the class action will target the company as the terms of the statute make it the primary contravenor. Furthermore, the statute is crafted so that civil penalty and compensation claims can succeed against the corporation without proving intent or fault. Infringement notices, which may only be brought against the company, equally have no intent or fault requirement. The situation is different for criminal prosecutions where a fault element is required.[63] However, for individuals such as directors, criminal, civil penalty and compensation actions can only be pursued by some form of accessorial liability,[64] which requires the proof of additional elements, such as, intentional participation with actual knowledge of the elements constituting the contravention by the corporation.[65] In short, it is easier to succeed against the corporation than a director. However, in addition to the continuous disclosure regime, a civil action may be brought against the company or the directors in relation to misleading or deceptive conduct. However, only compensation for loss or damage is available.

Second, when the goal is a large payment for compensation, the company is usually the preferred target as it has greater resources to afford the payment without facing insolvency. This includes Side C of D&O insurance which responds to securities claims against the corporation. Side C usually has the same amount of coverage as Sides A and B, which apply to the directors so that the full limit of the policy can be obtained through pursuing the company alone.[66]

Despite the additional difficulties in pursuing directors, it is clear that they can be pursued, although with ASIC better placed to be able to deter individuals than the class action because of the greater range of enforcement tools at its disposal. ASIC has acknowledged that imprisonment is a significant deterrent for white-collar criminals,[67] but ASIC can only act against directors for breach of continuous disclosure regime where they are an accessory to a breach. Alternatively, ASIC needs to reconfigure its allegation as a criminal contravention of another statutory provision.[68] ASIC may also pursue banning orders, civil penalties and civil proceedings. ASIC may also enter into an enforceable undertaking with an individual, although the individual would need to do so voluntarily. However, as explained above, ASIC may have other objectives, such as changing corporate culture, that involve focusing on the corporation.

[62] Ch 5, section II.A.i (referring to Centro and Leighton directors and executives being forced to resign).

[63] Ch 2, section II.D.

[64] As explained in ch 2, accessorial liability for a criminal offence comes from the Criminal Code, s 11.2 and for a civil penalty provision from Corporations Act 2001 (Cth), ss 674(2A), 675(2A). There is also a due-diligence defence for civil penalty liability pursuant to Corporations Act 2001 (Cth), ss 674(2B), 675(2B). Compensation actions require a contravention of the civil penalty provision which can only occur through accessorial liability for the individual.

[65] Robert Austin and Ian Ramsay, *Ford, Austin and Ramsay's Principles of Corporations Law* (LexisNexis Online, 2018) [9.284]; Stephen Odgers, *Principles of Federal Criminal Law*, 3rd edn (Thomson Reuters, 2015) 168–88.

[66] Ch 5, section II.B.vi.

[67] Senate Economics References Committee, (n 13) [4.32].

[68] See, eg, Corporations Act 2001 (Cth), ss 1041E (false or misleading statements), 1041F (inducing persons to deal).

The lack of enforcement action against individuals may be the result of difficulties of proof and the additional costs associated with those difficulties, or the elements of the law simply not being able to be made out in relation to an individual, or the legitimate pursuit of other objectives that involve directing enforcement action at the corporate entity. However, ASIC's successful action against the directors in the Centro case study using the statutory provisions addressing directors' duties demonstrates that these difficulties can be overcome.

I. The Paradox of Insurance

Chapter three raised as a concern for the achievement of deterrence utilising financial costs the possibility that deterrence may be undermined if those costs could be dispersed through passing them onto others. Chapter five examined the concern through the most common form of dispersion in securities enforcement and litigation, D&O insurance.

The current state of the law, as explained in chapter five, is that insurance can undermine deterrence in relation to penalties, where no personal responsibility (for example, *mens rea*) or moral blame is an element, and for civil claims, as insurance is permitted in these circumstances.

For ASIC to achieve deterrence, it needs to rely on the impact on reputation, as it does, or seek to use criminal prosecutions or disqualification/banning orders to a greater extent. For class actions which can only pursue civil claims, the entire payment may in theory be covered by insurance, although a large payment may exceed the amount of insurance coverage provided by the policy. The severity of deterrence achieved by class actions may be diminished.

While this state of affairs in relation to deterrence might suggest that the availability of D&O insurance should be more restrictive, a different approach is suggested when looked at from the perspective of compensation. The availability of insurance and its ability to spread risk means that a larger pool of funds may be available to respond to a contravention, in particular, the payment of compensation to those harmed. While insurance may undermine deterrence, it may also facilitate compensation.[69] Consequently, the requirements for effective deterrence and compensation are in conflict when it comes to insurance.

Prohibiting insurance is argued to not be a feasible response as the increased exposure to liability would discourage qualified persons from becoming directors, or at least cause greater risk aversion amongst boards of directors.[70] In addition, without insurance there may also be insufficient funds to pay compensation to investors that have suffered loss, which further undermines the goal of complete recovery. As a result, the focus has been on attempting to identify how insurance can continue but with deterrence being maintained. The main approach has been for the insurer to take steps to achieve deterrence through ensuring that policy pricing (premiums and deductibles) reflects the risk of contraventions occurring. Higher insurance costs should encourage firms to reduce that cost by reducing the risk of contraventions.[71]

A range of factors influence policy pricing not just the risk of class actions, such as the industry or sector a company is in, business strategy, financial position/market capitalisation, share price volatility, corporate governance and the range of possible causes of director liability.[72]

[69] Vanessa Finch, 'Personal Accountability and Corporate Control: the Role of Directors' and Officers' Liability Insurance' (1994) 57 *Modern Law Review* 880, 891; Colin Baxter, 'Demystifying D&O Insurance' (1995) 15 *Oxford Journal of Legal Studies* 537, 546, 560.

[70] Tom Baker and Sean Griffith, *Ensuring Corporate Misconduct* (University of Chicago Press, 2010) 221.

[71] ibid, 78, 97.

[72] ibid, 86, 95; AON, 'Directors & Officers (D&O) Insurance Market update' (2017).

Furthermore, the competitive nature of the insurance market can mean that higher prices for higher risks may not be able to be passed on because other insurers will offer cheaper policies.[73] One interviewee familiar with the D&O insurance market in Australia was of the view that despite the payments made in class actions, the premiums for D&O insurance had not increased during the period covered by the case studies due to intense competition in the insurance market.[74] However, more recent reports suggest that D&O insurance costs have increased as a direct result of class actions, and that there is some differentiation in pricing due to different sectors and the risk of the corporation.[75] Nonetheless, the multiple factors that affect pricing (which are discussed above) suggest that the pricing of D&O insurance policies is insufficiently linked to securities enforcement action and class actions for it to exert a strong deterrent effect.[76]

J. Summary of the Effectiveness of ASIC Enforcement and Class Actions

The above discussion has explained the effectiveness of ASIC and the class action, compared to each other, in the areas of deterrence and compensation. The discussion sets out why deterrence (broken down along the three dimensions of reputation, direction sanctions and indirect costs) and compensation may or may not be achieved and the factors that mediate or influence that outcome. To facilitate comprehension, the findings are summarised in Table 6.2.

Table 6.2 Relative effectiveness of ASIC enforcement and class actions in achieving deterrence and compensation

	ASIC enforcement	**Class action**
Deterrence – reputation	Higher Because: ➢ Independent body accountable to Parliament ➢ Reputation important to corporations and individuals ➢ Expressing society's expectations of acceptable conduct But: ➢ Impact varies with enforcement tool employed and whether finding of contravention ➢ Individuals rarely pursued but they could be	Lower Because: ➢ Pursuing private interests ➢ Deterrence is indirect ➢ Motivation linked to lawyer and funder profits ➢ Resolved through settlement ➢ Individuals rarely pursued

(continued)

[73] Baker and Griffith (n 70) 99–100.

[74] Interview Multiplex solicitor, 11. See also Herbert Smith Freehills, 'Change in D&O Market Conditions' (13 April 2017) ('D&O insurance premiums have not increased significantly during the last 10 years').

[75] Alice Uribe and James Frost, 'Directors hit in class action surge', *The Australian Financial Review* (4 January 2018) 1, 4; Chris Merritt, 'Class actions fuel insurance rates' *The Australian* (23 March 2018) 27.

[76] Sean Griffith, 'D&O insurance and the ability of shareholder litigation to deter' in Claire Hill and Brett McDonnell (eds), *Research Handbook on the Economics of Corporate Law* (Edward Elgar, 2012) 343.

Table 6.2 ***(Continued)***

	ASIC enforcement	**Class action**
Deterrence – direct sanctions	Lower Because: ➢ Smaller quantum linked to low statutory penalties/fines ➢ Rarely pursues criminal actions ➢ Greater emphasis on celerity, so as to address market integrity, results in non-litigious enforcement choices ➢ Insurance may reduce deterrence but criminal sanctions avoid this if pursued	Higher Because: ➢ Larger quantum as a result of seeking compensation But: ➢ Deterrence is incidental ➢ Focus is only on contraventions with large losses ➢ No ability to bring criminal actions ➢ Insurance may reduce deterrence
Deterrence – indirect costs	Lower Because: ➢ Smaller costs as ASIC is required to use resources efficiently	Higher Because: ➢ Larger costs as lawyers more expensive
Compensation	Lower Because: ➢ Rare to seek compensation unless in public interest But: ➢ Transaction costs borne by ASIC not shareholder	Higher Because: ➢ Provide access to justice ➢ Maximising payouts is in group members', lawyers' and funders' interest But ➢ Rare for complete compensation to be paid due to settlements and risk of failing to prove elements of case ➢ High transaction costs ➢ Circularity problem – diversified shareholders pay diversified shareholders ➢ Not pursued for smaller claims where potential recovery is uneconomic for a litigation funder to finance

III. Ramifications of ASIC Enforcement and Class Actions Coexistence

The advent of both ASIC and the shareholder-initiated class action as actors in the field of securities enforcement has given rise to regulatory pluralism. Chapter three developed a number of values or norms of a good regulatory process which chapter five then considered through the lens of the case studies. Consequently, this text has examined ASIC and the class action by reference to those values. It has also considered how overlapping enforcement impacts on those values and on the other actor. This section discusses the ramifications of overlapping enforcement.

A. Regulatory Pluralism

Regulatory pluralism was introduced in chapter three as an explanation for why private enforcement may be adopted.[77] It provides a way of thinking about the effect of public and private enforcement on the regulated entity, on society and the impact of public and private enforcement on each other. In short, these are the advantages and disadvantages to coexistence and they may be applied to the addition of class actions to a regulatory field that was previously the sole province of a government regulator, such as ASIC.

The advantages are that the additional knowledge and expertise of the class action proponents, not just ASIC, can be brought to bear. This allows for multiple viewpoints on what is a desirable regulatory outcome and how to achieve that outcome.[78] The need for private enforcement through the class action may be economic. The state may choose not to expend the resources necessary for adequate enforcement, or due to fiscal constraints be unable to adequately resource a regulator. ASIC's enforcement budget is discussed below, but ASIC has been subject to government cuts for a number of years that reduce resources.[79] Private enforcement can fill the gap. Public enforcement may also not proceed due to risk aversion, regulatory capture or ineptitude. Private enforcement can be a response to deficiencies in public enforcement.[80] The different incentives and accountability mechanisms for private enforcement, that is, being free of the bureaucratic hurdles that regulators must clear, can allow it to be more responsive to contraventions.[81]

However, simply adding regulatory instruments to an existing regulatory model may have a variety of effects, not all of which may be positive or helpful, and many may be unforeseen when initially adopted.[82] Regulatory pluralism can result in the 'fragmentation of the exercise of power and control' over enforcement.[83] The existence of public and private enforcement may result in a major and permanent realignment of roles and responsibilities.

B. What is the Public Interest?

A legislatively created, but independent, regulator such as ASIC is expected to act in the public interest. The class action, in contrast, pursues primarily private interests. However, seen through a regulatory lens, the collective pursuit of those private interests may be in the public interest.

Identifying what action is in the public interest may be open to debate. There may be agreement on what actions promote the public interest, but equally there could be differing

[77] Ch 3, section IV.B.iii.

[78] Orly Lobel, 'The Renew Deal: The Fall of Regulation and the Rise of Governance in Contemporary Legal Thought' (2004) 89 *Minnesota Law Review* 342, 373.

[79] Lexi Metherell, 'Budget 2014: ASIC's funding cut in move away from financial sector oversight', *ABC News*, 15 May 2014 (ASIC budget reduced by $120 million over five years).

[80] Kent Roach and Michael Trebilcock, 'Private Enforcement of Competition Laws' (1996) 34 *Osgood Hall Law Journal* 461, 472, 481.

[81] Barry Boyer and Errol Meidinger, 'Privatizing Regulatory Enforcement: A Preliminary Assessment of Citizen Suits Under Federal Environmental Laws' (1985) 34 *Buffalo Law Review* 833, 838, 870; Matthew Stephenson, 'Public Regulation or Private Enforcement: The Case for Expanding the Role of Administrative Agencies' (2005) 91 *Virginia Law Review* 93, 108–09, 110; Samuel Issacharoff, 'Class Actions and State Authority' (2012) 44 *Loyola University Chicago Law Journal* 369, 385–86.

[82] Boyer and Meidinger (ibid) 837; Neil Gunningham and Darren Sinclair, 'Regulatory Pluralism: Designing Policy Mixes for Environmental Protection' (1999) 21 *Law & Policy* 49, 50.

[83] Julia Black, 'Decentring Regulation: Understanding the Role of Regulation and Self-Regulation in a "Post-Regulatory" World' (2001) 54 *Current Legal Problems* 103, 108.

views of what action the public interest requires. Depending on the viewpoint adopted, the class action may assist pursuing the same vision of the public interest as ASIC holds. Alternatively, the class action may take a different view of what the public interest requires. The idea in regulatory pluralism of there being multiple viewpoints accepts this. Indeed, the class action may empower shareholders, who would otherwise have to accept ASIC's regulatory response, to engage the disclosing entity and challenge ASIC's approach. The most obvious example of this in the current context is that ASIC does not pursue compensation. The class action procedure, with the aid of lawyers and funders, may be seen as a vehicle for shareholders to pursue compensation rather than lobbying ASIC or members of Parliament for such action to be taken. The class action may be championed on the basis that it advances the public interest through obtaining compensation for those that suffered loss and indirectly achieving deterrence. Equally, if the public interest is best achieved by having a government regulator that can calibrate its response to wrongdoing, then a class action that is outside the control of the regulator may be seen as contrary to the public interest, as discussed further in section III.C below.

The Multiplex case study illustrates the tension over what is in the public interest, or whether class actions are pursuing public or private interests. In Multiplex, ASIC was able to secure the creation of a compensation fund as part of an enforceable undertaking that balanced, or traded off, various regulatory goals. In contrast, the proponents of the class action and the group members' interest was to seek compensation for a broader group of shareholders. The private interests of those group members in obtaining recovery is advanced, but so also is the public interest in ensuring that those who suffer loss due to another's wrongdoing are compensated. Indeed, the legislature specifically granted standing for those who suffer loss to seek compensation.[84] Other public interest concerns were highlighted in Multiplex when ASIC refused to disclose documents that would have revealed the identity of whistleblowers by relying on public interest immunity, as it wanted to protect whistleblowers and encourage them to come forward. Public interest immunity as a doctrine involves conflicting public interests – 'whether the public interest which requires that the document should not be produced outweighs the public interest that a court of justice in performing its functions should not be denied access to relevant evidence'.[85] The class action applicant's challenge to ASIC's position may be seen as siding with the public interest in placing relevant evidence before a court. However, it can also be seen through the lens of private interests – the applicant, as representative for the group members, trying to improve prospects of success without having to incur its own investigation costs to find alternative methods of proving its case.[86]

ASIC's enforcement choices and the commencement of a private class action can be combined so as to pursue the public interest in harmony. Alternatively, ASIC's enforcement actions and the class action may give effect to different or conflicting visions of what is required to promote the public interest.

C. Regulator Discretion and the Enforcement Pyramid

Chapter two explained that ASIC's approach to enforcement was to employ a range of regulatory tools through responsive regulation as typified by the enforcement pyramid.[87] ASIC,

[84] Ch 2, section II.V.
[85] *Sankey v Whitlam* (1978) 142 CLR 1, 38–39 (Gibbs ACJ).
[86] Ch 4, section IV and Ch 5, section IV.B.
[87] Ch 2, sections IV.A, IV.B.

like other government regulators, can adjust its approach to enforcement, moving between persuasion and deterrence as circumstances require.[88] Indeed, ASIC may seek to achieve behavioural and cultural change, compliance and education, as well as deterrence. Furthermore, where regulators have continuing or frequent engagement with regulated entities, negotiated outcomes may be possible, even desirable, as a way to minimise cost and craft bespoke regulatory responses.[89] The regulator is also able to adjust its response or approach based on the behaviour or capacity of the regulated entity.[90] Regulator discretion is aimed at allowing for multi-factorial decision-making.

In a world of regulatory pluralism, the enforcement pyramid is three-dimensional and takes account of additional actors.[91] In the current scenario, they are the proponents of the shareholder class action. Regulatory responses may come from either ASIC or the class action's proponents. However, the escalation or 'tit-for-tat' response in responsive regulation where a regulated entity fails to respond to lower order regulatory instruments can only be employed by ASIC as it has multiple enforcement responses that it can draw upon. The class action as an individual regulatory instrument is more static than dynamic so that it cannot be calibrated to take account of how a regulated entity responds to allegations of wrongdoing.[92] It cannot relent or reward a positive response. Equally it cannot move to a criminal footing for a negative response. In a plaintiff-defendant setting, the room to move is often only around the quantum of compensation and how quickly and willingly the defendant responds to the plaintiff's claim.

Private enforcement also impacts the regulator's use of the enforcement pyramid and regulatory discretion by seeking to maximise the amount of damages that can be recovered.[93] A 'graduated, responsive and interactive enforcement strategy' by the regulator may be problematic where the class action offers a static response.[94] Regulated entities may have no incentive to negotiate or cooperate with a regulator where substantial private damages claims may still follow.[95] The class action cannot be avoided by accepting a lower order enforcement tool because ASIC does not control the class action. Cooperative relationships between regulators and regulated entities may be disrupted.[96] This in turn means that the regulatory message to be communicated to the regulated entity may become confused or subject to interference.[97]

[88] Harry Kalven Jr and Maurice Rosenfield, 'The Contemporary Function of the Class Suit' (1940–41) 8 *University of Chicago Law Review* 684, 719; Boyer and Meidinger (n 81), 881–82; Rose, (n 48) 1329–30.

[89] Colin Scott, 'Enforcing Consumer Protection Laws' in Geraint Howells, Iain Ramsay and Thomas Wilhelmsson with David Kraft, *Handbook of Research on International Consumer Law* (Edward Elgar, 2010) 553–54.

[90] Robert Kagan and John Scholz, 'The "Criminology of the Corporation" and Regulatory Enforcement Strategies' in Keith Hawkins and John Thomas (eds), *Enforcing Regulation* (Kluwer-Nijhoff Publishing, 1984) 86; Black (n 83) 108.

[91] Ch 3, section IV.B explaining Neil Gunningham and Peter Grabosky, *Smart Regulation* (Oxford University Press, 1998), which advocates a three-dimensional pyramid where the three sides of the pyramid represent the government acting as regulator; business acting as a self-regulator; and commercial and non-commercial third parties.

[92] See Gunningham and Grabosky (ibid) 403 (static instruments 'cannot be tailored to ascend or descend [the expanded enforcement pyramid] depending on the behaviour of specific firms'); Neil Gunningham and Darren Sinclair, 'Smart Regulation' in Peter Drahos (ed), *Regulatory Theory: Foundations and Applications* (ANU Press, 2017) 138.

[93] Richard Nagareda, 'Class Actions in the Administrative State: Kalven and Rosenfield Revisited' (2008) 75 *University of Chicago Law Review* 603, 616–18.

[94] Gunningham and Grabosky (n 91) 402. See also Robert Baldwin and Julia Black, 'Really Responsive Regulation' (2008) 71 *Modern Law Review* 59, 65.

[95] Stephen Burbank, Sean Farhang and Herbert Kritzer, 'Private Enforcement' (2013) 17 *Lewis & Clark Law Review* 637, 669; Australian Competition & Consumer Commission, 'Submission to the Competition Policy Review – Response to the Draft Report' (26 November 2014) 80.

[96] Boyer and Meidinger (n 81) 841, Jody Freeman, 'The Private Role in Public Governance' (2000) 75 *New York University Law Review* 543, 662; Stephenson (n 81) 114.

[97] Baldwin and Black (n 94) 63 (discussing responsive regulation where there are multiple regulators).

The impact on regulator discretion may be illustrated by reference to deterrence as there are now two sources of deterrence. This can be positive as it can improve detection and prevent under-deterrence. However, it can also result in over-deterrence, or double deterrence, where a regulated entity is subject to two sets of deterrence, one from ASIC and one from the class action, although the latter is indirect. The regulated entity may then overinvest in compliance systems or adopt a defensive disclosure mindset due to concern about legal liability. If ASIC determines that it has correctly calibrated the level of deterrence required, then a class action will alter or distort the severity of the deterrence imposed.[98]

The case studies found that corporations were very concerned that information provided to ASIC or formal admissions could be used to assist the proponents of class actions. However, the corporate response was more subtle and strategic than might first be thought. The corporations did not become outright obstructive or withhold cooperation in their dealings with ASIC. The Multiplex and Leighton case studies show corporations being prepared to agree to lower-level enforcement responses as a way to minimise the assistance given to class action proponents. Multiplex accepted an enforceable undertaking with a novel compensation scheme so as to avoid admissions that would accompany the settlement of a civil penalty proceeding.[99] Multiplex paid more through the enforceable undertaking than if it had paid a civil penalty. Leighton accepted an enforceable undertaking and three infringement notices as part of a cooperative approach that minimised the creation of documentation that may assist the proponents of a class action.[100] It appears that the prospect of a class action results in cooperative behaviour aimed at minimising the quantum of its impact.

The case studies suggest that ASIC can leverage the possibility of a class action to extract cooperation. However, ASIC must be aware that it faces a corporation acting in a strategic manner. The voluntary provision of information may be about seeking to narrow ASIC's line of enquiry, which may not be conducive to obtaining a complete understanding of what conduct occurred and why. This in turn may hamper the selection of the correct enforcement approach or tool. If ASIC wanted to use an enforcement tool that involved admissions, such as a civil penalty, this may see the corporation be less cooperative because it could assist a class action. ASIC needs to be careful that it does not mistake (or reward) cooperation when in fact the corporation is attempting to manipulate the outcome.

For ASIC to be the enforcer whose actions are the most important in the corporate calculus, it needs to be willing to impose sanctions that have greater gravity than the quantum of a class action. The regulator may need to demonstrate a willingness to use even more potent remedies, such as requiring admissions of wrongdoing which have a greater reputational impact, a focus on individuals so that sanctions are felt directly (subject to the operation of insurance), and the use of the top of the pyramid, including criminal sanctions.

Centro may be seen as an example of ASIC seeking to assert its role as the dominant enforcement mechanism through prosecuting a civil penalty proceeding through to judgment against individual directors. ASIC obtained declarations of contravention with associated reputational harm, but only minor penalties. However, if the chosen enforcement action and resulting penalties, indirect costs and reputational impact achieved the necessary level of deterrence, then the follow-on class action, which imposed costs comprised of \$200m compensation (including

[98] See ch 5, section II.B.ii.
[99] Ch 5, section IV.B.
[100] Ch 5, section IV.B.ii.

the applicant's legal fees and funding fees), Centro legal fees of an estimated $30–50 million as well as other indirect costs and reputational harm, may have undermined that calculation. It may be observed that ASIC and the class action proponents chose different causes of action to pursue from the same factual matrix: ASIC focused on directors' duties in relation to financial statements and the class action focused on continuous disclosure. Consequently, it might be said that there is no crossover. However, ASIC could have chosen to pursue contraventions of the continuous disclosure regime, but in the exercise of its discretion, did not as it was focused on directors' responsibility to be financial literate.[101] Nonetheless, ASIC loses the fullness of the discretion that it had over enforcement of the continuous disclosure regime prior to the advent of shareholders being given standing to bring class actions. It is no longer the sole decider as to what claims may be pursued, if any, or as to the sanctions (including compensation) to pursue or accept.[102]

The adoption of private enforcement can also mean 'not only that the state shares power over the enforcement of the law but also that it loses some control over its growth'.[103] Private parties can determine which cases are decided/litigated or avoided/settled in addition to ASIC. Where these decisions 'are based on private motives rather than public agendas, they can easily push the law's development in directions that differ from the preferences of government authorities'.[104]

The class action can develop the law in ways that favours the interests that control it, namely making proof of a contravention and establishment of causation easier, while seeking an expansive measure of loss. Judgments on the continuous disclosure regime or prohibitions on misleading conduct can create precedent that binds others, including ASIC. To date, class action proponents' development of the law in those areas has been muted because of the preference for settlement. Nonetheless, ASIC may take a different view as to how the law should develop between the interests of the 'disclosing entity' and the market. For example, the class action proponents' preference for a lower threshold in relation to causation – reliance on the market rather than direct reliance – has developed through interlocutory judgments.[105] ASIC may see this as fostering market integrity, or it could take the view that such an approach is undesirable because it discourages people from making informed decisions about investments and engaging with the company in which they are a shareholder.[106] Where different interests and preferences exist for ASIC compared to the proponents of class action, ASIC can chose to intervene in such litigation.[107] Intervening allows ASIC to be heard on matters that are significant to its statutory objectives, the exercise of

[101] For an example where ASIC pursued both breaches of directors duties and the continuous disclosure regime arising from the same factual matrix, see ASIC, 'ASIC takes further action against Rio Tinto Limited and its former CEO and CFO' (Media Release, 18-119MR, 1 May 2018) (civil penalty proceedings commenced including claims against Rio Tinto Limited for contravention of the Corporations Act 2001 (Cth), s 674(2) of and against the former Chief Executive Officer and former Chief Financial Officer for breach of s 180).

[102] ASIC ALRC Submission (n 10) [47] (ASIC would not have 'a monopoly on legal action').

[103] Mathias Reimann, 'Private Enforcement in the United States and in Europe – A Comparative Perspective and Potential Lessons for Asia' in Robin Huang and Nicholas Howson (eds), *Enforcement of Corporate and Securities Law: China and the World* (Cambridge University Press, 2017) 33.

[104] ibid. See also David Freeman Engstrom, 'Agencies and Litigation Gatekeepers' (2013) 123 *Yale Law Journal* 616, 637–41; Burbank, Farhang and Kritzer (n 95) 668.

[105] See, eg, *Caason Investments Pty Ltd v Cao* [2015] FCAFC 94 (indirect causation was found to be arguable for the purpose of an interlocutory pleading dispute in a shareholder class action). Developments in relation to causation are discussed further in ch 7.

[106] Damian Grave, Ken Adams and Jason Betts, *Class Actions in Australia*, 2d edn (Thomson Reuters, 2012) 907–08.

[107] Corporations Act 2001 (Cth), s 1330.

its functions and powers, and important issues of statutory interpretation affecting the legislative policy of a provision or to ASIC's powers or ability to administer a provision.[108] There is also Parliament's ability to legislate an approach contrary to that which develops through litigation. This could favour ASIC or the class action's proponents, but importantly the outcome is determined by democratic means. However, where ASIC or the Parliament acts to assert a different view of the public interest, those actions expend public resources. Empowering shareholders to bring class actions is not without costs.

D. Accountability

ASIC is subject to a range of accountability mechanisms as outlined in chapter three, and as specifically explained in relation to the case studies in chapter five. In contrast to public regulators, a private enforcer is not accountable for the social impact of its decisions.[109] The focus is instead on the internal operation of the class action. The internal operation of the class action is concerned with the accountability of the lawyer, and to a lesser extent the litigation funder, as well as due process in the technical sense of the court ensuring that procedural fairness is extended to not just the representative party but also group members. These internal accountability and due process mechanisms are crucial to the protection of the participants in the class action. The effectiveness of these internal mechanisms will affect the legitimacy of the class action.[110] However, there is no accountability mechanism in relation to the broader public interest or through a requirement for compliance with a legislative mandate as there is for ASIC.

Regulatory pluralism suggests that 'transparency, accountability and discipline' are maintained through 'benchmarking comparisons and regulation through benchmarking'.[111] Various forms of enforcement can be compared with each other. ASIC and the class action no longer operate in silos. Rather, the suggestion is that the two forms of enforcement – public and private – can aid in achieving effective accountability through one being available for comparison or benchmarking with the other.

This text has as a central component the comparison of ASIC and the class action through the four case studies. Tables 4.3, 4.4 and 4.5 in chapter four summarise the comparisons based on outcome, cost and time. Those same elements could be employed as benchmarks, although further analysis is needed as demonstrated by the detailed evaluation in the text. As a starting point, the contraventions or losses (alleged or proven), outcomes achieved and whether that be a fine, enforceable undertaking or compensation, and costs incurred should be publicly available. For comparisons to be helpful and fair, there would need to be some explanation as to why the outcomes were acceptable. The comparison allows for the testing of such explanations. A parliamentary committee could ask ASIC why it chose a particular enforcement approach when the class action achieved 'x' compensation at 'y' cost. A court conducting a class action settlement

[108] ASIC, 'Information Sheet 180 – ASIC's approach to involvement in private court proceedings' (June 2013) 3.

[109] Boyer and Meidinger (n 81) 842; Freeman (n 96) 662–63, W Kip Viscusi (ed), *Regulation through Litigation* (AEI-Brookings Joint Center for Regulatory Studies, 2002) 3, 42–50; Stephenson (n 81) 119.

[110] Julia Black, 'Constructing and Contesting Legitimacy and Accountability in Polycentric Regulatory Regimes' (2008) 2 *Regulation & Governance* 137, 141.

[111] Bradley Karkkainen, '"New Governance" in Legal Thought and in the World: Some Splitting as Antidote to Overzealous Lumping' (2004) 89 *Minnesota Law Review* 471, 485.

approval may ask about the size of legal fees and funding fees where ASIC had undertaken an investigation and provided its materials. Explanations will exist, but accountability may require that they be supplied.[112]

Alternatively, where a particular class action raises matters that impact the regulation of continuous disclosure, including matters going to deterrence or compensation, ASIC could use its power to intervene in the proceedings. In a financial product/service class action, ASIC intervened and appealed in relation to the terms of settlement and the distribution of compensation.[113] In a different context, the court has requested ASIC to provide information on the fees charged by receivers.[114] As a result, ASIC could play a role in holding the class action accountable.

E. Efficiency

From a regulatory pluralism perspective, the existence of private enforcement allows for the state to supplement its enforcement efforts. The class action does not just provide a mechanism for seeking compensation, but also provides a further way to detect misconduct and impose sanctions which assists with deterrence.

The Parliamentary inquiry into ASIC found that 'ASIC's enforcement special account appears inadequate for allowing ASIC to fund large and complex cases' and that ASIC was an agency 'that receives far more reports of misconduct that it could possibly investigate'.[115] The Australian Shareholder Associations has linked the low penalties obtained by ASIC to ASIC having insufficient resources.[116] There is also a concern that regulators are unable to match the resources of corporate defendants with 'deep pockets' when it comes to enforcement involving litigation.[117] Private funding of enforcement offers the legislature a way in which to increase the resources available for enforcing its legislation. This follows from the lawyers and funders being able to profit from bringing cases. The solicitor for the applicant in the Leighton class action opined that 'shareholder class actions can really amplify the effect of the regulatory spend'.[118] Likewise, the solicitor for the applicant in the Multiplex class action described the issue as follows:

> It is one thing for the regulator to … get an enforceable undertaking. That will involve one level of public expenditure. It is another thing to run a fully blown class action seeking damages and full compensation. Such cases are very expensive and the question arises as to why the regulator [should] spend public money … on such a case if other lawyers will do it competently.[119]

Implicit in this rhetorical question is the view that government which exists to provide public goods such as regulation and enforcement is relieved from doing so where a private

[112] An explanation may derive from ASIC and the class action reacting to each other. ASIC may choose a lower level enforcement tool on the basis that it expects a class action to be brought for substantial damages and it is factoring the indirect deterrence effect of that into its approach. Similarly, the class action may craft pleadings and discovery based on what ASIC did or did not do.

[113] *ASIC v Richards* [2013] FCAFC 89.

[114] *Australian Executor Trustee Ltd v Provident Capital Ltd* (2018) 125 ACSR 133, 134–35 [5] (Rares J).

[115] Senate Economics References Committee, 'Performance of the Australian Securities and Investments Commission' (June 2014) 278, 292.

[116] Senate Economics References Committee (n 13) [3.26].

[117] Senate Economics References Committee (n 115) 400.

[118] Interview Applicant's solicitor Leighton, 23.

[119] Interview Applicants' solicitor Multiplex, 17.

alternative exists. Indeed, ASIC is clearly aware of the private avenues for seeking compensation.[120] The ability to save resources and leave seeking compensation to shareholders themselves appears to be keenly appreciated, but other ramifications, such as those discussed above, like interference with regulator discretion and double deterrence, do not seem to be as well understood, or given the same significance as reducing government expenditure on enforcement.

While private enforcement transfers the cost of enforcement from the state to litigants, lawyers and funders, there is still at a societal level the consumption of resources.[121] Society may legitimately be concerned to ensure that the consumption of those resources is undertaken efficiently. In particular, some of the resources consumed will still be provided by the taxpayer, such as the court system, so that an even more direct link may be established.

Chapter five discussed the efficiency of ASIC and the class action with the information available from the case studies. While ASIC is generally able to achieve enforcement outcomes more cheaply than class actions, particularly because it has non-litigation tools at its disposal, measuring efficiency is very difficult. As explained in relation to deterrence, the class action generally imposes higher financial sanctions. However, there are other outcomes that are very important, but difficult to measure, such as the intangible costs associated with reputational harm. In addition, the class action achieves compensation which would largely not occur if no class action was commenced. Equally, a large amount of the compensation achieved is consumed by transaction costs.

The one case study where a comparison of the efficiency of ASIC and the class action can occur is in relation to Multiplex and the compensation achieved. ASIC's expenditure of $500,000[122] resulted in a $32 million compensation fund of which $20 million was disbursed. The class action saw a gross recovery of $110 million but with expenditure of $46 million. Although ASIC recovered half as much as the class action, its recovery per dollar spent is significantly higher. The class action recovered about $2.40 for each $1.00 spent. ASIC recovered $64 for each $1.00 spent focusing on the fund created, or $40 for each $1.00 spent focusing on the portion of the fund claimed. This case study suggests that ASIC is more efficient than the class action, which owes much to ASIC's lower costs and the different incentives faced by the two. The higher fees in the class action reflect higher revenues for the lawyer and funder. Higher charges or costs for ASIC do not have this revenue component. In contrast, ASIC must work within the confines of its budget. Consequently, the transaction costs in class actions which reduce group member compensation, as discussed above, may also mean the class action is inefficient at a societal level when compared to ASIC.

F. Summary of ASIC Enforcement and Class Actions Coexistence

The above discussion demonstrates that the coexistence of ASIC and the class action complicates the regulatory landscape and offers both benefits and detriments, including in relation to their impact on each other. To facilitate comprehension of the advantages and disadvantages of combining public and private enforcement the above findings are summarised in Table 6.3.

120 Alex Boxsell, 'Regulators praise private court actions', *The Weekend Australian Financial Review* (5–9 April 2012) 59; ASIC Information Sheet 151 (n 52) 6.

121 John Coffee, 'Rescuing the Private Attorney General: Why the Model of Lawyer as Bounty Hunter is not Working' (1983) 42 *Maryland Law Review* 215, 226 fn 24.

122 ASIC's expenditure is estimated based on information from other enforcement actions: ch 5, section IV.D.i.

Table 6.3 Summary of effects of coexistence of ASIC enforcement and class actions

	Advantages	**Disadvantages**
Regulatory process	Greater resources, knowledge and expertise is available for enforcement Multiple viewpoints on whether and what regulatory action should be taken and how law should develop Class actions provide another perspective on what is in the public interest – public interest is contestable Class action can provide a check on regulator inaction due to risk aversion, regulatory capture or ineptitude ASIC and class action decisions/ outcomes are comparators or benchmarks for each providing a potential additional form of accountability ASIC can leverage follow-on class action to obtain cooperation from regulated entities	Regulator loses control, discretion over enforcement, including ability to calibrate a response through the enforcement pyramid ASIC loses ability to develop law through strategic litigation and may need to expend resources responding to precedent setting class action litigation Fragmentation of regulatory responses Class actions pursuit of private interests and accountability mechanisms aimed at the internal operation of the class action may negatively affect public interest ASIC actions taken due to its view of the public interest (eg, not disclosing whistleblower identities or not creating written records of investigations) may hamper pursuit of private interests and the public interest in compensation Regulator may cede area of regulation/ enforcement to private parties Corporations may decline or limit cooperation with ASIC due to follow on class action
Deterrence	Deterrence bolstered by having two sources of detection/action – averts under-deterrence	Over-deterrence
Compensation	Shareholders can pursue private rights/interests, ie able to obtain compensation without relying on ASIC (the state)	Compensation operates on a user-pays model with class actions more costly for shareholders and society (legal costs and litigation funding fees) than if regulator took action

IV. Conclusion

This chapter has sought to address two main questions. First, are ASIC enforcement and the shareholder class action, compared to each other, effective in achieving deterrence and compensation in relation to a particular category of Australia's securities law, namely the continuous disclosure regime? Second, what are the ramifications of ASIC enforcement and shareholder class actions coexisting: how does their coexistence impact on the values of a 'good' regulatory process, and do they help or hinder each other in the achievement of their objectives?

A. Effectiveness of ASIC Enforcement and the Class Action – Outcomes

The first question focused on effectiveness of the outcomes achieved through a comparison of ASIC enforcement and the class action. The findings of the thesis may be summarised as follows.

i. ASIC

Deterrence is a key objective for ASIC. ASIC seeks to achieve deterrence through impacting reputation and direct sanctions. However, an objective review of the enforcement tools used by ASIC in the continuous disclosure area demonstrates that ASIC relies heavily on administrative enforcement tools (infringement notices, disallowing the use of a reduced content prospectus and enforceable undertakings) rather than the litigation tools of civil penalty and criminal proceedings as set out in Table 6.1. ASIC's objective does not appear to align with its actual conduct in terms of the choice of enforcement tools. Indeed, the choice of enforcement tools was crucial to whether and how deterrence could be achieved.

The case studies found that ASIC is able to be more effective than the class action in achieving deterrence through reputational sanctions because ASIC is an independent, accountable body. However, the extent of the impact on reputation appears to vary depending on the enforcement tool employed and the outcome achieved. Tools that have no finding of wrongdoing, such as the much-used administrative tools, seem to have less impact than those tools that do, namely the litigation tools. But administrative tools are not without impact because reputation is important to corporations and individuals, and ASIC's status lets it communicate its findings and concerns to the market.

The case studies also found that ASIC's effectiveness in achieving deterrence through direct sanctions such as fines, civil penalties and criminal penalties was seen as lower than that achieved by the class action in the case studies. This was because ASIC rarely used the litigation tools which could result in the imposition of criminal and civil penalties. Of course, if ASIC actually used criminal sanctions, something that the class action cannot achieve, it would place deterrence on an entirely different plane than is possible with the class action.

ASIC's choice of enforcement tools to achieve the deterrence objective necessitated consideration as to how this approach arises. The conclusion is that ASIC's approach to deterrence is subject to a number of self-imposed and external constraints that influence how ASIC operationalises its objective.

In the continuous disclosure area, ASIC places significant importance on using deterrence to ensure market integrity. As chapter two explained, continuous disclosure is designed to ensure that price-sensitive information is made public so that the market is informed. When ASIC detects conduct that is antithetical to prompt disclosure of price-sensitive information, it has determined that it needs to act quickly to inform the particular entity, but also (importantly) other participants in the market, that it regards the conduct as contrary to the law. This approach is supported by using enforcement tools that can be promptly applied, certainty and celerity in classical deterrence terms, which are the administrative remedies. Litigation-based enforcement tools, by their nature, involve greater delay.

ASIC's concern to promote market integrity may also require a focus on objectives related to or supportive of deterrence, such as achieving behavioural and cultural change, compliance and education. While ASIC and the class action overlap on deterrence, ASIC has a larger remit. The multiple enforcement tools and ability to combine them in an enforcement pyramid reflect that ASIC does more than just deter. As a result, an enforceable undertaking that directly mandates corporate policy or governance changes may be a more effective tool for what ASIC seeks to achieve in relation to market integrity. ASIC's enforcement choices may be seen as the considered use of regulator discretion aimed at achieving the multitude of objectives that it is tasked with.

ASIC must also operate with the regulatory resources at its disposal so that the cost of regulatory tools also plays a role. Administrative tools at the bottom of the enforcement pyramid are cheap, compared to the cost of higher order tools involving hard fought, adversarial litigation with its various procedural protections for defendants. ASIC's use of litigation-based enforcement tools may also be hampered by low penalties.

The continuous disclosure regime is also structured so as to make the use of higher order sanctions against individuals difficult, due to additional elements that must be proved compared to proceedings against the corporation. Accordingly, individuals are not typically targeted for enforcement action despite recognition that the threat of personal liability, especially criminal sanctions, can achieve effective deterrence. In addition, civil penalty and compensation claims against directors may be alleviated through D&O insurance so that the director does not feel the financial cost directly.

ASIC rarely seeks compensation, and appears to give this goal lower importance in relation to continuous disclosure for two main reasons: the focus on market integrity discussed above; and the presence of the class action. ASIC places greater importance on achieving market integrity through deterrence than on obtaining compensation, and shareholders have a route to compensation through the class action. However, in relation to the latter reason, class actions may not always be commenced, especially if the claim is considered uneconomic for a litigation funder to finance. Nonetheless, the class action is typically more effective at achieving compensation than ASIC.

ii. Class Actions

The main goal of the proponents of class actions is to pursue compensation which often results in large monetary payments. Class action litigation can achieve access to justice that would not otherwise be possible, including because ASIC makes compensation a low priority. However, the headline figure obscures the true outcome, which needs to factor in that the compensation recovered is rarely equivalent to the losses suffered and there are significant deductions for legal fees and litigation funding fees. Class actions have also been subject to criticism due to the circularity problem, which 'in shorthand' is shareholders paying themselves compensation. The criticism is a concern at a theoretical level but the extent of its application in practice is difficult to ascertain, and it can be avoided through the participation of non-diversified shareholders in the class action and by the inclusion of claims that go beyond the corporation to include directors and advisers. However, the class action may have little incentive to pursue directors as it can access their D&O insurance through pursuing the company, as Side C extends the same quantum of coverage to the company. Compensation is a worthy goal, as established by both the objective of the legislation and corrective justice, but in practice it may not make the person 'whole' by achieving full compensation.

Class actions, in contrast to ASIC, typically impose significant financial sanctions through the indirect effect of compensation payments. Class actions also impose significant indirect costs through the use of civil litigation. From a deterrence perspective it does not matter where the money extracted from a defendant (compensation or costs) goes, only that the defendant pays it. D&O insurance can relieve the defendant from paying some or all of a compensation payment. In financial terms, the class action imposes greater sanctions and therefore deterrence than ASIC, but subject to the effect of insurance. However, the class action is a blunter tool than ASIC, as by its nature it only has costs to impose. Furthermore, as the class action's real goal is to maximise compensation it has little concern in trying to calibrate the deterrence achieved with the seriousness of the wrong committed. The private nature and financial incentives embedded in class actions, as well as the focus on settlement, may undermine deterrence through impact on reputation as compared to ASIC.

iii. Re-examining Effectiveness after Changes in Policy Settings and Legal Requirements

The third question is whether changes in policy settings and legal requirements can encourage or discourage public and private enforcement, and consequently impact the effectiveness of public and private enforcement in achieving deterrence and compensation. This is a re-examination of the first question through the lens of actual policy changes in Australia post-31 December 2017, including changes to ASIC's resourcing and enforcement approach, and regulation of litigation funding. This analysis, including drawing on further empirical examination of the enforcement undertaken by ASIC and class action activity, is set out in chapter seven.

B. Ramifications of ASIC Enforcement and Class Actions Coexistence – Process

The second question was directed at the regulatory process. The coexistence of ASIC action and the class action complicates the regulatory landscape and offers both benefits and detriments, including in relation to the impact of each on the other.

The benefits are greater resources for enforcement, added expertise, multiple viewpoints on desirable responses to contraventions, and an additional or replacement source of deterrence and compensation. The detriments are largely for the regulator, which loses its dominant position, its ability to define the actions that the public interest requires, its exercise of discretion drawing on its expertise and powers, including being able to deploy enforcement tools consistent with responsive regulation, and its development of a consistent regulatory framework.

These pros and cons also illustrate the societal calculus that government and the legislature have made, perhaps without expressly knowing that they were. The shareholder class action was borne from a combination of the grant of standing to shareholders to pursue their losses from a contravention of the continuous disclosure regime, enactment of a class action procedure, and the advent of litigation funding. Private citizens were given the means, albeit at considerable cost, to take action to pursue compensation and, indirectly, deterrence. The state is relieved, to some degree, from the provision of what was previously a public good, enforcement (especially in relation to obtaining compensation, but also deterrence), and instead a user-pays principle applies. However, societal consumption of resources to obtain compensation may actually be higher due to the cost of lawyers in private practice and litigation funding. Private enforcement also has an entrepreneurial element with class action lawyers and litigation funders, although primarily concerned with access to compensation for group members, determining what cases are brought and where duplication may occur with ASIC, based on their own financial imperatives. The lower accountability of private actors may mean less oversight of how enforcement is carried out. In summary, the shareholder class action may advance or harm the public interest depending on the particular circumstances in which it is brought.

The regulatory process is no longer a straight line between regulator identification of contraventions and the choice of a suitable enforcement tool based on the regulator's objectives and interactions with the regulated entity. Regulation of continuous disclosure is now a triangle of interactions between the regulator, the regulated entity and the class action. Each is trying to take account of, or pre-empt, what another may do. However, ASIC's enforcement approach appears to be affected to a greater extent by the class action, than the proponents of class actions are affected by ASIC and its enforcement strategy.

The ramifications of co-existence may have received scant consideration when class actions were enacted, but in light of the findings in the text it is now necessary to take a more considered and structured approach to factoring coexistence into the operation of the regulatory process for the enforcement of the continuous disclosure regime. This issue is addressed in chapter eight.

7

Public and Private Enforcement Recalibrated

I. Introduction

The case studies and conclusions reached in the earlier chapters were based on the substantive law, Australian Securities and Investments Commission (ASIC) regulatory enforcement practice and class actions approach prior to 31 December 2017. This chapter examines changes, or proposed changes, to that state of affairs from 2018 to 2021. The existence of these reforms is of significance because it illustrates that both public and private enforcement can be encouraged or discouraged based on the settings of a range of policy levers and legal developments. This in turn may impact the effectiveness of ASIC and the class action, in particular, in achieving deterrence and compensation.

The reforms that are analysed are the changes to ASIC's approach to enforcement which has been invigorated through a new 'Why not litigate?' approach, the adoption of an industry funding model, and increased powers and penalties. Shareholder class actions and litigation funding have also been the subject of legal developments through case law and law reform recommendations. In the case of litigation funding, the previous light touch regulatory approach has been replaced with more stringent regulation. Lastly, the continuous disclosure laws have been the subject of reform with measures to add an intention or fault requirement, as existed before 2002, adopted in a bid to make it more difficult to prove a civil contravention.

II. ASIC's Enforcement Approach Revisited

The invigoration of ASIC's approach to enforcement has been driven by three developments. The first was the Royal Commission into Misconduct in the Banking, Superannuation and Financial Services Industry (Financial Services Royal Commission) which embodied a critical examination of ASIC's regulatory enforcement practice. The Royal Commission's recommendation was that ASIC should take as its 'starting point' the question of 'whether a court should determine the consequences of contravention'.[1] This has given rise to an enforcement approach know as 'Why not litigate?'. The second was the Australia Parliament's adoption of an industry funding model for ASIC which replaced the previous taxpayer-funded model. The industry funding model holds out the prospect of greater resources for ASIC, but this is subject to the executive retaining control

[1] Royal Commission into Misconduct in the Banking, Superannuation and Financial Services Industry, 'Final Report – Volume 1' (2019) ('Final Report') 446, recommendation 6.2; Royal Commission into Misconduct in the Banking, Superannuation and Financial Services Industry, 'Interim Report – Volume 1' (2018) ('Interim Report') 278.

over ASIC's budget. The third was the Australian Parliament's enactment of legislation to increase the quantum of penalties for criminal offences and civil penalties as well as adding a new power for the making of relinquishment orders.

A. ASIC's Approach to Misconduct and Choice of Enforcement Tools

The Financial Services Royal Commission was the culmination of concerns about misconduct in Australia's financial sector, including by the major banks. The Australian Government had sought to avoid a Royal Commission with its wide-ranging powers due to fears that its outcome may have unforeseen political and economic ramifications. Ultimately, just as a range of parliamentary backbenchers and the opposition obtained the numbers to pass the necessary resolution, the then Prime Minister, Malcolm Turnbull, announced that the examples of misconduct required a Royal Commission.[2]

The Royal Commission was not addressing continuous disclosure, or even the securities market more generally. The focus was firmly on banking and financial services. However, the Terms of Reference included requiring the Commissioner, Kenneth Hayne (former justice of the High Court of Australia), to inquire into 'the effectiveness and ability of regulators of financial services entities to identify and address misconduct by those entities', and whether there needed to be changes to the financial regulators to minimise the likelihood of misconduct.[3] ASIC was one of those financial regulators, in addition to being the regulator responsible for securities regulation, including the continuous disclosure regime that is of interest here.

Concerns about ASIC's ability to regulate financial services, especially the well-resourced banks and financial services companies, may be linked back to the Senate Economics References Committee's inquiry into the performance of ASIC.[4] ASIC was characterised as 'a timid, hesitant regulator' that was too ready to trust the representations of the entities regulated.[5] Moreover, the Committee found that 'ASIC's enforcement role is one of its most important functions. ASIC needs to be respected and feared'.[6] Consequently, the enforcement approach of ASIC, not just the misconduct of regulated entities, came in for close scrutiny as part of the Royal Commission.

i. The Interim Report and ASIC's Response

In the Interim Report that was tabled in Parliament on 28 September 2018, ASIC's response to misconduct was summarised as: 'When banks have disclosed, or ASIC has otherwise learned of, misconduct, ASIC has almost always sought to negotiate what will be done in response. … Rarely has ASIC gone to court to have the defaulting party penalised'.[7] The Interim Report went on to state that 'When deciding what to do in response to misconduct, ASIC's starting point appears to

[2] Michael Roddan, *The People vs The Banks* (Melbourne University Press, 2019) 1–8.

[3] Letters Patent, Royal Commission into Misconduct in the Banking, Superannuation and Financial Services Industry (14 December 2017) 3.

[4] Adele Ferguson, *Banking Bad* (ABC Books, 2019) 107 (describing the inquiry as 'the first brick in the wall for a royal commission into banking and the financial services sector').

[5] Senate Economics References Committee, 'Performance of the Australian Securities and Investments Commission' (June 2014) xviii.

[6] ibid xxi.

[7] Interim Report (n 1) 271.

have been: How can this be resolved by agreement?'[8] Further the report opined that this cannot be the starting point for a conduct regulator. Rather the regulator needs to determine 'whether it can make a case that there has been a breach and, if it can, then ask why it would not be in the public interest to bring proceedings to penalise the breach'.[9]

The Interim Report clearly disapproved of ASIC's negotiated outcome approach to enforcement and indicated that ASIC 'must' consider whether legal proceedings should be initiated. However, the Interim Report accepted that negotiation and persuasion were important regulatory tools, and recognised the role of the enforcement pyramid.[10] In particular the report emphasised the need for escalating up the pyramid and that it is enforcement which allows for persuasion to be effective.[11]

ASIC provided a response to the Interim Report which stated:

> The enforcement pyramid model of sanctions of escalating severity has been found to be a sound foundation for enabling a regulator to address corporate misconduct – particularly by larger financial institutions.
>
> ASIC perceives the Interim Report's central criticism of its regulatory approach to identified actual or potential misconduct, and then enforcement practice, to be as follows: ASIC's starting point with potential or actual contraveners is too often either persuasion and education or negotiation and settlement. It too rarely or too slowly moves away from either, even in the face of unsatisfactory responses or outcomes, and cedes some level of control over consequences to the contraveners themselves in so doing. Given that the Braithwaite model's effectiveness to regulate behaviour – particularly here to prevent potential misconduct – relies on agile movement up the enforcement pyramid or the real threat of the same, then ASIC does not optimise the model and accordingly does not adequately deter or punish misconduct or modify behaviours giving rise to that misconduct.
>
> ASIC accepts that it must alter its enforcement priorities and practices within the financial sector – and particularly for larger financial institutions – to be more agile in initiating and prosecuting court action, and in many instances even commencing with it. ASIC acknowledges that for larger financial institutions it should deploy enforcement tools towards the apex of the enforcement pyramid more frequently, particularly criminal and civil court actions. Strategic regulation can only work where the regulator evidences a clear willingness to employ severe sanctions to punish those who commit serious or repeated violations.[12]

ASIC went on to add that it 'recognises that its enforcement priorities must change to emphasise deterrence and public denunciation more strongly in its use of various regulatory tools (inside and, where applicable, outside court) as mechanisms by which to change behaviours'.[13] ASIC said that it now accepts that, when considering enforcement measures, it should start with the question 'why not litigate?'.[14] However, ASIC also noted that it is not possible to operate near the peak of the pyramid all the time because it would 'unaffordable, unworkable and counterproductive'.[15]

[8] ibid 277.
[9] ibid.
[10] ibid 287.
[11] ibid.
[12] ASIC, Submission to Royal Commission into Misconduct in the Banking, Superannuation and Financial Services Industry, 'ASIC Response to Interim Report' (2 November 2018) 5.
[13] ibid 9.
[14] ibid.
[15] ibid 5–6.

ii. *The Final Report*

In the Final Report Commissioner Hayne affirmed his approach from the Interim Report. This included three 'basic points':

- that 'there can and will be some cases of contravention of the law in which the outcome is negotiated between contravener and regulator';
- remediation, or compensation for losses, for consumers is an important goal, but ASIC does not have to choose between remediation and enforcement; and
- the regulator needs to aim to ensure that breach of the law is not profitable.[16]

However, these points were qualified by the view that 'In the end, the critical question whenever ASIC is considering any contravention of the law must be the question ASIC now accepts must be asked: "Why not litigate?"'.[17]

Commissioner Hayne went on to explain why settlement may not be a desirable outcome in relation to enforcement:

> Litigation takes time. It costs money and often great effort. There is always some uncertainty. What is to be made of time, cost and uncertainty? All three considerations will always be there. Why not avoid them? If a compromise can be reached without those risks, why not take it?
>
> The answer lies in recognising that litigation of the kind now under consideration is the exercise of public power for public purposes. It is litigation by a public authority to enforce the law. A private plaintiff can always choose not to pursue, to abandon or to compromise that plaintiff's private rights. A private plaintiff may take any of these steps for any reason or no reason. But altogether different considerations arise in connection with the public enforcement of the law.
>
> Breach of the law carries consequences. Parliament, not the regulators, sets the law and the consequences. There are cases where there is good public reason not to seek those consequences. Prosecution policies have always recognised that there may be good public reasons not to pursue a particular case. But the starting point for consideration is, and must always be, that the law is to be obeyed and enforced. The rule of law requires no less. And, adequate deterrence of misconduct depends upon visible public denunciation and punishment.[18]

Commissioner Hayne concluded that 'unless and until it is plain that the public interest requires that there be no litigation, all forms of regulatory enforcement must remain under active consideration'.[19] This approach culminated in Recommendation 6.2, namely that, 'ASIC should adopt an approach to enforcement that: takes, as its starting point, the question of whether a court should determine the consequences of a contravention'.[20]

iii. *ASIC's Response*

ASIC's response to the final report included adopting guiding principles and operational guidelines for a new internal Office of Enforcement, which 'have as their predicate a focus on

[16] Final Report (n 1) 426–27.
[17] ibid 427.
[18] ibid 432–33.
[19] ibid 427–28. See also 436.
[20] ibid 446. See also 433.

deterrence, public denunciation and punishment of wrongdoing by way of litigation'.[21] Moreover, the principles include:

> Principle One: Where a possible breach of the law is known to ASIC, ASIC will undertake an assessment and, if appropriate, conduct an investigation by reference to the facts and law. Once ASIC is satisfied that breaches of law are more likely than not, it will ask itself: why not litigate?
>
> Principle Two: Any public interest in pursuing a (non-court) negotiated outcome is weighed against the clear benefits of a judgment and imposition of a prison sentence, civil penalty or other court-based outcome with a negotiated outcome pursued only where objective assessment weighs in favour of the negotiated outcome …[22]

The then chair of ASIC, Mr James Shipton, informed the Australian Parliament's Senate Economics Legislation Committee of the creation of the Office of Enforcement and the adoption of the why-not-litigate-enforcement stance as part of ASIC's accountability requirements.[23] The position was reiterated by the then deputy chair, Mr Daniel Crennan, who advised that there would be 'a very strong focus on litigation', and that a negotiated outcome would only be adopted in 'quite a limited range of enforcement matters' and only after enforcement had been considered.[24]

The media has described ASIC's new approach as a 'litigate first strategy'.[25] However, Mr Shipton refuted this characterisation, stating that 'Why not litigate?' is 'a very different concept to a "litigate first" or a "litigate everything" strategy'.[26] Mr Shipton reiterated the approach set out in the guiding principles and operational guidelines for ASIC's Office of Enforcement that are set out above.

ASIC's approach is to start with determining if litigation is possible, based on whether a breach of the law is more likely than not, and then weighing the 'clear benefits' of a court pronouncement and punitive sanctions, against a negotiated outcome.[27] The approach has been described by ASIC as involving a 'procedural discipline', or asking the correct questions, in determining the enforcement approach to adopt for a particular contravention.[28] It is also arguably an enforcement approach that adopts a more comprehensive view of deterrence as it recognises the importance of direct sanctions but also expressive deterrence as 'wrongdoing [will be] publicly denounced through the courts'.[29]

While the Royal Commission was aimed at the banking, superannuation and financial services sector, ASIC's response, including its Office of Enforcement and its operationalisation of 'Why not litigate?', applies to all of ASIC's areas of responsibilities.[30] Indeed, in a continuous disclosure case brought by ASIC against a chief executive officer and chief financial officer post-Royal Commission, the court recognised 'there is a public interest in the adjudication of

[21] Australian Securities and Investment Commission, 'ASIC update on implementation of Royal Commission recommendations' (Media Release 19-035, 19 February 2019) 13.

[22] ibid.

[23] Evidence to Senate Economics Legislation Committee, Parliament of Australia, Canberra (20 February 2019) 85, 88 (James Shipton, chair, ASIC) ('Shipton Evidence to Senate Economics Legislation Committee').

[24] Evidence to Senate Economics Legislation Committee, Parliament of Australia, Canberra (20 February 2019) 87–88 (Daniel Crennan, deputy chair, ASIC).

[25] Tony Boyd, 'Beware ASIC's litigate first strategy' *The Australian Financial Review* (26 March 2019) 48.

[26] James Shipton, ASIC chair, 'The fairness imperative', AFR Banking and Wealth Summit, Sydney (27 March 2019).

[27] 'ASIC update' (n 21) 13.

[28] Sean Hughes, 'ASIC's Approach to Enforcement after the Royal Commission', 36th Annual Conference of the Banking and Financial Services Law Association, Gold Coast (30 August 2019).

[29] ibid.

[30] ASIC, 'Annual Report 2019–20' 7, 41–43; ASIC, 'REP 691 Regulator Performance Framework: ASIC self-assessment 2019–20' (26 May 2021) [109].

allegations of significant wrongdoing concerning the conduct of Australian companies involving their directors and officers'.[31]

Further, ASIC's previous approach of negotiated outcomes may also be seen as characterising its approach to enforcement of the continuous disclosure regime as shown by its use of enforcement tools in chapter six, Table 6.1.

iv. Revisiting the Enforcement Pyramid

Neither Commissioner Hayne nor ASIC sought to disavow the enforcement pyramid or responsive regulation. Yet in the former's recommendations and the latter's response there is a clear shift to starting with consideration of whether a court-determined outcome should be sought; an enforcement tool, depending on whether it is a civil or criminal, that is in the middle or toward the top of the enforcement pyramid.

John Braithwaite has explained that 'The idea of the pyramid is that our presumption should always be to start at the base of the pyramid first. Then escalate to somewhat punitive approaches only reluctantly and only when dialogue fails'.[32] Indeed, even with the most serious matters, the approach is to maintain the course and adopt the presumption that 'it is better to start with dialogue at the base of the pyramid'.[33] The presumption is only overridden in rare situations where there are compelling reasons.[34] Some harms may be so great, or some contraventions so significant, that they warrant an immediate response from the top of the pyramid such as criminal sanctions or licence revocation. Step-by-step escalation up the pyramid may not be appropriate.[35] Exactly how harmful or serious is not specified.

The approach taken by the Royal Commission and by ASIC of first asking 'Why not litigate?' does not sit comfortably with either the presumption of starting at the base of the pyramid, or the rare exception of an immediate response from the top of the pyramid. However, the enforcement pyramid and the 'Why not litigate?' approach may be capable of being reconciled.

The main aim of the 'Why not litigate?' approach was to reinvigorate the enforcement pyramid in a context where regulated entities had not been deterred from misconduct due to ASIC's approach of negotiated outcomes.

For regulators to be able to speak softly because they carry 'big sticks', the regulator must create a credible impression that it will use the big stick when required. Credibility follows from escalation up the pyramid occurring when needed, including using the most severe sanctions at times.[36] Indeed, the regulator must 'respond aggressively and punitively toward … the most intransigent actors'.[37] Put another way, carrying the big stick is not enough; the regulator must effectively wield it sometimes so that its threats are credible.[38] John Braithwaite has stated that the 'fundamental resource of responsive regulation is the belief of citizens in the inexorability of escalation if problems are not fixed'.[39]

[31] *Australian Securities and Investments Commission v Helou* (2019) 139 ACSR 489, 518 [199] (Beach J).

[32] John Braithwaite, 'The Essence of Responsive Regulation' (2011) 44 *University of British Columbia Law Review* 475, 482.

[33] ibid 483.

[34] ibid.

[35] Robert Baldwin and Julia Black, 'Really Responsive Regulation (2008) 71 *Modern Law Review* 59, 62–63.

[36] Michael Legg, 'Regulatory Theory, Litigation and Enforcement' in Michael Legg (ed), *Regulation, Litigation and Enforcement* (Thomson Reuters, 2011) 20.

[37] Cristie Ford, *Innovation and the State – Finance, Regulation and Justice* (Cambridge University Press, 2017) 86.

[38] Dimity Kingsford Smith, 'A Harder Nut to Crack? Responsive Regulation in the Financial Services Sector' (2011) 44 *University of British Columbia Law Review* 695, 726.

[39] Braithwaite (n 32) 489, 501.

The Interim Report cited academic literature that warned that 'a pure "advise and persuade" or compliance oriented strategy of enforcement, [can] fail to deter those who have no interest in complying voluntarily'.[40] In the Final Report ASIC was found to have failed to utilise the peak of the pyramid effectively:

> [I]t is wholly consistent with the analyses that are expressed by the metaphor of the regulatory pyramid, that serious breaches of law by large entities call for the highest level of regulatory response. And that is what has been missing. Too often serious breaches of law by large entities have yielded nothing more than a few infringement notices, an enforceable undertaking (EU) not to offend again (with or without an immaterial 'public benefit payment') or some agreed form of media release.[41]

An argument may be made that ASIC had spoken softly so frequently and, coextensively, failed to escalate up the pyramid, that the pyramid no longer worked in the banking, superannuation and financial services sector. Indeed the former ASIC chair interpreted the Royal Commission's findings as indicating that ASIC as an organisation 'should never be reticent or afraid of going up towards the top of [the enforcement] pyramid' and that if enforcement is not used 'other regulatory tools lack … credibility and can't be backed up'.[42] On this basis, the 'Why not Litigate?' approach is an attempt to reboot the pyramid rather than replace or up-end it.[43]

'Why not litigate?' does not speak to any new desire within ASIC to litigate all matters or to operative exclusively in the top levels of the enforcement pyramid. Rather, 'why not litigate?' is literally to be the first question that ASIC officers and lawyers ask themselves when confronted with an alleged contravention of the law. Importantly, by starting with 'why not litigate?', ASIC commences with an open question, meaning that it can and presumably will, identify numerous circumstances in which litigation should *not* be its response. In these circumstances, ASIC will continue to use its compliance measures and/or negotiated outcomes, but critically, only if those responses are in the public interest and only after considering and determining that litigation is *not* the more appropriate response. It cannot be presumed that ASIC *will* litigate first, although it seems clear ASIC will litigate more often than in the past.

However, as the 'Why not Litigate?' approach is still in its infancy it is unclear whether ASIC will reboot the enforcement pyramid and then return to an approach consistent with responsive regulation, or whether ASIC may adopt an enforcement strategy that consistently relies more heavily on litigation.[44] The Royal Commission clearly depicted litigation and deterrence as being in keeping with the public interest and the rule of law.[45] But with the COVID-19 pandemic the Australian Government has indicated that it expects ASIC to support Australia's economic recovery.[46] This is turn has prompted questions as to whether government will seek to discourage a 'Why not Litigate?' approach.[47]

[40] Interim Report (n 1) 287 citing Neil Gunningham, 'Compliance, Deterrence and Beyond' in LeRoy Paddock ed, *Compliance and Enforcement of Environmental Law* (Edward Elgar Publishers, 2017) 63, 66.

[41] Final Report (n 1) 433.

[42] Shipton Evidence to Senate Economics Legislation Committee (n 23) 86–87.

[43] Michael Legg and Stephen Speirs, '"Why not litigate?" – The Royal Commission, ASIC and the Future of the Enforcement Pyramid' (2019) 47 *Australian Business Law Review* 244.

[44] Vicky Comino, 'Life after the Banking Royal Commission: Is the Royal Commission a "game-changer" for the financial services sector in Australia?' (2020) 35 *Australian Journal of Corporate Law* 381, 399.

[45] Final Report (n 1) 432–33.

[46] The Hon Josh Frydenberg, Treasurer, 'Appointment of new Chairperson and Deputy Chairperson to the Australian Securities and Investments Commission' (Media Release, 29 April 2021) ('the Government expects ASIC to support Australia's economic recovery from the COVID pandemic').

[47] Michael Roddan, John Kehoe and Michael Pelly, 'Cleaned-out ASIC charged with aiding recovery' *The Australian Financial Review* (29 April 2021) (reporting on the appointment of a new ASIC chair and observing that ASIC 'now faces a shift to a more business-friendly footing' and 'ASIC will likely be dissuaded from Royal Commissioner Kenneth Hayne's

B. Industry Funding of ASIC

The insufficient funding of ASIC had been a longstanding problem, especially as its areas of responsibility increased.[48] During the Royal Commission ASIC's then chairman was asked how the level of resourcing affected the way ASIC performed its functions and exercised its powers. The response was:

> [I]t weighs very heavily on the regulatory choices that we have to make … We are constrained in probably every aspect of our regulatory work. Certainly in investigations, certainly in other matters relating to enforcement …[49]

In 2017 the Australian Parliament passed legislation that adopted a cost recovery model that required market participants to reimburse the 'regulatory costs' of ASIC's activities. 'Regulatory costs' is defined as the amount determined in a legislative instrument by ASIC. Regulatory costs are 'the costs relating directly or indirectly to the regulation of leviable entities', and may include, without limiting the above definition, education, surveillance, guidance, engagement with industry and policy advice.[50]

This reform was in response to the recommendation of the Financial System Inquiry (FSI) that the Government recover the cost of ASIC's regulatory activities directly from industry participants through fees and levies calibrated to reflect the cost of regulating the different industry sectors that ASIC regulated.[51] Industry funding was adopted as it was consistent with the user-pays principle, ie those that drive the need for regulation pay for the regulation, and to free up government resources for other activities.[52] It was also seen as promoting efficiency and accountability – efficiency being that industry has an incentive to organise and conduct itself so as to minimise regulatory costs.[53] The funding mechanism envisaged was also said to promote accountability to industry as industry could comment on whether funding levels were appropriate.[54] The idea of making ASIC accountable to industry was a pre-Royal Commission idea and seems inappropriate in light of the Royal Commission's findings. Downwards accountability allows for the regulator's constituents to have a voice and could include regulated entities, but there is a clear danger to effective enforcement if regulated entities are permitted to influence the funds that can be provided to enforce the law that governs those same regulated entities.

Prior to July 2017, when the regulator took some form of enforcement action the cost was borne by the taxpayer. Since July 2017, under the cost recovery model, enforcement costs are included in the regulatory costs charged to industry. In the Treasury's Consultation Paper on the industry funding model for ASIC the Government made clear the regulatory activities that the Government would seek to recover the costs of included enforcement.[55]

"why not litigate?" war-footing, with a revamped formal statement of expectations that will "make clear that the government expects ASIC to support Australia's economic recovery from the COVID pandemic"."). However, ASIC has indicated that it will continue to pursue enforcement through litigation but will seek to select the most appropriate enforcement tool, which may include an enforceable undertaking where speed of resolution or flexibility of remedies is important: Michael Pelly, 'We love litigation, say new ASIC chiefs' *The Australian Financial Review* (3 September 2021).

[48] Roddan (n 2) 301 ('when the watchdog had failed to bark, it was because the government had muzzled them'); Ferguson (n 4) 316.

[49] Royal Commission into Misconduct in the Banking, Superannuation and Financial Services Industry, Transcript of Cross-Examination of Mr James Shipton (22 November 2018) 6906–07.

[50] ASIC Supervisory Cost Recovery Levy Act 2017 (Cth), s10.

[51] Commonwealth of Australia, 'Financial System Inquiry Final Report' (2014), recommendation 29; ASIC, 'Cost Recovery Implementation Statement: ASIC industry funding model 2019–20' (June 2020) [40].

[52] The Australian Government the Treasury, 'Consultation Paper – Proposed Industry Funding Model for the Australian Securities and Investments Commission' (28 August 2015) 4.

[53] ibid.

[54] ibid 23.

[55] ibid 5–6.

While the cost recovery model may increase the resources available to ASIC, the amount of the costs recoverable cannot exceed 'the sum of all amounts appropriated by the Parliament for the purposes of ASIC for the financial year'.[56] Consequently, government still sets the annual budget for ASIC and ASIC must still operate within the budget set by the Parliament.

However, as a consequence of the Royal Commission, ASIC's budget was increased to allow it to 'strengthen and intensify [its] approach to enforcement'.[57] This included funding for an accelerated enforcement strategy that is guided by the 'Why not litigate?' approach to enforcement discussed above.[58]

Cost recovery was sought for the first time when levy invoices were issued in January 2019 for the 2017–18 year. For the 2,177 listed corporations (which are subject to the continuous disclosure regime), the cost to be recovered was $50.415 million and the levy was calculated as follows: 'Minimum levy of $4,000, plus $0.30 per $10,000 of market capitalisation above $5m. The maximum levy is $605,317 for entities with a market capitalisation of $20bn or more'.[59] For the 2018–19 year for the 2,177 listed corporations (which are subject to the continuous disclosure regime), the cost to be recovered was $63.825 million and the levy was calculated as follows: 'Minimum levy of $4,000 plus $0.39 per $10,000 of market capitalisation above $5m. The maximum levy is $774,157 for entities with a market capitalisation greater than $20bn'.[60]

C. Increased Penalties and Powers

After the Royal Commission, Parliament enacted the Treasury Laws Amendment (Strengthening Corporate and Financial Sector Penalties) Act 2019 (Cth), which increased the maximum penalties for criminal offences and for civil penalties. It also expanded the enforcement options available to ASIC. The penalties reform was the culmination of recommendations by the ASIC Enforcement Review Taskforce in late 2017.[61] The legislation took effect from 13 March 2019.

The criminal penalties for contraventions of the continuous disclosure provisions are still set out in Schedule 3 of the Corporations Act. Schedule 3 only lists the provisions that apply to the reporting entity, ie ss 674(2), (5), 675(2) and not the provisions applicable to individuals, ie ss 674(2A), 675(2), which are only civil penalty provisions.[62] As a body corporate cannot be imprisoned the penalty units applicable are calculated according to a new formula – term of imprisonment expressed in months multiplied by 10 to obtain the amount of penalty units (which also applies to individuals) and then multiplied by 10 again for a body corporate.[63] The provisions containing the new formula replaced s 1312 which had allowed a court to impose a penalty of five times the amount specified in Schedule 3 for a corporation.

[56] ASIC Supervisory Cost Recovery Levy Act 2017 (Cth), s 10(3).

[57] Hon Josh Frydenberg, Treasurer, 'Record funding and resources for ASIC and APRA to help restore trust in Australia's financial sector' (Media Release, 22 March 2019) (in the 2019–20 Budget 'The Australian Securities and Investments Commission (ASIC) will be provided with more than $400 million in additional funding, representing on average a 25 per cent increase in its annual funding compared to 2017–18.').

[58] ASIC, 'Cost Recovery Implementation Statement: ASIC industry funding model 2019–20' (June 2020) [32], [36].

[59] ASIC, 'ASIC industry funding: Summary of 2017–18 levies' (December 2018). The costs incurred by ASIC that were recovered through the levies are set out in ASIC, 'Annual Dashboard Report for 2017–18'.

[60] ASIC, 'ASIC industry funding: Summary of 2018–19 levies' (December 2019). The costs incurred by ASIC that were recovered through the levies are set out in ASIC, 'Annual Dashboard Report for 2018–19'.

[61] Revised Explanatory Memorandum, Treasury Laws Amendment (Strengthening Corporate and Financial Sector Penalties) Bill 2018, 5.

[62] In ch 2, section II.D.i it was explained that directors, officers and advisers may also be criminally liable if they aid, abet, counsel or procure the disclosing entity's contravention but pursuant to the Criminal Code s 11.2 not Corporations Act 2001 (Cth), ss 674(2A), 675(2A).

[63] Corporations Act 2001 (Cth), ss 1311, 1311A, 1311B (penalty for an individual), 1311C (penalty for a body corporate).

Prior to the amendment that was 200 penalty units, or 1,000 penalty units for a corporation, for s 674(2).

Table 7.1 Criminal penalties for continuous disclosure offences

Provision	**Schedule 3 penalty**	**Conversion of term of imprisonment to penalty units**	**Penalty units for a body corporate**
Section 674(2)	Five years' (60 months') imprisonment	600	6,000
Section 674(5)	Two years' (24 months') imprisonment	240	2,400
Section 675(2)	Five years' (60 months') imprisonment	600	6,000

The substantive sections of Chapter 6CA, namely ss 674(2), (2A), 675(2), (2A), are financial services civil penalty provisions which attract pecuniary penalties. The maximum amounts are set out in Table 7.2. Prior to 13 March 2019, the court could order the payment of a pecuniary penalty of $200,000 for an individual and $1 million for a corporation.

Table 7.2 Pecuniary penalties for continuous disclosure civil penalties[64]

Individual – Greater of:	**Corporation – Greater of:**
5,000 penalty units	50,000 penalty units
if the court can determine the benefit derived and detriment avoided because of the contravention, that amount multiplied by three	if the court can determine the benefit derived and detriment avoided because of the contravention, that amount multiplied by three
	(i) 10 per cent of the annual turnover of the body corporate for the 12-month period ending at the end of the month in which the body corporate contravened, or began to contravene, the civil penalty provision; or (ii) if the amount worked out under subparagraph (i) is greater than an amount equal to 2.5 million penalty units: 2.5 million penalty units

Between 1 July 2017 and 30 June 2020 a penalty unit was $210. From 1 July 2020 the value of one penalty unit was $222.[65] Consequently, the highest criminal penalty for a corporation under the old law was 1,000 penalty units multiplied by $210 or $210,000, while under the new law the highest criminal penalty is 6,000 penalty units multiplied by $222 or $1,332,000. For a corporation facing a civil penalty proceeding, the pecuniary penalty under the old law was $1,000,000 compared to now where using penalty units it would be 50,000 multiplied by $222, or $11,100,000.

The enforcement options available to ASIC for a contravention of a financial services civil penalty provision were set out in chapter 2 and included pecuniary penalty orders and compensation orders. The Treasury Laws Amendment (Strengthening Corporate and Financial Sector Penalties) Act 2019 (Cth) added relinquishment orders and gave ASIC standing to apply to the

[64] Corporations Act 2001 (Cth), s 1317G.

[65] Crimes Act 1914 (Cth), s 4AA; Crimes Legislation Amendment (Penalty Unit) Act 2017 (Cth).

court for these orders. The Corporations Act states that a court may order a person to pay the Commonwealth 'an amount equal to the benefit derived and detriment avoided because of a contravention of a civil penalty provision if a declaration of contravention by the person has been made'.[66] A relinquishment order can be made in addition to a pecuniary penalty order. The amount owing under a relinquishment order is a debt payable to ASIC on behalf of the Commonwealth.

The aim of a relinquishment order is to prevent the unjust enrichment of those who contravene a civil penalty provision by removing any financial benefits that arise through requiring any benefit derived or detriment avoided be disgorged.[67] The Revised Explanatory Memorandum noted:

> On some occasions, it can be difficult to identify those who have suffered losses or damages at the hands of wrongdoers. In those situations, and unless those who have suffered losses or damages commence compensation proceedings, the financial benefit gained from misconduct could still remain with the wrongdoer as they would only be subject to a financial penalty.[68]

The relinquishment order is therefore a tool to try and more perfectly achieve deterrence by ensuring that misconduct addressed through a pecuniary penalty order is not nonetheless still profitable.

The new legislation also amends the law to ensure that when a court considers that it is appropriate to make a pecuniary penalty order or relinquishment order in respect of breaches of civil penalty provisions, or impose a fine in relation to the commission of an offence, the court must (1) give consideration to the effect of the orders/fine on the amount available to pay a compensation order; and (2) give preference to making an appropriate amount available for compensation. The court is then granted power to make 'such orders as the court thinks fit for the purpose of ensuring that the [appropriate] amount remains available for the payment of' compensation.[69] Where a defendant is able to pay the amounts imposed by the orders/fine and compensation, the provision will have no work to do. But for defendants with lower levels of financial resources where there are significant penalties/fines as well as losses by shareholders then the court may need to make orders to ensure that an appropriate amount remains available for compensation.

The former ASIC chair, James Shipton, opined that 'ASIC's adoption of the "Why not litigate?" enforcement stance is strengthened with the expansion of penalties and powers recently available to ASIC'.[70] This makes intuitive sense as a higher maximum penalty allows for greater deterrence where needed. It also means that when ASIC weighs the cost of enforcement action against the benefit that can be achieved, including deterrence, taking court-based action is able to achieve an outcome that will give effect to ASIC's objectives. Higher penalties may also assist in conveying the seriousness of the misconduct to the regulated population, but also the community more generally.[71]

[66] Corporations Act 2001 (Cth), s 1317GAB.

[67] Revised Explanatory Memorandum, Treasury Laws Amendment (Strengthening Corporate and Financial Sector Penalties) Bill 2018, 57. The relinquishment order is similar to the Proceeds of Crimes Act 2002 (Cth), where property can be forfeited to the Commonwealth to deprive persons of any financial benefits or profits from committing criminal offences: ibid 58.

[68] Revised Explanatory Memorandum, Treasury Laws Amendment (Strengthening Corporate and Financial Sector Penalties) Bill 2018, 57.

[69] Corporations Act 2001 (Cth), s 1317QF.

[70] Shipton (n 26).

[71] Hughes (n 28).

III. Class Actions Revisited

The large monetary payments achieved by shareholder class actions and the high transaction costs, especially litigation funding fees, which are documented in this text,[72] have attracted a range of interests seeking to restrain or promote shareholder class action activity.

A. ALRC Inquiry into Class Actions and Litigation Funding

The Australian Law Reform Commission (ALRC) released the report from its year-long inquiry into class actions and litigation funding on 24 January 2019.[73] The reference to the ALRC was a response to concerns that the social utility and legitimacy of the class action regime was being undermined because the interests of claimants, and society more generally, was taking a backseat to profit generation for lawyers and funders.[74]

During the conduct of the inquiry the ALRC found that several issues relating to the way in which the class action regime in Part IVA of the Federal Court of Australia Act 1976 (Cth) ('FCA Act') was operating were confined largely to issues relating to shareholder claims. The ALRC found that shareholder class actions constituted one-third of all Federal Court class actions filed in the period March 2013 to March 2018, they were always funded and they rarely went to trial.[75] Moreover, for all finalised shareholder claims between 2013 and 2018, the median percentage of the settlement used to pay (a) legal fees was 26 per cent, and (b) litigation funding fees was 23 per cent, with the result that the median percentage of settlement paid to group members was 51 per cent.[76] In short, half of the recovery was consumed by transaction costs.

i. Oversight of Legal Costs

The ALRC recommended that three practices dealing with settlement be included in the Federal Court's practice note on class actions:

- appointment of a referee to assess the reasonableness of legal costs;[77]
- permitting the use of a tender process for appointing a settlement administrator;[78] and
- requiring the settlement administrator to provide a report on the key elements of the administration, such as cost and time elapsed.[79]

The recommendations have been previously raised by academic commentators[80] and have to a limited extent been considered or adopted by Federal Court judges. For example, Lee J and Murphy J have been advocates for the appointing a referee to inquire and provide a report on

[72] See eg ch 6, section II.F.

[73] Australian Law Reform Commission, 'Integrity, Fairness and Efficiency – An Inquiry into Class Action Proceedings and Third-Party Litigation Funders' (Report No 134, December 2018) ('ALRC 2018 Class Actions Report').

[74] ibid [1.7]–[1.13].

[75] ibid [3.1].

[76] Ibid Table 3.8.

[77] ibid Recommendation 8.

[78] ibid Recommendation 9.

[79] ibid Recommendation 10.

[80] See eg, Michael Legg 'Class action settlements in Australia – the need for greater scrutiny' (2014) 38 *Melbourne University Law Review* 590.

legal costs, the selection of cost-effective settlement administrators and reporting by administrators to the Court.[81] Inclusion in the practice note would assist in increasing the adoption of these practices to reduce costs.

ii. Class Action Contingency Fees for Lawyers

The ALRC proposed that the currently illegal practice of a contingency-based legal fee be permitted within the confines of a class action.[82] The ALRC did not recommend the legalisation of contingency fees more broadly.[83] Further, such a legal fee would require court approval and be subject to judicial variation.[84]

Contingency fees can provide for alignment of lawyer and client interests, as both are interested in maximising recovery at a minimum cost.[85] A contingency fee may also provide proportionality between the fee charged by the lawyer and the recovery achieved, which has been problematic in relation to class actions with smaller recoveries.[86] However, allowing contingency fees might exacerbate unethical lawyer behaviour. The ALRC recommended that if a contingency fee is used by a lawyer, the lawyer must advance any disbursements and provide security for costs.[87] When combined with the lawyer's interest in the contingency fee, the lawyers may frequently have a greater financial interest in the outcome of the litigation than any group member. To be weighed against the concern of unethical behaviour is the existing Australian Solicitors' Conduct Rules, fiduciary obligations and duties to clients and duties to the court.[88] Additionally court approval and oversight of the fee awarded would be a crucial consumer protection especially for absent group members.

While the ALRC approach affords greater protections for clients, it is nonetheless highly likely to stimulate further class actions. Indeed, the ALRC acknowledged that its aim was to make the funding of medium-sized actions, which are not of interest to funders, more viable.[89] The ALRC's proposal for a contingency fee was aimed at providing more funding options and promoting access to justice.[90] However, the likely outcome is also an increase in the number of class actions.[91]

[81] See *Lifeplan Australia Friendly Society Limited v S&P Global Inc* [2018] FCA 379 [36], [41] (Lee J); *Dillon v RBS Group (Australia) Pty Limited (No 2)* [2018] FCA 395 [19], [64]–[67] (Lee J); *Caason Investments Pty Limited v Cao (No 2)* [2018] FCA 527 [104]–[105], [111]–[124] (Murphy J); *Money Max Int Pty Limited (Trustee) v QBE Insurance Group Limited* (2018) 129 ACSR 1, 36–39 [160]–[180] (Murphy J). See also Michael Legg and John Emmerig, 'Australian Federal Court Reforms Class Actions Settlement Practice' (2018) 46 *Australian Business Law Review* 262.

[82] ALRC 2018 Class Actions Report (n 73) [7.75].

[83] The ALRC approach may be contrasted with the Victorian Law Reform Commission (VLRC), 'Access to Justice – Litigation Funding and Group Proceedings', Report (2018) Recommendation 7, which supported the lifting of the ban on contingency fees more generally through a coordinated approach amongst the Australia states, and Recommendation 8, which put forward the use of a contingency fee (called a litigation services fee) in class actions.

[84] ALRC 2018 Class Actions Report (n 73) [7.82], [7.83].

[85] See Michael Legg, 'Contingency fees – Antidote or poison for Australian civil justice?' (2015) 39 *Australian Bar Review* 244, 250.

[86] See *Petersen Superannuation Fund Pty Ltd v Bank of Queensland Limited (No 3)* (2018) 132 ACSR 258, 286 [129] (Murphy J).

[87] ALRC 2018 Class Actions Report (n 73) [6.43]. See [7.104]. See also Appendix H, s 33WB for suggested legislative amendments.

[88] Legg (n 85) 258–61; VLRC (n 83) 61.

[89] ALRC 2018 Class Actions Report (n 73) [1.7], [7.3].

[90] ibid [1.33].

[91] ibid [2.5], [7.66], [9.20].

iii. Litigation Funding

The ALRC discussion paper initially addressed concerns over litigation funding through recommending that funders must obtain a licence which would include conditions such as character, capital adequacy and managing conflicts of interest.[92] The ALRC final report abandoned this approach in favour of giving greater powers and responsibility for the supervision of litigation funding to the Federal Court. As a result, the pre-existing regulatory regime that provided that litigation funders are not required to hold an Australian Financial Services Licence (AFSL) as long as they have adequate practices in place to manage conflicts of interest was to remain.[93]

Concerns over capital adequacy and insolvent funders initiating litigation but then being unable to honour indemnities to the representative party (and group members) were addressed through recommending a statutory presumption that litigation funders provide security for costs.[94] The concern with such an approach is that it is common practice that the amount of security that a court requires to be posted is substantially lower than the costs actually incurred by the defendant.

The lack of a licensing regime would continue under the ALRC approach so that anyone or any entity could fund class actions in Australia. The conditions of a licence can include specified levels of competency (such as education) and restrictions based on status or background (such as criminal record, bankruptcy). None of this would be required to fund litigation in Australia. As the Productivity Commission stated, licensing helps ensure that 'only reputable and capable funders enter the market'.[95] However, there is a need to balance consumer protection with regulatory burdens that may create barriers to entry, which may then increase the funding fee charged.[96]

The ALRC did however, recommend a suite of statutory powers be given to the Federal Court:

- litigation funding agreements with respect to class actions are enforceable only with the approval of the Court;
- the Court has an express statutory power to reject, vary, or amend the terms of such litigation funding agreements;
- litigation funding agreements for class actions must provide expressly for a complete indemnity in favour of the representative plaintiff against an adverse costs order; and
- Australian law governs any such litigation funding agreement and the funder submits irrevocably to the jurisdiction of the Court.[97]

A number of Federal Court judgments have addressed the issue of whether litigation funding fees can be altered by the Court, with reliance being placed on FCA Act, s 33V(2) (if the Court makes an order approving a settlement 'it may make such orders as are just with respect

[92] Australian Law Reform Commission, 'Inquiry into Class Action Proceedings and Third-Party Litigation Funders' (Discussion Paper No 85, June 2018), proposals 3-1, 3-2.

[93] Corporations Act 2001 (Cth), s 911A; Corporations Regulations 2001 (Cth), regs 7.1.04N, 7.6.01(1)(x), 7.6.01(1)(y), 7.6.01AB. See also Australian Securities and Investments Commission, 'Regulatory Guide 248 – Litigation Schemes and Proof of Debt Schemes: Managing Conflicts of Interest' (April 2013). See ch 3, section IV.D.iii discussing regulation as a form of achieving accountability.

[94] ALRC 2018 Class Actions Report (n 73) Recommendation 12 [6.48]–[6.53].

[95] Productivity Commission, 'Access to Justice Arrangements – Inquiry Report No 72' (September 2014) 632.

[96] ibid.

[97] ALRC 2018 Class Actions Report (n 73) Recommendation 14.

to the distribution of any money paid under a settlement') and s 33ZF ('the Court may, of its own motion or on application by a party or a group member, make any order the Court thinks appropriate or necessary to ensure that justice is done in the proceeding').[98] In *Liverpool City Council v McGraw-Hill Financial, Inc (now known as S&P Global Inc)*, Lee J accepted that in an appropriate case, the Court may refuse to approve a settlement because a funding commission is excessive or disproportionate.[99] However, after reviewing the heads of power, his Honour doubted that power existed for the Court to interfere and vary funding agreements in the context of a settlement by altering the contractual promises of group members to pay commission.[100] The expression of different views by single judges of the Court has left the question uncertain.[101]

The powers recommended by the ALRC would address the conflict in the above judicial decisions and provide the Federal Court with the necessary powers to protect the interests of group members. Litigation funders who wished to fund class actions would need to subject their funding agreements, in particular the fees that were to be charged, to court oversight.

iv. Shareholder Class Actions

The ALRC identified that there were a range of substantive legal issues that were significant shareholder class action drivers, in particular:

- the current lack of any need to prove any element of fault or intention, which raises whether the original requirement of 'intentionally, recklessly or negligently' failing to comply with the listing rules should be reinstated;
- uncertainty over the causation requirement and whether 'market-based causation' or a presumption of reliance is sufficient or the law requires proof of individual reliance on the alleged misconduct;
- uncertainty over the measure of loss; and
- lack of defences for the corporation, such as due diligence.[102]

The ALRC canvassed the arguments on both sides of the above issues, but concluded that a further evidence-based review directed to the substantive law was warranted. Consequently, the ALRC recommended as follows:

> The Australian Government should commission a review of the legal and economic impact of the operation, enforcement, and effects of continuous disclosure obligations and those relating to misleading and deceptive conduct contained in the Corporations Act 2001 (Cth) and the Australian Securities and Investments Commission Act 2001 (Cth).[103]

The most contentious argument, as it transpired, was in relation to the addition of a requirement for fault or intention. The arguments raised on this issue are discussed below in section IV in relation to reformulating the continuous disclosure laws.

[98] See *Earglow Pty Ltd v Newcrest Mining Limited* [2016] FCA 1433 [133]–[158] (Murphy J); *Blairgowrie Trading Ltd v Allco Finance Group Ltd (Receivers & Managers Appointed) (In Liq) (No 3)* (2017) 118 ACSR 614, 642 [101] (Beach J); *Mitic v OZ Minerals Limited (No 2)* [2017] FCA 409 [26]–[32] (Middleton J).

[99] *Liverpool City Council v McGraw-Hill Financial, Inc (now known as S&P Global Inc)* [2018] FCA 1289, [22] (Lee J).

[100] ibid [47].

[101] *Endeavour River Pty Ltd v MG Responsible Entity Limited (No 2)* [2020] FCA 968 [4]–[5] (Murphy J).

[102] ALRC 2018 Class Actions Report (n 73) [9.69]–[9.80].

[103] ibid Recommendation 24.

B. First Continuous Disclosure Class Action Judgment

Despite the fact that the Australia class action regime has been in place since 1992 and the first shareholder class action was brought in 1999,[104] until the decision in *TPT Patrol Pty Ltd as trustee for Amies Superannuation Fund v Myer Holdings Limited*,[105] all shareholder class actions resolved, chiefly by settlement, before reaching judgment.[106] The Myer class action went to judgment on the common questions.

The Myer class action was launched in late 2016 by TPT Patrol, as trustee of the Amies Superannuation Fund against retail chain Myer. At the centre of the case was a representation made by then Myer CEO Bernie Brookes on 11 September 2014 that Myer expected that net profit after tax (NPAT) in financial year 2015 (FY15) would exceed NPAT in financial year 2014 (FY14) by stating that: 'We will therefore not only have anticipated sales growth, but anticipated profit growth this year' (the 11 September 2014 representation). About six months later, when reporting Myer's half-year results on 19 March 2015, Brooke's replacement as CEO, Richard Umbers, stated that its NPAT would fall between $75 million and $80 million in FY15 (excluding one-off costs) (the 19 March 2015 correction).

Beach J delivered judgment on 24 October 2019 finding that on seven different occasions after 11 September 2014, Myer should have corrected the 11 September 2014 representation as a number of reforecasts had been prepared internally which indicated that NPAT for FY15 was below the budgeted amount and meant that Myer ought to have known that the assertion that Myer would materially exceed FY14 NPAT was no longer sustainable. Contravention of the continuous disclosure and misleading or deceptive conduct provisions was proved.

Beach J then turned to causation and loss. An ongoing issue in shareholder class actions, as raised by the ALRC, was the appropriate approach to causation under the statutory provisions. Defendants had generally argued that only direct reliance by each group member was sufficient. This would make causation an individual issue and require all group members to adduce evidence to prove that they relied on the alleged statement or omission. This would make shareholder class actions more forensically difficult and time-consuming to run. Moreover, given that many shareholders do not read every corporate statement, proving that a particular misrepresentation was relied on by each shareholder would be difficult in many cases, inevitably reducing the quantum of claims and possibly making a class action commercially unviable for litigation funders. Plaintiffs, aware of these difficulties, sought to plead causation as a common issue. Originally, resort was made to the US fraud on the market doctrine,[107] but this was adapted to take account of the Australian statutes and case law to become market-based causation.[108]

Beach J found that the wording 'by' and 'resulted from' in the continuous disclosure and misleading or deceptive conduct provisions did not require direct reliance and the purpose of

[104] *King v AG Australia Holdings Ltd (formerly GIO Australia Holdings Ltd)* [2003] FCA 980.

[105] *TPT Patrol Pty Ltd as trustee for Amies Superannuation Fund v Myer Holdings Limited* (2019) 140 ACSR 38.

[106] See ch 2, section V.C.vi and Appendix 2 Table 3.

[107] The doctrine relies on the 'efficient capital markets hypothesis' and states that if a market is efficient, then misrepresentations or omissions by a company affect the market price by artificially inflating or reducing the price. If investors rely on the integrity of the market price when purchasing shares, a misrepresentation causing artificial inflation of the shares causes them loss through their mere action of purchasing the shares, negating the need for proof of individual reliance on the misrepresentation. Fraud on the market has been endorsed in the United States in *Basic Inc v Levinson* 485 US 224 (1988); *Halliburton Co v Erica P John Fund Inc* 134 S Ct 2398 (2014). For Australian cases see eg *P Dawson Nominees Pty Ltd v Multiplex Limited* (2007) 242 ALR 111, [9]–[10] (Finkelstein J); *Bonham v Iluka Resources Limited* [2015] FCA 713, [71] (Kerr J).

[108] See eg *Caason Investments Pty Ltd v Cao* (2015) 236 FCR 322, 332–335 [59]–[80] (Gilmour and Foster JJ), 352–353 [153]–[158], 354–355 [169] (Edelman J); *Masters v Lombe (Liquidator); In the Matter of Babcock and Brown Limited (In Liq)* [2019] FCA 1720, [362]–[381] (Foster J). See also Corey Byrne and Michael Legg, 'Market-based causation after TPT Patrol Pty Ltd v Myer Holdings Limited' (2020) 37 *Company & Securities Law Journal* 295, 296–306.

the provisions were not inconsistent with an indirect causation theory being 'embedded within the statutory language'.[109] Beach J also distinguished market-based causation from the US fraud on the market doctrine, dismissing the latter as 'irrelevant' to Australia, inconsistent with the statutory language and based on US legal idiosyncrasies.[110]

Beach J recognised three 'well-established mechanisms' for causation: direct causation; passive indirect causation; and active indirect causation. His Honour found that the shareholders could prove their claim on the basis of active indirect causation, which was:

> [T]he scenario where a respondent's misleading conduct induces some reaction in X, and the applicant would have acted differently but for that reaction by X. There is no additional requirement that the applicant was aware of or relied on the respondent's conduct. It is enough that X relied, and that the applicant would have acted differently but for that reliance by X. Or in other words, it is enough that the applicant relied on X.[111]

In the above example, X is the securities market. Beach J endorsed the theory of market-based causation and found that, theoretically, shareholder group members could suffer loss merely by purchasing shares whose value had been inflated by misrepresentations or omissions made by the defendant company to the securities market.

While TPT Patrol had been successful in showing a contravention and in having market-based causation endorsed, there would be no compensation. This was because, based on the manner in which loss was pleaded and the expert evidence constructed, no share price inflation was demonstrated at each of the seven dates, so that if Myer made the required disclosure it would not have affected the share price.[112] *Myer* may have been an unusual case in that its expected NPAT, although lower than what it had disclosed, was not materially different from the market consensus as to the expected NPAT figure was. In short, the market was already sceptical that the forecast NPAT would be met. Beach J left open whether some shareholders may have been able to prove loss under a different approach, however, this was not resolved as the matter settled.[113]

C. Regulation of Litigation Funding

On 22 May 2020, the federal treasurer announced that litigation funders would be required to hold an Australian financial services licence (AFSL) from 22 August 2020, which would mean they were regulated by ASIC.[114] Litigation funders were also required to comply with the requirements of the Managed Investment Scheme (MIS) regime under the Corporations Act.[115]

[109] *TPT Patrol Pty Ltd as trustee for Amies Superannuation Fund v Myer Holdings Limited* (2019) 140 ACSR 38, 293 [1526] (Beach J). See ch 2, section B.iv.c, section III.D.

[110] ibid 294–95 [1532]–[1535].

[111] ibid 316–17 [1659].

[112] ibid 325 [1712]. The loss measure used was the so-called inflation-based measure, ie the difference between the price at which the shareholder bought his or her interest and the market price that would have prevailed but for the contraventions. Other measures include: (1) the 'true value' measure: the difference between the price at which the shareholder acquired their interest and the true value of that interest; (2) the 'left in the hand' measure: the difference between the price paid for the shares and whatever is left in hand upon a sale of the shares; and (3) the 'no transaction' measure: the difference between the position the shareholder is in at the date of the trial as a result of acquiring the shares and the position they would have been in if he had not acquired the shares. See ch 5, section III.B.

[113] Dominic Powell, 'Landmark Myer class action settled after shareholders unable to prove loss' *The Sydney Morning Herald* (6 May 2020).

[114] The Hon Josh Frydenberg, Treasurer, 'Litigation funders to be regulated under the Corporations Act' (Media Release, 22 May 2020); Corporations Amendment (Litigation Funding) Regulations 2020 (Cth).

[115] Corporations Act 2001 (Cth), Ch 5C. The application of the MIS regime to a class action with litigation funding initially occurred in *Brookfield Multiplex Limited v International Litigation Funding Partners Pte Ltd* (2009) 180 FCR 11, but was overridden by regulation. See Michael Legg, Edmond Park, Nicholas Turner and Louisa Travers, 'The Rise and Regulation of Litigation Funding in Australia' (2011) 38 *Northern Kentucky Law Review* 625, 662–70.

AFSL holders are obliged to:

- act honestly, efficiently and fairly in providing financial services;
- ensure the applicant is a fit and proper person (which allows for regard to be had to criminal convictions and insolvency);
- maintain an appropriate level of competence to provide financial services;
- have adequate financial, technical and human resources to provide the financial services covered by the licence;
- have appropriate arrangements for managing conflicts of interests;
- comply with licence conditions and financial service laws;
- ensure representatives are adequately trained and competent;
- have adequate risk management systems;
- be a member of the Australian Financial Complaints Authority;
- maintain an internal dispute resolution procedure;
- hold adequate coverage of professional indemnity insurance; and
- notify ASIC of licensee breaches.[116]

MISs traditionally provided a mechanism for investors to pool their funds or use them in a common enterprise to create an investment scheme from which they acquire rights to benefits.[117] Examples include raising funds for primary production (such as forestry, food and flower plantations, and animal breeding), film production and collective investment in land, company securities and other securities.[118] The MIS regime seeks to protect investors by requiring that there be a responsible entity that is a public company and holds an AFSL.[119] The responsible entity also has particular obligations, such as a duties to act honestly, with care and diligence and to act in the best interests of the scheme's members. Further, if there is a conflict between the members' interests and the responsible entity's interests, the members' interests take priority.[120] MISs must be registered if they have more than 20 members or are promoted by a person in the business of promoting MISs.[121] A registered MIS has a constitution which must make adequate provision for:

- the consideration to be paid to acquire an interest in the scheme;
- the powers of the responsible entity to make investments of, or otherwise dealing with, scheme property, including powers to borrow or raise money for the scheme;
- the method for dealing with member complaints;
- any rights of members to withdraw from the scheme;

[116] Corporations Act 2001 (Cth), ss 912A, 912D, 913B, 913BA, 913BB.

[117] Corporations Act 2001 (Cth), s 9.

[118] Robert Austin and Ian Ramsay, *Ford, Austin and Ramsay's Principles of Corporations Law* (LexisNexis Online, 2018) [22.470.3].

[119] Corporations Act 2001 (Cth), s 601FA.

[120] Corporations Act 2001 (Cth), s 601FC. The obligations also apply to officers of a responsible entity: s 601FD.

[121] Corporations Act 2001 (Cth), s 601ED.

- rights of the responsible entity to any fees, remuneration, expenses or indemnity; and
- winding up of the scheme.[122]

There are also requirements for a compliance plan, compliance committee, auditing of the compliance plan and rights of withdrawal for members.[123]

While the need for licensing of a litigation funder has been accepted, the application of the MIS regime has attracted criticism as the requirements were not designed for a class action or litigation more generally.[124] Consequently, ASIC granted relief from some obligations, such as the need to give a Product Disclosure Statement (PDS) (as an interest in a MIS is also a financial product) to some members, some content requirements of a PDS; modification of the withdrawal procedures for scheme members; and obligations for the valuation of scheme property.[125]

The short-term impact of the regulations was a decline in all class action filings. In the five months since the litigation funding regulations came into effect, six class actions were commenced in the Federal Court of Australia, while 32 class actions were commenced in the preceding eight months. Indeed, with the new requirements commencing on 22 August 2020, three claims were filed on 20 August and eight claims on 21 August.[126]

D. Group Costs Orders in Victoria

On 30 June 2020, the Justice Legislation Miscellaneous Amendments Act 2020 (Vic) commenced. This introduced a new section 33ZDA to the class actions regime in the State of Victoria, which provided for 'group costs orders'. Section 33ZDA permits a plaintiff in a class action to apply to the court to make an order that:

(a) the legal costs payable to the law practice representing the plaintiff and group members be calculated as a percentage of the amount of any award or settlement that may be recovered in the proceeding; and
(b) liability for payment of the legal costs and all group members.

The court may make such an order if satisfied that 'it is appropriate or necessary to ensure that justice is done in the proceeding'. The court may also amend a group costs order, including, but not limited to, amendment of any percentage ordered, during the course of the proceeding.

If a group costs order is made:

(a) the law practice representing the plaintiff and group members is liable to pay any costs payable to the defendant in the proceeding;[127] and
(b) the law practice representing the plaintiff and group members must give any security for the costs of the defendant in the proceeding that the court may order the plaintiff to give.

[122] Corporations Act 2001 (Cth), s 601GA.
[123] Corporations Act 2001 (Cth), ss 601HA, 601HG, 601JA, 601KA.
[124] Parliamentary Joint Committee on Corporations and Financial Services, Litigation funding and the regulation of the class action industry hearing, *Hansard* (13 July 2020) 34 (Professor Michael Legg), 50 (Andrew Saker, Omni Bridgeway Limited); Ronald Mizen, 'New rules could see funded class actions grind to halt' *The Australian Financial Review* (29 July 2020).
[125] ASIC Corporations (Litigation Funding Schemes) Instrument 2020/787, 21 August 2020; Australian Securities and Investments Commission Corporations (Litigation Funding Schemes) Instrument 2020/787, 'Explanatory Statement' (21 August 2020).
[126] Michael Pelly, 'Pandemic surge in class action' *The Australian Financial Review* (21 May 2021) 17.
[127] In Australia the usual costs rule is that costs follow the event or loser pays; ch 2, section V.E.

The media has referred to group costs orders as giving rise to the legalisation of contingency fees in Australia.[128] However, the amendment is much more similar to a common fund order. Contingency fees are typically contractual – the client agrees that the lawyer can take a percentage of the recovery if the claim is successful. That is not the case here – the court makes an order that binds all group members regardless of any contract, including setting the amount of the percentage to be charged. Further, the court can only make the order if it is satisfied that it is 'appropriate or necessary to ensure justice is done'. The group cost order is therefore closer to the US common fund order for legal fees in American class actions which were adopted because the lawyers could not contract with all group members in an opt-out class action.[129] Further, as a condition of a group costs order the plaintiff law firm must not only take on the risk of the plaintiff's costs of the class action if unsuccessful, but is also liable for any costs payable to the defendant, and any security for costs order made in the defendant's favour if the claim fails.

Group costs orders are not available in other jurisdictions in Australia. Accordingly, these reforms introduce a significant difference in what was previously a relatively homogenous class action regime across Australia. It may be that class action plaintiff lawyers will see the Supreme Court of Victoria as a more attractive forum for commencing class action litigation. This is illustrated by continuous disclosure class actions that traditionally have been brought in the Federal Court, migrating to the Supreme Court of Victoria. Class actions against Treasury Wines (April and May 2020),[130] Arrium (August 2020), G8 Education (November 2020), Freedom Foods (December 2000 and February 2021) and Crown Resorts (February 2021) were all commenced in Victoria.[131] However, it is not clear that a group costs order will be more lucrative than a lawyer billing by the hour with a litigation funder paying the bill. Much will depend on what fees the Victorian courts allow.

There is also a question as to the impact of group costs orders on the future of litigation funding. As explained in chapter two, section V.E, litigation funding was a response to lawyers being unable to charge a fee by reference to a percentage of the recovery achieved, but also the Australian costs rule that the loser pays the winner's costs. Section 33ZDA allows lawyers to charge by reference to a percentage of the recovery and its requirements include that the lawyer bear the risk of the case failing, and provide any security for costs. As such, this would seem to make funding unnecessary. However, that may not be the case. The lawyer needs to obtain the financing or some form of insurance to be able to meet those requirements. The legislation does not specify or proscribe how that may be done. Litigation funding may then still have a role, but of a secondary character dealing with the lawyer rather than group members. There is also the fact that group costs orders are not compulsory. For some cases, lawyers may not be able to bear the risk of having to pay the defendant's costs or they may prefer to be paid an hourly rate as they go. Litigation funding will be the solution. However, group costs orders clearly introduce more competition into the litigation funding market as demonstrated by the shift in continuous disclosure class action filings to Victoria.

[128] Jennifer Hewett, 'Legal bid for bigger slice of class actions' *The Australian Financial Review* (17 June 2020), 2 (referring to the bill for 'the right to charge contingency fees in the booming and lucrative arena of class actions'); Chris Merritt, 'Contingency fee shift courts conflict' *The Australian* (20 June 2020) 15.

[129] A common fund in generic terms, is where one person (eg a litigant or a lawyer) who recovers a fund for the benefit of persons other than himself or his client, is entitled to a reasonable fee from the fund: Michael Legg, 'Reconciling Litigation Funding and the Opt Out Group Definition in Federal Court of Australia Class Actions – The Need for a Legislative Common Fund Approach' (2011) 30 *Civil Justice Quarterly* 52, 63–64.

[130] *Stallard v Treasury Wine Estates Ltd and Napier v Treasury Wine Estates Ltd* [2020] VSC 679 [14] (Nichols J) (although both class actions were filed before the enactment of group costs orders 'it was anticipated that the Justice Legislation (Miscellaneous Amendments) Bill 2019 (Vic) would be passed in the near future').

[131] See Appendix 2, Table 3. The first decision considering group costs orders is *Fox v Westpac Banking Corporation* [2021] VSC 573.

E. Second Continuous Disclosure Class Action Judgment

Worley Limited was a provider of professional project and asset services in the energy, chemicals and resources sectors. On 14 August 2013, it stated via the ASX in a written announcement that it expected its net profit after tax (or NPAT) in FY2014 to exceed that of FY2013, which was $322 million. More specifically, the announcement included the statement, 'While recognizing the uncertainties in world markets, we expect our geographic and sector diversification to provide a solid foundation to deliver increased earnings in FY2014'.

On 9 October 2013, Worley announced to the market that its first-half result would be lower than in FY2013, but affirmed the August 2013 earnings guidance statement. On 10 and 15 October 2013, Worley repeated its August 2013 earnings guidance statement.

On 20 November 2013, Worley announced that it expected its NPAT to be $260 to $300 million for FY2014, which was 7–17 per cent less than its NPAT in FY2013. This caused Worley's share price to fall approximately 26 per cent.[132]

Mr Crowley commenced a class action on behalf of all persons who purchased Worley shares in the period of 14 August to 20 November 2013 and who allegedly suffered loss due to Worley failing to comply with the continuous disclosure regime and for engaging in misleading or deceptive conduct.

Worley's statement on 14 August 2013 of expected NPAT growth was based on a budget, which had been prepared by Worley, but not released to the public. Central to much of Mr Crowley's case was that this budget did not provide reasonable grounds for an expectation of NPAT growth. He alleged that a reasonable budget would have forecast NPAT of $260 to $300 million for FY2014, which was less than the FY2013's NPAT of $322 million.

Mr Crowley alleged Worley contravened the continuous disclosure laws and prohibition on misleading conduct based on three allegations:

- The 'budget case': Worley did not have a reasonable basis for its earnings guidance statement to the market on 14 August 2013.[133]
- The 'performance case': in the alternative, from 14 August 2013 and, on 9, 10 or 15 October 2013, due to Worley's actual performance in the early months of FY14, Worley lacked a reasonable basis for maintaining the FY14 guidance representation and, by failing to correct the August 2013 earning guidance statement (or the 9 October 2013 announcement), Worley engaged in conduct that was misleading or deceptive or likely to mislead or deceive.[134]
- The 'consensus case': Worley was aware of analysts' consensus expectation that Worley would deliver between approximately $354 and $368 million in NPAT for FY14, and ought to have known its earnings were likely to fall materially short of the consensus expectation (as opposed to the earnings guidance) from 14 August 2013. Failing to disclose that earnings would fall short contravened the continuous disclosure requirements.[135]

On 22 October 2020 Gleeson J delivered judgment finding no contraventions. The class action was unsuccessful for two primary reasons. First, in relation to the budget case and the performance case, the court concluded that, on 14 August 2013 and all other relevant times, Worley did have a reasonable basis for stating that it expected its NPAT to be in excess of $322 million.

[132] *Crowley v Worley Limited* [2020] FCA 1522 [1]–[5], [313], [567]–[568] (Gleeson J).
[133] ibid [20].
[134] ibid [53]–[54].
[135] ibid [55].

Central to this finding of the court was that the budget for FY2014 and its preparation were reasonable. Second, assuming that a consensus expectation existed, the consensus case failed because it required the applicant to demonstrate that Worley knew or ought to have known that its FY14 earnings would fall materially short of the predicted range. The court was not satisfied that any relevant officer of Worley, whose state of mind was to be attributed to Worley, had or ought to have had that knowledge or belief at any relevant time.[136]

As the applicant failed to establish that Worley had engaged in unlawful conduct, the court did not consider the appropriate method for establishing causation or proving and measuring loss in a shareholder class action.

The outcome in *Worley* did not require any major development in the law. Rather it turned primarily on the evidence presented not making out the case pleaded. The documentary evidence and the evidence given by Worley's witnesses, whom the court found to be credible, was consistent with the budget and related disclosures being reasonable. The evidence the claimants put forward was 'mostly hindsight and not supported by detail that might have contradicted the evidence of [Worley's] witnesses'.[137]

However, the judge arguably set the evidentiary bar higher than it had previously been understood to be, by holding that 'The allegation that a publicly listed company did not have reasonable grounds for its earnings guidance is a relatively serious one', which therefore attracts the *Briginshaw* standard.[138] Under *Briginshaw*, although the evidentiary standard of proof remains the ordinary civil standard (the balance of probabilities), the strength of the evidence necessary to establish a fact or facts can rise depending on the seriousness of the allegation or consequences. Consequently, a court should not lightly make a finding of serious misconduct.[139] However, the holding was in a context where the causes of action relied on, namely misleading conduct and contravention of the continuous disclosure regime did not require proof of any intent or standard of misconduct such as negligence or fraud. Nonetheless, if the applicability of the *Briginshaw* standard continues then proving a contravention of the continuous disclosure regime is made more difficult.

F. Parliamentary Joint Committee on Corporations and Financial Services

On 13 May 2020, the Attorney-General referred to the Parliamentary Joint Committee on Corporations and Financial Services (PJC) an inquiry into litigation funding and the regulation of the class action industry. To a significant extent it was a replay of the ALRC 2018 inquiry. The PJC delivered a 400-plus-page report on 21 December 2020.[140] The PJC's general view was that 'the class action system needs to be reformed to reflect the underlying tenets of its original intent: that is, to deliver reasonable, proportionate and fair access to justice in the best interests of class members'.[141] However, while the range of recommended reforms certainly provided greater

[136] ibid [13]–[15], [429], [501]–[502], [617]–[620], [646]–[651].

[137] ibid [69].

[138] ibid [58]–[59] citing *Briginshaw v Briginshaw* (1938) 60 CLR 336, 361–362 (Dixon J).

[139] *Neat Holdings Pty Limited v Karajan Holdings Pty Limited* (1992) 67 ALJR 170, 171 (Mason CJ, Brennan J, Deane J, Toohey J and Gaudron J).

[140] Parliamentary Joint Committee on Corporations and Financial Services, Litigation funding and the regulation of the class action industry (December 2020).

[141] ibid xvi.

protection of group member interests, the PJC's recommendations also provided greater protections for defendants, in particular listed corporations the target of continuous disclosure class actions.

i. Oversight of Legal Costs

The PJC made two main recommendations in relation to the oversight of legal costs, although its focus was directed more to the costs of litigation funding. First, the PJC endorsed the use of referees and contradictors in relation to court supervision of deductions for legal costs, but also litigation funding charges.[142] Second, the PJC also recommended the more frequent use of contradictors as a procedure for protecting group member interests, including from excessive costs. The PJC also recommended the adoption of a procedure to facilitate communication of group members' concerns about a settlement to a contradictor, where appointed.[143]

ii. Contingency Fees and Group Costs Orders

The PJC also considered the potential impact of proposals to allow contingency fees. The PJC was critical of proposals to allow lawyers to charge contingency fees in the class action context, stating that it was not persuaded that doing so would 'lead to reasonable, proportionate and fair outcomes'.[144] The PJC pointed to a number of factors that supported its conclusion. There was a concern that contingency fees created too great a risk that lawyers could compromise their ethical and professional obligations to the court and to the client if they have a direct financial interest in the outcome. The potential for contingency fee arrangements to increase access to justice was doubted on the basis that only a small number of law firms would have sufficient capital to undertake the risk required to compete for larger cases that are typically funded by litigation funders, and the funds recoverable from smaller class actions would be less likely to compensate firms for the risk taken. Further there was a possibility that group members may be charged for both a contingency fee and a litigation funding fee, which would increase costs. The PJC also observed that if law firms were providing a funding service then it may be that they should be subject to similar regulatory arrangements as third-party litigation funders.[145]

The PJC then made two recommendations that may have the effect of restricting the impact of the Victorian group costs order. Recommendation 30 was that the Federal Government should amend the Corporations Act and the ASIC Act to confer exclusive jurisdiction to hear class actions arising under that legislation on the Federal Court.[146] If adopted, this recommendation would have the effect that shareholder class actions could not be brought before the Supreme Court of Victoria (or any other state Supreme Court), and could therefore not be subject to group costs order in Victoria.

Recommendation 21 was that the Federal Government review the feasibility of applying the AFSL and MIS regimes to lawyers operating on a contingency fee arrangement in class actions, which would cover group costs order arrangements in Victoria.[147] The PJC considered that this would achieve consistent regulation for entities undertaking similar commercial activities,

[142] ibid 162–65.
[143] ibid 183, 186–87.
[144] ibid 248.
[145] ibid.
[146] ibid 351.
[147] ibid 250–51.

being the financing of class action litigation. The heightened regulatory burden for lawyers may dissuade the use of the group costs order.

iii. Litigation Funding Regulation

The PJC adopted the ALRC recommendations on statutory powers for the Federal Court in relation to enforcement of funding agreements and the ability to reject, vary or amend their terms.[148] The PJC reviewed the change to litigation funding regulation discussed above and noted the various concerns about whether the MIS regime was fit for purpose. The PJC's Recommendation 28 was that:

> The committee supports the regulations issued by the Treasurer which clarify that litigation funders require an Australian Financial Service License and that they be regulated as Managed Investment Schemes. Noting that ASIC has provided relief from a number of MIS requirements, the committee recommends the Australian Government legislate a fit-for-purpose MIS regime tailored for litigation funders.[149]

In December 2020, the Australian Labor Party moved to disallow the funding regulations on the basis that they were not 'fit for purpose' and 'will only make it more difficult for ordinary Australians to access justice against deep-pocketed corporates'.[150] The motion was narrowly defeated in the Senate with a 32-vote tie (a clear majority is required to pass a motion in the Senate). One Nation Senator Pauline Hanson (a member of the cross-bench) voted against the motion, but has indicated that she will work with the Australian Government to introduce amendments to the regulatory regime in 2021, including to exempt class actions from the MIS requirements if the funder commits to giving at least 70 per cent of the damages or settlement sum to class members.[151] The Government has continued to examine this option.[152]

IV. Reformulating the Continuous Disclosure Laws

A. ALRC Inquiry into Class Actions and Litigation Funding

As explained in section III.A above, the ALRC recommended an evidence-based review of the continuous disclosure regime and related prohibitions on misleading conduct. One of the issues raised was whether to reinstate a requirement for intent or fault as existed in the continuous disclosure regime pre-2002.[153] A number of relevant submissions were made on this issue.

[148] ibid 158.

[149] ibid 312.

[150] Deborah O'Neill (NSW, Australian Labor Party), Senate debates (2 December 2020).

[151] Ronald Mizen, 'Litigation funding rules survive after 11th-hour One Nation backdown' *The Australian Financial Review* (4 December 2020).

[152] Australian Treasury and Attorney-General's Department, 'Consultation Paper – Guaranteeing a minimum return of class action proceeds to class members' (June 2021); Corporations Amendment (Improving Outcomes for Litigation Funding Participants) Bill 2021 (maintaining MIS based regulation, proposing rebuttable presumption that less than a 70% recovery for group members is not reasonable, granting courts power to amend a funder's fee to ensure it is fair and reasonable).

[153] See ch 2, section II.D.ii citing Corporations Law 2001 (Cth), s 1005; *Jubilee Mines NL v Riley* (2009) 40 WAR 299, 318–19 [69]–[71] (Martin CJ); *Grant-Taylor v Babcock & Brown Limited (in liq)* (2016) 245 FCR 402, 421 [102] ('Chapter 6CA (as it now operates) however generally widened the scope of the continuous disclosure provisions, as compared with the prior provisions, by removing the elements required of intentional, reckless or negligent non-disclosure.') (Allsop CJ, Gilmour and Beach JJ).

ASIC in its submission to the ALRC stated:

> Market integrity is fundamental to investor confidence and a well-developed financial market. Financial markets cannot fund the economy without trust and confidence. As set out at paragraph 2 of Report 487 Review of Australian equity market cleanliness (REP 487), confidence in market integrity:
>
> (a) encourages investor participation;
> (b) contributes to liquidity;
> (c) stimulates more competitive pricing; and
> (d) leads to a lower cost of capital.
>
> Financial markets can only operate fairly when the information they rely on is accurate, useful and available to all. If investors perceive they are not being appropriately informed or that they are at an exploitable information disadvantage, they tend to protect themselves by reducing their exposure to the market. They also demand a higher return or invest in other markets with better integrity and fair access to information.[154]

ASIC was of the view that the 'economic significance of fair and efficient capital markets dwarfs any exposure to class action damages'.[155]

In contrast, the Australian Institute of Company Directors (AICD) argued that the prevalence of shareholder class actions risked 'a "chilling effect" on the ability of listed companies to attract investment, both domestically and from overseas markets, or to engage in mergers and acquisitions activity'.[156]

The availability and pricing of directors' and officers' insurance (D&O insurance) was also argued to be negatively impacted by shareholder class actions.[157] The AICD submitted that the active shareholder class actions market had resulted in 'an unsustainable rate of increase in the cost of Directors' and Officers' insurance … for all listed companies, with reports suggesting there has been an alarming 200% increase in annual D&O premiums over the last 12 to 18 months'.[158] The Insurance Council of Australia was of the view that D&O insurance market was now unprofitable and the current premium pool inadequate to cover claims, with the result that 'insurers [were] required to significantly increase premiums or exit this sector of the insurance market'.[159]

B. Requiring Intention or Fault for Liability – Interim Measures

The COVID-19 pandemic saw corporate Australia raise the uncertainty created from border and business closures[160] as necessitating changes to continuous disclosure laws and class actions.[161]

[154] Australian Securities and Investments Commission (ASIC), Submission No 72 to Australian Law Reform Commission, 'Inquiry into class action proceedings and third-party litigation funders' (September 2018), [25]–[26].

[155] ibid [4].

[156] AICD, Submission No 35 to Australian Law Reform Commission, 'Inquiry into class action proceedings and third-party litigation funders' (September 2018) 3.

[157] ALRC 2018 Class Actions Report (n 73) [9.81]–[9.88]. See ch 6, section II.I identifying that rising insurance costs did not occur until 2018.

[158] AICD Submission No 35 (n 156) 3.

[159] Insurance Council of Australia Ltd, Submission No 47 to Australian Law Reform Commission, 'Inquiry into class action proceedings and third-party litigation funders' (September 2018) 2.

[160] The ways in which COVID-19 might give rise to market-sensitive information include: ongoing and further government intervention; capital management events; operational impacts; material changes in business fundamentals; mitigation and response actions; changes in law; employee safety issues; changes in demand for products; and impacts on material contracts. See Charles Ashton and Vijay Cugati, 'Continuous disclosure during COVID-19: shining the spotlight on earnings and debt', Allens (6 April 2020).

[161] Patrick Durkin, 'Treasurer considers class action freeze', *The Australian Financial Review* (9 April 2020). An AICD survey found that one third of listed company directors want a total ban on class actions: Sally Patten, 'Company directors call for a ban on class actions', *The Australian Financial Review* (11 June 2020).

After sustained lobbying from the Business Council of Australia and AICD, the Federal treasurer used the COVID-19 powers under s 1362A of the Corporations Act to amend the continuous disclosure laws for a six-month period from 26 May 2020.[162]

The treasurer's determination has the effect that listed entities' decisions on continuous disclosure do not attract liability under s 674(2) unless they knew or were reckless or negligent with respect to whether information would, if it were generally available, have a material effect on the price or value of the entities' securities. The link between altering the continuous disclosure regime and class actions was made express by the treasurer in his media release:

> The heightened level of uncertainty around companies' future prospects as a result of the crisis also exposes companies to the threat of opportunistic class actions for allegedly falling foul of their continuous disclosure obligations if their forecasts are found to be inaccurate. …
>
> The changes announced today will make it harder to bring such actions against companies and officers' during the Coronavirus crisis and while allowing the market to continue to stay informed and function effectively.[163]

However, as discussed in chapter two, the broad misleading or deceptive conduct provisions, such as s 1041H of the Corporations Act, do not have any fault or intention element and are also pleaded as the basis for a class action claim. These provisions would circumvent the effectiveness of any changes to the continuous disclosure regime.[164]

The AICD CEO, Angus Armour, welcomed the higher requirements for proving a breach of the continuous disclosure laws, but took issue with the ability of shareholders to bring a class action alleging misleading and deceptive behaviour by directors but with no need to prove fault or intent.[165] The existence of 'strict' liability provisions such as 1041H were targeted for reform.[166]

The changes to the continuous disclosure laws also applied to civil penalty actions brought by ASIC. However, the then deputy chair of ASIC, Daniel Crennan QC, responded to the change by pointing out that the change only impacted civil claims and that the requirements for ASIC to bring criminal proceedings remained the same.[167] Criminal proceedings have always necessitated a showing of some form of state of mind.[168] Mr Crennan also noted that the obligations for disclosure in the ASX listing rules had not changed.[169]

On 23 September 2020 the treasurer announced that the Government would be extending the temporary continuous disclosure provisions for a further six months until 23 March 2021.[170] The temporary measures ceased to apply from 23 March 2021.

[162] Corporations (Coronavirus Economic Response) Determination (No 2) 2020 (Cth); Michael Pelly, Patrick Durkin and John Kehoe, 'Chairman cheers disclosure freeze amid investor concerns', *The Australian Financial Review* (26 May 2020).

[163] The Hon Josh Frydenberg, Treasurer, 'Temporary changes to continuous disclosure provisions for companies and officers' (Media Release, 25 May 2020).

[164] James Thomson, 'Disclosure changes hurt investors' *The Australian Financial Review* (27 May 2020) 40.

[165] Patten (n 161).

[166] Will Heath, Nigel Hunt and David Friedlander, 'Continuous disclosure relaxation causes joy and despair – who's right?', *The Australian Financial Review* (28 May 2020).

[167] Michael Pelly, 'Crennan warns directors on disclosure laws', *The Australian Financial Review* (5 June 2020). See also Corporations (Coronavirus Economic Response) Determination (No 2) 2020 (Cth), reg 9.

[168] ch 2, section II.D.i.

[169] Pelly (n 167). The requirement in ASX Listing Rule 3.1 remained that once an ASX listed entity 'is or becomes aware of any information concerning it that a reasonable person would expect to have a material effect on the price or value of the entity's securities, the entity must immediately tell ASX that information'.

[170] The Hon Josh Frydenberg, Treasurer, 'Extension of temporary changes to continuous disclosure provisions for companies and officers' (Media Release, 23 September 2020); Corporations (Coronavirus Economic Response) Determination (No 4) 2020 (Cth).

C. Parliamentary Joint Committee on Corporations and Financial Services

The PJC report referred to above split along party lines in relation to continuous disclosure. The PJC report, authored by a majority of members who were from the conservative Liberal National Party, endorsed the changes made to the continuous disclosure regime and recommended that they should be made permanent.[171] However, a minority report by Labor members rejected this recommendation.[172]

The majority view was that 'shareholder class actions are generally economically inefficient and not in the public interest'.[173] The majority supported its position by reference to high transaction costs, the circularity problem, 'those responsible for continuous disclosure breaches do not receive timely sanctions or bear the full costs of their actions' and the undesirable effects on the availability and cost of D&O insurance, which discourages qualified persons from becoming directors.[174]

These criticisms have been previously made and are discussed in chapter three and critiqued in chapters five and six utilising the case studies. Of note here is that the PJC's majority view does not recognise that its arguments may conflict. Responsible individuals do not bear the full costs of their actions because of D&O insurance,[175] but more readily available insurance is argued to be desirable. Moreover, if an intent or fault requirement is added to the continuous disclosure regime, this may trigger exclusions for insurance coverage at law and in the policy.[176]

The PJC then turned to the continuous disclosure regime. The committee recognised that continuous disclosure is an important mechanism in the efficient operation of the market, but opined that returning to the pre-2002 position, where a fault element was required for a contravention, achieved a better balance between fostering market integrity and increasing the difficulty of bringing shareholder class actions.[177]

The minority report saw the changes as being politically motivated and contrary to ASIC's advice that 'The economic significance of fair and efficient capital markets dwarfs any exposure to class action damages'.[178] The minority instead endorsed the ALRC's recommendation that the Australian Government should commission a review of the legal and economic impact of the operation, enforcement, and effects of continuous disclosure obligations and those relating to misleading and deceptive conduct, rather than seeking to make an emergency measure law without proper study.[179]

D. Requiring Intention or Fault for Liability – Permanent Measures

The Treasury Laws Amendment (2021 Measures No 1) Bill was introduced to Parliament on 17 February 2021 to: (1) make permanent the temporary changes to the continuous disclosure

[171] PJC (n 140) 351 (Recommendation 29).
[172] ibid 363.
[173] ibid 348.
[174] ibid 348–49.
[175] ch 5, section II.B.vi.
[176] ibid. Insurance may not be available or will be found to be illegal as a matter of public policy in relation to criminal liability or liability for a civil penalty where the conduct was intentional or morally offensive: Robert Merkin and Ian Enright, *Sutton on Insurance Law*, 4th edn (Thomson Reuters, 2015) [23.1860].
[177] PJC (n 140) 350–51.
[178] ibid 362–63.
[179] ibid 364.

obligations in ss 674 and 675 of the Corporations Act which were introduced in May 2020 under Corporations (Coronavirus Economic Response) Determination (No 2and (2) to align s 1041H of the Corporations Act and s 12DA of the ASIC Act with the new ss 674 and 675 such that corporations and their directors and officers will only be liable for misleading or deceptive conduct for failing to disclose material information where they have acted with knowledge, recklessness or negligence.

The purpose of the Bill was expressed to be the raising of the liability standard so that companies and their officers can 'more confidently provide guidance to the market without exposing themselves to the risk of opportunistic class actions'.[180]

The Bill amends the existing legislation to create separate criminal offences and civil penalty provisions. Previously there was only a single provision, but it was subject to dual track enforcement. The changes do not affect the Commonwealth's ability to prosecute criminal breaches, with their associated fault elements. The civil penalty provisions remain financial services civil penalty provisions under section 1317E and contraventions can in turn be the basis for ASIC enforcement through a pecuniary penalty order, disgorgement order and compensation order (as explained in section II.C above), but also a compensation order sought by a person who suffered damage as a result of the contravention. However, the Bill adds a fault or intention requirement to the civil penalty provisions through s 674(2) so that it reads:

> (2) If:
>
> (a) this subsection applies to a listed disclosing entity; and
> (b) the entity has information that those provisions require the entity to notify to the market operator; and
> (c) the information is not generally available; and
> (d) the entity knows, or is reckless or negligent with respect to whether, the information would, if it were generally available, have a material effect on the price or value of ED securities of the entity;
>
> the entity must notify the market operator of that information in accordance with those provisions. (emphasis added)

Prior to the proposed amendment, s 674(2)(d) above was s 674(2)(c)(ii), where the requirement was that 'a reasonable person would expect' the information to have a material effect. In short, the change has been explained as a move from a strict liability standard to a fault standard.[181]

ASIC may also continue to issue infringement notices under Part 9.4AA of the Corporations Act. However, the Bill seeks to retain the existing no-fault requirement, ie the pre-Bill position, so that ASIC does not need to be satisfied of any intent or state of mind to have reasonable grounds to believe there has been a contravention.[182]

In March 2021, the Senate Standing Committee on Economics released a report in which the conservative coalition Government majority recommended that the Treasury Laws Amendment (2021 Measures No 1) Bill be passed without amendment.[183] The report captured the range of arguments for and against the amendments. Submissions in support of the Bill argued that it would address the following matters:

- the low threshold for commencing shareholder class actions for an alleged breach of continuous disclosure and the consequent high incidence of class actions in Australia;

[180] The Hon Michael Sukkar MP, House of Representatives, *Hansard* (17 February 2021) 10. The Bill also responded to the PJC's Recommendation 29 that the interim measures be made permanent.

[181] Evidence to Senate Economics Legislation Committee – Estimates, Parliament of Australia, Canberra, 25 March 2021, 10 (Ms Cathie Armour, ASIC Commissioner) ('Armour Evidence to Senate Economics Legislation Committee').

[182] Senate Standing Committee on Economics, 'Report on Treasury Laws Amendment (2021 Measures No 1) Bill' (March 2021) [1.48]–[1.49].

[183] ibid [2.138]. The Labor and Greens party members of the Committee recommended that the Bill not be passed.

- the impact of continuous disclosure shareholder class actions on the limited availability and high cost of D&O insurance;
- the risk-aversion of company boards and officers as a result of shareholder class actions;
- the ineffectiveness of shareholder class actions due to the circularity problem and costs involved.[184]

This was effectively a summary of the PJC report. Key reasons for opposition to the amendments included: negative impacts on market integrity; trust and reputation; the impact on investors; and a weakened ability of ASIC to regulate effectively.[185]

On 16 March 2021, the Senate again referred the Bill to a committee, this time the Senate Economics References Committee, for inquiry and report. The majority of this committee was composed of the Labor opposition and minor parties who recommended that the Bill not be passed as the arguments in favour of the Bill were not supported by evidence and were unpersuasive.[186] The arguments for an against the Bill were again canvassed. It was noted that adding a fault element would make proving contraventions more difficult, which may dissuade shareholders from using the provision to bring proceedings.[187] There were also competing submissions as to whether there is a direct connection between Australia's existing continuous disclosure laws, class action numbers, D&O insurance price increases, and the limited availability of D&O insurance.[188] Other factors, such as decreased competition in the D&O market and other risks were also at play.[189]

The Bill was directed at class actions but due to the provisions providing for both public and private enforcement the amendments would also impact ASIC. ASIC's officers explained that the impact was effectively two-fold when appearing at a Senate Estimates committee hearing. First, the addition of a fault/intent element would be a new element that ASIC had not previously had to investigate or prove, which would mean that investigations would need to be altered to address the new requirement.[190] This could in turn mean that more time would need to be devoted to each incident with the effect that less cases may be pursued.[191] Second, while ASIC's ability to issue infringement notices does not change, the regime is structured so that acceptance of the notice by the reporting entity is voluntary. If the infringement notice is rejected then ASIC would need to pursue a civil penalty with the new fault/intent element.[192] The disclosing entity may rationally choose not to pay the infringement notice because it knows that ASIC will have a higher hurdle to clear for a civil penalty.[193] Operationally this may impact how ASIC chooses to investigate and enforce the continuous disclosure regime, including starting with civil penalties.[194] Commencing with civil penalties may be seen as consistent with a 'Why not litigate?'

[184] ibid [2.59].

[185] ibid [2.100].

[186] Senate Economics Reference Committee, 'Report on Treasury Laws Amendment (2021 Measures No 1) Bill' (June 2021) [2.195], [2.216]. The conservative coalition Government members recommended that the Bill be passed.

[187] ibid [2.134], [2.173], [2.176].

[188] ibid [2.155]–[2.162].

[189] See eg Marsh and McLennan, 'Directors and Officers Liability (D&O) 2020 Australian Insurance Market Recap Series' (December 2020) 2.

[190] Armour Evidence to Senate Economics Legislation Committee (n 181) 6. ASIC would also face an enforcement landscape where the changes to the misleading or deceptive conduct provisions in relation to continuous disclosure cases would create a different standard compared to when the misleading or deceptive conduct provisions are used in other areas that ASIC regulates. See also Senate Economics Reference Committee (n 186) [2.186], [2.190].

[191] ibid.

[192] Corporations Act 2001 (Cth), ss 1317DAF, 1317DAG. See ch 2, section II.D.iv.

[193] This concern was the motivation behind ASIC issuing a warning rather than an infringement notice in the Telstra case study: see ch 4, section III.A; ch 5, section II.A.iii.

[194] Armour Evidence to Senate Economics Legislation Committee (n 181) 6–7.

enforcement approach, but inconsistent with government policy, if that be the policy, of reducing reliance on litigation. Further, if the proof needed for civil penalty cases (intent/fault being added to the *Briginshaw* standard) is closer to the proof needed for a criminal prosecution then the latter may be preferred.

On 9 August 2021 the Bill was passed by the Senate and finally passed by both Houses on 10 August 2021. Consequently, a fault/intent requirement has been added to s 674(2) as explained above, with ramifications for the elements to be proved and evidence to be gathered, for both class actions and ASIC.

V. ASIC Enforcement and Continuous Disclosure Class Actions Post-2017

To address whether there has been a change in the pattern of ASIC enforcement and class actions post 2017 it is instructive to start by reviewing the key dates.

The Financial Services Royal Commission was established on 14 December 2017. The Interim Report of the Financial Services Royal Commission was tabled in Parliament on 28 September 2018. ASIC's Response to Interim Report was completed and dated 2 November 2018. The final report was tabled in Parliament on 4 February 2019. The 'Why not litigate?' approach as a response to criticism of ASIC's negotiated outcomes approach was in play by the second half of 2018.[195] ASIC first levied invoices pursuant to Parliament's industry funding model in January 2019 for the 2017–18 year. The increased penalties and powers applicable to the continuous disclosure regime took effect from 13 March 2019.

In the class actions arena litigation funding regulation was announced on 22 May 2020 with the new regulatory regime coming into effect on 22 August 2020. Group costs orders became available in Victoria from 30 June 2020. The *Myer* decision was handed down on 24 October 2019 and the *Worley* decision on 22 October 2020.

For both ASIC and class action proponents, the federal treasurer's interim amendments to the continuous disclosure regime operated from 26 May 2020 until 23 March 2021. The permanent measures took effect from 14 August 2021.

A. ASIC Enforcement

i. *ASIC Enforcement Activity Post-2017*

From the perspective of ASIC enforcement across all of its areas of responsibility there was a definite increase in litigation-based enforcement. ASIC has reported that a comparison of the 2018 and 2020 calendar years reveals that ASIC has recorded a 64 per cent increase in civil penalty proceedings as well as a 36 per cent increase in the number of criminal proceedings commenced.[196] ASIC's former deputy chair has also explained that 'in the post-royal commission world, enforceable undertakings were "fairly unlikely to be provided" … because they do not require an admission of liability'.[197]

[195] Hughes (n 28) as an ASIC Commissioner stating that 'In October 2018 we adopted the Why Not Litigate? Enforcement approach'.

[196] ASIC, 'REP 688 ASIC Enforcement Update: July to December 2020' (April 2021) 3.

[197] Misa Han, James Eyers and Edmund Tadros, 'ASIC: deals unlikely in post-Hayne world', *The Australian Financial Review* (17 May 2019) 21.

In relation to enforcement of the continuous disclosure regime ASIC explained to the Senate Economics Committee that 'most of our activity has been through using infringement notices and civil penalties'.[198] This is borne out by ASIC's enforcement actions since 2017 where it has issued three infringement notices, with associated ineligibility to issue a reduced-content prospectus, and six civil penalty proceedings. There have been no warnings, no enforceable undertakings, but also no criminal prosecutions.

The infringement notices are listed in Schedule 2, Table 1. The three entities were Gold Mountain Limited, Byte Power Group Limited and Regional Express Holdings Limited. Turning to civil penalties, there was one action that was commenced on 30 September 2016 but not finalised until 2019 so that it was not included in the pre-2017 analysis in chapters two to six. ASIC successfully brought proceedings against Vocation Limited (in liquidation – declarations but no pecuniary penalty) and the company's former executive managing director (disqualified from managing corporations for six years and pay a pecuniary penalty in the amount of $70,000), non-executive chairman (disqualified from managing corporations for two years and pay a pecuniary penalty in the amount of $25,000), and company secretary and chief financial officer (CFO) (disqualified from managing corporations for three years and pay a pecuniary penalty in the amount of $30,000.[199]

On 2 March 2018 ASIC commenced civil penalty proceedings against Rio Tinto Limited (RTL) and its former CEO and CFO. A number of causes of action in relation to financial statements and director's duties were relied on. However, on 1 May 2018 the proceedings were amended and RTL was alleged to have contravened the continuous disclosure regime by failing to disclose a substantial impairment in the carrying value of the operating assets of one of its wholly owned subsidiaries in its 2012 Interim Financial Statements.[200]

On 8 March 2018, ASIC commenced civil penalty proceedings against Antares Energy Limited and one of its directors, the former CEO and chairman. Judgment in ASIC's favour was delivered on 12 October 2020.[201]

On 14 June 2018 ASIC commenced civil penalty proceedings against the former managing director of Quintis Limited for failing to discharge his duties as a director under s 180 of the Corporations Act. The breach of director's duties relied on the managing director causing Quintis to breach its continuous disclosure obligations.[202]

On 14 September 2018 ASIC commenced civil penalty proceedings against Australia and New Zealand Banking Group Limited (ANZ) for an alleged continuous disclosure breach in relation to a $2.5 billion institutional share placement undertaken by the ANZ in 2015.[203] The action

[198] Armour Evidence to Senate Economics Legislation Committee (n 181) 6. See also Evidence to Senate Economics Legislation Committee – Estimates, Parliament of Australia, Canberra, 25 March 2021, 9 (Mr James Shipton. ASIC chair).

[199] ASIC, 'ASIC commences civil penalty proceedings against Vocation Limited (in liquidation)' (Media Release 16-334, 30 September 2016); *Australian Securities and Investments Commission v Vocation Limited (In Liquidation)* (2019) 371 ALR 155; *Australian Securities and Investments Commission v Vocation Limited (In Liquidation) (No 2)* (2019) 140 ACSR 382.

[200] ASIC, 'ASIC takes action against Rio Tinto and its former CEO and CFO for misleading and deceptive conduct' (Media Release 18-061, 2 March 2018); ASIC, 'ASIC takes further action against Rio Tinto Limited and its former CEO and CFO' (Media Release 18-119, 1 May 2018). Proceedings were adjourned due to the COVID-19 pandemic: *Australian Securities and Investments Commission v Rio Tinto Limited* [2020] FCA 1721.

[201] ASIC, 'ASIC takes civil action against Antares Energy and a director' (Media Release 18-067, 8 March 2018); *Australian Securities and Investments Commission v Big Star Energy Limited (No 3)* (2020) 148 ACSR 334.

[202] ASIC, 'ASIC launches civil penalty proceedings against former Quintis managing director Frank Wilson' (Media Release 18-174, 14 June 2018). Proceedings were adjourned due to the COVID-19 pandemic: *Australian Securities and Investments Commission v Wilson* (2020) 146 ACSR 149.

[203] ASIC, 'ASIC commences civil penalty proceedings against ANZ for alleged continuous disclosure breach in relation to 2015 institutional equity placement' (Media Release 18-268, 14 September 2018).

was stayed until the hearing and final determination of criminal cartel proceedings brought by the Australian Competition and Consumer Commission against ANZ and its group treasurer at the time.[204]

On 22 February 2019 ASIC filed civil penalty proceedings against Getswift Limited and three directors – the executive chairman, managing director and legal counsel – for contraventions of the continuous disclosure regime and the prohibitions on misleading conduct. ASIC also alleged breach of director's duties and sought orders disqualifying the directors from managing a corporation.[205] The proceedings went to trial and concluded on 30 September 2020.[206]

The civil penalty proceedings against MG Responsible Entity Limited (MGRE) that settled pre-31 December 2017[207] then had related litigation commenced on 20 June 2019. ASIC commenced proceedings against former managing director and chief financial officer of MGRE and Murray Goulburn Co-operative Co Limited (MG) in relation to breach of their directors' duties and their 'involvement' (s 674(2A)) in MGRE's continuous disclosure failure. This was not a civil penalty proceeding, but rather ASIC sought declarations and orders disqualifying them from managing a corporation due to repeated contraventions of the Corporations Act.[208]

The action against the managing director and CFO is interesting as they made an application to permanently stay or dismiss the proceeding against them as an abuse of process because of prior regulatory suits against the company, two class actions and delay in the proceedings being brought against them.[209] A number of arguments were put forward, including that ASIC's decision to institute the present proceeding had been predominantly motivated by the publication of the final report of the Financial Services Royal Commission, ASIC's need to respond to criticism of its previous enforcement approach and the 'Why not litigate?' approach to enforcement.[210] Counsel submitted that this was a collateral and improper purpose, ie it is an abuse of process. Beach J rejected the characterisation. However, his Honour did note 'this all highlights a broader problem that needs to be addressed concerning the coordination and disposition of multiple regulatory actions and class actions concerning the same events, circumstances and parties'.[211] A matter that is taken up in chapter eight. Ultimately, the proceedings settled and the managing director and CFO admitted contraventions and were disqualified from managing corporations for three years and four years respectively.[212]

On 10 June 2021 ASIC commenced civil proceedings against shipbuilder Austal Limited for continuous disclosure and misleading conduct breaches, and against Austal's CEO for his involvement in Austal's continuous disclosure contravention (s 674(2A)), and for failing to exercise reasonable care and diligence as a director of Austal.[213] On 4 August 2021 ASIC commenced

[204] *Australian Securities and Investments Commission v Australia and New Zealand Banking Group Limited* (2019) 138 ACSR 42.

[205] ASIC, 'ASIC commences civil penalty proceedings against GetSwift Limited and its directors Bane Hunter and Joel Macdonald' (Media Release 19-039, 22 February 2019); *Webb v GetSwift Limited (No 5)* [2019] FCA 1533 [3], [11]–[12] (Lee J).

[206] Getswift was subject to ASIC proceedings and three class actions (two were stayed) that were initially to be heard sequentially by the same judge and with judgment delivered in both once both trials had concluded. This case management approach was overturned on appeal: *GetSwift Limited v Webb* (2021) 388 ALR 75. The trial judge for the ASIC proceedings was then able to prepare a judgment.

[207] See ch 2, section IV.C.iii.

[208] ASIC, 'ASIC commences Federal Court action against former Murray Goulburn executives Gary Helou and Bradley Hingle' (Media Release 19-152, 25 June 2019).

[209] *Australian Securities and Investments Commission v Helou* (2019) 139 ACSR 489.

[210] ibid 532 [280] (Beach J).

[211] ibid 533 [291].

[212] *Australian Securities and Investments Commission v Helou (No 2)* [2020] FCA 1650.

[213] ASIC, 'ASIC commences civil proceedings against shipbuilder Austal Limited for continuous disclosure breach' (Media Release 21-128, 10 June 2021).

civil proceedings against Hollista CollTech Limited for continuous disclosure and misleading conduct breaches in relation to sanitiser products marketed in the context of the Covid-19 pandemic, and against Hollista's CEO for failing to exercise reasonable care and diligence as a director of Hollista.[214]

From 2003, when the first civil penalty was imposed, to end of 2017 (a 15-year period) ASIC had brought civil penalty proceedings against nine corporate entities/directors[215] and then from 2018 to August 2021 (a 3½-year period) it brought another seven civil penalty proceedings against corporate entities/directors.

ASIC's enforcement tool usage is summarised in Table 7.3, which evidences a clear shift from a regulator preferring negotiated outcomes to a regulator that is more litigation-focused. However, infringement notices and settlement of litigation are still on the table.

Table 7.3 ASIC enforcement tool usage pre- and post-31 December 2017

Enforcement Tool	**ASIC usage as at 31 December 2017 based on matters commenced**	**ASIC usage post-2017 at 4 August 2021 based on matters commenced**
Warning	1	0
Infringement notices	37	3
Disallowing the use of a reduced content prospectus	10	3
Enforceable undertakings	11	0
Civil penalty proceedings	9 (7 successfully completed, 1 ongoing and 1 unsuccessful)	7 (2 successfully completed (1 commenced pre-31 December 2017) and 6 ongoing)
Criminal proceedings	2 (1 unsuccessful)	0

ii. Effectiveness of ASIC

Deterrence remains a key objective for ASIC and is better supported by the policy changes discussed in this chapter, namely the 'Why not litigate?' approach, increased penalties and increased funding.

In the timeframe examined above it is the 'Why not litigate?' approach that has had the greatest impact. The 'Why not Litigate?' approach champions the determination by a court of whether conduct contravenes the law. This enforcement approach is more supportive of deterrence, as broadly defined in this text, as it involves a greater emphasis on court-based enforcement tools, which by their nature result in a finding of contravention, direct sanctions and an impact on reputation through public denunciation. It is also likely that a resort to litigation may increase indirect costs imposed on defendants through the greater costs associated with the adversarial nature of litigation, but also the higher stakes. It is too soon to say whether this 'procedural discipline' will ultimately become part of responsive regulation and guide the use of the enforcement pyramid, or become a new regulatory approach. Either way, it has reinvigorated regulatory enforcement.

[214] ASIC, 'ASIC takes Holista CollTech Limited and its CEO to Court over COVID-19 product claims' (media Release 21-202, 4 August 2021).

[215] See ch 2, section IV.c.iii listing eight completed civil penalty proceedings and with *Vocation* there are nine.

Higher penalties for court-based actions also promotes deterrence. Deterrence is built on persons seeking to avoid harm or loss. The greater the harm or loss, the greater the desire for avoidance. The potential severity of sanctions has increased because the maximum penalties are significantly higher. However, for higher penalties to translate into deterrence they must actually be imposed. The 'Why not litigate?' approach and greater resourcing makes the likelihood of the increased penalties being employed higher as cases will be brought before the court.

Greater resources allow for ASIC to conduct more investigations and bring more enforcement actions. The certainty of sanctions being imposed should be greater because contraventions are more likely to be detected. The 'Why not litigate?' approach should see more of these contraventions prosecuted. The speed of imposition or celerity of sanctions may also improve if greater resources are available to move alleged contraventions through the court system.

In classical deterrence terms, certainty, severity and celerity can all be improved in a court-based enforcement approach by the above policy changes.

However, ASIC's previous approach relied heavily on administrative enforcement tools which prioritised detection of a contravention and timely imposition of sanctions. This was because of ASIC's desire to act quickly to protect market integrity.[216] While the Financial Services Royal Commission was critical of ASIC's negotiated outcome approach, it did not state that such an approach was never appropriate, but rather that it needed to be in the public interest to forego litigation and adopt a negotiated outcome. Speed is important in the area of continuous disclosure because of the need to ensure that the market is informed and efficient. As a result, an enforcement approach that supports prompt action may be in the public interest. This could include infringement notices and enforceable undertakings. If the above policy changes have the effect of overly promoting reliance on litigation, such as for civil penalties, which involve delay, then market integrity may be harmed contrary to the purpose of continuous disclosure. ASIC's effectiveness necessitates being able to reconcile prompt action with ensuring specific and general deterrence. There may be a number of ways to creatively utilise enforcement tools to achieve this.[217]

ASIC has also shown a willingness to pursue individuals, rather than just entities. Five of the six civil penalty proceedings included a claim against an individual. Moreover, ASIC effectively went back to the misconduct involving MG Responsible Entity Limited and had two individuals disqualified. Pre-31 December 2017, ASIC had also brought civil penalty proceedings against corporations that included claims against individuals.[218] The 'Why not Litigate?' approach in increasing the use of litigation rather than administrative enforcement tools has created the opportunity to hold more individuals to account. Chapter three explained that sanctions aimed at individuals are supported from a deterrence perspective because the decision to contravene the law is ultimately made by individuals. The threat of personal liability for misconduct provides a direct incentive to ensure compliance as the negative effect of sanctions will be felt by the individual. But the positive deterrence effects may be undone if insurance can be drawn on to pay penalties and costs. Criminal prosecutions would remove the operation of any insurance.

[216] ch 5, section II.C.iii.

[217] Examples may include being prepared to utilise an infringement notice or enforceable undertaking for the entity but using litigation for the individuals. This may be problematic where the individuals continue to control the entity, but each should have separate legal representation. Utilising civil penalties to reboot the enforcement pyramid but when it comes to the penalties, either through settlement or judgment, making submissions to the court that an important factor requiring a higher amount is any delay caused by the respondent leading to the market not being informed of illegal disclosure practices.

[218] See ch 2, section IV.c.iii, referring to Padbury Mining Ltd and two of its executives, and Sino Australia Oil and Gas Ltd and its CEO.

The impact of the interim changes to the substantive law is difficult to discern where there is a six-year statute of limitations that at the time of writing had only just begun and the additional elements may require more time be devoted to investigation and assessment of prospects of success. All the civil penalty proceedings, except Hollista, related to conduct prior to 2020. Hollista addressed conduct that partially occurred during the operation of the interim changes with the result that it was pleaded that Hollista knew or was reckless or negligent in relation to the representations made during the time period covered by the interim changes.[219] In terms of infringement notices, only the one issued to Regional Express Holdings Limited involved 2020 conduct, but the relevant dates were outside the time period covered by the interim changes.[220] Nonetheless, it is to be expected that additional requirements for proving a contravention may impact how ASIC chooses to investigate and enforce the continuous disclosure regime. This may slow ASIC's ability to take action with adverse effects for promptly deterring others in the market. Additional requirements may also see less litigation and associated deterrence if a case is harder to prove. However, if ASIC can prove negligent, reckless or intentional behaviour, this should attract higher direct sanctions and reputational harm as the misconduct is more egregious.

The policy changes have not altered ASIC's approach to compensation in the timeframe under study.[221] However, the Financial Services Royal Commission did make the point that compensation for losses is an important goal and ASIC does not have to choose between remediation and enforcement. Indeed, as the text has argued, compensation can achieve deterrence, albeit incidentally. Further, the Treasury Laws Amendment (Strengthening Corporate and Financial Sector Penalties) Act 2019 (Cth), in putting the issue of compensation before the court as part of the considerations relevant to the orders to be made in civil penalty and criminal proceedings, may encourage change by making the availability of compensation a more salient issue.

B. Continuous Disclosure Class Actions

i. Continuous Disclosure Class Action Activity post-2017

The continuous disclosure class action picture is far less clear than the situation with ASIC. As chapter six and Appendix 2, Table 3 set out, there were 43 corporations and associated persons/entities subject to shareholder class actions involving an alleged contravention of the continuous disclosure regime as at 31 December 2017. Ten of these were filed in 2017.[222] The number of class actions is based on the event giving rise to the alleged contravention. Where there are multiple class action filings arising from the same event this does not increase the number of class actions included.

In subsequent years, adopting the same approach, the filing of shareholder class actions involving an alleged contravention of the continuous disclosure regime were seven (2018), four (2019), nine (2020) and one (2021), ie 21 in total. If multiple class actions in relation to the same event are added then this can have a dramatic effect due to the growth in competing class actions,

[219] *ASIC v Holista CollTech Limited*, 'Concise Statement', Federal Court of Australia, WAD177/2021 (4 August 2021).

[220] ASIC, 'REX pays $66,000 penalty for alleged continuous disclosure breach' (Media Release 21-105, 18 May 2021) (the allegation was a breach of continuous disclosure obligations from 11 May 2020 to 12 May 2020 by failing to disclose that it was considering the feasibility of commencing domestic operations in addition to its regional operations).

[221] See Senate Economics Reference Committee (n 186) [2.172] (citing ASIC's General Counsel, Chris Savundra's evidence to the Committee: 'we're in the business of deterrence and imposing penalties to deter behaviour; we're not in the business in this space of seeking to recover compensation').

[222] Note that this increase in class action filings occurred in the year prior to the increase in D&O insurance premiums.

with 22 (2018), six (2019), 12 (2020) and two (2021) class actions respectively.[223] These numbers demonstrate a lull in 2019 and again in 2021 rather than a decreasing or increasing trend.

Litigation funding regulation would have acted as an initial break on class actions that needed third-party funding, especially as applications for an AFSL needed to be lodged and granted, but also to take the necessary steps to adhere to the requirements for an MIS. Group costs orders, on the other hand, would have incentivised plaintiffs' lawyers to take the lead on providing funding for class actions. While *Myer* aided continuous disclosure class actions through recognising market-based causation, two unsuccessful outcomes from the only trials of continuous disclosure class actions may have highlighted the difficulties in bringing such actions, which may dampen the number of claims. The reasoning in *Worley* and the adoption of the higher *Briginshaw* standard of proof would also be expected to cause the proponents of class actions to pause. The willingness of defendants to take continuous disclosure class actions to judgment with the prospect of the loser being liable for their opponents' costs should cause a closer assessment of a case's merits.

Litigation is not just about obtaining a remedy in the instant case, but also to create precedents, with both plaintiff lawyers/litigation funders and defendants having sought to develop helpful precedent in the past.[224] Market causation in *Myer* and the *Briginshaw* standard in *Worley* appear to be further examples. Unlike legislation, seeking reform through the courts is less certain. However, judge-made law is an important contributor to the setting of policy levers. In Australian class actions that has certainly been the situation as the underlying legislation, Part IVA of the Federal Court of Australia Act 1974 (Cth), has not been amended in its near 30-year history despite developments such as litigation funding.

However, the 2019 lull predates all of the above events, except *Myer*, which was handed down at the end of October 2019. A potential explanation is that class action firms and funders switched their attention to other forms of class action. For example, the misconduct identified by the Financial Services Royal Commission became a fertile source of class actions.[225] The misconduct would have been further elaborated on by ASIC investigations and enforcement action in relation to that conduct. There may therefore have been a waiting period in which prospects of success were considered with the benefit of the Royal Commission and ASIC actions. It may also have been the case that the capacity for private enforcement had been reached due to a high number of filings in 2017 and 2018, including many competing class actions.

The return to higher filings in 2020 may be linked to developments in litigation funding regulation. As discussed above, in relation to class action filings generally, the litigation funding regulation spurred a rush to file prior to the regime coming into effect on 22 August 2020, but then a slowing of filings. Equally the group costs order regime in Victoria attracted a surge in continuous disclosure class actions in that jurisdiction in 2020–21.

The slow pace of continuous disclosure class actions in 2021 may be linked to the treasurer's interim measures that added an intention/fault requirement from 26 May 2020 to 23 March 2021. Equally, the uncertainty from the pandemic itself would have altered corporate assumptions so

[223] A similar trend exists in the empirical research of Professor Vince Morabito in relation to shareholder class action filings (a broader category than continuous disclosure class actions which also includes all competing class actions): 25 (4 March 2018–3 March 2019), 11 (4 March 2019–3 March 2020), 14 (4 March 2020–3 March 2021). Vince Morabito, 'Courts see record number of class actions as shareholder proceedings drop in significance' *Lawyerly* (20 May 2021).

[224] Examples include cases interpreting s 33C of the Federal Court of Australia Act 1974 (Cth) (eg *Wong v Silkfield Pty Ltd* (1999) 199 CLR 255, *Cash Converters International Limited v Gray* (2014) 223 FCR 139) and seeking and challenging common fund orders (*Money Max Int Pty Ltd v QBE Insurance Group Ltd* (2016) 245 FCR 191; *BMW Australia Ltd v Brewster* [2019] HCA 45; 94 ALJR 51).

[225] Jones Day, 'White Paper – Australia Financial Services Industry Royal Commission Leads to Class Actions Boom' (August 2020).

that previous disclosures to the market were no longer valid and updates and forecasts would be qualified by reference to available information.[226] Also, as explained in relation to ASIC, the impact on filings of needing to prove additional elements is unclear, but likely to reduce the number of actionable claims.

The longer-term effect of these combined developments will depend on the costs they impose or increased returns they permit, including the degree of uncertainty that is created. Class action lawyers and funders can adapt to changes in the class actions and continuous disclosure landscape through altering the mix of cases they have in their portfolio and the fees that they charge. If continuous disclosure class action become more difficult to prove then choices can be made as to which cases to commence, tending towards those with stronger prospects of success considering the elements that must be proved, and the fee that will be charged, with greater risk attracting a higher fee. However, restrictions on increasing fees due to regulation or competition can restrict this response.

ii. *Effectiveness of Shareholder Class Actions*

The goal of the class action has not changed, with maximising compensation still in the interests of the representative party, group members, lawyers and funders. Class action settlements have remained substantial,[227] with the largest settlement post-31 December 2017 being the Spotless class action that was commenced in 2017 and settled in 2020 for $95 million.[228] There have been no developments aimed at capping recoveries or otherwise limiting the amount of compensation that could be claimed. Indeed, the class action's access to justice objective appears to be unchallenged.

However, policy changes have been directed to reducing the number of class actions through making proof of a contravention more difficult. The steps discussed above involved the adoption of the *Briginshaw* standard and the Bill to add fault or intention elements. The *Myer* case that went to trial also highlights the difficulty in proving loss. Equally, *Myer* also found that market-based causation was permissible, which makes proof of a contravention causing loss easier to establish. If the elements of the law that must be established to obtain compensation are made more or less difficult to prove then this may have a flow on effect as to the number of viable class actions and the compensation that may be recovered. Equally it must be remembered that compensation only arises where a wrong has caused loss. If the law is amended so that no wrong is committed, there is no compensation due and no class to be brought.

Effective compensation requires full recovery and minimising of transaction costs. The policy changes aimed at reducing group members costs also impact on the profitability of class actions for litigation funders and lawyers. There has been a focus on more independent assessment of lawyer and litigation funder fees so as to reduce transaction costs which would improve the compensation received by group members. The introduction of a cap on the return that litigation funders may receive also aids in reducing transaction costs.

The enactment of group costs orders by the State of Victoria's legislature has been seen as making class actions more profitable for lawyers, but the court's role in setting the fee may mean a reduction in legal fees. Group costs orders also create risks for lawyers, such as recovering no fee when a case is unsuccessful and being liable for a defendant's costs, that will need to be

[226] See ASIC, 'COVID-19 implications for financial reporting and audit: Frequently asked questions (FAQs)', 10 June 2021.
[227] Appendix 2, Table 3.
[228] *Court v Spotless Group Holdings Limited* [2020] FCA 1730.

factored into determining the percentage that can be charged. How the group costs order legislation impacts costs and efficiency will require court judgments applying the statute.

These efficiency-enhancing developments would also be factored in to whether a lawyer and funder would be prepared to invest their labour and funds in a class action. The risk-return analysis may see some class actions not be pursued if the fee that can be earned does not reflect the risk or work to be undertaken. Most likely the lawyer and funder would seek to pursue other class actions without these restrictions, if possible. For example, if group costs orders are not more profitable for lawyers then they may use conditional fees or continue to work with a funder that pays legal fees as the case progresses as the fee proposition is less risky. The most likely outcome is that lawyers will make a case-by-case assessment as to the fee model to employ.

Similarly, regulation of litigation funding which can protect group member interests may also increase compliance costs which make the litigation funding fee higher, or where fees are regulated, the class action may become an unattractive investment. Much may turn on the litigation funder's cost of capital and desired return on investment.

In short, the class action procedure's ability to deliver compensation is directly linked to the risks and returns that class action proponents face.

Class actions on behalf of shareholders achieve deterrence through the imposition of direct costs in the form of compensation and indirect costs associated with defending and settling litigation. This deterrence remains incidental, as it is not the main goal, but also of a quantum greater than what ASIC has achieved, although the increased penalties have not yet taken effect. The same factors that impact the ability of the class action to achieve compensation also impacts the incidental deterrence that is achieved. Less class actions means less deterrence. Whether that is positive or negative depends on whether the class action is preventing under deterrence or causing over deterrence. The reputational impact of a class action on a corporation and directors is arguably more problematic due to the heightened criticism of lawyers' and funders' motivation and fees. While some of this has been partisan and may be given less credence as a result, it has been raised by independent entities such as the courts and the ALRC.[229]

VI. Conclusion

This chapter has explained how the mix of public and private enforcement may be influenced based on the settings of a range of policy levers and legal developments. A jurisdiction that sought to encourage or discourage public or private enforcement may draw on the learning in this chapter to recalibrate regulatory enforcement and/or class action activity.

In summary, greater regulatory enforcement can be encouraged through the endorsement and adoption of a robust enforcement approach, increased resourcing and increased penalties and powers. It also follows that moving in the opposite direction on each of these elements – enforcement approach, resourcing, penalties and powers – will discourage enforcement.

Turning to class actions, while many of the policy changes were directed at reducing the number of class actions, there were also changes that encouraged the bringing of class actions. However, none of the measures prevent class actions, as would be the case, for instance, if standing

[229] See eg *Endeavour River Pty Ltd v MG Responsible Entity Limited* [2019] FCA 1719, [30] (Murphy J) (a funding rate of 32% of the gross settlement was sought, but the court stated that it was 'not fair and reasonable'); *Endeavour River Pty Ltd v MG Responsible Entity Limited (No 2)* [2020] FCA 968, [22], [26], [41]–[47] (Murphy J) (funder offered to consent to an order approving a funding commission fixed at 28% of the gross settlement, and then offered 25% which was approved by the court).

to sue was removed. Consequently, how the forces of encouragement and discouragement ultimately play out is not clear. But regulation of litigation funders through licensing and oversight of fees may achieve better results for group members. Care must be taken that these measures do not become excessive and make litigation funding of class actions uneconomic.

Further, making the substantive law more difficult to prove, such as through adding additional fault or intention elements, may discourage both ASIC enforcement and class actions. However, it may be more accurate to state that such an amendment to the law will reduce the number of contraventions, which in turn will see fewer cases brought. There is a much larger policy question that has not been adequately grappled with, but which the ALRC identified, ie whether the continuous disclosure regime as currently configured achieves the objective of market integrity and investor protection.[230]

The developments discussed in this chapter have generally had the aim of making public enforcement more effective. ASIC is in a much stronger position to enforce the continuous disclosure laws than it was prior to 31 December 2017. If the public regulator is more active, more likely to utilise litigation and is able to seek higher penalties, it may more effectively achieve deterrence, both through direct sanctions and impact on reputation. However, the experience documented here also demonstrates that there has not been an increase in ASIC's preparedness to seek compensation. The class action remains the more effective vehicle for obtaining compensation. The reforms aimed at reducing transaction costs may even improve that effectiveness. Equally, if fewer class actions are brought then there is the prospect of shareholders who suffered loss being without an avenue for recovery.[231] The future effectiveness of the class action is unclear, but a focus on effectiveness needs to balance adequate returns for lawyers and/or funders with improving efficiency so as to better compensate those who have suffered loss.

In relation to the effects of coexistence of ASIC enforcement and class actions discussed in the earlier chapters, despite policy changes that could diminish the frequency of class actions, coexistence remains the position. Moreover, the ability of class actions to provide access to justice remains the accepted position. Consequently, the interaction between public and private enforcement from a regulatory process perspective continues and is addressed in chapter eight.

[230] ALRC 2018 Class Actions Report (n 73) Recommendation 24, [9.6]–[9.11]. See also ch 2, section II.A setting out the purpose and background of continuous disclosure.

[231] See ch 6, Table 6.2.

8

Coordination of Public and Private Enforcement

I. Introduction

The rise of the shareholder class action has given rise to overlapping enforcement of the continuous disclosure laws by the public regulator, the Australian Securities and Investments Commission (ASIC), and private citizens with the assistance of lawyers and litigation funders. Chapters five and six explained the ramifications of this overlap for deterrence, compensation and regulation drawing on the analytical framework and case studies developed in this text. The logical next step from the coexistence of public and private enforcement is to consider if they can be more effectively combined through some form of coordination.

This chapter briefly recounts the ramifications of overlapping enforcement and then situates the need for coordination within 'regulatory pluralism' scholarship which argues that law may be employed to provide the mechanisms for orchestration or coordination. The traditional or existing mechanisms for coordinating enforcement in Australia, particularly in the courts, are reviewed in order to establish a baseline of coordination mechanisms. The chapter then turns to examine coordination mechanisms from four regulatory regimes in the United States: environmental citizen suits; employment discrimination claims; *qui tam* and the Class Action Fairness Act of 2005 (CAFA). These examples serve to demonstrate that public and private enforcement may be combined and, through drawing on previous academic analysis, how that combination may be achieved. It also serves to illustrate the concerns that coordination raises.

These examples as well as existing procedures are then drawn upon to suggest two potential coordination strategies for the public and private enforcement of securities regulation generally, and the continuous disclosure regime specifically. These two approaches are an information-sharing approach and a 'regulator as gatekeeper' approach.

The design of the strategies for coordination depends on the objective of the coordination. The focus in this text has been on the effective achievement of deterrence and compensation through ASIC enforcement and the shareholder class action (outcomes), and the promotion of values that support a 'good' regulatory process (process). Consequently, when considering coordination the approaches designed here again adopt this focus.

II. Why Coordination?

The coexistence of ASIC enforcement action, including litigation, and class actions has ramifications for deterrence, compensation and regulation. These ramifications are discussed in chapter six and summarised here. Moreover, the discussion in earlier chapters focused on the overlap between ASIC enforcement and the class action, with the result that they are seen as alternatives to, or competitors with each other. Another approach is to see them as cooperating, or at least as being subject to mechanisms that take account of their coexistence and how they can be more effectively combined.[1]

A. Overlapping Deterrence and Compensation

ASIC and the class action may overlap in relation to the pursuit of deterrence and compensation as potential outcomes.

In relation to deterrence, because sanctions are at the heart of deterrence and 'can include, in principle, anything that exacts a cost',[2] then penalties, compensation and even reputational harm, can have a cumulative deterrent effect. As these sanctions are typically pursued by different parties without coordination, there is a risk of over-deterrence. Equally, if the regulator refrained from taking action out of an expectation that a class action would be brought and that did not transpire then there may be under-deterrence.

Prior to 2017 ASIC tended to utilise administrative remedies, such as infringement notices and enforceable undertakings, and rely primarily on deterring through the impact of regulatory action on reputation.[3] The class actions' large compensation payments and litigation costs achieved deterrence, albeit incidentally rather than as an explicit goal, through the imposition of direct sanctions.[4] However, since 2017 ASIC has greater resources, broader powers and increased penalties, as well as a revamped regulatory approach that all point to ASIC making greater use of civil penalty proceedings.[5] In the same period class actions have been subject to increased criticism and greater scrutiny, including regulation of litigation funding, that cumulatively are designed to reduce shareholder class action activity but may not transpire due to the incentives for seeking compensation continuing.[6] Consequently the likelihood of both ASIC and the class action imposing direct sanctions through extracting large financial payments, as well as reputational and indirect costs has increased. Indeed, overlapping ASIC enforcement and class actions has continued since the end of 2017, with class actions brought in relation to Vocation Limited, Quintis Limited, Getswift Limited and MG Responsible Entity Limited/Murray Goulburn Co-operative Co Limited.[7]

In terms of compensation, both ASIC and a person who suffers damage from contraventions of the continuous disclosure regime and prohibitions on misleading conduct have standing to seek compensation. The double recovery rule guards against a defendant being required to pay twice. The High Court of Australia, in explaining the compensatory principle, which was discussed in chapter three, added 'Cognate with this concept is the rule, described … as universal, that a plaintiff cannot recover more than he or she has lost'.[8] Duplicative compensation is not permitted. However, there may still be significant costs and inefficiencies if both the regulator and the class action sought compensation for the same contravention, even if for different shareholders.[9]

[1] Samuel Issacharoff, 'Class Actions and State Authority' (2012) 44 *Loyola University Chicago Law Journal* 369, 390.

[2] David Kennedy, *Deterrence and Crime Prevention* (Routledge, 2009) 32. See ch 3 section II.C.

[3] Ch 6, sections II.A and IV.A.i.

[4] Ch 6, section II.D.

[5] Ch 7.

[6] Ch 7.

[7] See ch 7 and Appendix 2, Table 3.

[8] *Haines v Bendall* (1991) 172 CLR 60, 63 (Mason CJ, Dawson, Toohey and Gaudron JJ).

[9] See in relation to overlapping civil penalty and class action proceedings: *Webb v GetSwift Limited (No 5)* [2019] FCA 1533, [31]–[32] (Lee J) ('There are great economies likely to be achieved by the one docket judge case managing both

In short, 'multiplicity is a harm to society's legitimate interest in judicial efficiency'.[10] However, ASIC has tended not to seek compensation in relation to continuous disclosure contraventions and, since the advent of the class action, to leave the obtaining of compensation to the class action. This state of play is purely discretionary on the part of ASIC and could change due to an alteration in policy, including because ASIC typically incurs less transaction costs that reduce the compensation paid to shareholders.[11]

B. A Regulatory Process Perspective

The coexistence of public and private enforcement impacts the values of a 'good' regulatory process. Private enforcement can add additional expertise and resources that may provide for more comprehensive enforcement. Private enforcement may also provide additional views about what is in the public interest and the capacity to act on those views. It can also provide an accountability mechanism through being available for comparison with the regulator's achievements. But is can also create duplicative, or even conflicting, enforcement. If the public interest is best achieved by having a government regulator that can calibrate its response to wrongdoing, including being able to move up and down the enforcement pyramid in response to the regulated entities' reaction and reward cooperation, then a static class action that seeks to maximise the compensation paid relative to risks assumed and is outside the control of the regulator may be counterproductive. Indeed, it may undermine the regulator's enforcement approach. Cooperation from regulated entities may be more difficult to achieve resulting in more costly enforcement approaches from higher up the enforcement pyramid, or prolonged engagements as the regulated entity seeks to manage regulatory enforcement and a class action. Greater resources may be expended not just by the regulated entity, but by society as a whole, due to the dual track of public and private enforcement.

C. Regulatory Pluralism and Coordination

The desire and need for coordination may be situated within 'regulatory pluralism' scholarship. As explained in chapter three, a core belief is that the state no longer has a monopoly on regulation and there is a need to harness multiple regulatory agents as a broader range of regulatory actors will produce better regulation than a government-only approach. Regulation is no longer a bipartite process involving government as the regulator and business as the regulatee. Other actors, including the class action which has been the subject of study here, may also play a regulatory role.[12] Regulatory responses may therefore come from a number of sources. However, the

regulatory proceedings and a class action if they involve consideration of the same underlying facts.'); *GetSwift Limited v Webb* [2021] FCAFC 26, [5] (Middleton, McKerracher and Jagot JJ); in relation to competing class actions where there may be a duplication of procedural steps and legal costs: *McKay Super Solutions Pty Ltd (Trustee) v Bellamy's Australia Ltd* [2017] FCA 947, [44] (Beach J) (setting out nine 'examples of the type of potential duplicated costs and expenses'); *Wigmans v AMP Ltd* [2019] NSWSC 603, [347] (Ward CJ in Eq) ('the continuation of more than one of the competing [class actions] would be inimical to the facilitation of the just, quick and cheap resolution of the real issues in these proceedings').

[10] Richard Freer, 'Avoiding Duplicative Litigation: Rethinking Plaintiff Autonomy and the Court's Role in Defining the Litigative Unit' (1989) 50 *University of Pittsburgh Law Review* 809, 832.

[11] ch 6, section II.F and II.G.

[12] See Neil Gunningham and Peter Grabosky, *Smart Regulation* (Oxford University Press, 1998), Lester Salomon, 'The New Governance and the Tools of Public Action' (2001) 28 *Fordham Urban Law Review* 1611, Orly Lobel, 'The Renew

ideal situation is said to be one which uses a combination of instruments to achieve a coordinated and connected response.[13]

In the mid-1980s Barry Boyer and Errol Meidinger commented that:[14]

> In short, experience has shown that both an extensive system of private prosecution and a public monopoly in criminal enforcement are susceptible to abuse. What is needed is the appropriate mix of public and private enforcement that will fit the particular times and its social needs, together with adequate systems of accountability to prevent abuse.

Similarly, Professors Neil Gunningham and Peter Grabosky explain: 'The challenge is to harness the constructive elements of private enforcement, neutralize those elements which might be counterproductive, and combine them systemically with public enforcement'.[15] More recently, 'the institutional design challenge' has been identified as 'not choosing between public and private enforcement', but instead determining 'how to coordinate multiple, overlapping, and interdependent enforcement mechanisms'.[16]

Regulatory pluralism suggests a move from competitive to coordinated decision making. It requires ongoing communication mechanisms. This of course raises the more practical question of how should communication and coordination be achieved.[17] An answer is that law is no longer seen as only the conclusion as to what is allowed or prohibited, but rather as also providing a procedure for orchestration or coordination of the multiple actors that are employed as part of regulatory pluralism.[18]

III. Existing Coordination Mechanisms

The starting point for coordination is to first consider the existing, but limited, mechanisms that may be employed to coordinate ASIC enforcement actions and class actions.

A. Case Management

In civil litigation, including litigation involving civil penalties, the courts aim to avoid a multiplicity of suits.[19] Court rules as to joinder of parties and cause of action seek to give effect to the need

Deal: The Fall of Regulation and the Rise of Governance in Contemporary Legal Thought' (2004) 89 *Minnesota Law Review* 342, Bradley Karkkainen, '"New Governance" in Legal Thought and the World: Some Splitting as Antidote to Overzealous Lumping' (2004) 89 *Minnesota Law Review* 471; Scott Burris, Michael Kempa and Clifford Shearing, 'Changes in Governance: A Cross-Disciplinary Review of Current Scholarship' (2008) 41 *Akron Law Review* 1.

[13] Gunningham and Grabosky (ibid) 400.

[14] Barry Boyer and Errol Meidinger, 'Privatizing Regulatory Enforcement: A Preliminary Assessment of Citizen Suits Under Federal Environmental Laws' (1985) 34 *Buffalo Law Review* 833, 956–57.

[15] Gunningham and Grabosky (n 12) 14–15, 106.

[16] David Freeman Engstrom, 'Agencies and Litigation Gatekeepers' (2013) 123 *Yale Law Journal* 616, 623.

[17] W Kip Viscusi, 'Overview' in W Kip Viscusi (ed), *Regulation Through Litigation* (AEI-Brookings Joint Center for Regulatory Studies, 2002) 3.

[18] Lobel (n 12) 400, Kenneth Abbott and Duncan Snidal, 'Strengthening International Regulation Through Transnational New Governance: Overcoming the Orchestration Deficit' (2009) 42 *Vanderbilt Journal of Transnational Law* 501, 520–21.

[19] Federal Court of Australia Act 1976 (Cth), s 22 ('The Court shall, in every matter before the Court, grant, either absolutely or on such terms and conditions as the Court thinks just, all remedies to which any of the parties appears to be entitled in respect of a legal or equitable claim properly brought forward by him or her in the matter, so that, as far as possible, all matters in controversy between the parties may be completely and finally determined and all multiplicity of proceedings concerning any of those matters avoided.'). The provision was modelled on the English Supreme Court

to avoid a multiplicity of proceedings, subject to concerns about fairness and efficiency.[20] Courts also have a number of case management mechanisms such as a stay, consolidation and joint trials to avoid duplication.[21] These mechanisms have been used in relation to competing class actions in Australia.[22] The High Court of Australia in dealing with five overlapping class actions observed that a:

> [M]ultiplicity of proceedings is not to be encouraged and that competing representative proceedings run by different firms of solicitors, with different funders, may in principle be inimical to the administration of justice. But, as was earlier stated, there is no 'one size fits all' approach. Multiplicity may be addressed by a variety of means …[23]

Those means are: (1) a permanent stay of all but one of the proceedings; (2) the proceedings could be consolidated; (3) an order could be made under s 33N(1), colloquially known as a declassing order, which would prevent all but one proceeding from continuing as a class action; (4) an order could be made closing the class in all but one proceeding, so that there would be a single open class action, with a joint trial; and (5) a joint trial of all proceedings.[24]

The Australian courts have also sought to grapple with overlapping regulatory suits and class actions through case management. The hearing of the related proceedings which arise from the same underlying facts together, or sequentially, by the same judge has been considered due to potential efficiency gains. However, such an approach has also been met with concerns about judicial bias.

In the Centro proceedings, Middleton J who had heard ASIC's civil penalty proceedings and was due to hear the class action disqualified himself due to an objection on the basis of an apprehension of bias.[25] The test for apprehended bias is whether a fair-minded lay observer might reasonably apprehend that the judge might not bring an impartial mind to the resolution of the question he or she is required to decide.[26] The concern with the sequential approach arises from the extent to which previous findings in the civil penalty proceedings may, in the eyes of the fair-minded lay observer, impact on the judge's ability to decide the class action other than on its merits.

In contrast to the sequential approach, in relation to the Volkswagen emissions defeat device as it impacted Australian consumers, Foster J case managed and heard seven separate proceedings (five class actions and two civil penalty proceedings by the Australian Competition and Consumer Commission) brought against corporate defendants together. In an endeavour to 'hear and determine all of the above proceedings … expeditiously, efficiently and fairly', Foster J ordered that 12 separate factual questions that were common to all seven proceedings be heard and determined before all other questions in the proceedings. A trial of a second set of common

of Judicature Act 1873, s 24(7). See *Philip Morris Inc v Adam P Brown Male Fashions Pty Ltd* (1981) 148 CLR 457, 505 (Mason J) ('a provision which was designed to eliminate multiplicity of actions').

[20] Federal Court Rules 2011 (Cth), Pt 9. See eg *Bishop v Bridgelands Securities* (1990) 25 FCR 311, 314 (Wilcox J) ('the Court should take whatever course seems to be most conducive to a just resolution of the disputes between the parties, but having regard to the desirability of limiting, so far as practicable, the costs and delay of the litigation').

[21] See eg Federal Court of Australia Act 1976 (Cth), ss 22, 23; Federal Court Rules 2011 (Cth) rr 30.11; *Commissioner of the Australian Federal Police v Zhao* (2015) 255 CLR 46, 61 [48] (French CJ, Hayne, Kiefel, Bell and Keane JJ).

[22] Michael Legg, 'Competing Class Actions: A Suggested Solution through Certification' (2018) 7 *Journal of Civil Litigation & Practice* 38.

[23] *Wigmans v AMP Limited* [2021] HCA 7; 95 ALJR 305, [106] (Gageler, Gordon and Edelman JJ).

[24] ibid. See also *McKay Super Solutions Pty Ltd (Trustee) v Bellamy's Australia Ltd* [2017] FCA 947, [9] (Beach J).

[25] *Kirby v Centro Properties Limited (No 2)* [2011] FCA 1144.

[26] *Ebner v Official Trustee in Bankruptcy* (2000) 205 CLR 337, 344–45 [6] (Gleeson CJ, McHugh, Gummow and Hayne JJ); *CNY17 v Minister for Immigration* (2019) 268 CLR 76, 87 [17]–[18] (Kiefel CJ and Gageler J); 96–97 [50] (Nettle and Gordon JJ); 118 [132] (Edelman J).

questions and then a third trial addressing the remaining issues was planned. The first hearing in respect of the initial 12 questions was conducted with judgment reserved. Before judgment could be delivered all seven proceedings settled by way of agreement between the parties.[27]

Returning to continuous disclosure, Lee J was assigned to oversee two separate proceedings commenced against GetSwift Limited, one being a regulatory proceeding seeking civil penalties brought by ASIC and the other a shareholder class action brought by a Mr Webb. The GetSwift proceedings were both allocated to the docket of Lee J following the commencement of the ASIC proceedings against the company and the staying of two other competing class actions against the company.[28]

Lee J proposed that although he would first hear the ASIC proceeding then the class action, evidence that the parties sought to rely upon would need to be adduced separately in each proceeding. Lee J would only consider the evidence and submissions made in each separate proceeding and clear his mind of the evidence and submissions made in the other.[29]

The respondents to both proceedings appealed Lee J's decision to the Full Court with ASIC's support and unopposed by the class action representative party, Mr Webb. The appellants argued that a fair-minded lay observer might reasonably apprehend that the primary judge, consciously or subconsciously, might be influenced by extraneous information from the ASIC proceeding.[30]

While a judge is assumed to be capable of putting irrelevant and immaterial matters to one side as part of their assumed abilities as a professional decision-maker, the Full Court allowed the appeal. In the class action the primary judge would be required to ignore the evidence of up to 33 lay witnesses, an expert and the submissions in the ASIC proceeding, and would similarly in the ASIC proceeding have to ignore evidence of four experts and submissions made in the class action. The Court considered that the hypothetical observer may look to the reality of the process and the potentially conflicting evidence, and reasonably apprehend that the primary judge may be influenced subconsciously by the extraneous information.[31]

For completeness it should be noted that the GetSwift proceedings could not utilise an approach similar to Volkswagen as there were individual defendants in the ASIC proceeding who had the benefit of the privilege against self-exposure to a penalty.[32] The privilege means that individuals are excused from filing and serving any affidavits, substantive defence, or answers to interrogatories, until the close of the regulator's case.[33] In comparison in *Australian Securities and Investments Commission v Helou*, where ASIC sought to disqualify directors for continuous disclosure contraventions after having settled civil penalty proceedings against the Murray Goulburn corporate entities, but with a class action on foot, Beach J observed: 'there is no good reason why there cannot be a joint trial of ASIC's claims with the claims in the Webster class action'.[34] This was because Mr Helou, who was a common defendant in both proceedings did not

[27] See *Australian Competition and Consumer Commission v Volkswagen Aktiengesellschaft* [2019] FCA 2166, [6]–[13], [20], [22], [24]–[31] (Foster J).

[28] *GetSwift Limited v Webb* [2021] FCAFC 26, [7]–[9] (Middleton, McKerracher and Jagot JJ).

[29] *Webb v GetSwift Limited (No 5)* [2019] FCA 1533, [4] (Lee J).

[30] *GetSwift Limited v Webb* [2021] FCAFC 26, [13] (Middleton, McKerracher and Jagot JJ). The appellants also argued that a fair-minded lay observer might reasonably apprehend that, in hearing, considering, and forming views about the material in the ASIC proceeding, the primary judge might have prejudged the resolution of issues common to both proceedings. However, the Full Court did not focus on this ground: [14].

[31] ibid [47]–[48].

[32] *Webb v GetSwift Limited (No 5)* [2019] FCA 1533, [5] (Lee J).

[33] *Pyneboard Pty Ltd v Trade Practices Commission* (1983) 152 CLR 328, 335–36 (Mason ACJ, Wilson and Dawson JJ); *ASIC v Mining Projects Group Ltd* (2007) 164 FCR 32, 36 [7] (Finkelstein J); *Meneses v Directed Electronics OE Pty Ltd* (2019) 273 FCR 638, 660 [87] (Moshinsky, Wheelahan and Abraham JJ).

[34] *ASIC v Helou* [2019] FCA 1634, [289] (Beach J).

have the benefit of any penalty privilege because s 1349 of the Corporations Act 2001 (Cth) had the effect of abrogating the penalty privilege in proceedings in which ASIC sought declarations and a disqualification order only.[35]

The case management of regulatory suits and class actions together provides an opportunity for coordination, but only after litigation is commenced and subject to the exigencies of avoiding the perception of judicial bias and giving effect to the penalty privilege.

B. Intervention

The court rules also provide for a person to apply to intervene in proceedings 'with such rights, privileges and liabilities (including liabilities for costs) as may be determined by the Court'.[36] The court determines whether leave to intervene is granted and on what terms. A person granted the right to intervene on whatever terms is not a party.[37] The court may also appoint an *amicus curiae*. The High Court of Australia has explained that intervention is permitted in the following circumstances:

> A non-party whose interests would be directly affected by a decision in the proceeding, that is one who would be bound by the decision, is entitled to intervene to protect the interest likely to be affected. A non-party whose legal interest, for example, in other pending litigation is likely to be affected substantially by the outcome of the proceedings in this Court will satisfy a precondition for leave to intervene. Intervention will not ordinarily be supported by an indirect or contingent affection of legal interests following from the extra-curial operation of the principles enunciated in the decision of the Court or their effect upon future litigation.[38]

Further, where the party seeking to intervene 'can show that the parties to the particular proceedings may not present fully the submissions on a particular issue, being submissions which the court should have to assist it to reach a correct determination' the court may exercise its jurisdiction to grant leave to intervene.[39]

Intervention provides a mechanism where if there are overlapping actions and a decision in one will impact the other, the court may receive submissions so as to be able to take account of the effect of its decision.

ASIC is granted an additional statutory right to intervene in proceedings relating to a matter arising under the Corporations Act.[40] As an intervener, ASIC is taken to be a party to the proceeding and, subject to the Act, has all the rights, duties and liabilities of such a party. As a result ASIC is able to cross-examine witnesses, adduce evidence and make submissions.[41] The existence of the intervention power has been interpreted as 'Parliament intended to give ASIC

[35] ibid [212], [289].

[36] Federal Court Rules 2011 (Cth), r 9.21.

[37] *Caason Investments Pty Ltd v International Litigation Partners No.3 Ltd* (2018) 265 FCR 487, 499 [53] (Allsop CJ, Middleton and Perram JJ).

[38] *Roadshow Films Pty Ltd v iiNet Ltd* (2011) 248 CLR 37, 38–39 [2] (French CJ, Gummow, Hayne, Crennan and Kiefel JJ).

[39] ibid 39 [3].

[40] Corporations Act 2001 (Cth), s 1330 provides that 'ASIC may intervene in any proceeding relating to a matter arising under this Act'. ASIC's approach to intervening is set out in ASIC, 'ASIC's Approach to Involvement in Private Court Proceedings' (Information Sheet 180, June 2013). See also Joanna Bird, 'ASIC's Role as Intervener: When Should the Regulator Intervene in Private Litigation?' (2010) 28 *Companies and Securities Law Journal* 460.

[41] Corporations Act 2001 (Cth), s 1330(2); *Lock, in the matter of Cedenco JV Australia Pty Ltd (in liq) (No 2)* [2019] FCA 93, [10] (Besanko J); *Tonto Home Loans Australia Pty Ltd v Tavares (No 2)* [2012] NSWCA 129, [5] (Allsop P).

an important role'.[42] ASIC has utilised this power in relation to class actions, but in the financial services area not in relation to continuous disclosure.[43] ASIC's concern was with the calculation of the litigation funding fee.[44] ASIC has also appealed where its intervention did not achieve the outcome sought.[45]

The right to intervene creates a staging post for the regulator to initiate communications with class action proponents which may permit coordination, or if not, the placing of the regulator's views before the court.

C. *Res Judicata*, Estoppel and Abuse of Process

In both civil and criminal litigation the doctrines of *res judicata* and issue estoppel are designed to avoid a multiplicity of actions by avoiding relitigation of decided cases and decided issues of fact or law.[46] However, central to the operation of these doctrines is that they apply not just to the same party, but also extend to a privy in interest so that an individual who claims through another is subject to all estoppels affecting the person through whom that individual claimed.[47] Abuse of process may also be raised where the use of a court's procedures would be unjustifiably oppressive to a party or would bring the administration of justice into disrepute, such as through the relitigation of previously decided matters.[48] In the criminal law the doctrine of double jeopardy and pleas of autrefois acquit and autrefois convict also operate.[49]

In the current context the plaintiffs and the causes of action in an ASIC enforcement action and a shareholder class action are usually different, although the underlying factual matrix is the same. The effect of the above doctrines is that where different parties that are not 'privies in interest' bring different causes of action then the doctrines of *res judicata* and issue estoppel do not apply. For example, for the same conduct, ASIC may pursue a civil or criminal penalty and a class action may pursue compensation. However, an argument based on abuse of process may be available in some situations, such as when the later proceeding seeks to prove essential facts contrary

[42] *Carey v ASIC* (2008) 169 FCR 311, 313–14 [9] (Finkelstein J).

[43] *Richards v Macquarie Bank Ltd [No 4]* [2013] FCA 438, [17] (Logan J).

[44] The class action was unusual in that it was funded by some of the group members, and to varying degrees. At settlement the applicant sought a 'funder's premium' of 35% for those group members who cofunded the litigation. This meant that group members who contributed to the legal costs and disbursements involved in running the class action recovered 42% of their losses, while those who did not contribute only recovered 17.602% of their losses.

[45] *ASIC v Richards* [2013] FCAFC 89 overturning the settlement and the 35% uplift in recovery for group members who self-financed the cost of prosecuting their class action.

[46] *Tomlinson v Ramsey Food Processing Pty Ltd* (2015) 256 CLR 507, 516–518 [20]–[22] (French CJ, Bell, Gageler and Keane JJ) (discussing *res judicata* (an exercise of judicial power determining a cause of action finally resolves that cause of action and it cannot be relitigated), merger of judgment (rendering of a final judgment causes the rights and obligations in controversy, as between those persons, to cease to have an independent existence and to merge in that final judgment), cause of action estoppel (precludes assertion in a subsequent proceeding of a claim to a right or obligation which was asserted in the proceeding and which was determined by the judgment), issue estoppel (precludes the raising in a subsequent proceeding of an ultimate issue of fact or law which was necessarily resolved as a step in reaching the determination made in the judgment) and Anshun estoppel (precludes the assertion of a claim, or the raising of an issue of fact or law, if that claim or issue was so connected with the subject matter of the first proceeding as to have made it unreasonable in the context of that first proceeding for the claim not to have been made or the issue not to have been raised in that proceeding)).

[47] ibid 520 [28].

[48] *R v Carroll* (2002) 213 CLR 635, 670 [118], 673 [130]–[131] (McHugh J); *Tomlinson v Ramsey Food Processing Pty Ltd* (2015) 256 CLR 507, 518–519 [25]–[26] (French CJ, Bell, Gageler and Keane JJ).

[49] *R v Carroll* (2002) 213 CLR 635, 643–644 [22]–[23] (Gleeson CJ and Hayne J); *Island Maritime Ltd v Filipowski* (2006) 226 CLR 328.

to an earlier judicial determination. In practice it is unlikely that either ASIC or a class action applicant would bring further proceedings if a court had found that the continuous disclosure regime had not been contravened by a defendant in earlier proceedings.[50]

As explained in chapter two, both ASIC and a class action may pursue compensation for shareholders who suffered loss due to a contravention of the continuous disclosure regime. Here, both claims may be able to be brought by ASIC and a representative party in a class action, but they could not recover the same compensation for the same persons.[51]

D. Access to ASIC Investigations

As explained in chapter four section IV.B.ii, ASIC has the power to conduct oral examinations and obtain books and documents in relation to compliance with continuous disclosure.[52] ASIC may release transcripts of oral examinations conducted by it and related books to a person's lawyer if the lawyer satisfies ASIC that the person is carrying on, or is contemplating in good faith, a proceeding in respect of a matter to which the examination related.[53] ASIC also has a general power to give any person a transcript of an oral examination and related books but the power is subject to the confidentiality regime in the Australian Securities and Investments Commission Act 2001 (Cth).[54] Class action proponents have also sought to access transcripts and documents through use of a subpoena. While the statutory provisions only address the sharing of information in the direction from ASIC to the class action, these interactions can open channels for dialogue and possible coordination.

IV. Coordination in Other Regulatory Regimes

Further inspiration as to how to coordinate ASIC enforcement and class actions may be drawn from a number of US regulatory regimes that explicitly provide mechanisms for public and private enforcement to be coordinated.

A. Environmental Law Citizen Suits

Each substantive environmental statute enacted by the US Congress between 1970 and 1980 contains a provision for the commencement of citizen suits. The citizen suit provisions are

[50] See eg *ASIC v Westpac Banking Corporation* (2020) 277 FCR 343 (ASIC unsuccessful in pursuing contraventions of responsible lending requirements in s 128 of National Consumer Credit Protection Act 2009 (Cth) against Westpac); *Tate v Westpac Banking Corporation (No 2)* [2020] FCA 1374 (class action against Westpac based on contraventions of responsible lending requirements in the National Consumer Credit Protection Act 2009 (Cth) discontinued).

[51] *Tomlinson v Ramsey Food Processing Pty Ltd* (2015) 256 CLR 507, 526 [47] (French CJ, Bell, Gageler and Keane JJ) (finding that Mr Tomlinson was not a privy in interest with the Fair Work Ombudsman who had brought previous proceedings so that no estoppel applied but stating that Mr Tomlinson would be prevented from personally pursuing Ramsey for the same amount as a 'result of the operation of the distinct rule against double recovery'.).

[52] Australian Securities and Investments Commission Act 2001 (Cth), ss 19, 29, 30, 33 and 35.

[53] ibid s 25(1); *Boys v Australian Securities Commission* (1998) 80 FCR 403, 420 (Heerey J).

[54] Australian Securities and Investments Commission Act 2001 (Cth), ss 25(3), 127; Johns *v ASIC* (1993) 178 CLR 408, 425 (Brennan J).

modelled on s 304 of the Clean Air Act.[55] The statute allows 'any person' to commence a civil action on his own behalf against any person

> who is alleged to have violated (if there is evidence that the alleged violation has been repeated) or to be in violation of (A) an emission standard or limitation under this chapter or (B) an order issued by the Administrator or a State with respect to such a standard or limitation.[56]

The US Supreme Court has observed that 'The 1970 Clean Air Amendments contained a new concept – the statutory authorization of "citizens suits," allowing private citizens to sue any person violating the Clean Air Act'.[57] Shortly after the enactment of the citizen suit in the *Clean Air Act*, federal courts observed:

> In enacting s 304 of the 1970 Amendments, Congress made clear that citizen groups are not to be treated as nuisances or troublemakers but rather as welcomed participants in the vindication of environmental interests. Fearing that administrative enforcement might falter or stall, 'the citizen suits provision reflected a deliberate choice by Congress to widen citizen access to the courts, as a supplemental and effective assurance that the Act would be implemented and enforced.[58]

The citizen suit is a prominent example of legislation empowering private enforcement to pursue regulatory contraventions.[59] While Congress granted 'any person' the right to sue under the Clean Air Act, those persons must still satisfy standing requirements. For a citizen suit standing requires the satisfaction of three elements: (1) the plaintiff must have suffered an 'injury in fact' – which need not be a property interest or personal injury but may include recreational, aesthetic and health effects; (2) there must be a causal connection between the injury and the conduct complained of; and (3) it must be 'likely', as opposed to merely 'speculative', that the injury will be 'redressed by a favorable decision'.[60] Further, the violation must be continuing or repeated. A citizen suit cannot be brought for a past violation where there is no reasonable likelihood of recurrence. Once violations cease the third element of standing, redressability, cannot be satisfied.[61]

Citizen suits do not generally provide for compensation. Rather, the remedies that can be sought are typically a civil penalty, to be paid to the United States Treasury, injunction forbidding continued violations and injunctions requiring steps to achieve compliance[62] If a plaintiff wishes to seek compensation, they must bring proceedings relying on a different cause of action. Indeed, the citizen suit legislation typically contains a savings clause which states that 'Nothing

[55] Stephen Fotis, 'Private Enforcement of the Clean Air Act and the Clean Water Act' (1985) 35 *American University Law Review* 127, 136; Jeffrey Miller, 'Theme and Variations in Statutory Preclusions Against Successive Environmental Enforcement Actions by EPA and Citizens Part One: Statutory Bars in Citizen Suit Provisions' (2004) 28 *Harvard Environmental Law Review* 401, 416.

[56] Clean Air Act § 304, 42 USC § 7604(a). The legislation also permits proceedings against the 'Administrator' being the regulator, ie the US Environmental Protection Agency 'where there is alleged a failure of the Administrator to perform any act or duty under this chapter which is not discretionary with the Administrator'.

[57] *Ruckelshaus v Sierra Club*, 463 US 680, 692 fn 13 (1983). See also 693 ('the authorization of citizen suits under the Clean Air Act, which was seen as an "unprecedented" innovation'). The citizen suit concept is usually said to have its origins in Joseph Sax, *Defending the Environment: A Strategy for Citizen Action* (Knopf, 1971).

[58] *Friends of the Earth v Carey*, 535 F2d 165, 172 (2d Cir 1976) citing *Natural Resources Defense Council Inc v Train*, 510 F2d 692, 700 (DC Cir 1975).

[59] David Markell and Robert Glicksman, 'Dynamic Governance in Theory and Application, Part I' (2016) 58 *Arizona Law Review* 563, 626–27.

[60] *Lujan v Defenders of Wildlife*, 504 US 555, 561 (1992); *Friends of the Earth, Inc v Laidlaw Environmental Services (TOC) Inc*, 528 US 167, 183 (2000).

[61] *Gwaltney of Smithfield, Ltd v Chesapeake Bay Foundation Inc*, 484 US 49, 58–63 (1987); *Steel Co v Citizens for a Better Environment* 523 US 83, 109 (1998).

[62] Karl Coplan, 'Citizen Enforcement' in Leroy Paddock, Robert Glicksman and Nicholas Bryner (eds), *Decision Making in Environmental Law* (Edward Elgar, 2016) 424.

in this section shall restrict any right which any person (or class of persons) may have under any statute or common law to seek enforcement of any emission standard or limitation or to seek any other relief'.[63]

The Clean Air Act § 304, 42 USC § 7604 also provides:

> No action may be commenced–
>
> (1) under subsection (a)(1)–
>
> (A) prior to 60 days after the plaintiff has given notice of the violation (i) to the Administrator, (ii) to the State in which the violation occurs, and (iii) to any alleged violator of the standard, limitation, or order, or
>
> (B) if the Administrator or State has commenced and is diligently prosecuting a civil action in a court of the United States or a State to require compliance with the standard, limitation, or order, but in any such action in a court of the United States any person may intervene as a matter of right.

A similar provision exists in all US environmental law citizen suit provisions, namely to require plaintiffs to provide the Federal Government/regulator, the relevant state, and the alleged violator with 60 days' notice of the asserted violation, although the time period may vary.[64] The US Environmental Protection Agency has issued federal regulations concerning the service and contents of notices of intent to sue under the statutes. These regulations require prospective citizen plaintiffs to identify the specific standards violated and the time, place and manner of the violations.[65] Where a citizen suit is commenced within the notice period the courts will dismiss the suit.[66] The US Supreme Court has held that the 60-day notice period is a 'mandatory, not optional, condition precedent for suit'.[67]

The notice requirement is seen to serve three related purposes. First, by notifying enforcement agencies of alleged violations this may result in enforcement action without the citizen needing to litigate. Second, the 60-day waiting period guarantees that the Government will have an opportunity to enforce the law before a private Attorney-General.[68] Third, it allows a violator to address the alleged contravention with a view to establishing that the violation is not continuing, nor will it be repeated, so that litigation is not needed.[69] The citizen suit is meant to spur both the regulator and the regulated entity into action.[70]

If the Government commences a civil or criminal action, or under some statutes, an administrative enforcement proceeding, and is 'diligently prosecuting' it, a citizen suit cannot be filed.[71] However, the Government claim must cover the same ground as the citizen suit for the citizen suit to be unable to proceed.[72] The US Supreme Court has commented that:

> The bar on citizen suits when governmental enforcement action is under way suggests that the citizen suit is meant to supplement rather than to supplant governmental action. The legislative history of the

[63] Clean Air Act § 304, 42 USC § 7604(e).

[64] Coplan (n 62) 423 (the Resource Conservation and Recovery Act specifies 90 days).

[65] 40 CFR § 54.3(b). See also 40 CFR § 54.2 (the method of service).

[66] See eg *Hallstrom v Tillamook County* 493 US 20 (1989) (in relation to the Resource Conservation and Recovery Act of 1976); *Coalition Against Columbus Center v City of New York* 750 F Supp 93 (SDNY 1990) (in relation to the Clean Air Act).

[67] *Hallstrom v Tillamook County* 493 US 20, 26 (1989).

[68] Fotis (n 55) 136.

[69] *Steel Co v Citizens for a Better Environment* 523 US 83, 109 (1998).

[70] Fotis (n 55) 136.

[71] Barton Thompson, 'The Continuing Innovation of Citizen Enforcement' (2000) *University of Illinois Law Review* 185, 193; Coplan (n 62) 425.

[72] See *Adkins v VIM Recycling, Inc* 644 F3d 483, 487 (7th Cir 2011); Connor Adamson, 'Lowering the Bar?: Reevaluating the Diligent Prosecution Bar in Light of the Gold King Mine Spill' (2019) 30 *Villanova Environmental Law Journal* 77, 84.

> Act reinforces this view of the role of the citizen suit. The Senate Report noted that '[t]he Committee intends the great volume of enforcement actions [to] be brought by the State," and that citizen suits are proper only "if the Federal, State, and local agencies fail to exercise their enforcement responsibility.[73]

Consequently, the regulator has the ability to influence the availability of citizen suits through its own actions, such as taking enforcement action that operates to preclude a citizen suit.

B. Employment Discrimination Claim

Title VII of the Civil Rights Act of 1964 is intended to prohibit practices which create inequality in employment opportunity due to discrimination on basis of race, religion, sex or national origin.[74] The enforcement of unlawful employment discrimination involves a combination of private action and action by the Equal Employment Opportunity Commission (EEOC).

The enforcement provision, Civil Rights Act, 42 USC § 2000e-5, provides for a 'charge' to be filed by a member of the EEOC or 'by or on behalf of a person claiming to be aggrieved' alleging 'an unlawful employment practice'. A charge from a person must be filed within 180 days after the alleged unlawful employment practice occurs. No claim may be brought unless the alleged discrimination is first made the subject of a charge.[75]

Ginsburg J, writing for a unanimous Supreme Court, held that Title VII's charge-filing requirement is not a jurisdictional prerequisite, but rather a mandatory claim processing rule.[76] Consequently, an objection based on a mandatory claim-processing rule not being complied with may be forfeited due to delay, waiver or estoppel.[77] Equally a defendant who promptly raises non-compliance with the charge-filing requirement will be able to have the matter dismissed.[78]

Charges must 'be in writing under oath or affirmation and … contain such information and be in such form as the Commission requires'.[79] The regulations require the name and contact details of the charging party and the person against whom the charge is made. Further the charge must contain 'A clear and concise statement of the facts, including pertinent dates, constituting the alleged unlawful employment practices', although the regulations go on to state that 'a charge is sufficient when the Commission receives from the person making the charge a written statement sufficiently precise to identify the parties, and to describe generally the action or practices complained of'.[80] The US courts have identified 'the crucial element of a charge [as being] the factual statement contained therein'.[81]

The above explanation of the procedural steps suggests that the aggrieved person is responsible for drafting the charge. However, it appears that the EEOC may have a more active role as it employs a two-step filing procedure utilising an intake questionnaire, which solicits preliminary information, and then the formal charge. The questionnaire asks for the information required for the charge, but based on this information an EEOC official determines whether grounds exist

[73] *Gwaltney of Smithfield, Ltd v Chesapeake Bay Foundation Inc*, 484 US 49, 60 (1987).

[74] *Franks v Bowman Transportation Co*, 424 US 747, 763 (1976); *Lenzi v Systemax Inc*, 944 F3d 97, 110 (2d Cir 2019).

[75] Civil Rights Act, 42 USC § 2000e-5(b); *Fort Bend County, Texas v Davis*, 139 S Ct 1843, 1846 (2019). The filing of a charge may be relied on by another person in multi-plaintiff litigation and by group members in a class action: Lex Larson, *Larson on Employment Discrimination* (LexisNexis Online) § 70.03[2].

[76] *Fort Bend County, Texas v Davis*, 139 S Ct 1843, 1850–1851 (2019).

[77] *Zipes v Trans World Airlines, Inc*, 455 US 385, 393 (1982); *Hardaway v Hartford Public Works Department*, 879 F.3d 486, 489–490 (2d Cir 2018).

[78] See eg *Sughrim v New York*, 2020 WL 7047697, *18 (SDNY 30 November, 2020).

[79] Civil Rights Act, 42 USC § 2000e-5(b); 29 CFR § 1601.9.

[80] 29 CFR § 1601.12.

[81] *Sanchez v Standard Brands, Inc*, 431 F2d 455, 462 (5th Cir 1970); *Price v Southwestern Bell Telephone Co*, 687 F2d 74, 78 (5th Cir 1982).

for the filing of a formal charge, drafts the charge and provides it to the aggrieved person for approval and signature under oath.[82]

The regulations also provide that a charge may be amended to cure technical defects or omissions, and permits 'amendments alleging additional acts which constitute unlawful employment practices related to or growing out of the subject matter of the original charge' as the amendments will relate back to the date the charge was first received.[83]

Upon receiving a charge, the EEOC notifies the employer and investigates the allegations. The investigation may consist of written requests for information, questionnaires or interrogatories to the respondent, and an on-site visit.[84] If the Commission finds 'reasonable cause to believe the charge is true', the Civil Rights Act instructs the EEOC to 'endeavor to eliminate [the] alleged unlawful employment practice by informal methods of conference, conciliation, and persuasion'. These informal methods are conducted confidentially and cannot be used as evidence in a subsequent proceeding without the written consent of the persons concerned. When informal methods do not resolve the charge, the EEOC has the option to bring a civil action against the employer in court.[85]

If a charge filed with the EEOC is dismissed by the Commission, or if within 180 days from the filing of the charge the Commission has not filed a civil action under this section a complainant is entitled to a 'right-to-sue' notice. Within 90 days following such notice, the complainant may commence a civil action against the allegedly offending employer.[86]

The scope of the civil action is determined by the charge filed with the EEOC.[87] Otherwise the EEOC is not afforded an opportunity to resolve the claim as instructed by the Civil Rights Act. Consequently, the underlying question for the courts is whether the EEOC had the opportunity to resolve the claims. A suit may include all claims within the scope of the investigation that could reasonably be expected to grow out of the administrative charge. There must be a reasonable relationship between the allegations in the charge and those in the complaint, and the claim in the complaint could reasonably be expected to be discovered in the course of the EEOC's investigation.[88]

C. *Qui Tam*

The False Claims Act creates a civil cause of action for the Attorney-General or a private citizen, the *qui tam* relator, that may be commenced against persons who commit certain fraudulent acts against the US Federal Government.[89] Many of the *qui tam* provisions in the False Claims Act address the interaction between the Government and the relator.

[82] Laurie Stegman, 'An Administrative Battle of the Forms: The EEOC's Intake Questionnaire and Charge of Discrimination' (1992) 91 *Michigan Law Review* 124, 126. See also www.eeoc.gov/filing-charge-discrimination ('A Charge of Discrimination can be completed through our EEOC Public Portal after you submit an online inquiry and we interview you.').

[83] 29 CFR § 1601.12(b).

[84] Michael Mankes, 'Combatting Individual Employment Discrimination in the United States and Great Britain: A Novel Remedial Approach' (1994) 16 *Comparative Labor Law Journal* 67, 71.

[85] Civil Rights Act, 42 USC § 2000e–5(b), (f)(1); *Fort Bend County, Texas v Davis*, 139 S Ct 1843, 1847 (2019).

[86] Civil Rights Act, 42 USC § 2000e–5(b), f(1); 29 CFR § 1601.28; *Fort Bend County, Texas v Davis*, 139 S Ct 1843, 1847 (2019).

[87] *Thornton v United Parcel Service Inc*, 587 F3d 27, 31 (1st Cir 2009); *Peters v Renaissance Hotel Operating Co*, 307 F3d 535, 550 (7th Cir 2002).

[88] *Littlejohn v City of New York*, 795 F3d 297, 322 (2d Cir 2015).

[89] Unlike citizen suits above where the plaintiff must demonstrate that they have standing, the relator has standing via the government's injury because their entitlement to a bounty is a partial assignment of the claim to the relator: *Environment Texas Citizen Lobby, Inc v ExxonMobil Corp*, 968 F3d 357, 364 (5th Cir 2020).

The key provision of the False Claims Act imposes civil liability on 'Any person who – knowingly presents, or causes to be presented, a false or fraudulent claim for payment or approval'.[90] A claim is any request or demand for money or property presented to an officer, employee or agent of the United States.[91] The cause of action has three core elements:

- the person must present, or cause another person to present, a claim for payment or approval to the United States;
- the claim must be false or fraudulent; and
- the person must act knowing that the claim is false.[92]

Another frequent source of liability is the making or using of false records in support of a false claim.[93]

Actions under the Act, though filed by private citizens, are 'brought in the name of the Government'. The False Claims Act contains express filing and service requirements that govern the initiation and early stages of a *qui tam* action. In particular, 'A copy of the complaint and written disclosure of substantially all material evidence and information the person possesses shall be served on the Government'. Further the complaint 'shall be filed in camera, shall remain under seal for at least 60 days, and shall not be served on the defendant until the court so orders'.[94] Within 60 days the Government must:

- elect to intervene and take over the action;
- notify the court that it declines to intervene, permitting the relator to conduct the action;
- move to dismiss the action; or
- attempt to settle the action prior to formal intervention.[95]

The reasons for the combination of confidentiality and service on the Government given by Congress were to allow the Government to ascertain privately 'whether it was already investigating the claims stated in the suit and then to consider whether it wished to intervene', to 'prevent wrongdoers from being tipped off that they were under investigation' and 'to protect the defendant's reputation from the taint associated with being a defendant in a lawsuit ostensibly brought by the United States, when the United States had yet to decide whether the allegations have any merit'.[96] The main issue for present purposes is that the procedure allows for the Government to assess the claim and how it wishes to respond before the claim is made public. It should be noted that the Government does not just receive the complaint, which is a form of pleading, but also 'substantially all material evidence and information the person possesses' which aids the Government's investigation and decision-making. If the Government elects to intervene, the Government conducts and controls the action.[97]

[90] False Claims Act, 31 USC § 3729(a)(1)(A).
[91] ibid § 3729(b)(2)(A).
[92] See eg *Blusal Meats Inc v United States*, 638 FSupp. 824, 827 (SDNY 1986), aff'd, 817 F2d 1007 (2d Cir 1987).
[93] False Claims Act, 31 USC § 3729(a)(1)(B). It is important to note that liability under that subsection is dependent on a violation of subsection (a)(1)(A).
[94] ibid § 3730(b)(2).
[95] ibid §§ 3730(b)(4)(A), 3730(b)(4)(B), 3730(c)(2)(A); John Boese and Douglas Baruch, *Civil False Claims and Qui Tam Actions*, 5th edn (Wolters Kluwer, 2020) § 4.04.
[96] Boese and Baruch (n 95) § 4.03. See also *United States ex rel Pilon v Martin Marietta Corp*, 60 F3d 995, 998 (2d Cir 1995).
[97] False Claims Act, 31 USC § 3730(b)(4).

A relator is entitled to conduct the action only if the Government declines to intervene. If the Government declines to take over the matter, it may still require that it be served with copies of all pleadings filed and deposition transcripts in the case. This continued monitoring is 'an attempt to avoid adverse developments in individual cases, but also to prevent the development of negative precedent that may have significantly broader implications'.[98] At a later date even though the Government declined to intervene within the 60-day period, it may intervene 'upon a showing of good cause'.[99] The Government may also move to have the complaint dismissed. This can be because the claim is thought to be unmeritorious or on public interest grounds such as where the defendant voluntarily disclosed a contravention and was cooperating with the Department of Justice.[100] The Government regards such a motion as mandatory, but some courts have held that is subject to judicial review.[101]

A unique aspect of the *qui tam* suit is that the legislation specifies a range of percentages of recovery that are paid to the relator where there is a successful outcome. If the Government intervenes, the relator receives 15–25 per cent of the recovery or settlement amount. The amount paid to the relator 'depend[s] upon the extent to which the person substantially contributed to the prosecution of the action'.[102] However, this recovery is subject to a proviso – where the court finds that the relator was not the original source of the information that led to the successful action, the court awards between zero and 10 per cent, 'taking into account the significance of the information and the role of the person bringing the action in advancing the case to litigation'.[103] If the Government declines to proceed with the action, the relator receives 'an amount which the court decides is reasonable for collecting the civil penalty and damages' but between 25 and 30 per cent of the recovery or settlement amount.[104] The legislation also addresses the situation where the relator participated in the wrongdoing by allowing the court to reduce the percentage of recovery, except where the relator has been convicted of a crime in relation to the underlying claim and the statute specifies that no recovery may be made.[105] As the loss and therefore any payment belongs to the Government, the actual percentage of recovery is typically a product of negotiation between the Government and the relator.[106]

D. Class Action Fairness Act of 2005

The Class Action Fairness Act of 2005 (CAFA) was enacted to curb perceived class action abuses in state courts and attempts by class action lawyers to avoid class actions being adjudicated in

[98] Boese and Baruch (n 95) §4.04[E].

[99] False Claims Act, 31 USC § 3730(c)(3). See *United States ex rel. Eisenstein v City of New York*, 556 US 928, 932–933 (2009).

[100] Pamela Bucy, 'Private Justice' (2002) 76 *Southern California Law Review* 1, 70–72.

[101] Boese and Baruch (n 95) §4.05; *United States ex rel. Sequoia Orange Co v Sunland Packing House Co*, 151 F3d 1139 (9th Cir 1998).

[102] False Claims Act, 31 USC § 3730(d)(1).

[103] ibid § 3730(d)(2). The lack of an original source of information is expressed in the statute as 'Where the action is one which the court finds to be based primarily on disclosures of specific information (other than information provided by the person bringing the action) relating to allegations or transactions in a criminal, civil, or administrative hearing, in a congressional, administrative, or Government Accounting Office report, hearing, audit, or investigation, or from the news media'.

[104] *Vermont Agency of Natural Resources v United States ex rel Stevens* 529 US 765, 768–770 (2000); Christopher Martin, Jr, 'Reining in Lincoln's Law: A Call to Limit the Implied Certification Theory of Liability Under the False Claims Act' (2013) 101 *California Law Review* 227, 236.

[105] False Claims Act, 31 USC § 3730(d)(3).

[106] Boese and Baruch (n 95) §4.09.

federal court through amending the requirements for diversity jurisdiction and removal to federal court.[107] However the statute also addresses class action settlements and includes a requirement that:

> Not later than 10 days after a proposed settlement of a class action is filed in court, each defendant that is participating in the proposed settlement shall serve upon the appropriate State official of each State in which a class member resides and the appropriate Federal official, a notice of the proposed settlement[108]

The appropriate federal official is the Attorney-General of the United States or, in cases involving depository institutions, the person 'who has the primary Federal regulatory or supervisory responsibility with respect to the defendant, if some or all of the matters alleged in the class action are subject to regulation or supervision by that person'. The appropriate state official is

> the person in the State who has the primary regulatory or supervisory responsibility with respect to the defendant, or who licenses or otherwise authorizes the defendant to conduct business in the State, if some or all of the matters alleged in the class action are subject to regulation by that person

If no such regulator exists, the appropriate state official is the state's Attorney-General.[109]

The statute specifies eight pieces of information that are to be provided to the government officials:

> (1) a copy of the complaint and any materials filed with the complaint and any amended complaints;
> (2) notice of any scheduled judicial hearing in the class action;
> (3) any proposed or final notification to class members of the right to request exclusion (opt out) or that such right does not exist, and of any proposed settlement;
> (4) any proposed or final class action settlement;
> (5) any settlement or other agreement made between class counsel and counsel for the defendants;
> (6) any final judgment or notice of dismissal;
> (7) the names of class members, or if that is not feasible an estimate of the number of class members, who reside in each State and the estimated proportionate share of the claims of such members to the entire settlement; and
> (8) any written judicial opinion relating to the materials described under subparagraphs (3) through (6).[110]

CAFA then states that the court may not issue an order finally approving the proposed settlement until 90 days after the last government official receives notice.[111]

The purpose of CAFA's notice provision has been described as 'obscure' as the statute does not require the government officials that receive the notice to do anything.[112] Indeed, it explicitly states that 'nothing in this section shall be construed to expand the authority of, or impose any obligations, duties, or responsibilities upon, Federal or State officials'.[113] The effect of the notice requirement is that if it is not complied with then 'a class member may refuse to comply with and may choose not to be bound by a settlement agreement or consent decree in a class action'.[114]

[107] The Committee on the Judiciary, 'Class Action Fairness Act of 2005, Senate Report 109-14', S Rep No 14, 109th Congress, 1st Sess 2005 ('Committee on the Judiciary CAFA Report').
[108] Class Action Fairness Act, 28 USC § 1715(b).
[109] ibid § 1715(a); William Rubenstein, Alba Conte and Herbert Newberg, *Newberg on Class Actions*, 5th edn (Thomson Reuters, 2011) § 8:19.
[110] Class Action Fairness Act, 28 USC § 1715(b).
[111] ibid § 1715(d).
[112] Rubenstein, Conte and Newberg (n 109) § 8:18.
[113] Class Action Fairness Act, 28 USC § 1715(f).
[114] ibid § 1715(e).

However, the aim of the provision was set out in the US Senate's Committee on the Judiciary Report as follows:

> New section 1715 is designed to ensure that a responsible state and/or federal official receives information about proposed class action settlements and is in a position to react if the settlement appears unfair to some or all class members or inconsistent with applicable regulatory policies. ...
>
> [F]ederal and state officials will be notified about proposed settlements and have an opportunity to get involved if they think it is appropriate but will not be required to do so.[115]

The Senate Report goes on to say that 'the Committee believes that notifying appropriate state and federal officials of proposed class action settlements will provide a check against inequitable settlements in these cases'.[116] Despite the reference to regulatory policies it is not further elaborated upon. The goal appears to be group member protection rather than concerns about the interaction between public and private enforcement.

E. Taxonomy of Coordination Mechanisms

The above regulatory regimes, except for CAFA, have been used to construct a taxonomy of coordination mechanisms.[117] The mechanisms offer design choices for structuring the role of the regulator or government in relation to the private party.

A regulator may be given affirmative or residual authority to control or terminate private enforcement. Affirmative authority means that the regulator has power to determine if a private action can be filed or can require that after a proceeding is filed it must be dismissed. Residual authority refers to powers granted pursuant to court legislation or rules for a regulator to become involved in private litigation. For example, rules permitting a regulator to intervene or appear as an amicus.[118] Both the Civil Rights Act and the False Claims Act give the regulator affirmative authority to control or terminate private enforcement. The taxonomy also refers to whether the affirmative authority operates at a 'retail' or 'wholesale' level, meaning the regulator considers private actions on a case-by-case basis, or it can determine that all private rights of action in a particular area may not be pursued.[119] Each of the regimes adopts a retail approach.

The mechanisms employed may then be either advisory or binding. Advisory involves merely communicating the regulator's view as to whether a claim is meritorious or should proceed, but without the power to give effect to that view. A binding decision in contrast allows or prevents a claim from proceeding. The EEOC in being required to issue a right to sue letter regardless of its views on the merits is only advisory. The Department of Justice has binding decision-making under the False Claims Act and can have claims dismissed by a court.[120]

[115] Committee on the Judiciary CAFA Report (n 107) 32; *Garner v State Farm Mutual Auto Insurance Co*, 2010 WL 1687832, *14 (ND Cal 22 April 2010) ('Although CAFA does not create an affirmative duty for either state or federal officials to take any action in response to a class action settlement, CAFA presumes that, once put on notice, state or federal officials will raise any concerns that they may have during the normal course of the class action settlement procedures.'); *Acosta v Frito-Lay Inc*, 2018 WL 2088278, *9 (ND Cal 4 May 2018).

[116] Committee on the Judiciary CAFA Report (n 107) 35.

[117] Freeman Engstrom (n 16) 645–46 Table 1, Table 2.

[118] ibid 647.

[119] ibid 647–48. See also Joseph Grundfest, 'Disimplying Private Rights of Action Under the Federal Securities Laws: The Commission's Authority' (1994) 107 *Harvard Law Review* 961 who argues that in the US where the judiciary implied a private right of action in SEC Rule 10b-5 the SEC could disimply such a cause of action.

[120] ibid 649–50.

The regimes may also be classified based on whether they employ a 'passive gate', where the regulator can simply authorise or not authorise a private action, or 'active displacement', which means that the regulator can only stop private enforcement if it takes action. The Department of Justice is a 'passive gate' in relation to the False Claims Act as it can simply have claims dismissed. However, it can also take over a private claim. Citizen suits under the environmental laws can only be prevented by the regulator taking action, ie 'diligently prosecuting' an action.[121]

The taxonomy also refers to veto or licence in relation to regimes that are affirmative and binding. A veto operates so that a private suit may continue unless affirmatively prevented by the regulator. A licence operates so that a private suit can be commenced if the regulator provides permission. All of the above regimes employ a veto.[122]

In summary, in the current context, the taxonomy suggests giving ASIC affirmative power to control or terminate private claims. Residual authority, as explained above, already exists. The retail/wholesale dichotomy is not applicable as it is the Australian legislature that creates or removes private rights of action, as shown by the continuous disclosure and misleading conduct causes of action under study which were created by Parliament. If the legislature desired to have no private enforcement then it could remove the grant of standing. The way in which an affirmative power would operate is a matter for further analysis below. The power could be advisory or binding, and if binding could be passive (no action needed by ASIC) or active (ASIC must take action). Further, if binding, the private action may need to seek permission or a licence first, or the private action may be commenced but ASIC could veto its continuation. The regime created by CAFA adds an additional approach of sharing information but without any affirmative power to control or terminate private claims.

V. Concerns with Coordination

Before suggesting models of coordination, it is prudent to consider the concerns that the literature has identified in relating to coordination.

There is a price for government in reserving a pre-eminent role for the regulator. The regulator must consider the merits of the private suits brought to its attention and determine how to respond. Coordination involves the use of already scarce regulator resources in evaluating the merits of private actions. In relation to US employment discrimination it has been argued that a lack of sufficient funding frustrated the EEOC's ability to perform such a function.[123] Further, cost and delay was also imposed on claimants with the coordination regime described as 'an administrative obstacle course' that 'plac[es] the EEOC at the courthouse door'.[124] Consequently individuals needed to perform additional steps and wait longer before receiving an adequate remedy.[125] The CAFA notice provision has been largely ineffective, with the outgoing Associate Attorney-General at the Department of Justice stating in February 2018 that the Department of Justice received over 700 CAFA notices every year, but had only participated in two cases due to delays in processing the notices.[126] Regulatory oversight may see increased bureaucratisation of

[121] ibid 650–51.
[122] ibid 654.
[123] Mankes (n 84) 78; Sean Farhang, *The Litigation State* (Princeton University Press, 2010) 131.
[124] Stegman (n 82) 125.
[125] Mankes (n 84) 75–76.
[126] Rachel Brand, US Department of Justice, 'Remarks to the Washington, DC Lawyers Chapter of the Federalist Society (15 February 2018) cited in Amanda Rose, 'Cutting Class Action Agency Costs: Lessons from the Public Company (2020) 54 *UC Davis Law Review* 337, 430.

the litigation initiation process with a resulting loss of speed and flexibility in private enforcement.[127] Further, there may be a risk that a regulator is overwhelmed with private claims to review so that it may be unable to properly investigate those claims that truly merit consideration.[128]

The regulator may lack expertise in considering private suits.[129] For example, a regulator may have significant expertise and experience in investigating, finding and proving contraventions, but little in proving causation and damages that are necessary elements for compensation. This could make an accurate assessment of the merits difficult.

Where the regulator has the authority to authorise or veto class actions it places the power over private enforcement completely with the regulator and risks losing the advantages that private enforcement provides, such as overcoming regulatory capture and resource constraints.[130] Private litigation that relies on lawyers and funders making calculated investments of time and money based on a risk calculus may cease to make those investments because the regulator can set the return at zero by not allowing a class action to proceed.[131]

A key argument for allowing private enforcement is that allowing the pursuit of private interests can also advance the public interest through the enforcement of society's laws.[132] Rather than a single regulatory agency determining what is in the public interest there can be multiple viewpoints put forward, albeit through the single avenue of commencing litigation in the courts. Where the regulator has the authority to authorise or veto class actions, those multiple viewpoints may be lost and the public interest may be defined solely by the regulators' views. This in turn raises concerns 'about whether agencies can or will deploy such powers in ways that serve rather than undermine the public good' and whether 'they may privilege pursuit of political rewards over welfare-maximizing regulation of private enforcement efforts'.[133] Equally, it must be remembered that coordination has been argued to be necessary because private enforcement 'may be motivated by private interests that diverge from the "public interest"'.[134]

VI. Coordination Strategies for Securities Regulation

The strategy for coordination to be adopted in relation to ASIC and the class action depends on the objective of the coordination. The focus in this text has been on the effective achievement of deterrence and compensation through ASIC enforcement and the shareholder class action (outcomes) and the promotion of values that support a 'good' regulatory process (process). Consequently, when considering coordination the approach here is to again adopt this focus.

Before examining two strategy options it needs to be recalled that, as explained in chapter three, achievement of the objectives is difficult to ascertain. While the goal of deterrence

[127] James Park, 'Rules, Principles, and the Competition to Enforce Securities Laws' (2012) 100 *California Law Review* 115.

[128] 'Recent Legislation' (2011) 124 *Harvard Law Review* 1829, 1835 (examining the operation of whistleblowing requirements under the Dodd–Frank Wall Street Reform and Consumer Protection Act).

[129] Freeman Engstrom (n 16) 663, 671–72.

[130] Park (n 127); J Maria Glover, 'The Structural Roles of Private Enforcement Mechanisms in Public Law' (2012) 53 *William and Mary Law Review* 1137, 1159–60; John Coffee, *Entrepreneurial Litigation: Its Rise, Fall and Future* (Harvard University Press, 2015) 226.

[131] Glover (n 130) 1215; Adam Zimmerman, 'Mass Settlement Rivalries' (2013) 82 *University of Cincinnati Law Review* 381, 402.

[132] William Rubenstein, 'On What a "Private Attorney General" Is – And Why It Matters' (2004) 57 *Vanderbilt Law Review* 2129, 2147.

[133] Freeman Engstrom (n 16) 621.

[134] Markell and Glicksman, (n 59) 619.

is clear – avoidance of misconduct through fear of the perceived consequences of engaging in the misconduct – ascertaining if the goal has been achieved is more challenging. Deterrence is clearly observable and has been found through empirical studies. However, whether sufficient deterrence has been achieved is difficult to measure as it is unclear 'How much deterrence we get from a combination of sanctions'.[135] The aim of compensation is to make the injured person whole through full compensation. If they are given more than that, they have been over-compensated, and if given less, under-compensated.[136] Full compensation is in theory more ascertainable than deterrence because it equates with the loss suffered. While the law provides guidance as to the measurement of loss it must still be applied to the specific facts. Moreover, as set out in chapter three, there are limits to achieving full compensation such as uncertainty of outcome which can promote negotiated settlements that are less than full compensation. Finally, in looking at procedural values, and in particular the public interest and efficiency, these values may be contested or conflicting with different interests affording them more or less importance.

A. Information-sharing Approach

A minimalist coordination strategy would be to focus on the sharing of information. This approach draws on the CAFA model discussed above and the use of notices in each of citizen suits, employment actions and *qui tam*, but significantly modifies them. From a regulatory pluralism perspective, the law would orchestrate the sharing of information but not what is to be done in response to the receipt of that information.

A person proposing to commence a class action could be required to notify ASIC of that intention and to provide information as to the respondents (company, directors, advisers), the causes of action, the group definition (the time period to which the claim applies) and the relief sought, including the alleged harm suffered and the quantum of compensation that would be owed. The notice would need to include assumptions such as when disclosure was required by the continuous disclosure regime, the extent to which shares were overvalued and the volume of shares traded. The class action proponent is required to share information that it already requires to assess prospects, obtain litigation funding and commence proceedings.

Under this approach there is no scope for ASIC to prevent or stop a class action because it is viewed as unmeritorious or as undermining ASIC's regulatory approach, such as taking a more lenient approach to contravention in exchange for cooperation. Rather, ASIC is able to use the information provided to assist it in determining what its regulatory response should be. The existence of the class action becomes something ASIC factors into the likely levels of deterrence that may follow as a result of compensation being paid. As the class action typically focuses on the corporation and seeks only a monetary payment, ASIC may consider focusing on different parties and using different enforcement tools. ASIC may take enforcement action against directors, officers or advisers rather than the corporation. ASIC may seek direct changes to policies and procedures through seeking an enforceable undertaking from the company. ASIC may determine that criminal proceedings are warranted because the compensation payments that would flow from a class action are insufficient to deter. ASIC and the legislature would have to accept that most of the time ASIC would operate at either the base of the enforcement pyramid or at its peak, as the middle ground of monetary payments would be the province of the class action.

[135] Peter Cleary Yeager, 'The Practical Challenges of Responding to Corporate Crime' in Shanna Van Slyke, Michael Benson and Francis Cullen (eds), *The Oxford Handbook of White-Collar Crime* (Oxford University Press, 2016) 654.

[136] Ch 3, section III.D.

However, if no class action is filed then ASIC may need to take on the role of seeking compensation or using another tool to achieve deterrence.

While this approach allows ASIC to better calibrate its response, it must be recognised that ASIC may feel compelled to act prior to receiving the class action information. As ASIC has responsibility for market integrity and governance which necessitates prompt actions that deter and educate, ASIC needs to identify and stop contraventions expeditiously.[137] It may also be the case that class action proponents seek to draw on ASIC's actions as part of the due diligence of determining whether to bring suit. The litigation strategy may be to ride on ASIC's coat tails or at least have the benefit of knowing that ASIC has taken action before commencing a class action. The rise of competing class actions has reduced the availability of this strategy as waiting may undermine the likelihood of being able to pursue a class action when others are already before the court.

ASIC could also use the information provided and its analysis to strategically intervene in class actions. Where a class action goes to trial, ASIC may wish to make submissions on novel areas of law so that the court is informed as to the ramifications of various interpretations for enforcement more generally. The Full Court of the Federal Court has previously identified 'the public interest in the proper interpretation of an important provision of the Act' as warranting ASIC's intervention.[138] Where a class action settles, development of the law is less of an issue, but ASIC may still wish to assist the court by providing submissions on some aspects of the settlement, such as prospects of success vis-à-vis the settlement amount, or on the transaction costs incurred in bringing the class action (legal fees and litigating funding fees) because they reduce the compensation payable to group members.[139]

This approach would also maintain the ability of class action proponents to seek information from ASIC. Indeed, if ASIC is told about planned class actions and given the information set out above, its officers may be able to incorporate that information into their own thinking about what to investigate and the types of materials to gather as evidence. Indeed, one class action lawyer interviewed as part of the case studies thought that ASIC should consider how its regulatory tools and actions could be deployed so as to assist people harmed by a contravention to obtain a private remedy.[140] However, it is the nature of investigations that they are usually the first step ASIC takes and they may have been completed before any class action is contemplated.

ASIC may also assist shareholders by maintaining a register of class actions, similar to the register of enforceable undertakings, so that there is a central repository of information that potential claimants could consult to see if a class action was on foot. The register would also contain historical information that would record the outcome of class actions, including the fees charged by lawyers and funders.[141]

[137] Interview ASIC Executive Telstra/Multiplex; Interview ASIC Executive Leighton, 4.

[138] *Bacnet Pty Ltd v Lift Capital Partners Pty Ltd (in liq)* (2010) 183 FCR 384, 405 [142] (Keane CJ and Jacobson J).

[139] Ch 6, section III.D.

[140] Interview applicant's solicitor Leighton, 15. See also John Coffee, 'Rescuing the Private Attorney General: Why the Model of Lawyer as Bounty Hunter is not Working' (1983) 42 *Maryland Law Review* 215, 224–25 ('it often may be more efficient for public agencies to concentrate on detection (an area where they have the comparative advantage because of their superior investigative resources) and leave the actual litigation of the case to private enforcers, who are frequently more experienced in litigation tactics').

[141] Similar suggestions for a repository of information have been made by Australian Law Reform Commission, 'Integrity, Fairness and Efficiency – An Inquiry into Class Action Proceedings and Third-Party Litigation Funders', Report No 134 (2018) 151–52, 263 (recommending that the Federal Court of Australia collect 'critical information for a "class action database"'), Parliamentary Joint Committee on Corporations and Financial Services, 'Litigation funding and the regulation of the class action industry' (December 2020) [11.112]; Amanda Rose, 'Classaction.gov' (2021) 88 *University of Chicago Law Review* 487, 495–96 (summarising US literature calling for a repository of class action outcomes).

Although the strategy involves a minimalist approach, it will still involve some cost. The class action proponents need to provide information and ASIC needs to review it. Further costs may flow depending on the action ASIC takes. Without adequate resourcing the advantages for ASIC would not materialise. This strategy maintains the advantages of the class action. It allows ASIC to draw on the ability of private actors to fund the enforcement of regulation and therefore supplement the resources available to ASIC. However, it does not remove the class action's impact on regulatory discretion and the regulator's ability to effectively use the enforcement pyramid to escalate and deescalate in response to the regulated entities actions.

This regime of notice and consideration of claims by the regulator means that the regulator and private plaintiff have the opportunity to communicate, and possibly coordinate their approaches. The opportunity to interact allows each to educate the other. This provides an opportunity for both to inform the other of their concerns and priorities.[142] Ultimately, though, public and private enforcement determine for themselves how they will proceed. This will always be the case unless the regulator is granted the ability to veto or licence the use of the class action.

B. Gatekeeper Approach

A more intrusive form of coordination would be to establish ASIC as a gatekeeper for class actions. The approach developed below provides ASIC with authority to determine if a class action may be commenced. Without ASIC approval the class action cannot be filed. From a regulatory pluralism perspective the law would give ASIC authority to act as the orchestrator or conductor of all enforcement mechanisms. In terms of the taxonomy explained above, this approach may be described as one with 'affirmative authority', a 'licence' and as 'binding'. Further, there is no 'active displacement' adopted here. Active displacement would mean that ASIC can only prevent a class action where it takes some form of enforcement action, or a specific type of action, namely seeking compensation. However, one of the outcomes of coordination may be that no action is needed which would not be available under an active displacement approach.

i. Deterrence

One approach put forward in the United States in relation to securities regulation has been to focus on deterrence and, in particular, avoiding over-deterrence.[143] This approach starts by explaining that oversight of shareholder class actions has not previously been given serious attention because compensation was seen as the goal of class actions, and interposing a government agency was inconsistent with corrective justice.[144] The argument then proceeds on the basis that if this goal is disputed because compensation is said not to be achieved, due to arguments of pocket-shifting and low recovery rates, then the focus can shift to class actions achieving deterrence only. Moreover, the shareholder class action can also be argued to be analogous to citizen suits and *qui tam* actions where compensation is also not the goal.[145]

[142] Bucy (n 100) 69; John Braithwaite, *Regulatory Capitalism* (Edward Elgar, 2008) 70.

[143] Amanda Rose, 'Reforming Securities Litigation Reform: Restructuring the Relationship Between Public and Private Enforcement of Rule 10B-5' (2008) 108 *Columbia Law Review* 1301, 1354.

[144] ibid 1349–50.

[145] ibid 1313, 1350–52.

Under this model ASIC would determine what enforcement tools were suitable based on its view of the public interest and the exercise of regulatory discretion, including taking account of cooperation. ASIC's view of the public interest, based on the interviews from the case studies, is likely to be ensuring market integrity and good governance.[146] In terms of securing cooperation, arguably this could mean that ASIC would have the class action, as well as criminal action, as 'big sticks' that could be wielded if the regulated entity did not respond in a manner judged appropriate by ASIC. Class actions that were permitted to be brought by ASIC would not just impose direct costs, but in having the imprimatur of the regulator may also carry greater reputational impact in terms of deterrence. Regulated entities would have an incentive to negotiate or cooperate with ASIC so as to avoid the substantial damages claims that would otherwise follow. The concern with this approach is that the advantages of the class action may be lost because ASIC trades them away as part of its regulatory discretion. There would be a risk of regulatory capture or inertia. Although, at least in the civil penalty and criminal litigation spheres the court must approve a civil penalty settlement[147] and it is the court that determines the sentence in a criminal prosecution.[148] The judicial system provides a form of oversight as to regulatory discretion in these circumstances. However, there is no equivalent in relation to enforceable undertakings, infringement notices, or when no action is taken.

ii. Deterrence and Compensation

The above approach sidelines compensation, but compensation is a clear goal of the continuous disclosure regulatory regime with both ASIC and individuals granted standing to pursue compensation. An 'ASIC as gatekeeper' approach to coordination needs to embrace the complete range of remedies available, including compensation.[149] ASIC needs to take account of both deterrence and compensation.

The difficulty in calibrating deterrence and compensation arises because the payment of compensation may also deter.[150] If it is assumed that there is an optimal or sufficient amount of deterrence and ASIC has achieved this alone then allowing a class action to seek compensation

[146] Interview ASIC Executive Telstra/Multiplex; Interview ASIC Executive Leighton, 4.

[147] *Commonwealth v Director, Fair Work Building Industry Inspectorate* (2015) 258 CLR 482 (a court asked to approve a civil penalty settlement may receive submissions on the appropriate penalty from the regulator and the defendant but such submissions are to be considered on their merits and the court must be persuaded that it is an appropriate remedy in all the circumstances.) See also *Volkswagen Aktiengesellschaft v Australian Competition and Consumer Commission* [2021] FCAFC 49, [129] (Wigney, Beach and O'Bryan JJ) ('The regulator's submissions, or joint submissions, must be assessed on their merits, and the Court must be wary of the possibility that the agreed penalty may be the product of the regulator having been too pragmatic in reaching the settlement.').

[148] *Barbaro v The Queen* (2014) 253 CLR 58, 76 [47]–[49] (French CJ, Hayne, Kiefel and Bell JJ) ('it is for the sentencing judge, alone, to decide what sentence will be imposed' and that the prosecution is not permitted to provide the court with a statement as to the bounds of the available range of sentences). See also [30] where French CJ, Hayne, Kiefel and Bell JJ acknowledge that 'the prosecution may have a view of the available sentencing range which gives undue weight to the assistance which the offender has given or promised'.

[149] See Glover (n 130) 1178, 1189 (arguing for the avoidance of 'remedial gaps' as well as 'remedial overkill'); Royal Commission into Misconduct in the Banking, Superannuation and Financial Services Industry, 'Final Report – Volume 1' (2019) 3–4 ('The Australian community expects, and is entitled to expect, that if an entity breaks the law and causes damage to customers, it will compensate those affected customers. But the community also expects that financial services entities that break the law will be held to account. The community recognises, and the community expects its regulators to recognise, that these are two different steps: having a wrongdoer compensate those harmed is one thing; holding wrongdoers to account is another.').

[150] Ch 6, section II.A.

would result in over-deterrence. Equally, preventing the class action from being brought results in under compensation, or no compensation. This can be illustrated through Table 8.1.

Table 8.1 Deterrence and compensation coordination options

	ASIC	Class action	Outcome
1	Sufficient deterrence	No compensation	Sufficient deterrence/under compensation
2	Sufficient deterrence	Compensation	Over-deterrence/compensation
3	Insufficient deterrence	No compensation	Under-deterrence/compensation
4	Insufficient deterrence	Compensation	Sufficient deterrence/compensation

To avoid the over-deterrence or under-compensation outcome, ASIC has two options. First, as suggested by the fourth line in Table 8.1, it could factor in the compensation and incidental deterrence that the class action would achieve and seek a lower level of deterrence so that in total there is sufficient deterrence and compensation. This is similar to how ASIC would use the information-sharing approach. However, like that approach, and as show in the third line in Table 8.1, it has the drawback that ASIC does not know if a class action will be brought, and if it is not brought there arises both under-deterrence and under-compensation. Moreover, in all scenarios where ASIC relies on the class action to achieve compensation it does not know the quantum of compensation and there is a risk that the class action will settle for too little.

Alternatively, ASIC could seek compensation as part of seeking deterrence and aim for both sufficient deterrence and full compensation. No class action would be required. ASIC could obtain compensation through either civil litigation[151] or through the corporate entity and/or accessories 'volunteering' to provide a redress scheme to investors who suffered loss.

It is unrealistic to expect ASIC to approach deterrence and compensation as though it can be reduced to a mathematical equation. As explained at the beginning of this section, accurately determining deterrence and compensation can be difficult. Rather, the above analysis means that ASIC's approach to coordination needs to factor in compensation, and whether it or the class action should be tasked with obtaining it. The ASIC interviewees, while acknowledging that compensation could be pursued by ASIC in appropriate situations, stated that it was not ASIC's main objective.[152] This view is borne out by the case studies with ASIC only seeking compensation in relation to Multiplex and by ASIC's post-2017 enforcement approach. Much may turn on whether obtaining compensation for harmed shareholders is seen as being in the public interest, or as the pursuit of a private interest. ASIC has previously indicated that it 'will ordinarily only take action to recover damages … on a person's behalf if this would be in the public interest, beyond the interests of the affected consumers'.[153] However, once compensation is seen as not just a desirable objective for the shareholders who have suffered loss, but as also achieving indirect deterrence, ASIC may need to reconsider what the public interest requires. In doing so, ASIC should weigh up what is the most cost-effective manner in which to

[151] As explained in ch 2, ASIC is able to pursue a compensation order where there is a contravention of a financial services civil penalty provision or can rely on the 'other orders' catch-all provision as both apply to the continuous disclosure regime. See Corporations Act 2001 (Cth), ss 1317HA(1), 1317J, 1325. ASIC may also bring an action in the name of a person to recover damages for fraud, negligence, default, breach of duty or other misconduct where that person consents. See Australian Securities and Investments Commission Act 2001 (Cth), s 50.

[152] Interview ASIC Executive Telstra/Multiplex; Interview ASIC Executive Centro, 3; Interview ASIC Executive Leighton, 3.

[153] ASIC, 'Information Sheet 151 – ASIC's approach to enforcement' (September 2013) 6. See ch 2, section IV.C.iv.

achieve compensation. If ASIC has sufficient resources to pursue compensation for shareholders but with lower transaction costs than a class action, that should be part of the coordination considerations.[154]

It may be said that such an approach will remove the incentives for class actions, with adverse effects on class action lawyers and litigation funders. Such a criticism is accepted. However, the legislative provisions for compensation were never designed to achieve remuneration for lawyers and funders: they were designed to compensate those who suffered loss due to contraventions of the legislation. If ASIC can deliver adequate compensation with lower transaction costs, it should. Equally, if the class action is better placed to achieve compensation and incidental deterrence, through providing additional regulatory resources and expertise, then ASIC should facilitate its use.

However, under the gatekeeper model, even if ASIC is pursuing compensation rather than permitting a class action by private parties, there may still be a role for class action lawyers. A further suggestion from the academy aimed directly at securities enforcement is for the regulator to retain class action lawyers to bring suit using a contingency fee – converting the 'pirate' to a 'privateer' who is retained and accountable to the public regulator.[155] The approach allows the regulator to obtain greater resources, access lawyers with a specialised skill set, share the risk of the litigation and introduce greater accountability for class action lawyers.[156] In Australia, ASIC has previously used private law firms to bring continuous disclosure civil penalty proceedings. In the James Hardie case ASIC retained the private law firm Clayton Utz, and in the Fortescue case ASIC retained the private law firm Mallesons Stephen Jaques, now King & Wood Mallesons.[157] However, neither firm were class action plaintiff lawyers or paid on a contingency fee basis (which was illegal in Australia). ASIC obtained additional skills but not greater resources or risk-sharing.

Additional steps could be taken to address resourcing and risk-sharing. ASIC could be prepared to pay part of the lawyers' fees as the case progressed, with the remaining fees payable upon a successful outcome – an approach that litigation funders have previously used.[158] ASIC may also wish to consider whether it should be able to recover for funding any litigation or redress negotiation, albeit at a much lower level than commercial litigation funders, to address resourcing. Alternatively, ASIC may bring proceedings in the State of Victoria and endorse the lawyers seeking group costs orders.[159] However, all of these measures may be unnecessary under the industry funding model that applies to ASIC where it can recoup enforcement expenses from industry.[160] Further, the suggested measures may increase the transaction costs for seeking

[154] See Steven Malech and Robert Koosa, 'Government Action and the Superiority Requirement: A Potential Bar to Private Class Actions' (2005) 18 *Georgetown Journal of Legal Ethics* 1419; Zimmerman (n 131) 402 (US class actions may be denied certification where government proceedings are pursuing the same claims because the class action is not 'superior' as required by Federal Rules of Civil Procedure r 23(b)(3) because the government suit is a more economical and manageable method of obtaining relief).

[155] Coffee (n 130) 175, 227, 234; John Coffee, *Corporate Crime and Punishment: The Crisis of Underenforcement* (Berrett-Koehler Publishers, 2020) 100–07. The concept draws on US state Attorney-Generals employing private lawyers to bring tobacco litigation and the use by the Federal Deposit Insurance Corporation, Federal Housing Finance Agency and National Credit Union Administration of private attorneys.

[156] Coffee (n 130) 180–83.

[157] See *Australian Securities and Investments Commission v Macdonald (No 11)* [2009] NSWSC 287; *Australian Securities & Investments Commission v Fortescue Metals Group Ltd [No 5]* [2009] FCA 1586. Both cases are referred to in ch 2, section IV.C. In Australia all parties are also able to obtain access to expertise through the independent bar which provides advocacy and advice.

[158] Michael Legg, 'The pros and cons of different types of fee arrangements' (2021) 74 *Law Society Journal* 82, 83.

[159] See ch 7, section III.D.

[160] See ch 7, section II.B.

compensation and therefore undermine the reason for ASIC taking on the compensation role in the first place.

Under the gatekeeper model ASIC needs to employ a combination of enforcement tools, including potentially permitting a class action, to achieve both deterrence and compensation. This requires ASIC to ensure a clear-eyed approach to its own strengths and weaknesses, most importantly, where it has expertise and where it needs to acquire it. From a regulatory pluralism perspective, ASIC's role includes facilitating the class action where needed, including to expand regulatory resources, share the regulatory burden and coordinate the use of enforcement tools to achieve the desired outcome.[161]

The main risk is that ASIC's gatekeeper role may see the loss of additional and different viewpoints as to what the public interest requires in relation to how enforcement should be configured. Multiple viewpoints can still be expressed in that approval for a class action can be sought from ASIC. The seeking of approval allows for the voicing of perspectives on what the public interest requires. An applicant would not just ask for approval but demonstrate why the class action needed to be commenced. The application and approval process may also provide for even more perspectives on what is desirable in the public interest, including from the identified defendants and possibly from interest groups. The public interest may also receive greater consideration and articulation through requiring ASIC to provide reasons. However, the process must not become unwieldy and excessively costly. Ultimately, if ASIC does not grant approval then the competing views supporting a class action are not translated into action.

VII. Conclusion

This text has examined the coexistence of public and private enforcement in the form of ASIC and the continuous disclosure class action. Moreover, the text has explained the ramifications of this overlap for deterrence, compensation and regulatory process values. The effect of this examination is that ASIC and the class action may help, but also hinder each other. Having identified that ASIC and the class action may negatively impact each other, and the achievement of desirable regulatory values, this chapter examined a range of coordination mechanisms from other regulatory regimes to design strategies for coordination.

This chapter put forward two potential coordination strategies: the information-sharing approach and the 'regulator as gatekeeper' approach.

The information-sharing approach requires a person who is proposing to commence a class action to notify ASIC of that intention and to provide specified information. ASIC is then able to use that information to assist in determining the enforcement action it will take. ASIC can take account of the class action in relation to the availability of compensation and the associated indirect deterrence that may follow. This approach does not restrict the commencement of a class action or subject it to conditions so that this strategy does not address the detrimental effects on the regulatory process, such as the class action's impact on regulatory discretion.

The gatekeeper approach provides ASIC with the authority to determine if a class action may be commenced. ASIC performs the role of enforcement coordinator and needs to determine the combination of enforcement tools that should be employed, including potentially permitting a

[161] Neil Gunningham and Darren Sinclair, 'Smart Regulation' in Peter Drahos (ed), *Regulatory Theory: Foundations and Applications* (ANU Press, 2017) 139.

class action, to achieve both deterrence and compensation. This approach addresses the negative impacts of the class action on the regulatory process. However, such an approach creates a risk that additional and different viewpoints as to what the public interest requires in relation to how enforcement should be configured may be lost.

Each approach brings with it advantages and disadvantages that may be ameliorated or accentuated depending on their actual implementation.

Appendix 1

I. Interview Questions for ASIC

(1) What enforcement action was taken?
(2) Why was that enforcement action taken? What was the goal of the enforcement action?
(3) Did the goal include deterrence? Why/why not?
(4) Who was to be deterred? [general/specific, company/individuals]
(5) How was deterrence to operate in this instance? [monetary/non-monetary (reputation)]
(6) Did the goal include compensation? Why/why not?
(7) Was the goal achieved? Was the outcome viewed as a success by ASIC?
(8) What was the cost of the enforcement action to ASIC?
(9) How much time elapsed from contravention to sanction?
(10) Could ASIC have used its powers/resources more effectively?
(11) In this instance, what role did the class action, or prospect of a class action, play in ASIC's thinking/approach?
(12) More generally, does ASIC consider how a class action may impact on ASIC's approach to enforcement?
(13) If ASIC knew that a class action would be undertaken would that have changed ASIC's enforcement approach?
(14) Is ASIC able to assist in the bringing of a class action or more efficient conduct of the class action?
(15) Do class actions assist or hinder ASIC in the achievement of its goals?
    (a) Better deterrence or over-deterrence?
    (b) Compensation?
    (c) More resources for enforcement?
    (d) Detection of misconduct more likely?
    (e) More or less cooperation from regulated entities?
    (f) Greater availability of expertise/knowledge?
    (g) Promote the public interest?
    (h) Accountability for approach/results?

II. Interview Questions for Class Action Applicants, Litigation Funders and their Lawyers

(1) Why was the class action commenced? What was the goal?
(2) Did the goal include deterrence? Why/why not?
(3) Who was to be deterred? [general/specific, company/individuals]
(4) How was deterrence to operate in this instance? [monetary/non-monetary (reputation)]

(5) Did goal include compensation? Why/why not?
(6) Was the goal achieved? Was the outcome viewed as a success? What is the criteria for success? (quantum of losses suffered by group members)
(7) What was the cost of the class action?
(8) How much time elapsed from contravention to settlement?
(9) In this instance, what role did ASIC's enforcement approach play in your thinking/approach?
(10) More generally, do you consider how ASIC's approach to enforcement may impact the need for a class action?
(11) If ASIC took no action would that have changed your decision to bring a class action?
(12) Is ASIC able to assist in the bringing of a class action or more efficient conduct of the class action?
(13) Do class actions assist or hinder ASIC in the achievement of its goals?
    (a) Better deterrence or over-deterrence?
    (b) Compensation?
    (c) More resources for enforcement?
    (d) Detection of misconduct more likely?
    (e) More or less cooperation from regulated entities?
    (f) Greater availability of expertise/knowledge?
    (g) Promote the public interest?
    (h) Accountability for approach/results?

III. Interview Questions for Regulated Entity/Class Action Respondents' Directors/Officers and their Lawyers

(1) What were the ramifications of ASIC's enforcement action?
(2) Impact on:
    (a) Governance practices (ie internal procedures/compliance mechanisms)?
    (b) Going concern (solvency of corporation)?
    (c) Share price?
    (d) Corporate reputation?
    (e) Individual directors/officers?
    (f) Costs? Legal fees, diversion of management (ability to quantify), insurance.

(3) What were the ramifications of the class action?
(4) Impact on:
    (a) Governance practices (ie internal procedures/compliance mechanisms)?
    (b) Going concern (solvency of corporation)?
    (c) Share price?
    (d) Corporate reputation?
    (e) Individual directors/officers?
    (f) Costs? Legal fees, diversion of management(ability to quantify), insurance.

(5) How did/does the existence of both ASIC enforcement powers and class actions impact decision-making when a potential contravention was/is identified?

IV. Summary of Interviews

Case study	ASIC	Company	Class action lawyer/funder
Telstra	1* (19 April 2016)	3 Former senior executive interviewed (3 December 2015) Two external lawyers interviewed (9 February 2016)+	2 Two class action lawyers interviewed (7 December 2015) No funder in class action
Multiplex	1* (19 April 2016)	3 External lawyer interviewed (22 December 2015) Two external lawyers interviewed (9 February 2016)+ No response from former general counsel	1 Class action lawyer (18 February 2016) Funder declined
Centro	1 (31 March 2016)	5 Former General Counsel interviewed (3 December 2015) Two external lawyers interviewed (9 February 2016)+ Two other external lawyers interviewed (4 December 2015)	2 Funder interviewed (10 December 2015) Class action lawyer interviewed (19 February 2016).
Leightons	1 (25 May 2016)	0 External lawyer and inhouse counsel declined.	1 Class action lawyer interviewed (4 April 2016) Funder declined

* the former ASIC officer interviewed for these two case studies is the same person.
+ the external lawyers interviewed for these three case studies are the same persons.

V. Interviews with Short Title

Summary of interview with ASIC senior executive involved in the Telstra and Multiplex enforcement actions (19 April 2016) ('Interview ASIC Executive Telstra/Multiplex').

Summary of interview with two participants in the Telstra class action, Multiplex class action and Centro class action (9 February 2016) ('Interview Lawyer Participants Telstra/Multiplex/Centro').

Transcript of interview with a solicitor for the applicant in Leighton class action (4 April 2016) ('Interview Applicant's solicitor Leighton').

Transcript of interview with ASIC senior executive involved in the Leighton enforcement action (25 May 2016) ('Interview ASIC Executive Leighton').

Transcript of interview with former ASIC senior executive involved in Centro civil penalty proceedings (31 March 2016) ('Interview ASIC Executive Centro').

Transcript of interview with former Centro senior executive (3 December 2015) ('Interview Centro Executive').

Transcript of interview with former Telstra senior executive (3 December 2015) ('Interview Telstra Executive').

Transcript of interview with litigation funder involved in Centro class action (10 December 2015) ('Interview Centro funder').

Transcript of interview with participants in Centro class action (4 December 2015) ('Interview Lawyer Participants Centro').

Transcript of interview with solicitor for Multiplex (22 December 2015) ('Interview Multiplex solicitor').

Transcript of interview with solicitor for the applicant in Centro class action (19 February 2016) ('Interview Applicant's solicitor Centro').

Transcript of interview with solicitor for the applicant in Multiplex class action (18 February 2016) ('Interview Applicants' solicitors Multiplex').

Transcript of interview with solicitors for the applicant in Telstra class action (7 December 2015) ('Interview Applicant's solicitors Telstra').

Appendix 2

Table 1 Continuous disclosure infringement notices from 1 July 2004 to 30 June 2021

No	Date of media release	Date of issue of infringement notice by ASIC	Entity	No of infringement notices	Total penalty	Media release
1.	1 August 2005	14 June 2005	Solbec Pharmaceuticals Limited	1	$33,000	05-223
2.	16 February 2006	20 December 2005	QRSciences Holdings Limited	1	$33,000	06-042
3.	21 April 2006	–	SDI ltd	1	$33,000	06-124
4.	15 May 2006	18 April 2006	Avastra Limited	1	$33,000	06-156
5.	16 July 2006	21 June 2006	Astron Limited	1	$66,000	06-242
6.	8 December 2006	13 November 2006	Avantogen Limited	1	$33,000	06-428
7.	20 March 2007	21 February 2007	Promina Group Limited	1	$100,000	07-69
8.	1 August 2007	18 June 2007	Raw Capital Partners Limited	1	$33,000	07-207
9.	12 March 2008	12 February 2008	Centrex Metals Limited	1	$33,000	08-50
10.	5 June 2008	10 April 2008	Rio Tinto Limited	1	$100,000	08-117
11.	29 April 2008	16 April 2008	Sub-Sahara Resources NL	1	$33,000	08-87
12.	14 October 2009	–	Commonwealth Bank of Australia	1	$100,000	09-199MR
13.	22 September 2010	19 August 2010	Citigold Corporation	1	$33,000	10-198AD
14.	1 December 2010	30 November 2010	Nufarm Ltd	1	$66,000 and ASIC accepted an enforceable undertaking	10-255AD

(continued)

Table 1 ***(Continued)***

No	Date of media release	Date of issue of infringement notice by ASIC	Entity	No of infringement notices	Total penalty	Media release
15.	12 August 2011	27 July 2011	Nexbis Limited	1	$33,000	11-168AD
16.	8 March 2012	–	BC Iron Limited	1	$66,000	12-43AD
17.	8 March 2012	–	BioProspect Limited	1	$33,000	12-42AD
18.	18 March 2012	–	Leighton Holdings	3	$300,000 and ASIC accepted enforceable undertaking	12-53MR
19.	15 June 2012	–	Navigator Resources Limited	1	$33,000	12-130MR
20.	19 December 2012	–	Northern Iron Limited	1	$66,000	12-324MR
21.	20 September 2013	12 August 2013	ZYL Limited	2	$66,000	13-262MR
22.	14 October 2013	19 September 2013	Central Asia Resource Limited	1	$33,000	13-274MR
23.	3 December 2013	–	Stone Resources Australia Limited	1	$33,000	13-323MR
24.	10 February 2014	–	Diploma Group Limited	1	$33,000	14-025MR
25.	13 June 2014		Reward Minerals Ltd	1	$33,000	14-126MR
26.	10 June 2015		Rhinomed Limited	1	$33,000	15-144MR
27.	3 July 2015	–	Coal Fe Resources Ltd	1	$33,000	15-171MR
28.	27 July 2015	–	Waterberg Coal Company Limited and 45.88% controlled entity Firestone Energy Limited	2	$33,000 each	15-191MR
29.	18 December 2015		Living Cell Technologies Limited	1	$33,000	15-402MR

(continued)

Table 1 ***(Continued)***

No	Date of media release	Date of issue of infringement notice by ASIC	Entity	No of infringement notices	Total penalty	Media release
30.	25 January 2016	18 December 2015	ZhongHuanYun Holdings Group	1	$33,000	16-013MR
31.	25 January 2016	18 December 2015	Australia Samly Holdings Limited	1	$33,000	16-012MR
32.	10 June 2016	–	Rhinomed Limited	1	$33,000	16-190MR
33.	20 September 2016	23 August 2016	Sanhe Building Materials Technology Company Limited	1	$33,000	16-319MR
34.	20 September 2017	–	Sirtex Medical Limited	1	$100,000	17-320MR
35.	11 October 2017	–	Bellamy's Australia Limited	1	$66,000	17-342MR
36.	20 October 2017	–	Adairs Limited	1	$66,000	17-352MR
37.	11 December 2017		Murray River Organics Group Limited	1	$33,000	17-427MR
38.	7 August 2018		Gold Mountain Limited	1	$33,000	18-228MR
39.	12 February 2019		Byte Power Group Limited	1	$33,000	19-026MR
40.	18 May 2021		Regional Express Holdings Limited	1	$66,000	21-105MR

Table 2 Continuous disclosure enforceable undertakings – 1998 to 30 June 2021

Entity subject to enforceable undertaking and date	Summary of undertakings
ASIC, Enforceable Undertaking: Crown Casino Ltd, Document No 008 547 289 (11 September 1998)	Crown to provide quarterly financial reports to the ASX for three years. Crown to adopt written compliance programmes which including training directors/senior officers in continuous disclosure obligations, create a compliance officer position, cause the external auditor to review the compliance system and procedures for information to be internally reported for consideration for compliance with continuous disclosure obligations. Crown to make files and documents available to ASIC for inspection upon request.

(continued)

Table 2 ***(Continued)***

Entity subject to enforceable undertaking and date	Summary of undertakings
ASIC, Enforceable Undertaking: Pahth Telecommunication Ltd, Document No 008 547 505 (2 February 2001)	Pahth to review corporate governance practices including providing for monthly meetings of directors and consideration of compliance with continuous disclosure obligations. Pahth to adopt written compliance programs which including training directors/senior officers in continuous disclosure obligations, create a compliance officer position, cause the external auditor to review the compliance system and procedures for information to be internally reported for consideration for compliance with continuous disclosure obligations. Pahth to provide a copy to ASIC.
ASIC, Enforceable Undertaking: Plexus International Ltd, Document No 008 547 509 (30 March 2001)	Plexus to review corporate governance practices including providing for monthly meetings of directors and consideration of compliance with continuous disclosure obligations. Plexus to adopt written compliance programmes which including training directors/senior officers in continuous disclosure obligations, create a compliance officer position, cause the external auditor to review the compliance system and procedures for information to be internally reported for consideration for compliance with continuous disclosure obligations. Plexus to provide a copy to ASIC.
ASIC, Enforceable Undertaking: SMEC Holdings Ltd, Document No 008 547 519 (4 June 2001)	SMEC to adopt written compliance programmes which including training directors/senior officers in continuous disclosure obligations and procedures for information to be internally reported for consideration for compliance with continuous disclosure obligations.
ASIC, Enforceable Undertaking: Uecomm Ltd, Document No 017 029 061 (17 October 2002)	External consultant to review, recommend amendments to, and report on implementation of recommendations to continuous disclosure policies and procedures. Uecomm to adopt written compliance programmes which including training senior officers in continuous disclosure obligations and procedures for information to be internally reported for consideration for compliance with continuous disclosure obligations. Uecomm to provide a copy to ASIC. Uecomm unable to rely on Corporations Act 2001 (Cth) provision reducing disclosure obligations in a prospectus for 12 months.
ASIC, Enforceable Undertaking: Multiplex Ltd, Document No 017 029 205 (20 December 2006)	Multiplex to procure early payment of $50 million indemnity from Roberts family who had originally established company. Multiplex to use best efforts to procure within 12 months a majority of independent directors on the board. Multiplex to establish a $32 million fund to compensate stapled security holders and provide report from third party as to the amount claimed. External consultant to review, recommend amendments to, and report on implementation of recommendations to continuous disclosure policies and procedures. Multiplex unable to rely on Corporations Act 2001 (Cth) provision reducing disclosure obligations in a prospectus until external consultant reviews and reports are completed.

(continued)

Table 2 ***(Continued)***

Entity subject to enforceable undertaking and date	Summary of undertakings
ASIC, Enforceable Undertaking: TZ Limited, Document No 017029221 (3 July 2008)	External consultant to review, recommend amendments to, and report on implementation of recommendations to continuous disclosure policies and procedures.
ASIC, Enforceable Undertaking: Nufarm Ltd, Document No 026 113 023 (1 December 2010)	External consultant to review, recommend amendments to, and report on implementation of recommendations to financial reporting and continuous disclosure systems. Nufarm to conduct training on continuous disclosure obligations. Nufarm unable to rely on various Corporations Act 2001 (Cth) provisions or ASIC class orders reducing or removing disclosure obligations in relation to the offer or issue of securities until undertakings complied with and nine months has elapsed since the date of the enforceable undertaking. Nufarm also subject to an infringement notice.
ASIC, Enforceable Undertaking: Leighton Holdings, Document No 027 714 755 (16 March 2012)	External consultant to review, recommend amendments to, and report on implementation of recommendations to continuous disclosure policies and procedures. External consultant to carry out annual review of continuous disclosure policies and procedures for three years. Leighton Holding also subject to infringement notices.
ASIC, Enforceable Undertaking: NuSep Holdings Ltd, Document No 029169364 (18 December 2014).	NuSep to continue procedures being implemented – changing composition of board and appointing a company secretary with relevant qualifications; adopting procedures to ensure accurate minutes of meetings; adopting effective record-keeping practices Appointment of an independent compliance expert nominated by ASIC within 30 days of the undertaking, who in relation to continuous disclosure will be required to identify any deficiencies in NuSep's disclosure systems and recommend improvements which are consistent with industry best practice for a company of NuSep's size and kind that are reasonably required to ensure that they meet the requirements of the continuous disclosure obligations. A timelines is provided for the independent compliance expert to commence its review and to report to the board and to ASIC. Recommendations in the report are to be implemented within 270 days of the undertaking. Further reviews are to be undertaken for the next two years. NuSep to ensure that its compliance procedures for continuous disclosure include procedures to ensure that each NuSep officer is made aware on an ongoing basis of NuSep's continuous disclosure obligations, to require the reporting of material information to the NuSep officer responsible for communicating with the ASX, to ensure the accuracy of information released to the market, and maintenance of records of all disclosure matters. (Note the enforceable undertaking also addressed other corporate governance issues arising from alleged contraventions of other provisions in the Corporations Act 2001 (Cth).)

(continued)

Table 2 *(Continued)*

Entity subject to enforceable undertaking and date	Summary of undertakings
ASIC, Enforceable Undertaking: Rhinomed Ltd, Document No 029622129 (9 June 2016, varied on 23 December 2016)	Rhinomed to appoint an independent expert from a list of three provided by ASIC that meet certain criteria. The independent expert is to review Rhinomed's practices, policies, procedures and resources for dealing with its continuous disclosure obligations, identify any deficiencies and recommend amendments which are consistent with industry best practice for a company of Rhinomed's size and kind that are reasonably required to ensure that they meet the requirements of the continuous disclosure obligations. A timeline is provided for the independent expert to commence its review and to report to the board and to ASIC. A further timeline is provided for Rhinomed to implement the recommendations of the independent expert. Rhinomed to conduct training on continuous disclosure obligations. Rhinomed unable to rely on Corporations Act 2001 (Cth) provision reducing disclosure obligations in a prospectus until independent expert has reported to ASIC and provided an opinion that its recommendations have been implemented.

Note: ASIC, Enforceable Undertaking: Nomura International Plc, Document No 008 547 314 (16 February 1999) is often listed as relating to continuous disclosure. However, on the face of the enforceable undertaking, Nomura was dealing with securities on the ASX in relation to closing out its arbitrage position and no reference is made to continuous disclosure.

Table 3 Continuous disclosure class actions – 2002 to 30 June 2021

	Company	Parties	Commenced	Litigation funding	Settlement details
1	*Harris Scarfe Holdings Ltd* *(ABN 25 009 476 073)*	Directors	June 2002	No	Settled for \$3 million in October 2006. *Guglielmin v Trescowthick (No 5)* [2006] FCA 1385 (12 October 2006)
2	*Concept Sports* *(ABN 11 005 973 133)*	Company, directors in 2004, auditor	21 December 2004	No	The terms of the settlement are confidential but believed to have been for \$3m.
3	*Aristocrat Leisure Ltd* *(ABN 44 002 818 368)*	Company	November 2003	Yes	Settled for \$144.5 million (including costs) settlement on 28 August 2008. *Dorajay Pty Ltd v Aristocrat Leisure Ltd* [2009] FCA 19 (21 January 2009)
4	*Telstra Corporation Ltd* *(ABN 33 051 775 556)*	Company	20 January 2006	No	Settled December 2007 for \$5 million. *Taylor v Telstra Corp Ltd* [2007] FCA 2008 (13 December 2007)

(continued)

Table 3 ***(Continued)***

	Company	Parties	Commenced	Litigation funding	Settlement details
5	*Downer EDI Ltd* *(ABN 97 003 872 848)*	Company	Not commenced	Yes	Confidential settlement in October 2008 believed to be $20 million.
6	*Multiplex Ltd* *(ABN 96 008 687 063)*	Company	2006	Yes	Settled for $110 million (including costs), in July 2010. *P Dawson Nominees Pty Ltd v Brookfield Multiplex Limited (No 4)* [2010] FCA 1029 (21 September 2010)
7	*AWB Ltd* *(ABN 99 081 890 459)*	Company	17 April 2007	Yes	Settled for $39.5 million (including costs) in April 2010. No settlement approval judgment published
8	*Village Life (Fig-tree Developments)* *(ABN 47 081 797 033)*	Company Directors	May 2007	Yes	Settlement of $3 million approved May 2009. *Vernon v Village Life Ltd* [2009] FCA 516 (12 May 2009)
9	*GPT Group Pty Ltd (ABN 88 073 246 009)*		27 February 2008	Yes	Settled in May 2013 for $75 million (including costs) and approved in June and November 2013 after further inquiry into legal costs. *Modtech Engineering Pty Ltd v GPT Management Holdings Limited* [2013] FCA 626 (21 June 2013) *Modtech Engineering Pty Ltd v GPT Management Holdings Ltd (No 2)* [2013] FCA 1163 (7 November 2013)
10	*Centro Properties Ltd (ACN 078 590 682)* *Centro Retail Australia Ltd (ACN 149 781 322)* *Centro MCS Manager Ltd (ACN 054 494 307* *Centro MCS Manager Ltd (ACN 051 908 984)* *('Centro Entities')*	Company Responsible entity Directors Auditor	May 2008	Yes	Settlement in June 2012 for three class actions for $200 million (including costs). *Kirby v Centro Properties Ltd (No 6)* [2012] FCA 650 (19 June 2012)

(continued)

Table 3 ***(Continued)***

	Company	Parties	Commenced	Litigation funding	Settlement details
11	*Credit Corp Group Ltd* *(ABN 33 092 697 151)*	Company	23 December 2008	Yes	Conditional settlement 12 December 2011. Settlement approved 13 March 2012. Settlement scheme $6.5 million (including costs). *Clime Capital Ltd v Credit Corp Group Ltd (No 3)* [2012] FCA 218 (13 March 2012)
12	*Oxiana Limited* *(ABN 40 005 482 824)* *and successor entity OZ Minerals Limited* *(ABN 40 005 482 824)*	Company	24 August 2010 in NSWSC Transferred to FCA	Yes	The Federal Court approved settlement on 1 July 2011 for the Hobbs Anderson proceedings of $39 million (including costs). The Court also approved the Scott and Taws proceeding settlement for $21 million (including costs) on 1 July 2011. *Hobbs Anderson Investments Pty Ltd v Oz Minerals Ltd* [2011] FCA 801 (1 July 2011)
13	*Sigma Pharmaceuticals Ltd* *(ABN 15 088 417 403)*	Company	29 October 2010	Yes	Settled for $57.5 million (including costs). *Earglow Pty Ltd v Sigma Pharmaceuticals Limited* [2012] FCA 1496 (19 December 2012)
14	*National Australia Bank Ltd* *(ABN 12 004 044 937)*	Company	November 2010	Yes	Settlement of $115 million (including costs) agreed November 2012 and approved 19 December 2012. *Pathway Investments Pty Ltd v National Australia Bank Limited (No. 3)* [2012] VSC 625 (19 December 2012)
15	*Trans Pacific Industries Group Pty Ltd* *(ABN 82 001 774 438)*	Company	Not commenced	Yes	Settlement 10 April 2012. Settlement amount $35 million.
16	*Gunns Ltd* *(ACN 009 478 148)*	Company	20 April 2011	Yes	Gunns went into voluntary administration in September 2012.
		Directors	22 December 2015	Yes	Second class action settled 21 March 2016 for confidential amount. *Foley v Gay* [2016] FCA 273 (21 March 2016)

(continued)

Table 3 ***(Continued)***

	Company	Parties	Commenced	Litigation funding	Settlement details
17	*Nufarm Limited* *(ABN 37 091 323 312)*	Company	12 August 2011	Yes	Two class actions consolidated. Settlement of $43.5 million (including costs) in principle August 2012. Settlement approved 28 November 2012. *Hadchiti v Nufarm Limited* [2012] FCA 1524 (28 November 2012)
18	*Arasor International Ltd*	Directors Auditors	11 October 2012	Yes	Class action settled in July 2017 for $19.25 million (including costs) *Caason Investments Pty Limited v Cao (No 2)* [2018] FCA 527 (16 April 2018) *Caason Investments Pty Ltd v International Litigation Partners No 3 Ltd* [2018] FCAFC 176 (18 June 2018)
19	*Allco Finance Group Ltd*	Company Auditor Executive chairman	8 August 2013	Yes	Class action settled in November 2016 for $40 million (including costs) *Blairgowrie Trading Ltd v Allco Finance Group Ltd (Receivers & Managers Appointed) (In Liq) (No 3)* [2017] FCA 330 (31 March 2017)
20	*Leighton Holdings Ltd*	Company	30 October 2013	Yes	Class action settled for $69.45 million (including costs). *Inabu Pty Ltd v Leighton Holdings Ltd* [2014] FCA 622 (6 June 2014) *Inabu Pty Ltd v Leighton Holdings Ltd (No 2)* [2014] FCA 911 (25 August 2014)
21	*Treasury Wine Estates Limited*	Company	4 November 2013 (Vic) stayed 2 July 2014 (Fed Ct)	Yes	Class action settled in August 2017 for $49 million. No settlement approval judgment published. orders dated 10 November 2017.
22	*Worley Parsons Limited*	Company	18 December 2013 (Vic) – stayed 27 October 2015 (Fed Ct)	Yes	Trial – claim unsuccessful

(continued)

Table 3 ***(Continued)***

	Company	Parties	Commenced	Litigation funding	Settlement details
23	*Oz Minerals Limited*	Company	24 February 2014	Yes	Class action settled in June 2016 for $32.5 million (including costs) *Mitic v OZ Minerals Limited (No 2)* [2017] FCA 409 (21 April 2017)
24	*Newcrest Mining*	Company	21 July 2014	Yes	Class action settled for $36 million (including costs) *Earglow Pty Ltd v Newcrest Mining Limited* [2016] FCA 1433 (28 November 2016)
25	*Forge Group Limited*	Company Directors	23 December 2014	Yes	Settled in July 2019 for $16.5 million (including costs) *Rushleigh Services Pty Ltd v Forge Group Limited (in liquidation) (Receivers and Managers appointed)* [2019] FCA 2113 (9 December 2019)
26	*Billabong International Limited*	Company	24 March 2015	Yes	Class action settled for $45 million (including costs) *Newstart 123 Pty Ltd v Billabong International Ltd* [2016] FCA 1194 (7 October 2016)
27	*Vocation Limited*	Company Auditor Directors Law firm	26 February 2015 (Vic) 20 August 2015	Yes	Two class actions consolidated. Class action settled on 30 November 2020. The respondents and cross-respondents will pay a total of $50 million, inclusive of interest and costs *Whittenbury v Vocation Limited (in liquidation)* [2021] FCA 829 (23 July 2021)
28	*QBE Insurance Group Limited*	Company	9 September 2015	Yes	Class action settled in December 2017 for $132.5 million (including costs) *Money Max Int Pty Ltd (Trustee) v QBE Insurance Group Limited* [2018] FCA 1030 (9 July 2018)
29	*Macmahon Holdings Limited*	Company	4 November 2015	Yes	Settlement of $6.7m (including costs) *Hopkins as Trustee of David Hopkins Super Fund v Macmahon Holdings Ltd* [2018] FCA 2061 (12 December 2018)

(continued)

Table 3 ***(Continued)***

	Company	Parties	Commenced	Litigation funding	Settlement details
30	*Slater & Gordon*	Company Auditors Law firm	12 October 2016 20 June 2017 31 July 2018 13 September 2019	Yes	Claim against company settled in July 2017 for $36.5m. Company subject to schemes of arrangement *Hall v Slater and Gordon Ltd* [2018] FCA 2071 (21 December 2018)
31	*CIMIC Group Limited*	Company	23 November 2016	Yes	Settled in December 2019 for $32.4 million (including costs) *Inabu Pty Ltd as trustee for the Alidas Superannuation Fund v CIMIC Group Ltd* [2020] FCA 510 (28 April 2020)
32	*Ashley Services Group Limited*	Company Directors Participants involved in preparation of prospectus	1 December 2016	Yes	Settled in April 2019 for $14.6 million (including costs) *Bradgate (Trustee) v Ashley Services Group Limited (No 2)* [2019] FCA 1210 (13 June 2019)
33	*Myer*	Company	25 March 2015 (S Ct Vic) stayed 29 December 2016 (Fed Ct)	No	Trial with contraventions found but no loss. Settled on basis of each party to pays its own costs.
34	*Sirtex Medical Limited*	Company	9 February 2017 15 December 2017	Yes	Two class actions consolidated. Settled in June 2019 for $40 million (including costs) *Kuterba v Sirtex Medical Limited (No 3)* [2019] FCA 1374 (23 August 2019)
35	*Bellamy's Australia Limited*	Company	23 February 2017 7 March 2017	Yes	Two class actions (one open and one closed) case managed together. Settled in November 2019 for $49.7 million (including costs) *McKay Super Solutions Pty Ltd (Trustee) v Bellamy's Australia Ltd (No 3)* [2020] FCA 461 (13 March 2020)

(continued)

Table 3 *(Continued)*

	Company	Parties	Commenced	Litigation funding	Settlement details
36	*Murray Goulburn Co-operative Co Limited*	Company, responsible entity and directors.	9 May 2017 (commenced May 2016 in S Ct Vic and transferred) 16 August 2018		Two class actions. Webster – settled in April 2019 for $37.5 million (including costs) Endeavour River – settled in June 2019 for $42 million (including costs) *Webster (Trustee) v Murray Goulburn Co-Operative Co. Limited (No 4)* [2020] FCA 1053 (9 April 2020) *Endeavour River Pty Ltd v MG Responsible Entity Limited (No 2)* [2020] FCA 968 (9 July 2020)
37	*Spotless Group Holdings Limited*	Company	25 May 2017	Yes	Settled in May 2020 for $95 million (including costs) *Court v Spotless Group Holdings Limited* [2020] FCA 1730 (9 September 2020)
38	*Surfstitch Group Limited*	Company Director	22 May 2017 (commenced in S Ct Qld and transferred) 28 June 2017 (S Ct NSW)	Yes	Two class actions settled in September 2019 for $8.31 million and Convertible Notes, estimated to have a value of between $0 and approximately $3.24 million. Company placed in administration. *TW McConnell Pty Ltd as trustee for the McConnell Superannuation Fund v SurfStitch Group Ltd (administrators appointed) (No 4); Nakali Pty Ltd v SurfStitch Group Ltd* [2021] NSWSC 121 (19 February 2021)
39	*Quintis Ltd*	Company	7 September 2017 9 November 2017 23 May 2018	Yes	Three class actions commenced but two stayed. Application to approve a settlement in the matter was adjourned by Lee J on 3 July 2020 due to uncertainty as to the extent of insurance coverage

(continued)

Table 3 ***(Continued)***

	Company	Parties	Commenced	Litigation funding	Settlement details
40	*DSHE Holdings Ltd*	Company Directors Underwriters Insurers	28 September 2017 16 February 2018	Yes	Three class actions settled in December 2020 for $25 million. *Findlay v DSHE Holdings Ltd; Mastoris v DSHE Holdings Ltd; Mastoris v Allianz Australia Insurance Ltd* [2021] NSWSC 249 (17 March 2021)
41	*Commonwealth Bank of Australia*	Company	9 October 2017 29 June 2018	Yes	Two class actions (one open and one closed) case managed together ongoing.
42	*Crown Resorts Limited*	Company	4 December 2017	Yes	Ongoing
43	*UGL*	Company	18 December 2017	Yes	Settled in August 2019 for $18 million. *Clime Capital Limited v UGL Pty Limited* [2020] FCA 66 (5 February 2020)
44	*GetSwift Ltd*	Company Director	20 February 2018, 26 March 2018, 13 April 2018		Three class actions commenced but two stayed. Settlement agreed on 13 July 2021 involving a modest cash contribution and then further sums as a capped percentage of any capital raisings (or a capped percentage of company revenue as a backstop if no or limited funds are raised) over a 3-year period. Subject to court approval
45	*Iluka Resources Ltd*	Company	11 April 2018	Yes	Ongoing
46	*AMP Limited*	Company	9 May 2018 (2) 25 May 2018 5 October 2018 (2)	No for class action not stayed	Five competing NSW Supreme Court shareholder class actions after four class actions were transferred from the Federal Court to the NSW Supreme Court. All stayed except one. Ongoing
47	*BHP*	Company	31 May 2018 24 September 2018		Two class actions commenced. Initially consolidated into one proceeding but subsequently continued separately. Another class action stayed. Ongoing

(continued)

Table 3 ***(Continued)***

	Company	Parties	Commenced	Litigation funding	Settlement details
48	*Brambles Limited*	Company	8 August 2018 14 August 2018	Yes	Two class actions commenced and consolidated.
49	*Woolworths Group Limited*	Company	10 September 2018	Yes	Settlement agreed on 29 January 2021 for $44.5 million (including costs) but subject to court approval
50	*RCR Tomlinson*	Company Directors	16 November 2018	Yes	Three class actions commenced. One proceeding with two litigation funders
51	*Sims Limited*	Company	15 February 2019	Yes	Ongoing
52	*IOOF Limited*	Company	12 April 2019	Yes	Discontinued after unsuccessful case brought by Australian Prudential Regulation Authority in relation to superannuation obligations: *Australian Prudential Regulation Authority v Kelaher* [2019] FCA 1521.
53	*Lendlease Group*	Company	18 April 2019	Yes	Two class actions commenced and consolidated. Ongoing
54	*Vocus Group*	Company	24 April 2019	Yes	Settled in December 2019 for $35 million. *Fisher (trustee for the Tramik Super Fund Trust) v Vocus Group Limited (No 2)* [2020] FCA 579 (4 May 2020)
55	*IOOF Limited*	Company	28 February 2020		Ongoing
56	*Wellard*	Company	12 March 2020	Yes	Ongoing
57	*Boral Limited*	Company	19 March 2020 28 May 2020 21 August 2020	Yes	Three class actions commenced, one stayed and the other two case managed (one open and one closed) Ongoing
58	*Treasury Wine Estates Limited*	Company	April 2020 1 May 2020 (Vic)	No	Two class action commenced and consolidated. Ongoing
59	*Ardent Leisure Limited*	Company Director	17 June 2020	Yes	Ongoing

(continued)

Table 3 ***(Continued)***

	Company	Parties	Commenced	Litigation funding	Settlement details
60	*Arrium Corporation Limited*	Directors Auditor	14 August 2020 (Vic)	Yes	Ongoing
61	*Cimic Group Limited*	Company	21 August 2020	Yes	Ongoing
62	*G8 Education Limited*	Company	20 November 2020 (Vic)	Not at commen-cement	Ongoing
63	*Freedom Foods*	Company Auditor	December 2020 February 2021 (Vic)	Yes	Ongoing
64	*Crown Resorts Limited*	Company	25 February 2021 (Vic)	No	Ongoing

Note: The following two group actions although considered to be class actions by some commentators are not included as continuous disclosure class actions because they were pursued through an insolvency process.

Company	Parties	Commenced	Litigation funding	Settlement details
Sons of Gwalia Limited	Company Directors Auditor	Pursued through insolvency process.	Yes	Settled for $178 million (directors and auditors). Company in administration
ION Limited	Company	30 July 2010 Pursued through insolvency process.	Yes	Confidential settlement Company in administration

BIBLIOGRAPHY

'9 trends that are changing Australia's equity markets', *Company Director Magazine* (1 September 2019).

Abbott, Kenneth and Snidal, Duncan, 'Strengthening International Regulation Through Transnational New Governance: Overcoming the Orchestration Deficit' (2009) 42 *Vanderbilt Journal of Transnational Law* 501.

Access to Justice Taskforce, Federal Attorney-General's Department, 'A Strategic Framework for Access to Justice in the Federal Civil Justice System' (September 2009).

Adamson, Connor, 'Lowering the Bar?: Reevaluating the Diligent Prosecution Bar in Light of the Gold King Mine Spill' (2019) 30 *Villanova Environmental Law Journal* 77.

American Law Institute, 'Principles of the Law of Aggregate Litigation' (2010).

AON, 'Directors & Officers (D&O) Insurance Market update' (2017).

Apel, Robert and DeWitt, Samuel, 'Informal and Formal Sanctions' in Daniel Nagin, Francis Cullen and Cheryl Lero Jonson (eds), *Deterrence, Choice, and Crime: Contemporary Perspectives* (Routledge, 2018).

Arensen, Kenneth and Bagaric, Mirko, *Criminal Processes and Investigative Procedures: Victoria and Commonwealth*, 4th edn (LexisNexis, 2019).

Arlen, Jennifer and Carney, William, 'Vicarious Liability for Fraud on Securities Markets: Theory and Evidence' [1992] *University of Illinois Law Review* 691.

Ashton, Charles and Cugati, Vijay, 'Continuous disclosure during COVID-19: shining the spotlight on earnings and debt', Allens (6 April 2020).

ASIC Capability Review Panel, 'Fit for the future: A capability review of the Australian Securities and Investments' (December 2015).

'ASIC's Corporate Plan 2018–22'.

Askew, Kate, 'ASIC looking under the lid', *The Age* (26 March 2005).

ASX, 'Australian Investor Study 2020'.

'ASX Listing Rules Guidance Note 8 – Continuous Disclosure: Listing Rules 3.1–3.1B' (11 May 2018).

ASX Listing Rules.

ASX, 'Historical Market Statistics' (December 2020).

Austin, Janet, 'Does the Westpoint litigation signal a revival of the ASIC s 50 class action?' (2008) 22 *Australian Journal of Corporate Law* 8.

Austin, Robert and Ramsay, Ian, *Ford, Austin and Ramsay's Principles of Corporations Law* (LexisNexis Online, 2018).

Australian Broadcasting Corporation, 'ASIC lets Telstra off', *The 7.30 Report* (14 December 2005) (Senator Stephen Conroy).

—— 'Corporate watchdog in crackdown on disclosure breaches', *AM* (19 March 2012) (Greg Medcraft, ASIC Chairman).

Australian Competition & Consumer Commission, 'Submission to the Competition Policy Review – Response to the Draft Report' (26 November 2014).

Australian Government, Department of Finance, 'Resource Management Guide No 200 – General duties of accountable authorities' (June 2014).

—— 'Statement of expectations: Australian Securities and Investments Commission' (February 2007).

—— 'Statement of expectations: Australian Securities and Investments Commission' (July 2014).

—— 'Statement of expectations: Australian Securities and Investments Commission' (April 2018).

Australian Government the Treasury, 'Consultation Paper – Proposed Industry Funding Model for the Australian Securities and Investments Commission' (28 August 2015).

Australian Institute of Company Directors, Submission No 35 to Australian Law Reform Commission, 'Inquiry into class action proceedings and third-party litigation funders' (September 2018).

Australian Law Reform Commission, 'Compliance With The Trade Practices Act 1974' (Report No 68, 1994).

—— 'Grouped Proceedings in the Federal Court' (Report No 46, 1988).

—— 'Inquiry into Class Action Proceedings and Third-Party Litigation Funders' (Discussion Paper No 85, June 2018).

—— 'Integrity, Fairness and Efficiency – An Inquiry into Class Action Proceedings and Third-Party Litigation Funders' (Report No 134, 2018).

—— 'Principled Regulation: Federal Civil and Administrative Penalties in Australia' (Report No 95, 2002).
Australian National Audit Office, 'Administration of Enforceable Undertakings' (2 June 2015).
Australian Securities and Investments Commission, 'Annual Report 2013–2014'.
—— 'Annual Dashboard Report for 2017–18'.
—— 'Annual Report 2016–2017'.
—— 'Annual Report 2019–20'.
—— 'ASIC: A guide to our regulatory documents' (June 2007).
—— 'ASIC accepts an enforceable undertaking from the Multiplex Group' (Media Release 06-443, 20 December 2006).
—— 'ASIC commences civil penalty proceedings against ANZ for alleged continuous disclosure breach in relation to 2015 institutional equity placement' (Media Release 18-268, 14 September 2018).
—— 'ASIC commences civil penalty proceedings against GetSwift Limited and its directors Bane Hunter and Joel Macdonald' (Media Release 19-039, 22 February 2019).
—— 'ASIC commences civil proceedings against shipbuilder Austal Limited for continuous disclosure breach' (Media Release 21-128, 10 June 2021).
—— 'ASIC commences civil penalty proceedings against Vocation Limited (in liquidation)' (Media Release 16-334, 30 September 2016.
—— 'ASIC commences Federal Court action against former Murray Goulburn executives Gary Helou and Bradley Hingle' (Media Release 19-152, 25 June 2019).
—— 'ASIC commences proceedings against current and former officers of Centro' (Media Release 09-202AD, 21 October 2009).
—— 'ASIC enforcement outcomes: January to June 2017 – Report 536' (August 2017).
—— 'ASIC enforcement report – July to December 2013' (Media Release 14-018MR, 31 January 2014).
—— 'ASIC Enforcement Update: July to December 2020 – Report 688' (April 2021).
—— 'ASIC industry funding: Summary of 2017–18 levies' (December 2018).
—— 'ASIC industry funding: Summary of 2018–19 levies' (December 2019).
—— 'ASIC launches civil penalty proceedings against former Quintis managing director Frank Wilson' (Media Release 18-174, 14 June 2018).
—— 'ASIC restricts Axiom Mining from issuing a reduced content prospectus' (Media Release 17-210, 28 June 2017).
—— 'ASIC restricts Continental Coal from issuing reduced content prospectus following disclosure and financial reporting failures' (Media Release 16-061, 4 March 2016).
—— 'ASIC settles in Storm Financial proceedings' (Media Release 13-122MR, 29 May 2013).
—— 'ASIC takes action against Rio Tinto and its former CEO and CFO for misleading and deceptive conduct' (Media Release 18-061, 2 March 2018).
—— 'ASIC takes civil action against Antares Energy and a director' (Media Release 18-067, 8 March 2018).
—— 'ASIC takes further action against Rio Tinto Limited and its former CEO and CFO' (Media Release 18-119MR, 1 May 2018).
—— 'ASIC update on implementation of Royal Commission recommendations' (Media Release 19-035, 19 February 2019).
—— 'ASIC warns Telstra on Disclosure Procedures' (Media Release 05-391, 14 December 2005).
—— 'Centro civil penalty proceedings' (Media Release 11-188, 31 August 2011).
—— 'Continuous Disclosure Obligations: Infringement Notices, An ASIC Guide' (May 2004).
—— 'Cost Recovery Implementation Statement: ASIC industry funding model 2019–20' (June 2020).
—— 'COVID-19 implications for financial reporting and audit: Frequently asked questions (FAQs)', 10 June 2021.
—— 'Decision in Centro civil penalty case' (Media Release 11-125, 27 June 2011).
—— 'Enforceable Undertaking: Leighton Holdings Limited, Document No 027714755' (16 March 20120.
—— 'Enforceable Undertaking: Multiplex Ltd, Document No 017 029 205' (20 December 2006).
—— 'Enforceable Undertaking: Rhinomed Ltd, Document No 029622129 (9 June 2016, varied on 23 December 2016).
—— 'Enforceable Undertaking: Stephen John Cougle, Document No 027 958 710' (19 November 2012).
—— 'Former Harts executives charged with continuous disclosure breach' (Media Release 06-176, 2 June 2006).
—— 'Information Sheet 151 – ASIC's approach to enforcement' (September 2013).
—— 'Information Sheet 180 – ASIC's approach to involvement in private court proceedings' (June 2013).
—— 'Leighton Holdings complies with three ASIC infringement notices for alleged continuous disclosure breaches and ASIC accepts compliance enforceable undertaking' (Media Release 12-53MR, 18 March 2012).
—— 'Penalties for Corporate Wrongdoing – Report 387' (March 2014).
—— 'Prosecution of Brisbane man discontinued' (Media Release AD09-06, 22 January 2009).
—— 'Regulator Performance Framework: ASIC self-assessment 2019–20 – Report 691' (May 2021).
—— 'Regulatory Guide 62 – Better disclosure for investors' (August 2000).
—— 'Regulatory Guide 73 – Continuous disclosure obligations: infringement notices' (October 2017).

—— 'Regulatory Guide 100 – Enforceable Undertakings' (February 2015).
—— 'Regulatory Guide 248 – Litigation Schemes and Proof of Debt Schemes: Managing Conflicts of Interest' (April 2013).
—— 'Review of Australian equity market cleanliness – Report 487' (August 2016).
—— 'REX pays $66,000 penalty for alleged continuous disclosure breach' (Media Release 21-105, 18 May 2021).
—— 'Senate Inquiry into the Performance of the Australian Securities and Investments Commission – Main Submission by ASIC' (October 2013).
—— 'Statement of Intent – Australian Securities and Investments Commission' (July 2014).
—— Submission No 72 to Australian Law Reform Commission, 'Inquiry into class action proceedings and third-party litigation funders' (September 2018).
—— Submission to Royal Commission into Misconduct in the Banking, Superannuation and Financial Services Industry, 'ASIC Response to Interim Report' (2 November 2018).
—— 'Verdict on charges against former Hart executives' (Media Release AD08-26, 25 September 2008).
—— 'Waratah Resources' former executive chairman convicted and sentenced for misleading the market' (Media Release 17-018MR, 30 January 2017).
Australian Treasury and Attorney-General's Department, 'Consultation Paper – Guaranteeing a minimum return of class action proceeds to class members' (June 2021).
Ayres, Ian and Braithwaite, John, *Responsive Regulation* (Oxford University Press, 1992).
Baer, Miriam, 'Choosing Punishment' (2012) 92 *Boston University Law Review* 577.
—— 'Linkage and the Deterrence of Corporate Fraud' (2008) 94 *Virginia Law Review* 1295.
Bagaric, Mirko, 'Incapacitation, Deterrence and Rehabilitation: Flawed Ideals or Appropriate Sentencing Goals?' (2000) 24 *Criminal Law Journal* 21.
Baker, Tom, and Griffith, Sean, *Ensuring Corporate Misconduct* (University of Chicago Press, 2010).
Baldwin, Robert and Black, Julia, 'Really Responsive Regulation' (2008) 71 *Modern Law Review* 59.
Baldwin, Robert, Cave, Martin and Lodge, Martin, *Understanding Regulation*, 2nd edn (Oxford University Press, 2012).
Barrymore, Karina, 'Call out to join a Leighton suit', *Herald Sun* (2 September 2011) 71.
Bartholomeusz, Stephen, 'Leighton covers its indecent disclosure', *Business Spectator* (online) (27 March 2012).
Bathurst, TF, 'Insurance Law – A View from the Bench' (2014) 25 *Insurance Law Journal* 94.
Baxt, Robert, 'Editorial' (2006) 24 *Company and Securities Law Journal* 73.
—— 'Infringement Notices – It's Time to Scrap Them' *Company Director*, 1 April 2006.
Baxt, Robert, Black, Ashley and Hanrahan, Pamela, *Securities and Financial Services Law*, 9th edn (LexisNexis, 2017).
Baxter, Colin, 'Demystifying D&O Insurance' (1995) 15 *Oxford Journal of Legal Studies* 537.
Beach, Jonathan, 'Class Actions: Some Causation Questions' (2011) 85 *Australian Law Journal* 579.
—— 'Structural and Forensic Developments in Securities Litigation', International Commercial Law Conference, Inner Temple, Inns of Court, London (29 June 2016).
Becker, Gary, 'Crime and Punishment: An Economic Approach' (1968) 76 *Journal of Political Economy* 169.
Bednall, Tim and Hanrahan, Pamela, 'Officers' liability for mandatory corporate disclosure: Two paths, two destinations?' (2013) 31 *Company and Securities Law Journal* 474.
Beisner, John, Shors, Matthew and Davidson Miller, Jessica, 'Class Action "Cops": Public Servants or Private Entrepreneurs' (2005) 57 *Stanford Law Review* 1441.
Bird, Helen, Gilligan, George and Ramsay, Ian, 'The who, why and what of enforceable undertakings accepted by the Australian Securities and Investment Commission' (2016) 34 *Company and Securities Law Journal* 493.
Bird, Joanna, 'Regulating the Regulators: Accountability of Australian Regulators' (2011) 35 *Melbourne University Law Review* 739.
Black, Bernard, Cheffins, Brian and Klausner, Michael, 'Outside Director Liability' (2006) 58 *Stanford Law Review* 1055.
Black, John, Hashimzade, Nigar and Myles, Gareth, *A Dictionary of Economics*, 4th edn (Oxford University Press, 2013).
Black, Julia, 'Constructing and Contesting Legitimacy and Accountability in Polycentric Regulatory Regimes' (2008) 2 *Regulation & Governance* 137.
—— 'Decentring Regulation: Understanding the Role of Regulation and Self-Regulation in a "Post-Regulatory" World' (2002) 54 *Current Legal Problems* 103.
Blackburn, Maurice, 'Leighton reaches swift $69.45m class action settlement' (Media Release, 16 May 2014).
—— 'Record-Breaking $200m Centro Class Action Win' (Media Release, 9 May 2012).
Bloch, Merav, Weatherhead, James and Webster, Jon, 'The Development and Enforcement of Australia's Continuous Disclosure Regime' (2011) 29 *Company and Securities Law Journal* 253.
Boese, John and Baruch, Douglas, *Civil False Claims and Qui Tam Actions*, 5th edn (Wolters Kluwer, 2020).
Boros, Elizabeth, 'Public and Private Enforcement of Disclosure Breaches in Australia' (2009) 9 *Journal of Corporate Law Studies* 409.

Bovens, Mark, 'Analysing and Assessing Accountability: A Conceptual Framework' (2007) 13 *European Law Journal* 447.
Bowers, Samantha and Murphy, Jason, 'Centro case makes directors sit up', *The Australian Financial Review* (29 July 2011) 23.
Boxsell, Alex, 'IMF profits from Centro case', *The Australian Financial Review* (24 August 2012) 44.
—— 'Regulators Praise Private Court Actions', *The Weekend Australian Financial Review* (5–9 April 2012) 59.
Boxsell, Alex and Bowers, Samantha, 'Ruling boosts class actions', *The Australian Financial Review* (1 July 2011) 56.
Boyd, Tony, 'Beware ASIC's litigate first strategy' *The Australian Financial Review* (26 March 2019).
Boyd, Tony and Crowe, David, 'ASIC gives Telstra a yellow card', *Australian Financial Review* (15 December 2005) 4.
—— 'Failure to disclose was within the law', *Australian Financial Review* (8 September 2005) 16.
Boyer, Barry and Meidinger, Errol, 'Privatizing Regulatory Enforcement: A Preliminary Assessment of Citizen Suits Under Federal Environmental Laws' (1985) 34 *Buffalo Law Review* 833.
Braithwaite, John, *Corporate Crime in the Pharmaceutical Industry* (Routledge & Kegan Paul, 1984).
—— *Regulatory Capitalism* (Edward Elgar, 2008).
—— 'The Essence of Responsive Regulation' (2011) 44 *University of British Columbia Law Review* 475.
Brand, Rachel, US Department of Justice, 'Remarks to the Washington, DC Lawyers Chapter of the Federalist Society' (15 February 2018).
Bratton, William and Wachter, Michael, 'The Political Economy of Fraud on the Market' (2011) 160 *University of Pennsylvania Law Review* 69.
Bronitt, Simon and McSherry, Bernadette, *Principles of Criminal Law*, 3rd edn (Thomson Reuters, 2010).
Brunet, Edward, 'Debunking Wholesale Private Enforcement of Environmental Rights' (1992) 15 *Harvard Journal of Law & Public Policy* 311.
Bucy, Pamela 'Private Justice' (2002) 76 *Southern California Law Review* 1.
Buell, Samuel, 'The Blaming Function of Entity Criminal Liability' (2006) 81 *Indiana Law Journal* 473.
Burbank, Stephen, Farhang, Sean and Kritzer, Herbert, 'Private Enforcement' (2013) 17 *Lewis & Clark Law Review* 637.
Burris, Scott, Kempa, Michael and Shearing, Clifford, 'Changes in Governance: A Cross-Disciplinary Review of Current Scholarship' (2008) 41 *Akron Law Review* 1.
Butler, Ben, 'ASIC attacked on Multiplex deal' *The Sydney Morning Herald* (22 July 2010).
Butler, Ben and Ferguson, Adele, 'Disclosure rules need more bite – ASIC', *The Sydney Morning Herald* (19 March 2012) 1.
Butler, Ben, Wood, Leonie and Wilkins, Georgia, 'Centro $200m legal deal a record', *Sydney Morning Herald* (9 May 2012) 2.
Byrne, Corey and Legg, Michael, 'Market-based causation after TPT Patrol Pty Ltd v Myer Holdings Limited' (2020) 37 *Company & Securities Law Journal* 295.
Cairns, Bernard, *Australian Civil Procedure*, 10th edn (Thomson Reuters, 2014).
Cameron, Camille, 'Litigation as "core business": Analysing the access to justice and regulatory dimensions of commercially funded class actions in Australia' in Deborah Hensler,
Cane, Peter, *Atiyah's Accidents, Compensation and the Law*, 8th edn (Cambridge University Press, 2013).
Cappelletti, Mauro, 'Alternative Dispute Resolution Processes Within the Framework of the World-Wide-Access-To-Justice Movement' (1993) 56 *Modern Law Review* 282.
Cashman, Peter and Abbs, Ross, 'Prospects and problems for investors in class action proceedings' in KE Lindgren (ed), *Investor Class Actions* (Ross Parsons Centre, 2009).
Cassidy, Andrew and Chapple, Larelle, 'Australia's Corporate Disclosure Regime: Lessons from the US model' (2003) 15 *Australian Journal of Corporate Law* 1.
Centro Properties Group, 'Centro Group announces restructure agreement' (ASX/Media Release, 9 August 2011).
Centro Retail Australia, 'Conditional Settlement of class actions' (ASX/Media Release, 10 May 2012).
Chalfin, Aaron and McCrary, Justin, 'Criminal Deterrence: A Review of the Literature' (2017) 55 *Journal of Economic Literature* 5.
Chamblee Burch, Elizabeth, 'Securities Class Actions as Pragmatic Ex Post Regulation' (2008) 43 *Georgia Law Review* 63.
Charles, Matthew and Leyden, Fleur, 'Two class actions loom against embattled Telstra', *The Courier-Mail* (16 September 2005) 29.
Chawla, Jennifer, 'Criminal Accountability and Wall Street Executives: Why the Criminal Provisions of the Dodd-Frank Act Fall Short' (2014) 44 *Seton Hall Law Review* 937.
CIMIC Group Limited, 'Change of Name to CIMIC Group Limited (CIM)' (ASX Announcement, 22 April 2015).
Cleary Yeager, Peter, 'The Elusive Deterrence of Corporate Crime' (2016) 15 *Criminology & Public Policy* 439.
—— 'The Practical Challenges of Responding to Corporate Crime' in Shanna Van Slyke, Michael Benson and Francis Cullen (eds), *The Oxford Handbook of White-Collar Crime* (Oxford University Press, 2016).
—— 'Understanding Corporate Lawbreaking: From Profit Seeking to Law Finding' in Henry Pontell and Gilbert Geis (eds), *International Handbook of White-Collar and Corporate Crime* (Springer, 2007).
Clough, Jonathan and Mulhern, Carmelm, *The Prosecution of Corporations* (Oxford University Press, 2002).

Coffee, John, 'Class Action Accountability: Reconciling Exit, Voice, and Loyalty in Representative Litigation' (2000) 100 *Columbia Law Review* 370.

—— *Corporate Crime and Punishment: The Crisis of Underenforcement* (Berrett-Koehler Publishers, 2020).

—— *Entrepreneurial Litigation: Its Rise, Fall and Future* (Harvard University Press, 2015).

—— 'Law and the Market: The Impact of Enforcement' (2007) 156 *University of Pennsylvania Law Review* 229.

—— '"No Soul to Damn: No Body to Kick": An Unscandalized Inquiry into the Problem of Corporate Punishment' (1981) 79 *Michigan Law Review* 386.

—— 'Reforming the Securities Class Action: An Essay on Deterrence and Its Implementation' (2006) 106 *Columbia Law Review* 1534.

—— 'Rescuing the Private Attorney General: Why the Model of Lawyer as Bounty Hunter is not Working' (1983) 42 *Maryland Law Review* 215.

—— 'The Regulation of Entrepreneurial Litigation: Balancing Fairness and Efficiency in the Large Class Action' (1987) 54 *University of Chicago Law Review* 877.

—— 'Understanding the Plaintiff's Attorney: The Implications of Economic Theory for Private Enforcement of Law Through Class and Derivative Actions' (1986) 86 *Columbia Law Review* 669.

Coffey, Josephine, 'Enforcement of Continuous Disclosure in the Australian Stock Market' (2007) 20 *Australian Journal of Corporate Law* 301.

Coleman, Jules, 'The Practice of Corrective Justice' in David Owen (ed), *Philosophical Foundations of Tort Law* (Clarendon Press, 1995).

Collins, Hugh, 'Ascription of Legal Responsibility to Groups in Complex Patterns of Economic Integration' (1990) 53 *Modern Law Review* 731.

Comino, Vicky, 'Australia's 'Company Law Watchdog' – ASIC and Corporate Regulation' (Thomson Reuters, 2015).

—— '"Corporate Culture" Is the "New Black" – Its Possibilities and Limits as a Regulatory Mechanism for Corporations and Financial Institutions' (2021) 44 *UNSW Law Journal* 295.

—— 'Life after the Banking Royal Commission: Is the Royal Commission a "game-changer" for the financial services sector in Australia?' (2020) 35 *Australian Journal of Corporate Law* 381.

Commonwealth of Australia, 'ASIC Enforcement Review Taskforce Report' (December 2017).

—— 'Financial System Inquiry Final Report' (1997).

—— 'Financial System Inquiry Final Report' (November 2014).

Commonwealth Treasury, 'Review of Sanctions in Corporate Law' (2007).

Companies and Securities Advisory Committee, 'Report on an Enhanced Statutory Disclosure System' (1991).

Cooper, Edward, 'The (Cloudy) Future of Class Actions' (1998) 40 *Arizona Law Review* 923.

Cooper, Jeremy, Deputy Chairman, ASIC, 'Corporate wrongdoing: ASIC's enforcement role' (Speech, International Class Actions Conference 2005, Melbourne, 2 December 2005).

Cooper Alexander, Janet, 'Rethinking Damages in Securities Class Actions' (1996) 48 *Stanford Law Review* 1487.

Cooter, Robert and Ulen, Thomas, *Law and Economics*, 5th edn (Pearson, 2007).

Coplan, Karl, 'Citizen Enforcement' in Leroy Paddock, Robert Glicksman and Nicholas Bryner (eds), *Decision Making in Environmental Law* (Edward Elgar, 2016).

Cornell, Andrew, 'More than a reprimand needed to appease suspicions' *Australian Financial Review* (15 December 2005) 4.

Cornerstone Research, 'Securities Class Action Filings – 2017 Year in Review' (2018).

Cornwall-Jones, Jason, 'Breach of Contract and Misleading Conduct: A Storm in a Teacup' (2000) 24 *Melbourne University Law Review* 249.

Corporate Law Economic Reform Program, 'Corporate Disclosure: Strengthening the Financial Reporting Framework' (Proposals for Reform: Paper No 9, September 2002).

—— 'Fundraising – Capital Raising Initiatives to Build Enterprise and Employment' (Proposals for Reform: Paper No 2, April 1997).

Cox, James, 'Making Securities Fraud Class Actions Virtuous' (1997) 39 *Arizona Law Review* 497.

—— 'Private Litigation and the Deterrence of Corporate Misconduct' (1997) 60 *Law & Contemporary Problems* 1.

—— 'The Social Meaning of Shareholder Suits' (1999) 65 *Brooklyn Law Review* 3.

Cox, James and Thomas, Randall, 'SEC Enforcement Heuristics: An Empirical Inquiry' (2003) 53 *Duke Law Journal* 737.

Crutchfield, Philip and Button, Catherine, 'Men overboard: The burden of directors' duties in the wake of the Centro case' (2012) 30 *Companies and Securities Law Journal* 83.

Cummins, Carolyn, 'Auditors strike back at Centro claim', *The Sydney Morning Herald* (13 June 2009) 3.

—— 'Centro in court over $1bn class action', *The Age* (25 August 2008) 3.

D'Aloisio, Tony, Chairman, ASIC, 'Responding to the global financial crisis: the ASIC story' (Speech, Trans-Tasman Business Circle, 30 November 2010).

Dal Pont, GE, *Lawyers' Professional Responsibility*, 6th edn (Thomson Reuters, 2017).

Dam, Kenneth, 'Class Actions: Efficiency, Compensation, Deterrence and Conflict of Interest' (1975) 4 *Journal of Legal Studies* 47.

Danckert, Sarah, 'Half of $200m Centro judgment will go in costs', *The Australian* (20 June 2012) 22.

Davidoff, Steven and Zaring, David, 'Regulation by Deal: The Government's Response to the Financial Crisis' (2009) 61 *Administrative Law Review* 463.

Degeling, Simone and Legg, Michael, 'Fiduciaries and Funders: Litigation Funders in Australian Class Actions' (2017) 36 *Civil Justice Quarterly* 244.

—— 'Fiduciary Obligations of Lawyers in Australian Class Actions: Conflicts between Duties' (2014) 37 *University of New South Wales Law Journal* 914.

Desai, Aakash and Ramsay, Ian, 'The Use of Infringement Notices by ASIC for Alleged Continuous Disclosure Contraventions: Trends and Analysis' (2011) 39 *Australian Business Law Review* 260.

Dictionary of Accounting, 4th edn (Oxford University Press, 2015).

Dietrich, Joachim and Middleton, Thomas, 'Statutory remedies and equitable remedies' (2006) 28 *Australian Bar Review* 136.

Dixon, Olivia, 'Corporate Criminal Liability: The Influence of Corporate Culture' in Justin O'Brien and George Gilligan, *Integrity, Risk and Accountability in Capital Markets: Regulating Culture* (Hart Publishing, 2013).

Donnan, Julian, 'Class Actions in Securities Fraud in Australia' (2000) 18 *Company and Securities Law Journal* 82.

Dorf, Michael and Sabel, Charles, 'A Constitution of Democratic Experimentalism' (1998) 98 *Columbia Law Review* 267.

Duffy, Michael, 'Australian Private Securities Class Actions and Public Interest – Assessing the Private Attorney-General by Reference to the Rationales of Public Enforcement' (2017) 32 *Australian Journal of Corporate Law* 162.

Dunckley, Mathew, 'More join Wider Multiplex action' *The Australian Financial Review* (25 September 2008) 11.

Dunlevy, Maurice, 'ASIC ramps up Centro probe', *The Australian* (19 November 2010) 21.

—— 'Centro class action zeroes in on insurance', *The Australian* (6 March 2009) 19.

—— 'Decision on PwC lawsuit in weeks' *The Australian* (23 September 2010) 31.

Durie, John, 'ASIC has hit the spot this time', *The Australian* (22 October 2009) 32.

Durkin, Patrick, 'Centro Investors Vent Anger at "Injustice"', *The Australian Financial Review* (1 September 2011) 9.

—— 'Treasurer considers class action freeze', *The Australian Financial Review* (9 April 2020).

Edwards, Amy, '"Financial Consumerism": citizenship, consumerism and capital ownership in the 1980s' (2017) 31 *Contemporary British History* 210.

Emmerig, John and Legg, Michael, 'Twenty Five Years of Australian Class Actions – Time for Reform' (2017) 36 *Civil Justice Quarterly* 164.

Encyclopaedic Australian Legal Dictionary (LexisNexis).

Evidence to Joint Committee on Corporations and Financial Services, Parliament of Australia, Canberra (11 March 2011) (Mr Tony D'Aloisio, ASIC Chairman).

Evidence to Parliamentary Joint Committee on Corporations and Financial Services, Parliament of Australia, Melbourne (17 August 2018) (Mr James Shipton, ASIC Chairman).

Evidence to Senate Economics Legislation Committee – Estimates, Parliament of Australia, Canberra (16 February 2006) (Mr Jeffrey Lucy, ASIC Chairman).

Evidence to Senate Economics Legislation Committee – Estimates, Parliament of Australia, Canberra (16 February 2006) (Mr Jeremy Cooper, ASIC Deputy Chairman).

Evidence to Senate Economics Legislation Committee – Estimates, Parliament of Australia, Canberra (12 October 2011) (Mr Greg Medcraft, ASIC Chairman).

Evidence to Senate Economics Legislation Committee – Estimates, Parliament of Australia, Canberra (20 November 2013) (Mr Greg Medcraft, ASIC Chairman).

Evidence to Senate Economics Legislation Committee – Estimates, Parliament of Australia, Canberra (20 February 2019) (Daniel Crennan, Deputy Chair, ASIC).

Evidence to Senate Economics Legislation Committee – Estimates, Parliament of Australia, Canberra (20 February 2019) (James Shipton, Chair, ASIC).

Evidence to Senate Economics Legislation Committee – Estimates, Parliament of Australia, Canberra (25 March 2021) (Mr James Shipton. ASIC Chair).

Evidence to Senate Economics Legislation Committee – Estimates, Parliament of Australia, Canberra (25 March 2021) (Ms Cathie Armour, ASIC Commissioner).

Farhang, Sean, *The Litigation State* (Princeton University Press, 2010).

Ferguson, Adele, '$400m lawsuit turns spotlight on issues of governance', *The Sydney Morning Herald* (1 September 2011) 7.

—— *Banking Bad* (ABC Books, 2019).

—— 'Class actions on the increase', *The Australian* (4 January 2008) 15.

—— 'Leighton class action', *The Age* (1 September 2011) 1.

—— 'Multiplex settlement is a bitter-sweet victory', *The Age* (22 July 2010) 9.
—— 'Wrong signal to let Leighton off lightly', *The Sydney Morning Herald* (19 March 2012) 5.
Ferran, Eilis, 'Dispute resolution mechanisms in the U.K. financial sector' (2002) 21 *Civil Justice Quarterly* 135.
Financial Crisis Inquiry Commission, 'The Financial Crisis Inquiry Report' (2011).
Finch, Vanessa, 'Personal Accountability and Corporate Control: the Role of Directors' and Officers' Liability Insurance' (1994) 57 *Modern Law Review* 880.
Fisch, Jill, 'Confronting the Circularity Problem in Private Securities Litigation' [2009] *Wisconsin Law Review* 333.
Fisse, Brent and Braithwaite, John, *Corporations, Crime and Accountability* (Cambridge University Press, 1993).
—— *The Impact of Publicity on Corporate Offenders* (State University of New York Press, 1983).
Fitzpatrick, Brian, *The Conservative Case for Class Actions* (The University of Chicago Press, 2019).
Fleming, John, 'The Role of Negligence in Modern Tort Law' (1967) 53 *Virginia Law Review* 815.
Fletcher, George, 'Fairness and Utility in Tort Theory' (1972) 85 *Harvard Law Review* 537.
Ford, Cristie, *Innovation and the State – Finance, Regulation and Justice* (Cambridge University Press, 2017).
—— 'New Governance in the Teeth of Human Frailty: Lessons from Financial Regulation' [2010] *Wisconsin Law Review* 441.
Ford, HAJ and Austin, RP, *Principles of Corporations Law*, 7th edn (Butterworths, 1995).
Fotis, Stephen, 'Private Enforcement of the Clean Air Act and the Clean Water Act' (1985) 35 *American University Law Review* 127.
Fox, Merritt, 'Why Civil Liability for Disclosure Violations When Issuers Do Not Trade?' [2009] *Wisconsin Law Review* 297.
Freeman, Jody, 'Extending Public Law Norms Through Privatization' (2003) 116 *Harvard Law Review* 1285.
—— 'Private Parties, Public Functions and the New Administrative Law' (2000) 52 *Administrative Law Review* 813.
—— 'The Private Role in Public Governance' (2000) 75 *New York University Law Review* 543.
Freeman Engstrom, David, 'Agencies and Litigation Gatekeepers' (2013) 123 *Yale Law Journal* 616.
—— 'Private Enforcement's Pathways: Lessons from Qui Tam Litigation' (2014) 114 *Columbia Law Review* 1913.
Freer, Richard, 'Avoiding Duplicative Litigation: Rethinking Plaintiff Autonomy and the Court's Role in Defining the Litigative Unit' (1989) 50 *University of Pittsburgh Law Review* 809.
Freiberg, Arie, *Regulation in Australia* (The Federation Press, 2017).
—— *The Tools of Regulation* (The Federation Press, 2010).
Frydenberg, MP, Josh, 'Appointment of new Chairperson and Deputy Chairperson to the Australian Securities and Investments Commission' (Media Release, 29 April 2021).
—— 'Extension of temporary changes to continuous disclosure provisions for companies and officers' (Media release, 23 September 2020).
—— 'Government consults on stronger penalties for corporate and financial sector misconduct' (Media Release, 26 September 2018).
—— 'Litigation funders to be regulated under the Corporations Act' (Media Release, 22 May 2020).
—— 'Record funding and resources for ASIC and APRA to help restore trust in Australia's financial sector' (Media Release, 23 March 2019).
—— 'Temporary changes to continuous disclosure provisions for companies and officers' (Media Release, 25 May 2020).
Funnell, Warwick and Cooper, Kathie, *Public Sector Accounting and Accountability in Australia* (UNSW Press, 1998).
Gibson, Belinda, ASIC Commissioner, 'Disclosure and the Role of ASX and ASIC' (Speech, Listed Companies Conference, 26 March 2008).
Gibson, Belinda, Deputy Chairman, and John Price, Commissioner, ASIC, 'Continuous disclosure: Guidance Note 8 rewrite' (Speech, ASX Forum, 22 and 29 April 2013).
Garner, Michael and Mould, Helen, 'Measuring and Proving Loss in Securities Class Actions' in Damian Grave and Helen Mould (eds), *25 years of class actions in Australia: 1992–2017* (Ross Parsons Centre, 2017).
Garrett, Brandon, *Too Big to Jail* (Harvard University Press, 2014).
Garth, Bryant, 'Conflict and Dissent in Class Actions: A Suggested Perspective' (1982) 77 *Northwestern University Law Review* 492.
Gerring, John, 'Case Selection for Case Study Analysis: Qualitative and Quantitative Techniques' in Janet Box-Steffensmeier, Henry Brady and David Collier (eds), *The Oxford Handbook of Political Methodology* (Oxford University Press, 2008).
Gilligan, George, Birdm Helen and Ramsay, Ian, 'Civil Penalties and the Enforcement of Directors' Duties' (1999) 22 *University of New South Wales Law Journal* 417.
Glover, J Maria, 'The Structural Roles of Private Enforcement Mechanisms in Public Law' (2012) 53 *William and Mary Law Review* 1137.
Gluyas, Richard, 'Corporate regulator urges tougher disclosure penalties', *The Australian* (19 March 2012) 2.
Gold, Russell, 'Compensation's Role in Deterrence' (2016) 91 *Notre Dame Law Review* 1997.

Golding, Greg, 'Tightening the Screws on Directors: Care, Delegation and Reliance' (2012) 35 *University of New South Wales Law Journal* 266.

Golding, Greg and Kalfus, Natalie, 'The Continuous Evolution of Australia's Continuous Disclosure Laws' (2004) 22 *Company and Securities Law Journal* 385.

Goldsmith, Jack and Vermeule, Adrian, 'Empirical Methodology and Legal Scholarship' (2002) 69 *University of Chicago Law Review* 153.

Goldwasser, Vivien, 'The Enforcement Dilemma in Australian Securities Regulation' (1999) 27 *Australian Business Law Review* 482.

Goodin, Robert, 'Theories of Compensation' (1989) 9 *Oxford Journal of Legal Studies* 56.

Gordley, James, 'Tort Law in the Aristotelian Tradition' in David Owen (ed), *Philosophical Foundations of Tort Law* (Clarendon Press, 1995).

Grabosky, Peter, 'Beyond Responsive Regulation: The Expanding Role of Non-State Actors in the Regulatory Process' (2013) 7 *Regulation & Governance* 114.

Grasmick, Harold and Bursik, Robert, 'Conscience, Significant Others and Rational Choice: Extending the Deterrence Model' (1990) 24 *Law & Society Review* 837.

Grave, Damian, Adams, Ken and Betts, Jason, *Class Actions in Australia*, 2nd edn (Thomson Reuters, 2012).

Grave, Damian, Watterson, Leah and Mould, Helen, 'Causation, Loss and Damage: Challenges for the New Shareholder Class Action' (2009) 27 *Company & Securities Law Journal* 483.

Griffith, Sean, 'D&O insurance and the ability of shareholder litigation to deter' in Claire Hill and Brett McDonnell (eds), *Research Handbook on the Economics of Corporate Law* (Edward Elgar, 2012).

Grundfest, Joseph, 'Disimplying Private Rights of Action Under the Federal Securities Laws: The Commission's Authority' (1994) 107 *Harvard Law Review* 961.

Gunningham, Neil, 'Enforcement and Compliance Strategies' in Robert Baldwin, Martin Cave and Martin Lodge (eds), *The Oxford Handbook of Regulation* (Oxford University Press, 2010).

Gunningham, Neil and Grabosky, Peter, *Smart Regulation* (Oxford University Press, 1998).

Gunningham, Neil and Sinclair, Darren, 'Regulatory Pluralism: Designing Policy Mixes for Environmental Protection' (1999) 21 *Law & Policy* 49.

—— 'Smart Regulation' in Peter Drahos (ed), *Regulatory Theory: Foundations and Applications* (ANU Press, 2017).

Halsbury's Laws of Australia (LexisNexis, 2017).

Han, Misa, Eyers, James and Tadros, Edmund, 'ASIC: deals unlikely in post-Hayne world', *The Australian Financial Review* (17 May 2019) 21.

Hargovan, Anil and Harris, Jason, 'Sons of Gwalia and statutory debt subordination: An appraisal of the North American experience' (2007) 20 *Australian Journal of Corporate Law* 265.

Harland, David, 'The statutory prohibition of misleading or deceptive conduct in Australia and its impact on the law of contract' (1995) 111 *Law Quarterly Review* 100.

Hastings, Luke, 'Enforcing the Continuous Disclosure Regime' in Michael Legg, *Regulation, Litigation and Enforcement* (Thomson Reuters, 2011).

Hawkins, Keith and Thomas, John, 'The Enforcement Process in Regulatory Bureaucracies' in Keith Hawkins and John Thomas (eds), *Enforcing Regulation* (Kluwer-Nijhoff Publishing, 1984).

Heath, Will, Hunt, Nigel and Friedlander, David, 'Continuous disclosure relaxation causes joy and despair – who's right?', *The Australian Financial Review* (28 May 2020).

Hensler, Deborah, Pace, Nicholas, Dombey-Moore, Bonita, Giddens, Beth, Gross, Jennifer and Moller, Erik, *Class Action Dilemmas – Pursuing Public Goals for Private Gain* (RAND Institute for Civil Justice, 2000).

Herbert Smith Freehills, 'Change in D&O Market Conditions' (13 April 2017).

Herzberg, Abe and Anderson, Helen, 'Stepping Stones – From Corporate Fault to Directors' Personal Civil Liability' (2012) 40 *Federal Law Review* 181.

Hewett, Jennifer, 'Legal bid for bigger slice of class actions' *The Australian Financial Review* (17 June 2020).

Hill, Jennifer, 'Centro and the Monitoring Board – Legal Duties Versus Aspirational Ideals in Corporate Governance' (2012) 35 *University of New South Wales Law Journal* 341.

Hodges, Christopher and Tzankova, Ianika (eds), *Class Actions in Context* (Edward Elgar, 2016).

Hodges, Christopher and Voet, Stefaan, *Delivering Collective Redress* (Hart, 2018).

Honore, Tony, 'The Morality of Tort Law – Questions and Answers' in David Owen (ed), *Philosophical Foundations of Tort Law* (Clarendon Press, 1995).

House of Representatives Standing Committee on Legal and Constitutional Affairs, Parliament of the Commonwealth of Australia, 'Corporate Practices and the Rights of Shareholders' (1991).

Howells, Geraint, Ramsay, Iain and Wilhelmsson, Thomas, 'Consumer Law in its International Dimension' in Geraint Howells, Iain Ramsay and Thomas Wilhelmsson with David Kraft, *Handbook of Research on International Consumer Law* (Edward Elgar, 2010).

Hughes, Sean, 'ASIC's Approach to Enforcement after the Royal Commission', 36th Annual Conference of the Banking and Financial Services Law Association, Gold Coast (30 August 2019).
Huisman, Wim, 'Offender Decision Making in Corporate and White-Collar Crime' in Wim Bernasco, Jean-Louis van Gelder and Henk Elffers (eds) *The Oxford Handbook of Offender Decision Making* (Oxford University Press, 2017).
Humphrey, John and Corones, Stephen, 'Forrest v ASIC: A "perfect storm"' (2014) 88 *Australian Law Journal* 26.
IMF (Australia) Ltd, 'ASIC Centro Win Bolsters Class Actions' (Newsletter, 24 May 2013).
IMF (Australia) Ltd, Submission No 103 to Productivity Commission, 'Access to Justice Arrangements' (18 November 2013).
Insurance Council of Australia Ltd, Submission No 47 to Australian Law Reform Commission, 'Inquiry into class action proceedings and third-party litigation funders' (September 2018).
International Monetary Fund, 'Australia: IOSCO Objectives and Principles of Securities Regulation – Detailed Assessment of Implementation', IMF Country Report No 12/314 (November 2012).
IOSCO, 'Credible Deterrence in the Enforcement of Securities Regulation' (June 2015).
—— 'Methodology For Assessing Implementation of the IOSCO Objectives and Principles of Securities Regulation' (May 2017).
—— 'Objectives and Principles of Securities Regulation' (May 2003).
—— 'Objectives and Principles of Securities Regulation' (May 2017).
Issacharoff, Samuel, 'Class Actions and State Authority' (2012) 44 *Loyola University Chicago Law Journal* 369.
—— 'Governance and Legitimacy in the Law of Class Actions' [1999] *Supreme Court Review* 337.
Issacharoff, Samuel and Klonoff, Robert, 'The Public Value of Settlement' (2009) 78 *Fordham Law Review* 1177.
Jackson, Howell, 'Variation in the Intensity of Financial Regulation: Preliminary Evidence and Potential Implications' (2007) 24 *Yale Journal of Regulation* 253.
Jackson, Howell and Roe, Mark, 'Public and Private Enforcement of Securities Laws: Resource-Based Evidence' (2009) 93 *Journal of Financial Economics* 207.
John, Stephen, Chairman, Leighton Holdings, 'Address to Shareholders' (Presentation to 51st Annual General Meeting of Leighton Holdings Limited, 22 May 2012).
Jones Day, White Paper – Australia Financial Services Industry Royal Commission Leads to Class Actions Boom (August 2020).
Kagan, Robert, 'On Regulatory Inspectorates and Police' in Keith Hawkins and John Thomas (eds), *Enforcing Regulation* (Kluwer-Nijhoff Publishing, 1984).
—— 'Regulators and Regulatory Processes' in Austin Sarat (ed), *The Blackwell Companion to Law and Society* (John Wiley & Sons Ltd, 2008).
Kagan, Robert and Scholz, John, 'The "Criminology of the Corporation" and Regulatory Enforcement Strategies' in Keith Hawkins and John Thomas (eds), *Enforcing Regulation* (Kluwer-Nijhoff Publishing, 1984).
Kahan, Dan, 'The Secret Ambition of Deterrence' (1999) 113 *Harvard Law Review* 413.
—— 'What Do Alternative Sanctions Mean?' (1996) 63 *University of Chicago Law Review* 591.
Kalajdzic, Jasminka, Cashman, Peter and Longmoore, Alana, 'Justice for Profit: A Comparative Analysis of Australian, Canadian and U.S. Third Party Litigation Funding' (2013) 61 *American Journal of Comparative Law* 93.
Kalven Jr, Harry and Rosenfield, Maurice, 'The Contemporary Function of the Class Suit' (1940–41) 8 *University of Chicago Law Review* 684.
Karkkainen, Bradley, '"New Governance" in Legal Thought and in the World: Some Splitting as Antidote to Overzealous Lumping' (2004) 89 *Minnesota Law Review* 471.
Keay, Andrew, 'The Public Enforcement of Directors' Duties: A Normative Inquiry' (2014) 43 *Common Law World Review* 89.
Keane, Patrick, 'Access to Justice and Other Shibboleths' (Speech, JCA Colloquium, 10 October 2009).
Kennedy, David, *Deterrence and Crime Prevention* (Routledge, 2009).
Khanna, VS, 'Corporate Criminal Liability: What Purpose Does it Serve?' (1996) 109 *Harvard Law Review* 1477.
King, Agnes, 'Red faces, not red ink at PwC audit', *The Australian Financial Review* (14 May 2012) 56.
King & Wood Mallesons, 'The Review – Class Actions in Australia 2016/2017' (2018).
Kingsford Smith, Dimity 'A Harder Nut to Crack? Responsive Regulation in the Financial Services Sector' (2011) 44 *University of British Columbia Law Review* 695.
—— 'Financial Services Regulation and the Investor as Consumer' in Geraint Howells, Iain Ramsay and Thomas Wilhelmsson with David Kraft, *Handbook of Research on International Consumer Law* (Edward Elgar, 2010).
—— 'Regulating Investment Risk: Individuals and the Global Financial Crisis' (2009) 32 *UNSW Law Journal* 514.
Koeck, WJ, 'Continuous Disclosure' (1995) 13 *Company and Securities Law Journal* 485.
Korobkin, Russell and Ulen, Thomas, 'Law and Behavioral Science: Removing the Rationality Assumption from Law and Economics (2000) 88 *California Law Review* 1051.
Kraakman, Reinier, 'Corporate Liability Strategies and the Cost of Legal Controls' (1984) 93 *Yale Law Journal* 857.

Kruger, Colin, 'Investors sue Telstra to recoup $300m', *Sydney Morning Herald* (21 January 2006) 29.
Kumar Katyal, Neal, 'Conspiracy Theory' (2003) 112 *Yale Law Journal* 1307.
Landes, William and Posner, Richard, 'The Private Enforcement of Law' (1975) 4 *Journal of Legal Studies* 1.
Langevoort, Donald, 'On Leaving Corporate Executives "Naked, Homeless and Without Wheels": Corporate Fraud, Equitable Remedies and the Debate Over Entity Versus Individual Liability' (2007) 42 *Wake Forest Law Review* 627.
Larson, Lex, *Larson on Employment Discrimination* (LexisNexis Online).
Latimer, Paul, 'Compensation of investors for failure of a securities industry licensee' (1997) 15 *Company and Securities Law Journal* 495.
Law, Jonathan (ed), *A Dictionary of Business and Management*, 5th edn (Oxford University Press, 2009).
Le Mire, Suzanne, '"It's Not Fair!": The Duty of Fairness and the Corporate Regulator' (2014) 36 *Sydney Law Review* 445.
—— 'Low penalties, high costs: ASIC needs legislative reform', *The Conversation* (20 February 2014).
Lederman, Eliezer, 'Criminal Law, Perpetrator and Corporation: Rethinking a Complex Triangle' (1985) 76 *Journal of Criminal Law and Criminology* 285.
Legg, Michael, 'A Comparison of Regulatory Enforcement, Class Actions and Alternative Dispute Resolution in Compensating Financial Consumers' (2016) 38 *Sydney Law Review* 311.
—— 'ADR and Class Actions Compared' in Michael Legg (ed), *The Future of Dispute Resolution* (LexisNexis, 2013).
—— 'Class Actions and Regulating Culture in Financial Organisations: Observations from a Comparison of US and Australian Bank Class Actions' in Justin O'Brien and George Gilligan (eds), *Integrity, Risk and Accountability in Capital Markets* (Hart, 2013).
—— 'Class action settlements in Australia -the need for greater scrutiny' (2014) 38 *Melbourne University Law Review* 590.
—— 'Coercive Investigatory Powers of ASIC, ACCC and ATO' in Michael Legg (ed), *Regulation, Litigation and Enforcement* (Thomson Reuters, 2011).
—— 'Contingency fees – Antidote or poison for Australian civil justice?' (2015) 39 *Australian Bar Review* 244.
—— 'Entrepreneurs and Figureheads – Addressing Multiple Class Actions and Conflicts of Interest' (2009) 32 *University of New South Wales Law Journal* 909.
—— 'Funding a Class Action through Limiting the Group: What does Part IVA of the Federal Court of Australia Act 1976 (Cth) permit?' (2010) 33 *Australian Bar Review* 17.
—— 'Institutional Investors and Shareholder Class Actions: The Law and Economics of Participation' (2007) 81 *Australian Law Journal* 478.
—— 'Judge's role in settlement of representative proceedings: Lessons from United States class actions' (2004) 78 *Australian Law Journal* 58.
—— 'Litigation Funding of Australian Class Actions after the High Court Rejection of Common Fund Orders' (2020) 39 *Civil Justice Quarterly* 305.
—— 'Misleading and Deceptive Conduct in Prospectuses' (1996) 14 *Company and Securities Law Journal* 47.
—— 'Public and Private Enforcement: ASIC and the Shareholder Class Action' in Michael Legg, *Regulation, Litigation and Enforcement* (Thomson Reuters, 2011).
—— 'Ramifications of the Recognition of a Common Fund in Australian Class Actions: An Early Appraisal' (2017) 91 *Australian Law Journal* 655.
—— 'Reconciling Litigation Funding and the Opt Out Group Definition in Federal Court of Australia Class Actions – The Need for a Legislative Common Fund Approach' (2011) 30 *Civil Justice Quarterly* 52.
—— 'Regulatory Theory, Litigation and Enforcement' in Michael Legg (ed), *Regulation, Litigation and Enforcement* (Thomson Reuters, 2011).
—— 'Securities Regulation in Australia: The Role of the Class Action' in Robin Huang and Nicholas Howson (eds), *Enforcement of Corporate and Securities Law: China and the World* (Cambridge University Press, 2017).
—— 'Shareholder Class Actions in Australia – The Perfect Storm?' (2008) 31 *University of New South Wales Law Journal* 669.
—— 'The Aristocrat Leisure Ltd shareholder class action settlement' (2009) 37 *Australian Business Law Review* 399.
—— 'The Leighton class action settlement: managing a need for speed' (2015) 2 *Australian Alternative Dispute Resolution Bulletin* 19.
—— 'The pros and cons of different types of fee arrangements' (2021) 74 *Law Society Journal* 82.
—— 'Was Peter Thiel's funding of the Gawker case an abuse of legal process?' *The Conversation* (31 May 2016).
Legg, Michael and Emmerig, John, 'Australian Federal Court Reforms Class Actions Settlement Practice' (2018) 46 *Australian Business Law Review* 262.
Legg, Michael and Hickey, Samuel, 'Finality and Fairness in Australian Class Action Settlements' (2019) 41 *Sydney Law Review* 185.
Legg, Michael and Jordan, Dean, 'Disclosure Needs Special Care', *The Australian Financial Review* (14 February 2007) 55.
Legg, Michael and McInnes, Ross, *Australian Annotated Class Actions Legislation*, 2nd edn (LexisNexis, 2018).

Legg, Michael and Mirzabegian, Sera, 'Appropriate Dispute Resolution and the Role of Litigation' (2013) 38 *Australian Bar Review* 55.
Legg, Michael, Park, Edmond, Turner, Nicholas and Travers, Louisa, 'The Rise and Regulation of Litigation Funding in Australia' (2011) 38 *Northern Kentucky Law Review* 625.
Legg, Michael and Speirs, Stephen, '"Why not litigate?" – The Royal Commission, ASIC and the Future of the Enforcement Pyramid' (2019) 47 *Australian Business Law Review* 244.
Leighton Holdings, 'Conditional Settlement of Leighton Class Action' (Media Release, 16 May 2014).
—— 'Leighton appoints Ernst & Young as independent reviewer' (ASX Announcement, 17 May 2012).
—— 'Leighton completes sale of John Holland to CCCI' (ASX Announcement, 20 April 2015).
Leighton Holdings Ltd, 'Concise Annual Report for the 2011 Transitional Financial Year' (30 March 2012).
Lemos, Margaret and Minzner, Max, 'For-Profit Public Enforcement' (2014) 127 *Harvard Law Review* 853.
Lenaghan, Nick, 'Alarm as Centro moves to sue its auditors', *The Australian Financial Review* (27 May 2009) 50.
—— 'Centro: the mother of class acts', *The Australian Financial Review* (12 May 2012) 54.
—— 'PwC wrangle threatens deal', *The Australian Financial Review* (23 November 2011) 50.
—— 'Trust seals its recovery', *The Australian Financial Review* (16 April 2013) 29.
Letter from Douglas Gration, Company Secretary, Telstra Corporation Limited to The Manager, Company Announcements Office, ASX (7 September 2005).
Letter from Tony D'Aloisio, Chairman, ASIC to Peter Costello, Treasurer, 'ASIC Statement of Intent' (27 June 2007).
Letters Patent, Royal Commission into Misconduct in the Banking, Superannuation and Financial Services Industry (14 December 2017).
Leung, Tim, and Webster, Jon, 'Directors' duties, financial literacy and financial reporting after Centro' (2012) 30 *Companies and Securities Law Journal* 100.
Levitin, Adam, 'The Politics of Financial Regulation and the Regulation of Financial Politics: A Review Essay' (2014) 127 *Harvard Law Review* 1991.
Liamputtong, Pranee, *Qualitative Research Methods*, 3rd edn (Oxford University Press, 2009).
Lim, Shueh Hann, 'Do Litigation Funders Add Value to Corporate Governance in Australia?' (2011) 29 *Company and Securities Law Journal* 135.
Lobel, Orly, 'The Renew Deal: The Fall of Regulation and the Rise of Governance in Contemporary Legal Thought' (2004) 89 *Minnesota Law Review* 342.
Lodge, Martin and Wegrich, Kai, *Managing Regulation: Regulatory Analysis, Politics and Policy* (Palgrave Macmillan, 2012).
LoPucki, Lynn, 'The Death of Liability' (1996) 106 *Yale Law Journal* 1.
Low, Hannah, 'ASIC a class act in Centro case', *The Australian Financial Review* (30 June 2011) 10.
Macey, Jonathan and Miller, Geoffrey, 'The Plaintiffs' Attorney's Role in Class Action and Derivative Litigation: Economic Analysis and Recommendations for Reform' (1991) 58 *University of Chicago Law Review* 1.
MacNamara, Lisa, 'Leighton's ASIC penalty more fuel for class action', *The Australian* (20 March 2012) 23.
Macquarie Dictionary.
Majewski, Teresita and Schiffer, Michael Brian, 'Beyond Consumption: Toward an Archaeology of Consumerism' in David Gaimster and Teresita Majewski (eds), *International Handbook of Historical Archaeology* (Springer, 2009).
Malech, Steven and Koosa, Robert, 'Government Action and the Superiority Requirement: A Potential Bar to Private Class Actions' (2005) 18 *Georgetown Journal of Legal Ethics* 1419.
Mankes, Michael, 'Combatting Individual Employment Discrimination in the United States and Great Britain: A Novel Remedial Approach' (1994) 16 *Comparative Labor Law Journal* 67.
Mann, Peter, 'Directors' and Officers' Insurance in the Regulatory Litigation Context' in Michael Legg, *Regulation, Litigation and Enforcement* (Thomson Reuters, 2011).
Markell, David and Glicksman, Robert, 'Dynamic Governance in Theory and Application, Part I' (2016) 58 *Arizona Law Review* 563.
Marsh and McLennan, 'Directors and Officers Liability (D&O) 2020 Australian Insurance Market Recap Series' (December 2020).
Martin, Jr, Christopher, 'Reining in Lincoln's Law: A Call to Limit the Implied Certification Theory of Liability Under the False Claims Act' (2013) 101 *California Law Review* 227.
May, Peter, 'Regulatory Regimes and Accountability' (2007) 1 *Regulation & Governance* 8.
Mayanja, James, 'Enhancing Private Enforcement of Australia's Corporate Continuous Disclosure Regime: Why Unshackling Litigation Funders Makes Eminent Sense' (2010) 25 *Australian Journal of Corporate Law* 48.
McCubbins, Mathew, Noll, Roger and Weingast, Barry, 'Administrative Procedures as Instruments of Political Control' (1987) 3 *Journal of Law Economics & Organization* 243.
McLaughlin, Eugene and Muncie, John, *The Sage Dictionary of Criminology*, 2nd edn (Sage, 2006).

McLean, Adam, 'Centro, PwC take record $200m legal hit', *The Australian Financial Review* (9 May 2012).
Merkin, Robert and Enright, Ian, *Sutton on Insurance Law*, 4th edn (Thomson Reuters, 2015).
Merritt, Chris, 'Class action "mates" too powerful', *The Australian* (31 October 2014) 27.
—— 'Class actions fuel insurance rates' *The Australian* (23 March 2018) 27.
—— 'Contingency fee shift courts conflict' *The Australian* (20 June 2020) 15.
—— 'Fear of class actions grows', *The Australian* (13 June 2014) 31.
—— 'Funder sitting pretty thanks to Centro suit', *The Australian* (11 May 2012) 34.
—— 'Second wave of litigation looms', *The Australian* (25 July 2014) 27.
—— 'Securities class actions just blackmail suits', *The Australian* (6 June 2014) 33.
Metherell, Lexi, 'Budget 2014: ASIC's funding cut in move away from financial sector oversight', *ABC News* (15 May 2014).
Miller, Daniel, 'Consumption as the Vanguard of History: A Polemic by Way of an Introduction' in Daniel Miller (ed), *Acknowledging Consumption: A Review of New Studies* (Routledge, 1995).
Miller, Jeffrey, 'Theme and Variations in Statutory Preclusions Against Successive Environmental Enforcement Actions by EPA and Citizens Part One: Statutory Bars in Citizen Suit Provisions' (2004) 28 *Harvard Environmental Law Review* 401.
Miller, Lisa, 'The Use of Case Studies in Law and Social Science Research' (2018) 14 *Annual Review of Law and Social Science* 381.
Miller, Paul, 'Shareholder class actions: Are they good for shareholders?' (2012) 86 *Australian Law Journal* 633.
Mitchell, Gregory, 'Case Studies, Counterfactuals and Causal Explanations' (2004) 152 *University of Pennsylvania Law Review* 1517.
Mitchell, Lawrence, 'The "Innocent Shareholder": An Essay on Compensation and Deterrence in Securities Class-Action Lawsuits' [2009] *Wisconsin Law Review* 243.
Mizen, Ronald, 'Litigation funding rules survive after 11th-hour One Nation backdown' *The Australian Financial Review* (4 December 2020).
—— 'New rules could see funded class actions grind to halt' *The Australian Financial Review* (29 July 2020).
Morabito, Vince, 'An Empirical Study of Australia's Class Action Regimes – First Report' (December 2009).
—— 'An Empirical Study of Australia's Class Action Regimes – Second Report' (September 2010).
—— 'An Empirical Study of Australia's Class Action Regimes, Third Report: Class Action Facts and Figures – Five Years Later' (November 2014).
—— 'An Empirical Study of Australia's Class Action Regimes – Fifth Report' (July 2017).
—— 'Contingency Fee Agreements with Represented Persons in Class Actions – An Undesirable Australian Phenomenon' (2005) 31 *Common Law World Review* 201.
—— 'Courts see record number of class actions as shareholder proceedings drop in significance' *Lawyerly* (20 May 2021).
—— 'Judicial Responses to Class Action Settlements that Provide no Benefits to some Class Members' (2006) 32 *Monash University Law Review* 75.
—— 'Replacing Inadequate Class Representatives in Federal Class Actions: Quo Vadis?' (2015) 38 *University of New South Wales Law Journal* 146.
Moran, Susannah, 'Telstra class action payout fair, says judge', *The Australian* (14 December 2007) 25.
—— 'Telstra offers 5c to settle class action', *The Australian* (13 November 2007) 3.
—— 'Telstra settles class action with investors', *The Australian* (12 November 2007) 1.
Murphy, Bernard, 'Shareholder class actions: are you vulnerable?' (June 2007) *Keeping Good Companies* 275.
Murphy, Bernard and Cameron, Camille, 'Access to Justice and the Evolution of Class Action Litigation in Australia' (2006) 30 *Melbourne University Law Review* 399.
Murphy, Bernard and Watson, Andrew, 'Negotiations and Settlement – 2010 Multiplex Debrief' LexisNexis Shareholder Class Action Masterclass, Sydney (18 October 2010).
Nagareda, Richard, 'Class Actions in the Administrative State: Kalven and Rosenfield Revisited' (2008) 75 *University of Chicago Law Review* 603.
Nagin, Daniel, 'Deterrent Effects of the Certainty and Severity of Punishment' in Daniel Nagin, Francis Cullen and Cheryl Lero Jonson (eds), *Deterrence, Choice, and Crime: Contemporary Perspectives* (Routledge, 2018).
Narburgh, Guy and Ivimey, Sally-Anne, 'Side by Side (A, B and C): Securities Class Actions and D&O Insurance' in Damian Grave and Helen Mould (eds), *25 years of class actions in Australia: 1992–2017* (Ross Parsons Centre, 2017).
National Australia Bank, 'Class action Settlement' (ASX Announcement, 9 November 2012).
Nehme, Marina, Hyland, Margaret and Adams, Michael, 'Enforcement of Continuous Disclosure: The Use of Infringement Notice and Alternative Sanctions' (2007) 21 *Australian Journal of Corporate Law* 112.
Nicolae, Maria, 'The Liability-Sanction Relationship: A Case Study in the Effectiveness of the Corporate Regulatory Regime' (2013) 31 *Company and Securities Law Journal* 365.
North, Gill, 'A Call for Bold and Effective Corporate Disclosure Regulatory Framework' (2010) 28 *Company and Securities Law Journal* 331.

Note, 'Class Actions – Presumption of Reliance Under SEC Rule 10B-5 – Halliburton Co v Erica P John Fund Inc' (2014) 128 *Harvard Law Review* 291.

Note, 'Congress, The Supreme Court, and the Rise of Securities-Fraud Class Actions' (2019) 132 *Harvard Law Review* 1067.

Note, 'Developments in the Law-Corporate Crime: Regulating Corporate Behavior Through Criminal Sanctions' (1979) 92 *Harvard Law Review* 1227.

Odgers, Stephen, *Principles of Federal Criminal Law*, 3rd edn (Thomson Reuters, 2015).

Ogus, Anthony, *Regulation – Legal Form and Economic Theory* (Clarendon Press, 1994).

Owen, David, 'Why Philosophy Matters to Tort Law' in David Owen (ed), *Philosophical Foundations of Tort Law* (Clarendon Press, 1995).

Oxford English Dictionary.

Park, James, 'Rules, Principles and the Competition to Enforce Securities Laws' (2012) 100 *California Law Review* 115.

Parliamentary Joint Committee on Corporations and Financial Services, 'Litigation funding and the regulation of the class action industry' (December 2020).

—— 'Litigation funding and the regulation of the class action industry hearing' *Hansard* (13 July 2020).

—— 'Statutory oversight of the Australian Securities and Investments Commission' (13 March 2012).

—— 'Statutory oversight of the Australian Securities and Investments Commission' (21 June 2010).

Paternoster, Ray, 'How Much do we Really Know About Criminal Deterrence?' (2010) 100 *Journal of Criminal Law and Criminology* 765.

Paternoster, Ray and Bachman, Ronet, 'Perceptual Deterrence Theory' in Francis Cullen and Pamela Wilcox, *The Oxford Handbook of Criminological Theory* (Oxford University Press, 2013).

Paternoster, Ray and Simpson, Sally, 'Sanction Threats and Appeals to Morality: Testing a Rational Choice Model of Corporate Crime' (1996) 30 *Law & Society Review* 549.

Patten, Sally, 'Company directors call for a ban on class actions', *The Australian Financial Review* (11 June 2020).

Payne, Brian, 'Effects on White-Collar Defendants of Criminal Justice Attention and Sanctions' in Shanna Van Slyke, Michael Benson and Francis Cullen (eds), *The Oxford Handbook of White-Collar Crime* (Oxford University Press, 2016).

Pearson, Gail, 'Risk and the Consumer in Australian Financial Services Reform' (2006) 28 *Sydney Law Review* 99.

Pelly, Michael, 'Crennan warns directors on disclosure laws', *The Australian Financial Review* (5 June 2020).

—— 'Pandemic surge in class action' *The Australian Financial Review*, 21 May 2021.

Pelly. Michael, Durkin, Patrick and Kehoe, John, 'Chairman cheers disclosure freeze amid investor concerns', *The Australian Financial Review* (26 May 2020).

Perino, Michael, 'Enron's Legislative Aftermath: Some Reflections on the Deterrence Aspects of the Sarbanes-Oxley Act of 2002' (2002) 76 *St John's Law Review* 671.

Perry, Stephen, 'The Moral Foundations of Tort Law' (1992) 77 *Iowa Law Review* 449.

Pitt, Harvey and Groskaufmanis, Karl, 'Minimizing Corporate Civil and Criminal Liability: A Second Look at Corporate Codes of Conduct' (1990) 78 *Georgetown Law Journal* 1559.

Polinsky, A Mitchell and Shavell, Steven, 'The Economic Theory of Public Enforcement of Law' (2000) XXXVIII *Journal of Economic Literature* 45.

Posner, Richard, 'An Economic Theory of the Criminal Law' (1985) 85 *Columbia Law Review* 1193.

Powell, Dominic, 'Landmark Myer class action settled after shareholders unable to prove loss' *The Sydney Morning Herald* (6 May 2020).

Price, John, Commissioner, ASIC, 'Continuous Disclosure' (Speech, Chartered Secretaries Australia 2012 Annual Conference, 3 December 2012).

Productivity Commission, 'Access to Justice Arrangements' (Report No 72, 5 September 2014).

Ramsay, Iain, *Consumer Law and Policy*, 3rd edn (Hart Publishing 2012).

—— 'Consumer Law, Regulatory Capitalism and the "New Learning" in Regulation' (2006) 28 *Sydney Law Review* 9.

—— 'Enforcement of Continuous Disclosure Laws by the Australian Securities and Investments Commission' (2015) 33 *Company and Securities Law Journal* 196.

'Recent Legislation' (2011) 124 *Harvard Law Review* 1829.

Redish, Martin, 'Class Actions and the Democratic Difficulty: Rethinking the Intersection of Private Litigation and Public Goals' (2003) *University of Chicago Legal Forum* 71.

Reimann, Mathias, 'Private Enforcement in the United States and in Europe – A Comparative Perspective and Potential Lessons for Asia' in Robin Huang and Nicholas Howson (eds), *Enforcement of Corporate and Securities Law: China and the World* (Cambridge University Press, 2017).

Reiss Jr, Albert, 'Consequences of Compliance and Deterrence Models of Law Enforcement for the Exercise of Police Discretion' (1984) 47 *Law and Contemporary Problems* 83.

—— 'Selecting Strategies of Social Control Over Organizational Life' in Keith Hawkins and John Thomas (eds), *Enforcing Regulation* (Kluwer-Nijhoff Publishing, 1984).

Roach, Kent and Trebilcock, Michael, 'Private Enforcement of Competition Laws' (1996) 34 *Osgood Hall Law Journal* 461.

Roberts, Tracey, 'Innovations in Governance: A Functional Typology of Private Governance Institutions' (2011) 22 *Duke Environmental Law and Policy Forum* 67.

Robinson, Paul, 'Strict Liability's Criminogenic Effect' (2018) 12 *Criminal Law and Philosophy* 411.

Robinson, Paul and Darley, John, 'Does Criminal Law Deter? A Behavioral Science Investigation' (2004) 24 *Oxford Journal of Legal Studies* 173.

Roddan, Michael, *The People vs The Banks* (Melbourne University Press, 2019).

Roddan, Michael, Kehoe, John and Pelly, Michael, 'Cleaned-out ASIC charged with aiding recovery' *The Australian Financial Review* (29 April 2021).

Romzek, Barbara and Dubnick, Melvin, 'Accountability in the Public Sector: Lessons from the Challenger Tragedy' (1987) 47 *Public Administration Review* 227.

Rose, Amanda, 'Classaction.gov' (2021) 88 *University of Chicago Law Review* 487.

—— 'Cutting Class Action Agency Costs: Lessons from the Public Company (2020) 54 *UC Davis Law Review* 337.

—— 'Reforming Securities Litigation Reform: Restructuring the Relationship Between Public and Private Enforcement of Rule 10B-5' (2008) 108 *Columbia Law Review* 1301.

—— 'The Multienforcer Approach to Securities Fraud Deterrence: A Critical Analysis' (2010) 158 *University of Pennsylvania Law Review* 2173.

Royal Commission into Misconduct in the Banking, Superannuation and Financial Services Industry, 'Final Report – Volume 1' (2019).

—— 'Interim Report – Volume 1' (2018).

—— Transcript of Cross-Examination of Mr James Shipton (22 November 2018).

Rubenstein, William, 'On What a "Private Attorney General" Is – And Why It Matters' (2004) 57 *Vanderbilt Law Review* 2129.

Rubenstein, William, Conte, Alba and Newberg, Herbert, 3 *Newberg on Class Actions*, 5th edn (Thomson Reuters 2011).

Salomon, Lester, 'The New Governance and the Tools of Public Action' (2001) 28 *Fordham Urban Law Review* 1611.

Sax, Joseph, *Defending the Environment: A Strategy for Citizen Action* (Knopf, 1971).

Schwartz, Gary, 'The Ethics and the Economics of Tort Liability Insurance' (1990) 75 *Cornell Law Review* 313.

Schwartz, Warren, 'An Overview of the Economics of Antitrust Enforcement' (1979) 68 *Georgetown Law Journal* 1075.

Scott, Colin, 'Accountability in the Regulatory State' (2000) 27 *Journal of Law and Society* 38.

—— 'Enforcing Consumer Protection Laws' in Geraint Howells, Iain Ramsay and Thomas Wilhelmsson with David Kraft, *Handbook of Research on International Consumer Law* (Edward Elgar, 2010).

Securities Exchange Commission, 'Statement of the Securities Exchange Commission Concerning Financial Penalties' (4 January 2006).

Senate Economics References Committee, '"Lifting the fear and suppressing the greed": Penalties for white-collar crime and corporate and financial misconduct in Australia' (23 March 2017).

—— 'Performance of the Australian Securities and Investments Commission' (June 2014).

—— 'Report on Treasury Laws Amendment (2021 Measures No. 1) Bill' (June 2021).

Senate Standing Committee on Economics, 'Report on Treasury Laws Amendment (2021 Measures No. 1) Bill' (March 2021).

Sexton, Elisabeth, 'Watchdog ruling shakes up boardrooms', *The Sydney Morning Herald* (8 July 2011) 7.

Shapira, Roy, 'Reputation Through Litigation: How the Legal System Shapes Behavior by Producing Information' (2016) 91 *Washington Law Review* 1193.

Shapiro, David, 'Class Actions: The Class as Party and Client' (1998) 73 *Notre Dame Law Review* 913.

Shavell, Steven, 'Liability for Harm versus Regulation of Safety' (1984) 13 *Journal of Legal Studies* 357.

—— 'The Fundamental Divergence Between the Private and the Social Motive to Use the Legal System' (1997) 26 *Journal of Legal Studies* 575.

—— 'The Judgment-Proof Problem' (1986) 6 *International Review of Law and Economics* 45.

Shipton, James, 'A New Era for Conduct Regulation in Australia', Thomson Reuters Australian Regulatory Summit (11 April 2018).

—— 'The fairness imperative', AFR Banking and Wealth Summit, Sydney (27 March 2019).

Simons, Helen, 'Case Study Research: In-Depth Understanding in Context' in Patricia Leavy (ed), *The Oxford Handbook of Qualitative Research* (Oxford University Press, 2014).

Simpson, Sally, 'Making Sense of White-Collar Crime: Theory and Research' (2011) 8 *Ohio State Journal of Criminal Law* 481.

Slater & Gordon, 'Court Orders Telstra to pay $5 million to Settle Class Action' (Media Release, 13 December 2007).

—— 'New Centro Class Action Issued' (Press Release, 25 May 2008).

—— 'Thousands of mum and dad investors poised to share in Australia's biggest shareholder class action settlement' (Media Release, 9 May 2012).

Spender, Peta, 'Securities Class Actions: A View from The Land of the Great White Shareholder' (2002) 31 *Common Law World Review* 123.

Stegman, Laurie, 'An Administrative Battle of the Forms: The EEOC's Intake Questionnaire and Charge of Discrimination' (1992) 91 *Michigan Law Review* 124.

Stephenson, Matthew, 'Public Regulation or Private Enforcement: The Case for Expanding the Role of Administrative Agencies' (2005) 91 *Virginia Law Review* 93.

Stevens, Matthew, 'Centro in line to become ultimate testbed for board behaviour', *The Australian* (22 October 2009) 21.

Stewart, Claire, 'Peril of disclosure rush raised', *The Australian Financial Review* (20 March 2012) 17.

Stewart, Richard and Cass Sunstein, 'Public Programs and Private Rights' (1982) 95 *Harvard Law Review* 1195.

Stone, Christopher, 'The Place of Enterprise Liability in the Control of Corporate Conduct' (1980) 90 *Yale Law Journal* 1.

Summers, Robert, 'Evaluating and Improving Legal Processes – A Plea for "Process Values"' (1974) 60 *Cornell Law Review* 1.

Sunstein, Cass, 'On the Expressive Function of Law' (1996) 144 *University of Pennsylvania Law Review* 2021.

—— 'The Limits of Compensatory Justice' in John Chapman (ed), *Compensatory Justice – NOMOS XXXIII* (New York University Press, 1991).

Sutherland, Edwin, 'Is "White Collar Crime" Crime?' (1945) 10 *American Sociological Review* 132.

—— *White Collar Crime* (Holt, Rinehart and Winston Inc, 1949).

—— 'White-Collar Criminality' (1940) 5 *American Sociological Review* 1.

Tang, Edmund, 'Sound fundamentals: Australia now home to world's 4th largest pension assets', Australian Trade and Investment Commission (14 April 2020).

Taub, Daniel and Maguire, Fergus, 'Brookfield Asset Buys Australia's Multiplex for A$4.2 Billion', *Bloomberg* (11 June 2007).

Telstra Corporation Limited, 'Class action dismissed' (Media Release 296/2007, 13 December 2007).

—— 'Court asked to approve class action settlement' (Media Release 263/2007, 12 November 2007).

—— 'Telstra statement on ASIC' (Media Release 352/2005, 14 December 2005).

Thompson, Barton, 'The Continuing Innovation of Citizen Enforcement' (2000) *University of Illinois Law Review* 185.

Thompson, Larry, Deputy Attorney General, US Department of Justice, Memo to Heads of Department Components, US Department of Justice (20 January 2003).

Thomson, James, 'Disclosure changes hurt investors' *The Australian Financial Review* (27 May 2020) 40.

Tilbury, Michael, *Civil Remedies – Volume 1 Principles of Civil Remedies* (Butterworths, 1990).

Tomasic, Kathyrn, 'Australian Securities and Investments Commission v Healey: Implications for the directors' duty of care and diligence' (2011) 26 *Australian Journal of Corporate Law* 234.

Urban, Rebecca, 'Leighton fine "a timely message"', *The Australian* (24 March 2012) 31.

Uribe, Alice and James Frost, 'Directors hit in class action surge', *The Australian Financial Review* (4 January 2018) 1, 4.

van Rooji, Benjamin and Fine, Adam, 'Toxic Corporate Culture: Assessing Organizational Processes of Deviancy' (2018) 8 *Administrative Sciences* 23.

Velikonja, Urska, 'Public Compensation for Private Harm: Evidence from the SEC's Fair Fund Distributions' (2015) 67 *Stanford Law Review* 331.

Victorian Law Reform Commission, 'Access to Justice – Litigation Funding and Group Proceedings' (Report, 2018).

—— 'Civil Justice Review' (Report No 14, 2008).

Viscusi, Kip, (ed), *Regulation through Litigation* (AEI-Brookings Joint Center for Regulatory Studies, 2002).

Walker, John, Khouri, Susanna and Attrill, Wayne, 'Funding Criteria for Class Actions' (2009) 32 *University of New South Wales Law Journal* 1036.

Waters, Cara, 'The new class conflict: The efficacy of class actions as a remedy for minority shareholders' (2007) 25 *Company and Securities Law Journal* 300.

Waye, Vicki, 'Conflicts of Interests Between Claimholders, Lawyers and Litigation Entrepreneurs' (2007) 19 *Bond Law Review* 225.

Weinrib, Ernest, 'Corrective Justice in a Nutshell' (2002) 52 *University of Toronto Law Journal* 349.

Weiss, Elliott and John Beckerman, 'Let the Money Do the Monitoring: How Institutional Investors Can Reduce Agency Costs in Securities Class Actions' (1995) 104 *Yale Law Journal* 2053.

Welsh, Michelle, 'Enforcing contraventions of the continuous disclosure provisions: Civil or administrative penalties' (2007) 25 *Company and Securities Law Journal* 315.

Welsh, Michelle and Morabito, Vince, 'Public v Private Enforcement of Securities Laws: An Australian Empirical Study' (2014) 14 *Journal of Corporate Law Studies* 39.

Welsh, Michelle, Spender, Peta, Lynch Fannon, Irene and Hall, Kath, 'The end of the "End of History for Corporate Law"?' (2014) 29 *Australian Journal of Corporate Law* 147.
Wen, Philip, 'Big investors in Leighton consider joining class action', *The Age* (2 September 2011) 1.
West, Michael, 'Off the Hook, With Barely a Slap', *Sydney Morning Herald* (3 September 2011) 2.
White, Rob and Haines, Fiona, *Crime & Criminology*, 4th edn (Oxford University Press, 2008).
White, Robert, Tranter, Bruce and Hanson, Dallas, 'Share Ownership in Australia – The Emergence of New Tensions?' (2004) 40 *Journal of Sociology* 99.
Wiggins, Jenny, 'ASIC gets tougher on disclosure', *The Australian Financial Review* (19 March 2012) 1.
Wiggins, Jenny, 'Class action alleges CIMIC misled investors on cash flow' *The Australian Financial Review* (26 August 2020).
Wood, Leonie, 'Follow-up case launched in Centro class action', *The Age* (2 December 2010) 2.
—— 'Laptop vital evidence, court told', *The Age* (10 August 2011) 5.
Wright, Richard, 'Right, Justice and Tort Law' in David Owen (ed), *Philosophical Foundations of Tort Law* (Clarendon Press, 1995).
Yeung, Karen, 'Quantifying Regulatory Penalties: Australian Competition Law Penalties in Perspective' (1999) 23 *Melbourne University Law Review* 440.
Yin, Robert, *Case Study Research: Design and Methods*, 5th edn (Sage, 2014).
Zimbardo, Philip, *The Lucifer Effect – Understanding How Good People Turn Evil* (Random House, 2008).
Zimmerman, Adam 'Mass Settlement Rivalries' (2013) 82 *University of Cincinnati Law Review* 381
Zipursky, Benjamin, 'Civil Recourse, not Corrective Justice' (2003) 91 *Georgetown Law Journal* 695.

INDEX

Lightning Source UK Ltd.
Milton Keynes UK
UKHW032310111022
410343UK00003B/280

9 781509 941513